Nuclear Logics

PRINCETON STUDIES IN
INTERNATIONAL HISTORY AND POLITICS

SERIES EDITORS

G. John Ikenberry and Marc Trachtenberg

A list of titles in this series appears at the back of the book

Nuclear Logics

CONTRASTING PATHS IN

EAST ASIA AND THE MIDDLE EAST

Etel Solingen

PRINCETON UNIVERSITY PRESS

PRINCETON AND OXFORD

Requests for permission to reproduce material from this work should be sent to
Permissions, Princeton University Press

Published by Princeton University Press, 41 William Street, Princeton, New Jersey 08540

In the United Kingdom: Princeton University Press, 3 Market Place, Woodstock,
Oxfordshire OX20 1SY

Library of Congress Cataloging-in-Publication Data

Solingen, Etel, 1952–
    Nuclear logics : contrasting paths in East Asia and the Middle East / Etel L. Solingen.
        p. cm.—(Princeton studies in international history and politics)
    Includes bibliographical references and index.
    ISBN–13: 978-0-691-13147-4 (hardcover : alk. paper)
    ISBN–13: 978-0-691-13468-0 (pbk. : alk. paper)
    1. Nuclear nonproliferation—East Asia.   2. Nuclear nonproliferation—Middle East.
3. Nuclear nonproliferation—International cooperation.   4. Security, International.
I. Title.
    JZ5675.S665 2007
    355.02'17095—dc22   2007008396

British Library Cataloging-in-Publication Data is available

This book has been composed in Sabon

Printed on acid-free paper. ∞

press.princeton.edu

Printed in the United States of America

10 9 8 7 6 5 4 3 2 1

To Clara Fanny and Fito,
parents, friends, teachers

Contents

Preface   ix

PART ONE: *Introduction and Conceptual Framework*   1

CHAPTER ONE
Introduction   3

CHAPTER TWO
Alternative Logics on Denuclearization   23

PART TWO: *East Asia: Denuclearization as the
Norm, Nuclearization as the Anomaly*   55

CHAPTER THREE
Japan   57

CHAPTER FOUR
South Korea   82

CHAPTER FIVE
Taiwan (Republic of China)   100

CHAPTER SIX
North Korea   118

PART THREE: *The Middle East: Nuclearization as the
Norm, Denuclearization as the Anomaly*   141

CHAPTER SEVEN
Iraq   143

CHAPTER EIGHT
Iran   164

CHAPTER NINE
Israel   187

CHAPTER TEN
Libya   213

CHAPTER ELEVEN
Egypt   229

PART FOUR: *Conclusions*   247

CHAPTER TWELVE
Findings, Futures, and Policy Implications   249

Notes   301

References   351

Index   385

Preface

THIS BOOK'S OBJECTIVE is twofold: to help understand why states seek or renounce nuclear weapons and to relate the question to the general study of international relations. Policy-oriented studies have often understated the value of international relations theory to this subject matter. International relations theory has generally treated the topic as poor ground for theorizing, a puzzling fact considering voluminous efforts devoted to deterrence and superpower nuclear interaction. This book is an effort to bridge that gap. Readers, scholars, and practitioners less interested in theoretical disciplinary debates may turn directly to the empirical historical chapters and policy conclusions. Teachers and students of international relations may find the more theoretical sections useful for the classroom.

Three features of this book reflect these dual objectives of explaining nuclear behavior and revisiting the way we study it. First is the effort to harness recent advances in the study of globalization, international institutions, norms, and democratization to further our understanding of different logics underlying nuclear choices. This is done in a way that takes account of both strengths and deficiencies in each approach while suggesting directions for future research. A second feature is the focus on the riddle of diverging nuclear trajectories in East Asia and the Middle East. Despite the centrality of these two regions to the policy debate and despite methodological advantages inherent in the comparison, dedicated studies along these lines have been rare if not nil. A third trait lies in the inclusion of fresh arguments that have been largely overlooked as explanations of nuclear behavior. As the book's title suggests, different logics can explain why states acquire or refrain from acquiring nuclear weapons. Understanding nuclear choices as the sole reflection of international power considerations has come at a high cost, analytically and politically. The most important frontier in the study of nuclear choices is the relationship between regime and state security, or internal and external political survival. Construing nuclear aspirants as monolithic states is both analytically deficient and can subvert the successful design of positive and negative inducements regarding nonproliferation.

By contrast, identifying the domestic conditions underlying nuclear decisions takes us several steps beyond conventional studies largely concerned with external security. Nuclear weapons programs have been more likely to emerge, on average, from domestic political landscapes dominated by hostility to economic openness. Conversely, leaders oriented to economic growth via the global political economy have, by and large, created conditions that reined in nuclearization. A systematic understanding of the relationship between domestic models of political survival and nuclear policy is both timely and analytically indispensable. These models may not capture all the correlates of nuclear preferences and are, after all, only ideal-types or conceptual constructs, but they do propose a comparative framework capable of reducing complex reality down to some fundamentals. They can explain why different *actors* within the same state vary in their approaches and preferences regarding nuclear policy; why nuclear policies within states may vary *over time* as a function of the relative power of particular domestic forces; and why different *states* vary in their commitment to increase information, transparency, and compliance with the nonproliferation regime.

The inclusion of different brands of international relations theory and their application to nine empirical cases—all in a single book—allowed no more than a condensed treatment of each perspective and each case study. Readers interested in further elaborations of these theories or cases will find citations for further reading. Although the nine country-chapters are based on far more extensive background sources, space limitations precluded anything beyond succinct historical overviews of each case. What may have inevitably been left out in historical detail should hopefully be offset through concise and disciplined accounts following a common conceptual structure. Furthermore, although nuclear outcomes often result from interplay between political intentions and technical capabilities, my emphasis here is far more on the former than the latter. Technical aspects can be gleaned from various declassified sources and from academic and NGO studies cited throughout, whereas understanding intentions still lags in disciplined analysis.

Although when I embarked on this project I had a clear sense that the theme was a timely one, I could not have foreseen the density of events related to nuclear proliferation that has occurred over the past two years. This manuscript goes to press under the fog of North Korea's nuclear test, the first such test among the nine cases reviewed here, and it is too early to evaluate its repercussions. Furthermore, various Middle East countries have been scrambling to respond to what they perceive as Iran's defiant nuclear behavior. If the book's theme was a moving target when I began writing it, it has become an accelerating runaway object at the end of the process. As a consequence, and given the length of the publication process, it is likely that some of the material will be superseded by more recent events. The conception of this book as a primer for understanding nuclear behavior through theoretical lenses, however, makes the runaway nature of events an extremely useful natural experiment for gauging the advantages and limitations of different theories. The guidelines for research, scenarios for testing theories, case studies for teaching, and topics for theses and dissertations thus provide helpful tools for making sense of emergent events. These advantages of unfolding reality for social science research do not offset the net disadvantages, in the eyes of many, for international security.

Research on intentions is burdened by the secrecy that often envelops nuclear policies. Efforts to reconstruct the history of these programs can yield no more than an approximation of events, subject to endless revision as new documents emerge. The incompleteness of the data renders the *Roshomon* feature of the analysis quite appropriate, with different theories highlighting different dimensions of the total picture. I rely on primary data where available, including personal interviews, declassified documents, historical archives, public speeches, interview transcripts, memoranda, oral communiqués, cabinet discussions, personal memoirs, legislative records, published accounts of defectors, and secondary sources. Particularly useful were declassified documents available from the National Security Archives, the U.S. National Archives, and the Cold War International History Project (Woodrow Wilson International Center for Scholars), which includes declassified documents from the former Soviet Union. Some leaders left more elaborate records about their objectives and aspirations—whether real ones or justifications—than others. South Korea's President Park Chung Hee and Prime Ministers Yoshida Shigeru, Nakasone Yasuhiro, Tanaka Kakuei, David Ben-Gurion, and Shimon Peres, among others, wrote memoirs, as did foreign ministers and personal secretaries such as Kusuda Minoru, Yigal Allon, and President Gamal Abdul Nasser's close advisor Mohamed Hasnayn Haykal. Presidents Hashemi Rafsanjani and Mahmoud Ahmadinejad, as well as other Iranian officials, have not shied away from publicly expressing their views on nuclear matters. Indeed, for all their visceral hatred of Western values, Khamene'i and Ahmadinejad have readily exploited Western technology to advocate their views through personal blogs. Similarly, North Korea's home-page offers a window into Internet-savvy Kim Jong-Il. Qadhafi's evolving thinking may be gathered from his Green Book, extensive recent press interviews, and his personal website. The Iraq Survey Group (2004) provided a window into Saddam Hussein's beliefs about nuclear weapons and those of his close associates. Published interviews with, and memoirs by, nuclear scientists such as Iraq's Ja'afar Dhiya Ja'afar, Hussain Al-Shahristani, Mahdi Obeidi, Khidir Hamza, and Imad Khadduri, Libya's Muhammad Izzat Abd-al-Aziz, and Taiwan's Wu Ta-you all provide additional sources.

The nine cases account for a large share of nuclear aspirants in the second nuclear age and serve well the logic of comparing East Asia with the Middle East. Paraphrasing Meyer (1984), the nine cases allow us to study the forest and the trees, the more generic dynamics of nuclear decisions and the more specific details linking choices, decisions, actions, effects, and outcomes. Nine cases also constitute a formidable research challenge. Although I relied on expert knowledge on each country along the way, I alone am responsible for any remaining errors. The book took several years of research and writing and would have probably taken several more were it not because of the generosity of several agencies. A grant from the Japan Foundation Center for Global Partnership (CGP) allowed me to take two sabbatical quarters to complete the manuscript. The CGP also graciously hosted a stimulating academic workshop in Tokyo with the participation of experts on the Middle East and East Asia. I am grateful to CGP's Executive Director Taida Hideya as well as Hara Hideki, Chano Junichi, Carolyn Fleisher, and Goto Ai for their support. Special thanks go to Professors Takashi Inoguchi, Masashi Nishihara, and T. J. Pempel for commenting on the initial proposal and various chapters. A Social Science Research Council-Japan Foundation Abe Fellowship introduced me to the study of Japan and East Asian regional cooperation. Many of this book's ideas began germinating during an SSRC-MacArthur Foundation Fellowship on International Peace and Security, which allowed me to indulge in rare comparisons between East Asia and the Middle East. I also acknowledge support from the University of California's Institute on Global Conflict and Cooperation (IGCC), especially Director Peter Cowhey, and from the University of California's Pacific Rim Research Program. I am grateful to UC Irvine's Center for the Scientific Study of Ethics, especially Director Kristen Monroe, for sponsoring this project, to Dean Barbara Dosher for encouragement, and to Dave Easton for his infallible critical eye and unfailing support.

I also owe a debt of gratitude to many scholars and practitioners willing to discuss their views with me during visits to Japan, South Korea, Egypt, Israel, Taiwan, Jordan, and China, as well as to current and former U.S. and E.U. officials and NGO experts. Current and former government officials interviewed in East Asia and the Middle East helped interpret particular events that they witnessed. They include former prime ministers, foreign ministers, and defense ministers; their advisors; former director generals of Atomic Energy Commissions; high officials in National Security Councils and in defense academies; and ambassadors. I am beholden to them for their candid perspectives while respecting their request for anonymity. I benefited enormously from comments by seminar participants at Stanford University's Center for International Security and Cooperation, IGCC's Program on U.S. National Security at the University of California, San Diego, Arizona State University's Institute on Qualitative Research Methods, the Swiss Federal Institute of Technology/Center for Security Studies International Security Forum, UCLA's Von Grunebaum

Center for Near Eastern Studies, UCLA's Burkle Center for International Relations, Monterey Institute's Center for Nonproliferation Studies, UC Irvine's Center for the Scientific Study of Ethics and Center for Global Peace and Conflict Studies, and panels at annual meetings of the American Political Science Association, International Studies Association, CISS/ISA 2006 Millennium Series, International Political Science Association (Fukuoka, Japan), International Convention of Asia Scholars (Shanghai, China), and First Global International Studies Conference (Istanbul, Turkey).

As for the many scholars and experts who graciously provided useful suggestions on various chapters, I am especially indebted to Nobuyasu Abe, Asher Arian, Amatzia Baram, Hans Blix, Michael Brecher, William Burr, Leszek Buszynski, T. J. Cheng, Alan Dowty, Lynn Eden, Nabil Fahmy, Sung Chull Kim, Ellis Krauss, Akira Kurosaki, Wen-cheng Lin, Chih-cheng Lo, Yossi Melman, Abbas Milani, Chung-in Moon, Young-Kyu Park, Daniel Pinkston, William C. Potter, Mitchell Reiss, Richard Samuels, Jeffrey Richelson, Art Stein, Robert Wampler, Ren Xiao, Andrew Yang, Herbert York, and the late Shalhevet Freier. My apologies to those I may have accidentally left out. As tempting as it is to blame them for any residual errors, these remain my own. For superb research assistance, I am grateful to Maryam Komaie, Wilfred Wan, Colin Moore, Maria van Meter, Adam Martin, and Titus Chen. UCI librarian Dianna Sahhar provided very valuable help with difficult sources. I would also like to thank anonymous reviewers who offered very constructive suggestions. Chuck Myers at Princeton University Press was extremely supportive of this effort, for which I am most grateful, as I am to Linda Truilo for her careful editing and professionalism, and Nathan Carr for shepherding the manuscript to completion.

Last, but certainly not least, without the love and wonderful companionship of my husband Simon, this book might have been completed several years earlier, but with much less enjoyment. My children Aaron and Gaby are both the best teachers of high-theory and the best guides for down-to-earth fun I have ever met. I could have never completed this book without them. I dedicate this book to my mother Clara Fanny and my late father Fito, from whom I learned much more than all the basics.

The reader may be left with many more questions than those answered in this book. If so, I will feel rewarded by the effort. As 2004 Physics Nobel laureate David Gross once expressed, "The more we know, the more aware we are of what we know not. Indeed, the most important product of knowledge is ignorance."

PART ONE

Introduction and Conceptual Framework

CHAPTER ONE

Introduction

THE QUANDARY

WHY HAVE SOME STATES sought nuclear weapons whereas others have shunned them? Why has the Middle East largely evolved toward nuclearization whereas East Asia has moved in the opposite direction since the 1970s?[1] How have international power distribution, globalization, international institutions, or democracy affected those choices? Will these regional trends remain? This book seeks to answer these central questions in international politics by improving our understanding of "nuclear aspirants" or states that have considered, developed, abandoned, or acquired nuclear weapons programs since the conclusion of the Nonproliferation Treaty (NPT) in 1968, a period sometimes labeled the "second nuclear age."[2]

Beyond their immediate policy relevance, the contrasting nuclear trajectories of East Asia and the Middle East offer an important analytical puzzle worthy of systematic analysis. In the Middle East, for example, Iraq, Libya, Israel, and Egypt until 1971 have allegedly pursued nuclear weapons relentlessly, and Iran has been widely suspected of similar intentions on the basis of its violations of NPT commitments. Iraq was precluded from acquiring a nuclear device (1981, 1991) by military force. Some sources even include Saudi Arabia, Algeria, and Syria as plausible long-standing aspirants.[3] Since 1971 Egypt—a leader in the Arab world— became an important exception to the region's nuclearizing trajectory. Recent concerns with a defiant Iranian nuclear program have arguably led Turkey, Algeria, Egypt, Morocco, Saudi Arabia, Tunisia, and the United Arab Emirates (UAE henceforth) to embark on nuclear power programs that could constitute potential precursors of nuclear weapons (Campbell, Einhorn, and Reiss 2004). Saudi Foreign Minister Prince Saud al-Faisal declared, "We are urging Iran to accept the position that we have taken to make the Gulf, as part of the Middle East, nuclear-free and free of weapons of mass destruction. We hope they will join us in this policy and assure that no new threat or arms race happens in this region."[4] By contrast, ever since China acquired nuclear weapons in 1964, Japan, Taiwan, and South Korea renounced nuclear weapons and joined the NPT, while Southeast Asia established a nuclear weapon–free zone (NWFZ). North Korea has been the exception, testing a nuclear weapon in 2006, the first East Asian state to do so in forty-two years, since China's 1964 test. Even prior to its test, North Korea's nuclear defiance raised fears that it could galvanize support for reactive proliferation in South Korea, Japan, and Taiwan, thus ending East Asia's progression away from proliferation.[5] Yet the puzzle of contrasting historical trajectories across these two regions remains. Whereas the norm in East Asia has been an apparent evolution toward denuclearization, North Korea has been the anomaly. Conversely, the norm among core Middle East powers has been toward nuclearization, except for Egypt and, more recently, Libya. Egypt's Ambassador to the United States Nabil Fahmy described the Middle East as

> a poster boy for the failure of global and regional nonproliferation efforts. . . . Like most regions, the majority of its member states are card-carrying and committed members of this salient international nonproliferation regime and regulations. . . . Yet very significant questions remain outstanding regarding the present state of play of nuclear nonproliferation in that region. More than a decade ago, Iraq was caught violating its safeguard in NPT obligations. . . . Today, its neighbor Iran, also NPT member, has questions raised about its nuclear program and the degree of its respect of its safeguard obligations. (CEW)

Both traditional and novel theories of nuclear behavior can be applied to explain these diverging trajectories. Neorealist literature in international relations has often traced nuclearization to international structure, relative power, balance of power, and self-help. It is crucial to distinguish between neorealist theory in international relations scholarship, pivoted in the concepts of structural or relative power, international anarchy, and self-help on the one hand, and the common use of the word "realism" in American politics on the other. The latter is frequently applied to visions or policies that are "realistic" or "feasible." Yet, a policy that some may consider "realistic" in the more colloquial sense can be diametrically opposed to structural or neorealist understandings of international politics. Throughout this book the term neorealism refers to its use in international relations scholarship as a structural theory of politics (and in particular to offensive neorealism), not as a policy that seems "realistic." While some rely on neorealism as the theory that explains nuclear policy, concerns with existential security are never perfunctory reflections of structural considerations invariably leading to aggression or power maximization, but rather the product of domestic filters that convert such considerations into different policies. The extent to which *state*—rather than *regime* security—is invariably the dominant source of nuclear behavior may have been overestimated, precluding alternative—and perhaps more incisive—understandings of what drives the acquisition or renunciation of nuclear weapons.[6] One such alternative forces greater attention to domestic political considerations of nuclear aspirants. In particular, systematic differences in nuclear behavior can be observed between states whose leaders or ruling coalitions advocate integration in the global economy, and those whose leaders reject it. The former have incentives to avoid the political, economic, reputational, and opportunity costs of acquiring nuclear weapons because such costs impair a domestic agenda favoring internationalization.[7] Conversely, leaders and ruling coalitions rejecting internationalization incur fewer such costs and have greater incentives to exploit nuclear weapons as tools in nationalist platforms of political competition and for staying in power. This insight may be extended to explain differences between nuclear aspirants in East Asia and the Middle East over nearly four decades. East Asian leaders pivoted their domestic political control on economic performance and integration into the global economy. Middle East leaders relied on inward-looking self-sufficiency and an emphasis on domestic markets and nationalist values for their political survival.[8] These respective platforms created different incentives and constraints that influenced leaders' preferences for or against nuclear weapons.

Nuclear behavior should provide an *easy* arena for testing a theory uniquely pivoted on relative power and state security in an anarchic world, such as neorealism. Lying at the very heart of a state's security dilemma, nuclear policy loads the dice in favor of this approach. In other words, nuclear behavior provides the "most likely case" or most favorable domain for corroborating neorealist tenets. For that very reason nuclear behavior is perhaps *not* a crucial arena for validating those canons from a methodological standpoint. A good or crucial test of a theory is one that forces it to survive conditions that are *not* favorable to confirm it.[9] On this basis, too many deviations from neorealist predictions regarding nuclear policy constitute potentially significant challenges to the theory. Conversely, nuclear behavior provides an extremely *difficult* arena for testing theories of domestic political survival as the one offered here. Political leaders can only portray their decisions for or against nuclear weapons as dictated by "reasons of state" rather than by domestic political expediency. Precisely because decisions regarding nuclear weapons are "least likely" to validate the role of domestic politics, they provide a crucial and tough arena for investigating such effects. Thus, even partial substantiation uncovering an important role for domestic considerations in this "unfriendly" terrain, where evidence is much harder to garner, gains particular significance.

From a methodological standpoint, the ability to corroborate that domestic approaches to political survival are more relevant to nuclear behavior than often suspected might be akin to a "Sinatra inference" (Levy 2002): if the theory can make it here, it can make it anywhere. One should certainly not be carried away with this prospect, however. The empirical chapters certainly provide sufficient reason to pay far more attention to this rather understudied source of nuclear behavior. At the same time, each case is explored through a much broader theoretical repertoire to assess the relative advantages and limitations of each approach for improving our understanding of nuclear outcomes. This is not a strict effort to test theories (in no less than nine cases!) but rather to illustrate theory-driven analysis of nuclear decisions in a defined empirical domain. To reiterate, balance-of-power considerations are certainly important but a better understanding of nuclear behavior and outcomes requires theoretical recalibration and a closer examination of competing and complementary perspectives to avoid overestimation of some theories and underestimation of others. As an early study by Meyer (1984) suggested, it is quite likely that some assumptions from different perspectives are valid; the task is identifying when and why. Furthermore, in his view, all motives of nuclear behavior are, in the end, filtered through the domestic politics within which decisions are made. A systematic understanding of these effects makes this approach analytically indispensable in the study of nuclear aspirants.

NONPROLIFERATION: PAST PREDICTIONS AND PRESENT CONUNDRUM

Nuclear choices have wide-ranging implications for international security. The potential proliferation of nuclear weapons served as partial justification for the 2003 war in Iraq and continues to rank high in the foreign policy agenda of major powers and international institutions. The United States, the European Union, Japan, the G-8, and former U.N. Secretary General Kofi Annan have defined the problem as the preeminent threat to international security, with attending consequences for budgetary allocations and the need for collective action.[10] Although Iran and North Korea are now focal cases, many regard this as a much broader problem, regardless of political persuasions. The Bulletin of Atomic Scientists moved the minute hand of its "Doomsday Clock" from seven to five minutes, warning that "we stand at the brink of a second nuclear age." President George W. Bush has repeatedly asserted that more nations have nuclear weapons, and still more have nuclear aspirations.[11] Campbell et al. (2004) suggested that we may be approaching a "tipping point" that will unleash a proliferation epidemic, and that we now stand on the verge of a new nuclear age with potentially more nuclear-weapons-states (NWS) and a much greater chance that these weapons will be used. Others regard the nonproliferation regime (NPR) as poised for collapse and fear that the "domino theory" of the twenty-first century may well be nuclear.[12] Former director general of the International Atomic Energy Agency (IAEA) and chief U.N. weapons inspector Hans Blix declared that "certainly if Iran were to develop further in the wrong direction, there is a risk for other countries considering going for nuclear weapons. And if the North Koreans move on, well the risks are very, very great. If the North Koreans were to test a weapon, yes, it would be very, very serious" (ASAW). IAEA director general Mohammed El-Baradei declared that "we are reaching a point today where I think Kennedy's prediction is very much alive. Either we are going to . . . move to nuclear disarmament or we are going to have 20 or 30 countries with nuclear weapons, and if we do have that, to me, this is the beginning of the end of our civilization" (CNSW). In 2006 these concerns appeared even more real as North Korea tested a nuclear weapon and fear of a defiant Iran arguably led to declarations by six Middle East countries that they would pursue nuclear energy programs.[13]

Not all agree with this vision, and assessments of past progression vary with different benchmarks. President Kennedy's 1963 prediction of fifteen to twenty-five NWS by 1973 did not come about.[14] The past three decades reflected declining nuclear aspirations even by technically capable states. As Rosecrance (1964:300) correctly predicted, nuclear weapons did not spread "as ineluctably as the instruments of modern industrialism." Most states (189) joined the NPT, the most widely subscribed international treaty in existence, including some that had rejected it for decades, as did Argentina and Brazil. Some gave up nuclear weapons, including Ukraine, Belarus, Kazakhstan, and South Africa. Libya surrendered its program to U.S. and IAEA scrutiny in 2003. More states abandoned than acquired nuclear weapons programs during the past fifteen years (Roberts 1995; Wolfsthal 2005). Yet the number of NWS increased. India and Pakistan conducted tests in 1998 and, like Israel, remained outside the NPT. Israel's capabilities have been widely asserted although its formal policy of "not being the first to introduce nuclear weapons into the region" remains in place.[15] North Korea proclaimed possession of nuclear weapons in 2003 and tested one in 2006; Iran's record in acquiring weapons-suitable technologies has not been matched by dutiful reporting to the IAEA. Both North Korea and Iran are deemed to have breached their NPT commitments. The tally of NWS has thus risen from the five recognized by the NPT in 1968 (the United States, Britain, Russia, China, and France) to nine states in 2006.

What explains this variability in behavior, with some states renouncing nuclear weapons altogether, others reversing previous efforts in that direction, and yet others developing them in violation of international commitments? Three decades ago Economics Nobel laureate Thomas Schelling (1976:80) advised that "the emphasis has to shift from physical denial and technology secrecy to the things that determine incentives and expectations." Nearly three decades later Hans Blix recognized that the task of uncovering the sources of incentives for proliferation still constitutes a fundamental problem (CEW). As Brad Glosserman (2004) puts it, a key obstacle to efforts to counter nuclear proliferation is that "we still don't know why governments proliferate nuclear weapons. Several explanations have been offered . . . but no single explanation convinces. Until we know why governments acquire nuclear weapons, it will be difficult to stop them from doing so." The theoretical literature in international relations on this issue is much less copious than the studies on nuclear deterrence, tends to advance mono-causal explanations (a single factor explains it all), and frequently involves case studies by country experts.[16] This book's objective is to advance our understanding of nuclear behavior and revisit the way we study it. A controlled comparison between East Asia and the Middle East offers several advantages for achieving those objectives.

THE RESEARCH DESIGN

There are at least nine reasons why a focused comparison (George and McKeown 1985) between the two regions that is sensitive to methodological issues in comparative analysis, case selection, and research design, offers important benefits for improving our understanding of denuclearization:[17]

First, the two regions are at the forefront of policy debates as potential nuclear dominoes. The North Korean and Iranian crises will continue to shape—and perhaps shake—the foundations of regional and international security. *Both the Middle East and East Asia find themselves in the midst of a historical period with potentially profound transformational effects, providing a unique vantage point from which to evaluate the past and explore the future of nuclear proliferation.*

Second, the NPT's inception was a watershed that affected the balance of incentives and constraints regarding nuclear weapons, offering analysts the opportunity to gauge variability in outcomes against a common international institutional order represented by the NPR. Since 1968 about fourteen industrializing countries have been suspected of exploring or considering nuclear weapons, taking concrete steps in that direction, or outright producing them.[18] Nearly two-thirds of the cases were in the Middle East (five) and East Asia (four).[19] The concentration on East Asia and the Middle East therefore *(a) helps understand nuclear decisions while holding an important causal variable—international regime—constant;*[20] *and (b) enables a focused comparison of the two main regional concentrations of nuclear aspirants since 1968.*

Third, four decades ago these two regions experienced authoritarian rule, limited economic interdependence, regional security dilemmas, and state-building challenges. The contrasting subsequent evolution of their respective political-economy models offers an opportunity to examine background conditions leading to distinct nuclear policies. This evolution entailed wide variance in another causal variable (integration in the global economy), potentially explaining divergent nuclear policies.[21] This variance provides excellent conditions for a natural experiment: the two regions differed both on the causal and the dependent variable—nuclear outcomes (King, Keohane, and Verba 1994; George and McKeown 1985). Both regions are also subject to ongoing pressures that may alter those outcomes in the future, offering propitious conditions for assessing competing perspectives on the dynamics of proliferation. Hence, comparative process-tracing of nuclear behavior in the two regions generates additional methodological advantages:[22] *(a) the presence of similar initial background conditions across regions (approximating a "most similar case" design);*[23] *(b) subsequent wide variation in a specific causal variable of interest (particularly across regions but also within them); and (c) wide variation in the dependent variable.*

Fourth, both regions had hierarchic and multipolar power distributions, helping to control for a presumed prime causal variable. According to neorealist canons, comparable power distributions should lead to similar outcomes and clearly cannot account for differential outcomes (George and Bennett 2005:156). Furthermore, multipolarity itself has been hypothesized to enhance the likelihood of nuclearization (Mearsheimer 1990). Hence, not only should we have observed *similar* outcomes in both regions but also *nuclearization* in both cases. This has not happened yet and, as discussed in chapter 2, neorealist explanations habitually invoke auxiliary theories that are often rooted in domestic politics (Legro and Moravcsik 1999). Nonetheless, comparing these two regions *offers an opportunity to examine the effects of balance-of-power theories on different states, across regions as well as within them.*

Fifth, an early theory advanced that high preexisting industrial and technological infrastructures were a prerequisite for acquiring nuclear weapons (Meyer 1984). The post-1968 trajectories of these two regions, however, arguably call into question these expectations. East Asia developed dynamic industrial and technological infrastructures but refrained from applying them to nuclear weapons' development. The least industrially dynamic—North Korea—was the exception and was driven by political will rather than technological thrust. In the Middle East, Israel might suggest a better fit with technological determinism, but in the 1970s, states with much weaker industrial infrastructures (Libya, Iraq, and Iran) embarked on nuclear weapons programs, sometimes circumventing low indigenous capabilities by purchasing critical technologies "off the shelf" from the A. Q. Khan network. With perhaps better technical chances than these three, Egypt discontinued its quest for nuclear weapons. These comparisons between and within the two regions *help dismiss technological determinism by pointing to "most likely cases" in East Asia that abstained from acquiring nuclear weapons and "least likely cases" in the Middle East (from the standpoint of this argument) that sought them.*

Sixth, the two regions differed on the relationship between natural energy resources and nuclear technological capabilities, civilian and military. Japan, South Korea, and Taiwan were highly dependent on foreign natural resources and developed robust and sophisticated nuclear industries without converting them into weapons. The region's anomaly, North Korea, was also energy-poor but lagged in civilian nuclear energy while seeking nuclear weapons. Oil-rich Middle East powers such as Iraq, Libya, and Iran had dramatically lower incentives to develop nuclear industries at the outset, yet they allocated gargantuan resources to nuclear programs that had weapons applications, without ever achieving viable nuclear industries after decades of investment. Egypt had moderate oil endowments and a faltering nuclear industry, and it discontinued its nuclear weapons program. Israel lacked energy resources altogether and its non-NPT status burdened its ability to develop a nuclear industry but not a weapons program. These observations point to additional analytical benefits from comparing two regions that best exemplify special forms of capital accumulation related to natural endowments—Middle East rentier states versus East Asian developmental states: *(a) in the post-1968 era, oil wealth may be more of an enabling antecedent* (Van Evera 1997)—*albeit not a necessary condition—for nuclear weapons than wealth amassed from industrialization; and (b) an inverse relationship may be hypothesized between robust civilian nuclear industries and the pursuit of nuclear weapons.*[24]

Seventh, the scholarly literature on both regions tends to stress unique features, particularly evident in cultural understandings of each one. "Contextualized comparisons" of cases *within* each region enable tests of distinctive regional properties. At the same time, the inclusion of cases from both regions precludes excessive concentration on specificity that sometimes obscures useful cross-regional comparisons. A *focused comparison between the two regions advances the broader comparative politics agenda while circumventing fallacies of regional "exceptionalism."*

Eighth, most of the cases under study provide, in and of themselves, important tests of alternative theories. From one neorealist standpoint, Japan and Egypt are arguably "most likely" cases for acquiring nuclear weapons as major regional powers facing nuclear-armed neighbors, and Libya a "least likely" case. Yet the former two renounced nuclear weapons and the latter pursued them. Different identity-based arguments place different cases on the "most likely" and "least likely" lists for nuclearization.

Hypotheses linking relative closure to the global economy to nuclearization place North Korea, Libya, Iraq, and Iran in the "most likely" category and Japan, Taiwan, and South Korea in the "least likely." Both identity and political-economy arguments sometimes compete with alternative explanations. *The two regions thus provide useful cases that enable "crucial" or tough tests for corroborating or rejecting different theories.*[25]

Finally, despite these analytical and methodological advantages and policy relevance *there has been no systematic effort to explain divergent nuclear behavior in the two regions.* Where does one start?

CONCEPTUAL PERSPECTIVES

In an early study of nuclear proliferation, Rosecrance (1964:299) argued that although predictions regarding prospective nuclear aspirants are chimerical, "there are some guideposts on this otherwise perilous route." This book extracts potential guideposts from various schools of thought that might shed light on the complex phenomenon of denuclearization. No major school provides a satisfactory response to these differential paths. Nor have they ever been applied to controlled, systematic comparisons between our two regions of interest. This section introduces their essential premises and applicability to these cases leaving for chapter 2 a more thorough discussion of theoretical issues and specific applications to the Middle East and East Asia.

Structural Power (Neorealism)

An established school of thought in international relations advances that state insecurity drives the search for nuclear weapons. In its structural form, commonly referred to as neorealism, this view traces nuclear decisions to the balance of power and security dilemmas (Waltz 1981; Mearsheimer 1990).[26] The nuclearization (or potential nuclearization) of a state is thus expected to induce similar responses by its neighbors. In this view, the domestic nature of states, regimes, groups, or individuals is irrelevant to nuclear decisions and outcomes. Uniquely concerned with national security, neorealism has been granted pride of place in explaining nuclear behavior. As argued, were alternative theories to be found equally (or more) persuasive on nuclear issues, neorealism would be questioned in its home court, where it enjoys highest advantage for substantiating its tenets. The empirical studies indeed suggest that neorealism—although useful in some general sense—fails to explain some of the cases examined, is incomplete in explaining others, competes with alternative explanations in what should be its best arena of argumentation, suffers from underdetermination (leads to multiple possible outcomes), and may be unfalsifiable given that so many options can be made to fit vague notions of security maximization a posteriori. Beyond these generic deficiencies, discussed in chapter 2, neorealism suffers from several shortcomings in explaining nuclear trajectories in our two regions.

First, both regions had *hierarchic* and multipolar power distributions. Multipolarity should have encouraged nuclearization in both cases but led instead to nuclearization in much of the Middle East but not East Asia since 1964. Second, both regions lacked *robust and symmetric* distributions of nuclear capabilities, yet they led to different outcomes. Third, states presumably afflicted with intense security dilemmas abstained from acquiring nuclear weapons (Egypt, Japan, South Korea, Taiwan) whereas states with much lower existential threats (Libya, Iraq in the early 1970s) did not. U.S. commitments to East Asian allies were extremely important in addressing those dilemmas, but these were not absolute, inclusive, unlimited, or unconditional commitments that put security dilemmas entirely to rest under the anarchical conditions stipulated by neorealism. Fourth, U.S. commitments in the Middle East (or South Asia)—to Iran's shah, for instance (or Pakistan)—have mysteriously not had the same effect. Nor have Chinese and Soviet commitments to North Korea led to its denuclearization. As Waltz (2003:38) has persuasively argued, "in the past half-century, no country has been able to prevent other countries from going nuclear if they were determined to do so." Fifth, Egypt abandoned nuclear weapons designs in 1971 *without* the backing of an effective U.S. alliance even as its main adversary (Israel) was presumed to have them. Unsurprisingly, given all these anomalies, Levite (2002/03:83) finds that "there is no evidence to suggest . . . that the U.S. influence has ever been a sufficient factor for inducing reversal." Indeed, U.S. security guarantees do not account for most cases of nuclear reversal. Sixth, whereas changes in structural power would have predicted changes in nuclear policies, the rise of China, the collapse of the Soviet Union, the relative decline of Japan, and enhanced competition between China and the United States have not altered East Asia's nuclear trajectory thus far. Japan, Taiwan, and South Korea remained non-nuclear weapons states while North Korea continued on its nuclearizing path. Finally, is East Asia traversing a bipolar, hegemonic, or multipolar transition at the dawn of the twenty-first century?[27] Disagreements within neorealism over the actual nature and specific effects of power distribution on nuclear incentives provide uncertain grounds for explaining past, let alone predicting future, trajectories.

That security predicaments are important sources of nuclear behavior bears repetition. At the same time, reducing nuclear tendencies to this rubric, as is often done, leads to analytic overestimations of *state* security as the exclusive source of nuclearization. As Betts (2000) argues, insecurity is not a sufficient condition for acquiring nuclear weapons; many insecure states have not, from Vietnam to Singapore, Jordan, and many others. The earlier dominance of neorealism on this issue stemmed partially from inherent problems of epistemology and evidence collection, afflicting nonproliferation studies perhaps most severely.[28] Leaders and state officials have incentives to justify nuclear decisions in terms of "reasons of state," which both domestic and international audiences consider more legitimate than parochial internal reasons. Analysts thus find more "evidence" for the role of security concerns in leaders' statements and justifications along those lines, and the secondary literature reinforces that focus.[29] In-depth analyses of North Korea, Iraq, Libya, and arguably Iran after 1991 including those in this book clearly suggest that nuclear weapons programs were driven more by *regime* than by state insecurity. Yet the latter, not the former, is the staple of neorealist accounts of nuclearization. The analytic and policy implications of this distinction are only beginning to permeate academic and policy-oriented thinking on nuclear proliferation.[30] The most important frontier for understanding nuclear choices and outcomes is the relationship between regime and state, or internal and external political survival.

As will be clear throughout the chapters that follow, this book does not assert that U.S. alliances with Japan and South Korea and commitments to Taiwan are irrelevant. Indeed, such commitments provide an important explanatory layer for these countries' nuclear abstention. Yet understanding their relative receptivity to persuasive and coercive aspects of the U.S. alliance requires us to delve into their domestic politics. Nuclear weapons would have seriously undermined favored strategies of economic growth and regional and global access. The choice for alliance *itself* was the product of domestic models that favored it over other options, trumping internal demands for nuclear weapons and generating receptivity to hegemonic inducements. This argument thus qualifies the tendency to focus exclusively on alliances in three ways. First, the domestic argument provides a deeper understanding of nuclear preferences insofar as it can also explain why alliance was chosen to begin with. Second, alliances provide a more robust explanation *if* one can show that the net outcome of domestic political debates were forceful demands for nuclear weapons that were trounced by the United States. There is little evidence of such forceful demands, particularly in Japan but perhaps even in South Korea and Taiwan, despite some domestic proponents of nuclear weapons in all three countries. The net outcome of the domestic debate was in line with East Asia's favored domestic model of political survival, which nuclearization would have derailed. Third, other hegemonic defense pacts involving the United States and the Soviet Union did not induce abstention from nuclear weapons in too many other cases (Iran's shah, Israel, Pakistan,

North Korea, and Iraq among others). Indeed, if alliances told the tale, Britain (and arguably France) should never have gone nuclear. The role of alliances in the second nuclear age is mediated by the relative receptivity of domestic models to alliance and denuclearization. Absent such receptivity, alliances have played far less determining roles; in its presence, alliances have provided stronger incentives to abstain from nuclear weapons.

Neoliberal Institutionalism (Neoliberalism)

Neoliberal perspectives focus on the role of international institutions in mitigating security dilemmas by enhancing information about others' intentions and capabilities, and by monitoring and enforcing compliance (Keohane 1984; Gourevitch 1999; Kahler 2000; Inoguchi 1997). The emphasis is on *states'* rational incentives to choose particular institutional arrangements that leave all states better off (Pareto optimal). Some consider the network of institutions known as the NPR, including regional NWFZs, as serving that purpose. Accordingly, the NPT established a two-tier system: a small tier of five nuclear-weapons-states (NWS) and a large tier of states that renounced nuclear weapons in exchange for civilian nuclear technology. Although there has been no systematic collection of evidence corroborating that the NPT indeed accounts for nuclear choices made since 1968, this perspective has widespread appeal and strong intuitive plausibility. However, as Betts (2000:69) argued, "If the NPT or CTBT [Comprehensive Nuclear Test Ban Treaty] themselves prevented proliferation, one should be able to name at least one specific country that would have sought nuclear weapons or tested them, but refrained from doing so, or was stopped, because of either treaty. None comes to mind." Another prominent expert on the NPT, Egypt's ambassador to the United States, Nabil Fahmy, expressed that "in the spirit of candid and clear-sighted analysis, one must be obliged to acknowledge that very few non-nuclear weapons states—parties—actually joined the treaty because it responded to their immediate security concerns. Most of the parties that joined NPT did so for political or economic reasons or circumstances, or because they had no reason to pursue nuclear weapons or nuclear programs from the beginning" (CEW).

How does a neoliberal perspective fare in explaining differential trajectories in our two regions? First, state-centric rational-institutionalist perspectives prove compatible with a few cases but inadequate, incomplete, or unnecessary for explaining nuclear choices and outcomes in several others. Persuasive institutionalist accounts would have had to establish that—had the NPR not existed at the time—alternative decisions to develop nuclear weapons in Japan or South Korea would have obtained (Taiwan ceased to be an NPT party due to China's opposition). The historical record does not provide strong evidence for such a counterfactual. Second, the NPT clearly did not prevent Middle East nuclearization, as several parties defected from their commitments. East Asia exhibited far higher levels of compliance with the NPR (except North Korea) than the Middle East, which begs the question of what explains this disparate compliance. Third, East Asia lacked a regionally based nuclear regime that could account for its denuclearizing trajectory (Southeast Asia's NWFZ is rather recent, hence clearly not the cause of denuclearization in that region). Fourth, although the Middle East was home to the oldest regional institution, the Arab League played no effective role in nuclear policies. Israel and Iran provided convenient justification for the League's inaction on nuclear weapons programs in Iraq or Libya, but inter-Arab rivalries were no less crucial in paralyzing the League as an effective regional institution. Notwithstanding these points, the empirical chapters suggest that the NPR can be credited with some success in raising the costs of acquiring sensitive technologies and equipment, tightening inspection regimes in post-1991 Iraq, changing the context against which states formulated decisions regarding nuclear weapons, and offering new focal points such as the Additional Protocol. These achievements must be assessed against the fact that the NPR operated in the most thorny domain of national security, where the emergence and functioning of international institutions are most difficult. From this standpoint, rational institutionalist perspectives face vast disadvantages relative to neorealism as a theory that explains nuclear choices and outcomes.

Norms and Constructivism

The constructivist approach draws attention to how international norms emerge and converge around institutions, emphasizing socialization and normative pressure (Checkel 1997; Finnemore and Sikkink 1998; Barnett and Finnemore 1999; Johnston 2001). The NPR can be traced to anti-nuclear norms that developed after Hiroshima and Nagasaki. Despite the presumed rise of non-nuclear *use* norms (Schelling 1976; Tannenwald 2005), insufficient systematic evidence is available to ascertain whether a strong norm against nuclear acquisition developed as well. Furthermore, in the framework of deterrence theory, acquisition *circumvents* use and can conform to a "conditional morality" (Nye 1988). How can norms-based arguments be applied to explain differences in nuclear trajectories between the two regions? First, only East Asia since the 1970s may imply the possible operation of anti-acquisition norms, given nuclear restraint (except for North Korea). There is only limited evidence, however, for the impact of such norms even there, suggesting that they may have provided neither necessary nor sufficient conditions for denuclearization. Rational disincentives (including external coercion, alliances, or domestic politics) could have led to compliance with the NPT. Japan's unique experience makes it a "most likely case" to support normative accounts of non-acquisition, but its "nuclear embeddedness" under the U.S. umbrella and other considerations reveal a possible overstatement of the nuclear allergy. There is no evidence of norms-based constraints for Taiwan or South Korea (or for other cases of denuclearization including South Africa, Argentina, Brazil, Egypt, Ukraine, Belarus, and Kazakhstan, among others). Second, the Middle East's poor record of NPT-compliance (and actual *use* of chemical weapons) questions the possibility that such norms developed deep roots in this region. Indeed, alternative norms stemming from nationalist, religious, and other identities invested nuclear weapons with redemptive value as tools of modernization and defiance of the international order.

Constructivist accounts would be particularly valuable if they could isolate the effects of socialization from those of hegemonic coercion or rational nuclear learning. They could explore clustered behavior toward or away from nuclearization in different regions and why such differences obtain under the shadow of a presumably shared anti-nuclear-weapons-acquisition norm. A systematic application of norms-based approaches to explain these two regions must be complemented with a theory of domestic politics capable of explaining whose meanings are relevant to leaders' decisions to pursue or eschew nuclear weapons, who are the norm entrepreneurs promoting one set of values or the other and why, and, most importantly, what explains the relative receptivity to each path in different regions. As with security-related "reasons of state," leaders are arguably more likely to explain nuclear decisions by appealing to norms than by wielding parochial political considerations. In that sense, norms-based considerations should surface more easily in the effort to reconstruct such decisions.

Democracy and Nuclear Weapons

The perspective that democracies and non-democracies differ in their international behavior has blossomed in the study of international relations. The democratic peace hypothesis, for instance, seeks to explain why democracies do not wage wars against each other (Elman 1997; Russett and Oneal 2001; Lipson 2003) but has not been applied systematically to explain regional nuclear trajectories. Some may argue that since 1968, democracies have not acquired nuclear weapons as a means to cope with conflict with other democracies except for India. The non-democratic nature of states, however, cannot explain differences between East Asia and the Middle East. First, Taiwan, South Korea, and several Southeast Asian states were not democratic when they renounced nuclear weapons; most were dictatorships. Second, most autocracies in both regions did not embark on nuclear weapons programs. Third, while *most* nuclearizing states in the Middle East have been autocracies (Iraq, Libya, Iran, and Egypt under Nasser), some autocracies also reversed course and abandoned nuclear weapons programs (Egypt first, and most recently Libya) and others never pursued it (Jordan). Autocracies thus did not exhibit uniform nuclear behavior in the Middle East. Fourth, the only sustained democracy—Israel within 1967 borders—is attributed with robust nuclear capabilities. Regime-type theories might be extended to suggest that isolated democracies surrounded by adversarial autocracies have greater incentives to acquire nuclear weapons than democracies surrounded by democratic neighbors. This remains an untested theory that may be arguably supported by the Indian case but not by Japan (or South Korea and Taiwan since they became democracies).

In sum, given the historically mixed nature of regimes in both regions, the democratic peace would not be expected to apply to either case. Furthermore, the tendency between interactive democracies to dampen conflict may not necessarily be equivalent to the tendency to denuclearize, as France and Britain suggest (Lipson 2003).

Domestic Models: Orientations to the Global Economy and Nuclear Behavior

Domestic models of political survival and their orientations to the global political-economy have implications for nuclear trajectories. Leaders or ruling coalitions advocating economic growth through integration in the global economy have incentives to avoid the costs of nuclearization, which impair domestic reforms favoring internationalization. By contrast, nuclearization implies fewer costs for inward-looking leaders and for constituencies less dependent on international markets, investment, technology, and institutions, who can rely on nuclear weapons programs to reinforce nationalist platforms of political survival. *Hence, nuclearization has been much less attractive and far more costly for most East Asian leaders for domestic, regional, and international reasons,* which will be detailed further in the next chapter. Furthermore, the heavy regional concentration of internationalizing strategies in East Asia reinforced each state's incentives to avoid nuclearization. *Conversely, Middle East leaders faced lower domestic barriers to, and responded to stronger domestic incentives for, nuclearization than East Asian ones.* In addition, the heavy regional concentration of inward-looking strategies throughout the Middle East exacerbated mutual incentives to develop nuclear weapons.

Despite preliminary support for systematic differences in nuclear behavior traceable to domestic political survival, this hypothesis remains an understudied source of nuclear behavior.[31] This omission has important implications. A "missing" or "omitted" variable may lead to an overestimation of other causal variables, granting them too large an effect on the outcome while rendering at least some of their effects spurious (Brady and Collier 2004). Without taking into account domestic political survival models, one may not properly understand nuclear behavior or estimate the actual effects of balance of power, international norms and institutions, or democracy. Introducing a previously omitted variable does not imply that other variables are rendered irrelevant, but rather that we are better able to understand their relative impact on nuclear choices. Domestic political arguments help explain why security dilemmas are sometimes seen as more (or less) intractable, why some states rank alliance higher than self-reliance but not others, why nuclear weapons programs surfaced where there was little need for them, and why such programs were obviated where one might have expected them. Balance of power as well as norms and institutions may be more relevant than political survival in some cases and not others, but, in the aggregate, complete explanations of nuclear behavior must include all relevant variables for particular cases, a consideration that guides the empirical chapters in this book.

Political survival models provide valuable insights on the evolution of nuclear trajectories in East Asia and the Middle East. First, only staunch opponents of internationalization pursued nuclear weapons in East Asia: China (1950s–1960s) and North Korea. Second, all nuclear programs in the Middle East were launched by leaders steering import-substitution and relatively closed political economies (Iran, Iraq, Egypt until 1971, Israel, and Libya). Third, Japan, Taiwan, and South Korea, although afflicted with intense security dilemmas, support the hypothesis that internationalizing models create propitious conditions for denuclearization as do some Southeast Asian cases, notably Singapore (never considered a nuclear aspirant).

The proposition that domestic orientations to the global economy and nuclear policy may be linked is probabilistic, bounded, and refutable. It is probabilistic because it does not suggest an inevitable or deterministic outcome; very few social science theories can do that. It is bounded in three ways: conditions of necessity and sufficiency for nuclear weapons development, contingency on regional effects, and temporal sequences in the acquisition of such weapons. First, resistance to the global economy may provide only near-necessary but not sufficient conditions for the development of nuclear weapons programs.[32] Not all Middle East leaders who were wary of internationalization also developed nuclear weapons (Sudan and Syria did not, but acquired alternative weapons of mass destruction—WMD). Technical or other barriers could explain such abstention, but the absence of security dilemmas certainly could not. Internationalizing models may not be necessary but are likely to be sufficient for denuclearization, except in the next two circumstances.

Second, the proposition is bounded by the relative incidence of alternative models in neighboring states. The extent to which regions share congruent orientations toward internationalization (either positive or negative) modifies domestic preferences on nuclear issues. The collective evolution of East Asia toward internationalization reinforced *individual* incentives of leaders to avoid nuclearization to preserve regional stability, foreign investment, and domestic growth, despite China's 1964 tests. North Korea's closure made it more impermeable to these positive regional synergies. Most Middle East rulers retained relatively closed political economies, facing fewer domestic and international disincentives for nuclearization.[33] Leaders that might have otherwise favored internationalization faced an unwieldy neighborhood that actively discouraged it. Thus, inward-looking regimes seeking nuclear (or other WMD) weapons in the neighborhood constrain potential incentives for internationalizing leaders to denuclearize.

Third, the proposition may be bounded by temporal sequences in the acquisition of nuclear weapons. Disincentives related to internationalization may operate more forcefully in countries where nuclear programs have not yet yielded weapons (as in Japan, South Korea, Taiwan, Argentina, Brazil, Spain, and various pre-1968 cases not explored here). The impact of such disincentives may be lower—but not nonexistent—once nuclear thresholds have been crossed.[34] China developed nuclear weapons during the "first nuclear age" dominated by U.S.-Soviet rivalry, decades prior to its decision to integrate within the global economy. Israel's nuclear efforts were launched in an era of import-substituting and centralizing policies (1950s). Beyond their respective security concerns, both cases suggest that it may be far more costly politically to eliminate existing weapons than to abandon steps in that direction. As suggested by prospect theory, leaders value more what they already have ("endowment effect") than what they might get; hence they are more averse to losing what they possess than potential future gains (McDermott 1998; Levy 2000; Mercer 2005). If prospect theory holds, under otherwise similar circumstances leaders can be assumed to accept higher risks to retain existing nuclear weapons than to retain programs leading to their potential acquisition. Furthermore, the disincentives stemming from an internationalizing model may be stronger at deliberative or incipient stages of nuclear weapons consideration than after they have been acquired. When nuclearization precedes the inception of internationalizing models, subsequent denuclearization may arguably be less likely.

A final methodological point must be stressed. Leaders prefer to use "reasons of state" as justifications for favoring or renouncing nuclear weapons and are unlikely to expose narrow considerations of individual, political party, or regime survival. Such ulterior purposes may sometimes underlie intentions more accurately but are less legitimate, less likely to be formulated in public (and even private), and are consequently hard to sub-stantiate. A dictator's acknowledgment that he needs nuclear weapons to sustain his regime, although genuine, is unimaginable.[35] So are admissions by democratic leaders that nuclear decisions (in either direction) may be driven by the need to fashion supportive coalitions favoring economic choices or to maximize electoral support from special constituencies. Such reluctance to portray nuclear decisions in purely self-serving political terms applies both to those favoring or renouncing nuclear weapons. Con-sider the difficulty in suggesting that "we should avoid nuclear weapons because they would undermine our corporations' ability to access world markets," or certain constituencies' ability "to attract foreign investment," or "our party's model of economic growth." Such parochial calculations would be regarded with cynicism and disregard for "national security," and they would alienate even supporters of the favored nuclear policy (such as an anti-nuclear constituency that might otherwise reject the hid-den agenda). The political sensitivity of nuclear choices precludes candor to a greater extent than most other issues, yet domestic political consider-ations can weigh heavily on such decisions. Despite generic concerns with secrecy regarding nuclear decisions, democratic contexts provide better windows into such internal considerations than closed polities.

A Road Map

Chapter 2 provides an extensive analysis of different theoretical perspec-tives that can be marshaled to explain the nuclear evolution of the two regions, including more classical traditions focused on balance of power as well as more recent scholarship on international norms, institutions, democracy, and globalization. This overview analyzes both the logic of ne-orealist explanations as well as possible overestimations of their utility in our various cases. The analysis then turns to the merits and disadvantages of neoliberal institutionalism for advancing our understanding of nuclear choices and differential NPT-compliance patterns in the two regions. Next I discuss the potential role of anti-nuclear acquisition norms and alternative constructivist frameworks that could explain cross-regional differences. I subsequently explore the extent to which the democracy variable provides a useful foundation for understanding the cases under study. Last I examine the relationship between competing patterns of domestic political survival and divergent regional trajectories. The chapter ends with suggestions for a research agenda in the scholarly study of denuclearization.

The empirical chapters in parts 2 and 3 involve cases that differ in their nuclear behavior, ranging from those that only entertained theoretical possibilities for developing nuclear weapons to those that took concrete steps to develop them, those that acquired them (with or without testing), to those that renounced them after some consideration and those that reversed earlier decisions to acquire them. The chapters thus point to wide variability in the dependent variable—nuclear decisions for and against nuclear weapons—and relate the historical record to different theoretical expectations outlined in chapter 2. Each chapter explores how leaders sought to resolve balance-of-power dilemmas while addressing disincentives stemming from regional and international institutions, norms, the global political economy, and the challenges of autocracy and democracy. Given space limitations, each historical case should be read more as a search for theoretical progress than as a theory-testing exercise. What are the important things we can learn, as we move kaleidoscopically from one approach to the other, that might have remained hidden by conventional wisdom? The long period under review allows for within-case comparisons across changing conditions in power balances, regime type, evolving norms, and models of political survival. It also increases the number of observations (nuclear decisions) over time. The cases are grouped by region in a way that enables us to distill some commonalities but also understand potential within-region anomalies.

Part 2 analyzes the experience of Japan, South Korea, and Taiwan pointing to denuclearization as the norm since the 1970s and to North Korea as the regional anomaly. Insofar as all three cases were subject to significant external threats from their regional environment that required power balancing, their eventual decision against developing nuclear weapons (particularly Japan's) may constitute an anomaly for undiluted neorealist perspectives, although less so for neoclassical variants sensitive to domestic politics and the advantages of alliances. I explore how decision-makers in each country sought to resolve security predicaments over time, the role of the NPR in their nuclear choices, the relative importance of anti-nuclear acquisition norms in each case, the relationship between internationalizing models of regime survival and nuclear choices, and the effects of an eventual evolution from autocracy to democracy in Taiwan and South Korea. The commonalities across these cases contrast dramatically with the North Korean anomaly, rooted in an autarkic model of regime survival with implications for the effect of alliances, norms, and international institutions.

Part 3 examines the contrasting pattern of nuclearizing tendencies in Iraq, Israel, Iran, Libya, and Egypt until 1971, and Egypt's subsequent departure from that trend. By 2003, Libya too announced its exit from the nuclear path. The comprehensive overview of each case explores balance-of-power considerations, approaches to norms and international institutions, and the relationship between domestic political survival models and nuclear outcomes. The connection between inward-looking models and decisions to pursue nuclear weapons is particularly evident in this region. Autocratic states with entrenched *mukhabarat* mechanisms of repression, military-industrial complexes, and import-substituting priorities had a freer hand in steering nuclear programs in violation of NPT commitments. An entropic regional institution—the Arab League—reflected the character of its constituent units and was unable to prevent nuclearization throughout the region. The Multilateral Middle East Peace Process, underpinned by internationalizing leaders in selected Arab countries and Israel, became the most important effort to bring about a WMD-free-zone. Although stillborn and burdened with inward-looking pressures on all parties, as well as with continued threats from non-parties to the peace process, like Iran and Iraq, this process may have foreshadowed what the future may still deliver. For now, the Middle East remains the region with the highest barriers to denuclearization.

Part 4 distills lessons from both regions for analysis and policy, offering recommendations for improving the formulation of hypotheses in each conceptual tradition, and for outlining potential scenarios for the future. The first section evaluates the relative merits and applicability of conceptual approaches to nuclear choices examined in chapter 2 in light of the empirical cases in parts 2 and 3. It also explores the extent to which causal factors that may have persuasively explained the past are also likely to exert their influence on the future. Will past regional trajectories persist in light of evolving power balances, normative, institutional, and domestic circumstances? What processes or events might trigger possible discontinuities in nuclear courses? Will a failure to sway North Korea into a new path galvanize support for nuclearization among its neighbors (particularly Japan), ending East Asia's progression away from proliferation? Chapter 12 explores such scenarios by revisiting the power, institutional, and domestic considerations at play in the early twenty-first century. I end with some practical policy implications, including a call for particular sensitivity to domestic considerations, which, in the final analysis, define the paths of nuclear aspirants.

CHAPTER TWO

Alternative Logics on Denuclearization

WHY DO SOME STATES seek nuclear weapons, why do some reverse such decisions, and why do others never embark on such a quest? Singh and Way (2004) lament the lack of reliable knowledge on determinants of nuclear proliferation and the lack of agreement on the validity or generalizability of academic theories of nuclear proliferation. In an effort to shed light on this absence of consensus, this chapter explores the most important explanations for nuclear behavior, both favoring and renouncing nuclear weapons. Their respective shortcomings clearly explain some skepticism regarding any one theory's ability to account fully for outcomes. Yet extant literature offers important clues regarding incentives such as "the desire to intimidate and coerce rivals, the search for enhanced security against regional or international rivals, the status and prestige associated with mastering nuclear technology, and domestic politics and bureaucratic self-aggrandizement."[1] Disincentives include financial cost, technical difficulties, domestic and international opposition, damage to important bilateral relationships or collective security alliances, and global nonproliferation norms. Most academic studies of denuclearization involve policy-oriented, single-country, or mono-causal explanations. Much less effort has gone into deploying recent themes on globalization, international norms and institutions, and the role of democracy for the purpose of identifying nuclear patterns under particular global conditions, across regions and varying domestic circumstances.

This chapter's overview of conceptual approaches is geared to improve our understanding of nuclear trajectories in East Asia and the Middle East over the past three decades. The two regions not only offer important conceptual and methodological opportunities for this dedicated comparison, as outlined in chapter 1, but also account for nine of the fourteen most-studied nuclear aspirants since the NPT's inception in 1968. Understanding these two regions' experience with denuclearization is therefore essential for assessing the broader phenomenon. Notwithstanding its special focus on these two regions, the chapter includes the remaining cases in its overall appraisal of different theoretical strands. I begin with neorealism, which some consider the standard explanation for why states seek nuclear weapons. Next I focus on neoliberal-institutionalism and its premise that states create and join institutions such as the NPT on the basis of rational cost-benefit calculations. A third approach, rooted in constructivism, examines the emergence and diffusion of anti-nuclear acquisition norms that presumably affected state behavior, as well as competing norms that may have worked to promote nuclear proliferation. A fourth perspective explores potential links between democracy and nuclear outcomes. The fifth approach draws from the dense but understudied connections between domestic models of political survival and nuclear policies to propose alternative nuclear logics. The chapter's general purpose is fourfold: to clarify the theoretical foundations of each approach, summarize their main conceptual and empirical strengths and deficiencies, suggest an unorthodox logic underlying nuclear choices, and delineate the outstanding research agenda.

STRUCTURAL POWER—NEOREALISM

In a world lacking a recognized ultimate authority, international anarchy forces states to survive via self-help. As the organizing principle of neorealism, this zero-sum view expects states to strive to increase their power relative to others in a purely competitive international structure. In this "individualistic pursuit of security" (Jervis 1982) states take advantage of others' vulnerabilities, don't make more concessions than needed, and threaten to use force. The unintended consequence of this competition for security is a balance of power. In this view, domestic considerations, regime types, or personalities are irrelevant to nuclear decisions and processes. Nuclear weapons are considered to be well suited to secure survival by generating caution, rough equality, and clarity of relative power.[2] Neorealist interpretations of nuclear decisions were applied to some of the first nuclear weapons states, including the United States, the Soviet Union, and arguably China. France and Britain after World War II (two of five cases) were better explained by the search for prestige, grandeur, and great power status than by neorealism (Rosecrance 1964; May 1994).[3] Our focus here, however, is nuclear behavior under a different world-time characterized by fledgling multilateral institutions such as the NPT and a rapidly integrating global political economy since the 1960s. Nuclear aspirants such as Taiwan, Israel, and Pakistan were often cited as states with existential vulnerabilities to massive conventional attacks (Harkavy 1981; Dunn 1982; van Creveld 1993). Others, including Iran during its war with Iraq, were assumed to have sought nuclear weapons in response to their rivals' prior or prospective acquisition, in a pattern of "reactive proliferation."

Yet several acutely vulnerable states have not acquired nuclear weapons, nor have several states whose rivals had either already acquired them or were on that path. The many anomalies in these categories include Taiwan,

South Korea, Egypt, Japan, and countries in other regions, as well as too many "dogs that didn't bark" or states that faced analogous vulnerabilities but presumably didn't actively consider nuclear weapons, such as Vietnam, Jordan, Turkey, Saudi Arabia, Syria, Singapore, Chile, and many others.[4] Typical explanations for these anomalies invoke the role of alliances, which enable vulnerable states to renounce indigenous nuclear weapons in exchange for hegemonic protection. Coercion is another tool for powerful states to squash allies' nuclear aspirations. These may be important in explaining South Korea, Japan, and Taiwan to different degrees but hegemonic protection and coercion has had checkered effects in many other cases (Harkavy 1981; Dunn 1982). U.S. and Soviet commitments to client states (North Korea, Iraq, Israel, and Pakistan) did not lead these states to renounce nuclear weapons. Nor did the absence of security guarantees play any role in decisions by Egypt (1971), Libya (2003), South Africa, Argentina, or Brazil to reverse nuclear ambitions.[5] Indeed, if U.S. alliances told the tale, Britain and France would have arguably never gone nuclear (Rosecrance 1964). U.S. security guarantees do not account for most cases of nuclear reversal. Furthermore, U.S. coercion—short of war—failed to denuclearize non-allies such as North Korea, India, Iran, and Iraq for many decades. Waltz (2003:38) makes an even sharper case, arguing that "in the past half-century, no country has been able to prevent other countries from going nuclear if they were determined to do so." The empirical record thus suggests that neither hegemonic protection nor coercion seem necessary or sufficient for nuclear aspirants to forgo nuclear weapons.

Beyond these empirical inconsistencies, neorealism raises additional conceptual difficulties. First, the quintessential logic of survival assumed to operate in the nuclear realm trumps the notion that states can substitute self-help with external protection. Even robust formal U.S. alliances with Japan and South Korea raise perennial questions of commitment, which surfaced even in the context of NATO allies. Reliance on alliances is particularly incongruent with the logic of self-help where technical nuclear capabilities are high and as hegemonic commitments decline.[6] Both conditions applied to Japan, South Korea, and Taiwan, particularly following Nixon's Guam doctrine, when all three were weighing NPT ratification. U.S. commitments to Taiwan, particularly following U.S.-China normalization and abrogation of the Washington-Taipei Mutual Security Treaty, were certainly not comparable to those granted Japan and South Korea, yet Taiwan too renounced nuclear weapons. Second, experts disagree widely over thresholds of vulnerability that might lead states to opt for nuclear weapons. This is unsurprising given inherent difficulties in defining power, relative power, balance of power, and hence the nature and extent of states' "exposure" (Haas 1953). Focusing on "threats" rather than power (Walt 1987) raises the question of who defines threats, a question that often leads into domestic politics. Nuclear aspirants like Taiwan and Israel are often considered more clear-cut instances of extreme vulnerability than Libya (or Argentina, Brazil, or South Africa), who nonetheless pursued nuclear weapons. Yet given anarchy, the logic of self-help, elusive thresholds of vulnerability, and the unilateral pursuit of security, why have more states not sought nuclear weapons? Third, a neorealist logic is inconclusive, open ended, and, despite its prima facie simplicity, less parsimonious than often assumed.[7] Different states adopted contrasting portfolios under comparable circumstances regarding power balances. Furthermore, single states changed nuclear policies over time—toward or away from nuclearization—even as external security considerations remained unchanged.

The logic of self-help clearly points to wide-ranging options. Consider the menu of means it finds suitable for addressing intense security vulnerabilities: straightforward acquisition and testing of nuclear weapons (Pakistan), hegemonic guarantees in lieu of indigenous nuclear weapons (Japan, South Korea), ambiguous nuclear stances outside the NPT (Israel), formal NPT membership cum flagrant violations of its principles (Iraq, Libya, North Korea, Iran), and renunciation of nuclear weapons to avoid arms races (post-1970s Egypt). This last option has presumably been embraced by many others among the nearly 180 states that fulfilled NPT commitments largely in the absence of hegemonic guarantees. If self-help can drive states to such a wide array of nuclear choices—from straightforward acquisition to straightforward renunciation—its tenets are indeterminate, hardly a reliable guide to *anticipate* what states might actually do. Neorealism is thus afflicted with the problem of multifinality, suggesting many outcomes consistent with a particular value of one variable.[8] This raises the question of whether neorealist explanations are falsifiable, given that so many options can be made to fit vague notions of security maximization a posteriori, and given the tendency to explain away anomalies through mechanisms extraneous to self-help (Legro and Moravcsik 1999). Among neoclassical realists who have seriously addressed such deficiencies, Glaser (2000:256) acknowledged that "if external/rational models leave a state's options indeterminate, internal-sources models could be useful for understanding how states choose among the range of rational options."[9] This leads naturally to the possibility that *state* security has been overestimated—and *regime* security has been underestimated—as sources of nuclear behavior. Understanding regime security requires domestic theories of international behavior.

Summing up, security predicaments and existential vulnerabilities are certainly not figments of neorealist imagination. They have a natural prima facie appeal, and may explain some cases reasonably well, if incompletely, as the empirical chapters suggest. At issue is not the theory's valuable insights but their unquestioned acceptance as the driving force of all nuclear decisions despite significant shortcomings: too many anomalies of insecure states forgoing nuclear weapons (Betts 2000); the reality of an overwhelming majority of states renouncing them despite uncertainty, anarchy and self-help; elastic and subjective definitions of self-help, vulnerability, and power itself; inconclusive, open-ended operational implications of self-help for nuclear behavior; hegemonic protection as neither necessary nor sufficient for nuclear abstention; overestimation of "state" at the expense of "regime security"; and concerns with falsifiability. While noting the simplicity and elegance of neorealism, Schweller (2006) acknowledges that they come "at the expense of its explanatory and predictive accuracy, that is, its empirical fit. . . . States confronted by similar threats and opportunities may not respond in the same way or with the same degree of effectiveness." Similarly, Ogilvie-White (1996:3) argued that neorealism "can only explain some of the dynamics of nuclear proliferation, leading to a distorted and over-simplified view of nuclear decision-making and nuclear behavior." Some of these shortcomings are evident in explaining diverse nuclear paths in East Asia and the Middle East.

First, both regions shared hierarchic and multipolar power distributions, which should have led to *similar* and *nuclearized* outcomes in both cases since the 1960s. Yet the Middle East evolved toward nuclearization whereas East Asia, except North Korea, did not. Multipolarity, a presumed engine of nuclearization (Mearsheimer 1990), yielded such a result only in one region. Both the continuity of these outcomes for over thirty years, as well as any changes in these long-term trends—such as a possible nuclearization of East Asia—would have to be explained by relative power considerations to remain consistent within a neorealist framework. Second, both regions lacked robust and symmetric distributions of nuclear capabilities, yet each evolved in entirely different directions. Third, some states afflicted with intense vulnerabilities renounced nuclear weapons (Egypt, Japan, South Korea, Taiwan, Jordan, and others). U.S. commitments to East Asian cases, though important in addressing their vulnerability, were far from absolute, complete, unlimited, irreversible, or unconditional in ways that put security concerns to rest particularly in a neorealist world. They were most fragile for Taiwan. U.S. commitments to Iran's Shah and Israel (or Pakistan) puzzlingly did not have the same effect. Neither did Soviet and Chinese commitments to North Korea. No comparable commitments existed for Egypt and Jordan (or Argentina, Brazil, and South Africa), hence these cannot account for their denuclearization. Other insecure states denuclearized without hegemonic commitments. This checkered pattern requires a theory of domestic politics capable of explaining relative receptivity to the kind of alliances that facilitate denuclearization. Fourth, states with lower existential threats than

Egypt or Jordan (Libya, arguably Algeria, and 1970s Iraq) coveted nuclear weapons. Fifth, changes in East Asia's power distribution in the 1990s (China's rise, Soviet collapse, Japan's decline, growing China-U.S. and Japan-China competition) did not alter the region's nuclear trajectory. Disagreements on the very nature of power distribution in East Asia at the turn of the century (bipolar, hegemonic, multipolar?) and their implications for instability hardly provide a solid foundation for predicting nuclear outcomes (Ikenberry and Mastanduno 2003). These problems warn against overestimation of power balancing as a source of nuclear behavior and encourage efforts to develop more complete understandings of nuclear aspirants. As Rosecrance (1966:35) argues, "nuclear weapons, then, may not be valuable for states seeking to improve or maintain a material international position."

NEOLIBERAL INSTITUTIONALISM

Rationalist (neoliberal) institutionalism assumes that states advance their interests through international institutions that manage growing interdependence, overcome collective action problems, reduce uncertainty, lower transaction costs that impede cooperation, enhance information about preferences and behavior, monitor compliance, detect defections, increase opportunities for cooperation, reduce the costs of retaliation, facilitate issue-linkages, and provide focal points or salient solutions (North 1981; Keohane 1984; Lipson 1984; Gourevitch 1999). Institutions constrain states' behavior and can change strategies and beliefs over outcomes. States join institutions because they would be worse off without them. Significantly, institutions have emerged even where egoistic pursuits of self-interest would have questioned their value, such as in nonproliferation. As Nye (1988) argued, "That most states adhere to a regime [NPT] in which they foreswear the right to use the ultimate form of self-help in technological terms is quite an extraordinary situation." Contra neorealist tenets, neoliberalism foresees situations where joining institutions is less costly than unilateral pursuits of security. In particular, the NPT presumably enables an escape from "prisoner's dilemmas" or incentives to defect, by reassuring states through mutual scrutiny.

The NPT has been the core of a regime—nested institutions, treaties, and agreements including the International Atomic Energy Agency (IAEA) and the Nuclear Suppliers Group—preventing the spread of nuclear weapons.[10] Its centerpiece is a "grand bargain" epitomizing the notion that institutions facilitate issue-linkages: the first five acknowledged nuclear-weapons-states (NWS) commit to advance nuclear disarmament (Article VI); all other states renounce nuclear weapons in exchange for the "inalienable right" to develop civilian nuclear energy (Article IV). Members agree not to transfer nuclear weapons to non-nuclear weapon states, not to produce them (unless they already had them by 1967), or export nuclear materials without safeguards. The IAEA was entrusted with monitoring these commitments through inspections designed to detect diversions from facilities declared by host states. "Full-scope-safeguards" required placing all present and future facilities under IAEA oversight. Traditional safeguards typically avoided "asking too many questions" and focused on only one of five potential paths to weapons (Bunn 2004). They could not prevent states a priori from removing weapons-grade material from safeguarded facilities and could detect diversion only a posteriori. Article X acknowledged the right to withdraw from the NPT with three months' advance notification, which North Korea exercised and Iran has threatened to invoke.

Export controls tightened over the years as the London Suppliers Group agreed on a code of conduct (1977) restraining transfers of sensitive technologies—uranium enrichment and waste reprocessing—suitable for weapons-grade materials. Only in 1992, following the discovery of Iraq's pre-1990 clandestine efforts, the group imposed full-scope safeguards on recipients and covered dual-use items. Some developing countries regarded the London "Club" as a cartel preserving technological and commercial monopoly. The Missile Technology Control Regime (MTCR) emerged to control exports of nuclear-capable missiles. The 1990s marked some successes with formal NPT accessions by South Africa, Ukraine, Belarus, Kazakhstan, Argentina, Brazil, France, and China; Program 93+2 (1992) enhancing IAEA prerogatives to conduct "special inspections" of undeclared sites based on all available intelligence; and the NPT's indefinite extension (1995). In 1996, NWS and Israel (but not India, Pakistan, or North Korea) among 175 signatories signed the Comprehensive Test Ban Treaty (CTBT) prohibiting nuclear tests, although the United States, China, Israel, and others have failed to ratify it, obstructing the treaty's entry into effect. A Southeast Asian NWFZ entered into force (1997), joining the existing treaties of Antarctica, Tlatelolco, and Rarotonga. An Additional Protocol (1997) required NPT members to go beyond full-scope safeguards and submit declarations of all past, present, or future nuclear-related activities, peaceful or otherwise, whether or not nuclear materials were involved. IAEA inspectors were to be granted access to any nuclear-related facility, including educational or military. In 2004 U.N. Security Council (UNSC) Resolution 1540 required members to enforce nonproliferation through national legislation. By 2005, 102 members had signed the Additional Protocol and sixty-two of them had entered into force (see www.iaea.org).

Despite these accomplishments, debates over the IAEA's ability to enhance information and monitor compliance raged after failure to detect

Iraq's weapons program prior to 1991, Iran's alleged violations since the 1980s, and Libya's program.[11] The IAEA did detect North Korea's reprocessing at Yongbyong and U.N. weapons inspectors accurately assessed UNSCOM's dismantling of Saddam's program after 1991 (which followed the first Gulf war rather than routine inspections). Yet the problem of clandestine technology and material transfers from first- or second-tier nuclear suppliers, converging on the A. Q. Khan network, poses strong challenges to supply-side efforts, which are the core of the NPR (Braun and Chyba 2004). Additionally, NWS have failed to comply with Article VI, which calls upon them to reduce nuclear arsenals and move toward disarmament. The Indian and Pakistani 1998 tests, including the mild international reaction to them, provided another blow to the regime as did a subsequent U.S. agreement to supply India with nuclear technology (Perkovich et al. 2004) and U.S. plans for bunker-busting nuclear weapons. Finally, political barriers have precluded effective UNSC collective action against violators for many years, with moderate successes on North Korea and Iran in early 2006 but much less impressive in the aftermath of North Korea's nuclear test and Iran's continued defiance.

In sum, neoliberalism offers an elegant model for why states cooperate through institutions even when it implies renouncing nuclear weapons. The NPR enhanced information about preferences and behavior by forcing states to debate whether or not to sign and ratify the NPT. Subsequent compliance patterns clarified preferences and behavior further. IAEA monitoring arguably raised the costs of clandestine technology acquisition—an important institutional success—and reduced uncertainty relative to a world of over 180 states without such institutions (uncertainty can never be completely eliminated). NPT Review Conferences, UNSC resolutions, and related NGO activities arguably changed the context against which states formulated decisions regarding nuclear weapons. Meetings and interaction in the broader NPR context increased opportunities for cooperation and offered focal points such as the Additional Protocol, the NPT's indefinite extension, and the CTBT. NPT membership reached 188 states. More countries ratified the NPT than any other arms-control and disarmament agreement.[12] The 2005 Nobel Peace Prize awarded to Secretary General El-Baradei and the IAEA signaled efforts to strengthen the NPR.

This perspective, however, also suffers from inadequacies in explaining states' nuclear decisions. First, it is quite difficult to research and document all states' cost-benefit calculations underlying NPT creation, and to confirm that benefits exceeded transaction costs entailed in negotiation and enforcement for each case. Such systematic empirical evidence has not yet been collected for most states. Only such evidence can validate the claim that states' cost-benefit calculations—rather than norms, great powers, or domestic politics—led to the NPT's conclusion in 1968 and to its continued existence. Second, nor is there evidence available to confirm that such calculations—rather than other variables—have underpinned compliance and led to the NPR's purported effects. Perhaps the very conditions that led states to sign and ratify the NPT, although not always directly observable (or measurable), can also explain subsequent compliance better than the NPT itself.[13] Third, states' calculations must also be able to explain challenges to the NPT (such as the New Agenda Coalition). These may be otherwise rooted in normative trends, including the potential decline of nuclear acquisition "taboos," or in shifting power relations among nuclear "have-nots." Separating states' interest-based motivations from principled claims is never easy, but at least some states have questioned the NPR on grounds other than their own right to acquire weapons. Fourth, states are presumed to create international institutions with Pareto-improving distributional effects that leave everybody better off. The lack of progress on Article VI weakens the assumption that the NPT embodies such features and may validate neorealist claims that power distribution—rather than reductions in transaction costs—explains the nature of the NPT. The nuclear "haves" have yet to disarm. Fifth, neoliberalism has treated *states* as monolithic abstractions without defining how state interests are constituted. Yet domestic actors underlying nuclear decisions are vital for understanding states' incentives to join, comply with, or reject institutions. Sixth, asserting that the NPR accounts for progressive denuclearization is inherently difficult, because its effects must be weighed relative to hypothetical histories (counterfactuals) without the NPT.[14] This alternative path of history is hard to know. Would more states have opted for nuclear weapons had the NPT never been concluded? Not necessarily, particularly if neorealist, constructivist, or domestic politics arguments could explain many cases that did not covet nuclear weapons. Leaders might have renounced such weapons for other normative or instrumental reasons. The NPT may not have been necessary for most states to renounce nuclear weapons.

These conceptual, methodological, and empirical difficulties, as with other perspectives, carry over onto the analysis of nuclear trajectories in our two regions. First, we still lack systematic evidence that most East Asian states drew a positive calculation about the merits of the NPT that, in turn, led them to renounce nuclear weapons. Normative, domestic, or hegemonic considerations might have driven them toward denuclearization, and as a corollary, to sign and abide by the NPT. It is plausible that these states would have remained non-nuclear even in the absence of the NPT. Second, North Korea and various Middle East cases drive home the need to understand the domestic sources of state behavior to explain compliance patterns. Third, regional security institutions (ASEAN Regional Forum, KEDO, and Six Party Talks) did not come into being until the 1990s in

East Asia, and thus cannot explain the pattern of avoiding nuclearization that unfolded since the 1970s. Nor can these weak institutions created in the 1990s account for denuclearized trajectories since that time. Fourth, regional institutions have not been sufficient to stem nuclearization in the Middle East. The world's oldest regional institution, the Arab League, played no role in enhancing conditions for regional denuclearization.[15] Arab-Israeli, inter-Arab, and Arab-Iranian rivalries rendered regional institutions—including the League and the 1990s Multilateral Middle East Peace Process—impotent.

NORMS AND CONSTRUCTIVISM

Constructivism studies institutions and norms as socialization processes in which a "logic of appropriateness," not interests or rational expectations, determines institutional purpose and shapes compliance (Checkel 1997; Finnemore and Sikkink 1998; March and Olsen 1998; Johnston 1999; Klotz and Lynch 2007). Institutions both reflect and imprint collective identities of member states, and change actors' beliefs and identities, thus altering their definition of interests. Institutions, in Barnett and Finnemore's (1999) formulation, "constitute and construct the social world." This approach requires the identification of constitutive rules or norms, and knowledge about the historical context and actors' common purposes, beliefs, shared meanings, and learning processes. In this view, the NPR stems from the evolution of an anti-nuclear weapons global norm embedded in the NPT, which both reflects and sustains this norm.[16] The NPR arguably socialized nuclear and non-nuclear bureaucracies, created new expectations and habits, and transformed states' beliefs about the ethical status of nuclear weapons, thereby leading to near-universal compliance. As Schelling (2000:1) suggested, nuclear weapons remain under a curse, ever more heavily, because they "are unique, and a large part of their uniqueness derives from their being *perceived* as unique. We call most of the other weapons *conventional*, in the sense of something that arises as if by compact, by agreement, by *convention*. It is an established convention that nuclear weapons are different." Yet Schelling (1976:80) also made clear that "the most severe inhibitions are undoubtedly those on the actual use of nuclear weapons, not on the possession of them."

Indeed, the proposition that the *acquisition* of nuclear weapons has been relegated to the dustbin of history is contested. Within two decades following Hiroshima and Nagasaki, the Soviet Union, China, France, and Britain acquired nuclear weapons and several states—including Sweden, Norway, Yugoslavia, and Switzerland—contemplated them, possibly until the 1960s. Pakistan, India, and Israel joined the list of NWS; the first two conducted very public nuclear tests in 1998 (India had also tested in 1974). At least another fifteen states sought to acquire weapons-related capabilities up until the 1990s and some even later, arguably including Iran. North Korea tested a nuclear weapon in 2006. Some maintain that several cases of nuclear "reversal" and "restraint" might simply be instances of "virtual" NWS, with unassembled capabilities that can quickly be converted into weapons.[17] Indeed Japan—the ultimate subject of normative explanations for nuclear weapons abstention—informed the International Court of Justice in 1994 that it did not necessarily consider the use of nuclear weapons to be illegal.[18] Finally, many believe that a nuclearized Iran could trigger nuclear dominoes in Saudi Arabia, Syria, Turkey, and Egypt, and that North Korea's nuclearization could drag Japan, South Korea, and Taiwan into nuclear weapon status (Campbell et al. 2004). Collectively, the examples included in this paragraph cast some doubt on the strength of a norm that arguably dissuades states from considering or acquiring nuclear weapons. Indeed, Secretary-General Kofi Annan pointed out that "the international community seems almost to be sleep walking" down a path where, after living a long time without nuclear weapons, states now feel compelled to revisit their logic.[19]

Furthermore, nuclear weapons continue to be included in strategic doctrines. The United States has only committed to "no first use" under certain conditions (vis-à-vis an NPT member, if the latter does not attack the United States or its allies). The Clinton administration's 1994 Nuclear Posture Review reaffirmed the role of nuclear weapons and did not rule out "first use." The 2002 review instructed the Department of Defense to draft contingency plans for using nuclear weapons even against non-nuclear states. A 2005 draft revising the 1995 doctrine on nuclear use ("Doctrine for Joint Nuclear Operations") contemplated reliance on nuclear weapons to preempt attacks by state or non-state actors and to destroy enemy stockpiles of nuclear, biological, or chemical weapons. Russia reversed Soviet no-first-use commitments. China committed to "no first use" as did India. Despite subsequent retractions, China's strategy became mired in doubt when the dean of National Defense University General Zhu Chenghu expressed in 2005 that China could launch a nuclear attack on "hundreds" of U.S. cities if the United States interfered militarily in a confrontation over Taiwan.[20] China's military planners perceive nuclear weapons as useful for enhancing international status and prestige, beyond their military utility (Johnston 1995). Pakistan has not embraced the "no first use" principle. President Chirac expressed that he would consider a nuclear response to a large *state-backed* terrorist strike against France.[21]

Over 76 percent of Russians polled in a survey were convinced that Russia needs nuclear weapons.[22] Overwhelming domestic support for nuclear weapons in India and Pakistan—over 1.4 billion of humanity—does not signal shame or contempt for nuclear weapons (Betts 1980:138). Nor does the world's meek response to the 1998 tests and their inclusion in strategic doctrines conjure up the image of revulsion that taboo violations would normally provoke.[23] Despite initial protests, neither country attracted universal opprobrium, severance of diplomatic relations, or extensive and lasting sanctions. The United States went on to promote close strategic relations with both and many other countries courted one or the other, particularly emerging India. Southeast Asian states rushed to invite India and Pakistan to partake in the ASEAN Regional Forum, the Treaty of Amity and Cooperation, and free-trade areas. The view that India and Pakistan, as Israel, have not violated international commitments (as non-NPT members) provides a partial explanation for this acquiescent response. Many countries, however, also continue to tolerate and woo NPT members widely suspected of coveting nuclear weapons, like Iran. Nor does the initial international reaction to North Korea's 2006 nuclear test seem like a powerful reaffirmation of anti-nuclear norms.

The absence of universal embrace does not invalidate a norm's existence. Indeed, the existence of "norm-violators" endows normative arguments with a refutable quality, protecting it from allegations of non-falsifiability or tautology. Yet this overview points to significant "anomalies" or departures from a non-acquisition norm, perhaps questioning the existence of a taboo beyond "non-use."[24] One observer goes further, noting that, at best, the past sixty years may suggest that a "nuclear taboo" may have taken root, but "it is not a taboo that prohibits use of nuclear means because atomic weapons are evil, because the possibility of nuclear warfare is inconceivable, or because the authority that decides on their deployment surely must be mad. The 'nuclear taboo' exists today because possessors of atomic weapons—and their general populations—condemn those who would consider their use on any but the most extreme occasion" (Gehring 2004). A 1996 advisory opinion of the International Court of Justice on the Legality of Nuclear Weapons appears to support this bounded notion of a nuclear-use taboo. The court's internal division is reflected in a decision that deemed the threat or use of nuclear weapons to "generally be contrary to the rules of international law" but also stipulated that "the Court cannot conclude definitively whether the threat or use of nuclear weapons would be lawful or unlawful in an extreme circumstance of self-defence, in which the very survival of a State would be at stake."[25] This ambiguity has parallels in religious positions. Pope John Paul II stated that "in current conditions 'deterrence' based on balance, certainly not as an end in itself but as a step on the way toward a progressive disarmament, may still be judged morally acceptable. Nonetheless, in order to ensure peace, it is indispensable not to be satisfied with this minimum, which is always susceptible to the real danger of explosion."[26] The U.S. Catholic Bishops' Pastoral Letter on

War and Peace echoes this view: "in concert with the evaluation provided by Pope John Paul II, we have arrived at a strictly conditional moral acceptance of deterrence. We cannot consider such a policy adequate as a long-term basis for peace." A comprehensive philosophical treatise on the morality of nuclear weapons informed by keen familiarity with nuclear deterrence and just war theory (Nye 1986) found nuclear deterrence to be "conditionally moral" while specifying what those conditions are. Finally, 2005 Nobel Peace laureate El-Baradei acknowledges that we face a reality where "nuclear weapons have continued to have a position of prominence as the currency of ultimate power" (CEW), a remark that questions the status of nuclear acquisition as a deeply ingrained taboo.

Indeed, competing normative perspectives view nuclear weapons as enormously attractive for their symbolic value and prestige (Husbands 1982; O'Neill 1999), particularly for states seeking the trappings of modernity through the "ultimate" weapon. This incentive is not new. As Rosecrance (1966:35) argued, "[P]restige may be the signal operative motivation for the acquisition of a nuclear capability." Nationalisms of all stripes and religious or ethnic-based identities have also been wielded as driving aspirations for nuclear weapons.[27] From this standpoint, prestige is not sought primarily as a deterrent but *in its own terms,* with possible ancillary security benefits. Prestige was considered the main driver of French, British, Indian, Egyptian, Argentine, and Brazilian pursuit of nuclear weapons.[28] Research along these lines is sometimes burdened by the reluctance of some decision-makers to acknowledge that prestige alone justifies gargantuan economic and political costs associated with developing weapons and delivery systems. Furthermore, the argument also requires a model of domestic politics that explains relative receptivity to nuclear weapons for prestige enhancement, without which it is unclear why many leaders renounce the same nuclear card that others consider a conduit to prestige.

Summing up, analyses of the ethics of nuclear weapons (inter alia Nye 1986; Hardin 1985) preceded the constructivist wave in international relations, but constructivism has enhanced sensitivity to the role of norms and identity in non-conventional weapons (Price 1997; Berger 1993; Tannenwald 2005; Freedman 2004). As with other approaches, however, important conceptual and methodological problems remain. First, studies must clarify potential differences between norms against nuclear weapons consideration and acquisition (the subject of this book), and nuclear use. Acquisition and use may be indivisible and morally equivalent in some accounts (Schell 1984), whereas for others, rooted in nuclear deterrence and rationality, acquisition *circumvents* use and is thus considered a "great force for peace."[29] Second, some trace the presumed devalued status of nuclear weapons as guarantors of security since the 1960s not to norms but to rational disincentives to acquire them because of high reputational, political, and economic costs, or hegemonic coercion.[30] Third, the concealed nature of some nuclear weapons programs may have partly resulted from efforts to avoid international opprobrium but also to prevent "reactive proliferation" or arms races with neighbors or other adverse effects. Rational "nuclear learning" (Nye 1987) may explain avoidance of overt nuclear postures. Fourth, empirical research on normative sources regarding nuclear acquisition or abstention since the 1960s is sparse, far from systematic, and often more concerned with global norms than with the domestic political processes that underpin them. Studies of Argentina, Brazil, Ukraine, Belarus, Kazakhstan, South Africa, Libya, Taiwan, South Korea, and even Japan often advance alternative, utilitarian explanations for denuclearization.[31] Fifth, norm-based studies must address the extent to which norms condemning the consideration, development, acquisition, or transfer of nuclear weapons have developed and evolved, what their origins might be, how they diffused (or failed to diffuse) from state to state, why they may have diffused to some states but not others, why they may have declined or atrophied, and how and when do we know that this has taken place (or what constitutes a critical mass of anomalies). Sixth, such studies must also explain, from ethnic, religious, and other identity viewpoints, sudden departures from a norm and the emergence of competing norms valuing nuclear weapons.

Some of these general points carry over into the application of constructivism to the focused comparison between East Asia and the Middle East. First, assuming that a universal norm against acquisition developed since the 1960s, the theory must explain extensive departures from the norm in the Middle East but not in East Asia. Second, normative explanations have been used to explain Japan's "nuclear allergy" but they compete with other accounts of the rationale for Japan's abstention, as reviewed in chapter 3. Third, no "nuclear allergy" accounts are available for Taiwan or South Korea that might explain their denuclearization. Fourth, normative accounts must also be able to explain regional anomalies such as North Korea. Fifth, "nuclear allergy" arguments collide head on with other norms which place high value on nuclear weapons in the Middle East. Indeed, since Hiroshima and Nagasaki, the Middle East has been the only region worldwide where WMD have been used.[32] No systematic effort to explain this relative normative receptivity to WMD is yet available. Sixth, abstention from nuclear weapons by Egypt, Jordan, and others in the Middle East questions the existence of normative convergence favoring nuclear weapons, at least at the decision-making level. Finally, important constructivist insights, whether pointing to a penchant for—or revulsion from—nuclear weapons must be complemented with a theory of domestic politics. Whose meanings, values, and interpretations are relevant to leaders' decisions to pursue or eschew nuclear weapons?

Who are the agents that promote one set of values or the other, and why? And, most important, what explains the relative receptivity to each path in different regions? Nuclear taboos may be the result of leaders' unwillingness to raise extremely divisive issues in particular domestic political contexts. This may be most particularly the case for two democracies—Japan and Israel—that nonetheless followed different paths.[33] Does democracy make a difference?

DEMOCRACY AND NUCLEAR POLICY

The democratic peace hypothesis—democracies do not wage wars against each other—has led to an explosion in research on whether and how democracies differ from autocracies in their international behavior.[34] The inclusion of the democracy variable in our conceptual survey is dictated not just by its centrality in recent academic scholarship but also by its presumed policy relevance since the 1990s. The Clinton administration made democratic enlargement a significant part of its foreign policy doctrine, and the Bush administration identified the "axis of evil" as both autocratic and nuclear-prone. Have autocracies been more prone to acquire nuclear weapons in the second nuclear age, and if so, why or why not?

There are several ways of extending theories about democracy and foreign policy to account for decisions favoring or renouncing nuclear weapons. According to Kantian conceptions of citizens' consent, the legitimacy granted by the domestic public of one liberal democracy to the elected representatives of another has a moderating effect away from violent solutions (Doyle 1983, 1986). Free speech, electoral cycles, and the public-policy process arguably restrain democratic leaders from pursuing extreme policies toward fellow democracies (Bueno de Mesquita and Lalman 1992; Russett and Oneal 2001). Since nuclear weapons symbolize most violent and extreme solutions, democracies may arguably shy away from acquiring nuclear capabilities to resolve disputes with fellow democracies. Furthermore, mutual and complementary efforts to minimize heavy losses in life and property may exist among citizens of liberal democracies.[35] Such restraint, however, might not operate when democracies face autocratic adversaries. First, as information-rich societies that maximize transparency, democracies are assumed to be less prone to violate international agreements than non-democracies. Yet the absence of transparency in autocracies trumps efforts to detect defections from international agreements. Second, high levels of open mutual communication among democracies facilitate international agreements among them (Keohane 1984). Autocracies' lower record of compliance with international agreements (Gaubatz 1996), however, arguably deters democracies

from concluding agreements—particularly on denuclearization—with autocracies. Third, stable democracies bind successive governments to international agreements, whereas successive coups in autocracies can lead to
reshuffles in their international commitments. Thus, facing problems of
uncertainty over ratification and implementation, liberal democracies are
strikingly mistrustful of non-liberal states (Doyle 1983) and possibly less
inclined to relinquish nuclear weapons when threatened by autocracies,
particularly if the latter are nuclear-armed. By contrast, stronger mutual
credibility and transparency among democracies arguably makes them
more hospitable to mutual nuclear disarmament and NWFZs that can
protect them from the risk of total devastation.

During the first nuclear age—not the focus of this book—three democracies acquired nuclear weapons (United States, France, Britain), which
may be construed as an effort to confront autocratic rivals (fascism first,
communism later), although the French and British cases are better explained by the search for prestige and grandeur (Rosecrance 1964). The
availability of a nuclear umbrella from a fellow democracy certainly did
not preclude the acquisition of a British and French deterrent.[36] Of all nuclear aspirants in the second nuclear age, no democracy appears to have
considered or acquired nuclear weapons for the purpose of deterring
other democracies. Some may debate whether India and Pakistan conform
to this generalization, since both shared democratic regimes at least part
of the time, but only India remained consistently democratic while developing nuclear weapons. In the Southern Cone the joint renewal of democracy in the 1980s in Argentina and Brazil overlapped with periods of
ambiguous nuclear programs until the early 1990s. The democratic administrations of Alfonsín and Sarney made joint declarations of peaceful
intentions and exchanged visits to sensitive facilities but did not abandon
opposition to the NPT, refusals to ratify Tlatelolco, rights to peaceful nuclear explosions, and development of delivery systems. As Carasales
(1995:42) points out, the words "inspection," "control," and "safeguarding" were absent in documents signed by democratic administrations in
the 1980s. Explicit denuclearization came about only as part of internationalizing models of political survival in the early 1990s, including the
first unequivocal renunciation of nuclear weapons, mutual verification and
inspection, the creation of an Agency for Accounting and Control of Nuclear Materials, and a Quadripartite Agreement with the IAEA, steps that
culminated in NPT ratification.

Beyond the democratic peace theory, other hypotheses addressing
regime type can be construed. First, many international regimes, including
the NPT, are subscribed to by various regime types. Second, NWFZs were
concluded in temporal and spatial domains with few democracies (Latin
America, the South Pacific, Africa, and Southeast Asia). Third, autocratic

leaders initiated unilateral denuclearization in Argentina, Brazil, Egypt, Kazakhstan, Belarus, Ukraine, South Korea, Taiwan, and other cases. Fourth, the vast majority of democracies and autocracies have abided by their NPT commitments. Although most *known* NPT violators were autocratic (Iraq, Iran, North Korea, and Libya), both democracies and autocracies have failed to abide by Article VI. Fifth, at least two out of three non-NPT states are long-standing democracies—India and Israel (Pakistan was democratic only intermittently)—although as non-members they can't be said to have violated the NPT. Sixth, democracies may approach the nuclear question under strong domestic taboos (Japan) or under widespread domestic support (India). Seventh, both democracies and autocracies acquired nuclear weapons, but democracies are considered less prone to transfer them to terrorist organizations (although private firms in democratic states have been involved in clandestine nuclear trade). Finally, nuclear behavior between democracies and autocracies may be more strongly affected by relative power, models of political survival, or norms unrelated to regime type.

Some of these hypotheses can be examined through the focused comparison between our two regions since 1968. First, during the period under consideration, only two democracies—Japan and Israel—considered or acquired nuclear weapons, and neither one did so while facing democratic adversaries. However, since both regions included mixed clusters of democratic and autocratic regimes, the democratic peace hypothesis may be less relevant in either case. One might have expected, however, a comparable mixed cluster to have led to similar trajectories regarding denuclearization. That was not the case. Second, Taiwan, South Korea, and several Southeast Asian states were autocracies when they denuclearized, and they largely abided by their NPT commitments. Third, most autocracies avoided nuclearization in both regions. Fourth, although most nuclear aspirants in the Middle East were autocracies (Iraq, Libya, Nasser's Egypt, Iran), some reversed course and abandoned nuclear weapons programs (Egypt, Libya). Autocracies have thus not exhibited uniform nuclear behavior in this region. Fifth, the only continuous Middle East democracy—Israel within 1967 borders—is attributed with robust nuclear capabilities, providing some support for the hypothesis that democracies, deeply distrustful of autocracies, may opt for nuclearization. This tendency may be even stronger for democracies surrounded by autocracies that threatened them with extinction at various points.[37] Yet Japan, and democratic South Korea and Taiwan since the late 1980s, did not develop nuclear weapons, despite North Korea's threats to reduce the first two to "a sea of fire" and China's threats to Taiwan. The U.S. alliance is often invoked to explain restraint in these three cases. Sixth, most NPT violators have been autocratic (Iraq, Libya, North Korea, and arguably Iran). Finally, although democracies and autocracies may respond differently to international sanctions and positive inducements, their behavior may also reflect different ties to the global political economy.

DOMESTIC POLITICS, MODELS OF POLITICAL SURVIVAL, AND NUCLEAR PREFERENCES

The bulk of the nonproliferation literature has paid inadequate attention to the effects of internationalization on domestic politics and nuclear policy. This gap is rather curious in light of an important tradition in international relations sensitive to the links between political-economy and security.[38] When mentioned, domestic political-economy considerations are included only as afterthoughts, rarely underpinned by a coherent framework. What makes this perplexing, as Bueno de Mesquita et al. (1993:311) argue, is that "even when a state has decided to acquire nuclear weapons it must create a domestic coalition to support the expense of a nuclear weapons program. Nations which cannot build such a coalition will be unable to build nuclear weapons. Determining which nations will choose to proliferate requires answering these questions." Furthermore, as Kahler (2002:81) argues, the discipline has fairly superseded efforts to black-box states, and understanding state behavior requires theoretically informed taxonomies of sub-state actors.

An effort in this conceptual direction begins with the premise that the kinds of ties linking leaders, groups, sectors, parties, institutions, and state agencies to international processes and institutions affect those actors' conceptions of interests.[39] Openness to global markets, capital, investments, and technology affects individuals and groups through changes in employment, incomes, returns on assets, prices of goods and services consumed, and the provision of public services (Nelson 1992). Internationalization affects different groups differently, some favorably (internationally competitive sectors or industries), others adversely (uncompetitive ones). Because the latter stand to lose from economic openness, at least temporarily, they have incentives to pressure governments for protection and import-substitution.[40] Export-intensive sectors and their suppliers, consumers of imported products, and large banks already involved in foreign activities tend to favor openness. Yet the economic and political impact of internationalization is far more complex and contingent on many factors, mediated by the institutional context, how actors predict potential gains and losses, and which coalitions leaders are able to logroll (Gourevitch 1978, 1986; Keohane and Milner 1996). This political landscape enables some trade-offs regarding nuclear decisions but not others. For example, actors seeking access to international markets, capital, investments, and technology fear potential losses accruing from leaders' violation or defiance of NPT commitments, which invite possible sanctions. Actors interested in importing highly sophisticated computers or dual-use equipment can be adversely affected if suppliers restrict exports. International sanctions can deprive domestic actors of many goods and services, including some that might be unrelated to nuclear programs.[41] Indeed, the potential threat of sanctions can be sufficient to limit investments and other economic exchange. Conversely, sanctions and isolation can strengthen domestic monopolies and state agencies that manage production and distribution, as in Iraq, Iran, and North Korea. Such trade-offs between political-economy and nuclear policy draw together constituencies that might otherwise have paid little attention to their leaders' nuclear preferences, but grow more attentive once their own interests become entangled with nuclear decisions. Both democratic and autocratic leaders are arguably sensitive to potential responses of different constituencies to such decisions.

The effects of internationalization are not restricted to political-economy. They are also felt by groups, cultures, social movements, and political leaders who perceive internationalization and crude market forces as threatening their values or identities. These movements appeal to communal "organic" values, often appropriate long-standing critiques of international capitalism as purely harmful, and they regard international ("Western") institutions as mere extensions of that system. Others foresee positive influences from the growing authority of international institutions in human, minority, and women's rights and other protections sought by IGOs and NGOs (Keck and Sikkink 1998; Finnemore and Sikkink 1999). Different groups and "norm entrepreneurs" consequently develop varying positions toward global regimes, including the NPR, the presumed right to acquire nuclear technology for energy purposes, and the consequences of NPT compliance or defiance. Political leaders understand the mobilizing capacity of prevailing norms, identity concepts, and historical myths no less than the mobilizing capacity of promises and myths about global markets.

While brokering supportive coalitions, leaders embrace models of political survival suitable to the state and societal constituencies that they seek to attract. Different models have different implications for nuclear weapons. Three ideal-typical models capture the essence in a far more diverse empirical variety: internationalizing, inward-oriented, and compromise-hybrid. Inward-looking leaders adopt models that resist integration into the global political economy through extensive trade protection, import-substitution, and state entrepreneurship to shield favored constituencies, including uncompetitive and protected industries, the associated military-industrial complex, civic-nationalists, ethnic-religious groups, and state bureaucracies threatened by internationalization, underemployed intelligentsia, and scientists and technologists highly dependent on state subsidies and military procurement. These coalitions reject economic reforms and conditions imposed by international institutions such as the IMF, WTO, and the World Bank, and they scorn international regimes portrayed as Western creations that curtail national sovereignty. The political profile and policies of various Middle East countries have approached many of these characteristics.

This model's affinity with nuclear weapons as ultimate technological and political tools stems from three main rationales. First, nuclear weapons programs enable the construction of a dense scientific, technological, industrial, military, and bureaucratic complex that can dwarf other economic endeavors—state and private—and attracts additional constituencies that have vested interests or values in that complex.[42] Second, the complex can operate autonomously, without formal budgetary oversight, sometimes even under democratic rule (Sagan 2003). Third, the complex's actual or imaginary output ("the bomb") is a powerful source of myths ripe for exploitation by inward-oriented leaders for domestic as much as external purposes, as Saddam Hussein and his lieutenants, Mu'ammar Qadhafi, and various Iranian leaders unabashedly admitted (see chapters 7, 8, and 10). From Argentina under Perón to Pakistan, North Korea, and the Middle East, leaders have explicitly wielded nuclear myths of invincibility and modernity to boost domestic appeal (Lavoy 1993). The natural side effects of this penchant for military-industrial complexes and inward-oriented economic policies are regional insecurity and competition, which, in a boomerang effect, strengthen the rationale for such complexes. By contrast, cooperative regional policies would thwart military expenditures and protection of state and private enterprises in the name of security, and the ability to manipulate nationalist, ethnic, and religious mythmaking as political currencies. Thus, inward-looking political survival entails policies that are mutually enhancing or synergistic across domestic, regional, and global levels. *Nuclear aspirants are more likely to emerge from domestic political landscapes dominated by inward-oriented coalitions than from their alternatives.*[43]

In contrast, leaders who stake their political survival on economic growth and internationalization advance policies of economic reform and export-led industrialization. This path requires expanding private economic activities and foreign investment, controlling military expenditures, reducing barriers to trade, and abiding by international institutions that validate and promote those choices. These leaders seek allies among export-intensive sectors and firms, highly skilled labor in competitive industries or firms, mobile capital, professionals oriented toward an open global economic and knowledge/technology system, consumers of imported products, ethnic and religious groups thriving under openness, and state bureaucracies steering economic reform. Over time successful economic growth yields resources that can be used to compensate groups and institutions that might be adversely affected by increased openness. Internationalizing models of political survival require macroeconomic and political stability, which reduces uncertainty, encourages savings, and enhances domestic and foreign investment. These are well served by cooperative, stable, and nonviolent regional environments that minimize resource mobilization for potential military conflict. Regional cooperation undercuts inward-oriented beneficiaries of state rents in the military-industrial complex and circumvents oversized, unproductive, and inflation-inducing military investments that drain budgets under the cloak of "national security." Stable and less militarized regional environments also send positive signals to the global political economy, minimize risk, enable foreign investment, decrease the likelihood of sanctions, reinforce ties to international institutions, and enhance countries' reputations as credible members of the international community. The domestic, regional, and international dimensions of internationalizing policies are mutually enhancing or synergistic. *Despite significant differences among them, most East Asian leaders approximated this model, more so than any other industrializing region. North Korea is an important exception.*

Policies of nuclear assertion or ambiguity are expected to introduce tensions at all levels of internationalizing models. Nuclearization could damage efforts to boost competitiveness and global access to markets, technology, investments, foreign aid, and external political support for policies underpinning such models. These external resources help broaden domestic political backing for more open economies and for strengthening domestic institutions favoring reform. Internationalizing leaders thus are likely to devalue large-scale, ambiguous, or unbounded nuclear weapons programs, which deplete the domestic economy, detract from reform priorities, and revitalize opponents of global integration.[44] Denuclearization is more likely to enhance international access, diminish regional tensions, and help contain inward-oriented forces at home. As Keller (2003) suggests, the quest for nuclear weapons has often involved serious impediments for admission into the Western world: "If you wanted to join the party, you checked your nukes at the door."

A third model of political survival—a hybrid of the first two—emerges when leaders must build compromise-coalitions in societies deeply divided with respect to internationalization, economic reform, foreign investment, and the role of nationalism, sovereignty, and military power. Under such conditions, different partners to the coalition carve out state agencies under their control, sometimes excluding other agencies from any oversight of their own fiefdoms. The Islamic Republic of Iran has intermittently illustrated hybrid dynamics where one camp favors economic opening (*Baz-Sazi*, rebuilding), regional stability, and international normalization and the other resists all three. The sustained struggle between these camps explains Iran's schizoid foreign policy in the past two decades. Whereas reformers sought domestic change and external compromise, radicals nurtured a secret nuclear program, allegedly violating NPT commitments for over eighteen years. By 2004 these radical inward-looking forces, which controlled state enterprises, foundations (*bonyads*), and banks, and which were allied with the Revolutionary Guards and the legal system, grew stronger and got President Mahmoud Ahmadinejad elected in 2005. Although many Iranians are said to support the nuclear energy program—to which developing countries are entitled as long as they abide by their NPT commitments—wide domestic differences over the political, economic, and social merits of an Iranian nuclear bomb arguably remain, although such differences are hard to gauge in a tightly controlled state.

Three important considerations must be stressed in applying this framework to understanding nuclear choices. First, the three models are "ideal-types" (Weber 1949), not historical or "true" realities but conceptual constructs or limiting concepts against which real situations are compared.[45] Real world leaders and coalitions can exhibit profiles and policies that bestride different ideal-types, although some fall closer to either end of the spectrum, given their core domestic alliances and constituencies. Thus, most East Asian leaders—although to varying degrees—advanced political survival strategies emphasizing international markets, private entrepreneurship, literacy and education, land reforms, export incentives, and foreign and domestic investment (Sen 1999). Most Middle East leaders relied on different combinations of import-substitution, state entrepreneurship, oil rents, and diminished incentives to foreign investors, policies that preserved the domestic political order that kept them in power (Richards and Waterbury 1990). A second consideration highlights two constraints on leaders' ability to implement their models: (a) the relative political strength vis-à-vis that of their domestic competitors (the more challenged they are at home, the less able they are to advance their preferred objectives); (b) the nature and strength of models in neighboring states (isolated internationalizing leaders encircled by inward-looking ones are less able to realize their favored policies). Jordan and Lebanon at the height of Nasserite models in Egypt, Iraq, and Syria are examples of such dilemmas, as was Sadat's isolation upon inception of economic reform (*infitah*) and compatible regional and global strategies. Israel's Labor-led coalition and counterparts in Palestine, Jordan, and Egypt advanced economic and peace initiatives during the Oslo process, but these were defeated by powerful domestic and regional opponents of the "new (internationalizing) Middle East." Conversely, an isolated inward-oriented leader preserving an autarkic economy (*juche*) and "military first" (*songun*) policies in North Korea has faced other pressures and incentives from a surrounding internationalizing region. A third consideration relates to the institutional context within which models of political survival must be crafted: democratic versus autocratic, presidential versus parliamentary, and predatory versus developmental states, whether led by party, military, or religious authority. Developmental states led by military autocrats (South Korea in the 1960s) and predatory states led by religious figures (Iran post-1979) might have both been autocratic but they presented different challenges for advancing their respective models of political survival.

Preliminary qualitative and quantitative studies validate the need to pay greater attention to the links between the domestic politics of internationalization and security policies.[46] The connection between models of political survival and nuclear policies finds support in systematic observations across different regional security contexts, diverse associations with hegemonic powers, and over successive leaderships within the same state. First, every case of denuclearization entailed a domestic evolution toward internationalization. Of all nuclear aspirants in the past three decades, not one endorsed denuclearization—fully and effectively—under domestic regimes that shunned integration in the global political economy. Only leaders and ruling coalitions advancing their political survival through export-led industrialization undertook effective commitments to denuclearize (Japan, Taiwan, South Korea, Egypt under Sadat, South Africa, Brazil, and Argentina). Nuclear decisions were nested in a broader shift toward internationalization in economics and security. Second, where internationalizing leaders and coalitions became stronger politically, as in Japan, South Korea, and Taiwan, the departure from nuclear claims was maintained even as their security context deteriorated (as in the Korean peninsula and the Taiwan Straits, at various points). This is also illustrated by the timing of rolling back nuclear ambitions in Argentina under Menem, South Africa, Libya (see chapter 10), Algeria, and Spain's accession to the NPT preceding E.U. membership. Third, in situations where leaders and coalitions favoring internationalization were weaker, as was the case historically in Argentina and Brazil until the early 1990s, the more politically constrained they were in curbing nuclear programs. This may also have been the case in Iran and Pakistan. Fourth, most (albeit not all) defiant nuclear courses have been unmistakably embraced by autarkic or inward-oriented models, from Perón's Argentina to North Korea, Iraq, Iran, and pre-2003 Libya. Indonesia's Sukarno—suspected of coveting nuclear weapons—fits this model as well. Fifth, even advocates of internationalizing models may have to contend with a dangerous region where neighboring leaders endorse alternative economic and nuclear policies. This problem is less intractable in East Asia, where export-led industrialization spread from Japan to most neighboring countries (except North Korea), than in the Middle East.

Summing up these observations, *in a minimalist formulation, internationalizing models of political survival make the development of nuclear weapons less likely than inward-looking models. Inward-looking models approximate necessary if not sufficient conditions for nuclear weapons programs. Internationalizing models are not necessary but likely to be sufficient for denuclearization except under two circumstances: (a) when neighboring inward-looking regimes seek nuclear weapons (or other WMD); and (b) when nuclear weapons were acquired prior to the inception of internationalizing models.*[47] As suggested by prospect theory, eliminating existing weapons may be politically more costly.[48] Furthermore, incentives from internationalization operate more forcefully at early stages of nuclear weapons development. These propositions find support in East Asia and the Middle East since the 1970s. First, Japan, Taiwan, and South Korea adopted internationalizing models receptive to denuclearization via alliances and hegemonic commitments during deliberative or incipient stages of nuclear weapons consideration. Internationalizing models and alliances were mutually enabling. The Southeast Asian "tigers" (including Singapore, afflicted with security dilemmas) avoided nuclear weapons despite inferior or no hegemonic commitments. Second, only models advancing autarky—such as North Korea (and China in the 1950s–1960s)—developed nuclear weapons in East Asia since the 1970s. Third, all nuclear programs in the Middle East were advanced by leaders and ruling coalitions steering import-substitution and relatively closed economies, some in conjunction with radical nationalist or religious agendas (Iraq, Libya, Egypt in the 1960s, Iran, and Israel in the 1950s–1960s fall under one or both categories). Fourth, the considerable strength of inward-looking models in the Middle East fueled Arab-Israeli, inter-Arab, and Arab-Iranian nuclear competition, raising significant barriers for internationalizing models that might have otherwise preferred denuclearization. Fledgling internationalizing coalitions nurtured the Oslo and Multilateral Middle East Peace processes during a brief interlude in the 1990s. The prospects for an eventual NWFZ—higher at that time than any time before or since—were overwhelmed by weighty inward-oriented forces within the region.

In sum, the relationship between domestic models of political survival and nuclear policies gains support from different regions, is analytically indispensable, and should be integral to explanations of denuclearization. As noted earlier, research on this approach is burdened in ways that other approaches are not. Leaders are far more likely to cast their decisions favoring or rejecting nuclear weapons as "reasons of state," invoking national security, incentives related to international institutions, and normative considerations (for or against such weapons) rather than ulterior domestic political motivations. Hence, available historical sources are likely to document "reasons of state," or norms, more frequently and thoroughly, loading the evidentiary dice against crude justifications of domestic politics. Leaders' reluctance to acknowledge political survival as motives for their behavior more generally, *but in the realm of nuclear weapons most particularly,* makes this an arena least conducive to finding corroborative evidence for this argument. Thus, even partial substantiation uncovering an important role for domestic considerations in this "unfriendly" terrain gains particular significance. In other words, some may argue that the threshold for gaining confidence in this argument should arguably be lower than for theories advantaged by the imperative to wield "reasons of state" as justifications for nuclear choices and by the special place of nuclear weapons in national security. And yet, both the aggregate observations in previous paragraphs, and the empirical probes in parts 3 and 4, strengthen our confidence that models of political survival and nuclear policies are not merely loosely associated but joined at the hip.

This approach is not without shortcomings, as will be evident throughout the chapters that follow. First, some cases compatible with political survival arguments can also be explained by neorealist, institutionalist, or normative considerations. Others cannot. I address the issue of complementarity, compatibility, subsidiarity, and inconsistency with other explanations in this chapter's conclusions. Second, the propositions are probabilistic, as are most statements in the social sciences. Internationalizing leaders may embrace nuclear weapons;[49] inward-oriented leaders may decide to abandon them. Both instances would prove the propositions refutable (i.e., they can be contradicted empirically), a healthy attribute provided that anomalies do not overwhelm corroborations. I explore these possibilities in chapter 12. Third, the propositions are bounded, as noted in chapter 1, with respect to conditions of necessity and sufficiency in developing nuclear weapons, the incidence of compatible models in the region, and temporal sequences in the acquisition of nuclear weapons. These scope conditions imply that it may be far more costly politically to eliminate existing weapons than programs in that pathway; and that the incentives of a global political economy may operate more forcefully at earlier stages in the inception of internationalizing models and early stages of consideration of nuclear weapons.

Conclusion

This chapter examined potential explanations for nuclear decisions in the second nuclear age, ranging from security predicaments, to the role of norms, international institutions, democracy, and domestic political survival models. As a critical overview, it highlighted both these theories' contributions and shortcomings, and explored their applicability to explaining nuclear trajectories in East Asia and the Middle East. This section distills some conclusions that might guide a future research agenda.

Structural realism directs our attention to balance-of-power mechanisms as driving the acquisition of nuclear weapons. These are undoubtedly critical considerations under anarchic international conditions that require states to engage in "self-help." Yet the many operational corollaries of self-help lead us back to the place we started: Why do some states cope with threats to their existence through nuclear weapons whereas others don't? Self-help is underdetermining or afflicted with the problem of multifinality, where various behavioral possibilities or outcomes—from seeking to renouncing nuclear weapons—are consistent with its premises of alleviating existential vulnerabilities. This problem precludes a priori inferences about which logics will prevail in particular cases. Furthermore, several acutely vulnerable states, including some whose rivals had already acquired or were developing nuclear weapons, did not respond in kind, such as Egypt, Vietnam, Taiwan, South Korea, Japan, Jordan, Turkey, Singapore, arguably Saudi Arabia, and many others in various regions. By contrast, states at much lower levels of vulnerability in balance-of-power terms did consider or embrace nuclear weapons programs, including Libya, South Africa, Argentina, and Brazil, among others. Hegemonic protection presumably obviated the need for nuclear weapons in Japan, South Korea, and Taiwan but not in several other cases: North Korea, Iraq, Israel, Iran under the Shah, and Pakistan (or Britain and France!), among others. Nor did security guarantees play any role in decisions by Egypt, Libya, South Africa, Argentina, or Brazil to reverse nuclear ambitions. U.S. coercion—short of war—failed to denuclearize non-allies such as North Korea, India, Iran, and Iraq for many decades. The record thus suggests that neither hegemonic protection nor coercion seem necessary or sufficient for nuclear aspirants to relinquish nuclear weapons. Indeed, as will become evident in part 2, hegemonic protection alone provides an incomplete account even for Japan, South Korea, and Taiwan, requiring an understanding of the domestic political conditions that made them more receptive to external protection and persuasion than others. In sum, a structural realist research agenda probing into nuclear behavior must do the following:

- cast the argument precisely and in falsifiable terms
- specify further the conditions under which hegemonic guarantees account for nuclear outcomes
- explain variation in nuclear behavior independently of domestic or auxiliary considerations extraneous to structural power

Neoliberal institutionalism provides a window into an important dimension weighing on nuclear decisions since the NPT was concluded in 1968. After all, the overwhelming majority of states has come to abrogate the right to acquire nuclear weapons by ratifying the NPT. However, there is no systematic empirical evidence that the NPT, rather than other external or domestic considerations of individual states, has driven decisions for or against nuclear weapons. The NPT may have been as important as, or perhaps even more so than hegemonic coercion but future research must validate this claim with systematic empirical evidence. Undoubtedly the NPT compelled states to make decisions (to sign/ratify/extend the NPT or abstain from all three). Those decisions, however, might have derived from prior nuclear choices, undertaken for normative, security-related, or domestic considerations. The very conditions that led states to sign and ratify the NPT, even if not always directly observable, can also explain subsequent compliance better than the NPT itself. Additional research can help disentangle these effects. Furthermore, institutional approaches must be able to explain different patterns of compliance, given that NPT violations have been concentrated in the Middle East, except for North Korea. Such approaches must also avoid state-centric perspectives, which are not as useful to decode variance in compliance across states and regions, in favor of a better understanding of domestic conditions. Finally, counterfactual analysis may help assess the claim that there would have been more nuclear aspirants in both regions had the NPT not existed. In sum, a neoliberal institutionalist research agenda for advancing understanding of nuclear behavior must do the following:

- undertake systematic studies able to validate the premise that state-level rational calculations accounted for progressive denuclearization and NPT-compliance, independently of normative or relative power considerations
- explain what has changed in those state-level calculations that may clarify the regime's alleged deterioration
- revisit the presumption of Pareto-optimality, that the NPT has left everybody better off, a presumption often challenged by some developing and developed countries
- conduct controlled counterfactual analysis of nuclear decisions in the hypothetical absence of the NPT

The presumed development of a nuclear taboo after Nagasaki, the subsequent inception of the NPT and its ability to attract a vast membership and widespread compliance, provide important foundations for exploring the role of norms in decisions to acquire or abstain from nuclear weapons. Yet further systematic research is required to establish unambiguously that most decisions to join and comply with the NPT can be traced to norms against acquisition. Indeed, several indicators suggest that the non-acquisition norm may not be universal at best, or that it faces potentially serious competitor norms at worst. Over thirty states actively considered nuclear weapons after Nagasaki (several after the NPT's conclusion), some violated NPT commitments; and the South Asian 1998 tests, North Korea's 2006 test, and Iran's nuclear defiance have been met with widespread moral indifference. The challenge from competing norms or beliefs ranges from those who endorse nuclear deterrence (i.e., acquisition) as a means to prevent nuclear use to those who advocate nuclear weapons for redemptive, identity-based values and purposes. Finally, norm-based accounts of WMD were often more concerned with the genesis of global norms than with the domestic political processes that explain their uneven diffusion. Constructivism may examine these issues without strictly dwelling on causal explanations (Kratochwil and Ruggie 1986) but could contribute to an improved understanding of nuclear behavior with a research agenda along the following lines:

- more systematic understandings of how the NPR has helped socialize some members into anti-acquisition norms but not others, and how it has done so independently of hegemonic coercion or rational nuclear learning[50]
- conceptual discrimination between norms against use and norms against acquisition (given some beliefs that acquisition *circumvents* use through deterrence)
- understanding the sources—and potential decline—of anti-acquisition norms, and their competition with norms advocating acquisition
- explaining clustered behavior toward or away from nuclearization in different regions, arguably under the shadow of the same international norm (or, why has the norm diffused selectively)
- complementing normative accounts of nuclear weapons acquisition or rejection with a theory of domestic politics (or what explains domestic receptivity to some norms but not others)

Democratic institutions have been found to affect foreign policy, particularly in relations with other democracies. But are democracies necessary for mutual commitments to denuclearize? The NPR and NWFZs came about through joint efforts by democracies and autocracies. Both regime types endorsed denuclearization, in some cases under weighty security predicaments, as in the cases of Taiwan and South Korea. Furthermore, the vast majority of democracies and autocracies have abided by NPT commitments. Have democracies (beyond the first-tier nuclear powers) been less prone to acquire nuclear weapons in the past four decades? India, Israel, and Japan have been the only sustained democracies among fourteen presumed nuclear aspirants since 1968. Democracies, however, have also been rare in most of the world over the same period. Furthermore, of three outstanding non-NPT members, two (India and Israel) are democracies (Pakistan only intermittently so). Most known NPT violators have been autocracies, but both regime types among nuclear weapons states have failed to make progress toward nuclear disarmament. Most states accounting for Middle East nuclearization have been autocracies, arguably influencing the nuclear choices of Israel as the sole democracy for many years. Yet three East Asian democracies facing intense security dilemmas (Japan and Taiwan and South Korea since the 1990) remained non-nuclear, an outcome often traced to extended deterrence. A research agenda integrating democratic theory in the analysis of nuclear aspirants might include the following:

- systematic studies on the relationship between regime type and the choice to acquire nuclear weapons, particularly when the regime already enjoys conventional military superiority
- a better understanding of the conditions under which democracies develop nuclear weapons when threatened by autocracies, under different relative power scenarios
- an in-depth inquiry into the extent to which there may be higher international toleration for nuclear weapons in the hands of democracies rather than autocracies

The relationship between domestic models of political survival and nuclear policies has been understudied despite its vital importance for understanding denuclearization. Its omission as a significant variable may have led to an overestimation of other causal variables and to potential spurious effects (Brady and Collier 2004). Its inclusion may improve our understanding of the actual effects of relative power, international norms, and institutions when interacting with domestic models (see later discussion). Leaders vary in their tolerance for domestic and international, political, and economic (including opportunity) costs entailed by nuclear weapons, an insight gleaned from the experience of an overwhelming number of nuclear aspirants. Internationalizing models make the development of nuclear weapons less likely than inward-looking models. The choices of all nine nuclear aspirants in the Middle East and East Asia are compatible with this hypothesis. Of the remaining five, Argentina, Brazil, and South Africa arguably corroborate the argument as well.[51] Internationalizing models are not necessary but likely to be sufficient for denuclearization except under two circumstances: (a) when neighboring inward-looking regimes seek nuclear weapons (or other WMD); and (b) when nuclear weapons were acquired prior to the inception of internationalizing models. Inward-oriented models are fairly close to providing necessary but not sufficient conditions for nuclear weapons programs. These hypotheses can be further refined in future research by taking the following steps:

- exploring the conditions under which internationalizing models may no longer provide sufficient conditions for continued denuclearization

(East Asia provides a good test case) and conditions that override the expectations that inward-looking models tend to provide necessary conditions

- specifying the precise domestic mechanisms that trigger reversals, particularly in cases where the same leaders who hitherto leaned on inward-looking models later shifted to internationalizing ones (could North Korea or Iran follow Libya?)
- improving our understanding of the relationship between democratization and internationalization. If internationalization requires democratization to sustain itself in the longer term, democracy could be found to have a positive but indirect effect on denuclearization.

This concluding section has thus far suggested ways in which each research program could remain true to its basic premises while advancing the common agenda of explaining nuclear choices. A more creative research path might be envisaged by relaxing some of those premises to accommodate complementary perspectives (March and Olsen 1998). For instance, one might hold a particular argument to be central but requiring auxiliary information from another. Structural realism often operates in this way implicitly, whereas neoclassical realism provides a more explicit incorporation of domestic conditions. A second possible analytical course may find one approach better suited to explain nuclear decisions at some points, whereas another approach may be better at explaining subsequent decisions. Efforts to avoid high costs of non-NPT membership may explain an initial decision to renounce nuclear weapons, but over time that consideration may be superseded by an evolving, now more engrained, normative commitment against acquisition. These and other possibilities could help us address the issue of equifinality, where many alternative causal paths appear to lead to the same outcome (George and Bennett 2005). Equifinality makes it harder to assess the causal weight and necessity of a given variable and leads to generalizations that are narrower or more contingent. Individual case studies may thus enable us to establish *whether* and *how* a variable mattered more than *by how much*. Collectively the nine cases included in this study can also reveal the extent to which the literature may have overstated some variables and understated others.

A domestic political survival account does not imply that nuclear weapons programs in every region have exactly the same political origins, although a remarkable proportion do. As argued, such accounts do not suggest that classical security considerations are irrelevant to nuclear postures. Rather, leaders and ruling coalitions interpret security issues through the prism of their own efforts to accumulate and retain power at home. Internationalizing leaders define economic growth and global access as crucial for advancing state security, rejecting nuclear weapons if the latter endanger those core objectives.[52] Conversely, inward-oriented leaders thrive by defining security as "self-help" while protecting and promoting constituencies that variously favor economic, political, strategic, religious, or cultural autonomy. Indigenous nuclear weapons are compatible with—albeit not necessarily a requirement of—such models. Put differently, domestic survival models may be seen as filters through which security is defined.[53] They thus provide a better handle on the operational implications of security predicaments than merely invoking "self-help." They help explain why security dilemmas were more intractable in some cases (Middle East) than others (East Asia), why some states ranked alliance higher than self-reliance (Japan, South Korea, Taiwan) or vice-versa (North Korea), why nuclear weapons programs surfaced where security considerations hardly justified them (Libya), and why such programs were obviated where one might have expected them (Egypt, Jordan, Turkey, among others). Without taking into account domestic political survival, the concept of relative power arguably fails to explain some cases, is incomplete in others, suffers from acute underdetermination, or competes with rival explanations in a domain (high security) where it would be expected to dominate without reservations. In sum, models of political survival avert the frequent overestimation of *state* security as a source of nuclear behavior, which often comes at the expense of underestimating *regime* security as a crucial driver of denuclearization. Parts 2 and 3 explore these dynamics in East Asia and the Middle East respectively.

PART TWO

East Asia:
Denuclearization as the Norm,
Nuclearization as the Anomaly

CHAPTER THREE

Japan

DURING WORLD WAR II (ca. late 1942) the Japanese army advanced an atomic weapons program—labeled *Ni-go Kenkyū* (NI) after its chief scientist, Nishina Yoshio, at its Tokyo Institute of Physical and Chemical Research (Riken). The navy, in furious competition, pursued its own program at Kyoto Imperial University under scientist Arakatsu Bunsaku. However, these programs—which requested uranium oxide from Germany and won strong support from Prime Minister Tōjō Hideki and the imperial princes—never came to fruition by war's end, partially due to inadequate technical, human, material, and industrial resources (Dower 1993; FASW). Following defeat in World War II, Japanese policymakers arguably faced successive external threats: possible Soviet invasion, blackmail, or nuclear attack; a nuclear-armed China (after 1964); a potentially unified and antagonistic Korean peninsula; potential interdiction of its vital sea lines; and a hostile nuclear North Korea.[1] Each of these threats could have led Japan to resort to indigenous nuclear weapons. Yet Japan signed the 1951 U.S.-Japan Mutual Security Treaty, which entered into force in 1952; the 1960 Treaty of Mutual Cooperation and Security; and a series of instruments that tied Japan's security to the U.S.-Japan alliance. Following the 1964 Chinese nuclear test, the 1965 Sato-Johnson communiqué reiterated the U.S. pledge to defend Japan against any outside aggression.

In 1968–70, under Prime Minister Sato Eisaku, the Cabinet Information Research Office asked experts to conduct a secret and unofficial study on the feasibility and desirability of nuclear weapons. This study, largely geared to deflate domestic pressures for nuclear weapons, concluded that *their domestic political and international diplomatic costs were too high* and that Japan's security would be far better advanced through political and economic efforts rather than a power-based approach (Kase 2001:58–59; Kurosawa 2004; Kamiya 2002–03; Hughes 2004:93). During the early 1970s, as NPT ratification was under consideration, the possibility that Japan might develop nuclear weapons remained a subject of extensive discussion. Much of the U.S. intelligence community, but not all, doubted that Japan would do so although by this time it had the industrial, scientific, financial, and technological resources to develop nuclear weapons if a political decision were made.[2] In 1976

Japan ratified the NPT, restating its Three Non-Nuclear Principles (*hikaku sangensoku*) not to possess, manufacture, or introduce nuclear weapons into Japan, enunciated by Premier Sato in 1967. Japan has remained a non-nuclear NPT member in good standing ever since. The Japan Defense Agency (JDA) conducted another study in 1995, reiterating the high costs of acquiring nuclear weapons. This nuclear evolution can be examined through competing and complementary perspectives analyzed in chapter 2.

STRUCTURAL POWER AND JAPAN'S DILEMMAS

Structural realism expects great powers like Japan to acquire nuclear weapons, particularly given the afore-mentioned strategic threats, its economic wherewithal, and abundant nuclear expertise.[3] Indeed, as early as 1957, Premier Kishi, Commerce and Industry minister during World War II, declared in the Diet that defensive nuclear weapons would not challenge Japan's Constitution.[4] Yet, Japan has not gone down that path, a fact that other versions of neorealism have traced to the U.S.-Japan alliance, which presumably obviated Japan's need for its own deterrent. Yet the reliability of the U.S. commitment has been a constant concern of Japanese policymakers, nuclear analysts, and the public at large. Furthermore, Japan did not even acknowledge an "alliance"—as opposed to a bilateral security treaty—until the 1980s, due to apprehension with nationalists on both the left (who called for the treaty's abrogation) and the right (who called for revisions). Concerns with the alliance's credibility reached a high point just as the NPT opened for signature and ratification in 1968. The July 1969 Nixon doctrine signaled greater U.S. disengagement in Asia, withdrawal of U.S. forces from Southeast Asia and South Korea, and greater burden-sharing by Asian allies. Nixon's 1971 visit to Beijing and the suspension of dollar convertibility into gold were announced without prior consultations with Japan despite their enormous ramifications for Japan's security. The Nixon shocks exacerbated Japan's perceived vulnerability, fueling persistent Japanese concern with evolving U.S.-China relations (Makoto 1978). This period was labeled the "nightmare of the Foreign Ministry" according to Sato's secretary Kusuda Minoru (cited in Tanaka and Murata 1995). Muramatsu Takeshi and others questioned U.S. ability to sustain its relative power worldwide and to protect Japan, concluding that Japan should arm itself with nuclear weapons jointly with the United States (Endicott 1975:6–7). Some pushed for enhanced autonomous defense production through progressive import-substitution of weapons systems (*kokusanka*). Others favored independent nuclear capabilities (a "free hand"), arguing that the United States would not risk a nuclear exchange with China or Russia to protect Japan (Akiyama 2003; Harrison 1996). Before becoming premier, Miyazawa Kiichi expressed in 1971 that "there is already a body of opinion in Japan which feels that dependence on the US nuclear umbrella is basically incompatible with our national sovereignty" and that the coming generations "may want to choose the lesser of two evils and opt to build their own umbrella . . . to be their own masters" (Harrison 1996:17–18).

Concerns with U.S. commitments never disappeared. When asked how he viewed the U.S. nuclear deterrent prior to Nixon's visit to China, Makoto Momoi, a former head of Japan's JDA Defense Research Institute, reportedly answered, "It's like a Bible. You may know every word in it, and believe it to be true, but can you really be sure of salvation?" In the aftermath of Nixon's trip to China, he replied to the same question as follows: "I think you can say that we've put the Bible away. It's something around the home, but the children don't read it any longer" (Ballard 1973). At the level of public opinion, two different surveys in 1969 (*Asahi*) and 1971 (*Yomiuri*) found that only about 30 percent of the public thought that the United States would defend Japan in case of emergency (Passin 1977:89). Former director of Japan's Ministry of Foreign Affairs (MOFA) Nuclear Energy Division, Kaneko Kumao (1996:8), stated that "assuming that Japan were to suffer a nuclear attack, the United States is highly unlikely to use its nuclear arms to defend Japan unless American forces in Japan were exposed to extreme danger." Premier Hosokawa Morihiro (1998:5) used the veiled threat of acquiring nuclear capabilities in order to ensure a U.S. commitment to extended deterrence: "It is in the interest of the United States, so long as it does not wish to see Japan withdraw from the NPT and develop its own nuclear deterrent, to maintain its alliance with Japan and continue to provide a nuclear umbrella." Only 49 percent of Japan's public felt confidence in U.S. commitments during the mid-1990s (Calder 1996:92). This perennial concern raises a fundamental problem for explanations of Japan's denuclearization that center on the alliance. In an anarchic world with no fool-proof security guarantees, why would a major power relinquish the ultimate guarantee? As one Japanese vice-admiral once put it, "The nuclear umbrella held by the U.S. must surely be useful, but for complete faith there is the nuclear umbrella opened by oneself" (Endicott 1975:63). The tension between self-reliant and alliance-reliant versions of neorealism is clear, although both stem from self-help considerations. Furthermore, a focus on strategic threats could have also led to the conclusion that Japan should *relinquish* nuclear weapons. At least four arguments along neorealist lines could point to non-nuclear solutions to Japan's power-balancing dilemmas.

The first, as we have seen, focuses on the U.S.-Japan alliance as a substitute for Japan's nuclear weapons, which would enable Japan to invest resources in the economic expansion that turned it into the second-largest economy worldwide. Yet problems of credibility and commitment question whether this option could be truly reconciled with undiluted premises of self-help. As Waltz (1993:66) argues, "The great powers of the world must expect to take care of themselves." Alliances create dilemmas of "abandonment" (failures to deliver, abrogating commitments) and "entrapment" (being dragged into conflicts that are more of an ally's priority than one's own, or *makikomare-ron*).[5] Alliances do not fundamentally resolve security dilemmas and give rise to alternative ones. Furthermore, if the alliance's strength mattered, the proclivity to develop nuclear weapons should decline as the perceived reliability of an ally's nuclear guarantee rises. However, relatively high levels of Japanese public support for the alliance—about 72 percent in 2003, up from 41 percent in 1969 and 50 percent in the 1990s—coincides with a perceived *weakening* of the so-called "nuclear allergy" (Hughes 2004:58). This might question a strong connection between the alliance's strength and Japan's openness to nuclear weapons or, at the very least, attenuates the alliance's role as the single driver of Japan's nuclear policy. The alliance was extremely important but must be seen through Japan's postwar domestic model, not as an end in itself. More on this later.

A second neorealist approach would reject the alliance regardless of its robustness and credibility. Self-help in this instance would deem nuclear weapons hazardous for Japan due to its small size, dense population, geographically concentrated industry, and close proximity to potentially hostile powers, all of which rendered it vulnerable to nuclear strikes. According to Kishida Junnosuke (1973), Japan's geographical liabilities and vulnerability to nuclear attack offset any advantages of nuclear weapons.[6] In an essay entitled "Heiwa no Daishō" (Compensation for Peace), Nagai Yōnosuke argued that a Gaullist autarkic nuclear deterrent would increase Japan's insecurity and vulnerability.[7] Some, particularly in opposition parties, regarded a non-nuclear status and equidistance from all nuclear powers as Japan's best option. A nuclear Japan, they feared, might trigger a nuclear South Korea (or unified Korea) and tensions with China and Russia, leaving Japan less secure than without nuclear weapons.[8] Countries interested in controlling Japan's industrial capabilities, others argued, would clearly not resort to nuclear weapons since they could potentially destroy Japan's industrial base (Imai 1975:25; Momoi 1978). Nuclear weapons were thus perceived to be unviable for Japan militarily, as the JDA's chief of the Defense Bureau declared in 1972, during the NPT ratification debate (Endicott 1975:94). Other views (Waltz 1993:69) counter such arguments with the rationale that territorial size is irrelevant and that invulnerability of second-strike delivery is the crucial consideration—not targets' dispersal—an issue that nuclear-armed submarines resolve.

A third neorealist variant focuses less on the extent to which the United States could or would supply security (i.e., its commitment to the alliance) and more on its supply of coercion (i.e., pressures to prevent Japan from going nuclear). This hegemonic explanation would be most persuasive if one could show that there was a *strong* demand for nuclear weapons from Japan, and that U.S. pressure succeeded in thwarting it. However, as we shall later see and despite periodic debates, Japan's domestic politics did not generate such demand. Sato may have conveyed to Ambassador Reischauer a personal preference for a nuclear Japan in December 1964 and may have expressed to President Johnson that if Communist China had nuclear weapons so should Japan. But he also added that he could mention that view only privately because his personal feelings were certainly not shared at home and the Japanese people felt that Japan should never possess such weapons.[9] Sato also conveyed to Dean Rusk that most Japanese felt their security rested with the alliance and that acquiring nuclear weapons "was not Japan's policy."[10] A pragmatist through and through, Sato made it his unequivocal objective to obtain Johnson's reassurance that Japan would be defended by nuclear means if necessary, a commitment that was not explicit in the bilateral treaty.[11] The Johnson-Sato communiqué fulfilled Sato's objective. In sum, this entire episode does not amount—by any stretch—to a strong demand for nuclear weapons that had to be met with a strong denial. Indeed, if Sato was as committed to a nuclear Japan—over and above other objectives—he might have pushed for it under the more receptive context of the Nixon administration. He did not.

At a January 1972 meeting with Sato, Nixon suggested that Japan faced an unacceptable choice either to develop "its own deterrent power however unpalatable vis-à-vis its neighbors, who are armed with nuclear weapons, or . . . [come] to an accommodation with them."[12] Sato replied that Japan's Diet had adopted a unanimous resolution on the Three Non-Nuclear Principles and therefore Japan had no recourse but to rely on the Mutual Security Treaty and the U.S. umbrella. Nixon also suggested that the United States was exerting no pressure on Japan to ratify the NPT and that, "*in fact, Japan might take its time, and thus keep any potential enemy concerned*" [emphasis added].[13] Nixon was reported to have immediately asked Sato to forget his preceding remark but insisted that Japan would be better off not telling its neighbors specifically what it would not do. Sato reportedly claimed later that Nixon "confused" him but U.S. diplomats subsequently "reassured" the Japanese that Nixon and Kissinger had been "misunderstood."[14] In any event, Sato's crucial objective at this point was the withdrawal of nuclear weapons from Okinawa, even while secretly agreeing to their return in an emergency. Okinawa's reversion to Japan had been Sato's foremost political purpose at home, one he was prepared to advance even by accepting formal adoption of the

Three Non-Nuclear Principles in exchange for the Diet's approval of his Okinawa agreement. I elaborate below on the domestic context against which these trade-offs were formulated.

On the U.S. side, Nixon may have signaled a possible forbearance regarding Japan's nuclearization. There were also scattered claims that Kissinger's National Security Council viewed Japan's own nuclearization as potentially helpful in dissipating concerns with U.S. nuclear weapons on Japanese soil.[15] It is difficult to assess how U.S. administrations might have responded to Japan's nuclearization.[16] The evidence suggests some U.S. ambivalence during the Nixon era, particularly in connection with U.S. efforts to enhance "burden-sharing." The same official that saw the need to dissuade Sato from pursuing nuclear weapons acknowledged that "we must recognize that Japanese domestic developments and international events, rather than U.S. desires, will be the prime determinant" of Japan's defense policies, and that the United States' "ability to influence the rate of Japan's defense expansion will continue to be marginal at best."[17] In the final analysis, it was reasonable for Japanese decision-makers to be concerned with potentially costly U.S. responses to a nuclear Japan. The declassified record, however, does not convey anything like a punishing hegemonic policy applied to counter a Japanese request at that time. In sum, there was neither demand for a Japanese deterrent nor supply of coercion.

A final neorealist variant could trace nuclear abstention to appropriate conventional capabilities (Nakagawa 1980). As Ryūkichi Imai (1975:25) argued, "If the country is concerned about its own military security, the alternative does not lie in seeking ways of nuclear armament. Military security for Japan is a matter of conventional defense." The National Defence Programme Outline of 1976 was designed to modernize air-defense and anti-submarine warfare (Sato 1982). While it is certainly the case that Japan evolved into the most sophisticated military force in East Asia, it lacked an independent military industrial base at the time of the NPT debates and even subsequently. Indeed, despite efforts by some strongly conservative politicians and some labor interests to advance kokusanka, Japan consciously avoided an autonomous military-industrial-complex for domestic reasons (Green 1995:78). Furthermore, plans for more expansive self-sufficient conventional weapons capabilities had *weakened* by the mid-1970s, when NPT ratification was highest on the agenda (Pempel 1998). Premier Miki Takeo introduced the 1 percent "ceiling" on defense expenditures in 1976, just as Japan ratified the NPT. Nor did Japan's constitution enable the buildup of strong conventional (offensive) deterrent forces independent of the United States. In any event, from an unalloyed neorealist standpoint, Japan's conventional forces and economic superiority over its rivals could not substitute for self-reliant nuclear weapons (Waltz 1993:69).

This overview suggests that competing injunctions can emanate from the same structural-power landscape: Japan should acquire nuclear weapons, should not acquire them, should rely on the U.S. nuclear umbrella, should not rely on it, should build extensive conventional capabilities as substitutes for nuclear weapons, could not rely on conventional deterrence, and so on (Makoto 1978). These various options drive home the open-ended nature of neorealism, where security dilemmas and self-help can lead to various, indeterminate solutions. Regardless of who holds decision-making authority, considerations of structural/relative power are presumed to drive decision-makers to *the* choice that maximizes a state's survival and integrity. Alas, such choice is often elusive and bears the marks of domestic considerations responding not merely to international power but also to international institutional constraints.

INTERNATIONAL INSTITUTIONS: FROM PROTRACTED NPT DEBATES TO FULL COMPLIANCE

Neoliberal-institutionalism assigns international regimes and institutions a significant role in influencing state decisions. In this view, Japan's choices would have been highly constrained by the conclusion of the NPT in 1968, particularly given overwhelming domestic consensus for a U.N.-oriented diplomacy. This orientation emerged from Japan's postwar search for reintegration into the international community, despite some reluctance regarding U.N.-centered multilateral security frameworks.[18] A persuasive institutionalist account would have to establish that—had the NPR not existed at the time—Japan's domestic politics would have yielded an alternative decision, that is, to develop nuclear weapons. The overview of the domestic context, described later in greater detail, does not support this contention. Indeed, Japan was privately studying the utility of nuclear weapons in the late 1960s and early 1970s even after signing the NPT, and the NPT itself had limited currency in Japan's domestic debate (Imai 1974). That Japan signed the NPT only in February 1970 (18 months after its adoption) and that it ratified it only in 1976, raised some doubts about its nuclear intentions as well. In particular, Japan attached a statement to its 1970 signature stipulating that the NPT should be the first step toward complete (universal) nuclear disarmament, that only such disarmament would remove the inequity between nuclear-weapons-states (NWS) and non-nuclear-weapon-states, that China and

France (as NWS) should sign the NPT too, and that non-nuclear-weapons-states should not be discriminated against in their efforts to develop peaceful nuclear technology. Finally, the statement explicitly noted the NPT's Article X allowing withdrawal by a country "when it is recognized that [the treaty] has endangered the supreme interests of the nation" (Endicott 1975:68).

A heated debate over NPT ratification ensued both within and beyond the Liberal Democratic Party (LDP), Japan's postwar leading but factionalized party. The LDP's ultraconservative Soshinkai (Pure Hearts Association), including the Ishii and the Seirankai factions, opposed NPT ratification.[19] Opposition parties also challenged the NPT to different degrees on the basis of its discriminatory nature. Ironically, opponents of ratification at both ends of the political spectrum shared some concerns while advancing different policies. Highly conservative forces opposed to mainstream LDP conservatives envisaged a nuclear-armed Japan, whereas the LDP's leftist opposition rejected the NPT in favor of universal nuclear disarmament. The Communist Party staunchly opposed the NPT, while the Socialists favored some positive aspects of an international agreement and distanced themselves from both the Communists and LDP's extreme conservatives. Movement toward ratification was slow and uneven. The LDP established a special NPT Committee in 1972, partially triggered by an uproar over a U.S. report suggesting that Japan could opt for nuclear weapons. Despite some initial ambiguity, the Japan Atomic Industrial Forum representing nuclear energy interests favored ratification. Others, including Foreign Minister Fukuda Takeo and Ministry of International Trade and Industry's (MITI's) Nakasone Yasuhiro (1972–74)—the architect of an ambitious kokusanka plan—were far more reluctant about immediate ratification. Fukuda declared that "now that Japan has signed the NPT, Japan cannot but ratify it. But we have no idea yet on when to ratify NPT" (Endicott 1975:70). Nakasone demanded a non-use declaration by NWS. Many criticized the IAEA safeguards agreement, demanding the same treatment granted to EURATOM (eventually granted to Japan in 1975). In 1974 Vice Foreign Minister Togo Fumihiko acknowledged the weight of conservative opposition to ratification within the LDP, adding that the NPT had nothing that would prevent Japan's ratification. Premier Tanaka reaffirmed the Non-Nuclear Principles, but Japan's delegate to the IAEA recognized in 1975 that lack of consensus within and beyond the LDP stood in the way of ratification.

Clearly, there was no agreement on whether the NPT should be the basis for Japan's nuclear policy. Few Japanese were enthusiastic about the NPT, and the response was a mixture of skepticism, reluctance, and outright resistance (Okimoto 1978:37). The debate was heated and, as Oros (2003:52) argues, "the outcome was not preordained." Only domestic dynamics can explain why a certain view prevailed over others leading to Japan's ratification in 1976, about six years after signature. Together with Article 96 of the constitution, which requires Japan to abide by its international treaty obligations, NPT ratification unquestionably raised barriers to Japan's nuclearization. Yet the option remained open, not least because Article X of the NPT allowed legal withdrawal three months after notification, which Japan had taken full notice of in its 1970 statement accompanying its signature.

The nuclear debate remained largely dormant after ratification but was reactivated by North Korea's nuclear program in the 1990s. Ministry of Foreign Affairs (MOFA) officials warned in 1993 that "if North Korea obtains nuclear weapons there will be a debate in Japanese public opinion . . . and this could weaken our commitment to the NPT" (Harrison 1996:29). Reacting to U.S. pressure to support the NPT's indefinite extension, MOFA officials expressed that such a move would "tie the hands of future governments in Tokyo if new security threats [should] arise" (Harrison 1993). In 1994 Japan informed the International Court of Justice that it did not necessarily consider the use of nuclear weapons illegal. This step raises important questions regarding the normative underpinnings of Japan's nuclear policy, widely considered to explain its non-nuclear status. These considerations too are best examined through Japan's domestic context. After significant tension with the United States over Article VI, Japan endorsed the NPT's indefinite extension in 1995, and ratified the Additional Protocol in 1999.

In sum, the NPT undoubtedly forced a heated debate in Japan, as in many other countries. For important actors in this debate, such as MOFA, adherence to the NPT was perceived as a critical component of Japan's international policies. Understanding NPT-induced pressures, however, is different from arguing that the NPT *determined* the content of Japan's decisions. Indeed, a deeper examination of the domestic debate reveals that NPT considerations played a marginal role.[20] Imai (1974:245) labels the NPT a "non-issue" during the mid-1970s and contends that few people opposed the NPT and even fewer actively promoted ratification. In his view, Japan could "afford to pay due respect to the architects of the NPT world order, *when and if it is required* [my italics]" (Imai 1974:251). The decision to remain non-nuclear was prior to, not a consequence of, the decision to ratify the NPT.[21] Japan's receptivity to NPT injunctions was thus a corollary of other domestic considerations, suggesting that Japan might have remained non-nuclear under the circumstances even in the absence of the NPT. What were the domestic conditions that drove Japan to sign, ratify, and fully abide by the NPT for over three decades?

DOMESTIC POLITICS: NUCLEAR ALLERGY, EMBEDDED
NUCLEARIZATION, AND THE YOSHIDA DOCTRINE

At least three interrelated domestic considerations influenced Japan's decisions to remain non-nuclear, which I label normative, institutional, and
political, respectively. First, the horror of Hiroshima and Nagasaki and
subsequent radioactive debris from U.S. hydrogen bomb tests at the
Bikini atoll in 1954 mobilized large public opposition to nuclear
weapons. The Fukuryu Maru incident, which had led to a fisherman's
death from radiation, triggered widespread anti-nuclear petitions with
perhaps 23–40 million signatories (Endicott 1975:91–100). This movement, including a large pacifist scientific and engineering community, became an agent of diffusion for Japan's "nuclear allergy," a term first used
by John Foster Dulles in 1954. Yet by the early 1960s the antinuclear
Gensuikyo (Japanese Council Against A and H Bombs) disintegrated into
three groups, and the movement lost public appeal.[22] Only one decade
after Hiroshima and Nagasaki, nearly a quarter of Japan's population favored acquisition of nuclear weapons (Calder 1988:419). According to
Okimoto (1978:322), after 1960 the weight of disarmament advocates
began to wane relative to ascending proponents of deterrence. In 1968,
between 51 and 66 percent opposed a nuclear-armed Japan, according to
various polls (Passin 1977:83). A 1969 Mainichi poll, however, found
only 46 percent to be opposed to developing nuclear weapons, and another poll, by Yomiuri Shimbun the same year, found that 77 percent predicted that Japan *would* have nuclear weapons by 2000.[23] Another study
found that 64 percent of college students expected Japan to have nuclear
weapons within twenty years or less (Okimoto 1978:218). Some of these
polls, together with the undertaking of internal government studies on the
potential role for nuclear weapons in Japan, cast doubt on the idea that
nuclear weapons were *unthinkable* at that critical time for NPT decisions
and for nuclear policy more broadly.[24] Though public opinion was certainly an important constraint, there was also popular distrust for the anti-
nuclear movement as being presumably captive to the Communist Party.
Proponents of disarmament were rather isolated (Okimoto 1978:322).
These appraisals should be viewed against the background of growing
Chinese nuclear capabilities and the "Nixon shocks."

A 1972 poll found that only 45 percent of LDP members thought Japan
should absolutely not arm itself with nuclear weapons, as opposed to 65,
68, and 80 percent respectively for Japan's Socialist Party, Komeito, and
Communist Party. The LDP also had the highest percentage (16 percent)
of respondents who thought Japan *should* get nuclear weapons in the
near future (as opposed to 10, 11, and 3 percent respectively). In the early
1970s, between 25 and 44 percent of those polled thought Japan *would*

go nuclear, whereas between 36 and 46 percent thought it would not, the latter declining to 30 percent in 1975 prior to NPT ratification.[25] A 1976 poll revealed that 48 percent of respondents felt "quite a bit" or "somewhat" uneasy about Japan *not* having nuclear weapons. As Kitamura (1996:13) argued, the nuclear allergy appeared to be "a flexible phenomenon." Okimoto (1978:219,483) found that public opinion polls may have been far more complicated and fluid, and that the debate over whether or not Japan should have nuclear weapons was "far from over and the option remain[ed] open to Japan in many ways." Endicott (1975:100) detected a growing "nationalistic pragmatism" that had by that time overcome "moral disgust" and increased the numbers of nuclear weapons advocates.[26] He estimated that a popular majority might have supported an LDP initiative for nuclear rearmament in the late 1960s in the aftermath of China's nuclear test. Intelligence documents confirmed that security issues were "no longer taboo in Japan" and that "in time [they] could lead to a more serious consideration of independent defense options, including eventually the nuclear option."[27] Yet they also cited domestic constraints that would curtail such developments in the short term, including public opinion and declining resources for defense spending. Opposition to nuclear weapons *grew* over the years, signaling that nuclear weapons acquisition would have become more politically prohibitive. By 1995, 80 percent opposed nuclear weapons and 89 percent expressed in 1998 that Japan did not "need" them (a formulation that does not discriminate between normative and pragmatic considerations regarding non-acquisition). Only 11 percent thought Japan would have nuclear weapons by 2000 (as opposed to 77 percent who thought so in 1969). Even after North Korea launched its Taepodong missile over Japan in 1998, a solid 79 percent advocated that all countries destroy nuclear weapons.[28]

Summing up, the nuclear allergy appears to have grown stronger in more recent times than it was during the first two decades of the postwar era.[29] The fateful decisions of the late 1960s and early 1970s, therefore, may not be traced as straightforwardly or uniquely to Hiroshima and Nagasaki as often assumed. Indeed, both proponents and opponents of nuclear weapons purportedly invoked memories of Hiroshima and Nagasaki (Harrison 2002:237). Furthermore, the very conduct of secret government studies on Japan's nuclear options suggests that a nuclear Japan may have been less than taboo at that time, particularly given the special sensitivity to secret contingency studies in the aftermath of the 1965 Three Arrows Study Incident (*Mitsuya Kenkyū Jiken*) concerning hypothetical war on the Korean peninsula (Okimoto 1978:152). There is little doubt that raising contingencies regarding nuclear weapons would have been politically risky, particularly given the preferences of influential players close to government circles, as discussed later. Secrecy, however, was the norm for most countries on nuclear issues. The stronger popular opposition to nuclear weapons in the 1990s than in the 1960s is an interesting puzzle if one assumes that the generation that witnessed Hiroshima and Nagasaki would have been *less* predisposed to nuclear weapons. In any event, it is difficult to extricate the normative from the rationalist sources of that opposition, given the continued political and diplomatic—domestic, regional, and international—risks and costs of nuclearization.

A second, related set of considerations draws attention to domestic legal barriers to nuclearization, even if their meaning was frequently contested.[30] Legal barriers can reflect prevailing norms, but they can also be imposed from above instrumentally by leaders bent on foreclosing present and future policy options. As Chai (1997) argues, Yoshida Shigeru and his allies did precisely that when they entrenched certain principles to minimize rearmament.[31] Whatever the precise source of such legal instruments, Article IX of Japan's 1947 Constitution—renouncing the "right of belligerency" and the right to assemble "war potential"—while not referring directly to nuclear weapons, nonetheless represented an institutional obstacle in the development of such weapons. Furthermore, Article 2 of the 1955 Atomic Energy Law stipulated that "the research, development, and utilization of atomic energy shall be limited to peaceful purposes."[32] Yet Kishi declared to the Diet in 1957 that defensive nuclear weapons would not challenge the constitution. The 1965 National Security Research Council report noted that China's nuclear test would increase pressures on Japan to respond, and a 1966 Council report revealed even more clearly the tensions between the ultraconservative Soshinkai—demanding not to foreclose Japan's nuclear option—and their opponents within the LDP.

Subsequent reports and declarations exposed continued tensions regarding the il/legality of nuclear weapons. In 1967, LDP Secretary-General Fukuda expressed that "the majority of the Liberal democrats see the need to outgrow the 'nuclear allergy'" (Harrison 1996:7). Premier Sato supported this statement initially but later announced Japan's Three Non-Nuclear Principles and subsequently presented the Four Nuclear Principles to the Diet, tying the former three to nuclear disarmament, reliance on the U.S. nuclear umbrella, and affirming the peaceful uses of nuclear energy.[33] In 1968 Agriculture and Forestry Minister Kuraishi Tadao was forced to resign following his statement that Japan needed to rearm with nuclear weapons if necessary, to protect Japanese fishermen from Soviet threats. In 1969, however, Sato himself proclaimed in the House of Councilors that Japan could possess nuclear weapons for defensive purposes.[34] Sato's meandering (despite a plausible personal preference for nuclear weapons) can be best explained by his efforts at political survival, discussed later. In 1970, the JDA's first White Paper declared that Japan cannot possess weapons posing threats of aggression but that purely defensive weapons were not unconstitutional. JDA Director-General (and later Premier) Nakasone ordered the 1970 secret study on the possibility of a nuclear-armed Japan. JDA military experts estimated that Japan could deploy nuclear weapons within five years at $555 million (1970 prices), although the absence of a testing ground was a problem. Nakasone declared that although he persistently opposed Japan's nuclearization, the removal of the U.S. umbrella could lead Japan "to consider various options including the possession of nuclear weapons."[35] Japan had signed the NPT earlier that year.

In 1971 the Diet formalized Sato's Three Principles in a resolution overwhelmingly supported by the LDP, Komeito, and the Democratic Socialist Party. The principles remained just that, a policy commitment (*kokuze*) rather than a legally binding or immutable instrument (Okimoto 1978:27). Yet in 1973 Premier Tanaka did not rule out defensive nuclear weapons, declaring that the constitution allowed tactical nuclear weapons. Soon thereafter he announced that nuclear weapons were generally considered to be offensive and hence would violate the constitution, adding that Japan should abide by the Three Principles. Subsequently, Tanaka reiterated that Japan could not hold offensive nuclear weapons but that this did "not mean that it will not be permitted to hold nuclear weapons at all" (Endicott 1975:43; Harrison 1996:42). As with Sato and others, Tanaka's tortuous argumentation on the nuclear issue reflected the lack of clarity embedded in Japan's legal instruments (except for the Atomic Energy Law). JDA Defense Bureau Director General Kubo Takuya and others considered nuclear mines and anti-air missiles to be defensive. These and subsequent statements reveal that institutional restraints had significant force, given the need to restate policies' compatibility with legal injunctions. There was continuous contestation, however, over these injunctions within and beyond the LDP.[36] Furthermore, nuclear weapons were routinely—if surreptitiously—introduced into Japan by U.S. warships in violation of non-nuclear principles.[37] The high potential for contestation explains why the Non-Nuclear Principles were never transformed into law (Chai 1997). As Mochizuki (2006) argues, "Japan's pacifism has always been pragmatic."

This open-endedness and evident political struggle over institutional injunctions suggest that understanding the fateful decisions of the 1970s requires greater attention to broader political conditions explaining the triumph of anti-nuclear weapons forces. Japan's postwar model of political survival constituted a third and crucial (necessary) barrier to nuclearization. In a specific rejection of the war-oriented autarkic and militarized model of the 1930s, Japan's postwar leaders sought domestic political legitimacy and electoral approval through export-led economic growth and recovery. As Berger (1998:29) notes, Japan's population at the time "was more concerned with the task of rebuilding the economy than dwelling on the past." This created significant receptivity to Yoshida Shigeru's model hinging on Japan as "merchant nation" (*chōnin kokka*), requiring a strong economic infrastructure, manufacturing capabilities, "putting the market in command," and swimming with (not against) the great tide of market forces (Kosaka 1982; Inoguchi 1993:x–xi, 10, 22–56; Samuels 2003). The Yoshida line was most vigorously contested during 1945–60, but following Kishi's resignation in 1960, Premier Ikeda Hayato's plan for doubling income within a decade marked the official reign of the Yoshida doctrine (Kosaka 1982; Inoguchi 2004). The LDP's "economy first" grand strategy had implications for domestic, regional, and international policies. Yoshida and his successors may have had varied positions on nuclear matters, but the economic dimension was primordial and dominated all others.[38] As Dower (1993:237) argues, the Yoshida doctrine was not primarily based on democracy, diplomacy, rearmament, or global leadership but on economic growth. "In the economic world," Yoshida (1962:159) argues, "nothing was more urgent than increased exports, and the improvement of Japan's position in world markets." There were explicit and implicit synergies among economic growth, global access, and relinquishing nuclear weapons.[39] The Yoshida doctrine became "the institutionalized center of Japan's political consensus" and "effectively set the terms of political debate for a half century" (Samuels 2003:223–24). Its success further reinforced its centrality for decades.

Since 1955, various LDP factions and the powerful bureaucracy brought together big business and finance, farming interests, and smaller and medium-sized business under the umbrella of rapid growth, exports, and economic protectionism.[40] Economic growth was at the heart of this model of political control and was a critical means to defeat perceived threats of communist subversion, particularly in the early postwar decades. The LDP's protracted factional conflicts included an ultra-conservative challenge to the Yoshida model that favored faster military buildup, resisted vigorously by Yoshida. The LDP presided over Japan's second wave of internationalization (Yoshida greatly admired Meiji), but this time defense-related production represented a small proportion of total industrial output, about 0.50 percent average.[41] This consensus favoring greater reliance on the global economy, including the highest business echelons—Yoshida's allies—overwhelmed kokusanka proponents. The constitution's Article IX was used to downsize the military and suppress advocates of rearmament. As Green (1995:21) suggests, kokusanka had high opportunity costs, negative macroeconomic and budgetary implications, and adverse consequences for U.S. alliance-related procurement and for "Japan's secure place in the global economy."

By the early 1950s Japan had joined the IMF, World Bank, General Agreement on Tariffs and Trade (GATT), U.N., and, in the 1960s, the Organization for Economic Cooperation and Development (OECD). Economic growth averaged 10 to 11 percent between 1952 and the mid-1970s—as high as 12 percent in real terms during the late 1960s, critical background information for decisions examined here—quadrupling Japan's share of global trade (Tanaka Kakuei 1973:170; Calder 1988; Inoguchi 1993:8; Pempel 1999). Japanese exports accounted for 3.5 percent of global exports in 1960, doubling to nearly 7 percent in 1970. The model consolidated in the 1960s under Premiers Ikeda and Sato. An economic "miracle" emerged out of food crises and extreme instability in the early postwar era, yielding both stability and continued LDP political dominance, the twin constitutive objectives of this model. The model had also made big business, conservative politicians, and the bureaucracy hypersensitive to threats of political change (Calder 1988). All partners in the ruling coalition were wary of political risks to the growth-orientation underlying corporate strategies. The stakes were high not only for individual corporate actors; Japan was already the third largest economy by the late 1960s. Nuclear weapons development would have created high uncertainty and posed major risks to the model's continuity and its related "peace diplomacy." They would have endangered an extant value—the economic miracle—for unknown future gains. Beyond destabilizing ripple effects, nuclear weapons would have also diverted from important economic sectors at a time when the LDP sought continued growth and resources to compensate sectors adversely influenced by internationalization. Japan's trading policy was already generating strong criticism and threatening exports that were already at risk due to the 1971 shock. Furthermore, the 1973–74 oil crisis and recession cast doubt on the sustainability of exports given much higher oil prices and growing protectionism. Sato conspicuously presented the Non-Nuclear Principles to the Diet's Budget Committee. As Reiss (1988:134) argues, key economic activities would have been brought "almost to a standstill as a result of Japan's emergence as a nuclear power."

The model's regional and international pillars, including the alliance, had important implications for the ability to maintain domestic growth and stability. As Kosaka (1986:123) argued, friendly relations with the United States and domestic stability were both necessary and sufficient conditions for security. The U.S. nuclear umbrella was a core foundation of the LDP's model, freeing it from the need to devote too many resources to security while facilitating Japan's access to global export markets, natural resources, and international institutions like the OECD, GATT, and the IMF.[42] Military expenditures remained at about 1 percent of GNP for decades since the 1950s and certainly lagged considerably relative to Japan's growing economic strength.[43] Successive leaders pledged against raising military expenditures above that threshold partly to reassure public opinion that rearmament would not endanger economic growth (or democracy).[44] Global, particularly U.S., markets facilitated absorption of ever-expanding Japanese exports that could also secure earnings for importing energy resources—amounting to over 90 percent of Japan's needs and 99.7 percent of its oil needs—a vital component in a model that sought to avoid the pitfalls of the prewar era.[45] Efforts to transcend such complete dependence on foreign oil led to an emphasis on the nuclear industry since 1956. Yet this industry too was particularly threatened by potential disruptions of fuel supplies, given Japan's heavy reliance on uranium imports, enrichment, and related services from the United States, Canada, Australia, Britain, France, and others. Nuclear weapons development would have triggered such disruptions, explaining the civilian nuclear sector's central role in NPT-related decision-making. As Imai (1975:25) argues, "If a Japanese intention to obtain nuclear weapons became known, the relationship with these countries could become so strained that the basic resources for nuclear power generation might no longer be available and the entire nuclear [energy] program would come to a complete stop." During discussions over NPT ratification, the Japan Atomic Industrial Forum stated that "the long term position of Japan's nuclear technology, industry, and resources will be better if the treaty is ratified before long."[46] MOFA also insisted that NPT ratification was critical to ensure stable nuclear fuel supplies.

In sum, given the international context at the time, Japan's nuclear energy program was arguably doomed without external support; Japan's economic miracle was doomed without nuclear energy; and the LDP was doomed without a sustained economic miracle. This analytical sequence illuminates how domestic considerations filtered and constituted international constraints. Significantly, Article 1 of the Atomic Energy Law makes it clear that the law's objective is to "secure energy resources in the future" and to contribute to "the elevation of the national living standard," the pivotal electoral consideration in the LDP's strategy (Endicott 1975:44). Additionally, the nuclear energy industry was arraying itself for potential exports in the 1970s, which would have been impossible without Japan's NPT ratification. Large industrial consortia with interests in the nuclear industry included Mitsubishi, Hitachi, Sumitomo, Mitsui, Toshiba, Furukawa, and Kawasaki. Together with the electric power companies—important sources of campaign funds for the LDP in their own right—these provided the backbone of Japan's miracle.[47] Unsurprisingly, the unofficial 1968–70 Cabinet Information Research Office study on the feasibility and desirability of nuclear weapons—largely geared to deflate domestic pressures for such weapons—concluded that their domestic political and international diplomatic costs were too high.

At a 1969 meeting with Keidanren (Federation of Economic Organizations) leaders, Sato revealed both his personal views and his understanding of these constraints: "Let me say this so that no one can misunderstand me: I do not regard it as a complete system of defense if we cannot possess nuclear weapons in the era of nuclear weapons. I will, nevertheless, adhere faithfully to the pledge I have made to the people. We will not possess, manufacture, or permit the introduction of nuclear weapons" (Harrison 1996:10). In 1971, during the ratification debate, Keidanren's chairman-elect Mitsubishi's Kono Fumihiko declared that "it is not necessary for Japan at all to arm itself with nuclear weapons" (Endicott 1975:89). Mitsubishi captured over 30 percent of defense procurement at the time. Kono was chairman of Keidanren's Defense Production Committee, representing the defense industry to a significant extent, and served on the Sanken (Industrial Problems Study Council), considered the high command of business and the strongest pressure group.

Japan's embrace of nuclear weapons would have also shattered the regional pillar of the LDP's model. In the 1950s–70s, Japan faced the task of reconstructing relations with neighboring countries through official development assistance, in an effort to transcend the historical legacy of World War II. Furthermore, continued growth and domestic political stability required market access to—and raw materials from—Asian neighbors, as well as a stable region enhancing economic expansion and attracting foreign investment. The 1968–70 study reportedly included an explicit reference to Japan's "trading state" requirements (Kase 2001:65). Diplomatic relations with South Korea were normalized in 1965, and, following normalization with China in 1972, industrial conglomerates began shifting their attention toward emerging trade relations with China and away from defense-related investments with adverse budgetary and regional effects.[48] A 1972 document detailing fundamental premises of the Fourth Defense Build-Up summarizes the "Foundation of National Defense" as follows: "our country's national defense . . . is to establish relations of friendship and cooperation with the many neighboring nations . . . that will lessen international tension and make necessary domestic policies for economic and social development."[49] This formulation makes the connections between the domestic and regional pillars of the LDP's model quite explicit. A nuclear-armed Japan would have reversed steady advances in normalization with regional partners and former adversaries, a vital component of the Yoshida model (Kishida 1973). As Makoto (1978:8) argued, "If Japan were to go nuclear, the hostility this would engender in the international environment would have the most serious implications for the economic relationships that are vital to Japan."

All these elements linking Japan's domestic model with its international and regional requirements clarify why nuclear weapons would have introduced levels of stress and divisiveness within a consensus-seeking society that no ruling coalition concerned with political stability and sustained growth could have afforded. The Yoshida doctrine was a " 'compromise' among the advocates of disarmed neutrality, unilateral rearmament, and disarmed economic (and technological) alliance with the United States—all of whom had to fit under the conservatives' ideological tent in order to achieve the political stability necessary for economic reconstruction" (Green 1995:26; Kosaka 1982). The alliance was but a *means* to accommodate this domestic compromise, which, from the perspective of nuclear opponents, was nothing but a case of "embedded nuclearization," whereby Japan's defense rested on U.S. nuclear weapons. Repeated violations of the principle not to introduce nuclear weapons into Japan were one expression of this "nuclear compromise." Even efforts to expand kokusanka in the area of conventional weapons triggered extensive political conflict and factional LDP infighting.

Japan's democratic institutions made public opinion, constitutionality, electoral considerations, and the costs and benefits of its model quite central to the LDP's survival. Despite its overall dominance since 1955, successive LDP coalitions have had to contend with pressures for unarmed neutrality and non-nuclear status, most prominently from Japan's Socialist Party but also the Communist Party, Komeito, and the Democratic Socialist Party. In particular, the LDP majority was slowly eroding throughout the 1960s, particularly after 1967. The opposition challenged the LDP on presumed violations of the Non-Nuclear Principles and pressed for alternative means of enhancing national security, such as poverty elimination.[50] This induced further pressure on the LDP for maintaining growth and socio-political compensatory mechanisms. The "nuclear compromise" was yet another form of compensation by conservative politicians interested in growth and stability.[51] Alluding to trade-offs between a growing economy and a nuclear program, Nakasone reportedly declared in 1970 that China opted for "going nuclear without pants," whereas Japan "has remained non-nuclear, preferring to be decently dressed" (Harrison 1996:12). As an earlier U.S. intelligence estimate put it, "Antimilitary, particularly antinuclear, attitudes remain extremely strong among the populace and susceptible to exploitation by socialists and Communists. The diversion of resources from development and welfare programs would not be politically feasible."[52] These links among socioeconomic and security—domestic, regional, and international—pillars of the LDP's model were evident in Japan's 1970 statement accompanying its signature of the NPT, noting that, between that time and such time when Japan decides to ratify the NPT, Japan "will investigate cautiously the rest of the problems which must be seriously considered in order to secure national *prosperity* [italics added]" (Endicott 1975:67).

The ratification debate took place against the background of successive political crises in the early 1970s (critical years for our purposes) and the continued erosion of the LDP's majority. Significant gains by opposition parties in the 1971 municipal elections and 1972 Lower House elections, the Nixon shocks, an abrupt yen revaluation in 1971, the 1973 oil crisis and ensuing hyperinflation, Tanaka's 1973–74 recession, corruption scandals, declining rates of economic growth, growing unemployment, Admiral Gene La Rocque's 1974 disclosures about nuclear weapons' passage in Japan, Miki's 1974 overtures to the opposition to split the LDP, and the Lockheed scandal all constituted potential threats to stability, unity, and LDP political control. As Inoguchi (1993:33) argues, "It looked during most of the 1970s as if the government might change hands at any moment." It had been possible to play positive-sum politics (expand the budget) in a positive sum (growing) economy during the 1960s, according to Curtis's (1984) succinct formulation. By the 1970s, the risks of playing positive-sum politics in a zero-sum economy were much higher. Under these conditions, and only a few months before general elections, Japan ratified the NPT in June 1976.

Nuclear policy must be examined within this context of political turbulence in which "intraconservative, left-right, and often foreign policy concerns interrelate," generating maximum political uncertainty for business, politicians, and bureaucrats (Calder 1988:39). Developing nuclear weapons, as Berger (1998:63) noted, "was certain to provoke political chaos at home and hostility abroad." This potential enabled Premier Miki to craft a broad coalition of moderate LDP factions (Shiina, Funada, Mizuta, Nakasone, and Ohira), opposition parties, MOFA and JDA leadership, high echelons of industry (Japan Atomic Industrial Forum), and the Atomic Energy Commission, in support of NPT ratification despite adamant opposition from Soshinkai, elements of the LDP's Sato, Fukuda, and Ishii factions, and the Communist Party (Endicott 1999). Miki was not popular even within his own party and had meager political accomplishments, but Diet support for NPT ratification stands out as an important instance of widespread—but not universal—political consensus at that time. This consensus reflected broad support for the general contours of the LDP's model of political survival, particularly after Ikeda's income-doubling plan.

Beyond this mainstream anti-nuclear weapons consensus, some conservative politicians and former military officers espoused greater sympathy for nuclear weapons. An early proponent in the late 1960s was Ishihara Shintaro, who openly questioned the credibility of the "broken" U.S. nuclear umbrella and proposed that Japan would command the world's respect only when she "let[s] loose at least one nuclear blast" (Kase 2001:67; Passin 1977:97). Ishihara also questioned other—including economic—pillars of the LDP's model, evident in his book *The Japan That Can Say No*. Sato himself, as we have seen, made conflicting statements on the nuclear issue that can be explained only by pressures from both the LDP's extreme conservative and left wings, which collaborated to oust him. The 1968–70 study to highlight the high costs of nuclear weapons for Japan took place under this unwieldy domestic context. The NPT was concluded in 1968, shortly after the LDP had launched a campaign to "rejuvenate the national spirit" and awaken "defense consciousness (*bōeiishiki*)" (Berger 1998:96). The campaign aimed at consolidating support for Sato, who polished his nationalist credentials by making Okinawa's reversion his foremost objective. Sato and Nixon agreed in 1969 to return Okinawa by 1972. Meanwhile, the campaign launched in 1968 acquired momentum under Nakasone's direction and the slogan "Independent Defense" (*Jishu bōei*). Serving as JDA director-general since January 1970, Nakasone supported the alliance and the Non-Nuclear Principles despite his highly nationalistic rhetoric. In February 1970 Japan signed the NPT, eighteen months after its conclusion. Backed by the LDP's mainstream, Sato blocked Nakasone's efforts to revise the 1957 Basic Principles of National Defense. The 1971 Diet resolution on the Non-Nuclear Principles resulted from a compromise: Sato sought the opposition's approval for the Okinawa agreement in exchange for the Diet's formal resolution on the Three Non-Nuclear Principles (Akiyama 2003). Unbeknownst to the public until 1974, Sato had agreed with Nixon to allow nuclear-armed ships to go through Okinawa in emergency situations, in violation of the Three Principles (Tanaka and Murata 1995). Despite continued efforts by pro-nuclear forces during the early 1970s, the LDP mainstream was able to retain its dominance. Following NPT ratification in 1976, the nuclear debate subsided as Japan's domestic politics became absorbed with maintaining, expanding, and later restoring the growth model that had come to a standstill.

By the 1990s, North Korea's violations of NPT commitments, its 1993 test of a Nodong missile in the the Sea of Japan, and its threatening statements toward Japan enhanced calls for more proactive Japanese policies.[53] Politicians such as Ozawa Ichiro (1994) began urging Japan's foreign policy to cease its captivity to domestic interests including big business, and to respond proactively according to "national interests." Ozawa suggested a new Fundamental Law for Peace and Security recognizing Japan's right to self-defense, political control over the military, global disarmament, elimination of nuclear weapons, and U.N. control of nuclear stockpiles. The JDA again concluded in 1995 that the political and financial costs of having nuclear weapons were too high and the adverse consequences for the Asian region too weighty.[54] The potential of nuclear weapons for triggering domestic confrontations was among those costs. North Korea's launching of a Taepodong 1 missile over Japan in 1998 revived calls for reconsidering Japan's ability to cope with such threats. In 1999, Vice Minister of Defense Nishimura Shingo expressed that Japan's failure to consider nuclear armament left it open to "rape" by China, and he was forced to resign immediately. Prior to the 2002 elections, Ozawa stated that "if China gets too inflated, the Japanese people will become hysterical in response," adding that "we have plenty of plutonium in our nuclear power plants, so it's possible for us to produce 3,000 to 4,000 nuclear warheads."[55] Ishihara, now Tokyo's governor, publicly welcomed such comments. Deputy-Chief Cabinet Secretary Abe Shinzo, citing Kishi's 1959 and 1960 arguments, maintained in 2002 that the constitution did not necessarily ban possession of nuclear weapons "as long as they are kept to a minimum and are tactical."[56] Abe denied advocating nuclear rearmament. Chief Cabinet Secretary Fukuda Yasuo suggested that Japan's Non-Nuclear Principles "are just like the Constitution . . . but in the face of calls to amend the Constitution, the amendment of the principles is also likely."[57] "Under Japanese law," Fukuda argued, "there is no reason to prevent Japan from arming itself with nuclear weapons. . . . If public opinion agrees with nuclear armament, the denuclearization principle can be revised."[58]

Legislators criticized Fukuda's remarks, and four major opposition parties demanded his resignation and a special parliamentary session with Premier Junichiro Koizumi, neither of which took place. Some Hiroshima victims demanded enshrinement of the Non-Nuclear Principles in the constitution. Koizumi declared that his government had no intention of seeking nuclear weapons and would abide by the Principles.[59] His spokesperson declared that Fukuda meant that "there is no law that specifically prohibits Japan from owning nuclear weapons," and Koizumi added, "It is significant that although we could have them, we don't."[60] Koizumi's statement reflected an understanding of the political-instrumental, normative, and institutional barriers that continued influencing Japan's nuclear weapons policy. At the annual Hiroshima ceremony in 2002, Koizumi reiterated that Japan would not alter support for the Non-Nuclear Principles. Endo Tetsuya, vice chairman of the Atomic Energy Commission, denied alleged Japanese intentions to acquire nuclear weapons, citing deeply rooted anti-nuclear sentiments, domestic statutes, international pacts on the peaceful use of nuclear power, the U.S. alliance, and the need to cooperate with Asian neighbors to nurture mutual trust and regional stability. The need to cite the entire repertoire of arguments against nuclear weapons suggests an effort to appeal to all elements of the anti-nuclear coalition. In 2002, Japan's diplomat Takehiro Funakoshi unambiguously reiterated Japan's

constraints viewed from an "economy first" model: "Japan is quite totally, economically interdependent with the international community . . .
so if we receive economic sanctions, that very weight will fall into a very
difficult situation."[61] A year later Professor Nishihara Masashi, president
of Japan's National Defense Academy, warned that Japan's nuclearization
would subject it to a worst-case scenario of economic sanctions and isolation (Kurosawa 2004:115).

The continued crisis with North Korea has kept the debate alive. An
overwhelming majority of LDP politicians favor constitutional reform but
a far smaller majority supports revision of Article IX (Pekkanen and
Krauss 2005). While LDP Diet member Kono Taro declared that "it's surprising how many lawmakers are in favor of having nuclear arms,"
Nishimura, now an opposition legislator, recognized that most Japanese
politicians continue to avoid this debate due to strong strains of pacifism
among voters (Sieg 2003). A Tokyo Shimbun poll found that only 83 of
724 Diet members publicly support Japan's nuclearization in response to
that of North Korea.[62] Nonetheless, even opponents of nuclear weapons
such as leading LDP legislator Takemi Keizo have warned that if the alliance's credibility is undermined, "more and more Japanese, including left
wingers and liberals as well as young Japanese, will advocate Japan's cut-
ting the alliance with the United States and taking its own approach in
international politics. Once that happens, Japan's possession of nuclear
weapons would be in sight."[63] These and other statements have fueled
speculation about the potential erosion of legal safeguards (*hadome*,
brakes) with respect to Article IX, collective defense, and arms exports,
among others. Furthermore, Japan's plutonium recycling, mixed uranium-
plutonium oxide fuel, and fast-breeder reactors have continued to stimu-
late suspicions inside and outside Japan (Takagi 1996; Mack 1996; Albright, Berkhout, and Walker 1997; Kurosawa 2004; Harrison 1996).

A foremost expert on Japan's nuclear history (Endicott 1999:2) asserted, however, that "there is no other peaceful nuclear power program
so thoroughly examined by the IAEA as Japan. It is by law open both by
the Basic Law and by international agreements, both bilateral and multilateral. I do not know how fissile materials in Japan would be channeled
into weapons programs without the world knowing." The IAEA announced in 2004 that it would halve the number of annual inspections in
Japan based on its conclusion that Japan has no intention to develop nuclear weapons.[64] Even Asahi Shimbun, otherwise often critical of government policies on national security, noted Japan's exemplary nonproliferation track record.[65] Former JDA Director-General Ishiba Shigeru
suggested that no outcome of the North Korean crisis will lead Japan to
enter a nuclear arms race in Northeast Asia."[66] At the 2003 Hiroshima
peace memorial service, Koizumi vowed to advance nuclear disarmament

and nonproliferation, urged early CTBT ratification, and reaffirmed his support for the Non-Nuclear Principles.[67]

CONCLUSION

If Japan ever considered nuclear weapons, it certainly relinquished them by joining, ratifying, and dutifully abiding by the NPT since the 1970s. Japan's sustained nuclear abstention is incompatible with unalloyed neorealism. Its predicted imminent transformation into a nuclear-weapon-state has not yet happened.[68] Rival neorealist perspectives predict various outcomes—nuclear and non-nuclear—highlighting neorealism's generic problem of underdetermination. Reliance on the U.S. alliance provides the best neorealist explanation but is somewhat limited and competes with other neorealist, normative, and domestic political considerations. The alliance-based explanation is incomplete because it begs the question of why alliance was adopted to begin with, requiring prior understanding of domestic considerations. From this standpoint, the alliance was a critical component of the Yoshida model of political survival, not an end in itself but a means to enable concentration on economic growth through global access while avoiding militarization.[69] Thus the alliance in and of itself may be insufficient for explaining Japan's nuclear choices. The domestic perspective endogenizes alliance, making it internal to the causal process and mechanisms explaining nuclear choices. In tension with neorealist expectations, Japan chose nuclear abstention at a time least conducive to reliance on U.S. commitments, following the Nixon shocks. Domestic considerations help explain why.

The Yoshida model and its legacy arguably constituted necessary conditions for Japan's non-nuclear status.[70] It is at least plausible that domestic considerations might have been *sufficient* in and of themselves to induce this outcome, although the alliance certainly made it easier to uphold the Non-Nuclear Principles. Advocates of a non-nuclear Japan (Nagai, Kōsaka, Kishida, and Momoi, among many others) could rely heavily on the alliance as disincentives to be emphasized in domestic debates.[71] Regardless of their deep personal preferences, nuclear weapons were a political liability for leaders advancing the postwar model, which defined national security as "economic in nature" (Inoguchi 1993:36). A 1957 NIE got it fundamentally right: "Japanese policy with respect to the production of nuclear weapons is likely to be determined primarily by domestic and regional considerations."[72] An expert on Japan's nuclear policy asserted that "for the Japanese people, nuclear issues were more or less subjects for domestic politics or domestic social movements, which seemed to be rather insulated from the reality of international security"

(Akiyama 2003:89). Another suggested that "Japan may have likely remained non-nuclear regardless of any external security developments" (Kase 2001:56). The Yoshida model, the nuclear allergy, and institutional restraints were all interrelated parts of the domestic landscape that trumped nuclearization.

In the end, our ability to evaluate the weight of the alliance alone in determining Japan's non-nuclear status would have been enhanced if, first, Japan had clearly and forcefully demanded nuclear weapons, and, second, such demand had been met by a no less forceful U.S. rejoinder. These two never happened, and their potential effects can only be studied counterfactually. Domestic demand for such weapons never crystallized in Japan. Although there were instances of ambiguous U.S. signals, particularly under Nixon, Japanese leaders understood the high risks that nuclearization entailed for continued access to foreign markets, nuclear materials, energy resources, and trade and stability in East Asia, all of which were critical inputs into export-driven economic growth and domestic stability. The compounded effect of the alliance, LDP's model of political survival, nuclear allergy, and institutional constraints made Japan's non-nuclear status virtually inevitable (overdetermined). Japan provides a case of equifinality, whereby many alternative causal paths led to the same outcome (George and Bennett 2005), making it harder for any single variable unequivocally to claim explanatory dominance. The Yoshida doctrine, however, as the heart of Japan's favored model of political survival, provided the glue that kept the anti-nuclear package together.

North Korea's nuclear program has imposed severe external shocks on Japan's security, reminiscent of Cold War Chinese and Soviet threats. At the height of the 1993 North Korean nuclear crisis, President Clinton expressed that Japan might feel "compelled to become a nuclear power" (Sigal 1998:68). Many observers have expressed similar views since. Continued test launching of missiles into the Sea of Japan, threats to reduce Japan to a "nuclear sea of fire," and the legacy of North Korea's abduction of Japanese civilians all made North Korea Japan's foremost menace.[73] From one neorealist standpoint, North Korea has pushed Japan toward greater "entrapment" in the U.S. alliance for fear of "abandonment" under conditions of enhanced threat. In turn, Koizumi did not veer very far from the "economy first" model that characterized Japan's postwar model of political survival. Norms and institutions have been in flux, given preparations for constitutional change. Some politicians asserted Japan's right to preempt imminent North Korean attack while acknowledging that Japan lacks the means to do so. Yet for over a decade, Japan's response to North Korea's escalation did not involve nuclearization. The 2006 missile and nuclear tests provide a new test to this long-standing commitment to denuclearization. As this book goes to press, an old/new nuclear debate is raging. Yet, Japan's immediate authoritative response, by none other than Premier Abe Shinzo (Kishi's grandson), unequivocally reaffirmed Japan's non-nuclear status: "I would like to clearly state that there will be no change regarding the Three Non-Nuclear Principles," Abe told the House of Representatives Budget committee.[74] Chapter 12 explores future scenarios stemming from the conceptual and historical considerations explored in this chapter.

CHAPTER FOUR

South Korea

ON JUNE 25, 1950, nearly one year following the removal of U.S. troops from South Korea, North Korea's superior military forces invaded South Korea, nearly swallowing it whole. The United States coalesced U.N. support for South Korea under the principle of collective security, leading to a reversal of battle and eventual military intervention by China. When the Armistice was signed in 1953, 700,000 civilians and 212,000 soldiers from South Korea, between one and three million North Koreans, and 52,000 U.S. soldiers had been killed (100,000 wounded), in addition to millions of displaced and maimed Koreans (Park 1971:83; Koh 1984:210; Cumings 2004). The war left an indelible imprint and a sense of utter vulnerability on South Korea, subsequently aggravated by perceived threats from an implacable North Korea backed by Soviet and Chinese allies and by continued mistrust of Japan, which had colonized Korea from 1910 to 1945. The perceived decline of U.S. commitments in the 1960s–1970s and North Korea's buildup of the sixth largest military force worldwide made the 1970s a particularly precarious time for South Korea, triggering its interest in nuclear weapons (Dunn 1982:57; Reiss 1988:82). This brief interlude provides some support for an unalloyed neorealism that regards alliances as problematic substitutes for self-help. South Korea, however, has relied primarily on the 1954 Mutual Defense Treaty with the United States for its own deterrence and defense for over fifty years. It ratified the NPT in April 1975, at the height of its fear of abandonment by the United States. Subsequently, South Korea acquired advanced nuclear industrial capabilities but, despite growing nuclear threats from the North, renounced the right to enrich uranium and reprocess waste and is acknowledged as a non-nuclear weapons state.[1] What explains this restraint?

STRUCTURAL POWER AND ALLIANCE DILEMMAS

As with other East Asian cases, different inferences from neorealism lead to different potential nuclear choices, all in the name of self-help. An unalloyed version regards anything less than a self-reliant nuclear deterrent as undermining state survival in the face of indisputable security threats.

Yet alternative neorealist perspectives hold nuclear abstention as the best guarantee of survival. These alternatives fall into four main categories.

The first suggests that South Korea's small size, dense population, geographically concentrated industry, and close proximity to hostile powers made nuclear weapons an irrational option, whereas the alliance could do the work. This alternative raises dilemmas of "abandonment" similar to those discussed for Japan, and captured by the following events. During the late 1940s the United States declared South Korea a financial drain and removed its troops in 1949, on the eve of the North's attack. Nixon's policies provided a renewed sense of abandonment, as the 1969 "Guam doctrine" called for greater self-reliance by Asian allies. The United States also responded reluctantly to North Korea's raids and its 1968 seizure of the USS *Pueblo*, removed forces from Indochina, unilaterally withdrew 24,000 troops (one of two infantry divisions) from South Korea in 1970, and officially informed South Korea of plans to reduce troops further in 1971. Nixon's 1972 surprise visit to China and the Shanghai Communiqué shocked South Korea no less than Japan. This sequence also drove home to South Korea the limits of U.S. commitments to Taiwan. President Jimmy Carter's 1977 announcement that remaining U.S. troops and nuclear weapons would be withdrawn from South Korea reportedly triggered Park Chung Hee's threat to develop an independent nuclear deterrent.[2] In 2003 the Pentagon announced its intention to redeploy its forces south of the demilitarized zone (DMZ), and in 2004 the United States announced a one-third reduction of its 36,000 troops in South Korea. Some U.S. commentators even called for removal of all U.S. forces in response to anti-American rhetoric in President Roh Moo-Huyn's campaign. All these substantiate South Korea's fears of abandonment, not to mention additional dilemmas of entrapment posed by the U.S. alliance.

A second neorealist variant suggests that nuclear abstention was less a consequence of an unreliable supply of U.S. security and more a result of U.S. coercion. The United States pressured South Korea to refrain from acquiring a French reprocessing plant in 1975–76, allegedly threatening it with canceling U.S. economic and military aid if South Korea developed nuclear weapons.[3] South Korea's domestic politics offer important insights on the precise sinews and effectiveness of hegemonic coercion, which, as argued in chapter 2, has proven futile with respect to many other nuclear aspirants, both allies and foes. Furthermore, U.S. influence on South Korea was high at some points but much lower at others, suggesting that domestic receptivity to U.S. coercion and inducements was an important intervening variable. I return to the foundations of domestic receptivity later. Beyond that, the domestic angle calls attention to the flip side of coercion: Park used some domestic demand for nuclear weapons to good effect, extracting more robust commitments from the United States. Park's model of political survival sheds light on why he may have preferred alliance over an indigenous deterrent, as discussed later.

The third neorealist alternative rejects both an indigenous deterrent and the alliance, as each could make South Korea more vulnerable. The former (in the absence of the latter) could have arguably invited a North Korean strike or a Japanese effort to develop its own deterrent (Yager 1980). Park conveyed that it would not be in South Korea's interest to acquire nuclear weapons, because China and the Soviets were neighboring nuclear powers (Reiss 1988:94). Furthermore, South Korea's small size and dense population made it especially vulnerable, although an alternative neorealist version (Waltz 1993:69) dismisses territorial size as irrelevant in the presence of invulnerable second-strike capabilities.

A final neorealist proposition views conventional superiority as obviating South Korea's need for nuclear weapons. The conventional balance on the Korean peninsula in the mid-1970s, when South Korea ratified the NPT, arguably favored the South only if one included U.S. troops. North Korea enjoyed formidable conventional strength, backed by Soviet and Chinese forces. U.S. direct military assistance to South Korea was extensive between 1953 and 1973 but declined sharply after 1969 and ceased completely in 1978. South Korea's Force Modernization Plan (1976–80) was designed to strengthen independent conventional capabilities. Average military expenditures grew from 4 to nearly 6 percent of GDP initially, decreasing to 5 percent by 1985 and to about 3.6 percent by the 1990s. As a percentage of GDP, military expenses were far lower than those of other states in high-conflict regions (in the Middle East such expenses ranged between 15 and 25 percent of GDP in the 1970s–80s).[4] While South Korea's GDP grew on average by 10 percent between 1965 and 1989 (lower in 1973–84, at 7.2 percent), military expenditures relative to GDP remained largely constant. A rising GDP enabled South Korea to modernize its military, capped at about 600,000 men. North Korea's People's Army had reached twice that size by 1958 (see chapter 6), but South Korea had a better-equipped force in addition to 40,000 U.S. troops. By the 1980s, South Korea's conventional forces were considered superior to North Korea's, fueled by its sustained economic growth (Hamm 2005).

This overview suggests that neorealism does not yield one but many a priori predictions about how South Korea could respond to balance-of-power considerations in its neighborhood. Given South Korea's technical prowess, regional power status, and serious threats from a nuclearizing North Korea, the unalloyed version would have predicted an indigenous South Korean nuclear deterrent to escape dilemmas of alliance commitment. An alternative view suggests that the benefits of alliance (and the supply of coercion) obviated an indigenous deterrent. Other variants suggested potential vulnerabilities of nuclear weapons acquisition and regarded the upgrading of conventional forces as effective substitutes for an indigenous nuclear deterrence. In sum, the problem of underdetermination, whereby one theory conjures a multiplicity of outcomes, rears its head, as is the case in too many other instances.

INTERNATIONAL INSTITUTIONS: NPT DEBATE AND BELATED COMPLIANCE

South Korea signed the NPT the day it opened up for signature (1968) and also signed an updated safeguards agreement with the IAEA in 1972, but it did not ratify the NPT until April 1975, nearly seven years after signing. Some justify South Korea's delay by China and North Korea's refusal to sign the NPT as well as by Japan's delays in ratification. Furthermore, the strategic retrenchment signaled by Nixon's policies undermined South Korea's faith in the alliance in the early 1970s. Indeed, South Korea's statement accompanying ratification clarified that NPT membership would be contingent on robust U.S. security commitments (Reiss 1988:92–108). Park's statements merely two months after ratification reiterated that South Korea would need its own deterrent if U.S. guarantees were removed. Efforts to acquire Belgian and French reprocessing facilities in the early 1970s were justified as means to ensure greater energy security and economic savings, considerations that had also driven Japan toward reprocessing, setting a precedent for South Korea. Reprocessing was also suitable for weapons-level plutonium production, although a clause in the 1975 agreement with France precluded South Korea's replication of the technology for twenty years. In September 1975, South Korea concluded a trilateral safeguards agreement with the IAEA and, after South Korea cancelled the reprocessing plant, a new agreement with the IAEA in November 1975 placed all its present and future nuclear facilities under international safeguards.

By the 1970s, South Korea had gone beyond its NPT commitments by agreeing not to develop indigenous enrichment or reprocessing facilities and paying for imported enriched uranium despite technical capabilities and strong economic incentives to produce it at home, in an energy-starved economy. South Korea accepted external limits on acquiring full fuel-cycle capabilities that were never applied to Japan or others. In 1999, it signed the Additional Protocol allowing even more intrusive, short-notice visits. Following its ratification in 2004, South Korea disclosed new information, as required by the Protocol, triggering concerns over small-scale experiments in chemical uranium enrichment (1979–81) and laser enrichment (2000), and unreported uranium conversion and plutonium separation activities (early 1980s), all without governmental authorization or knowledge.[5] The IAEA reprimanded South Korea for not reporting these activities but noted that the amounts of nuclear material were insignificant, that there were no indications that undeclared experiments had continued, and that South Korea had fully cooperated with IAEA inspections.[6] South Korea's overall commitment to the NPR did not appear in doubt; it established an independent agency for nuclear control and reaffirmed its commitments to denuclearization and transparency. Except for this incident, South Korea's record of compliance is considered excellent (Reiss 1988; Kang et al. 2005). Some suspect efforts to achieve an eventual "virtual" capability, albeit not a robust weapons program (Pinkston 2004). South Korea also ratified the Biological and Toxin Weapons Convention (BTWC) in 1987, joined the Australia Group in 1995, and ratified the Chemical Weapons Convention (CWC) in 1997.

There is no concrete evidence that the NPR itself played a major role in South Korea's decisions to ratify the NPT. Nor is there evidence of concerns with nuclear weapons' acquisition as a taboo. Many of the public statements discussed in this chapter pointedly suggest that nuclear abstention was linked to U.S. commitments or domestic considerations. As Japan, South Korea merely substituted U.S. nuclear weapons for its own, rendering a taboo argument problematic for explaining non-nuclear weapons status. Furthermore, despite kinship ties with North Korea, U.S. nuclear weapons remained the South's favored deterrent for decades, discounting concerns with common identity or ancestry between North and South Korea. Both significant delays and eventual ratification were punctuated by domestic and international events, including the Nixon shocks, concerns with neighbors' nuclear postures, potential U.S. reactions to South Korea's nuclearization, and domestic pressures on Park to abandon policies of international economic openness. The opposition to Park in the 1971 election campaign, and the various influential bureaucratic and military sectors poised to benefit from "industrial deepening" and expansion of the military-industrial-complex, demanded import-substitution, self-reliant defense, and other populist themes. Pressures to develop nuclear weapons were overlaid on this broader debate. Explaining South Korea's approach to the NPT thus requires attention to Park's dilemmas of political control in a highly contested domestic environment in the 1970s.

DOMESTIC POLITICS: "THINK EXPORT FIRST!" VERSUS "DEEPENING"

In the aftermath of the Korean War, Rhee Syngman maintained a corrupt model of extensive state entrepreneurship, protectionism, and import-substitution. Student protests in 1960 forced Rhee's resignation. His successor Chang Myon's brief tenure was punctuated by economic instability, widespread corruption, and mobilization of Communist and other groups demanding unconditional negotiations with the North. By the late 1950s, North Korea had achieved political consolidation and economic gains (Scalapino 1963a; Kuark 1963), fueling pro-unification demands within South Korea. When General Park seized power in 1961, he initially retained inward-looking policies, import licenses, and high tariffs.[7] However, against a background of protracted domestic instability, inflationary and balance-of-payment crises, the shadow of North Korea's significant economic performance, and the unfolding Japanese "miracle," Park replaced a brief episode of economic self-sufficiency with a growth-oriented export-led model of political survival in 1963–64.[8] Backed by junior officers, Park purged the bureaucracy, politicians associated with the old order, and the military itself. His new "sword-won" coalition included active and former military administrators; technocrats in the newly created Economic Planning Board (EPB) controlling the Ministry of Finance, the Bank of Korea, and all ministerial and state agencies; and big enterprises *(chaebol)*, which were coerced, subsidized, and induced into the new model (Jones and Sakong 1980; Cheng 1990; Moon 1990, 1994; Ogle 1990; Haggard 1995).

Strong incentives to export-oriented firms, guarantees for foreign investments and loans, tariff reductions, and sweeping improvements in tax collection followed. Some have traced Park's new model exclusively to U.S. pressures. In the 1950s, however, the United States had demanded that Rhee privatize state enterprises and banks, control inflation, reform exchange rate policy, and accept ceilings on its military, all to no avail (Cumings 1984, 1990; Haggard and Moon 1993; Haggard, Cooper, and Moon 1993). The United States also criticized Rhee's unmitigated hostility to normalization with Japan, a potential provider of new investment and aid. Rhee resisted these pressures, and Park moved toward new policies not in 1961 but in 1963–64. Rhee's absolute resistance and Park's variable receptivity (higher in 1964 than in 1961 or the 1970s) defy arguments that hegemonic diktats uniquely explain South Korea's export-led model.[9] Park's concerns with domestic political ferment, balance-of-payments deficits, inflation, and exhausted import-substitution, and with external U.S. and multilateral (IMF) pressures pushed in the same—export-led— direction. Many states facing comparable circumstances (including North Korea) did not follow that orientation, particularly in the 1960s, because their domestic political configurations were less conducive to such transformation (Solingen 2007a). Park assumed power following a coup and sought to gain domestic legitimacy through rapid economic growth (Oberdorfer 2001). The rationale he provided for his model was that "for a country like Korea, unendowed by nature and saddled with minuscule markets, only an external-oriented development strategy, making full use of the abundant human resources but aimed at exports, appeared relevant" (Park 1979:72). If successful, integration into the global economy would enhance domestic support for a weak, repressive regime with a hitherto unremarkable record. Park's regime's motto became "Nation Building Through Exports," and "Think Export First!"

The model leaned primarily on international markets, capital, technology, and extensive cooperation with raw material suppliers. An Open Door Policy was designed to strengthen global access through economic and political relations with all states regardless of ideological stripe. Park (1979:139) sought a new image for South Korea, away from the "unfavorable impression of being an extremely obstinate and inflexible anti-Communist state," and moved by a desire "not to run counter to world trends." Large-scale U.S. loans and grants had diminished by the early 1960s, and, as foreign aid declined sharply between 1959 and 1965, Park's efforts to attract Japanese capital and technology intensified.[10] Overriding nationalist opposition, Park ratified the treaty normalizing relations with Japan in 1965, securing $800 million in Japanese grants, loans, and credit over the following decade. Beyond immediate economic benefits, rapprochement with Japan was important to stabilize the region and enable domestic economic growth. Park's model required not only stability at home but also prevention of war "by all means," and "under any circumstances," because he regarded instability as "anathema to . . . development and progress" (Park 1979:94; 1976:118, 29–33). He abandoned the old Liberal Party's combative "Let Us March North" slogan and defined the search for unification with North Korea through peace and gradual mutual opening (Park 1971:99, 1979:50–56, 90). His model became his "compass of peace," emphasizing the synergies between domestic, regional, and international objectives (Park 1976:125–26).

The model barely began yielding fruit when the 1968 NPT's conclusion presented Park with a new dilemma. The model—dramatic growth in manufactured exports, close relations with the United States as market and ally, the rapprochement with Japan, increased reliance on international economic institutions, international access to raw material and technology suppliers, a massive diplomatic offensive, regional stability vis-à-vis the North, and lingering domestic ferment for reunification—dictated a restrained position on nuclear matters, leading Park to sign the NPT. The military was not particularly threatened by Park's objectives at this time. Its own institutional growth and political leverage were enhanced by massive U.S. military aid in the 1960s. Where internal cleavages surfaced, Park suppressed or muted them.[11] Park established the Atomic Energy Development Promoting Committee in 1968 under the chairmanship of the deputy prime minister, who was also economic planning minister, not under military control. The EPB was to have oversight over the nuclear energy industry and its external financing as well as over other ministries. As a zealous steward of the export-led model and macroeconomic stability, the EPB opposed large allocations to the military-industrial-complex.

The alliance provided, as in Japan, an opportunity to leap economically while restraining military expenditures that might compete with growth and thwart regional stability. However, a new confluence of domestic and international events in the early 1970s presented significant challenges for Park's model, emboldening domestic forces favoring greater economic and military self-reliance. External shocks included Nixon's 1969 Guam doctrine, the 1971 elimination of the gold standard, his surprise visit to China, and generalized fear of U.S. disengagement in the post-Vietnam era. Furthermore, growing protectionism overseas strengthened South Korea's inward-looking constituencies, including proponents of a more self-reliant military-industrial-complex. The repressed labor movement organized massive strikes in 1969–70, culminating in a worker's immolation (1970) and the harshly suppressed Kwangju uprising by the urban poor in Kyunggi province (1971). Stabilization efforts prodded by IMF standby agreements (1970–72) slowed down real growth and export expansion. New limits on textile exports mobilized the Federation of Korean Industries—representing the largest firms—to demand an end to economic contraction (Haggard 1994a:28–42). The opposition led by Kim Dae-Jung advanced populist themes in the 1971 electoral campaign, stressing equity, agricultural reforms, and support for the Cholla provinces, which had been disadvantaged relative to Park's native Kyongsang. Unsurprisingly, the 1971 elections yielded disappointing results for Park despite his alleged fraudulent intervention.

Park turned to more expansionist fiscal and monetary policies in 1972, reversing the financial liberalization of the mid-1960s, reinstating price controls, and introducing martial law under the October Revitalizing Reforms (*Siwol Yushin*) wrapped in juche (self-sufficiency) rhetoric, national identity, and national security in a sinister—if short-lived—effort to match North Korea's manipulation of juche. New import-substituting policies supported subsidies for heavy and chemical industrialization; provided protection to iron and steel, shipbuilding, oil refining, electronics, machinery, and petrochemical industries, among others; and emphasized self-sufficiency and "domestically producible" goods. Economic nationalists in the bureaucracy bypassed the EPB and the Ministry of Finance, which remained opposed to inward-looking industrial "deepening." Chaebols and conservative rural forces behind the Saemaul (New Village) Movement supported a return to authoritarianism and harsh repression. "Deepening" also favored military sectors pressing for homegrown military industrialization to replace U.S. imports and develop nonferrous metal industries (aluminum, copper, zinc, and lead) among others (Choi 1993; Haggard 1994b; Reiss 1988; Solingen 1998). Whereas military expenditures had declined by 20 to 30 percent in the 1960s, the Force Modernization Plan increased them by 25 to 50 percent yearly over the 1970s, from 5 to about 7.5 percent of GNP (Hwang 2003). The United States and the World Bank exerted significant political and economic coercion to block this turn toward deepening but were unable to prevent it, providing further evidence that international factors may be less determinative than often assumed (Cumings 1984; Haggard 1994a, 1994b).

Against this background of increased nationalist pressures for "deepening" and an expanding military-industrial-complex, Park created an Agency for Defense Development and a Weapons Exploitation Committee to study a nuclear option in 1970.[12] The committee allegedly recommended the development of nuclear weapons in 1972, and Park approved the purchase of a French reprocessing facility and a Canadian heavy-water reactor suitable for plutonium production (Pinkston 2004). The United States had decided to remove 20,000 troops by 1971, with potential further reductions once South Korea's troops returned from Vietnam, and pressed South Korea for voluntary export restraints on textiles.[13] Nixon's policies in economics and security reinforced domestic political, economic, and military constituencies favoring self-sufficiency. This turn had negative effects on the prospects of NPT ratification in the short term, as significant segments of the bureaucracy and the public opposed ratification (Reiss 1988). Some officials began uttering ambiguous statements about South Korea's nuclear options, countering official statements pledging support for nonproliferation. These inconsistencies reflected domestic divisions between supporters of Park's 1964 model and those favoring "deepening," tensions that grew stronger throughout the 1970s, when efforts to acquire dual-use facilities continued. Park's regime survival hinged on his ability to maneuver through this domestic divide.

On the one hand, suspicions about South Korea's nuclear intentions had to be put to rest if the export-led growth strategy was to have any chance. Greater transparency would stem adverse domestic, regional, and international consequences of nuclearization and protect the model's viability. The IMF (particularly the Oil Facility), the U.S. Export-Import Bank, and Japanese loans were crucial for balance-of-payments financing in 1974.[14] Export-oriented firms were critically dependent on primarily U.S. and Japanese investors, loans, and markets that could have curtailed and boycotted economic ties with a nuclear South Korea. Moreover, in an economy heavily dependent on foreign sources of energy, the promise of plentiful nuclear energy from Western-supplied power plants to fuel heavy industry and intermediary sectors was at risk if nonproliferation commitments were violated.[15] Foreign loans had increased tenfold between 1965 and 1970. Exports as a share of GDP had nearly tripled (from 10.4 to 29.1 percent) between 1966 and 1973. Manufactured goods—which accounted for 17 percent of exports in the early 1960s—had risen to 83 percent by the early 1970s. The incidence of poverty declined from more than 40 percent of all households in 1965 to 10 percent by the latter part of the 1970s. External borrowing allowed high levels of investment and savings. Yet South Korea counted on two weeks of oil reserves when the 1973 oil crisis erupted (Reiss 1988:78–108), seriously threatening Park's model (Krueger 1993; Haggard 1994a:39). Given this context, and Park's favored model, it is hardly surprising that Park was responsive to U.S. efforts to persuade South Korea to ratify the NPT in April 1975.

On the other hand, echoing proponents of an indigenous deterrent, Park warned in June 1975 that although South Korea was honoring NPT commitments, "if the U.S. nuclear umbrella were to be removed, we have to start developing our nuclear capability to save ourselves.[16] Park declared his faith in U.S. pledges but warned that "there were and still are quite a number of Koreans doubting the commitment of the United States" since the fall of Vietnam. A Korean opposition politician declared in the United States that South Korea could build nuclear weapons "whenever we want to," even if there were no plans at the time (Reiss 1988:85–86, 93–94). Park could wield this domestic opposition to extract stronger U.S. security commitments that would obviate the need for an indigenous deterrent. Studies of South Korea's nuclear policies emphasize Park's instrumental use of the threat to develop nuclear weapons—as a "bargaining chip"—to extract stronger U.S. commitments, more advanced weapons, support for its nuclear energy program, and improved access to Export-Import Bank financing for technology and military equipment (Ha 1978; Siler 1998). At the same time, in order to sustain the economic miracle, Park reassured the world that South Korea had no active plan to develop such weapons.[17] Thus Park made the most of the difficult external and domestic circumstances of the mid-1970s, pressing the United States for advanced weapons and technology and satisfying his home-grown military advocates of conventional deterrence without marring efforts to maintain international economic access. Park also linked any trade concessions to the United States with security offsets, demanding the retention of 43,000 U.S. troops in South Korea as well as U.S. reassurance of continuous commitments and military assistance.[18]

Clearly external constraints helped Park resolve domestic cross-pressures. Kissinger reportedly threatened a major break in bilateral economic relations—the lifeline of Park's "miracle"—unless South Korea ratified and implemented the NPT. The U.S. Congress introduced a joint resolution requesting that the Export-Import Bank withhold financing for South Korea's second nuclear reactor, and in late 1975 President Ford warned that acquiring the French reprocessing plant would lead to cancellation of Export-Import Bank loans for South Korea's nuclear energy program (Ha 1978; Siler 1998). The United States also threatened to delay Canada's delivery of a heavy-water reactor and to reconsider the entire spectrum of relations with South Korea, including security, if the latter developed nuclear weapons (Gleysteen 1999; Oberdorfer 2001). Without U.S. equipment and fuel supplies for South Korea's first nuclear plant, still under construction in 1975, the economy might have stalled at an already critical period following the oil crisis (Yager 1985). Nuclear power reactors under construction were being financed virtually entirely with foreign loans. The United States allegedly made financing of South Korea's second reactor contingent on its renunciation of reprocessing capabilities (Hayes 1993:51–52; Drezner 1999). Furthermore, the prospects for South Korea's nuclearization antagonized another major economic partner and old adversary: Japan. The United States and Japan accounted for 85 percent of all FDI in South Korea, for most of its foreign debt, and for over 60 percent of exports and imports. These pressures and constraints might have been less relevant (as indeed they were in many other cases) had Park not banked on a model of continued economic growth, domestic and regional stability, and access to global markets, oil, capital, and technology as his dominant priority. Nuclearization would have derailed Park's strategy in a regional environment already subjected to North Korea's destabilizing efforts. Park thus cancelled the reprocessing plant in January 1976 and proclaimed that South Korea had no nuclear weapons program (Meyer 1984; Spector and Smith 1990; Reiss 1988).

Throughout the 1970s, Park had also remained sensitive to preventing war with the North as a key requirement for maintaining stability and growth. His policy of "peaceful competition," launched in 1970, led to 1971 sessions between the Red Cross Societies of North and South, the 1972 July Fourth Joint Communiqué, and the formation of a North-South Coordination Commission. In 1973, Park followed up with a Foreign Policy for Peace and Unification vis-à-vis the North and initiatives to establish relations with communist countries and enhance regional stability. In a coherent specification of his objectives, Park (1976:125) expressed a self-binding commitment against the use of force: "I take this opportunity to make it clear once again to the North Korean side that violence or military force will never be employed by us in the pursuit of the goal of unification. That has been, and will continue to be, our fundamental position." Park and his technocratic and political allies opposed squandering resources crucial to the growth model (Jones and Sakong 1980; Gokarn 1995:51) and sought to check "the arbitrariness and rashness of the military officers" (Park 1971:107). Cultivating national strength meant "doing away with those activities that tend to drain or waste our natural resources in a broad sense" (Park 1976:171). Even after North Korea assassinated Park's wife in 1974, he continued to focus on the synergies between South Korea's economic vitality, regional stability, and a positive "recognition in the world community." Asked about his most significant achievement in fourteen years in office, Park cited the South's ability to excel over the North economically while avoiding a war of aggression.[19] He regarded the crossing of the $10 billion threshold in manufacturing exports in 1977 as a milestone, lifting South Korea's economy from seventy-second place in 1962 to twenty-eighth in 1976. South Korea had achieved that target—as Park emphasized in public speeches— in a shorter span than West Germany and Japan.

In 1977 Park stated unequivocally that South Korea would not pursue a nuclear deterrent even as fierce domestic competition between the two camps continued. Carter's early 1977 proposals to withdraw all U.S. troops and nuclear weapons from South Korea exacerbated this internal debate. South Korea's vice-premier and foreign minister speculated that certain circumstances could force the country to consider the nuclear option.[20] South Korea's minister of science and technology announced in August 1977 that South Korea would produce nuclear fuel domestically to guarantee fuel supply and, in 1978, that it would launch a massive plan for forty nuclear reactors by 2000. The National Unification Board released a report in early 1978 supporting South Korea's development of nuclear weapons. This nationalist resurgence resurfaced with the late 1970s oil crisis, which led to the highest inflation levels since the early 1960s, declining export performance, and political turmoil. Worsening economic and political conditions strengthened the opposition led by Kim Dae-Jung, backed by textile workers, small business, domestically oriented firms, impoverished urban and rural workers, and others adversely affected by Yushin reforms, the heavy industry drive, and stabilization efforts. Under the grim confluence of Carter's policies and domestic nationalist revival, South Korea allegedly continued efforts to master the nuclear fuel-cycle although there is no clear evidence for a full-fledged covert program.[21]

Park was assassinated in October 1979, at which time South Korea had a $20–38 billion external debt due largely to U.S. and Japanese banks.[22] South Korea also depended on the United States and Japan for half of its total trade, which had risen dramatically to over 50 percent of its GNP by the 1980s (Dunn 1982:108). Responding to widespread strikes, high inflation, and declining export performance—which had weakened promoters of industrial deepening—General Chun Doo-Hwan's coup bolstered the return of export-led growth. The EPB and their allies resumed bureaucratic controls, introducing Comprehensive Measures for Economic Stabilization. Chun introduced martial law to suppress demonstrations, notably at Kwangju, but also sought to attract support from what had become a large constituency of middle-class owners of small and medium-sized firms, professional, managerial, and technical workers, consumers, and savers.[23] Chun's forceful drive toward further integration in the global economy compelled him to nurture South Korea's nonproliferation credentials.[24] Public statements regarding the potential desirability of nuclear weapons subsided in late 1979 with the return of a full-fledged export-oriented model and cancellation of Carter's plans to remove U.S. troops from South Korea. In the 1980s, South Korea actively pursued a NWFZ despite enjoying unquestionable technical and industrial capabilities to overwhelm North Korea in a nuclear race.

TRANSITION TO DEMOCRACY: CHAEBOLS, "SEA OF FIRE," AND "SUNSHINE POLICY"

South Korea's transition to democracy did not alter the model that had lifted the country from abject poverty to advanced industrial status. Indeed, as the export-led model became more embedded in the 1980s, opposition to authoritarianism became more effective (Vogel 1987:59). Wider and stronger domestic constituencies favoring the growth model had emerged that, though opposed to authoritarian rule, supported liberalization, reduced state intervention, and Central Bank independence. A large middle class no longer faced the dilemma posed by a desire to eject authoritarianism and risk wrecking export-led growth. Yet residual defiance of economic openness and alignment with the United States and advocacy of immediate unification with the North remained important themes that gained greater political expression with the political opening that took place in mid-1987. Rho Tae-Woo assumed power in 1988, retaining an emphasis on exports and macroeconomic stability but also promoting housing, social spending, and greater responsiveness to societal demands (Moon 1994; Haggard and Kaufman 1995). Leaning on this politically inclusive domestic social agenda and strong export performance in the late 1980s, Roh announced his "Nordpolitik" dialogue as an "Economic Commonwealth" to promote trade and investment with the North, and normalization with the Soviet Union and China. South Korea's firms eyed opportunities to shift labor-intensive operations to North Korea (Pollack 1994) and supported Nordpolitik, which bolstered an internationalizing strategy while coopting the reunification theme from inward-looking nationalists (Choi 1993:42–3). Private investments were also expected to contribute to North Korea's China-style "soft-landing," a prospect that North Korea's old guard resisted forcefully (see chapter 6).

Further disclosures of North Korea's weapons program in the early 1990s and U.S. removal of tactical nuclear weapons from South Korea in

1990 tested—and confirmed—the latter's commitment to a non-nuclear trajectory. South Korea's defense minister was forced to retract a warning that his country might destroy the North's Yongbyong nuclear facilities.[25] Roh declared that South Korea "would no longer possess or store [other countries'] nuclear weapons on its soil" and that neither would it "manufacture, possess, store, deploy, or use nuclear weapons."[26] Although the removal of nuclear weapons was part of the George Bush Sr. administration's global strategy, it was also expected to reassure North Korea and facilitate IAEA inspections. Roh also proposed nuclear discussions with the North and mutual inspections of civilian and military facilities. The Koreas signed a "reconciliation and nonaggression pact" followed by a "Joint Declaration for a Non-Nuclear Korean Peninsula" in 1991, affirming commitments not to manufacture, store, receive, possess, deploy, or use nuclear weapons, and not to develop enrichment and reprocessing facilities. The South suspended 1992 Team Spirit exercises with the United States to signal its commitment to this process.

When Kim Young-Sam became the first democratically elected civilian president in early 1993, he pledged categorically that South Korea would never develop a nuclear arsenal, even though he feared a "chain reaction" leading from North Korea's nuclear program to Japan's nuclearization.[27] Following North Korea's unprecedented withdrawal from the NPT, Kim was reluctant to support President Clinton's offers to suspend 1993 Team Spirit exercises and offer diplomatic recognition and aid to the North in exchange for restoring its NPT commitments. Yet he also urged moderation after Clinton's stern warning to North Korea that it risked destruction. Kim had to navigate South Korea's new democratic waters, maintaining economic growth and stability while deflating domestic conservative—including military—opposition to propping up the North's regime.[28] This was no easy task given a North Korean official's warnings that it would "destroy Seoul in a sea of fire, like a rabid dog barking at the sky, unaware of the fate about to befall it."[29] Kim Young-Sam, the target of offensive remarks by North Korean leaders, also had to tolerate South Korea's marginalization from negotiations of the 1994 Agreed Framework, which nonetheless granted South Korea a central role in supplying two 1,000 MW nuclear reactors to North Korea. By 1994, leading business firms associated with the Korean Trade Promotion Corporation (KOTRA) were publicly urging the government to promote trade with the North despite the nuclear crisis, in line with government efforts to maintain low-key responses that would not damage foreign investment and tourism.[30]

In 1997 Kim Dae-Jung came to power after twenty-six years of imprisonment, torture, exile, and attempted murder by successive military regimes. Despite receiving strong support from labor and inward-looking economic nationalists, in his very first interview he pledged free markets to guarantee the safety of foreign investment, endorsed tight IMF conditions following the 1997 financial crisis, and vowed to tighten relations with the United States and Japan and improve dialogue with North Korea. "We are living," he said "in a globalized economy."[31] This was not a dramatically changed model of political survival from the one endorsed by his predecessors decades earlier, except for the striking improvement of relying on a liberal democracy to uphold the model. "Economic cooperation," argued Kim Dae-Jung, "benefits not only the North Korean economy, but our [South Korea's] economy as well."[32] He thus proposed a meeting with Kim Jong-Il and offered extensive economic benefits and humanitarian aid to North Korea through his "sunshine policy," culminating in the first inter-Korean summit held in Pyongyang in 2000. The summit was allegedly underwritten by hefty monetary transfers to Kim Jong-Il. South Korean officials acknowledged that promoting chaebol activities in the North was "an inexpensive insurance policy to calm investors, contributing to the $50 billion that has flowed into South Korea since 1997."[33] Ironically, the laboratory-scale enrichment experiment that tarnished South Korea's nonproliferation credentials in 2004 took place under Kim Dae-Jung's watch, although it was purportedly undertaken without knowledge of the science and technology minister or the president (Pinkston 2004).

Incoming president Roh Moo-Huyn strongly supported the "sunshine policy," re-labeling it "the peace and prosperity policy." Pyongyang's nuclear activities did not alter this policy of accommodation. Popular threat perceptions in South Korea appeared lower than ever just as North Korea acknowledged its growing nuclear potential.[34] Despite considerable difficulties imposed by North Korea, its low-wage labor force continued to provide incentives to chaebols backed by South Korea's Ministry of Finance and Economy. The Kaesong Industrial Park, originally launched by thirteen companies led by Hyundai-Asan, was planned to house 300 firms by 2007. It employed over 6,000 North Koreans in 2006 and is expected to employ 730,000 North Koreans and 100,000 South Koreans in more than 1,000 companies over the next twenty years, provided North Korea does not derail it and the United States and Japan don't boycott its output.[35] Beyond private prospects for sizable returns from exchanges with the North, South Korea expected these endeavors to yield a significant push for economic growth in the South. Chung In-Moon—former chairman of the Presidential Committee on Northeast Asian Cooperation Initiative, which promoted the Kaesong initiative—stated that "the success of Kaesong will have a real impact on the success of the South Korean economy."[36] A peaceful management of North Korea's continued provocations continues to be critical for South Korea's international economic standing, bond ratings, and appeal to foreign investors. Deputy finance minister Bahk Byong-Won acknowledged, in a year when South Korea's stock market was the world's ninth-worst performer, that North Korea "is one of the biggest areas of uncertainty about our [economic] outlook."[37] North Korea's behavior has inhibited investment not just in the North but also in South Korea, harming its currency sovereign ratings. Roh Moo-Huyn's "peace and prosperity policy" was expected to provide a stable environment that lowered military expenditures and, by subsidizing investments in North Korea, lowered the eventual costs of unification estimated at between $800 billion and $1.4 trillion.

Conclusion

Unalloyed neorealism would have expected a regional power like South Korea—one of the world's largest economies, with rising external threats from a nuclear North Korea, a declining U.S. alliance, and advanced technical capabilities—to have developed nuclear weapons. This has not happened. However, much as in our discussion of Japan, a much wider and open-ended range of nuclear policies by South Korea seemed compatible with neorealism. Whereas nuclear weapons might have addressed its vulnerability, they could have also exposed it more forcefully, all in the name of self-help. The alliance provides a sounder explanation for its denuclearization, particularly a posteriori, but leaves unexplained why South Korea was receptive to U.S. incentives and coercion whereas these two failed in other cases. Both the alliance and coercion may have been necessary for South Korea's denuclearization, but one can fully understand their role only in the context of domestic strategies of political survival. They explain why the U.S. alliance was chosen over North Korean-style juche (autarky, see chapter 6) in the first place, with ensuing consequences for relative receptivity to external inducements, both positive and negative. Would the same alliance have resulted had Park or any other leader relied on North Korea's brand of juche as his favored model? Can reliance on the United States at its lowest credibility point in the 1970s be understood without considering the alliance's broader purpose in Park's model?[38] Would the same policies have resulted had inward-looking "deepening" overturned Park's model lastingly in the 1970s?

For regimes taking cues from a strong military establishment (1960s–1980s) and under the ominous shadow of nuclear-capable neighbors, South Korea's denuclearization makes the role of domestic political-economy considerations in defining nuclear policies most remarkable. As Reiss (1988:95) argues, Park's goals "were twofold: to ensure political stability and to encourage economic growth. These goals were symbiotic: political tranquility would provide an environment attractive to investors, and a rising standard of living would help mollify internal discontent . . . it is possible that [nuclear weapons] would have been detrimental to these ends." An indigenous nuclear deterrent would have disrupted the 10 percent average annual growth rates that drew external support from allies, commercial partners, and international institutions. Park, reviled as an authoritarian, had made export-led growth the core of his domestic survival model. While not oblivious to potential advantages of nuclear weapons, he also tied their fate to that higher core objective. Park also used the threat of nuclear weapons development effectively as a bargaining tool to extract concessions from the United States, military and otherwise.

The politics of domestic survival thus help unpack South Korea's receptivity to external coercion, threats, and inducements. The threat from the North too was skillfully deployed as an efficient tool for mobilizing and consolidating domestic support for Park's model and suppressing internal dissent. "There is an even more important reason for seeking high economic growth, and that is the need for us to maintain a position superior to North Korea in our present state of confrontation. Already, the south's economic power is three times larger than that of the north, but the North Korean Communist regime, by concentrating its total resources on preparations for war, continues to present a serious military threat. . . . Unless a policy of high economic growth is sustained, there will be no way to meet increased defense spending."[39] "I have proposed to North Korea," Park explained, "to accept peaceful competition between our free system and theirs to determine which system can give the people a better life. The Republic of Korea is already emerging victorious from this competition and by fully making use of our talents as a people we should continue to sustain high growth to create in Korea an affluent, highly industrialized society."

Democratization helped consolidate the model and its fundamental nonproliferation commitments. By 2000, about 70 percent of South Korea's economy was tied to foreign trade. Widespread domestic support for this strategy had overwhelmed the few advocates of nuclear weapons.[40] Chaebols became main drivers but also instruments in the hands of South Korea's leaders to spearhead the transformation of North Korea. North Korea's nuclear threats made the relative stability, growth, and consolidation of this strategy all the more remarkable. Nuclearizing South Korea would have endangered the model, alienated domestic support, risked sharp economic decline, increased political and economic instability, and isolated its leaders from the market and institutional, regional and international forces that underpinned their model. A vibrant democracy made domestic considerations an even more central barrier to nuclearization, plausibly far more important than U.S. preferences on the matter.

The apparent decline in threat perceptions in South Korea cannot be explained by neorealism, given an ever more threatening North Korea disclosing nuclear capabilities. Ironically, more severe threats from a structural perspective were also met with dipping levels of support for the alliance.[41] Roh Moo-Huyn, presiding over South Korea's least friendly administration vis-à-vis the United States since the 1960s, reaffirmed that South Korea "has no intention of developing or possessing nuclear weapons."[42]

Meanwhile, the promising Six Party Talks statement of September 19, 2005, led experts at South Korea's brokerage firms to predict higher sovereign ratings for South Korea, improved performance of the undervalued local stock market, and new export markets for South Korean firms.[43] Business sectors hailed the statement as "a great achievement." The statement reaffirmed South Korea's assertion that it has no nuclear weapons and is committed not to receive or deploy them in accordance with the 1992 Joint Declaration on Denuclearization of the Korean Peninsula. Merely one day after, however, North Korea's retractions and ambiguity led credit-rating agency Moody's to suspend its planned raise in South Korea's credit rating.[44] The economic incentives of South Koreans are clearly intertwined with the vicissitudes of North Korea's nuclear policies and South Korea's responses to them.

North Korea's 2006 missile and nuclear tests were also tests for South Korea, with the potential for overturning the policies that South Korea has pursued thus far. After a unanimous UNSC resolution imposed arms and financial sanctions, North Korea warned the South that it would pay dearly if it implemented the sanctions.[45] Although South Korean polls after North Korea's nuclear test showed increased support for a South Korean nuclear deterrent, the Roh Moo-Huyn government's response was an affirmation of its policy of reconciliation and cooperation with North Korea, including the Kaesong and Kumgang projects and food aid, and a refusal to join the Proliferation Security Initiative to inspect vessels for weapons materials.[46]

CHAPTER FIVE

Taiwan (Republic of China)

IN 1949 Nationalist forces defeated by Chinese communists retreated to Taiwan and established the Republic of China (Taiwan henceforth).[1] In 1954 China bombarded Quemoy and Matsu triggering air strikes on the mainland, as ordered by President Chiang Kai-shek, which was followed by U.S. intervention in Taiwan's defense and the signing of a U.S.-ROC Defense Pact.[2] In 1958 China bombarded the islands again, prompting the Seventh Fleet into the Straits. President Chiang Ching-Kuo—Chiang Kai-shek's son—acknowledged in 1975 that Taiwan began efforts to acquire nuclear capabilities in the 1950s, acquiring basic capabilities by 1974 (Dunn 1982; Cooper 1979). Wu Ta-you (1988), former director of the Science Development Advisory Committee of Taiwan's National Security Council in the 1970s, admitted that China's 1964 nuclear test aggravated Taiwan's concerns. The Chungshan Institute of Science and Technology—founded in 1965 under Defense Ministry sponsorship—allocated $140 million to the "Hsin Chu" program in 1967 for acquiring a heavy-water reactor, a heavy-water production plant, a plutonium separation plant, and ballistic missile production. As his science advisor, Wu persuaded Chiang Kai-shek to reject this plan for its high (and underestimated) cost and its potential for alienating the international community and damaging Taiwan's security.[3] The military branded Wu a traitor, and he was no longer connected to the nuclear program after 1967. Nonetheless, according to Wu (1988), Chiang Kai-shek followed his advice to cancel the plan and Chiang never supported nuclear weapons development. According to declassified U.S. sources from 1966, however, Hsu Cho-yun, chairman of the history department at National Taiwan University—a man highly connected with Taiwan's national security bureaucracy—considered Chiang Kai-shek to have been fully behind it.[4]

In 1968 a civilian-controlled Atomic Energy Council (AEC) took over nuclear energy development, including Chungshan. However, Lt. Gen. Tang Chung-po, director of Chungshan's Preparatory Committee and Vice Minister of Defense, remained a council member. Although some considered Tang to be the driving force behind the nuclear weapons proposal, U.S. archival documents portray Tang as skeptical of Chiang Kai-shek's presumed nuclear designs.[5] Chungshan favored a heavy-water power reactor more suitable for fissile material production, whereas Wu allegedly proposed a safeguarded light-water reactor. Wu's recommendations were accepted, but the Institute for Nuclear Energy Research (INER, founded in 1968) adjacent to Chungshan also purchased a small heavy-water reactor from Canada in 1969, which was managed by Tang's deputy, Admiral Hsia Hsin.[6] Years later Wu declared that Chiang Ching-kuo—then a defense ministry official—decided to pursue plutonium separation secretly, without his father's knowledge, beginning in 1969 (Albright and Gay 1998). However, AEC's secretary general Victor Cheng countered that the fifteen grams of plutonium produced per year fell far short of what would have been required for nuclear weapons.

INER's fuel fabrication began in 1972 or 1973 and the heavy-water Taiwan Research Reactor (TRR) operated by 1973 but not at full capacity (Richelson 2006). AEC director Yen Chen-hsing acknowledged (in 1988) that INER had initially been engaged in nuclear weapons work. In 1973 AEC officials privately informed U.S. diplomats about plans for a "hot lab" at Chungshan. The United States warned Taiwan against acquiring a reprocessing plant (Burr 1999). Chungshan Director Chieng Chi-Peng, a former military man, was the major proponent of this purchase, which AEC members opposed. The United States pressured West German suppliers to abstain from transferring sensitive technologies and cautioned Taiwan that it should not create the impression that it was seeking nuclear weapons.[7] Taiwan's foreign minister confirmed that the reprocessing plant would not be acquired. A U.S. intelligence report concluded that, although Taiwan had no plans to develop nuclear weapons at that time, it could not rule out such a decision "at some future date."[8] Another memorandum cited the adamance of Aerospace Corporation's Dr. Bruce Billings, an advisor to the U.S. government, in assessing Taiwan's nuclear program as "absolutely open and non-military in its intent."[9] A late 1974 CIA report revived suspicions—buttressed by IAEA inspections—that Taiwan may have been seeking a nuclear weapons *option*, although no clear evidence emerged. The State Department issued a demarche through Ambassador Leonard Unger, demanding that Taiwan formally renounce nuclear weapons development.[10] The demarche's precise content remains classified, and it is unclear whether the document referred specifically to secret reprocessing activities. By September 1976 Taiwan provided an explicit commitment that "it has no intention whatsoever to develop nuclear weapons . . . or to engage in any activities related to reprocessing purposes," and dismantled the reprocessing laboratory as a token of good faith.[11]

Chiang Kai-shek died in 1975, and Chiang Ching-kuo became president in 1978, just as one member of the Kuomintang's (KMT) Central Committee urged Taiwan to acquire nuclear weapons. The vice foreign minister declared that Taiwan would not develop them, although some argue that efforts to produce plutonium continued through the 1980s.[12] In 1987 INER began construction of a multiple hot cell facility, presumably violating 1976 commitments. Chiang Ching-kuo died in January 1988 as the facility was allegedly being built. Some suggested that incoming Premier Lee Teng-hui probably did not know about it, but others contend Lee shut down the program.[13] U.S. officials visited the facility in early 1988 and arguably forced Taiwan to dismantle it, finding no evidence of plutonium separation. The IAEA demanded to inspect all Taiwan's nuclear facilities, installing additional cameras at the TRR and examining its plutonium-laden irradiated fuel. The United States also pressed Taiwan to return plutonium that the Americans had supplied for experimental purposes. Deputy chairman of Taiwan's cabinet-level AEC, Yang Chao-yie, declared that Taiwan "never made any plutonium separation experiments, not in the 1980s, and not earlier . . . the program was just research."[14]

Media reports suggested that Chungshan had only abandoned an active bomb-building program after its deputy director defected to the United States in 1988.[15] Col. Chang Hsien-yi was imputed with stealing documents containing evidence of Taiwan's suspicious activities. The Reagan administration allegedly pressured Taiwan to discontinue the presumed secret plutonium separation plant and to shut down TRR. The Defense Ministry denied that Taiwan ever manufactured nuclear weapons, and the cabinet denied that Chang was a CIA informant.[16] In 1999 retired Chief of General Staff (1981–89) General Hao Pei-tsun (Hao Po-ts'un) declared that Taiwan had been capable of developing nuclear weapons more than a decade earlier but never realized that potential. Hao also confirmed that Chungshan's main mission was to develop nuclear weapons but stopped the program once Taiwan signed the NPT.[17] Taiwan's 1988 commitments to the United States went beyond its NPT obligations (Mitchell 2004). Subsequently, Defense Minister Tang Fei declared that Taiwan had no ability to produce nuclear weapons "because all research work has been halted," and Taiwan "would never develop nuclear arms."[18]

This overview suggests that Taiwan allegedly engaged in early tentative efforts to develop nuclear weapons in the late 1960s and 1970s. Yet, despite its technical capabilities and existential vulnerability vis-à-vis China, it subsequently renounced them. A Russian Federation study of nuclear aspirants puts it quite succinctly: "Taiwan does not have nuclear weapons. . . . We can assert with sufficient confidence that officially imported nuclear technologies, knowledge, and equipment do not enable Taiwan to create nuclear weapons, but do provide it with the necessary know-how to do work in the nuclear field and may accelerate the country's own nuclear developments of a military nature, if such a decision is made."[19] Even Albright and Gay's (1998) cautious study defined Taiwan's nuclear status as "satisfactory," given that it never separated much, if any, plutonium. How do different perspectives described in chapter 2 explain this nuclear evolution?

STRUCTURAL POWER AND EXISTENTIAL THREATS

Taiwan provides a quintessential case of security vulnerability and should be rather easily explained by perspectives focusing on relative power and existential threats. China's persistent threats to invade Taiwan and its nuclear 1964 test were the first source of Taiwan's insecurity.[20] The second was Taiwan's concern with U.S. commitments to protect it. A secret cable from the U.S. embassy in Taipei discussed Chiang Kai-shek's deep feelings of insecurity in the aftermath of China's test: "We could be wiped out in one attack. . . . An attack on Taiwan would leave the island desolated and U.S. retaliation would be too late."[21] Remarkably, Chiang also discounted U.S. willingness to retaliate, particularly if its European allies opposed retaliation, noting that China was aware of that vulnerability and would use a nuclear success on Taiwan to intimidate the entire region. Chiang concluded with a plea for U.S. equipment and support (not troops) to enable Taiwan to destroy China's nuclear facilities, adding that the United States would certainly supply such support if they had "the firm friendship they professed" to have toward Taiwan. The document conveys Chiang's obsession with the insufficiency of the U.S. deterrent quite clearly. These doubts were not unfounded.

First, although the U.S.-Taiwan Defense Pact required the United States to defend Taiwan if attacked by China, in 1969 the United States withdrew for budgetary reasons the two destroyers patrolling the Taiwan Straits regularly since the Quemoy-Matsu incident. Seventh Fleet forces, to the extent that they were available, were to fulfill that task.[22] Second, by 1971 the U.N. had recognized the mainland as the sole legitimate representative of China, expelling Taiwan. Following President Nixon's 1972 visit to China and the Shanghai Communiqué recognizing "one China," Taiwan perceived a dangerous erosion of U.S. commitments. Third, in 1974 the United States withdrew nuclear weapons stationed in Taiwan to accommodate Beijing's demands.[23] Chiang Kai-shek requested a defense review and attempted to delay the removal of F4 aircraft. Fourth, in 1979 the United States severed diplomatic ties with Taiwan and normalized relations with China. The 1954 Defense Pact ceased to exist in 1980 and was unilaterally replaced by the United States with the Taiwan Relations Act (Bush 2004). Fifth, a 1982 Sino-U.S. communiqué reducing arms sales to Taiwan—with the eventual goal of eliminating them altogether—deepened Taiwan's perceptions of abandonment and betrayal. Sixth, in 2005 a senior

Pentagon official sharply criticized Taiwan's government for its limited military investments, suggesting at the annual U.S.-Taiwan Business Council-Defense Industry, attended by Taiwan's vice defense minister, that the United States might not defend Taiwan in a conflict with China unless Taipei boosted its defenses.[24] Clearly, Taiwan never got the sort of commitment embedded in the U.S.-Japan or U.S.-South Korean alliances. President Clinton (1994:703) acknowledged that the United States "had never said whether we would or wouldn't come to the defense of Taiwan if it were attacked."[25] General Hu Chen-pu, head of Taiwan's Ministry of Defense General Political Warfare Bureau, concluded that "the U.S. has never promised to come to Taiwan's aid in the event of cross-strait hostilities. Nor has Taiwan anticipated such aid from the U.S. for we can never be sure if it would render us assistance."[26]

These events and statements suggest competing neorealist logics for Taiwan's nuclear behavior. First, whereas Taiwan faced an existential threat from China, U.S. commitments to protect Taiwan were limited and uneven. An unalloyed neorealist perspective would expect a technically capable Taiwan to develop an indigenous deterrent; capable states are not assumed to place their very existence in the hands of less-than-resolute allies. Swings in U.S. policy toward Taiwan led some observers to argue that Taiwan's threat of a nuclear card was useful in forcing the United States to reaffirm its commitment to protect it, much as South Korea was doing at the time.[27] Taiwan's Ministry of Defense promptly reassured the world of Taiwan's firm policy not to research, develop, or produce chemical, biological, or nuclear weapons.[28] Reliable U.S. protection could have reduced Taiwan's incentives for going nuclear, but instead U.S. ambiguities heightened them. As a *Taipei Times* editorial stated it, "What Taiwan needs is the ability to stop Beijing from trying anything in the first place. . . . In the end this comes down to Taiwan's need for nuclear weapons."[29]

A second neorealist argument points to the supply of U.S. coercion as the source of Taiwan's nuclear weapons abstention. As the previous overview suggests, such pressures undoubtedly weighed heavily in dissuading some decision-makers. Yet, as we shall see below, whether or not there was consensus in Taiwan to develop nuclear weapons remains unclear. Furthermore, as noted in chapter 2, similar U.S. efforts to dissuade other nuclear aspirants failed. Such variability in responses to U.S. coercion compels us to delve into domestic factors that might have influenced Taiwan's choice to comply where others stood firm.[30] As Waltz (2003:40) has argued, the more vulnerable states feel, the more strenuously they will pursue a nuclear program. Yet, despite its technical capabilities and extreme vulnerability, Taiwan may not have pursued nuclear capabilities as strenuously as this approach would predict. Meyer (1984:132) classified

Taiwan's activities as geared to produce only a nuclear option rather than nuclear weapons. Yager (1985:193) goes even farther, arguing that Taiwan was never known to have had a program to produce nuclear weapons.

A third neorealist argument notes the political advantages of nuclear weapons for Taiwan's survival, independent of the reliability of U.S. commitments. Accordingly, nuclear weapons might have arguably increased the international credibility of a "pariah" state, as with North Korea, Libya, Iran, and Iraq.[31] Indeed Taiwan had arguably less to lose than these other cases, because its very statehood was internationally denied by the early 1970s. Nuclear weapons might have strengthened Taiwan's prospects for gaining recognition as a sovereign state (Cooper 1979). Furthermore, a transparent desperate commitment to defend the island with nuclear weapons might have arguably deterred China. This assumption follows the logic that seemingly "irrational" (emboldened, risk-averse) leaders or regimes often deter more effectively, as Kim Jong-Il arguably did. Such arguments address perceived political utilities of nuclear weapons for Taiwan but ignore their limited military utility in the Taiwan-China context (Betts et al. 1980:77). Yet Professor Chung Chien of the Atomic Science Faculty of Taiwan's National Tsinghua University proposed a revived nuclear program to provide Taiwan with "effective deterrence and reinforced defence."[32]

A fourth neorealist perspective notes that Taiwan had little alternative but to relinquish nuclear weapons as a self-help measure, regardless of U.S. pressures. Indeed Wu (1988:2), the chief scientist opposing the 1967 plan, asserted that "if we look at it from the perspective of pure strategic power, Taiwan could not use nuclear weapons for offense purposes; on the contrary, by possessing such weapons, we increase the possibility of an attack initiated by our enemy because they would be alarmed. Taiwan is a small place with no room for maneuver if it was attacked with a nuclear weapon, unlike those countries with vast land, which, even if they were attacked first, would still have the opportunity to counterattack. They could rely on that potential power to maintain balance."[33] Validating what had been a tacit assumption in previous decades, China confirmed in 1998 that Taiwan's nuclearization would trigger an attack on the island.[34] Ironically, as Mitchell (2004:303) argues, "in its search for the ultimate deterrent to [an] attack from the mainland, Taiwan may, in fact, provoke it." It is unclear, however, that China would have been able to act on such a threat in the 1960s and 1970s. Furthermore, unadulterated neorealism considers territorial size irrelevant and invulnerability of second-strike capabilities far more crucial (Waltz 1993).

A final neorealist perspective would trace Taiwan's abstention from nuclear weapons to conventional deterrence. China's armed forces were about ten times as large as Taiwan's in the 1970s but Taiwan's air force was qualitatively superior.[35] Taiwan's military expenditures over GNP were as high as 9 to 11 percent from 1951 to 1965, over and beyond U.S. supply of heavy equipment, including planes and ships. Expenditures declined to 8 percent on average between 1961 and 1987. Ironically for the argument that conventional strength might explain nuclear renunciation, Taiwan's conventional advantages were *declining* by the late 1960s, following China's 1964 test. U.S. military aid was subsiding and Taiwan's own military expenditures were declining relative to social, educational, and economic investments, a logic that I examine later. As Taiwan's leaders became more oriented to an export-led model of industrialization and political survival, military expenditures declined further, to 6 percent by the 1970s–1980s, and to 4 percent in the 1990s. The KMT was reluctant to finance expensive indigenous arms industries and the United States was equally reluctant to build a Taiwanese military-industrial-complex.[36] Although Taiwan was able to build modern conventional forces over time, its leaders were perennially concerned with a narrowing gap across the Straits. If this line of argumentation were correct, then one would expect Taiwan to reconsider nuclear weapons as the conventional balance tilts in China's favor.[37]

Some of these five viewpoints may be mutually compatible while others are clearly not, making it amply evident that neorealist interpretations of Taiwan's balance-of-power predicament yield competing injunctions: Taiwan should acquire nuclear weapons as a self-help measure, should not acquire nuclear weapons as a self-help measure, should rely on the U.S. deterrent, should not rely on vague U.S. commitments, and so forth. Despite its prima facie appeal and apparent simplicity, structural power considerations in a world of self-help have less-than-evident, less complete, and less coherent implications than is often assumed. Self-help becomes a rather vague pointer for likely behavior, unable to foretell whether nuclear weapons enhance or undermine security, leading to indeterminate forecasts that often require additional information unrelated to power balances, such as domestic politics.

INTERNATIONAL INSTITUTIONS: LIMITED INCENTIVES AND LIMITED TABOOS

Can the existence of a nuclear taboo explain Taiwan's decision to relinquish nuclear weapons? Yager (1980:70) reported that Taiwan used the immorality of nuclear weapons as one justification for not pursuing them, in addition to cost and other factors, but that, in any case, they could not be used against fellow Chinese. According to accounts reported in Taylor (2000:323), Chiang Kai-shek vetoed Chiang Ching-kuo's proposal because his government would never use nuclear weapons "to hurt our own countrymen." Yet the program allegedly carried on. Taiwan's 1976 commitment, mentioned earlier, stipulated that Taiwan would not develop nuclear weapons "because it did not want to use them for killing other Chinese."[38] Declassified U.S. historical documents make no specific reference to normative considerations by Taiwan's decision-makers even in the case of scientist Wu, who opposed nuclear weapons. One might infer from the 1976 declaration that there was perhaps a taboo proscribing the massive killing *of one's kin* but not necessarily a taboo against nuclear acquisition (as a deterrent) or against the nature of nuclear weapons per se. Furthermore, China's civil war, the KMT's massacre of 10,000 to 20,000 Taiwanese from the intellectual and social elite in 1947, and subsequent domestic executions and war plans against China question the extent to which even a kin-related taboo might have operated. Indeed, according to declassified documents, when John Foster Dulles told Chiang Kai-shek that only U.S. nuclear weapons could stop China from shelling Quemoy, Chiang responded that "the use of tactical atomic weapons might be advisable" (Taylor 2000:245). If nuclear *use* might have been advisable, nuclear acquisition would have arguably carried even lower taboo baggage, as a means to deter and avoid war.

Was a rational calculation to adhere to the NPT the underlying reason for Taiwan's abstention from nuclear weapons? Tracing Taiwan's nuclear behavior to incentives and injunctions from the NPR is elusive for several reasons. First, the NPT recognized China—Taiwan's main threat—as one of five legitimate nuclear-weapons-states (NWS) but prohibited others from acquiring them. The incentives to abide by an international regime that discriminated in favor of nuclear "haves" against nuclear "have-nots" could not have been very strong in this case, as it tied Taiwan's hands from acquiring its own deterrent against a neighboring territorial mammoth and nuclear armed adversary. The benefits of reciprocity, monitoring compliance, and detecting defections that are imputed to accrue from joining international institutions were arguably not there for Taiwan in the nuclear realm. Furthermore, the NPT was concluded in 1968, not long after China's 1964 nuclear tests and Taiwan's incipient consideration of a nuclear program. Yet Taiwan signed the NPT shortly after its 1968 conclusion and by 1970 began negotiating an IAEA safeguards agreement. In 1971 the U.N. (including the IAEA) recognized the mainland as China's sole representative, which would have further undermined Taiwan's incentives to cooperate with an institution that failed to even recognize it as a state (Taiwan was ousted as an IAEA member in 1971). Taiwan retained trilateral nuclear agreements with the United States and the IAEA predating the NPT, which provided the basis for safeguards on Taiwan's materials and facilities. As we have seen, renewed intentions to obtain reprocessing technology by some INER officers in the mid-1970s were countered *internally* by AEC members and others.

The IAEA clearly impressed the need for transparency on all of Taiwan's nuclear activities. Inspector General Rudolf Rometsch personally visited INER in May 1976 and asked Taiwan's officials to consider whether all nuclear activities were in their interests, urging them to avoid harming the reputation of safeguards procedures. A subsequent IAEA inspection in July 1976 upgraded the surveillance system, with Taiwan's agreement. Inspection of a reprocessing facility confirmed that its small size precluded production of weapons-suitable quantities of plutonium (Albright and Gay 1998). The INER research reactor and reprocessing facility were disassembled in the presence of IAEA and U.S. officials, who also inspected all other plants. INER became a research center focused on alternative energy resources. The 1980s Chang Hsien-yi events revived concern in some quarters but were not validated by IAEA assertions of noncompliance. Taiwan has not sought enrichment or reprocessing facilities since, remaining dependent on U.S. uranium enrichment services.

In sum, despite relatively high technical capabilities and a special security predicament, and although officially not an IAEA or NPT member, Taiwan adhered to NPT commitments, including the Additional Protocol, and offered appropriate access to IAEA inspections. The United States urged Taiwan in that direction but whether Taiwan would have otherwise acquired an indigenous deterrent remains a plausible but contestable hypothesis that requires analysis of the domestic context. U.S. coercion did not yield similar results elsewhere, begging an explanation of Taiwan's receptivity to U.S. coercion. Furthermore, the prior question of why Taiwan agreed to abide by NPT commitments in the first place is not resolved by an account that upholds international institutions as optimal means for guaranteeing states' security. Taiwan's incentives to join and abide by the NPT had little to do with the institution itself, which granted legitimate nuclear status to its arch-enemy but denied Taiwan not only nuclear weapons but statehood itself.[39] As a country condemned by China to progressive international marginalization, the prospects of alienating the U.N. and the IAEA might have certainly been a consideration. Yet an analysis of the particular model of domestic political survival adopted by Taiwan's leaders explains *why* avoiding international isolation was of the essence. Taiwan's nuclear policies and NPT compliance evolved in tandem with domestic considerations of economic growth that hinged on high dependence on international markets, technology, investments, and political support. In the absence of this model, Taiwan could have arguably gone the North Korean way, rebuking the IAEA despite its hegemons' best efforts.

DOMESTIC POLITICS: EVOLVING CONSTRAINTS AND INDUCEMENTS OF AN ECONOMIC TIGER

During its early years since its inception in 1949, Taiwan was a militarized, inward-oriented state, where the KMT monopolized power and forcefully repressed any opposition. Chiang Kai-shek assumed power in 1950, initially imposing a planned economy that emphasized import-substitution, heavy state intervention, and high military expenditures. Chiang also appointed a Central Reform Committee of younger party cadres untainted by defeat in the mainland. By the mid-1950s, reductions in U.S. aid deepened budgetary and balance-of-payments crises. Under Premier Chen Cheng, the KMT began charting a new model hinged on economic growth, price stability, egalitarian income distribution, and decentralized (small to medium) entrepreneurship. These political principles stemmed from the desire to avoid mistakes that had led to Nationalist defeat by mainland China: hyper-inflation, hyper-inequality, and hyper-corruption in business.

The KMT thus sought to secure its tenuous hold in power and to enhance its appeal across the Straits by nurturing a thriving economic system, one that was presumably superior to the mainland's "in improving the people's livelihood."[40] This strategy was at the core of the KMT's effort to stem domestic threats to its own survival, particularly from communist subversion and repressed native Taiwanese who supplied the regime with soldiers, taxes, and lower-level bureaucrats (Cliff 1998). To that effect the KMT coopted highly educated professionals and technicians (many economists and engineers) that had fled the mainland—and progressively native Taiwanese as well—into the bureaucracy's ranks. It also decimated the landlord class through land reform and kept private business at arm's length while creating conditions for their expansion. Most of this new political infrastructure of technocrats favored Taiwan's internationalization. The model required dramatic expansion of educational opportunities, including subsidies for primary education throughout the 1950s, phasing out state enterprises, and monitoring military expenses to maintain political and macroeconomic stability and maximize global access and appeal to foreign investors. Openness to FDI helped Taiwan break through its international isolation and ingratiated it with its principal benefactor, foreign investor, and preferential export market: the United States. Monetary, fiscal, trade, taxation, and foreign investment reforms were introduced in the late 1950s, as Chiang Kai-shek strengthened support for the reformist camp in a somewhat divided KMT.

KMT managers of state enterprises (largely inherited from the Japanese) and banks, as well as statist ideologues, resisted reforms because they were perceived to empower private entrepreneurs (including native Taiwanese) economically and politically. Thus, monopolistic firms remained under state control while anti-monopolistic practices were enforced on the private sector. In time, small and medium-sized firms flourished, thanks to extensive FDI and U.S. Agency for International Development (AID) conditionality, which helped smaller, component manufacturers (Gereffi 1990). State intervention had softened by the early 1960s and an export-oriented model was in place. Trade missions were sent to different continents, and free-port export processing zones became a priority (Cheng 1990; Jacoby 1966; Roy 2003; Nordhaug 1998; Amsden 1993). Exports by small and medium-sized firms were encouraged through bonuses and fees, whereas production for the domestic market was restricted. Export-processing zones attracted FDI in the 1960s, and another round of expensive educational reforms took place in 1969. In their discussions with the political leadership, state technocrats relied heavily on the centrality of avoiding inflation to sustain the model (prices rose only 2 percent between 1961 and 1970; see Cheng 1990; Jeon 1995). This would have important consequences for suppressing military expenditures, which were presumed to underpin a conventional deterrent.

Government officials and their societal allies who favored internationalizing economic reforms often pointed to U.S. AID pressures to advance *their own* preferences. At times, the United States clearly used aid to induce changes in Taiwan, as with the 19-Point Program of Economic and Financial Reform in 1960, although Nordhaug (1998) suggests that the domestic push for reform went even further than the United States had sought. Some small-scale conditionality was credible and applied in a few cases. U.S. threats to remove massive aid from Taiwan were not credible, however, given U.S. interests to strengthen Taiwan's stability and prosperity as a "showcase" for the region. Nor was there a compelling U.S. effort to condition military assistance on economic policies (and in any event such efforts failed to compel Rhee Syngman and many other leaders in cases from Pakistan to Latin America in the 1960s and 1970s). As an independent study by Jacoby (1966:132) suggests, "The major reason for the large measure of U.S. influence on Chinese [Taiwan's] economic policy was that there was agreement between the governments of the two countries on fundamental aims." Guided by lessons from defeat on the mainland and the imperatives of preventing internal subversion, the KMT pursued macroeconomic stability and land reform for its own reasons and only as circumstances dictated. U.S. influence was weakest on fiscal and monetary policies and strongest in impressing the merits of private investment.[41]

During Taiwan's early years, statism and militarization at home were accompanied by an aggressive posture toward the mainland. Indeed, in the early 1960s, Chiang Kai-shek and Chiang Ching-kuo proposed joint

U.S.-Taiwan actions—maritime raids, airdrops of paramilitary teams, and attacks on China's nuclear facilities and missile sites—to destabilize the mainland, then at the verge of testing nuclear weapons.[42] Yet KMT propaganda about an imminent invasion of the mainland subsided after 1963, when the new model required different regional conditions, including the expansion of trade and foreign investment and regional stability.[43] The bellicose positions of the early years were overshadowed by KMT's efforts to integrate Taiwan into the global economy, particularly as the new model began yielding fruit. Segments of the military initially felt threatened by potential effects of an export-led strategy that might endanger both economic self-sufficiency and war preparedness. Some members of the military—it is unclear how much support they had within the military itself—were reportedly also keen on developing nuclear weapons at this time (Yager 1980; Albright and Gay 1998). The 1967 nuclear proposal was the boldest alleged attempt to seek nuclear weapons by some military proponents and a small but powerful group within the KMT that allegedly supported development of a nuclear deterrent.[44] The proposal, however, was opposed both at home and internationally, and the military—tightly subordinated to the KMT in Leninist fashion—was ultimately unable to stem the internationalizing tide.

The KMT's largest faction favored concentration on economic development. Its overriding concern with retaining power through economic growth and political stability also compelled it to shift from rabid militarism in the early years to "an evermore absorbing interest in economic growth."[45] Thus, even against the background of what was at times a highly belligerent adversary across the Straits, Taiwan's leaders slowly dismantled the rhetoric of invading China. As Ward and Davis (1993:8) argue, "The military recovery of the mainland was eventually replaced by rising mass affluence as the chief source of regime legitimacy." Average growth rates of 10 percent (1963–67) granted Chiang a stronger hold on power by the late 1960s, but further growth remained contingent on exports expansion, given a small domestic market and limited natural resources, which required ample foreign reserves to pay for imports.[46] KMT technocrats feared that military expenditures might curtail sustained growth and limit its ability to apply economic resources to enhance relations with neighboring countries. The KMT thus progressively lowered defense allocations from about 11 percent of GNP in the early years to an 8 percent average between 1961 and 1987, declining by the 1970s and 1980s as the internationalizing model became more robust (Chan 1988, 1992; Cumings 1984; HDR 1994; IISS 1995/96). Military expenditures therefore played a minor and indirect role on Taiwan's GNP growth, export expansion, and improvement of income equality. The KMT opposed an expansive domestic military-industrial-complex that might have compromised the political economy of growth. Tight fiscal and monetary policy, high real interest rates, low money supply, stable foreign exchange rates, and continued access to international markets and foreign investment remained core instruments of KMT policy even during economic crises of the 1970s.

Chiang Kai-shek and the main architects of this model understood the links between the model's requirements and renouncing a nuclear competition with China. Scientist Wu's (1988:2) account of why he had opposed the 1967 nuclear proposal emphasized the need to consider "whether the economic and financial strength of our country in the near future will be capable of supporting the plan." Furthermore, he argued, "Given our country's current situation, the world's unfavorable reactions should be taken into consideration," and "given the current prospects for our country's economy, we will not have the necessary financial resources. We can only proceed in an orderly manner with our efforts to improve the national economy and people's livelihood, and to build up the scientific infrastructure." In the 1960s the model was only beginning to bear expected fruits. Exports as a percentage of GDP quadrupled from 11 percent in 1962 to 46.7 percent in 1973 and 52 percent by 1977, with industrial exports reaching 85 percent of total exports by 1973 (Chan and Clark 1992:84).

A particular Achilles heel for the model's continuity was Taiwan's dependence on external energy resources. In the 1970s, Taiwan imported over 80 percent of its energy needs, mostly oil, and nuclear power had become critical to the model's viability. By 1976 Taiwan's first two nuclear power plants were in advanced stages of construction and four additional ones were planned (Yager 1985). The possibility of endangering Taiwan's vital nuclear energy industry by seeking weapons-related technology was an important consideration in the effort to counter those segments of the military interested in nuclear weapons. Wu (1988) warned that a plutonium plant would awaken suspicion from the international community and advocated instead a plant that better matched peaceful use. The United States was not only Taiwan's main market, source of foreign investment, and provider of weapons and security guarantees, but also its principal supplier of low-enriched uranium for power reactors.[47] In 1976, U.S. officials emphasized that any violation of Chiang's commitment would "fundamentally jeopardize" nuclear energy cooperation (Albright and Gay 1998; Burr 1999). As Burr (1999:2) argues, Taiwan was generally responsive to U.S. pressures and "elements of the ROC elite were willing to pass on significant intelligence about Taiwan's nuclear plans."

Wu (1988) alluded to internal differences among government officials regarding the 1967 proposal. Indeed, not everyone in Chungshan was favorable to the proposal, as one can surmise from Wang Shih-chieh's effort, recounted earlier, to mobilize Hsu and a wider opposition to derail

the 1967 proposal *from within*. Subsequent efforts to obtain a reprocessing plant endangered IAEA willingness to conduct special inspections,
given existing Chinese pressures on the IAEA to withdraw inspections
from Taiwan altogether.[48] Without IAEA and U.S. endorsement, the nuclear energy program was threatened. Without energy and U.S. preferential trade status, the economic miracle was doomed. Without a sustained
economic miracle, the KMT's political prospects were fragile. Yen Chen-
hsing, chairman of the AEC of the Executive Yuan, made these connections
quite explicit when he asserted that nuclear energy in Taiwan was designed
to "make the country prosperous and the people rich. No nuclear weapons
will be manufactured."[49] Taiwan's official position on nuclear weapons was
presented as final, and the president's position as very firm (Yager 1980).
Following IAEA inspections of suspected reprocessing facilities in 1976
and continued U.S. pressure, Chiang Ching-kuo promised the U.S. ambassador that Taiwan would not engage in reprocessing activities. A
diplomatic note reinforced that commitment. Taiwan's research reactor
was disassembled in the presence of IAEA and U.S. officials, its facility for
handling plutonium was taken apart, all its power plants were appropriately inspected, and INER turned to research alternative energy sources
(Mitchell 2004:302).

Like South Korea's Park, Chiang and his successors at the same time understood the instrumentality of veiled threats to develop nuclear weapons
as a "bargaining chip" to extract stronger U.S. security and economic commitments, more advanced weapons, and support for the nuclear energy
program.[50] Chiang Ching-kuo reiterated in 1977 that although Taiwan had
"the ability and the facilities to manufacture nuclear weapons . . . we will
never manufacture them" (Yager 1980:70).

DEMOCRATIZATION

Chiang Kai-shek died in 1975. Chiang Ching-kuo, who had assumed the
premiership in 1972, the KMT's leadership in 1975, and the presidency in
1978, strengthened the bureaucratic-societal coalition favoring reform
and modernization (Rubinstein 1999). Between 1950 and 1990, Taiwan's
GNP grew by an 8.7 percent average, its exports expanding 20 percent
annually (Pempel 1999). Trade openness (imports plus exports as a percentage of GDP) tripled from 30 percent in 1960 to 89 percent in 1973
(Haggard 1995; Chan 1988; Bradford 1990; Cheng 2005; Jeon 1995). By
the 1980s, twenty-nine of the top fifty biggest enterprises in Taiwan were
private domestic firms, with the rest divided into ten state enterprises and
eleven foreign firms. Chiang Ching-kuo died in January 1988 and was replaced by native-born Lee Teng-hui, who maintained and enhanced his

predecessors' growth model. Taiwan's transition to democracy, however, exacerbated tensions with China as pro-independence forces acquired greater weight. In 1991, Lee expressed that Taiwan "should re-study the question [of nuclear weapons] from a long-term point of view," asserting that "everyone knows we had had the plan before."[51] However, he immediately moved to reaffirm that, despite Taiwan's capabilities, it "will never change its stance on developing nuclear weapons."[52] Following China's test-firing of missiles near Taiwan in 1995, a National Assembly deputy urged the government to consider nuclear weapons. Lee responded that "whether [we] need production of nuclear weapons takes long-term study" and that "Taiwan used to have the capability to make nuclear weapons but it caused international concern and damaged the country's image," reassuring that Taiwan will not develop a nuclear arsenal.[53]

The concern with image had a very specific referent, involving Taiwan's ability to retain global access and economic viability even as its diplomatic relations with the rest of the world had dwindled over the years under China's unrelenting pressure. On the one hand, Lee pronounced a "two states" principle that incensed China. On the other hand, efforts to retain international access dictated an ever tighter economic relationship with China that was capable of defusing tensions across the Straits. Since the 1980s economic ties between China and Taiwan grew dramatically. Over 60 percent of Taiwan's foreign investment was estimated to have found its way to China by the 1990s, and 500,000 to one million Taiwanese entrepreneurs (*Taishang*) contributed to the economic transformation of Taiwan's presumed archenemy. Taiwan became dependent on China for three-fourths of its exports, which garnered Taiwan a significant trade surplus, reaching a record high of $18.11 billion in the first half of 2006 (from $7 billion for all of 1990).[54] Important (and growing) domestic constituencies in Taiwan had strong economic incentives to ensure peaceful accommodation with China, though not necessarily unification (Bush 2004). These constituencies, particularly Taishang, had very strong political connections with Taiwan's leadership, bureaucracy, industrial associations, and parties (Cheng 2006). Politicians such as Lee Teng-hui and Chen Shui-bian favored a more internationalized set of economic partners over deepening reliance on China's markets for goods and investments.

The Democratic Progressive Party (DPP) led by Chen Shui-bian, which had campaigned as an advocate of Taiwan's independence, won the 2000 elections. By this time the military, a long-time partner in the KMT's ruling coalition and highly averse to war with China, was even less prepared to support nuclear weapons and became apprehensive about DPP intentions (Mitchell 2004). Chen's platform, however, explicitly rejected nuclear weapons and even nuclear power (although there are divisions within the DPP over nuclear energy), and sought to establish a "nuclear-free homeland." Commenting on North Korea's threats to test a nuclear weapon, Chen expressed that "it has always been the Democratic Progressive Party's policy to establish a nuclear-free homeland and to safeguard regional peace and stability. Our stance has not changed, despite North Korea's nuclear ambitions."[55] Only a small party, the Taiwan Independence Party, endorsed a nuclear weapons program. DPP Premier Yu Shyi-kun's statement at a government training seminar that Taiwan should be able to respond to Chinese missiles with missiles of its own prompted questions at the Legislative Yuan in 2004, but Yu denied Taiwan's development of medium-range cruise missiles or nuclear weapons.[56] Chen's formulations of separate statehood and his moves toward changing Taiwan's constitution and using referenda to address the threat of China's missiles along Fujian province alienated China's leadership (Christensen 2003). In March 2005, China's National People's Congress approved a law mandating the use of "nonpeaceful" means against Taiwan if it declares independence.

KMT leader Lien Chan met President Hu Jintao in a historical visit to China followed by James Soong of the People First Party (PFP). The popularity of this act of reconciliation with constituencies searching for compromise with China forced Chen Shui-bian into taking compromising steps of his own. Furthermore Chen was now operating within legislative constraints that forced his party into a limited alliance with the small PFP, which, in contrast with the DPP's pro-independence constituencies, held dramatically opposing views on cross-Straits relations. Chen's domestic considerations thus limited further his willingness to sacrifice Taiwan's economic relations with China on the altar of "independence now!"[57] Meanwhile, the KMT (and the PFP)—the "Blue" parties—have blocked Taiwan's purchase of F-16C/D fighter jets over fifty times since 2004, arguing that it supports only "reasonable arms purchases" that meet Taiwan's defense needs, are not a financial burden, and are supported by all citizens.[58] Nuclear weapons would be several steps removed from what is politically feasible in Taiwan for the foreseeable future, as long as a solid majority, including the most powerful elites, prefer the status quo with China.[59]

CONCLUSION

Taiwan meets most definitions of existential insecurity—spanning its entire experience as a separate political entity—in a way that few other cases do. Indeed, it does not even enjoy recognition as a state by most other states and international institutions. Yet it has not resorted to nuclear weapons. The United States applied considerable pressure to prevent its nuclearization but, as a known expert on Taiwan's nuclear program once put it, "The unanswered question is, Why did the ROC authorities yield so readily to U.S. demands?" (Yager 1985:192). The KMT and its successors' military, political, and economic dependence on the United States are central to understanding Taiwan's nuclear history. Nuclear decisions were embedded in a model of regime survival emphasizing economic growth, prosperity, stability, and the defeat of internal subversion, which explains widespread receptivity to U.S. demands and inducements. Nuclear weapons would have introduced massive stress at home, with neighboring countries and worldwide, with attending consequences for the model's viability.[60] KMT's leaders had strong incentives to avoid regional conflict and instability, dictated by the need to maintain domestic growth, political stability, attractiveness to foreign investors, controlled military expenditures, and ample foreign reserves, given Taiwan's international isolation. Access to preferential export markets, international capital, investments, and nuclear technology to fuel the economic miracle required nuclear restraint. Without it, the KMT's political prospects were fragile. Indeed, a senior Taiwanese official interviewed in the 1970s alluded to concerns that nuclear weapons might endanger those objectives, citing a Chinese proverb that "he who has no jade, has no guilt" (Yager 1980:70).

As Burr (1999) argues, "The inner history of the Taiwan nuclear program remains to be told." Yet events in the 1960s involving Wu Ta-You and later, in the 1980s, involving Chang Hsien-yi, Chungshan's deputy director, as well as others suggest there was domestic opposition to a nuclear weapons program that might derail the model. Although some military officers and segments of the KMT leadership might have valued nuclear weapons, the risks for their continued hold on power overwhelmed presumed advantages.[61] High KMT officials and advisors warned Chiang Ching-kuo that a nuclear program was economically and politically unsound and unwise (Taylor 2000:276). Exports, economic growth, and prosperity—which propelled Taiwan from the poorest to one of the top eighteen largest economies worldwide—were and remain the indisputable favored means for Taiwan's politicians to ensure their political survival; all other goals have been subordinated to these objectives. The model thus explains why U.S. pressures to deny Taiwan a nuclear deterrent have been more effective than in other cases, including ones where high levels of dependence on U.S. power have also been present. The model also explains subsequent severe anomalies for neorealism, such as Taiwan's impressive embrace of the mainland—its presumed archrival—as its vital trading partner. Over time, Taiwan's model itself became exportable. Its success stimulated Chinese leaders' emulation of economic prosperity as a ticket to regime survival. Democracy added an additional layer to the model, enabling Taiwan's leaders to buttress support at home and from democracies around the world. An internationalized democracy also made any secret nuclear program less plausible. While unveiling Taiwan's first formal national security policy, National Security Council Deputy Secretary-General Michael Tsai provided further reassurance about Taiwan's policy: "We're not pursuing preemptive capabilities, and we will not develop nuclear weapons or weapons of mass destruction."[62] Following North Korea's nuclear test, Premier Su Tseng-chang and Defense Minister Lee Jye assured the Executive Yuan that Taiwan will "definitely not" own, develop, acquire, stockpile, or use nuclear weapons.[63]

CHAPTER SIX

North Korea

THE NUCLEAR TRAJECTORY of the Democratic People's Republic of Korea (North Korea henceforth) diverged significantly from all other cases discussed in part 2. In the aftermath of World War II, North Korea became an indigenous adaptation of Soviet and Chinese models. Kim Il-Sung launched the Korean War and, following defeat, faced a massive U.S. presence across the border. Fearing the collapse of his regime, he turned North Korea into a military fortress heavily supported by Soviet and Chinese allies. His quest for nuclear weapons may have begun as early as the 1950s (Mazarr 1995a:93). Soon after China's 1964 test, he sent a delegation to Beijing requesting assistance in developing a parallel program (Oberdorfer 2001:252). The request was presumably denied, and yet both superpowers were unable to curtail North Korea's nuclear ambitions. By the 1970s, North Korea had already separated a small amount of plutonium from a Soviet-supplied research reactor. In the early 1980s, North Korea began construction of other plutonium-related facilities. In 1985, the Soviets ostensibly persuaded North Korea to sign the NPT.[1] By the end of the 1980s, North Korea was able to separate weapons-grade plutonium in sufficient quantities. In 1993, North Korea threatened to withdraw from the NPT, reversing itself soon thereafter. In the early 1990s, it also allegedly began negotiating uranium-enrichment technology transfers from Pakistan. In 2003, North Korea became the first state to withdraw from the NPT, following extensive violations of its 1985 ratification commitments (Pollack and Reiss 2004). North Korea threatened to convert South Korea and Japan into a "sea of fire." By 2005, it acknowledged possession of a "nuclear deterrent," estimated at four to six bombs by IAEA Director El-Baradei.[2] In 2006, North Korea tested a nuclear weapon, the first new East Asian state to do so in forty-two years, since China's 1964 test. Why has North Korea's nuclear path differed from the region's pattern of denuclearization since the 1970s?

DETERRING FRIENDLY AND RIVAL HEGEMONS?

North Korea undoubtedly faced a tenuous security context, as did all other cases discussed thus far. Applying an unalloyed neorealist logic to explain why North Korea developed and tested nuclear weapons, whereas the others did not, requires evidence that North Korea faced the most dire security predicament of any of the cases reviewed thus far, or indeed more dire than any other cases in this region, such as (North) Vietnam. This is not easy to establish, given the plasticity of concepts such as relative power or balance of power, as noted in chapter 2, a situation often leading to contestable interpretations. Even if this comparative vulnerability cannot be accurately ascertained, why was there strong demand for nuclear weapons in North Korea? Nuclear weapons arguably enabled North Korea to achieve superiority over South Korea, deter U.S. attacks, and carve independence from Soviet and Chinese patrons. Declassified secret correspondence between Kim Il-Sung and Stalin suggests that Kim was not concerned with potential use of nuclear weapons by the United States during the Korean War (Mansourov 1995). He later learned, however, that Truman did consider them. Subsequent statements such as that of Secretary of Defense James Schlesinger, claiming that the United States would not foreclose use of tactical nuclear weapons *in the event of North Korea's attack*, undoubtedly added to Kim's regime insecurity (Harrison 2002; Moon 2007). North Korea's inclusion in the 2002 "Axis of Evil" speech induced even greater concerns with regime survival. However, the argument that concerns with U.S. threats drove North Korea's search for nuclear weapons is not free of inconsistencies (Mazarr 1995c).

First, North Korea enjoyed hegemonic protection from not one but two superpowers, backed by respective mutual defense treaties signed in 1961, just as North Korea reportedly boosted its search for indigenous nuclear weapons. Second, North Korea's search intensified in the 1960s when the United States was least threatening, even by contemporary Soviet intelligence assessments conveyed to North Korea, which established that the United States "does not intend to increase tension in this region, and . . . nothing points to the conclusion that [the United States] really aims at starting a new Korean War. It is obvious that the various factors of the international situation of the USA, such as the Vietnam War, do not make the perspective of a new Asian war attractive for the United States."[3] Indeed, according to the same source, "On the basis of the evidence available to it . . . the Soviet Union has concluded that the majority of the incidents occurring along the demilitarized zone are initiated by the DPRK." Third, South Korea's nuclear program did not start until 1970 (see chapter 4), and could thus not explain North Korea's initial search for nuclear weapons as "reactive proliferation," suggesting more of a proactive program. Fourth, North Korea's 1970s demands that the United States remove tactical nuclear weapons from South Korea and pledge nuclear non-aggression, and that South Korea renounce nuclear weapons, had been fulfilled by the early 1990s. Yet North Korea engaged in ever-more elaborate nuclear schemes at that point. Fifth, the United States provided significant substance to North Korea's threat perceptions in 1994 when Defense Secretary William Perry declared that he would not rule out a preemptive military strike on North Korea.[4] Yet shortly thereafter, Kim Jong-Il signed the "Agreed Framework," a step few would trace to U. S. threats, which, more often than not, invited North Korea's defiance rather than submission. Thus, the prospects of material advantages that might sustain North Korea's regime seemed to have played a more critical role in accepting the Agreed Framework.[5]

Clearly, perceptions of relative power and threat could change quite rapidly, in tandem with regime calculations and domestic circumstances. Such sudden changes in behavior under conditions of unchanged external threats—including 40,000 U.S. troops in South Korea—reveal analytical tensions in structural-power interpretations of North Korea's behavior. Indeed, Kim Il-Sung told President Carter that his country was more interested in reductions of U.S. troops in South Korea than in their complete withdrawal, and Kim Jong-Il accepted Kim Dae-jung's views that U.S. troops were necessary.[6] Furthermore, some North Korean diplomats and generals reportedly told U.S. diplomats unofficially that U.S. troops should remain in the Korean peninsula (Oberdorfer 2001:402). According to a former secretary of North Korea's Workers Party who defected to the South, Hwang Jang-yop, "There are few in North Korea who really feel the danger of an invasion of the North by the South."[7] In the 2000s, the war on Iraq, the U.S. doctrine of preemption, and the Nuclear Posture Review's consideration of tactical nuclear weapons may have strengthened North Korea's search for deterrence in recent years but cannot be applied retroactively to explain its nuclear behavior over the preceding four decades.

Unalloyed structural perspectives also draw attention to dilemmas of abandonment that might have pushed North Korea toward self-reliant deterrence. The Sino-Soviet competition, however, may have enhanced North Korea's bargaining power vis-à-vis both patrons. Article I of its defense pact with the Soviet Union stipulated that any armed attack (and state of war) "afflicting either party would compel the other to extend immediate military and other assistance *with all the means at its disposal* [emphasis added]." The 1961 Sino-Korean Treaty on Friendship, Cooperation, and Mutual Assistance stipulated that if either party was subjected to armed attacks and thus involved in war, "the other Contracting Party shall immediately render military and other assistance by all means at its disposal."[8] North Korea was thus covered by two nuclear umbrellas (Mansourov 1995) and relations between China and North Korea were described being as close as "lips and teeth." China's performance during the Korean War provided credibility to that commitment. Notwithstanding these pledges to shield North Korea, Kim Il-Sung forcefully protected his independence, mistrusting superpowers' commitments despite general ideological (communist) affinities.[9] Furthermore, his determination to develop nuclear weapons became stronger in the 1970s, when U.S. power was dramatically curtailed and well before China's 1980s economic reforms and the Soviet demise exacerbated Kim's dilemmas of abandonment. However, even in the 1980s, when his nuclear program accelerated, Kim Il-Sung called his friendship with China "invincible" (Wampler 2003, document 3). Clearly China and the Soviet Union/Russia could neither persuade nor dictate North Korea to avoid nuclearization despite their crucial support for its regime, compelling the need to explain why alliances and hegemonic coercion fail to prevent nuclearization in some cases but not others.[10] The question of why dilemmas of abandonment should have pushed North Korea—but not others in the region—toward nuclearization can be answered only by analyzing the relative receptivity of different regimes to external guarantees of security. Most leaders may have arguably preferred to minimize such dependence, as previous chapters indicate, yet different domestic models of political survival allowed different compromises regarding external dependence. North Korea's regime had zero-tolerance for any policy short of self-help, integral to a model rooted in autarky and self-sufficiency (juche). As Kim Il-Sung's crucial instrument of domestic political control, juche precluded any perception of North Korea as subordinated to an external force.[11]

A competing neorealist account would find nuclearization as *increasing* North Korea's insecurity, given its relatively small size and population centers, assigning conventional superiority higher value for securing state survival.[12] The regime indeed built such superiority at the outset, devoting nearly one-fourth of its GDP to that effort (Reiss 1988:82) and amassing an estimated military force of 600,000 soldiers and 900 aircraft by 1958, rising to about 5 million soldiers (one-fourth of the total population) including the Korean People's Army (regular army) and other militias. Yet, notably from the standpoint of this argument, 1980s investments in the nuclear program coincided with the attainment of the most robust conventional force North Korea had ever assembled. Why such a strong conventional deterrent did not preclude parallel efforts to acquire nuclear weapons compels an explanation, and not just for this case. Beyond that, North Korea may have felt weak, isolated, and threatened (Waltz 2003) but the various options deducible from self-help principles—superpower alliances, conventional deterrence, self-reliant nuclear deterrence—make it difficult to explain why nuclear self-reliance dominated over other choices. An effort to understand North Korea's vocation for extreme self-reliance that led it down the nuclear path, and intermittent gyrations in its nuclear policy despite stable presumed threats, compels a better grasp of its domestic politics of *regime* survival. After all, as Oh and Hassig (2004) argue, "The ultimate goal of North Korea's nuclear weapons program is *to keep a Kim in power, not to assure the security of the North Korean state*" [emphasis added].

INTERNATIONAL INSTITUTIONS: REJECTING THE NPT AND CRAWLING TOWARD THE SIX-PARTY TALKS

North Korea's refusal to sign the NPT for many years may seem compatible with neoliberal institutional perspectives regarding the conditions under which states are likely to join institutions, insofar as the NPT granted nuclear status to its adversary, the United States, and two of its neighbors—even if they were also its protectors—while denying them to North Korea itself. At the same time, the NPT presumably tied major adversaries—South Korea and Japan—to non-nuclear status. Given North Korea's intentions to acquire nuclear weapons, it should not be surprising that it refused to sign the NPT until 1985, nearly seventeen years after its conclusion and only under alleged Soviet pressure. This late accession indicates that for many years Soviet pressures were insufficient to persuade North Korea to join the NPT. Furthermore, these were arguably the very years when superpower protection was least questionable (relative to the 1990s, for instance), presumably alleviating North Korea's concerns about NPT membership. The IAEA allowed eighteen months to negotiate and sign a safeguards agreement, but due to an error it extended the period for another eighteen months in 1987. Nonetheless, North Korea rejected full-scope IAEA inspections de facto and repudiated its commitments to conclude a safeguards agreement, leaving it suspended between formal accession, deficient compliance, and flagrant violations. Following 1990 IAEA resolutions asking North Korea to sign the safeguards agreement, it agreed to inspections after the United States removed nuclear weapons from South Korea. North Korea also demanded prerogatives to declare the agreement "null and void, depending on [its] evaluation of the attitudes" of NWS (CNSW). In 1991, South Korea's Rho Tae-Woo declared South Korea's commitment to a denuclearized Korean peninsula, removing another subterfuge used by North Korea to reject inspections. The Soviets and Chinese suspended nuclear cooperation with North Korea at that point. The Soviet collapse forced sharp adjustments in North Korea's domestic model and external relations. By the end of 1991, both Koreas signed the "Joint Declaration for the Denuclearization of the Korean Peninsula" stipulating verification through joint inspections independent of the IAEA.[13] North Korea finally signed the safeguards agreement in 1992, allowing official IAEA inspections for the first time. Regular inspections in 1992 uncovered inconsistencies in plutonium reprocessing, triggering IAEA demands for special inspections of North Korea's military facilities, the first ever in IAEA history (Goldschmidt 2003:24).

Military and Atomic Energy Minister Choe adamantly rejected such inspections and the party's daily *Nodong Sinmun* warned that forced inspections would unleash "the crushing calamities of war." Undeterred, the IAEA Board of Governors gave North Korea one month to comply. North Korea announced its intention to withdraw from the NPT in March 1993 and placed its armed forces in semi-war footing, triggering an international crisis. The IAEA Board reported North Korea's noncompliance to the UNSC (Samore 1994:25). North Korea later "suspended" its withdrawal not only as threats of U.S. sanctions loomed on the horizon but also in response to President Carter's visit, leading to the "Agreed Framework" in October 1994 (Wit, Poneman, and Gallucci 2004). The latter established gradual normalization, U.S. assurances not to use nuclear weapons against North Korea, replacement of North Korea's sensitive reactor with light-water reactors through the Korean Peninsula Energy Development Organization (KEDO), and provision of oil to North Korea in exchange for freezing its reprocessing facility, promising not to build new ones and store fuel rods, resuming talks with South Korea, and allowing unimpeded IAEA inspections. Both sides failed to fulfill some of these commitments. KEDO's reactors were delayed and the United States provided no assurances regarding nuclear weapons use.

Around 1998, North Korea reportedly began its secret uranium-enrichment activities as the plutonium program was frozen.[14] When a North Korean diplomat acknowledged that effort in October 2002, the United States abandoned the Agreed Framework and North Korea removed surveillance equipment and expelled IAEA inspectors. The IAEA condemned North Korea's violations in 2003, and North Korea announced its immediate withdrawal from the NPT and began reprocessing spent fuel rods, enough for six to eight additional weapons beyond the estimated two to six in its possession.[15] North Korea's officials variously proclaimed ownership of a "physical deterrent," a "nuclear deterrent," and "something even stronger than a nuclear deterrent" (Oh and Hassig 2004). There is no available evidence regarding whether or not international norms played any role in North Korea's nuclear decisions. One source (Mansourov 1995:30) contends that Kim Il-Sung may have considered nuclear *use* on South Korea to be counterproductive because it would alienate the Korean people, suggesting that this was largely an instrumental consideration. Acquisition was a different matter altogether and targeting Japan or U. S. forces reportedly was regarded as quite useful politically, at home and internationally.

Have other regional institutions fared better than the IAEA in influencing North Korea? The ASEAN Regional Forum (ARF) emerged in 1994 as the only inclusive multilateral security institution in the Asia-Pacific, eventually gathering twenty-four heterogeneous participants, including North Korea. The ARF's primary purpose was to facilitate communication, provide information, increase transparency, reduce uncertainty, advance economic prosperity, and avoid costly arms races (Shirk 1994; Johnston 1999; Solingen 2008). It was highly informal, lowly institutionalized, based on consensus, and lacked enforcement powers, hence a relatively "safe" institutional forum for North Korea with some utility for presenting its views. Although the ARF has advanced confidence-building through "White Papers" on defense policy and exchanges between military academies, it has no mechanisms for preventive diplomacy and has enabled only limited dialogue on North Korea's denuclearization at the margin of its meetings. Asia Pacific Economic Cooperation (APEC) gathers twenty-one Asian and Pacific Rim countries that largely share a broad commitment to economic liberalization, and hence exclude autarky-oriented North Korea. APEC has addressed North Korea more directly than the ARF by linking economic cooperation to the country's denuclearization and calling it to resume Six-Party Talks (SPT) negotiations. The SPT emerged in August 2003 as an even less structured institution than the others, with the participation of China, the United States, Japan, South Korea, North Korea, and Russia. Since the SPT are wholly dedicated to North Korea's complete and verifiable denuclearization, it should not be surprising that North Korea has searched for every ploy to stall its mission, demanding direct U.S.-North Korea negotiations instead. At the very first meeting of the SPT, North Korea announced its intention to test a nuclear weapon, carrying out its threat three years later. The five other parties have competing interests regarding the means for persuading North Korea to denuclearize, including the utility of sanctions and the desirability of "regime change." South Korea and China pressed for the most conciliatory positions vis-à-vis North Korea, the United States for the least conciliatory, and Japan and Russia somewhere in between.[16] The SPT were thus ridden with the very problems of collective action envisaged by the institutional theories that they were presumably designed to resolve. The overview of domestic developments, described later, returns to North Korea's approach to KEDO and the SPT.

In sum, North Korea has a rich history of eschewing the constraints of the NPR. It may have signed the NPT under the assumption that it could defect easily, clandestinely or openly, as it has indeed done (Harrison 2002:203). The IAEA upheld safeguards agreements and insisted on full-scope safeguards but, as has everyone else, it has thus far failed to denuclearize North Korea, which has also ignored bilateral denuclearizing commitments with South Korea and with various multilateral fora, including the ARF and the SPT. North Korea has not signed the CWC but has ratified the BTWC. A potential February 2005 SPT breakthrough has yet to yield fruit. Neoliberal institutionalist explanations of nuclear behavior (defection in this case) are most often cast at the level of nation-states as neorealist ones. North Korea's experience compels greater effort to examine the deeper sources of state behavior in, and compliance with, institutions, which may in turn explain why some states seek to solve dilemmas of cooperation while others don't. States' relative proclivities to join institutions that detect defections, monitor compliance, facilitate issue-linkages, and reduce the costs of retaliation must be found in domestic configurations of interests and beliefs.

DOMESTIC POLITICS: JUCHE AND THE KIMS' DILEMMA

A common misperception assumes that leaders heading strongly hierarchical regimes such as North Korea's are wholly unconstrained by political and bureaucratic power. Even highly centralizing leaders, however, must craft supportive clientelistic networks with stakes in regime maintenance. Kim Il-Sung and Kim Jong-Il gained and maintained power by navigating these domestic political vectors through the use of ruthless punishment and flexible rewards. Their model of political survival differed dramatically from that of most of their neighbors. After World War II, Kim Il-Sung's faction eliminated in Stalinist fashion all other factions opposing heavy industry and collectivization of agriculture, creating the unified Workers' Party (WP), backed by the Soviet-trained People's Army (Cumings 1990; Paige and Lee 1963; Kuark 1963). On June 25, 1950, Kim Il-Sung attacked South Korea, convinced that the invasion would ignite an uprising against Syngman Rhee, allowing North Korea to control the entire peninsula. Despite miscalculating U.S. resolve and despite his eventual defeat, Kim Il-Sung wielded the war as an instance of "heroic" leadership confronting an imperialist hegemon.[17] War and revolution—perceived external and internal threats—were intimately linked in Kim's design to buttress his nascent legitimacy.[18] Kim forged a regime characterized as "ideologically paternalistic, economically collectivist, ethnically racist, diplomatically isolationist, and culturally nationalist."[19] This militarized regime came to control every aspect of economic activity, emphasizing outright autarky or juche (self-sufficiency). Juche was already in use earlier but was more formally introduced by Kim in 1955, becoming far more prominent in the 1960s (Kim 2006). In Kim Il-Sung's words, "self-reliance in the economy [juche] is the material basis of chajusong (all-round independence in international relations)," and "economic dependence leads to political subordination."[20] The outcome of the Korean War provided a convenient springboard to deepening militarization and juche.

Juche was both the path to *charip kyongje* (self-dependent national economy), which was capable of producing virtually everything indigenously, and to *minjok tongnip* (national or ethnic independence). The nationalist character of juche replaced Marxism-Leninism, leading to friction even with the Soviets.[21] Juche was the quintessential essence of Kim Il-Sung's model of political control and vital to his own mythification and leadership cult. An obvious corollary of juche was North Korea's characterization of the South as *sadaejuui* (flunkey, "puppet"), a proxy of "imperialist USA" with joint proclivities to initiate wars, as they were imputed to have done in 1950. Vilification of the United States and imperialism made the non-aligned movement an appropriate international context for brandishing juche. The Sino-Soviet competition also offered the opportunity to advance juche and North Korea's unique path to communism. Juche drove the "hermit kingdom" to one of the lowest levels of foreign trade worldwide in an economy where the state dominated all industry and agriculture. Japan's occupation of Korea and war economy had left a relatively advanced heavy industry infrastructure. By 1946 Kim Il-Sung had nationalized over 1,000 industrial enterprises—90 percent of all industry—molding them to serve a militarized state. The military was his regime's backbone, a recipient of one-third of the budget, one-fourth of GNP since the 1960s, and considerable political autonomy. By 1950, North Korea's People's Army was 200,000 to 300,000 strong, armed with heavy weapons and tanks ready to invade South Korea.[22] Soviet military assistance helped build this vast military-industrial-complex that included most of the one hundred leading engineering enterprises. The military ruled over self-sustaining economic fiefdoms that produced their own foodstuffs and earnings from irrigation and other massive projects.

The First Five-Year Plan (1957–60) emphasized heavy industry—including machine-building, electricity, metallurgy, coal mining, and chemicals—a campaign metaphorically labeled "fleshing out the skeleton." Increased house construction and efforts to provide basic needs contributed to remarkable GNP growth (1953–62).[23] During this brief yet unique episode of North Korea's postwar economic growth—in the late 1950s—the military budget declined. Yet by 1958, North Korea had nonetheless already turned into one of the largest military forces in the industrializing world. The 1962 Fourth Congress of the Workers' Party (Rodongdang) adopted the "four great military policy-lines": arm the entire people, fortify the entire country, cadetify the entire army, and modernize the entire army (Baek 1988:168–86; Chung 1963; Trigubenko 1996). At this time North Korea also began cooperative training programs in nuclear science with the Soviets and Chinese, in 1959 signing bilateral protocols on peaceful uses of nuclear energy (CNSW). Militarization and war-readiness as mobilizing tools had a distinct "blowback" effect, persuading many in North Korea that invasion was imminent even after Park discontinued Rhee's policy of "Let's March North."[24] Until the 1960s, North Korea's economy had performed better than South Korea's, but Kim Il-Sung perceived Park's new model of integration into the global economy as a threat to his own (polar opposite) juche strategy. North Korea thus escalated hostility against the South throughout the 1960s and 1970s, repeatedly attempting to assassinate Park (eventually killing his wife), seizing the USS *Pueblo* in 1968, infiltrating South Korea's coasts, and excavating invasion tunnels under the DMZ.[25]

As Oh and Hassig (2004) argued, "given its national priorities, it would be surprising if North Korea's regime did not exploit its nuclear capabilities to make nuclear weapons." Kim Il-Sung requested assistance for nuclear weapons development from the Soviets and Chinese. Both reportedly refused, although the Soviets transferred a small research reactor in 1962 and agreed to train hundreds of nuclear researchers, and China provided assistance in uranium mining. Soviet-era archival sources reveal that by 1963 North Korea's officials pressed Soviet experts for additional help, insisting that they must extract large quantities of uranium ore and asking those experts whether they thought North Korea could produce atomic weapons (CWIHP, September 27 and October 16, 1963). Kim Il-Sung also allegedly sent a delegation to China in 1964 to appeal for help with a parallel nuclear program (Oberdorfer 2001), and requested explicit East German nuclear assistance in 1963, 1967, and 1981, insisting that "we need the atom bomb" (CNSW; CWIHP, August 26, 1963). In 1964, North Korea established the Yongbyong nuclear research facility, obtaining nuclear equipment from France and Austria among others. Unsurprisingly from the vantage point of the regime's model of political survival, the words *charyok kaengsaeng* ("independence" or "self-reliance"), a variant of juche, adorned the entrance of Yongbyong in gigantic letters (Kang 1998). In 1965 the Soviets provided a 2 MW research reactor and small critical assembly, which were placed under IAEA safeguards. In 1967 North Korea sought a 100 MW reactor, but the Soviets, who apparently were kept at some distance from the critical assembly, rejected that request.[26] Kim's declaration in 1967 reveals the links between a self-reliant economy and a self-reliant self-defense: "The government . . . will thoroughly implement the line of independence, self-subsistence, and self-defense to consolidate the political independence of the country, further strengthen the foundations of an independent national economy capable of ensuring the complete reunification, independence and prosperity of our nation, and *increase the defence capabilities of the country so as to reliably safeguard its security on the basis of our own forces* [emphasis added] by excellently materializing our Party's idea of Juche in all fields" (Mansourov 1995:29).

Meanwhile North Korea's GNP, roughly comparable to that of the South in 1960, declined to half that of South Korea's by 1970. Embryonic efforts to open up the economy in the late 1960s failed (Sigal 1998). Kim, ever-attentive to Park's successes as threats to his own regime, began testing policies of autonomous peaceful unification and minimal relaxation of North Korea's economic arm's-length relationship with the West.[27] Imports from Western countries into North Korea nearly doubled, reaching over half of all imports and turning Japan into the second largest trading partner by the mid-1970s. Kim sent signals via Japan of his interest in direct negotiations with the United States. In 1971 he had suspended the requirement that U.S. troops be removed as a condition for dialogue with South Korea, ushering in the North-South dialogue. Yet the domestic foundations for genuine reform were less than incipient in North Korea. Furthermore, the 1970s institutionalized the economic role of the military through the creation of a "Second Economy" for the military-industrial-complex, separate from the civilian economy. In April 1974, Kim reportedly requested Premier Zhou Enlai to assist North Korea in developing its nuclear program and supplying it with tactical nuclear weapons. Although there is no reliable information regarding China's response, it did agree to train North Korea's nuclear scientists.[28] Declassified Hungarian Foreign Ministry memoranda report that two officials from North Korea expressed in 1976 that "by now the DPRK also has nuclear warheads and carrier missiles, which are targeted on the big cities of South Korea and Japan, such as Seoul, Tokyo, and Nagasaki." When the Hungarian interlocutor asked the two whether the People's Army had received the warheads from China, they replied that "they had developed them unaided through experimentation, and they manufactured them by themselves."[29] A most certain empty boast, the episode reveals more about intentions than capabilities. Indeed, another 1976 document from the same source established that "at present the DPRK wants to construct nuclear reactors, it is having talks about this issue, in order to become capable of producing atomic weapons in the future."[30] In 1976, North Korea allegedly threatened to suspend economic relations with the Soviets unless it supplied it with a nuclear power plant, a demand that the Soviets again rejected. Czechoslovakia was approached with a similar request in 1979. Soviet bloc officials concluded that North Korea "tries to make up for her lag behind South Korea [in nuclear power plants] in this way, with the hidden intention that later she may become capable of producing an atomic bomb."[31] By the late 1970s, Kim authorized the Academy of Science, the army, and the Ministry of Public Security to launch a nuclear weapons program and expand the Yongbyong facility.[32] In 1979 Kim ordered the construction of an indigenously designed 5 MW gas-graphite reactor suitable for plutonium production.

The dual track of the 1970s—hostile actions and compromising initiatives—reflected incipient tensions between the party's old guard and timid forces advancing economic reform as an alternative strategy of regime survival. This tension was to remain a leitmotif in North Korea's policies, including nuclear ones, particularly once reforms were under way. China's own reformers buttressed North Korea's by supporting embryonic private activities in agriculture and services, and incipient foreign investments in special-export zones. In January 1980, North Korea submitted a proposal addressed to the "Republic of Korea," using the latter's official name for the first time ever (Koh 1984:141). The five-point proposal involved non-aggression commitments, troop reductions, and withdrawal of foreign troops and nuclear weapons from the peninsula. However, the same year—following Chun Doo-Hwan's takeover in South Korea—Kim unveiled his proposal for a Democratic Confederal Republic of Koryo to the party's Sixth Congress, emphasizing revolutionary action rather than negotiations (at www.uriminzokkiri.com). In 1984 Kim removed Ri Jong-ok, a career technocrat with reformist tendencies who had been appointed premier in 1977. The 1984 Joint Venture Law spearheaded by Kim's son and heir Kim Jong-Il to attract Western and Japanese capital and technology provided new opportunities for embryonic reform. A succession of proto-reformers in the 1980s included Kim's relative Kang Song-san, appointed premier in 1984 but replaced by Ri Kun-mo in 1986 who, in turn, was replaced in 1988 by Yon Hyong-muk. The first premier to visit South Korea in 1990, Yon also promoted the Rajin-Sonbong special free-trade zone to enhance foreign investment (Sano 2005). Yet the reigning autarkic model forced North Korea to discontinue paying foreign debts, which limited access to additional capital. Military systems and primary products (anthracite, iron ore, and cement) accounted for 80 percent of exports while oil and oil products dominated imports.[33] Military exports to Iran, Pakistan, Iraq, Libya, Egypt, Vietnam, and Syria, including unconventional technologies and missile systems, were bartered for oil. Soviet aid continued to strengthen state bureaucracies. The old guard remained hostile to South Korea, bombing and assassinating ministers in Rangoon in 1983 and destroying a civilian KAL aircraft in 1987, actions that neutralized efforts by reformers to attract foreign investment.

An indigenous nuclear reactor was completed in 1986, allegedly a virtual replica of a British reactor obtained from declassified designs, which could provide bomb-grade plutonium (CNSW). North Korea also signed agreements with the Soviets for a nuclear power plant, and for trade and economic cooperation, in exchange for North Korea's accession to the NPT (Oberdorfer 2001). There was arguably some domestic support from economic reformers for an NPT bid at this time, but hardliners had no intention to abide by it in any event. Indeed, North Korea made no effort to negotiate and sign a safeguards agreement within the eighteen months stipulated by the IAEA. In 1986–87, North Korea began construction of the Yongbyong reprocessing facility, which began operating in 1989. After extensive nuclear negotiations with Pakistan since the late 1980s, North Korea received uranium enrichment technology including centrifuges, as President Pervez Musharaf confirmed in 2005.[34] In 1987 China discontinued all nuclear technology cooperation with North Korea in response to Yongbyong's secret activities. Among other things, French satellites and Japanese researchers at Tokai University confirmed in 1989 that Yongbyong had a detonation test site and a reprocessing facility. North Korea, however continued to deny that it was developing nuclear weapons. At this time North Korea's conventional military capability was superior to South Korea's, with one-fourth of its population (about 5 million) serving in the Korean People's Army (regular army), the People's Safety Ministry forces, and the Soviet Red Army militia. Military budgets in the late 1980s amounted to an unwieldy 25 percent of GDP ($4.5 to $5.4 billion in a $21 billion GDP) (Sakai 1996:120; *IISS* 1995–96:266; Trigubenko 1996:150; Banchev 1996:195, 226; Solingen 2001a). These levels were particularly astounding, given a foreign debt that kept North Korea at the world's bottom in credit standing. The pillars of Kim's model—the Party and the military-industrial-complex—revealed remarkable staying power even in the midst of a liberalizing East Asia, which had by now become the locomotive of a global export-oriented bandwagon. The People's Army would continue to grow from 838,000 (1985) to over 1.1 million (1994).

By the late 1980s and early 1990s, both the Soviets and Chinese were pursuing closer relations with South Korea. The collapse of the Soviet Union and other communist states widened the domestic cleavage between juche adherents and incipient reformers. Kim Il-Sung observed the demise of close friends Erich Honecker and Nicolae Ceausescu—and the latter's execution—and enforced a personality cult in North Korea with new vigor. Yet the economy remained stagnant and the performance gap between South Korea's and Kim's model had become dramatic. By 1980, South Korea's GNP was nearly six times higher and, by 1990, sixteen times higher than North Korea's (Kang 1998:241). The opportunity costs of military investments for satisfying the population's basic needs increased significantly.[35] The Soviets now required payments in convertible currency, which North Korea lacked, driving its trade from $4.6 billion (1990) down to $2.6 billion (1991). Exports reaching about $2 billion in the late 1980s, declined to less than $1 billion by the mid-1990s, and GDP shrunk by 3.7 percent (1990), 5.2 percent (1991), and 5 percent (1992). Foreign trade amounted to 12.6 percent (1992) and 10 percent (1994) of GDP.[36] Kim could blame the Soviets for North Korea's domestic disarray in 1990 while justifying a turn to Japan and the United States for economic aid, normalization, and investment. The Soviets had also suspended all exports of nuclear equipment in 1990 until North Korea accepted full-scope safeguards. By 1991, following another trip to China, Kim created the Rajin-Songbong free-trade-and-investment-zone and enacted a new legal framework for foreign investment. Reformers now enjoyed slightly broader space to promote emulation of East Asia's economic "tigers" and, aware that the nuclear program posed a crucial barrier to liberalizing foreign economic policy, reportedly forced a showdown over nuclear policy at the WP Central Committee, winning a significant tactical victory (Harrison 2002:33).

Against this background Kim accepted the "One Country-Two Regions" solution—in effect two sovereign states—at least during transition toward unification. He also approved IAEA inspections of North Korea's facilities and, in another dramatic reversal, agreed to separate U.N. membership for North and South in 1991. By year's end both Koreas signed the "Agreement on Reconciliation, Nonaggression, and Exchanges and Cooperation" and the "Joint Declaration for the Denuclearization of the Korean Peninsula." In January 1992 the United States and North Korea inaugurated direct bilateral talks, a move strongly endorsed by reformers.[37] A revealing aspect of this evolution is the fact that nearly 40,000 U.S. troops were still in South Korea when the North began moving toward more cooperative positions. The imputed long-standing reason for North Korea's external vulnerability remained a constant while its policies were undergoing significant change. In 1992, Kang Song-san returned to the premiership with younger reform-oriented technocrats who crafted a new joint-venture law to attract foreign capital and technology. By 1994 they were seeking to expand special export zones from Nampo, Rajin, and Sonbong into Pyongyang itself.[38] Struggling reformers included Kim Dal-Hyon, the minister of foreign trade, who had proposed to IAEA Director Blix the joint construction of a light-water reactor with South Korea in 1992 (Oberdorfer 2001:290), and was later purged; his successor Kim Jong-U, who advocated North Korea's opening to the global economy and appealed for foreign investment from the United States and, more generally, at a Davos meeting; Yi Song-nok, chair of the Koryo National Industrial Development Council, who discussed investments with chaebol representatives from South Korea; and Kim Jong-Il's sister Kim Kyong-hui, head of the Light Industry Department, and her husband, Kim Jong-Il's chief lieutenant Chang Song-taek, a reformer in the otherwise conservative and powerful Organizational Guidance Department.[39]

Domestic cleavages were also affected by challenges of succession, which had started in the 1970s but now moved to the core. Support for Kim Jong-Il was strong among some 170,000 members of the Small Team

Campaign—young cadres mobilized into industrial leadership—which he had led in the 1970s. Other supporters included some of his father's comrades-in-arms and a mass movement that by the mid-1990s rallied under the banner *Comrade Oh Jung Heum* (commemorating an anti-Japanese war hero) and had attracted some young army leaders. Kim Jong-Il placed his allies in key positions, including the premiership, foreign ministry, Central Committee Secretary for Unification, and heads of police.[40] Although opposition to Kim Jong-Il was strong among older military officers, he was nonetheless appointed Supreme Commander of the armed forces in 1991, when he began promoting his own loyal generals. The succession process accelerated after 1992, deepening domestic divisions within the military and economic leadership, already strained by natural disasters, famine, and economic collapse.[41] Signs of starvation and domestic reshuffling were evident by mid-1993 when reformist Deputy Premier and Chief of State Planning Kim Dal-Hyon was purged. In June 1993, North Korea suspended its withdrawal from the NPT under the threat of sanctions. The old guard articulated the position that "sanctions mean war." The latter half of 1993 and early part of 1994 was a very tense period of haggling over a proposed nuclear "package" designed to satisfy both camps.[42] Opponents of concessions wielded the failure of U.S., South Korean, Japanese, and multilateral promises of improved economic ties to materialize. This failure undermined reformers willing to exploit the nuclear card to extract economic benefits. Meanwhile, Kim Il-Sung, resurfacing from a relatively inactive period, acknowledged the "grave" challenges facing the economy in a rare public admission during his 1994 New Year's address.[43] President Carter's visit in June 1994 buttressed reformers and yielded Kim Il-Sung's commitment to improve relations with the United States and South Korea, and allow resumption of IAEA inspections. On July 6, 1994, three weeks after meeting with Carter, Kim stated his economic priorities for North Korea at that time: "Agriculture first. Light industry first. Foreign trade first." And an urgent need for electric power.[44] This was to be one of his last activities.

Kim Il-Sung died on July 8, 1994, just as the United States and North Korea were converging on a "package." Kim Jong-Il inherited the highest post and was faced with the delicate task of navigating through key battlegrounds of economic reform, dwindling resources for his military, and pressures for denuclearization. Having straddled domestic divides for most of his career, Kim Jong-Il was not new to this game. He had been connected with rabid factions that executed two American soldiers in the DMZ in 1976, planted the 1983 bomb in Rangoon and the 1987 bomb on KAL, and forced North Korea's NPT withdrawal in 1993 (Wampler 2003, Document 3; Oberdorfer 2001). Kim Jong-Il introduced the policy of *son'gun chŏngch'i* ("military first") to replace juche and its promoters with a policy of *kangsŏngdaeguk* (Strong and Prosperous Great Power) to reassure the military. As enunciated by *Nodong Sinmun*, "Military-first ideology is an ideology that has inherited the theoretical and practical achievements of the chuch'e [juche] idea and that has developed and enriched them with new theories, and it is a militant banner that firmly guarantees the final victory of the chuch'e idea. The chuch'e idea is the root of Military-first ideology. . . . The initiation of military-first ideology was possible, for there was the chuch'e idea, and the demonstration of the great vitality of the chuch'e idea has been possible, for there has been military-first ideology."[45] Kim Jong-Il was also credited with spearheading special economic zones and ancillary policies favored by some of his reformist allies.[46]

Domestic cleavages during his tenure were echoed in apparently incoherent—sometimes schizoid—foreign policies, including those on the nuclear issue. On one hand, *ancien régime* supporters regarded nuclear weapons as the ultimate expression of juche, national independence, and technical achievement that could buttress the old model's viability. Nuclear weapons trapped in juche represented the means to prevent subordination to a foreign yoke forever, which would ensure continued payoffs to the restive military establishment and allies in the party, bureaucracy, and military-industrial-complex, while enhancing regime support not just within North Korea but from sympathetic nationalists in South Korea as well (Park 1996:224). According to one military defector from North Korea, there was strong support for nuclear weapons in the People's Army.[47] General Choe-Kwang, chief of the army, proclaimed the army's objective of "reunifying the fatherland with arms in the 1990s."[48] Furthermore, an independent nuclear deterrent symbolized the triumph of North Korea's model over that of a "dependent" South Korea, overriding the latter's presumed economic achievements (Mazarr 1995c). On the other hand, reformers regarded increased trade and economic openness as ways to overturn catastrophic economic conditions and enable the regime's "soft landing" à la China. To prevent regime collapse due to energy and food crises, Kim Jong-Il supported a new "economic policy for the period of adjustment (1994–1996)" signaling new priorities in agriculture, light industry, and foreign trade.[49] Kim Jong-Il also approved a nuclear "package" whose features had the imprint of his personal survival strategy, straddling between contending camps. In October 1994, as chairman of North Korea's National Defense Committee, Kim accepted the Agreed Framework, which normalized relations with the United States, replaced the sensitive graphite-moderated reactor with two light-water reactors, and pledged peace and security in the Korean peninsula and NPT compliance.[50] The old guard achieved some concessions with U.S. promises not to use or threaten to use nuclear weapons against North Korea, to allow spent fuel rods to remain in North Korea for five to nine years, and to avoid direct participation of sadaejuui in negotiations, a snub to South Korea. North Korea's reformers gained expanded trade and investment commitments and expected the downgrading of Team Spirit exercises to deprive domestic opponents of the Agreed Framework of subterfuges for defecting. Renewed access to energy resources, including oil and a proliferation-resistant nuclear reactor that would yield ten times the output of the graphite system, served both political camps well.[51] Both camps gained from direct negotiations with the United States, which heightened possibilities of domestic reform but also relegated South Korea to the sidelines to the glee of North Korea's party and military officials.[52]

The Agreed Framework's execution bore the signature of continued domestic tensions in North Korea, including the strengthening of military influence in late 1995 and early 1996, and the rise of the "Red Banner Philosophy" emphasizing martial and revolutionary spirit (Oberdorfer 2001:402). Between 580,000 and 1,120,000 people were estimated to have perished in famines since 1994, and foreign trade declined by 20 percent from 1993 to 1994, the fifth consecutive fall, reducing trade volume to less than half the levels of 1990.[53] GNP reportedly plummeted from $21.3 to $12.6 billion between 1994 and 1998. A television anchor began one report in 1996 with this statement: "Today I will introduce you to tasty and healthy ways to eat wild grass."[54] In 1997 the architect and ardent promoter of juche Hwang Jang-Yop defected to South Korea after proposing a "new juche" that called for the introduction of selected market principles.[55] Hwang had antagonized both supporters of the old juche and younger pragmatic proponents of reforms. In 1996 he renounced war and praised China's model, which led to his ousting from the inner circles. At risk of imminent purging, Hwang defected as military hardliners got stronger. In 1998, North Korea launched its Taepodong missile into the Sea of Japan (Koreans' East Sea), apparently for domestic reasons.[56] Later that year the Supreme People's Assembly enshrined Kim Jong-Il both as head of the National Defense Commission, which became North Korea's overriding authority (the presidency was forever relegated only to Kim Il-Sung), and as general secretary of the party. It also amended the constitution to adopt selected China-style reforms, took away the Central People's Committee's power to oversee technocrats responsible for economic management, and granted responsibility for light industries and cooperative farms to local governments (Dwor-Frécaut 2004).

Kim Jong-Il packed the Assembly with prominent military leaders and positioned himself to rule from a military post while setting the stage for moderate reforms with military backing (Oberdorfer 2001:415; Harrison 2002:37). By 1999 the economy expanded significantly (over 6 percent) largely due to China and South Korea's assistance, but at a much slower rate since (1 to 2 percent). Kim approved Hyundai's investment zone at Kaesong in 2000, visited Shanghai's stock exchange in 2001, and used *Nodong Sinmun* to prepare the ground for reforms, declaring that "things are not what they used to be in the 1960s. So no one should follow the way people used to do things in the past. . . . We should make constant efforts to renew the landscape to replace the one which was formed in the past, to meet the requirements of a new era."[57] In May 2002 Kim hosted a warm dinner reception for Park Keun-hye, late Park Chung-Hee's daughter, quite a shift from the days when Park's strategy was vituperated as a failed policy of corrupt sadaejuui. In July 2002 Kim launched the most comprehensive reforms ever, steered by Premier Hong Song-nam, including the first foreign onshore oil concession, monetization, price controls relaxation, devaluation (to attract foreign investment and promote exports), decentralization of decisions in agriculture and industry, and new special industrial, investment, and tourism zones (Shinuiju, Kaesong, Kumgang). These reforms, approved by segments of the military, came short of those that China or Vietnam had implemented, but nonetheless they led to small and incipient private activities. Chinese businessmen visiting North Korea observed accelerating change and growing availability of goods.[58] Reformers tended to be economic bureaucrats with foreign exposure that reflected the interests of new entrepreneurs and corporate elites from about one hundred of the largest combines and commercial enterprises. Beneficiaries of reform also included those with access to foreign currency, "Japanese Koreans," agencies in charge of licensing and distribution of foreign aid, export-oriented workers, IT professionals, and an emerging middle class (Mansourov 2006). Kim Jong-Il was careful to avoid formal doctrinal debates between the two camps that might have unraveled his regime, encouraging instead "reform by stealth."[59] Over three hundred general and private markets, a new source of state revenue, were in operation by 2005, selling agricultural surplus produce, handmade items, and products from China and Russia.

Economic reform also increased inflation, unemployment, urban poverty, and corruption, which had been a legacy of the 1990s.[60] Most negatively affected by extant reforms were lower-level military personnel; state employees in industrial enterprises; collective farms, workers in education, health, and administration; women and children; scientists and intellectuals; and the elderly. The public distribution system is unable to provide minimum subsistence requirements. Rigid regulations and damaging midstream changes in commercial agreements led several South Korean chaebol to retreat from initial investments. The limited success of special-industrial zones stemmed from party interference, absence of infrastructure and statistics, unclear property rights, and more attractive alternatives for FDI. A self-described businessman "with close ties to the government" assigned to attract foreign investment acknowledged the difficulties posed by his country's nuclear program.[61] North Korea had already received extensive foreign aid from China, South Korea, the United States, Japan, and the U.N. in the previous decade, which was estimated at $2.4 billion since 1995 according to South Korea's Unification Ministry, and had established diplomatic relations with fourteen Western countries. Exports revenues increased, particularly from nonferrous metals and mineral products, although a much larger proportion of revenues stemmed from exports of illicit drugs, missiles to Egypt, Pakistan, Iran, Libya, and Syria, conventional weapons, and counterfeiting (Wortzel 2003).

As a sign of Kim's straddling strategy, *Nodong Sinmun* cited him in 2003 ascertaining that "our party, as it implements military-first politics, puts the People's Army, not the working class, to the fore as the main force of the revolution."[62] The "military-first" (*songun*) policy had become Kim Jong-Il's trademark, and Kim awarded military personnel the highest wage increases allowed after the onset of monetization. Kim acknowledged to South Korean media chiefs that "my power comes from the military."[63] The military's warning against reforms could not be missed, despite *Nodong Sinmum*'s jumbled editorials: "military-first ideology . . . calls for giving priority to military issues over everything, and it is a line, strategy, and tactics of putting the Army before the working class in order to depend on the Army by putting it to the fore as a pillar and as a main force for the revolution."[64] The same source reiterated that these foundations are the "direct inheritance" from Kim Il-Sung, reminding everybody (including Kim Jong-Il) of the costs of departing from these roots: "whether one supports or stymies military-first [politics] serves as a litmus test for discriminating independence from flunkeyism, patriotism from betrayal."[65] The article also revealed the kind of competing priority likely to derail songun commitments: *an open economy.* "A powerful socialist state in the true sense of the term is one where economy develops dynamically . . . based on the self-reliant foundations that never swing in any global economic fluctuations. . . . Only a country that has the people equipped with the ideology of placing importance on military issues and that has a self-reliant economy—which can ensure a powerful military might materially and technologically—can fully step up the construction of a powerful state." The emphasis on songun was part of Kim Jong-Il's campaign to exploit cleavages between the military and the security apparatus and to strengthen the former. Kim exploited divisions within the military and security organs also to promote those more favorable to economic reforms.[66] As part of a conglomerate under Kim's control, military personnel came to manage important trading firms in opium, mineral resources, infrastructure construction, agriculture, supplies to the military, weapons-production, and missiles.[67]

Although North Korea's closed system has hampered more direct knowledge of its domestic politics, signs of tension along the lines suggested in this analysis emerge ever more clearly from *Nodong Sinmun*: "In the 1990s of the 20th century, the struggle to make a choice between independence and subjugation and between socialism and capitalism was more fiercely waged than ever before in the international arena, and our country had become a miniaturized ground of the struggle and a most acute, decisive battle site."[68] This statement can be interpreted only as an acknowledgement of serious domestic tensions between economic reformers and guardians of the ancien régime even within the military itself. A subsequent analysis elaborated what domestic priorities should be, given a closed economic system, stressing that the interests of the armed forces should come prior to those of workers: "What takes the leading position in the correlation between the army and economy is, however, still the army. It is the new principle illuminated by the military-first idea that only when we place importance on the gun barrel can we build an economically powerful state. If economic power is based on military power, military power is a guarantee for economic power and impetus for economic development. We cannot defend national industries nor ensure a peaceful environment for economy-building without strong military power."[69]

These statements can easily be construed as preemptive threats against modernizers appointed to key positions and against trading nuclear weapons in exchange for external help in economic reform. In 2004, reformist Pak Pong-Ju was appointed premier but denied control over foreign and defense policies and was excluded from the powerful National Defense Commission that Kim Jong-Il heads.[70] Reformist technocrats and the trickle of students sent on study tours of market economies can read the trade-offs between the nuclear program and economic reform quite clearly. In the words of an analyst from Barclays Capital Research, "Large-scale public or private flows are unlikely to reach North Korea until the nuclear issue is resolved. Without progress on the nuclear front, the opening of the Kaesong industrial zone at the border with South Korea could increase the scale, but not the nature (assembly work with limited impact on capital and technology) of investment in the DPRK."[71] Ironically, reformers who had worked (but failed) to attract foreign investment into Rajin-Sonbong, such as External Economic Cooperation Committee Vice-Chairman Kim Mun-Sung, were executed or, in the case of Professor Kim Su-Yong of Kim Il-Sung University, ousted. Kim Jong-Il also purged Kim Jong-U, Chairman of the Committee on Promotion of Cooperation with Foreign Countries, other officials responsible for economic exchanges with South Korea, and executed alleged reformist General Kim Yong-Ryong, first deputy minister of the State Security Agency, who acted as the minister of state security, for criticizing the slow pace of reforms.[72]

All these purges followed a single pattern: coup-wary Kim Jong-Il trying to retain control over an increasingly less coherent regime by removing challengers and paying off loyal allies.

Conclusion

The lack of systematic information about the internal operation of North Korea's regime, its politics and economics, makes it difficult to arrive at any definitive account of its nuclear program. With respect to some specific issues, like the prisoners in Plato's cave, we may be able to see only reflections on the cave's wall rather than true realities (particularly when reading *Nodong Sinmun*). It is possible, however, to reconstitute at least some general aspects of North Korea's nuclear behavior that help extract some broader conclusions.

As have other inward-looking regimes, North Korea has defied political and economic sanctions from great powers and international institutions, allowing state agencies and industries responsible for productive and distributive functions to benefit from international closure. Leaders' statements and the 2006 nuclear test do not reveal particular concerns with a nuclear acquisition "taboo." Indeed, threats to turn Seoul into "a sea of fire" do not even suggest a taboo based on kinship and family relations. The presence of 40,000 U.S. troops in South Korea (down to 29,000) for decades has remained a genuine concern. It is precisely this unchanged geopolitical feature that highlights the difficulty of reducing North Korea's nuclear behavior exclusively to paranoic security considerations. Against rather stable structural power conditions, North Korea has executed sharp policy turns, particularly since the 1990s. Domestic dynamics help explain these shifting positions, from threats to reduce enemies to a "sea of fire" at some points to more compromising positions at others, and back. North Korea's two-track (not to be confused with "track-two") policy cannot be understood without taking into consideration Kim's straddling of competing models of political survival in order to retain support from core domestic constituencies.[73]

Incipient efforts to reform the economy have been burdened by decades of ruling through juche. Discarding juche in practice if not in principle required an awesome societal transformation that risked Kim's own survival and his regime continuity. Nuclear weapons endowed Kim and key constituencies in the army and party with prestige, resources, and a raison d'être—particularly in the face of domestic economic hardship—that could fade away with true economic transformation.[74] By the turn of the century North Korea was reportedly spending up to 40 and perhaps 50 percent of GNP on Kim's trademark songun policy, with most of that money devoted to unconventional capabilities.[75] Despite sustained efforts by very powerful strategic allies and very powerful strategic adversaries, North Korea was not persuaded to relinquish nuclear aspirations for decades. Neither did the policy remain static, as suggested by North Korea's commitment-and-retraction sequences. As Oh and Hassig (2004:279) note, for Kim Jong-Il, "generating one crisis after another may be the best way to stay in power." Furthermore, in the words of a frequent visitor to North Korea who challenges the standard monolithic interpretation of its behavior (Harrison 2005:1), "The key reason for North Korean intransigence in the nuclear crisis . . . is that Kim does not have unchallenged control over foreign and defense policy."

Clearly nuclear weapons were conceived as tools of regime survival that enhanced domestic support, bargaining chips that maximized international concessions, and a potential deterrent against external threats. The problem of multifinality identified in chapter 2 emerges once again, pointing to multiple sources of North Korea's nuclearization. In a fundamental way, however, these sources can all be traced to juche as the guiding inward-oriented model of political control. From this standpoint, the nuclear program became a "flexible support system for the North's overriding goal of regime preservation," as Mazarr (1995a:100–101) argues, and whatever external security motivations may have been present in the early phases of the program were never satisfied with the removal of U.S. tactical nuclear weapons from South Korea, the latter's renunciation of a nuclear deterrent, or repeated U.S. pledges of nuclear non-aggression and no hostile intent (1993, 1994, 2005). The issue of differentiating state from regime survival surfaces in North Korea's February 10, 2005, statement describing U.S. "hostile policy" aimed at seeking "the [DPRK's] 'regime change'; . . . The U.S. disclosed its attempt to topple the political system in the DPRK at any cost, threatening it with a nuclear stick. This compels us to take a measure to bolster its nuclear weapons arsenal in order to protect the ideology, system, freedom and democracy chosen by [our] people. . . . We had already taken the resolute action of pulling out of the NPT and have manufactured nukes."[76] The same statement's tangential and disdainful reference to "peasant markets" in North Korea hinted at a negative undertone regarding economic reform by the architects of this particular policy step in the nuclear saga. At the same time, incipient reforms had already transformed the political landscape against which Kim continues to craft his own survival strategy (Mansourov 2004). North Korea's elite reformers and masses had become far more permeable to economic incentives and foreign influences, particularly from China's porous borders and from mobile phones and satellites. Cleavages over economic reform dealt a fatal blow to regime cohesion and to the old ideological pillar (juche). Most importantly, the absence of further reform had become an even greater danger to the regime than reform itself.

On September 19, 2005, the Six-Party Talks yielded an unprecedented joint statement where North Korea agreed to dismantle its nuclear program, return to the NPT, and allow IAEA monitoring. In turn, the five powers agreed to provide North Korea with energy, trade, and security guarantees, including normalization with the United States and Japan and U.S. confirmation that it had no intention to attack or invade North Korea with nuclear or conventional weapons. North Korea's structural power predicament had not changed at the eve of this particular regime's decision. Its adversarial nuclear-armed hegemon was deployed in the region much as it had been for decades. It seems far more fruitful to trace Kim Jong-Il's September 2005 decisions to shifting logics of political survival, which sometimes moved in the same direction as the rest of East Asia, and his subsequent retractions to a domestic backlash against nuclear concessions and economic reforms. Such backlash took place in 2006, when North Korea launched seven missiles into the Sea of Japan in July, and exploded a nuclear device in October. Both events took place around symbolic national anniversaries in North Korea. As an expert on North Korea's program suggests, the decision to test was "a purely political act" in revenge for financial sanctions imposed by the United States against illegal banking activities by Macau's Banco Delta Asia, that were "directly related to the personal income of the leadership in North Korea."[77] Chinese expert Shi Yinhong concurs: "The primary cause [was] that over the past few months North Korean domestic policy has changed. After the United States launched financial sanctions . . . any moderate elements in their policy ended. Extreme hardliners now have 100% control over policy making and . . . enormous political determination to launch their missiles, test their bombs and direct their nuclear arms programme. . . . By possessing nuclear weapons they can also show to their own people and army that they are strong and this can help solidify their domestic support."[78] North Korea's own statement regarding its nuclear test is transparent regarding the test's domestic audience: "The nuclear test was conducted with indigenous wisdom and technology 100%. It marks a historic event as it *greatly encouraged and pleased the KPA (Korean People's Army) and people that have wished to have powerful self-reliant defence capability*" [emphasis added].[79] Understanding North Korea's nuclear gyrations seems futile without further probing into how domestic considerations convert external pressures and inducements into policy. As of 2006, dim signals emerging from the hermit kingdom suggested that Kim Jong-Il still considered the effective introduction of markets as a significant threat to his hold on power.[80] The U.S. military, particularly after the Iraqi quagmire, was a distant second.

PART THREE

The Middle East:
Nuclearization as the Norm,
Denuclearization as the Anomaly

CHAPTER SEVEN

Iraq

IRAQ'S NUCLEAR ACTIVITIES began in 1956 with the establishment of the Iraqi Atomic Energy Commission (IAEC) with U.S. donations of unclassified reports from the Manhattan Project and training of Iraq's first generation of nuclear scientists. In 1959 Iraq sent 375 students to the Soviet Union for nuclear training, and in 1962 the Soviets supplied a 2 MW research reactor, which began operating around late 1967 (Richelson 2006:318). Iraq signed the NPT in 1968 and ratified it in 1969. In 1971 IAEC scientists began outlining a secret nuclear weapon program aimed at acquiring a safeguarded French reactor to be clandestinely duplicated and a plutonium reprocessing unit. In 1972, Vice President Saddam Hussein ordered the plan implemented immediately (NTIW, FASW; Hamza 1998). French Premier Jacques Chirac agreed to supply Saddam with the reactor in exchange for petroleum concessions. Saddam went to Paris in 1974 to conclude the transfer of Osiraq and Isis (Tammuz-1 and Tammuz-2), offering cheap oil as an inducement to ensure that only reactors with proliferation potential were supplied. In 1979 the Italian company SNIA-Techint supplied a pilot plutonium separation and handling facility ("hot cells"), and a uranium refining and fuel-manufacturing plant, none subject to IAEA safeguards. Iraq also obtained large amounts of unsafeguarded uranium from Portugal, Niger, and Brazil and sought depleted uranium metal suitable for plutonium production from a West German firm.

During the Iran-Iraq war (1980–88), Iran tried to obliterate Osiraq twice, unsuccessfully. In 1981 Israel destroyed it at sunset, when its civilian operators were absent and before it reached criticality so that no radiation was released (Khadduri 2003; Obeidi and Pitzer 2004). Both the war with Iran and Israel's attack exacerbated clandestine efforts to obtain enrichment technologies. In 1988 Saddam established deadlines to produce a nuclear device and in 1990 invaded Kuwait. Following U.S. deployment to the Gulf, Saddam ordered a "crash program" to build a nuclear weapon from safeguarded enriched uranium, including warheads and delivery systems, by 1991. Estimates about how close Iraq got to meeting those objectives vary from several months to three years. Details of this effort became evident only after Desert Storm when the U.N. Special Commission (UNSCOM) inspected and destroyed all facilities. Iraq remained under U.N. sanctions and subject to inspections, which Saddam sought to thwart. Several U.N. resolutions between 1991 and 2003 called on Iraq to abandon a pattern of deception regarding WMD programs. U.N. inspectors found no evidence of these programs but could not certify that Iraq had completely abandoned them (Blix 2005). The United States, Britain, and smaller contingents from other countries attacked Iraq on March 13, 2003. The CIA's Iraq Survey Group (ISG) search found no evidence of an active nuclear program.

IRAQ'S OR SADDAM'S SELF-HELP DILEMMAS?

Were neighbors immutable adversaries of the Iraqi state or specific targets of Saddam's hegemonic ambitions? Syria's Ba'th was Iraq's ideological kin but also a political adversary with a vast military machine that backed Iranian and Iraqi Shi'ites against Iraq's Ba'th. The latter, in turn, provided military assistance to Syria's Muslim Brotherhood and Lebanese Christians opposed to Syria's Alawite-dominated regime. Fertile Crescent designs in an earlier era, however, featured far closer relations among Iraq, Syria, and Jordan (Barnett and Solingen 2007). Jordan had royal historical links to the king whom Saddam had deposed, yet it sided with Iraq in 1991, aligning itself with the West in the war's aftermath. The Gulf States had limited military capabilities, but Saddam held them in high contempt for their oil assets and pro-Western orientation, particularly Kuwait and Saudi Arabia. Neither Syria's Ba'th nor less militarily endowed neighbors in the Gulf or Jordan could be construed as justifications for an Iraqi nuclear deterrent. Indeed, Saddam occupied Kuwait in 1990 within a few hours and only the U. S.-led military intervention saved Saudi Arabia from a similar fate.[1] Saddam's hegemonic ambitions, including control over the region's oil, shaped Iraq's relations with neighboring states.

Although Iran's oil resources were a target as well, its territory, population, and resources were three times larger than Iraq's (Baram 2001). Iraq had long-standing aspirations for Iran's oil-rich Khuzestan province, and the 1968 Ba'th coup began encouraging Iran's Arab minorities to revolt against the Shah. Animosity over the Shatt-el-Arab waterway acquired new salience after 1969 when Saddam began claiming all of it as Iraq's territory. In 1971 he claimed sovereignty over three islands in the Persian Gulf, expelled Iranians, and broke diplomatic relations with Iran. Most Arab states except Syria sided with Iran. A 1975 agreement conceded Iran's sovereignty over the eastern shore in exchange for discontinuing Iranian support for Iraqi Kurds and Shi'a. The 1979 Islamic revolution exacerbated Saddam's concerns with Iran's appeal to Iraqi Shi'a who were subjugated by a Sunni (particularly Tikriti) minority. Although Khomeini supported Shi'a demonstrations and civil unrest in 1979 and

1980, Iran was a diminished power absorbed with internal consolidation. Iraq declared the 1975 agreement null and void, unilaterally restoring a 1937 arrangement subjecting nearly all of the Shatt-el-Arab to Iraqi sovereignty (Walt 1996). In 1980 Saddam attacked Iran, announcing that he would be in Tehran within three days.

The logic of balancing Iran through a nuclear deterrent is far from unassailable. Saddam launched Iraq's nuclear weapons program in 1971, *after* Iran had signed (1968) and ratified (1970) the NPT and *prior* to the Shah's 1972 announcement of a large-scale nuclear energy program. Revolutionary Iran made it a more likely target of an Iraqi nuclear deterrent. However, whether the Iran-Iraq war (1980–88), initiated by Saddam, also made Iraq's reliance on nuclear weapons unavoidable remains contested. It is indeed the case that Iran was able to repel Iraq's invasion in 1982, driving it back behind its own borders and threatening Saddam's *personal* tenure (Iran demanded Saddam's removal).[2] Saddam's well-equipped and funded forces, however, were able to fend off Iran's massive response to Iraq's offensive. Military suppliers of Iraq included the Soviet Union, China, Egypt, Germany, and other Western countries, which also provided Iraq with biological and chemical weapons technology.[3] The United States provided Saddam with intelligence and economic aid. Despite heavy Iranian losses, its massive conventional "human waves" inflicted severe harm on Iraq's military. Saddam decided to use chemical weapons on Iranian troops and launched missiles on Tehran. Iran, as early as 1980, became the first state to bomb Osiraq, and it was unsuccessful.

Saddam used the war experience as justification for redoubling efforts to seek the "ultimate equalizer" against Iran: nuclear weapons. From Saddam's standpoint, as suggested in the ISG report, "The Persian menace loomed large and was a challenge to his place in history."[4] Iraqi nuclear scientist Khidir Hamza acknowledged that

> the Iran-Iraq war brought pressure on us from Saddam—pressure to increase the speed at which our program was developing. Why would Saddam want so many bombs? Israel is not that big, 3 or 4 bombs would do. With the pressure of the war with Iran, Saddam wanted to be a nuclear power, with a large arsenal and many options for possible use. We were handed requests for radiation weapons for the border. They were trying to draw the nuclear weapons program into the framework of that war, one way or another. With nuclear weapons Saddam felt that Iraq could hold its own in the long-term, even with two large aggressive neighbors like Iran and Turkey. He was also afraid of Turkey.[5]

Intensive efforts in the 1980s, recounted later, brought Saddam close to acquiring nuclear weapons by the end of the decade. His invasion of Kuwait and Desert Storm, however, ended this "crash program" by 1991.

Life under sanctions and IAEA inspections in the 1990s arguably enhanced Saddam's concerns with Iran. The Duelfer report (2004:29) cited Saddam's statement that, regarding his WMD efforts, "Iran was the main concern because it wanted to annex southern Iraq." Iraqi troops in the 1990s trained with the expectation that Iran would use chemical weapons if it invaded Iraq, but other Iraqi statements challenged this scenario. Interviews with Iraqi officials revealed that "no Iraqi decision-maker asserted that either country [Iran or the United States] was an imminent challenge between 1991 and 2003" and that "between 1998 and 2003, Iraqi leaders determined that Tehran was more of a long-term danger than an imminent one because of deficiencies in Iranian readiness and morale when compared against Iraqi training and preparedness" (ISG 2004:28–30). Over twenty years after Iran's revolution, Iraqi decision-makers continued to perceive their own military as superior to Iran's. Moreover, key Iraqi officers considered the worst-case scenario of Iranian chemical or biological attacks unlikely. Former Foreign Minister Tariq 'Aziz thought that U.N. monitoring provided Iraq with protection and, according to another former senior official, Saddam himself "felt that the United States would intervene to protect oilfields" (ISG 2004: 28–30). A former Iraqi defense minister cited Iraq's chief-of-staff statement that "Iran would have difficulty conducting a large surprise attack because Iraq would detect the extensive mobilization required for it. . . . Iraqi units were at least as good as their Iranian counterparts. . . . Iran enjoyed quantitative—not qualitative—ground superiority" (ISG 2004:30). Another senior official argued that although Iran's threat was real, Saddam always exaggerated it. These statements reveal distinct internal differences within Iraq regarding the need for a nuclear deterrent as the only means to cope with Iran, although such differences could not be expressed under Saddam's brutal rule. Meanwhile Saddam's nuclear ambitions fueled Iran's own program, which had been discontinued after the revolution. The fundamental question regarding the role of Iran in Iraq's nuclear designs is whether or not the nature of their respective regimes, more than simply an elusive balance of power, stimulated their nuclear one-upmanship.

Although not adjacent to Iraq, Israel was also considered a major ideological adversary, particularly after the Ba'th's ascent in 1968. Israel's alleged nuclear program in the 1970s was considered a secondary source of Saddam's efforts to develop his own (Dunn 1998). Prior to his 1975 trip to Paris to purchase Osiraq, Saddam told the Lebanese magazine *Al-Usbu al-Arabi* that the agreement with France would be "the first concrete step toward the production of the Arabic atomic weapon" and that Iraq needed help in obtaining nuclear weapons to counter Israel's nuclear arsenal.[6] Israel's 1981 attack on Osiraq added a personal affront to Saddam and his political allies and scientists. Yet Iraq's decision to launch a nuclear weapons program had its roots in 1971, a decade before Osiraq, as described later. About 4,000 scientists were recruited to work on "high-tech" projects—including the nuclear program—between 1974 and 1977 (Richelson 2006:319). Furthermore, it is impossible to separate the heavy nuclear investments of the 1980s from the fierce Iran-Iraq war. Indeed, it was in 1987, against the background of that brutal war, that Saddam's son-in-law and military industries czar Husseyn Kamil impressed on leading nuclear scientist Obeidi the urgency of obtaining nuclear weapons (Obeidi and Pitzer 2004:56,183). Kamil installed Obeidi as chief of an enrichment project that would remain secret even to the IAEC and also launched a weaponization program. When Obeidi suggested in 1987 that a basic prototype of a centrifuge might take one year to develop, Kamil replied, "That is not acceptable. . . . you have a month and a half. Nothing more. . . . It is an order" (Obeidi and Pitzer 2004:66). The immediate target was not in doubt. It was Iran.

Yet Israel provided an excellent rallying point to assert pan-Arab leadership for a leader who fashioned himself as the champion of liberating Palestine from the "river to the sea," a code-word for Israel's destruction. Whether Israel was a threat to Iraq geopolitically or to Saddam's regime and his efforts to acquire nuclear weapons can be gleaned from statements by Saddam's own officials. "All senior level Iraqi officials considered Iran to be Iraq's principal enemy in the region" and "generally ranked Tehran first and Tel Aviv as a more distant second as their primary adversaries" (ISG 2004:1, 28–30). According to former Vice President Taha Yasin Ramadan, "Saddam judged Israel to be a lesser adversary than Iran because Israel could not invade Iraq" (ISG 2004:31). Hamza initially thought Iraq would use nuclear weapons as a bargaining tool with Israel, but during the 1991 Gulf War Saddam stated that he was "going to drop it on somebody."[7] Saddam's most senior lieutenants, the so-called quartet members, were reported to have considered Israel "as a secondary threat compared to Iran. Israel had no land border with Iraq and was unlikely to mount a sustained attack on Iraq" (ISG 2004, Annex A:72). Kamil confirmed that Iran was the main threat.[8] Opposition to Israel "was ritualistic" (ISG 2004, Annex A:72), as described by Kamil, who questioned Saddam's anti-Israeli slogans following the Palestinian-Israeli Oslo agreements.[9] Saddam himself privately expressed to his top advisors on multiple occasions that "he sought to establish a strategic balance between the Arabs and Israel, a different objective from deterring an Iranian strategic attack or blunting an Iranian invasion" (ISG 2004:29). Yet a January 1991 audio tape recorded Saddam's hierarchy of targets for bacteriological weapons: "I need these germs to be fixed on the missiles . . . and I consider Riyadh as a target. . . . I want the weapons to be distributed to targets; I want Riyadh and Jeddah, which are the biggest Saudi cities with all the decision-makers, and the Saudi rulers live there. This is for the germ and chemical weapons. . . . Also, all the Israeli cities, all of them. Of course you should concentrate on Tel Aviv, since it is their center."[10]

A final argument might trace Saddam's nuclear weapons to U.S. threats, a plausible argument after 1990. Yet, as we have seen, the program was launched twenty years earlier in 1971, well before the more adversarial relationship with the United States that followed Iraq's invasion of Kuwait. The United States had supported Iraq during its war with Iran, despite its use of chemical weapons. Even the CIA's ISG (2004) report confirmed that Saddam and his chief advisors did not invariably regard the United States as an absolute military enemy. Furthermore, even after 1991, when Saddam considered a full-scale invasion by U.S. forces to be the most dangerous potential threat to the regime, "Saddam rated the probability of an invasion as very low" (ISG 2004:31). According to several regime figures, as late as the end of 2002, "Saddam had persuaded himself, just as he did in 1991, that the United States would not attack Iraq because it already had achieved its objectives of establishing a military presence in the region" (ISG 2004:32). Saddam believed the United States would avoid casualties at all costs and, even if it launched a war against Iraq it would circumscribe it to the South as in 1991, and would stop short of overthrowing him if it required an invasion. Interviews reportedly revealed that "no Iraqi decision-maker asserted that [the United States] was an imminent challenge between 1991 and 2003" and that Saddam saw U.S. air strikes as less of a worry than an Iranian land attack (ISG 2004: 28–30). Furthermore, Saddam's private statements, according to Tariq Aziz, revealed his confidence that France and Russia would prevent a U.S. invasion (Woods, Lacey, and Murray 2006).

An analysis of Iraq's nuclear program that leaves out Saddam's own personal calculation of regime survival is a rather poor guide for understanding the full range of choices that Iraq faced for thirty years. As the ISG report suggests, "The former Regime was Saddam, and he was the one person who made important decisions. It was his assessment of the utility of various policy options that was determinant. It was Saddam's calculations of risk and timing that mattered" (ISG 2004, TM:3). No less than Iraq's director of WMD programs, Saddam's own son-in-law, along with many other former officials, acknowledged that Iraq was the source of aggression on its neighbors.[11] Iran's revolution posed a particular *internal* threat to Saddam's Sunni Tikriti-based regime. Yet Saddam's decisions to seek nuclear weapons preceded the Islamic Republic's. Nor did Iran attack Iraq but vice versa.[12] Saddam's regime used Iran's threat effectively to justify military, including WMD, investments. Nuclearization could have variously been interpreted as increasing or decreasing Iraq's security, in yet another iteration of the open-endedness of structural power considerations as guides for action. Indeed, even during the difficult war with Iran, Saddam's cousin and former Minister of Defense Adnan Khayr Allah reportedly warned that a nuclear program made Iraq more vulnerable to attacks by Iran, Israel, and Turkey (Baram 2001:29). Beyond Iran, "the wish to balance Israel and acquire status and influence in the Arab world were also considerations, but secondary" (ISG 2004:1), and, as former Iraqi officials reported, such considerations were more of a tool to fuel Saddam's hegemonic aspirations in the Arab world than a response to existential fears about Iraq as a state. If relative power, balance of power, and existential dilemmas told the story, Egypt, adjacent to Israel and its adversary in several wars, was a more likely candidate to offset an Israeli deterrent. As Jones (1997a) suggested, "Arab-Arab and Arab-Iranian disputes have been at least as great a motivating force for the creation of these capabilities as any difference with Israel."

INTERNATIONAL INSTITUTIONS: FROM DECEPTION TO UNSCOM

Iraq signed the NPT in 1968, the year of the coup that consolidated the Tikritis in power, and ratified it in 1969. Despite these formal commitments, Iraq's weapons program was in place shortly after its accession to the NPT. As Hamza (1998) described it, "We decided to acquire a 40-megawatt research reactor, a fuel-manufacturing plant, and nuclear fuel-reprocessing facilities, all under cover of acquiring the expertise needed to eventually build and operate nuclear power plants and produce and recycle nuclear fuel. Our hidden agenda was to clandestinely develop the expertise and infrastructure needed to produce weapon-grade plutonium. . . . Iraq was careful to avoid raising IAEA suspicions; an elaborate strategy was gradually developed to deceive and manipulate the agency." In addition, as early as 1973, Saddam planted Iraqi officials within the IAEA to help steer Iraq's nuclear program from within the agency (NTIW). After attending an IAEA conference, Hamza and IAEC Secretary-General Moyesser Al-Mallah wrote a report to Saddam, who issued orders to limit contact with the IAEA that might reveal sensitive information about Iraq's designs. Saddam ordered Iraqi officials to penetrate this "intelligence-gathering organization" and get a seat for Iraq on the board. He sacked the Iraqi embassy in Vienna and staffed it with people instructed to carry out that mission. Hisham Al-Shawi, minister of higher education, was elected to the IAEA board and had Abdul-Wahid al-Saji appointed IAEA inspector. An independent account suggests that "intimate access to inside knowledge of IAEA operations proved invaluable in circumventing

IAEA's detection of Iraqi cheating."[13] Suroor Mahmoud Mirza, a brother of Saddam's senior bodyguard, was appointed "scientific attaché" to Vienna and was endowed with a generous budget to lubricate connections with IAEA employees and other delegations. According to Hamza (1998), Mirza "alerted us to the success of satellite remote sensing in uncovering clandestine, and especially underground, activities. As a result, Iraq built no underground facilities." Mirza also provided detailed reports on the role of inspectors in uncovering clandestine programs, on how information given to inspectors was controlled, on how limited the latter's leverage was, and on the need to engage Iraqis in inspections to gain greater access.

The IAEA thus provided training opportunities for Iraqi scientists and reportedly helped place them in ancillary organizations. Hamza (1998) described how during the 1980s,

> IAEA inspectors were carefully escorted along pre-designated paths that did not expose the new buildings in Tuwaitha. Questions by inquisitive inspectors were answered carefully to avoid revealing new information. Iraqi authorities spent considerable time before each inspection rehearsing answers to possible questions and planning the routes of the inspections. . . . Some of the EMIS [electromagnetic isotope separation] developmental activities were housed inside the same buildings that were inspected by the IAEA. . . . To avoid risk of discovery, workers were told to stay out of the building or remain behind locked doors during an inspection.

Hamza wondered why the absence of scientific publications by Al-Tuwaitha scientists failed to raise suspicions by IAEA and foreign intelligence organizations, why the IAEA's safeguards division showed little willingness to pursue leads (for instance regarding German participation in the centrifuge program), and why the IAEA appeared to have little interest in approaching scientists involved in Iraq's nuclear program to clarify questions regarding compliance.

In 1979 Iraq also began seeking calutrons for enriching uranium. Between 1979 and 1982 it purchased large quantities of uranium in various forms from several countries, reporting some transactions but not others. After Osiraq's destruction and in the midst of war against Iran, Iraq turned more forcefully to uranium enrichment as its preferred path to nuclear weapons, and explored gas centrifuge, chemical enrichment, ion exchange, and laser isotopic separation. It acquired yellowcake from Niger in 1981 and uranium dioxide from Brazil in 1982 without declaring either transaction to the IAEA. By late 1987, the construction of a large EMIS plant began at Tarmiya, and the gas centrifuge program acquired design information and assistance from Germany's MAN Technologie AG and from German documents on enrichment based on technology developed by the European consortium EURENCO. Activities on gaseous diffusion ended in 1989, and Iraq contracted to build the al-Furat facility for mass production of centrifuges. Weaponization activities were conducted at al-Atheer, and a site in the southwest was chosen for underground nuclear testing. The IAEA was unaware of most of these facilities until inspectors discovered them after the 1991 war.[14] These efforts were deemed likely to produce nuclear weapons under the very nose of the IAEA (and the United States) were it not that Saddam decided to invade Kuwait in August 1990. The U.S. response to the invasion and the potential for an allied counterattack led Saddam to order a "crash program" (Project 601) designed to divert safeguarded highly enriched uranium for nuclear weapons. During the war, Saddam showered Scud missiles on Israel despite the latter's abstention from the war. Desert Storm ended the "crash program" and enabled the outside world to learn about the extensive nuclear activities that Iraq had successfully hidden, including the EMIS program.[15]

U.N. Resolution 687 created UNSCOM, designed to verify Iraq's compliance with dismantling its WMD. The IAEA, entrusted with verifying compliance in the nuclear arena, found traces of indigenously produced, highly enriched uranium in 1991, forcing Iraq to disclose information selectively on enrichment to the IAEA. UNSCOM also destroyed nuclear-related sites, including the al-Athir weaponization and testing site, as well as chemical and biological weapons production sites. Iraq, however continued to hide facilities, thwart and delay inspectors' access, destroy documentary evidence, prevent inspectors from removing pertinent information, fire shots in the air, and physically intimidate U.N. inspectors (Blix 2005). UNSCOM chairman Richard Butler reported to the UNSC that Iraq's pattern of concealment could be traced to direct governmental orders issued in 1991. Defectors Kamil and Hamza confirmed this pattern of deception, which triggered contentious UNSCOM inspections in 1996, including showdowns over access to sensitive facilities (Hamza 1998). Following Kamil's defection, Saddam ordered the destruction of important WMD-related documents but also acknowledged that Iraq had filled warheads with biological agents and had started the crash program to develop nuclear weapons (Richelson 2006:468). In his 1996 report, IAEA Secretary-General Hans Blix declared that "all quantities of special nuclear material [highly enriched uranium or plutonium] found in Iraq have been removed and the industrial infrastructure which Iraq had set up to produce and weaponize special nuclear material has been destroyed" (NTIW). Yet Blix (2005:43) also declined to recommend that the nuclear dossier be closed. Saddam continued to defy UNSC resolutions, declaring in 1997 that his various presidential "palaces" were outside inspectors' limits.

Iraq suspended cooperation with UNSCOM and the IAEA in August 1998, later rescinding it. Butler, however, informed the UNSC in 1998 that Iraq's confrontational position prevented UNSCOM from performing its mandate. UNSCOM withdrew from Iraq in December 1998, which was followed by U.S. and British bombings of selected missile and WMD targets. Saddam unilaterally abrogated Iraq's compliance with U.N. resolutions—including the 1991 ceasefire—through a secret Revolutionary Command Council resolution, according to testimony by Presidential Secretary 'Abd Hamid Mahmud and Diwan President Ahmad Husayn Khudayr (ISG 2004:57). In 1999, UNSC Resolution 1284 disbanded UNSCOM, replacing it with UNMOVIC. Several UNSC resolutions had been approved since 1991, demanding Iraq's dismantlement of WMD—687 (April 1991), 707 (August 1991), 715 (October 1991), 1051 (March 1996), 1060 (June 1996), 1154 (March 1998), 1194 (September 1998), 1205 (November 1998), and 1284 (December 1999)—all under Chapter VII of the U.N. Charter allowing the UNSC to authorize military force to enforce resolutions. Both UNMOVIC's Executive Chairman Blix and IAEA Director General El-Baradei maintained that it was impossible to verify Iraq's compliance in the absence of inspections. Only in 2002, under U.S. threat of military action, did Iraq allow UNMOVIC to resume inspections.

UNSC Resolution 1441 (November 2002) acknowledged that Iraq was in "material breach" of obligations under previous resolutions but offered Iraq yet another chance to comply and provide a full and accurate account of WMD programs. Iraq submitted a declaration in December, and UNMOVIC and the IAEA resumed inspections. A 2003 UNMOVIC report declared that, in the absence of inspections between 1998 and 2002, UNMOVIC faced the same situation that the IAEA had faced in 1991. UNMOVIC was entrusted with verifying the absence of new activities or proscribed items but "the onus is clearly on Iraq to provide the requisite information or devise other ways in which UNMOVIC can gain confidence that Iraq's declarations are correct and comprehensive."[16] The report also suggested that "Iraq potentially could have made considerable advancements in that time, particularly in the biological and chemical fields." On March 7, 2003, El-Baradei reported to the UNSC that "after three months of intrusive inspection, we have to date found no evidence or plausible indications of the revival of a nuclear weapon program in Iraq."[17] Heated debates in the UNSC over Iraqi noncompliance precluded consensus over using force. Yet the United States recommended that inspectors leave Iraq and invaded it on March 17, 2003.

In the war's aftermath, the CIA's ISG was entrusted with establishing the facts about Saddam's WMD programs. Former U.N. weapons inspector David Kay and his successor, Charles Duelfer, headed the ISG, which conducted site visits, interviewed scientists and officials, and examined thousands of documents. In 2004 the comprehensive Duelfer report concluded that there was no evidence of an Iraqi coordinated effort to restart its nuclear program (ISG 2004). Iraq was able to conceal only some nuclear activities from IAEA inspectors, such as hiding documents and plans, but had not reconstituted its indigenous yellowcake production, converted uranium ore into a form suitable for enrichment, developed gas centrifuges or other forms of uranium enrichment, or handled fissile material for weapons production. The report found only evidence that Saddam intended to resume WMD activities once international sanctions had been lifted and that he invested heavily in retaining scientists and technologists at the IAEC, the Military Industrialization Commission (MIC), and ancillary activities so as to preserve the nuclear program's human infrastructure. The ISG (2004) also found a research facility at Al Quds Company—a MIC establishment created in 2002—capable of conducting explosives research applicable to both conventional and nuclear weapons research.[18]

In sum, Iraq violated its NPT commitments soon after ratifying it and consistently over time, launching its search for materials and technology for nuclear weapons in the early 1970s, evading IAEA detection. Saddam reportedly asked his senior nuclear advisor Ja'afar Dhiya Ja'afar, "If we stay in the NPT, will it in any way hinder the clandestine nuclear program?" Ja'afar reported his own answer to have been an immediate and unequivocal "no" (Kay 1993:88). According to Blix (2005:19–20), the IAEA Secretariat could have performed more frequent inspections on Iraq's facilities (inspections had been reduced to save resources) and could have enhanced its information-gathering capabilities regarding Iraq's sensitive imports. Those efforts, however, would not have led to discoveries in his view. Iraq's nuclear activities amounted to a colossal and successful deception enterprise that was derailed only by the 1991 Gulf War and constrained by unprecedented UNSCOM inspections thereafter. Defectors provided information that helped the IAEA push Iraq toward further disclosures, although not all information proved accurate (Richelson 2006). By 2002, some U.S., British, and German intelligence services suggested that Iraq could assemble nuclear weapons within months of obtaining fissile material. The ISG, however, found no indications supporting allegations that Iraq had obtained such material after 1991. Since 1991, following UNSC resolutions and sanctions on Iraq, the IAEA was better positioned to implement its mandate. The new safeguards system ("93+2") set up in 1993 strengthened the IAEA's mandate; UNSCOM effectively dismantled much of Iraq's nuclear infrastructure; and UNMOVIC's 2003 assessment of Iraq's capabilities proved right. These were significant achievements for an institution with an intrusive mandate in the most sensitive security domain. In many ways, the Iraqi experience is both one of institutional failures but also of learning and accomplishments. This experience also points to the analytical limits of focusing only on the international institutional supply of monitoring mechanisms. As Blix argues, the sources of domestic demand for nuclear weapons remain the most fundamental problem (CEW).

DOMESTIC POLITICS: "PARAMOUNT SHEIKH" AND GODFATHER OF THE NUCLEAR PROGRAM

The overview of Iraq's nuclear behavior thus far makes it clear that the nature of Saddam's regime was a main driver of nuclearization. The domestic conditions that enabled and underpinned this drive began with the takeover of power by Iraq's Ba'th ("resurrection" or "renaissance") party after several coups that placed Saddam Hussein and his Tikriti allies at the center of political life from 1968 to 2003. Iraq's ruling coalition approximated the economic inward-looking, state-entrepreneurial, nationalizing, militarized ideal-type model of political survival depicted in chapter 2 exceedingly well. The model was anchored in the entrenched combined power of militarized state bureaucracies and enterprises, import-substituting interests, the military-industrial-complex, and their respective beneficiaries in state-controlled professional, construction, and labor organizations. Saddam became vice chairman of the Revolutionary Command Council (RCC) and deputy to the president in 1969. After assuming the presidency in 1979, he also became chairman of the RCC, general-secretary of the Regional Leadership of the Ba'th, and commander-in-chief of the armed forces, personally overseeing the Republican Guard forces, Fedayeen Saddam, the Military Industrialization Commission (MIC), the four intelligence agencies, and the Al Quds Army. As with North Korea and Libya, Iraq under Saddam could be well depicted as *"l'état c'est lui."* Yet even extremely autocratic leaders must build supportive coalitions that share the benefits of the favored model of political survival.

The model combined repressive controls and abominable human rights abuses with redistributive patronage. Upon becoming president, Saddam ordered the execution of about 500 Ba'th members, including one-third of the RCC, thirty generals, and seven scientists and engineers.[19] Throughout the years he not only relied on extensive political terror, torture, and mass executions to control Iraqi society but also indulged about 700,000 Ba'th members as beneficiaries of the model.[20] Saddam's relatives and Tikriti (Sunni) clan members came to dominate the system over and beyond (and sometimes at the expense of) the Ba'th. He coopted (mostly Sunni) tribal leaders with weapons, cash, land, and authority.

Land reform, nationalizations, and Ba'th-styled state socialism introduced much-needed land distribution but also increased bureaucratic reg-
ulation of agriculture, turning a self-supporting country into one importing 70 percent of its food (Kedourie 1992; Marr 1985; al-Khalil 1989).
By the late 1970s, the regime's emphasis was not on agriculture but on
heavy industry (iron and steel, in an effort to diversify away from oil) and
military expenditures. Yet the primacy of oil was never challenged; oil
revenues enabled a massive weapons buildup and rewards for military
and civilian clientelistic networks. The prominence assigned to oil and the
military-industrial-complex trumped manufacturing and industrial diversification. Saddam introduced incipient economic reforms (*infitah*) during
the 1980s in the context of a power struggle with Ba'th rivals. The intelligence services (*al-Mukhabarat*) opposed economic reform and demanded protection money from entrepreneurs. Reforms were thus very
limited, not backed with appropriate financing, accompanied by suspicion of private business, and always sacrificed to maintain more important priorities, particularly the military-industrial-complex (Richards and
Waterbury 1990). Subsequently Saddam introduced Islam as an ideological ornamentation compatible with the Ba'th's basic rejection of economic liberalism. Given these inward-looking foundations, the state came
to account for over 80 percent of GDP in infrastructure, manufacturing,
trade, and services and 62 percent of gross output in large manufacturing,
while employing nearly half of the workforce. Despite Iraq's rich oil endowments, Ba'th inward-looking policies brought about a decline in trade
openness (imports plus exports as percentage of GNP) from 64 percent in
the early 1960s to 55 percent on average by the early 1970s. With expanding oil revenues in the late 1970s, trade openness rose to 71 percent,
declining to 47 percent by the mid-1980s, as state enterprises and the
military-industrial-complex absorbed progressively more resources.[21]

The ISG report provides a window into the regime's approach to political economy. Saddam reportedly ignored economic advisors in the Ministries of Finance and Planning and attacked Iran despite warnings about
economic consequences. His war decisions involved no plans for war-
financing; he was less concerned with the inflationary potential of his
policies or their implications for social stability; and he displayed little interest in economic policy except for siphoning off enormous resources to
sustain his inner circle and wider circles of patronage. A senior Finance
Ministry official revealed that the ministry drafted budgets in the 1980s
as if foreign debt did not exist. Internal debt was dealt with by printing
dinars and establishing artificial exchange rates. Hikmat Mizban Ibrahim
Al 'Azzawi, finance minister and later deputy prime minister and head of
the Financial Committee in the 1990s, reported directly to Saddam, who
instructed him on allocations for salaries, bonuses, farm subsidies, and

ration prices.[22] According to 'Abd-al-Tawab 'Abdallah Al-Mullah Huwaysh, former minister of military industrialization, Saddam was not preoccupied with fiscal policy or macroeconomic management even when Iraq suffered under constraining conditions imposed by international sanctions. The military-industrial-complex was the most prominent beneficiary of Saddam's inward-looking model. Iraq led the way in the Middle East with military expenditures as high as 51 percent of GDP (1973–85), about ten times an already high global mean of about 5 percent. Between 1982 and 1986 alone, during the war with Iran, Iraq imported weapons for at least $85 billion (against a total GDP of 47 billion in 1985).[23]

The external expression of this model was—despite few and marginal exceptions—an assault on the international economic order, reliance on the Soviet Union for arms purchases, advocacy of nonalignment, hardline positions within the Organization of Petroleum Exporting Countries (OPEC), opposition to Egypt's Camp David peace agreements, and rabid critiques of most international regimes and institutions as "lackeys" of the West (Ahmad 1991). Saddam's determination to maintain heavy state expenditures and patronage resources that were able to keep his regime in place were a critical consideration in launching wars against neighbors, far more so than the purely geo-strategic reasons outlined previously.[24] Prospects of maximizing oil revenues by defeating Iran backfired, leaving Iraq ever more dependent on outside forces, and with an external debt of $50 billion. The war absorbed $150 billion and was subsidized by Saudi Arabia, Kuwait, and the UAE, which provided $30 to $40 billion. Arms purchases alone, primarily Soviet and French, represented an estimated $54.7 billion (ISG 2004, chapter 2, Annex D: 2–3). The United States provided Iraq with intelligence information since 1984 and later with loan guarantees. Iraq never paid its debt to Western creditors, estimated between $35 and $45 billion. Saddam's incentives to attack Kuwait, according to Niblock (1993:77), stemmed from an effort to resolve this domestic political and economic conundrum by appropriating Kuwaiti oil assets. This would both cancel the debt to Kuwait and boost Saddam's patronage resources, domestic political control, and Iraq's share of worldwide oil resources. Even Tariq Aziz acknowledged the impact of accumulated debt from the war with Iran and declining oil revenues on the decision to invade Kuwait, confessing that "we were near the point of economic collapse" (Viorst 1991:66). Ironically Saddam's wars—designed to enhance his coffers—had the unintended effect of further sapping Iraq's economy from assets absorbed by the regime to preserve its constituencies.

Iraq's nuclear program both reflected and symbolized Saddam's inward-looking model, one extolling the virtues of state entrepreneurship and self-reliance. Saddam personally launched the secret nuclear weapons program in 1971 and prided himself of Iraq's nuclear accomplishments.

"I . . . am the Godfather of the IAEC and I love the IAEC," he boasted (ISG 2004:24–26, TM:3). In the mid-1970s Saddam transferred the IAEC to the RCC and appointed himself its chair, never disclosing it to the IAEA. The nuclear program was a tool for enhancing power and leverage *primarily at home* (ISG 2004:24), enabling Saddam to portray himself as a modernizing leader to relevant domestic constituencies while boosting his personal prestige and influence throughout the Arab world. Saddam regarded nuclear weapons as the most important ticket to the pantheon of venerated Mesopotamia rulers—from Hammurabi to Nebuchadnezzar—and of the Arab and Muslim world, evoking Tikriti-born anti-Crusader warrior Salah-al-Din (Baram 2001). Nuclear weapons would be the crowning achievement of "Paramount Sheikh," Saddam's self-appointed title, and the ultimate expression of a patronage system that coopted hundreds of thousands of Iraqis.

Former nuclear weapons scientist Hamza traced the program's beginnings to Saddam's direct orders in 1971, when he offered incentives to attract Iraqi scientists and engineers under intrusive security.[25] Saddam applied extensive coercion to discipline the nuclear workforce. At a 1974 meeting with IAEC staff he laid down the rules: all foreigners, including those representing international organizations, were to be considered spies; contact with them was to be very limited and reported in detail; unauthorized contacts with foreigners would be the equivalent of treason; an Office of Policy and International Relations within the IAEC was responsible for approving any contact with foreigners; non-Iraqi Arabs were considered foreigners; IAEC staff with foreign wives were ordered to divorce them. In April 1975, nuclear physicist Ja'afar returned to Baghdad to assume a leading role in the nuclear weapons program. In 1979 Hussein called a surprise meeting with Ja'afar and al-Shahristani, who headed the program at the time, asking them to begin extracting plutonium for a nuclear weapon. Al-Shahristani, who was accused of ties to Shi'a political movements, refused and was arrested by the feared *Mukhabarat* (Hamza and Stein 2000; Salama and Hunter 2005). When Ja'afar intervened on his behalf, he was arrested too, and both were tortured. Al-Shahristani spent eleven years imprisoned until he escaped during the 1991 Gulf War. Ja'afar allegedly gave in and returned to the IAEC to work on the clandestine nuclear program.[26] Saddam reportedly imprisoned and brutalized two-thirds of the nuclear program's senior leadership. After 1981, employees could not travel abroad with their families. Muayad Naji, a centrifuge program worker who left Iraq without authorization in 1992 to teach in Libya, was killed by Iraqi intelligence in Jordan.

These harsh conditions were offset by lucrative economic incentives and perks. The program grew from about 200 to 500 engineers and technicians in the early years to about 7,000 by 1982. By the early 1990s, it was estimated to have employed as many as 20,000 people. During the 1970s, the weapons program at al-Tuwaitha alone reportedly had spent about $750 million, including $300 million for Osiraq and $200 million for the fuel plant and plutonium separation facility. There were other nuclear weapons research facilities, however, some under complete isolation and secrecy from IAEC, as was the laser enrichment program launched in the late 1970s at the Al-Hazen Ibn Al-Haytham Center for Research, headed by Serwan al-Satidah (Hamza and Stein 2000:95–98). This program was sponsored within the Ba'th by Humam al-Ghafour, who had replaced Saddam as IAEC Chairman. By the early 1990s, the program reportedly had attracted $10 billion (Sayigh 1992; Kay 1993). The 1991 Gulf War and international sanctions brought about a drastic deterioration in nuclear employees' living conditions. Many professionals able to leave Iraq did so, and others already overseas did not return, including former IAEC chairman Al-Shawi, who had also been Iraq's ambassador to Britain and Canada.

Saddam appointed Husayn Kamil (married to his eldest daughter Raghad) as Overseer of Military Industrialization in 1987 and Minister of Industry and Military Industrialization (MIMI) in 1988, after acquiring the Ministries of Heavy Industry and Light Industry and supervising the Ministry of Petroleum, the IAEC, and "Petrochemical Complex 3" (Iraq's clandestine nuclear program). The military-industrial-complex (Military Industrialization Commission or MIC) under Kamil had oversight over all industries and most activities supporting research, development, production, and weaponization of WMD and missile systems. Saddam gave Kamil broad administrative and financial authority. The nuclear program, which had been separate from the MIC through much of its history, came under Kamil's control toward the end of the Iran-Iraq war in 1988. In the aftermath of the 1991 Gulf War, Kamil relied on the MIC to conceal banned weapons and deceive UNSCOM inspectors. In July 1991, he masterminded the undeclared destruction of large stocks of WMD and allegedly persuaded Saddam to hide and deny the nuclear program's existence, conceal the biological weapons program, and reject early U.N. offers to allow monitored oil sales to provide relief from sanctions. In 1995, reportedly due to a rift with Saddam's son Uday, Kamil fled Iraq and sought political asylum in Jordan with his brother Saddam Kamil, their wives and children (Saddam's grandchildren). Kamil disclosed hidden aspects of the nuclear and other WMD programs to U.N. officials. Under a promised pardon by Saddam, the Kamil families returned to Iraq, where the Kamil brothers, sister, father, and other family members were assassinated (Saddam's daughters and grandchildren were spared). The MIC was already on the verge of collapse as sanctions depleted its resources.

Tensions between maintaining WMD programs and eliminating international sanctions forced internal strain on Iraq. As WMD and MIC czar, Kamil opposed these programs' elimination in 1991 (ISG 2004, TM:9). Saddam regarded these programs as the centerpiece of his survival strategy, as he acknowledged in the ISG report, but he ordered the elimination of WMD stocks in 1991 to remove sanctions. He continued, however, to repudiate complete transparency over Iraq's WMD programs, retained some dual-use production facilities, and refused to admit that biological weapons had been produced. Kamil's defection and disclosures forced the destruction of some WMD documents initially, but subsequently Iraq transferred selected documents to UNSCOM in an effort to discredit Kamil. Sanctions had reached a critical point for Saddam's regime survival, with a decimated middle class, a collapsed dinar, and uncontrollable inflation (ISG 2004: 9–10). Until 1996 he had refused proposals to export oil in exchange for accepting constraints on revenues, fearing that such an arrangement would defuse international pressure on the UNSC to remove sanctions altogether. However, the economic crisis had weakened his power base—the army, the Sunni, his own family and tribe, and some Ba'th leaders—and had the potential for triggering coups (Baram 1998). These conditions led Saddam to accept UNSC Resolution 986 creating an Oil-for-Food program.

By January 1997 oil revenues began flowing in, increasing from $4.2 billion in 1997 to $5.11 billion in 1998 and $17.87 billion in 2000 (ISG 2004:60). The regime appropriated about $2.76 billion in 2001. The program's design enabled large-scale corruption involving U.N. officials and private firms from various countries, even though all UNSC members were responsible for approving transactions.[27] The Oil-for-Food program enabled Saddam to bolster his domestic and international influence by controlling contract allocations and revenue distribution. Iraqi oil was priced lower than market levels and attracted much interest, particularly from Russian and French firms. Buyers enjoyed wide margins of profit, and Saddam could select external beneficiaries that would help him undermine continued sanctions, particularly within the UNSC. Iraq played UNSC cleavages very effectively, prodding France, Russia, and U.N. Secretary-General Kofi Annan to dismantle sanctions. As sanctions eroded, the Bush administration proposed "Smart Sanctions" in early 2001, narrowing the targets but retaining overall support for sanctions. Iraq was able to circumvent Oil-for-Food regulations precluding its access to foreign exchange. Huwaysh, Kamil's successor as minister of Military Industrialization until 2003, presided over MIC budgets privileged by revenues from Oil-for-Food. These grew over forty-fold between 1996 and 2002, from 15.5 billion dinar to 1 trillion in 2003 (about $364 million in 2002), while Iraq's vulnerable population absorbed the brunt of the sanctions. MIC support for university projects rose from about forty projects in 1997 to 3,200 in 2002. Employees in MIC-related activities grew from 42,000 in 1999 to 63,000 in 2002. Saddam continued to offer senior nuclear scientists ample resources and privileges, improving IAEC funding and increasing its salaries tenfold between 2001 and 2003 (ISG 2004:59).

Oil-for-Food funds enabled sustained acquisition of dual-use research and development capabilities. U.S. and other Western intelligence agencies suspected that Saddam continued investments in WMD programs, but they had no concrete evidence that the nuclear program had been reconstituted, despite the Bush administration's efforts to emphasize such potential.[28] The war's aftermath confirmed that they had not been reconstituted. ISG's interviews with Saddam Hussein and his closest advisors corroborated that Saddam intended to resume a nuclear weapons program once sanctions were removed, just as Kamil had predicted.[29] While continuing to hinder UNSCOM inspections in 1997 and 1998, Saddam's strategy was to retain the human capacity to reconstruct programs after sanctions were lifted. Proscribed activities in long-range ballistic missiles continued even under the Oil-for-Food program. According to the ISG report, not a single senior official believed that Saddam had forsaken WMDs forever and most were certain he would have restarted WMD programs, beginning with the nuclear one, once resources became available. As for Saddam himself, "during a custodial interview, Saddam, when asked whether he would reconstitute WMD programs after sanctions were lifted, implied that Iraq would have done what was necessary" (ISG 2004, TM:9; Regime Strategic Intent:24, 49–51, 60). Tariq 'Aziz acknowledged that Saddam was fully committed to acquiring nuclear weapons even in the absence of an effective program after 1991. Huwaysh suspected—but provided no concrete evidence—that Saddam's increased interest in the IAEC after 1999 and the procurement of precise machine tools was part of an effort to restart the program with Fadil al-Janabi and Khalid Ibrahim Sa'id, who had participated in the pre-1991 endeavor (ISG 2004, vol. 2). Aziz suggested that Iraq could have acquired WMD within two years of the removal of sanctions, and, according to Saddam's science advisor 'Amir Hamudi Hasan Al-Sa'adi, Saddam had concluded by mid-to-late 2002 that sanctions had eroded and would inevitably be abandoned.

The Committee of Four, or Quartet, advising Saddam on foreign policy and other issues provides yet another window into the ruling coalition's inherently inward-looking makeup. Formed in 1996, the committee included Vice President Ramadan, RCC Vice Chairman 'Izzat Ibrahim Al-Duri, Deputy Prime Minister 'Aziz and Al-Majid (Chemical 'Ali). Ramadan and 'Aziz represented old-style Ba'thism in an organizational and philosophical sense, Ibrahim represented tribal and religious elements, and Al-Majid was Saddam's closest relative in government. The ISG report notes that

> the striking feature of the Quartet's members was their inward focus. They were certainly not cosmopolitan and their insularity hurt their ability to appreciate or assess what other countries saw as their interests and how Iraq's behaviour might create conflict. The Quartet, including 'Aziz, had a mindset of Iraq versus the world, rather than Iraq as part of the world. Even the globetrotting 'Aziz remained focused on Saddam's will and his exclusive power to determine Iraq's course. . . . The Quartet had little appreciation of global change since the end of the Cold War or how it affected Iraq's interests and options . . . They did not seek to capitalize on Iraq's potential significance in global trade through its place in the oil market. The Quartet never deliberated over globalization as a concept and how to position Iraq within it. (ISG 2004, Regime Strategic Intent Annex A: 71)

According to MIC Minister Huwaysh, Saddam's economic vision for Iraq's future (after the sanctions) was to re-create Iraq's industrial strength and a planned economy that would depend on neither oil exports nor an information-based or service sector nor tourism (Duelfer 2004, Regime Strategic Intent: 23).

Conclusion

As the chief of Iraq's centrifuge program Obeidi noted, "Sadam had always hungered for a nuclear weapon" yet his behavior did not match "basic scientific reasoning" and showed that "Iraq was in the grip of a delusional leader who lacked any long-term strategic thinking" (Obeidi and Pitzer 2004:xi, 135). The structure, function, budgets, and staffing of Iraq's nuclear program point to its central role in Saddam's model of regime survival against both domestic and foreign threats. As the ISG report suggests, Saddam's overriding objective was "the survival of himself, his regime, and his legacy. . . . Survival came first. This produced the multiple security organs, and their prime objective was protection of the leadership. It was natural that the objectives of United Nations inspectors collided with the security apparatus. Inspections aimed at deciphering the most sensitive weapons programs would transgress the security apparatus protecting the president. This was obvious and unavoidable if both objectives were pursued to the maximum" (ISG 2004, Regime Finance and Procurement: 5 and TM:6). WMD played a distinctive role in creating an aura of invincibility for Saddam, who feared internal coups more than external attacks.[30] When asked the question that was in so many minds—why was Saddam so concerned with inspections if there was nothing to hide?—a former official of Iraq's National Monitoring Directory replied that "any such meeting with foreigners was seen as a threat to the security of the Regime."[31] That WMD were principally designed to preserve Saddam and his regime rather than Iraq itself is also clear from Saddam's pre-delegation of authority to the Iraqi Special Security Organization, responsible for protecting Saddam himself. In 1991 these special units were ordered to launch chemical and bacteriological attacks on Saudi Arabia, Israel, and allied forces if communications with Saddam were broken and/or allied forces were close to occupying Baghdad (Ritter 1999; Baram 2001). This meant that, in the event that something happened to Saddam himself or that Baghdad fell, Iraq's WMD were to be launched, inviting potential nuclear retaliation and Baghdad's destruction. In other words, Saddam regarded the potential passing of his regime as coterminal with Iraq's integrity.

A second important function assigned to the nuclear program was arguably to deter Iran, whether or not nuclear weapons were the most effective means for that purpose. Iraqi officials confirmed that Iran was considered Iraq's principal enemy but differed on whether nuclear weapons were either necessary or sufficient to deter or contain Iran. For one, Iraq's nuclear endeavors accelerated Iran's own search for nuclear weapons (see chapter 8), increasing Iraq's insecurity. A desire to balance Israel and enhance Saddam's status in the Arab world provided a third layer of incentives. Nuclear weapons would enable Saddam, reportedly in his own words, to "protect the dignity of Iraq and Iraqis and the Arab nations."[32] Thus, to the extent that Saddam appealed to identity themes in support of nuclear weapons, these stood in sharp contrast to norms against nuclear acquisition. Rather, nuclear weapons were a means to endow his regime first, Iraq second, and the Arab world third, with prestige. The regime skillfully manipulated Arab identity against non-Arabs (Iranian, Israeli, Turkish), yet most regime leaders were not known for pan-Arab commitments such as Nasser's or Qadhafi's. Indeed, most other Arab regimes, fearful of Saddam's appeal to their own domestic base, responded with lukewarm support or outright opposition to Iraq's military and WMD adventures. In turn, Iraq's regime, especially the Quartet, did not consider the Arab world a "resource for Iraq, either to bolster efforts against Iran or to act as intermediaries with the West" (ISG 2004, Regime Strategic Intent, Annex A: 71). The Quartet is revealed to have shared Saddam's aversion to some Arab states, primarily Saudi Arabia but also Egypt. Even so, Al-Majid was surprised by what he regarded as Arab inaction against the 2003 attack on Iraq.

This ranking of nuclear weapons' instrumentalities for Saddam's regime raises an important quandary. The ISG reported that Saddam's only incentive to cooperate with ISG interviews was the possibility of shaping his legacy. The questioning indeed provided Saddam with an exceptional opportunity to explain his behavior *uniquely* in "national security" terms that might have (1) emphasized *only* selfless concern with Iraq's vulnerability and (2) helped Saddam wrap (spin) his designs as the product of external constraints. Yet Saddam's own account left little doubt regarding the centrality of his own survival and that of his regime as major drivers in his quest for WMD. While asserting that WMD helped him reverse the fate of wars (he had initiated), halt Iranian ground troops, and deter allied troops from entering Baghdad in 1991, he also acknowledged that the mere threat of chemical weapons helped him crush Shi'a revolts in Southern Iraq (ISG 2004, Regime Strategic Intent: 24–26). As Woods et al. (2006) argue, "Even with U.S. tanks crossing the Iraqi border, an internal revolt remained Saddam's biggest fear." Iraqi officials confirmed that Saddam wielded nuclear weapons as symbols of power designed to intimidate domestic rivals no less than foreign ones. Ironically, along the way, Saddam's fiercest adversaries in the Islamic Republic of Iran emulated his search for nuclear weapons as ultimate guarantees of regime survival.

CHAPTER EIGHT

Iran

IRAN'S SHAH purchased a 5 MW research reactor from the United States in the 1960s, signed the NPT in 1968, and ratified it in 1970. In 1972 he announced Iran's intention to build a large-scale nuclear energy program, and in 1974 he established the Atomic Energy Organization of Iran (AEOI) under his direct supervision. Several agreements with companies in France, the United States, and Germany arranged for the supply of power reactors. In 1975, the Shah stated that if other countries in the region were to acquire nuclear weapons, Iran would have to do likewise. Yet Iran's delegate to the Geneva Disarmament Conference reaffirmed his country's opposition to nuclear weapons, and the Shah himself declared the prospect of Iranian nuclear weapons "ridiculous" given the size of the superpowers' arsenals. In 1975 a U.S. NIE ranked the likelihood of Iran acquiring nuclear weapons lower than that of India, Taiwan, South Korea, Pakistan, or Indonesia.[1] Iran's efforts to purchase yellowcake from South Africa and other fuel cycle technology reportedly continued, and by the late 1970s U.S. intelligence services detected a potential clandestine program (Spector 1987:50–51). President Carter, heading an administration highly concerned with nonproliferation, granted Iran "most favored nation" status for spent fuel reprocessing in 1977 (Kibaroglu 2006). In 1978 the United States signed an agreement for the supply of several light-water nuclear reactors, but Iran's unstable domestic situation and accusations of mismanagement at the AEOI halted all proceedings.

In 1979 Ayatollah Khomeini deposed the Shah, and the Islamic Republic inherited two nuclear power reactors under German construction at Bushehr. The new regime discontinued many nuclear activities but retained Bushehr, which Iraq damaged heavily during the Iran-Iraq war in the 1980s. Most sources place the origins of Iran's Islamic Republic clandestine weapons program around 1984–1985.[2] In 1984, Khomeini ordered the construction of a new nuclear research center in Esfahan. The Soviet Union, China, Pakistan, West Germany, North Korea, Argentina, and Spain among others negotiated supplies of nuclear fuel cycle facilities and training. Between 15,000 and 17,000 students were sent abroad for related training. In 1987 President Ali Akbar Hashemi Rafsanjani allegedly ordered a nuclear weapons and delivery systems feasibility study.[3] A. Q. Khan reportedly visited Bushehr in 1986 and 1987. By 1992 the

CIA estimated that Iran was seeking nuclear weapons, and in 1996 Director John M. Deutsch confirmed it in congressional testimony.[4] Concerned with Iran's nuclear capabilities, President Bush included Iran among the "axis of evil" in his 2002 State of the Union address. Iran's infringements on its NPT commitments, reportedly since the 1980s, were validated by the IAEA only in 2003. In 2004, Blix argued that "the world is rightly concerned today that Iran might intend to make use of a capability to enrich uranium to make nuclear weapons."[5] In May 2005, he declared that Iran had acted in disregard of its safeguards obligations. It was not surprising, he added, that many countries suspected Iran of moving toward nuclear weapons, given that it had built an infrastructure in uranium enrichment while disregarding its IAEA obligations.[6] There is no direct positive evidence of Iran's development of nuclear weapons—a smoking gun—but there is reasonable evidence of a clandestine program. Why might have Iranian leaders advanced such a program?

Shifting Logics of Relative Power?

Neorealist perspectives trace Iran's nuclear ambitions mostly to rivalry with Iraq, competition for supremacy in the Persian Gulf, nuclear capabilities of Israel and Pakistan, and, particularly after the 2003 Iraq war, a perceived menace from the United States. These presumed threats developed sequentially, some of them dissipating over time to be replaced by others. The Shah had hegemonic ambitions and was clearly concerned with other regional nuclear aspirants. In 1974 he reportedly said that Iran would have nuclear weapons, "without a doubt and sooner than one would think," although Iran's embassy in France denied it (NTIW). The Shah cautioned that "not only Iran, but also other nations in the region should refrain from planning to gain atomic arsenals." In 1976 he became highly concerned with Pakistan's nuclear weapons efforts and offered to collaborate with the United States—Iran's closest ally at this time—to prevent such development.[7] The most defining threat from Iran's standpoint was Iraq's attack in 1980 and the prolonged war that ensued. Iraq's bombing of Tehran with Scud missiles and its use of chemical weapons against ever-younger Iranian soldiers—inflicting 50,000 casualties—compelled Iran to accept a cease fire, begrudgingly, in 1988. Iraq also bombarded the Bushehr site repeatedly. The speaker of Iran's parliament (*Majlis*) and commander-in-chief of the armed forces, Hashemi Rafsanjani, stated very explicitly that "with regard to chemical, bacteriological, and radiological weapons training, it was made very clear during the war that these weapons are very decisive. It was also made clear that the moral teachings of the world are not very effective when war reaches a serious stage and the world does not respect its own resolutions and closes its eyes to the violations and all the aggressions which are committed in the battle field. We should fully equip ourselves both in the offensive and defensive use of chemical, bacteriological, and radiological weapons. From now on you should make use of the opportunity and perform this task."[8] While deeply adversarial relations and a brutal war with Iraq played an important function in Iran's initial nuclear decisions, other considerations must be examined to establish the proper weight of structural power considerations on Iran's search for nuclear weapons.

First, the U.S. factor was clearly irrelevant for explaining the *origins* of Iran's program. The mutual hostility between the revolutionary regime and the United States following Iran's 1979 hostage-taking at the U.S. embassy was indeed a source of concern for Iran, but Khomeini discontinued nuclear activities at the time. The war with Iraq reactivated them since the mid-1980s and Iraq remained the target of Iran's deterrence until 2003. When asked in 1995 about the prospects for war between Iran and the United States, Foreign Minister 'Ali Akbar Velayati responded that "there is absolutely no reason for concern," contradicting Revolutionary Guards Chief Mohsen Rezai (DeSutter 1997:22). Inclusion of Iran in the "axis of evil" might have certainly exacerbated fears of U.S. activities geared to regime change. Iran's proscribed nuclear activities, however, reportedly preceded that speech by eighteen years (Normark et al. 2005). The intervention in Afghanistan brought the United States closer to Iran's border but also eliminated the Taliban, which had killed ten Iranian diplomats in 1998. Since the 1990s, the connections between Pakistan and (Sunni) Taliban and Pashtun in Afghanistan had enhanced Iran's competition with Pakistan, with Iran backing Afghanistan's Tajiks and Hazaras (Abedin 2006). Only after Saddam's removal from power in 2003 did the U.S. presence next-door emerge as a genuine concern for Iran, and only before U.S. forces found themselves challenged in Iraq's quagmire. In early 2005, after unconfirmed reports that U.S. commandos were selecting targets for air attacks on Iran, President Mohammed Khatami still considered the likelihood of a U.S. attack to be "very negligible."[9] Above all, in evaluating neorealist claims—which often ignore the internal nature of states—one must consider whether U.S.-Iranian relative power was different when the two were close allies prior to 1979 than subsequently. In 1959 Iran and the United States signed a defense pact committing the United States to help Iran resist foreign aggression and providing it with military and economic assistance under mutually agreed upon conditions. The pact was cancelled with the Islamic Revolution, which regarded the United States as an enemy because of its support for Muhammad Mossadegh's suppression in 1953, and for the Shah's despotic regime. Domestic considerations—the 1979 revolution—rather than changes in relative power global or regional transformed U.S.-Iranian relations into an adversarial one.[10]

Second, the same domestic considerations explain the transformation of Iranian-Israeli relations. The Shah's secular regime maintained extensive security cooperation with Israel. In the 1970s, Iran's Vice Minister of War Hasan Toufanian visited Israel's Foreign Minister Moshe Dayan, expressing keen interest in mutual reliance, including possible joint development of (nuclear-capable) Jericho II missiles.[11] The Islamic revolution severed relations with Israel and transformed it into a main target of vilification. Yet until the late 1980s, as the war with Iraq raged, Iran's nuclear concerns related largely to Iraqi NPT violations and only subsequently to Israel's non-NPT membership. In 1991, Deputy-President Ayatollah Mohajerani asserted that because Israel "has nuclear facilities, the Muslim states, too, should be equipped with the same capacity."[12] As Takeyh (2006b:141) argues, "For the Islamic Republic, Israel may be an ideological affront and a civilisational challenge, but it is not an existential threat mandating provision of nuclear weapons. . . . Terrorism and reliance on militant Islamic forces have always been Iran's preferred method of conducting its conflict with Israel." Israel featured in Iranian nuclear diplomacy, he contended, only in connection with the presumed "double standards" that allow Israel and India to be nuclear powers. That theme has proven very useful for mobilizing support among Muslim and non-aligned countries and softening criticism of Iran's program despite the fact that India and Israel, unlike Iran, never signed and hence never violated NPT commitments. Takeyh (2005) surveyed Iranian official speeches and commentaries on nuclear weapons and was surprised "by how seldom Israel actually features into these deliberations," and by how the clerics do not seem "inordinately concerned about Israel's nuclear monopoly." Rather, in his view, Iran's alarmist rhetoric about an "Israeli threat" was designed to satisfy extremist nationalist and anti-Israel domestic and regional constituencies, including Hezbollah. Jones (1998, 42) considers the Israeli argument to have "propagandistic elements and may not fully accord with Tehran's deepest threat perceptions." As Egypt's Ambassador Nabil Fahmy declared, "Iranian nuclear programs and the debate around them do not actually relate to the Middle East peace process and may be fueled by completely different anxieties or opportunities."[13]

Third, few dispute that if there ever was a guiding balancing logic to Iran's nuclear program, deterring Iraq was it (Jones 1998). The inadequacy of Iran's conventional forces presumably led to its inability to face up to the Iraqi onslaught in the 1980s. Iraq's use of WMD undoubtedly exacerbated Iran's incentives to respond in kind. Yet by 1991, Saddam was under U.N. containment, while Iran's nuclear efforts intensified in tandem with—rather than replacing—heavy conventional capabilities.

According to Chubin (2006), Iran's nuclear program in the 1990s was "in search for a rationale" not rooted in security imperatives but nationalism, prestige, and domestic drivers. The ousting of Saddam and Iraq's near-disintegration eradicated Iran's most prominent regional threat, in that these events led to a Shi'a dominated Iraqi neighbor. Meanwhile, Iran's massive conventional military machine became a significant force capable of addressing other potential threats. Whether or not deterring the United States—bogged down in Iraq—required a nuclear deterrent remains a matter of contention. Even Iranian leaders acknowledged that U.S. overextension (Afghanistan, Iraq, North Korea, and other challenges), the dispersal and secrecy of Iranian facilities, and concern with Iran's terrorist networks may be more powerful deterrents against U.S. attack than any emerging Iranian nuclear capabilities.

Fourth, the logic of deterrence against Iraq exacerbated the one-upmanship between Saddam's regime and that of the *mullhas*, leading to WMD races that ended only with Saddam's ousting. An important side effect of Iran's nuclear activities in response to Iraq was to heighten Israel's concerns with Iran's designs, particularly given the latter's support for radical terrorism and its rhetoric of eliminating Israel. By 2003, some Iranian and Israeli officials were exchanging threats regarding each other's nuclear facilities. Furthermore the potential for a nuclear-armed Iran began raising concerns that Egypt, Saudi Arabia, or Turkey might respond in kind.[14] Saudi Arabia, some argued, "could not tolerate the political, military, and diplomatic power that a nuclear weapon would give Iran."[15] Khalaf (2004) suggested that behind public silence from Sunni Arab officials lurked anxiety over Shi'ism's widening regional power from Southern Lebanon through Iraq to Iran and the Gulf, where Shi'a constitute a majority in Bahrain and minorities in Kuwait, the UAE, and Saudi Arabia. Furthermore, Iran and the UAE have long-standing territorial disputes over Persian Gulf islands. Abdul-Rahman bin Hamad al-Attiyah, secretary-general of the Gulf Cooperation Council (GCC), declared that Iran's nuclear armament is "unjustifiable."[16] Abd Al-Rahman Al-Rashed, director of Al-Arabiyya TV, was more forceful: "If you want to be foolish, you have to believe that Iran is producing its nuclear bomb in order to attack Israel; you'll turn into a complete idiot if you believe it's producing it in order to confront the United States. The Iranians are enriching uranium to produce nuclear weapons aimed, essentially, at its neighbors, mainly Pakistan. However, the danger encompasses the other neighboring countries as well, such as Saudi Arabia, Oman, Iraq, Afghanistan, Turkmenistan, and Azerbaijan."[17] Beyond Egypt, GCC countries, and Israel, Turkey too perceived Iran's Shahab-3 missiles and nuclear program as threats.[18] These mixed benefits of an Iranian nuclear deterrent were not lost on some Iranian decision-makers. Contradicting his earlier statements,

Rafsanjani declared in 1993 that nuclear weapons were not in anyone's interest, it would be irrational to use limited resources for nuclear weapons, which can never be used in the region, and Third World countries could never compete with the major nuclear powers.[19] Furthermore, Iran's nuclearization could lead to tighter cooperation between the United States and Iran's neighbors, leaving Iran more isolated. As Defense Minister Ali Shamkhani acknowledged, "Nuclear weapons will turn us into a threat that could be exploited in dangerous ways to harm our relations with the countries of the region."[20] Former IAEA delegate Ali Akbar Salehi warned that "[Iran] cannot buy security by having nuclear weapons which only invites more threats against [us]."[21] Other statements by Iranian officials suggested that nuclear weapons could increase Iran's vulnerability and provide pretexts for hostile powers, including that of a senior Iranian diplomat who noted the irony that Iran's nuclear program was precisely what might trigger an Israeli attack (ICG 2003:18). Despite tight control over public discourse in Iran, such views suggest that, from the standpoint of structural power, Iran's nuclearization was not an undiluted panacea. Indeed, structural conditions carried no unique prescriptions and were indeterminate as with other cases in this book.

Fifth, many believe that national pride, prestige, nationalism, cultural factors, and a desire to be seen as a dominant regional power drive Iran's nuclear program in its current phase (Takeyh 2006b; Perkovich 2005b; Chubin 2006). There is certainly much evidence to that effect from frequent statements by Iranian leaders. Supreme Religious leader Ayatollah Ali Khamene'i, for instance, suggested that Iran has the potential to become *the world leader in science* in fifty years and held the nuclear program as a symbol of scientific and technological prowess.[22] President Mahmoud Ahmadinejad argued that "the Iranian people—because of its past culture, its past civilization, its intelligent youth, its human and material potential—has the capacity to quickly become an invincible global power. This will happen as soon as it achieves advanced technologies."[23] Pride, nationalism, and *grandeur* are not strictly logics emanating from structural power and indeed can be tangential to military deterrence. They evoke either constructivist frameworks dealing with identity and normative receptivity to nuclearization or instrumental uses of identity and nationalism by particular ruling coalitions, or both. In this symbolic usage, nuclearization can be directed at domestic audiences but can also enhance leaders' appeal in the eyes of external ones. Ahmadinejad has skillfully broadened his allure among some Arab populations (but not their leaders) despite Iran's repression of its Arab minorities. The degree of domestic support for nuclear weapons based on prestige considerations within Iran itself is yet unclear, since limited freedom of expression compounds the difficulties in gauging public views on many topics.

Nuclear weapons on nationalist grounds may attract anti-U.S. and anti-Israeli audiences but also undermine relations with other states that accommodated Iranian policies in exchange for oil. Selective and opportunistic use of nationalism, Shi'ism, Islam, and other identity themes compels a theory of domestic politics able to explain why Iranian leaders may vary in their reliance on nuclear technology as a tool of political control.

In sum, whereas the war with Iraq may have sparked initial decisions to develop nuclear weapons in the mid-1980s, events since 1991 have arguably reduced such incentives. Iran's arch-enemy, Saddam, was first contained and later deposed, enabling unprecedented Iranian influence in Iraq and beyond. Pakistan and Israel are more removed from Iran's immediate environment and can hardly pose threats of Saddam's magnitude. As Chubin and Litwak (2003:105) argue, "Iran has no historic enemies; existential threats; or giant, hostile neighbors requiring it to compensate for a military imbalance with a nuclear program." Iran's progressive nuclearization has had stable political rather than security imperatives (Chubin 2006). Even if structural imperatives existed, various nuclear and non-nuclear means consistent with neorealism might have been adopted. In the end, the internal nature of Iran's regime is the critical consideration for how it has defined internal and external threats and crafted responses to them. Despite contested understandings of the internal workings of this regime, few doubt that they provide the main logic driving Iran's nuclear behavior. As one expert (Sick 1995) put it, "The regime in Tehran is its own worst enemy. There's nothing from the outside that's nearly as threatening to it as its own behavior at various times."

INTERNATIONAL INSTITUTIONS: THE ROAD TO DEFECTION

The Shah signed the NPT the day it opened for signature in 1968 and ratified it in 1970. The safeguards agreement with the IAEA entered into force in 1974 when the Shah also proposed a Middle East NWFZ at the UNGA. In 1978, the Shah accepted safeguards beyond IAEA requirements, demanded by President Carter in return for "most favored nation" status to obtain reprocessed fuel. Following the Islamic revolution, Iran discontinued its promotion of a NWFZ and, after a brief hiatus, some leaders began advocating nuclear weapons. In the statement cited earlier, Rafsanjani's reading of the global normative environment was quite removed from taboo notions of WMD. He pointed to Iraq's use of chemical weapons during the war as proof that the world did not abide by norms prohibiting their use, calling upon Iranians to seek WMD. Iran reportedly responded with chemical attacks that violated the 1925 Geneva Protocol (Spector 1990:209). Although Iran ratified the BTWC in 1973, it is suspected of developing dual-purpose biological weapon programs and maintaining significant stocks of chemical weapons despite strongly denying it and ratifying the CWC in 1997 (Cirincione, Wolfsthal, and Rajkumar 2005).

In 1987, the IAEA was unable to account for fissile material that Iran had moved to Bushehr from other facilities and had failed to declare to the IAEA (NTIW). In 1991, Blix expressed that he had "no cause for concern" regarding Iran, but that the IAEA would launch special inspections in "problem states" and Iran could become a possible test case.[24] In 1992, Iran declared to the IAEA for the first time the existence of its Isfahan facility, and AEOI Chief Reza Amrollahi invited the IAEA to visit six locations, three of which had never been inspected before. In 1992–93, IAEA inspectors found no evident violations at visited sites (Bushehr, Isfahan, Amirabad, Karaj, Saghand, and Moallem Kalayeh) but pronounced the visits inconclusive because of the facilities' large size and Iran's refusal to allow full access, including environmental probes (Albright 1995). IAEA Deputy Director Jon Jennekens declared that "we visited without any restriction everything we had asked to see. All nuclear activities in Iran are solely for peaceful purposes"(NTIW). Another IAEA inspector, however, called this report an "impudent and unfounded whitewash," arguing that inspectors had been led to decoy sites, a vacation resort named Moallem Kalayeh rather than a similarly named town housing uranium enrichment facilities.[25] Iran reportedly developed secret facilities and searched worldwide for proscribed nuclear components, missiles, and chemical and biological weapons (CEW; NTIW). During the early 1990s, Iran sought nuclear-capable ballistic missiles from Libya, North Korea, and China. North Korea supplied Iran with its 1,000 km-range Nodong 1 missile in exchange for long-term financing for its missile program (Spector 1990:213). Leading up to the 1995 NPT Review and Extension Conference, Iran threatened to withdraw from the NPT because of imputed U.S. violations of Article IV granting members full access to equipment, materials, and scientific and technological information for peaceful purposes. Iran withdrew its threat but warned that it would block consensus on the NPT's indefinite extension. Russia advised Iran to support extension to avoid delays in Russian nuclear reactor transfers to Tehran.

Begrudgingly Iran continued to proclaim adherence to selected international nonproliferation efforts. In 1993, U.N. representative Kamal Kharazi renewed calls for a Middle East NWFZ. In 1996, Iran signed the CTBT at the last moment, having supported India's objections until then and opposed Israel's role in representing the Middle East and South Asian region in the CTBT's Executive Council. Iran ceased to provide information to the CTBT Organization, arguing that the Majlis had doubts about international legal commitments, and it never ratified the CTBT. Meanwhile, proscribed nuclear activities allegedly proceeded apace. Reports of a Pakistani supply of highly enriched uranium surfaced as early as 1984, but subsequent reports by Malaysia's police traced centrifuge transfers by A. Q. Khan to the mid-1990s.[26] In 1996, CIA Director Deutsch suggested that there was no concrete evidence for the Pakistani connection.[27] In 2002, new revelations emerged from the National Council of Resistance of Iran associated with the exiled group *Mojahedin-e Khalq* (People's Holy Warriors). In February 2003, El-Baradei confirmed the existence of a previously undisclosed large-scale gas-centrifuge enrichment facility (Natanz) and a heavy-water production site (Arak). Iran had allegedly purified uranium with lasers since 1991, establishing an undisclosed pilot enrichment plant in 2000, and conducted research on polonium, a rare element suitable for nuclear weapons.[28] A June 2003 IAEA report stated that Iran had failed to fulfill some of its obligations, and July IAEA visits discovered traces of highly enriched uranium at Natanz, allegedly bearing Pakistani signature.[29] Iran denied enriching uranium and blamed traces on contamination of equipment supplies by "foreign intermediaries." IAEA reports cited Iran's acknowledgment that it had imported natural uranium hexafluoride, tetrafluoride, and dioxide from China, and that the 4.19 pounds of uranium hexafluoride that were once declared lost were instead used for research. Furthermore, contrary to Iran's declarations and NPT commitments, nuclear activities had taken place at military sites that were either beyond IAEA inspectors' reach or where access was frequently denied or delayed. Although in February 2003 Iran had pledged suspension of all uranium-enrichment activities to the IAEA, inspectors found that 285 new rotors for P-1 centrifuges had been assembled since. A September 2003 IAEA resolution asked Iran for full declaration of activities and unrestricted access by October 31, 2003. Prodded by the EU3 (Britain, Germany, and France), Iran supplied what it said was a comprehensive declaration, failing to address the enriched uranium's origin.

Under significant EU3 and IAEA pressure, Iran signed the Additional Protocol in December 2003, which would have enabled IAEA intrusive and spontaneous inspections of all nuclear-related facilities, but never ratified it. By early 2004, Iran was found to have had blueprints for an advanced centrifuge design for uranium enrichment (P-2), which previously had been hidden from inspections and allegedly kept separate from the Natanz facility. Iran repeatedly denied acquiring designs and key centrifuge components from Pakistan. The IAEA also found a document from A. Q. Khan offering assistance in shaping uranium metal into "hemispheric forms" required for nuclear bombs. Despite these reporting failures and inconsistencies, El-Baradei declared that "the jury is out on whether the program has been dedicated exclusively for peaceful purposes or if it has some military dimension" but that "it would be better not to refer the matter to the U.N. Security Council lest Iran opts out of the NPT, as did North Korea." He noted, however, that the inconsistencies suggested "a setback to Iran's stated policy of transparency."[30] Iran argued that its declaration was never intended to provide a "full picture" of past nuclear activities, contradicting its earlier October 2003 declaration of full disclosure.[31] In October 2004, Iran acknowledged that it had produced tons of hexafluoride gas suitable for uranium enrichment. The EU3 offered Iran access to nuclear fuel and technology, increased trade, and assistance with regional security concerns in exchange for freezing all enrichment activities. The United States removed its veto on Iran's potential accession to the WTO as an incentive added to the EU3 package.[32] Iran agreed to a temporary freeze. The IAEA's November 2004 report cited continued uncertainties surrounding Iran's enrichment activities.

In January 2005, Iranian officials showed IAEA inspectors a copy of an offer made by a foreign nuclear supplier to Iran in 1987 but refused to supply the document to the IAEA. Throughout the first half of 2005, Iran refused to provide information on P-2 or the source of nuclear contamination; prevented IAEA access to suspected facilities at Kalaye, Parchin, and Lavizan II; and threatened to unfreeze enrichment activities and withdraw from the NPT if the IAEA referred the case to the UNSC.[33] The IAEA reported that Iran misled the IAEA on plutonium reprocessing, which, rather than ceasing in 1993, continued through 1998.[34] Iran denied this, but El-Baradei defended IAEA's findings. Other IAEA reports cited concerns with the Green Salt Project, suggesting administrative interconnections between the conversion of uranium dioxide into $UF4$ ("green salt"), high explosives testing, and the design of a missile re-entry vehicle.[35] A new Ukrainian government acknowledged selling twenty-four nuclear-capable missiles to Iran (Milani et al. 2005:9). In August 2005, Iran restarted uranium conversion at a facility where it built a tunnel without informing the IAEA, which was discovered through satellite photos. Iran's chief nuclear negotiator declared (to domestic audiences) that EU3 negotiations had bought Iran one more year to complete the Esfahan facility.[36] The IAEA board voted to report Iran to the UNSC by November, due to its "history of concealment" and NPT violations, a step that El-Baradei characterized as "a message to Iran that [the international community] is not satisfied with the pace and level of cooperation with the IAEA."[37] Some Iranian leaders threatened to reject the Additional Protocol, withdraw from the NPT, and cut oil exports by 40 percent. Iran also punished states that endorsed the UNSC referral. In January 2006, El-Baradei reported that Iran decided to resume "research" enrichment activities while Iran declared its nuclear activities "irreversible."[38] In February the IAEA Board referred Iran to the UNSC, stating that the IAEA had no proof of diversion for nuclear weapons but that the nature and scope of Iran's program remained uncertain, including the origin of low and highly enriched uranium found at various locations and the extent of P-1 and P-2 activities.[39] A UNSC Presidential Statement urged Iran to suspend all enrichment and reprocessing, including research and development, and asked El-Baradei to report on Iran's compliance within thirty days. Just prior to El-Baradei's visit to Iran, Ahmadinejad announced that Iran had successfully enriched uranium, officially joining "the club of nuclear countries." His acknowledgment that Iran was conducting research on advanced P-2 centrifuges that could accelerate the production of enriched uranium contradicted previous Iranian denials that such research had been abandoned in 2003. Iran rejected IAEA requests to explain the inconsistency, fueling concerns of yet another undeclared facility. El-Baradei again reported that the IAEA could not provide evidence that Iran's nuclear program was exclusively for peaceful purposes, that Iran had not removed uncertainties, that it had banned access to certain military sites and had ceased implementation of the Additional Protocol, and that it had failed to reassure the IAEA regarding undeclared nuclear materials and activities.[40] Iran offered greater access on condition that the case be returned to the IAEA, but Britain and France presented a draft UNSC resolution calling for suspension of all enrichment and reprocessing, including research and development, and the construction of a heavy-water reactor. Ahmadinejad expressed that Iranians "do not give a damn about such resolutions."[41] Meanwhile, IAEA inspectors found new traces of highly enriched uranium on equipment from the military Physics Research Center at Lavizan-Shian, a base that Iran demolished in 2004.[42] Negotiations between the European Union and Iran failed to suspend sensitive activities.

In light of Iran's continued defiance of the August 2006 UNSC, in December 2006 the UNSC agreed unanimously to ban international trade in nuclear and missile technologies with Iran and to freeze foreign assets of twelve individuals and ten Iranian organizations. Ahmadinejad responded that the "U.N. resolution against Iran's atomic work has no validity for Iranians," describing the resolution as "a rusty instrument" that "has no effect," and proclaiming that "the resolution was born dead. . . . Even if they issue 10 more such resolutions it will not affect Iran's economy and politics." Ahmadinejad's depiction of the resolution as a "piece of torn paper," however, was met by a rejoinder by a conservative daily close to Khamene'i, positing that though the resolution was harmful for the country it was "too much to call it 'a piece of torn paper.' " In response to the resolution, the Majlis passed a bill asking the government to limit cooperation with the IAEA, barring thirty-eight inspectors from coming to Iran.[43]

This overview reveals extensive efforts to conceal information from the IAEA and exposes the breaching of NPT commitments. The NPR raised barriers to acquiring sensitive technologies but not high enough to prevent clandestine acquisitions, which appear to be significant. Iran's case also highlights a critical tension within the NPR: it allows enrichment and reprocessing provided they are transparent and open to IAEA inspections yet, as Carter (2004) suggests, under the guise of peaceful nuclear energy programs, cunning leaders can acquire paths to nuclear weapons. Indeed, some suspect that once past transgressions are "explained away, acknowledged and regretted, or simply excused," Iran may follow a "Japan model" to acquire all weapons-related technologies under legal cover.[44] Finally, Iran's policy gyrations warrant greater attention to domestic sources of selective NPT compliance. Vice President Mohajerani argued quite explicitly in 1992 that "Muslims must cooperate to produce an atomic bomb, regardless of U.N. efforts to prevent proliferation" (Hoodbhoy 1993:43). Rafsanjani unequivocally stated that although chemical and biological weapons were inhuman, "the war [with Iraq] taught us that international laws are only scraps of paper" (De Sutter 1997:44). Other Iranian officials favored a more compliant approach. Iran's domestic political landscape sheds light on these dynamics, on the general evolution of its nuclear policies, and on whether or not Iran is likely to remain in the NPT.

DOMESTIC POLITICS: "ISLAMIC BOMB" OR ECONOMIC REFORM?

A decade after the Shah assumed power in 1941, Premier Mosaddegh advanced a secular populist inward-looking program backed by a rising nationalist and anti-Western professional middle class. In 1953, the CIA supported a coup that ousted Mossadegh and reaffirmed the Shah's control. In the 1960s, the Shah launched a modernization plan promoting both primary and manufactured exports and import-substitution, creating large state enterprises but also promoting private firms (domestic and foreign), land reform, literacy, and profit-sharing in industry, all progressive policies for their time but undermined by unrelenting use of repression and torture. Oil and gas generated 75 percent of state revenue by the mid-1970s, buttressing the Shah's control over a rentier economy. His military consumed 40 percent of the budget (10 percent of GNP), a lower ratio of military expenditures to GNP than most of Iran's Arab neighbors. The state employed one-fourth of the non-agricultural workforce, much less than Iraq, Egypt, or Syria (Bill and Springborg 1990; Richards and Waterbury 1990). The Shah also promoted "aryan" ethnicity to differentiate Iran from the Arab world. His overall model of political survival relied heavily on the military-security apparatus and selected business interests, failing to broaden popular support. Heavy repression of the *ulema* (Muslim clergy) helped consolidate a formidable opposition, which recruited from poor and repressed masses. The 1978 decision to suspend a large-scale

nuclear energy program and channel funds for social spending was too little, too late. A coalition of religious, nationalist, and economic discontents
ousted the Shah in 1979. Details regarding his nuclear program remain
murky (Spector 1990) but overall he seemed much less willing to risk economic and political relations with the West than his successors.

After 1979, Iran's *nezam* (Islamic revolutionary system) came under the
control of the Supreme Islamic Jurisprudent (*velayat-e-faqih*), the Council
of Guardians (clerics selecting the faqih, or eminent religious leader), the
President, and the Supreme Defense Council, which commands the regular
armed forces and the Revolutionary Guards Corps (Pasdaran-e Enghelab-e
Islami). The faqih commands the military and intelligence systems, foreign
affairs, the judiciary and state propaganda machine; the president super-
vises the economy and social affairs. The revolution adopted a quintessen-
tially inward-looking model of political control expropriating industry,
creating large state enterprises, and redistributing wealth from the private
to public sector to attract populist support (Abrahamian 1993). A new
constitution granted state control over all major industries including oil,
petrochemicals, foreign trade, banking, mining, insurance, and trans-
portation. The state also controlled significant shares of construction,
manufacturing, and agriculture. Over 80 percent of the economy came
under the control of state enterprises and powerful tax-exempt foundations (bonyads) dominated by radical clerics or former military officers
appointed by Khamene'i. The Bonyad-e Mostaz'afi (Foundation for the
Oppressed) became the second-largest conglomerate after the National
Iranian Oil Company. Pasdaran acquired a military-industrial conglomerate ranked as the third largest. Although military expenditures listed
under the regular budget appeared moderate, bonyads with unpublished
budgets and accountable only to top clerics, and not to the Majlis or the
president, funded large-scale military programs.[45] Most bonyads subsidies benefited the middle class rather than the poor. A system of multiple exchange rates favored state agencies, bonyads, and a few privileged
businesses, undermining particularly private-sector exporters. Ironically, this inward-looking model made Iran more dependent on oil and
gas exports than under the Shah, representing the main source of state
revenues and foreign exchange (other exports include pistachio nuts,
carpets, and fruit).

The model's international pillars included contempt for Western political
and economic institutions, including diplomatic extraterritoriality, individual freedoms, and anti-terrorism. Regionally the regime belittled the Gulf
states as anti-Islamic Western "lackeys," exhorted Shi'ites to revolt against
them and against Saddam's secular regime, severed diplomatic relations
with Egypt following its peace treaty with Israel, and glorified Sadat's assas-
sin, naming a Tehran street after him. The revolution's radical religious pil-

lar turned Islam into a malleable guide for policy. In the early postrevolu-
tionary period, WMD were proclaimed contrary to Islam. Nuclear activities identified with the Shah were initially abandoned, particularly after
nearly 3,700 AEOI scientists—of 4,500—left Iran (DeSutter 1977). During
the 1980s debacle with Iraq, WMD programs became powerful tools of domestic survival, compatible with economic, political, military and technological self-reliance, anti-imperialism, sovereignty, and defiance of international regimes under presumed Western domination. Khomeini's close
advisor Ayatollah Mohammed Beheshti told Iranian scientist Fereydun Fesharaki that "it is your duty to build the atomic bomb for the Islamic Republican Party" (Spector 1990:208). Rafsanjani's deputy Mohajerani declared
that "because the enemy has nuclear facilities, the Muslim states too should
be equipped with the same capacity. . . . I am not talking about one Muslim
country, but rather the entirety of Muslim states."[46] At the height of the war
Khamene'i reportedly declared in a 1987 speech to the AEOI that "regarding atomic energy, we need it now. . . . The least we can do to face this danger is to let our enemies know that we can defend ourselves. Therefore every
step you take here is in defense of your country and your revolution. . . .
You should work hard and at great speed."[47] Many such statements on why
Iran should pursue WMD became part of the public record until 1991,
when the Gulf War and stringent controls over Iraq's WMD changed Iran's
rhetoric for English-speaking audiences. *Pasdaran* commander Rezai began
invoking morality, Iranian culture, and political logic as precluding such
weapons despite Iran's reported use of chemical weapons against Iraq
(CNSW; Cordesman 2000). Khamene'i asserted that "the Islamic Republic
of Iran, based on its religious and jurisprudence fundamental beliefs, would
never resort to the use of weapons of mass destruction" (ICG 2003:18). Yet
on December 14, 2001, Rafsanjani suggested that with an Islamic weapon,
"the imperialists' strategy will reach a standstill because the use of even one
nuclear bomb inside Israel will destroy everything." An Iranian official privately expressed that such statements were intended "for a domestic audience only" (Congressional Resolution 21 [2002]; ICG 2003:18).

Nuclear weapons development was steered by a radical network associated with Khamene'i, including the Ministry of Defense and special Pasdaran units with bonyad resources.[48] The Iranian constitution entrusted
the defense of Iran's territorial integrity to the military but assigned Pasdaran responsibility for protecting the Revolution itself, fueling rivalry
between the two. Pasdaran controls its own navy, ground troops, air
force, intelligence, missiles, and military-industrial-complex. Rafsanjani
chaired the Expediency Council, allegedly the driving force behind the
nuclear program. Dominant elements in the nuclear program challenged
commitments to international conventions, particularly the NPT, and were
involved in sponsoring terrorism and human rights abuses, subverting the

Middle East peace process, and intimidating Gulf sheikhdoms, leading
the Clinton administration to label Iran a "backlash state." As Majlis
speaker and acting Pasdaran commander, Rafsanjani openly called for nuclear weapons in a radio address to Pasdaran in 1988. Pasdaran also su-
pervised Iran's missile programs, including the Bandar-e-Abbas project,
which was to extend the range of Chinese Silkworm missiles and fit them
with nuclear warheads.[49] The nuclear network also created a vast scientific and technological constituency benefiting from special perquisites and
honors.

Power in Iran has been concentrated in a nomenklatura of about 5,000
clerical and lay officials from heavily intermarried families ruling over
the state, army, and rentier economy as an extended family (Halliday
2005:293). Yet Rafsanjani acknowledged in 1982 that two basic factions
vied for power: one supported nationalization, the other privatization
(Owen 2000:141). The reformist, "economy first," or "pragmatic" currents (*Baz-Sazi*, rebuilding) supported by some technocrats, younger entrepreneurs, and *bazaari* (bazaar) merchants and traders pressing for decreased state control, sought privatization, increased trade with Europe
and Asia, a utilitarian over an ideological approach to foreign policy, and
decreased tension with international institutions.[50] By the early 1990s
Rafsanjani introduced some structural adjustment and economic liberalization, lower trade restrictions, privatization, and reduction of subsidies
(Keddie 2006). Some Pasdaran commanders opposed Rafsanjani's reforms.
This evolving contest between radical and reformers helps explain duality
in Iran's nuclear behavior—a schizoid foreign policy—in the 1990s and
early 2000s. Deputy Foreign Minister Mahmud Vaezi asserted in 1992
that Iran opposed nuclear weapons, despite the contradicting statements
made by other officials.[51] In 1993, Rafsanjani denied that Iran was pursuing nuclear weapons, arguing that it could not afford them.[52] A wide
range of nationalist politicians, including some economic reformers, supported the nuclear energy program under IAEA supervision but not necessarily nuclear weapons or NPT defiance.[53]

The conservative Society of Combatant Clergy lost its majority in 1996
parliamentary elections when a centrist bloc—Servants of Reconstruction—
gained some ground. Moderate cleric Mohammed Khatami won the 1997
presidential elections with nearly 70 percent of the vote. Khatami's supporters included political and economic reformers—urging, among other
things, bonyads' accountability to elected officials—but also extreme conservatives from the Combatant Clerics of Tehran, whose leader 'Ali-Akbar
Mohtashemi declared that "only Iran's enemies . . . stress the primacy of
economic reconstruction . . . to divert attention from the more crucial issues of Iran's 'political and cultural independence'. . . . If you set the economy as the principle and sacrifice everything at its altar there would remain

nothing by which you could be powerful, free, and independent" (Menashri 1998:16). Under Khatami's rule, Pasdaran commander Yahia Safavi attacked "liberal" politicians warning that "we have to behead some and cut off the tongues of others. Our language is the sword," while making disparaging comments on the NPT and the CWC (Eisenstadt 1998:72,83). Khamene'i faithfully captured the views of opponents of globalization: "What is globalization? It means that a group of world powers . . . many those who have influence over the UN and mainly those countries which have been colonialists in the past—want to expand their culture, economy and traditions throughout the world. They want to set up a share-holding company in which they should hold 95% of its shares. . . . They want to have authority. They want to make decisions. That is what globalisation means" (Halliday 2005:315).[54] Given Khamene'i's control over vast portions of the state and bonyad apparatus thriving under his protectionist policies, Khamene'i's position on globalization is not surprising. His motions toward privatization are geared to transfer state enterprises to his protégés in bonyads and state banks (Khalaji 2006).

Khatami's hybrid coalition leaned on contradictory economic, social, and political forces vying for power within and outside the state (Milani 2005b). Despite Khatami's statements favoring globalization and privatization, his economic team retained basic commitments to a 1970s-style Islamist statist economy (O'Sullivan 2003). Expected political and economic changes at home or in policies toward terrorism, WMD, or the Middle East peace process never materialized despite some positive signals from the Clinton administration. In 1997 Khatami replaced Reza Amrollahi with Gholam Reza Aghazadeh as AEOI president and made him his vice president, actions interpreted either as signs of growing Majlis opposition to the costs of completing Bushehr ($800 million according to the AEOI) and a nod to replace it with Western technology (NTIW), or as a reaction to delays in the nuclear weapons program. During Khatami's presidency, Iran reportedly advanced the most daring technical and political phases of its clandestine nuclear program.[55] The 2001 elections reflected declining support for Khatami as his tepid policies disappointed erstwhile supporters. By the 2004 parliamentary elections, characterized by low turnout, reformists had been decimated through imprisonment, torture, and popular apathy. Hardliners from the radical conservative network Abadgaran (Developers of an Islamic Iran) now dominated the Majlis, encouraging increased political assertiveness by Pasdaran, opposing Turkish investments in telecommunications and airport management, French investments in automobiles, and all foreign investment in oil. Pasdaran opposed Turkish management of the airport ostensibly as "an affront to Iran's dignity" but more pertinently because one of its firms had sought the contract (Molavi 2004). Protectionist

Majlis legislators ousted the reformist Roads and Transport minister who had approved the agreement with the Turkish consortium. In June 2006, the Ministry of Oil awarded an inexperienced, Pasdaran-controlled firm (Ghorb) a $1.3 billion contract for a gas pipeline across Iran without a competitive tender, infuriating private construction companies. Inward-looking policies affected oil production and exacerbated unemployment (15 percent in 2006), inflation, corruption, and declining living standards. For all the Islamic Republic's populist rhetoric, income inequality remained at roughly the same level since 1979 as measured by Gini indices. Selected bonyads were "privatized" by handing them over to regime cronies (Milani 2005b:46).[56]

Ahmadinejad campaigned for redressing inequality and abolishing corruption, which he associated with Rafsanjani and Khatami among others, and he was elected president in July 2005 in tightly controlled elections with alleged interference from Khamene'i and his son Mojtaba, the Council of Guardians, and Pasdaran. Ahmadinejad's main constituencies were Pasdaran, its extensive economic and military fiefdoms, and paramilitary youth militias (*basiji*) who worked for Khamene'i as gangs and ideological storm troops, some conservative clergy, and segments of bazaari commerce and finance connected to the shady right-wing group Hojatiyye (Milani 2005b). Ahmadinejad promised employment to all *basijis* (his former comrades) and other unemployed and impoverished constituencies, and attracted social conservatives and nationalists rejecting Western culture and institutions, including *Mo'talefe*, a group formed by Bazaaris with strong ties to the clergy and Pasdaran, rooted in an old Islamic terrorist organization (Milani 2005b; Khosrokhavar 2004). Today Hojatiyye is led by Ayatollah Mesbah Yazdi, Ahmadinejad's spiritual mentor, who heads the Haggani school of radical Shi'ism, which is acerbically anti-democratic and anti-Western.[57] Mo'talefe's patronage stemmed from its control of retail and distribution networks and allocation of lucrative "special" permits and import licenses. Pasdaran enriched its coffers by importing banned and expensive commodities into private ports under their exclusive control. Closure to the global economy was vital to these groups' prosperity. Accordingly, Ahmadinejad's economic advisor Abumohammed Asgar-Khani pressed him to "go with techno-nationalism," import-substitution, and state control of the economy, and to keep foreign investors out.[58] Ahmadinejad deepened inward-looking policies including import-substitution, expanded state enterprises, and state monopoly over banking, and rejected reforms adversely affecting his core constituencies.[59] The day Ahmadinejad took office in August 2005, Iran rejected yet another EU3 proposal; that week he restarted uranium conversion in Isfahan, unleashing a dramatic deterioration in negotiations with the EU3 and IAEA.

According to Mohamed Semati from Tehran University, the hardline ruling coalition is stable and has been strengthened by U.S. coercive diplomacy. Similarly, Milani maintains that ostracism has advantaged those pursuing nuclear weapons, whereas engagement threatens the economic interests of beneficiaries of a closed economy, particularly state enterprises and bonyads.[60] Links between economic nationalism and nuclear defiance are evident in statements by Foreign Ministry Spokesman Asefi, who asserted that "we don't know with what language to tell the Europeans and Americans that Iran is not afraid of the U.N. Security Council. We have been subject to sanctions in the past. In the short term, it has put us under pressure. But in [the] long term, it has helped our economy to flourish."[61] Asefi's statement referred to a protectionist economy driven by inward-looking state agencies and bonyads controlled by Pasdaran and conservative clerics, which avoid taxes, competition, and state regulations and are inimical to reforms that threaten their power base (Khosrokhavar 2004). Milani identified serious cleavages even within the conservative coalition, with Pasdaran seeking more power from—and sharpening rifts within—the clerical hierarchy. Iranian leaders, in Milani's views, decided to assemble nuclear weapons not against the United States but against Iran's own democratic movement, as evidence of the regime's wherewithal and national achievement.[62] This interpretation that domestic considerations provide a strong rationale for nuclear weapons finds support in a statement by the alleged "father" of Iran's nuclear program Asgar-Khani, who, while citing the utility of nuclear weapons as a "minimum deterrent," acknowledged that they are "necessary not only as a substitute for fossil energy but also for Iran's social cohesion and prestige. . . . Internally Iran is in a state of disarray. I would now argue that, only by becoming a nuclear weapons state, can Iran consolidate its social coherence. Iran needs both soft and hard power to regain its national identity and prestige" (ICG 2003:18).

What is particularly illuminating in this statement is the fact that a presumed key figure in the weapons program concedes that they serve important domestic functions, a recognition that is hard to come by in most contexts—democratic or authoritarian—for reasons examined in part 1. Justifying nuclear weapons for "reasons of state" is usually considered more legitimate both domestically and internationally than are ulterior— often concealed—political purposes of regime survival. Mastery of the nuclear fuel cycle provides a valuable rallying nationalist theme, given that it requires vast investments in nuclear-bound human resources and technology, in the midst of economic stagnation, high inflation, and unemployment. Yet popular support for independent nuclear energy capabilities should not be confused with support for nuclear weapons.[63] The true extent of either cannot be ascertained in the absence of complete freedom of expression. At issue is not whether nationalist pride runs across the

Iranian political spectrum, which seems to be a safe assumption. What separates radicals from reformists is varying tolerance for the domestic political and economic costs, including opportunity costs entailed in massive and risk-prone nuclear undertakings by entrenched inward-looking forces.[64] The Guardian Council—which rejected Turkish investments in cellular phones and airport management—is headed by Ayatollah Ahmad Jannati, who argued that Iran should follow North Korea and leave the NPT (Shafer 2003:10; Nasr and Gheissari 2004). Pasdaran—which expanded economic controls and established monopolies over black market trade in embargoed goods such as consumer electronics, construction materials, and Western clothing—is headed by Safavi, who opposed negotiations with the EU3. As Nasr and Gheissari (2004) argue, these extremely lucrative independent sources of income enable extensive patronage and investments in military, including nuclear, programs. So vested is Pasdaran in nuclear weapons as guaranteeing its institutional survival that it opposes expansion of conventional forces as potential competitors. As a Pasdaran protégé, Ahmadinejad has offered to share nuclear technology with other Muslim nations.[65]

By contrast, pragmatists recognized that "integration into the international order and the global economy mandates accepting certain restrictions on [Iran's] nuclear programme" (Takeyh 2006a). Majlis Islamic Participation Front reformers advocated cooperation with the IAEA and EU3. Chairing the Majlis energy commission, Hossein Afarideh vigorously supported ratification of the Additional Protocol. The managing editor of a reformist publication went so far as to suggest that "we must not waste our time negotiating with European countries and insignificant players in the international relations arena. . . . The president can take the initiative and with the help of the Islamic Consultative Majlis Supreme Security Council and with the consent of the eminent leader, initiate fair talks with America, without any mediators, without any preconditions, and with full authority and resolution."[66] Some reformers reportedly favor "the Japanese model," which Semati (2004) describes as full access to fuel cycle capabilities and within half a step of producing nuclear weapons, but without actually producing them and allowing international inspections. How widespread this position is among reformers and whether or not it is a tactical preference under political hardship or a genuine strategic view remains unclear. Following their demoralizing electoral performance, reformers' incentives to publicize their preferences on foreign matters declined dramatically.[67] Reformers have been left out of all efforts to "control the nuclear crisis."[68] The prospects of extensive trade, European and U.S. support for Iran's WTO membership, transparent civilian nuclear technology, conventional weapons, and other incentives proposed by the EU3 entice those advocating an alternative model for Iran.

Hardliners allegedly pressured Iranian negotiators to retain full control of sensitive technologies.[69] Responding to these internal pressures, the long-standing Secretary of the High National Security Council Hassan Rowhani reiterated that suspension was not open-ended, warning that "if the Europeans do not respect their commitments or present an illogical or harsh resolution, Iran has already decided its response. . . . Iran will never compromise on its right to gain access to the complete nuclear fuel cycle."[70] Although arguably supportive of the EU3 plan, Khatami himself declared that Iran would resume enrichment if necessary and that the nuclear program would continue even if it meant an end to U.N. oversight, asserting that Iran abhorred nuclear weapons.[71] This rhetoric was largely responsive to a domestic audience that had become politicized by the nuclear stalemate with the IAEA. The strongly conservative Majlis introduced a bill forcing the resumption of enrichment and discontinuing U.N. inspections, violating Iran's commitments to the EU3.[72] A Majlis majority statement also declared that UNSC's invocations of Chapter VII would lead the Majlis to request that Iran abandon the NPT. In April 2006 Ahmadinejad announced that Iran "has joined the club of nuclear countries" by successfully enriching uranium for the first time. Prior to his dramatic speech, the regime orchestrated a show of traditional dancers waving allegorical enriched uranium vials in celebration of Iran's nuclear achievements, giving new meaning to displays of nuclear prowess for domestic audiences.

Ahmadinejad has distributed "justice shares" of state enterprises, but their poor performance and corrupt practices rendered them of limited value. Iran needs nearly one million annual new jobs to keep unemployment (11–15 percent in 2006) from rising further, yet unemployment rates reportedly increased sharply to 20–30 percent by 2007.[73] Rafsanjani, whom Ahmadinejad defeated in the 2005 elections, and others support Ahmadinejad publicly because their political survival hinges on competitive nationalist outbidding, but they and the business class, fearing the adverse impact of sanctions, have supported diplomatic solutions.[74] Rafsanjani reportedly impressed on Khamene'i the need to restrain Ahmadinejad, yet Khamene'i proclaimed Iran's willingness to supply nuclear technology and experience to Sudan, a country embattled with the U.N. on account of its genocide in Darfur. The largest reformist Participation Front has urged Ahmadinejad to stop the enrichment program. Technically, Ahmadinejad has limited, if any, direct control over nuclear policy, and hardline newspapers close to Khamene'i have called upon Ahmadinejad to distance himself from the nuclear issue. Khamene'i rules supreme, although in practice he must follow a consensus among the ruling coalition, and Ahmadinejad's effort to carve himself an important role on this issue affects the formation of a consensus. Former Pasdaran Commander

Rezai, now the Expediency Council's secretary, may have expressed these difficulties when rejecting concessions on the "peaceful" nuclear program but warning against "adventurism" rife with heavy political and economic costs (Abedin 2006).

The IAEA's September 2005 resolution referring Iran to the UNSC signaled to Iran's domestic constituencies that the regime's nuclear defiance could come at a high economic cost. Iran's stock market declined by 30 percent following the resolution, a phenomenon known as the "Black September" of Tehran's stock market, with investors transferring billions of dollars to Dubai. Capital flight in the first few months of Ahmadinejad's rule has been estimated at $200 billion.[75] Rafsanjani called for wisdom and diplomacy, "not slogans," in an elliptical reference to Ahmadinejad's confrontational UNGA speech preceding IAEA's decision. Ahmadinejad repeated calls for Iran to "wipe Israel off the map," arguing—accurately—that his comments reflected Iran's long-standing policy since Ayatollah Khomeini. Although not new, his comments provoked international concern with Iran's presumed nuclear intentions. Reformers denounced Ahmadinejad's statements as undermining Iran's interests and warned that international opposition to Iran was reaching alarming levels. Even Khatami acknowledged that "those words have created hundreds of political and economic problems for us in the world."[76] In October 2006, Rafsanjani published a previously undisclosed letter from the late Ayatollah Khomeini, written at the height of the was with Iraq, stating, "Now that our army and Revolutionary Guards officers, who are experts of war, clearly admit that the army of Islam will not register any victories soon, and due to the fact that the Islamic Republic's devoted military and political officers do not see the continuation of the war in the country's best interests. . . . I agree to the planned ceasefire."[77] Khomeini had also dismissed a dissenting letter from a Pasdaran commander who rejected the ceasefire and who suggested that Iran would be able to launch offensive operations with atomic weapons. In disclosing Khomeini's letter, Rafsanjani reminded Iranians of the cost of war and Khomeini's pragmatism in urging an end to it. Ahmadinejad's supporters attacked Rafsanjani as defeatist and removed references to the nuclear issue from a government website.

Oil windfalls have provided Ahmadinejad with surged revenues to finance his patrons and allies, but declining oil prices endanger his patronage resources. Some Iranian leaders have argued that although Iran has the second largest natural gas reserves worldwide and nearly 9 percent of oil reserves, nuclear energy will enable Iran's development by channeling natural resources into foreign markets. An ICG (2003) study, however, finds very limited economic rationale for the nuclear program. Furthermore, restructuring an inefficient oil sector would require $17 billion in FDI. These funds are also needed for expanding infrastructure for natural gas exports which require high initial investments and long-term contracts. The prospect of sanctions and U.S. retaliation for violating them has created too much uncertainty for investors to commit up-front capital resources in gas fields, particularly when Qatar, Oman, and the UAE offer greater stability and business advantages.[78] Even under continued oil revenues, Iranian economists warned, Ahmadinejad's programs are bound to saddle Iran with a case of "Dutch disease," a phenomenon typical of rentier economies with high inflation, declining competitive manufacturing exports, and resistance to change by political beneficiaries of oil rents.[79] An Iranian economist even dared to compare Ahmadinejad's populism with the Shah's last-ditch effort to stay in power in 1979.[80] Fifty prominent Iranian economists wrote an open letter to Ahmadinejad, the first of its kind, emphasizing that "the adoption of expansive monetary policies, and the existence of tension in Iran's international relations, [have] caused the investment atmosphere in the country to decline on a daily basis. By increasing risks and the expenses of the private sector, both foreign and domestic, private investment in the country has fallen sharply, while human and material resources are fleeing the country."[81] They also warned against the dangers of economic sanctions, the consequences of which, they argued, "are predictable. The rise in investment risk, disorder in foreign trade, reduction in the rate of profit from existing production capacity, slowdown in collecting capital, and the creation of deep inflation (stagflation) are among the harmful [effects] the country will have to bear in the event of a lack of constructive interaction with the global economy. . . . We insist your excellency and the regime's officials attend to a fundamental review of your economic policies and programs for the country." Even 150 Majlis legislators criticized Ahmadinejad's economic policies and failure to submit an annual budget on time. The December 2006 UNSC resolution also accelerated the stock market decline, with the number of traders decreasing by 46 percent. A group of powerful businessmen, the Islamic Coalition Party, met with a senior member of the Supreme National Security Council to urge moderation in the country's nuclear policies and avoid further harm to the economy. Nationwide elections for city councils in December 2006 dealt another blow to Ahmadinejad, whose allies won fewer than 20 percent of the seats. A former supporter explained the rejection of Ahmadinejad on the latter's "superstitious and populist tendencies."[82]

CONCLUSION

Four main points emerge from this analysis. First, to the extent that external threats drove Iran's search for nuclear weapons since the 1980s,

Iraq has been at their core. More recently, presumed vulnerability to rivals including the United States, Israel, or Pakistan are said to account for that search, but many in Iran disagree with the premise of these threats or how to cope with them, pointing to nuclear weapons as potentially undermining or enhancing security, depending on the eyes of Iranian beholders.[83] This open-endedness forces attention to other factors influencing Iran's nuclear behavior. In particular, while relative power considerations have remained the same, and may have even improved in Iran's favor, perceptions of threat have varied in response to domestic political alignments.[84] Second, Islam provided a flexible normative foundation that was marshaled to justify production and use of WMD at certain times but found incompatible with such weapons at other times.[85] Third, radical inward-looking leaders have approached international institutions and international law with contempt not just on nuclear matters. Pragmatic reformers endorse international institutions that can advance their positions at home. The IAEA's decision to refer Iran to the UNSC in 2006, and subsequent UNSC resolutions, conveyed the most powerful multilateral response thus far to an alleged long history of NPT violations. Fourth, radical forces behind Ahmadinejad regard nuclear weapons "as an insurance policy against a forced change in the government," or a guarantee of regime survival.[86] Takeyh (2004) argues that once coalitions and constituencies favoring nuclear weapons develop, "a state can cross the point of political no return [and] this phenomenon is becoming all too evident in the case of Iran."[87] However, the not-so-delicate dance between inward-looking radicals and economic reformers can yet change the odds that Iran's nuclear program will reach that point. Indeed, according to Milani (2005a:4), "As it is becoming more and more evident that the regime's pursuit of the bomb has only political self-preservation as its goal, popular support for the policy is also dissipating." While that may be the case, there were also reported indications in early 2007 that, with North Korea's help, Iran was preparing an underground nuclear test.[88] In a further sign of sharpening tensions between more pragmatic and more radical factions within Iran, former senior nuclear negotiator Hossein Mossavian, a critic of Iran's recent nuclear postures and a researcher at the Strategic Research Center headed by Rafsanjani, was reportedly arrested and charged with spying.

CHAPTER NINE

Israel

FOLLOWING THE 1947 U.N. PARTITION recognizing Zionist aspirations for a homeland and Israel's 1948 declaration of independence, five Arab countries attacked Israel in the first of several Arab-Israeli wars. In the war's aftermath, Arab states' refusal to recognize the new state and the Palestinian refugee problem kept Israel regionally isolated. Responding to clearly formulated threats of joint Arab efforts to obliterate Israel with Soviet support, Premier David Ben-Gurion ordered the construction of Dimona's nuclear complex in 1958, following the 1957 secret nuclear agreement with France supplying Israel with a 24 MW natural uranium/heavy-water reactor and a plutonium-reprocessing facility.[1] Although Charles de Gaulle halted construction of the plutonium facility in 1960, it was completed with the help of French technicians. Dimona became public only in December 1960 when Ben-Gurion, forced by a strongly worded query from U.S. Secretary of State Christian Herter, addressed Israel's Knesset (parliament), assuring the United States that Israel had no plans to develop nuclear weapons.[2] Successive leaders retained ambiguity about nuclear intentions and capabilities through a formula later codified by Deputy Defense Minister Shimon Peres (under Premier Levi Eshkol), who told President Kennedy in 1963 that "Israel would not be the first to introduce nuclear weapons to the Middle East."[3] This remained Israel's declared policy until today. By 1974, however, some U.S. intelligence services had concluded that Israel had nuclear weapons, based on its secret purchase of weapons-grade uranium, its refusal to allow thorough inspections, and its development of suitable ballistic missiles.[4] In 1986 nuclear technician Mordechai Vanunu declared that Israel had an arsenal of fifty to sixty nuclear weapons and a plutonium reprocessing facility.[5] By 2003, a nuclear "triad"—land, air, and sea-based—had allegedly secured Israel's second-strike capability (Cirincione et al. 2005).

Israel is often interpreted as one of the most straightforward cases among nuclear aspirants seeking *state* survival, and yet it presents an interesting riddle. If the purpose of nuclear weapons was to deter external attacks, why were they never acknowledged? The analytical frameworks outlined in chapter 2 provide different answers to this particular conundrum and to the more fundamental question of why Israel may have sought nuclear weapons.

INTERNATIONAL POWER: DILEMMAS OF SURVIVAL

Many studies suggest that Israel fits the neorealist model best insofar as it has faced an overwhelming threat to its survival from most neighbors, many of which rejected its very existence from the beginning and, in some cases, still do today (Dunn 1982; Sagan 1996–97; Feldman 1982; Normark et al. 2005; Cirincione et al. 2005, Dowty 2005). As Burrows and Windrem (1994:288) argue, "Israel's existence is guaranteed only by the force of its own arms." For Jones (1997b), Israel's position stemmed from its perception of existential threats from neighbors "prepared to threaten the use of weapons of mass destruction against it in support of their wider regional aims." Another leading study (Reiss 1988:138) argues that "few members of the international community have been confronted by such abiding animosity and pervasive threats to their security as Israel." Indeed, the external environment against which Ben-Gurion began weighing Israel's nuclear options included conventional Arab military superiority; a conventional arms embargo by major powers since 1950 that applied largely to Israel; extensive Soviet military and political support for Arab regimes; well-articulated commitments by Arab leaders to extirpate Israel from the region; related Israeli anticipation that these leaders would seek nuclear weapons to that effect; Arab states' search for missile and chemical weapons technology; Israel's isolation at the U.N., where oil-rich Arab and Islamic states rallied automatic condemnations of Israel; and Nasser's 1953 closure of the Straits of Tiran.[6] This standard interpretation gets further support from the fact that threats to Israel's survival were most acute during its early years—the 1950s—just as nuclear weapons were arguably envisaged. Moreover, initial decisions to acquire a nuclear capability were reportedly taken merely a decade after the Holocaust had decimated six million European Jewry. This consideration, however, has no relevance for a structural realist approach purely focused on balance of power rather than domestic characteristics, and is perhaps more consistent with categories of interest to constructivism, such as identity and historical memory.

Ben-Gurion doubted that Israel could sustain credible conventional deterrence against an overwhelming collective adversary involving several states with numerous times more territory, armed forces, population, and wealth. At his 1961 meeting with Kennedy, Ben-Gurion cited Egypt's military advantage vis-à-vis Israel—a 15:1 population ratio (30 versus 2 million) and a 3:1 weapons ratio—without taking into account other Arab states as well as Egypt's ability to acquire nuclear weapons.[7] Nasser had warned in 1960 that Arab states would invade Israel if it developed nuclear weapons, and he threatened to acquire nuclear weapons to maintain Egypt's "superiority."[8] Egypt's reported activities on missiles that were capable of carrying chemical warheads in 1963 buttressed those who doubted the value of conventional deterrence. Coupled with Nasser's rhetoric, Egypt's overflights over Dimona (1965–67) were perceived as possible reconnaissance for attacks on Dimona (Burrows and Windrem 1994:282; Brecher 1980:104, 230–31). Nasser threatened preventive war again in 1966 "to wipe out all that enables Israel to produce an atomic bomb," and closed the Straits of Tiran to Israeli navigation in 1967.[9] In the ensuing Six-Day War, Israel captured Sinai and the Golan Heights. In October 1973, Egypt and Syria launched the Yom Kippur surprise attack, inflicting a high level of Israeli casualties and a renewed sense of utter vulnerability.

Whether Israel's assumed nuclear capability played any effective deterrent role has been subject to intense academic debates. Some considered it a last resort to deter direct Soviet intervention or nuclear threats from Arab states.[10] Some traced Egypt and Syria's limited objectives in the 1973 war to fear of Israel's nuclear retaliation if certain thresholds were crossed.[11] There were unconfirmed reports that nuclear weapons were deployed during this war (Reiss 1988). Others argued that nuclear weapons played no role in 1973, as can be gleaned from Egyptian and Syrian war-planning documents (Evron 1994). Some interpreted Sadat's 1977 peace overture as underwritten by conviction that nuclear weapons made Israel invulnerable and only peace would lead to Israeli concessions. However, several competing explanations for Sadat's initiatives can be found.[12] Reluctance to use chemical weapons against Israel was also interpreted as evidence for a successful Israeli deterrent (Melman 2006), but others argued that Israel's deterrent failed when Saddam fired thirty-nine Scud missiles on Israel in seventeen separate instances during the 1991 Gulf War, in which Israel was not a party. Yet Iraqi defectors declared that Saddam had intended to fit chemical warheads on Scud missiles and was restrained only by fear of Israeli nuclear retaliation.[13] In 2003, Iraq refrained from attacking Israel despite repeated threats to do so prior to the war. Whether or not Israel's presumed deterrent helps account for these actions by neighboring states, many continue to impute deterrence effects to Israel's alleged arsenal.[14] Such views—even if lacking irrefutable validation—reproduce beliefs in nuclear deterrence among segments of the Israeli public, including some that are otherwise supportive of extensive territorial and political compromises. However, there is no indisputable evidence confirming that nuclear weapons account for Israel's continued existence.

A nuclear-armed, missile-capable Iran is perceived as Israel's newest strategic threat, accompanied by strong rhetoric that Israel "should be wiped off the map" and "is a 'cancerous tumor' that must be eradicated from the body of the *ummah*," and that "with the force of God behind it, we shall soon experience a world without the United States and Zionism."[15] Israeli officials cited Iran as the only U.N. member that has revealed its intention to destroy another member state, pointing to statements from both "moderates" and radicals threatening Israel's annihilation. President Khatami, a self-styled "reformer," retained sharply hostile anti-Israeli oratory even as a compromising Labor-led coalition signed the Oslo accords with Palestinian leaders.[16]

Existential threats have undoubtedly driven Israel's nuclear policies, particularly in the early years (Normark et al. 2005). Yet the question of whether nuclear weapons were the only solution to Israel's predicament from a strictly structural neorealist, self-help standpoint remains. Feldman (1982) argues that only an overt and explicit nuclear posture could provide security and that a second-strike capability would introduce stability. In other neorealist frameworks, merely keeping an adversary guessing provides enough deterrence (Waltz 2003; Shalom 1996:23; Peres, cited in Jabber 1971:40). Several arguments, however, have been advanced against the view that nuclear deterrence—implicit or explicit—was the best path to ensure Israel's existence. Some of these were wielded most prominently by selected cabinet members and by Israel's Committee for the Denuclearization of the Middle East in the 1960s. First, neighboring states could annul Israel's advantage by acquiring nuclear weapons, which would reactively lead to a nuclear arms race, as Yigal Allon, Israel Galili , and Meir Yaari contended (Evron 1994; Karpin 2006). Second, irrational leaders could erode the rationality of deterrence (Allon 1990:200; Reiss 1988; Beres 1986; Peres 1993; Dowty 2005). Third, Arab states could have launched a preemptive war to preclude Israel from becoming nuclear, an argument that Peres appeared to have accepted over time (Evron 1995; Cohen 1998:151). Fourth, minute Israel was vulnerable to first strikes, lacking adequate territory to secure second-strike capabilities. As Normark et al. (2005:15) argue, Israel is smaller than Wales. Fifth, even after acquiring second-strike capabilities, Israel could arguably not survive a small nuclear exchange (Brecher 1972:158). Israel's leading security analyst Ze'ev Schiff put this best recently in the context of Iranian threats: "What point is there in a counter-strategy after geographically minute Israel is destroyed?!"[17] Similarly, former member of Israel's Atomic Energy Commission (IAEC) Yuval Neeman said that Israel's small size could mean that a second-strike capability was irrelevant.[18] Clearly, there has been significant diversity regarding the merits of nuclear deterrence in this case, including a lively debate over whether or not deterrence can be achieved through explicit or implicit nuclear capabilities.

A second neorealist argument would hold Israel's relationship with the United States as obviating the need for an indigenous deterrent. U.S.-Israeli relations, however, were not close when Israel's vulnerability was at its highest, in its first two decades of existence. The United States maintained an arm's length relationship to ensure good relations with the Arab world and, as did other powers, abided by a conventional weapons boycott. Israel's requests for NATO security guarantees in 1957 went unanswered. Until 1966, the United States refused to supply Israel with aircraft and other important conventional weapons, let alone a nuclear umbrella. According to Dunn (1998:67), "Though Israel floated the idea of such a security guarantee in the 1960s at a time prior to the realization of its nuclear option, U.S. officials were unwilling to take that step." A declassified Israeli document reveals that Israel's decision-makers understood very well that Kennedy would not enter a formal alliance with Israel.[19] A declassified U.S. document acknowledged that "Israel does not consider present U.S. assurances adequate to protect Israel against attack" and that a "formal U.S. guarantee" might do so but could not be offered in order to "maintain a position of balance between the Arabs and Israel."[20] France supplied military aircraft in the 1960s, but de Gaulle downgraded the relationship, exacerbating Israel's sense of abandonment. U.S.-Israeli relations became far closer under the Johnson administration, but the "special relationship" was not institutionalized into the kind of alliance that formally extended the U.S. nuclear umbrella over Japan and South Korea.[21] As Reiss (1988:138) argues, "Israel has lacked a formal security guarantee with any other country."

A third neorealist consideration countering the need for an indigenous nuclear deterrent has less to do with U.S. supply of protection and more with its supply of coercion. Even as bilateral relations thawed in the 1960s, the United States pressured Israel for information on its nuclear reactor, forcing it to accept annual inspections of Dimona in order to reassure Nasser. President Kennedy clearly warned that Israel's nuclearization would have grave consequences for U.S.-Israeli relations and applied unrelenting pressure on Ben-Gurion, until the day he resigned, and on Eshkol, immediately after he assumed the premiership.[22] The United States also warned Eshkol not to link his response to Kennedy to a previous request by Ben-Gurion for a security guarantee, which Kennedy in any event rejected while repeatedly demanding that Israel sign the NPT (Shalom 1996:18–19). These pressures subsided, and inspections were discontinued in 1969 after a meeting between President Nixon and Premier Golda Meir (Dowty 1998). All U.S. bilateral cooperation with Israel on peaceful uses of nuclear energy ceased by 1975, but the United States arguably refrained from applying further pressure on Israel as long as other WMD programs in the region continued unabated. On this issue U.S. policy was not much different from that applied to Pakistan, India, and other nuclear programs where alternative considerations trumped nonproliferation policy (Gavin 2004–05). This was particularly the case under Nixon, at least until 1974. A declassified document from the Reagan administration reveals the issuing of export licenses for controlled nuclear technology to India, Israel, Argentina, and South Africa, although all refused to open facilities to international inspections at the time.[23]

A final neorealist argument countering the need for Israel's nuclear weapons points to conventional deterrence, which has in fact been the centerpiece of Israel's strategy (Freedman 1975; Yaniv 1987; Rabin 1993). However, as previous citations suggest, Ben-Gurion and others doubted that conventional superiority could last for long (see later discussion of domestic debates). First, there was the experience of conventional arms embargos, beginning with the U.N. embargo that forced Israel to fight its independence war with weapons supplied by Czechoslovakia with Soviet approval. That relationship ended in 1951. In 1967, France and the U.N. suspended military shipments to Israel. During the 1973 surprise attack by Egypt and Syria, the United States withheld military supplies. Second, a 1955 Soviet agreement tripled Egypt's military strength virtually overnight, just as Ben-Gurion was grappling with the nuclear question (Brecher 1972:42–43). The conventional balance in the mid-1950s favored Arab countries by twenty-five to one in troops and by three to one in military equipment (Normark et al. 2005:16). Massive Soviet military assistance to Arab states continued until 1989. Third, the United States began providing supplies of aircraft and tanks to Israel in the 1960s, but Kissinger withheld military supplies in the midst of Israeli efforts to repel the 1973 surprise attack.[24] Fourth, supplies of advanced military equipment to Egypt, Syria, and Saudi Arabia added to skepticism about sole reliance on conventional deterrence. Fifth, unlike Israel, most of its adversaries were blessed with abundant oil resources that could fund conventional modernization, leading to arms races that Israel could arguably only lose (Reiss 1988:143). Sixth, continued transfers of WMD, including nuclear and missile technologies in some instances to Iraq, Iran, Libya, Syria, Saudi Arabia, and others from such sources as Pakistan, China, and North Korea, fueled uncertainty about unexpected shifts in power balances. Saddam's 1991 missile attacks added to perceptions of declining conventional deterrence, enhanced vulnerability, and fears of abandonment, fueling arguments favoring nuclear deterrence. Seventh, Moshe Dayan and Shimon Peres initially thought that nuclear deterrence could provide the proverbial "more bang for the buck," thereby reducing conventional expenditures (Yaniv 1987; Evron 1991). Others, such as Galili and Allon, warned against a program that would siphon off resources from conventional weapons, making Israel more vulnerable.

The foregoing discussion suggests, as with other cases in this book, that balance-of-power considerations could lead to a wide range of outcomes: developing nuclear weapons as the ultimate self-help guarantee, revealing or hiding nuclear deterrent capabilities or withholding formal acknow-ledgment, avoiding nuclear weapons to preclude region-wide nuclear arms races that might leave Israel less secure and undermine relations with Western allies, and various other possibilities (Reiss 1988; Harkavy 1977a). Indeed, signing the NPT while developing nuclear options or weapons was another alternative in principle, practiced by Iraq, Libya, North Korea, and Iran. Furthermore, the NPT's opt-out prerogative in Article X was available, was used by North Korea, and was threatened to be used by Iran. The same structural vulnerability thus led to multiple op-erational prescriptions, an open-ended set. In the final analysis, decisions regarding nuclear weapons had to come to terms with both external and domestic considerations, which together explain the outcome: an ambigu-ous, never formally acknowledged nuclear program. Ambiguity (or the Hebrew expression "amimut") circumvented adverse U.S. and European reactions, which an overt deterrent might have unleashed, while insi-nuated a last-resort deterrent against overwhelming attacks by Soviet-backed Arab states (Dowty 1978; Beres 1986; Yaniv 1987; Evron 1991). Ambiguity also partially alleviated *domestic* pressures on neighboring states to match Israeli capabilities. Whether or not ambiguity thwarted es-calation and reciprocal WMD pursuits throughout the region remains an open question, although nuclear programs in Iraq, Iran, and Libya had independent rationales as well, as discussed throughout part 3. Nonethe-less, decisions favoring both nuclearization and ambiguity also had deep sources in other domains not reducible to elusive balance-of-power con-siderations.

INSTITUTIONAL SOLUTIONS? FROM U.N. AUTOMATIC MAJORITIES TO REGIONAL ALTERNATIVES

Soon after the 1967 war the conclusion of the 1968 NPT presented Israel with difficult choices. Rusk and other U.S. officials explicitly urged Israel to sign the NPT and implicitly linked delivery of F-4 Phantom fighters to NPT acceptance. As deputy premier, Allon reassured Rusk that Israel had no nuclear weapons and "would not be the first to introduce them" into the region, adding that Israel had not signed the NPT because it wanted to keep Egypt guessing about Israel's capabilities, and that it would sign "sooner or later." [25] Rusk also impressed on Foreign Minister Abba Eban that the nuclear issue affected the "fundamental relationship" between the two countries. Eban, a classic "dove," responded that there had not been a decision *not* to join the NPT up to that point, suggesting ongoing internal debate within the Israeli government. Meanwhile, the U.S. ambassador cautioned a high official in Israel's Foreign Ministry that their government should "not underestimate [the] depth of feeling on NPT at all levels [of the] [U.S. government]."[26] In November 1968, Israel conveyed to President Johnson that, given its unique security needs, it could not sign the NPT at that time (NTIW). Following the 1969 Nixon-Meir meeting, pressures to sign subsided.

Unlike Libya, Iraq, North Korea, and arguably Iran—which had signed and ratified the NPT but were later found by the IAEA to have dishonored their commitments—Israel never became an NPT member and was not legally bound by its tenets. Why did Israel abstain from joining the NPT? Non-membership arguably provided it with greater relative legal freedom to pursue nuclear weapons in the absence of a superpower protective umbrella. Even staunch *opponents* of a nuclear deterrent, however, were not strong advocates of the NPT, partly because of the U.N.'s long record of automatic—largely non-aligned and pro-Soviet—majorities endorsing anti-Israel positions advanced by Arab or Muslim blocs regardless of substantive merit.[27] Events leading to the 1967 war illustrated why Israel perceived a U.N. bias and why it did not trust the U.N. to prevent war more generally. Egypt's president Gamal Abdul Nasser closed the international waters of the Straits of Tiran to Israeli passage unilaterally in May 1967, called for removing U.N. peacekeepers from Sinai, and, in coordination with Syria and Jordan, amassed troops on Israel's borders (Reiss 1988). Secretary-General U Thant removed U.N. peacekeepers without delay, facilitating the outbreak of war.[28] As Quandt (1996:13) argues, it was Nasser who "took the initiative to turn a relatively quiescent front of the Arab-Israeli conflict into a battlefield." The Six-Day War preceded, and indeed led to, Israel's occupation of the West Bank and Gaza.

In 1974, Israel was expelled from UNESCO. Perceptions of existential viability were shaken further by the 1975 U.N. resolution equating Zionism—the basis for Israel's existence and its 1947 U.N. initial recognition—with "racism." The resolution was favored by seventy-two states and opposed by thirty-five (thirty-two abstained). From Israel's standpoint, U.N. antagonism rarely differentiated among successive governments with different proclivities, whereas habitual U.N. majorities sheltered Arab regimes from condemnation for massive human rights violations, including use of chemical weapons by three Arab states. Furthermore, as Reiss (1988:151) argues, "Israel had cause to doubt the impartiality of the IAEA," on whose board of governors it could have never gotten a seat, because members were elected by region. There were also concerns regarding NPT members who presumably sought access to civilian technology in order to bolster secret programs with military potential, such as Libya and Iraq (Freier 1985), concerns that proved accurate. IAEA failures to uncover and curtail illegal nuclear activities by Iraq, Iran, and Libya, particularly prior to the 1990s, also deepened universal concerns with the NPT. Furthermore, Libya, Iraq, Iran, Syria, and Egypt were believed to have chemical weapons (Cordesman 2004). Israel, Egypt, Lebanon, and Syria signed the Chemical Weapons Convention (CWC) but did not ratify it. U.N. experts confirmed that Iraq had biological warheads attached to Scud missiles during the 1991 Gulf War, which might have been used against Israel (Saddam had threatened to destroy "half of Israel" with chemical weapons in 1990).[29] Finally, Article X's opt-out option allowed NPT members to defect after acquiring nuclear weapons (Freier 1985).

As an alternative to the NPT, Israel began endorsing an NWFZ proposal that was first submitted to the UNGA by Egypt and Iran in 1974. A regionally based inspections regime was considered the best road to a NWFZ that could provide stronger guarantees against widely acknowledged NPT deficiencies. In 1980, Israel submitted a NWFZ proposal at the UNGA that did not require prior accession to the NPT. Arab states, however, balked at direct negotiations on a NWFZ that might imply recognition of Israel's existence.[30] With the Oslo peace process in the early 1990s, the Yitzhak Rabin government engaged Israel more seriously in the Multilateral Middle East Peace Process sponsored by major powers (1993–95). The Arms Control and Regional Security (ACRS) group held several plenary meetings and workshops on verification, onsite inspections, and declaratory confidence-building measures. Participants in the conceptual working group approved a "Declaration of Principles" on peace and security, including alternative versions of a future WMD-free zone.[31] Egypt demanded that WMDs be discussed at the outset and that Israel accede to the NPT immediately. Israel insisted that progress on broader security issues must precede NPT discussions, and it proposed regional alternatives particularly as outstanding nuclear aspirants—Iraq, Iran, and Libya among others—refused to participate in the multilateral process. Egypt's demands for Israel's immediate NPT accession were thus seen as politically prohibitive for the Labor-led coalition that had spearheaded the Oslo process with Palestinian partners.

Israel's position can be gleaned from its formal statement to the U.N. Disarmament Conference, where it welcomed ACRS as

> an essential pillar to support the peace process as a whole and an integral part of it. In this respect, the Middle East could certainly learn from the experiences of other regions—Europe, Latin America, Africa and the Pacific—where genuine efforts on the regional level have created mutually beneficial regional security frameworks. . . . Progress should be sought wherever and whenever possible—and its pace should be determined by conditions prevailing in the region. After peaceful relations and reconciliation are established among all states in the region,

Israel will endeavor to establish in the Middle East—through direct negotiations among all its members—a zone free of chemical, biological and nuclear weapons, as well as ballistic missiles, based on mutual and effective verification. No other fora . . . can bring about meaningful progress in realizing such an ambitious arms control agenda.[32]

In a region with significantly lower security threats—Latin America's Southern Cone—Argentina and Brazil reached a regionally based mutual inspections regime in the 1990s after decades of rejecting the NPT. This experience was observed with considerable interest in Israel and strengthened its position favoring mutual inspections in a region with far higher levels of mistrust and WMD activities than South America's.[33]

In early 1995, Egypt transferred the ACRS debate to the NPT Review and Extension Conference. To address Egypt's concerns, Premier Peres declared in late 1995 that Israel would endorse regional denuclearization two years after a comprehensive peace settlement was signed, stating publicly, "Give me peace, and we will give up the atom. That's the whole story. If we achieve regional peace, I think we can make the Middle East free of any nuclear threat."[34] This declaration was well received in Egypt, as Foreign Minister Ehud Barak learned during a visit to Cairo.[35] Israel sought to reassure ACRS participants that whatever capabilities Israel had were not meant as a threat to them but were instead a deterrent against non-ACRS third parties. Some Arab representatives, however, found it unacceptable to proceed with arms control while implicitly accepting Israel's continued nuclear ambiguity. Such recognition was politically untenable for Arab parties both domestically and from a bargaining standpoint, as it arguably removed Arab threats to Israel but not vice versa (Toukan 1997; Sayed 1997; Jones 1997a). In late 1995, Egypt suspended a scheduled ACRS meeting, alleging Israel's intractable position. As will be discussed in chapter 11, the Egyptian government was perceived to be responding to its own domestic demands to denuclearize Israel and to retain Egypt's leadership in the Arab world. ACRS unraveled as the one regional institutional framework with incipient potential for addressing collective-action problems in this difficult security arena.

In sum, Israel's behavior seems less consistent with a normative taboo against nuclear acquisition and more consistent with a neoliberal institutionalist logic that states would abstain from joining institutions unable or unwilling to monitor adequately other states' compliance, and hence likely to detract from their own security (Freier 1985). Israel's U.N. isolation over many decades also played a counterproductive role in nuclear decisions insofar as it arguably weakened domestic forces that may have considered denuclearization better in the longer run but found the U.N. not to be a dependable international mechanism.[36] To be sure, concerns with Soviet and Arab threats in the absence of external security guarantees might have remained. Nonetheless the NPT and demands for transparency certainly created significant pressures on Israeli leaders who, at least partly for domestic reasons explored later, had developed the compromise of nuclear ambiguity. Notably, Premier Eshkol's policies in 1966 arguably reined in a bureaucratically independent nuclear program, and those efforts preceded the NPT's conclusion in 1968.

DOMESTIC POLITICS: HOME ADVANTAGES OF "AMBIGUITY"?

Israel's domestic politics offer a critical window into nuclear decisions.[37] Coalitions led by the largest party—Mapai (Israel's Workers' Party)—and excluding the Communist Party and the right-wing Herut, prevailed for nearly three decades after independence. Ben-Gurion's slogan regarding coalitions was "No deals with Herut or the Communists" (Peres 1979:31). Despite common socialist platforms, significant differences existed across factions on domestic, guns-versus-butter, and foreign policy issues. The new state acquired extensive economic controls and promoted import-substitution but also depended on foreign capital and agricultural exports.[38] A small group centered around Ben-Gurion embodied *Mamlachtiut* (statism) and presumed autonomy from "sectarian" social forces and was also responsible for steering the nuclear program in the late 1950s and 1960s (Harkavy 1977a; Feldman 1982; Beres 1986; Aronson 1992). Ben-Gurion had to contend with the fragile nature of ruling coalitions where no single party could command a clear majority of popular votes. He would raise his frustration with Israel's electoral system (proportional representation) and its divisive features even amidst discussions of external threats to Israel's survival (Cohen 1998:42).

The coalitions' heterogeneity and the democratic institutions within which they operated rendered Ben-Gurion's model of political survival somewhat of a hybrid. On the one hand, state entrepreneurship (statism) and import-substitution were dominant in the 1950s and early 1960s, during the early stages of the nuclear program. Furthermore, Israel's founding fathers pivoted their platforms on explicit socialist principles that kept markets and private enterprise at arm's length. International market and institutional conditions, including widespread protectionism, were not as conducive to export-led models as they would become decades later. An emphasis on self-reliance was thus compatible with the economic foundations of Ben-Gurion's model, the fresh memory of the Holocaust, and the development of a military-industrial-complex after the 1948 war. As a country bereft of oil and water, Ben-Gurion regarded nuclear energy as a solution to both, providing electricity and desalinated water (Peres 1995:132). On the other hand, given Israel's minute size and small domestic market, external dependence was a given (Razin and Sadka 1993). The model thus relied on as much external aid and access to other international resources as was possible at the time. These were in limited supply, and Israel's desires for U.S. guarantees were rebuffed (Reiss 1988; Dunn 1998). Nor did Ben-Gurion expect them from the U.N. (Brecher 1972:139). The ruling coalition's political survival during those years thus hinged on the ability to provide both fail-safe assurances against external threats and adequate welfare for a population that included survivors of concentration camps and refugees from Arab states. Yet different factions translated the overall mission of providing both guns and butter into disparate policies that reflected alternative trade-offs between economic self-reliance and dependence, conventional and nuclear deterrence, and domestic versus external guarantees of survival.

Ben-Gurion and his followers, particularly Dayan and Peres, strongly advocated and steered the initial development of Israel's nuclear program under secrecy, avoiding discussions in full cabinet meetings to protect the program from opponents. Peres (1979:129) describes opponents as advocates of a "realistic" approach (not to be confused with a neorealist one, in the sense used in international relations theory), who argued that atomic energy was an idea, perhaps a hope in a distant future, but that realities of the moment—buying wheat and rice, in the words of a Knesset member—demanded that resources for technological dreams not be squandered. In addition, this group maintained, Israel had no scientific, administrative, or financial capacity to enter a field reserved for "the greatest of the world's nations," and that the great powers would "never forgive us if we try to embark on a programme that is beyond our capability as a small people," statements that Peres recalls were often heard in the Knesset. Furthermore, the finance minister (Eshkol) argued, "In Israel we are rationing eggs to one a week—and these people want atomic energy," presumably alluding to Ben-Gurion's group.

Leading Mapai cabinet members opposed Ben-Gurion's nuclear activities, including Finance Minister Eshkol, Foreign Minister Meir, Defense Minister Pinhas Lavon, Commerce Minister Pinhas Sapir, and Ambassador Eban (Pry 1984; Yaniv 1987; Raviv and Melman 1990; Peres 1995). Meir and Mossad chief Isser Harel were fuming at Peres for endangering relations with the United States when they thought a Soviet satellite had detected Dimona. Peres (1995:138–40) recounts this event as one time, among various others, when "our nuclear project was in danger of premature termination." Meir thought Israel should inform the United States of Dimona, pointing to its peaceful purpose while leaving room for future options (Karpin 2006). Leftist coalition partners Mapam and Ahdut-Ha'avoda enjoyed a strong base in the General Federation of

Labor (Histadrut), which Ben-Gurion attacked as a "state within a state" that challenged Mamlachtiut.[39] Ahdut-Ha'avoda and Mapam leaders, including Allon, Gallili, Meir Ya'ari, Yaacov Hazan, and Yair Zaban criticized the nuclear program. "If our hypothetical choice would be between a symmetrical ownership of nuclear weapons and a symmetrical absence of such weapons, *our choice should be a conventional balance over a nuclear one*," Allon (1990:91) argued.[40] The two parties—particularly Mapam, with its significant pro-Soviet constituencies—also opposed Ben-Gurion's efforts to seek treaties with the United States or NATO, and Peres's initiatives to obtain French and West German technical and defense cooperation. Popular opposition to closer relations (particularly military cooperation) with West Germany ignited cabinet crises and the fall of the government in 1957 over a proposed visit by Dayan to Germany. There were also sharp debates in 1963 in connection with German scientists' presumed participation in Egypt's development of missiles, and chemical and bacteriological weapons.

Prominent Israeli scientists opposed the nuclear program on various grounds. Six out of seven IAEC members resigned in 1957 arguably due to the opportunity costs of nuclear activities for advancing basic research, leaving only Ernst David Bergmann, founder of Israel Defense Forces (IDF) Science Corps (Hemed) and Ben-Gurion's principal nuclear advisor (Dowty 1978; Steinberg 1994). According to Peres (1979:126–27), Bergmann attracted unwarranted criticism from his fellow scientists because of his strong association with defense and his promotion of what they regarded as impractical and extremely costly projects (of which Dimona was only one). A distinguished scientist wrote a letter to Peres (1979:129–30) pointing out, in the context of nuclear energy, that under Israel's "present circumstances it is not within our power to solve this problem." The reference was a reaction to Bergmann's insistence on self-sufficiency, including building an indigenous Israeli nuclear reactor. In the matter of armaments, Peres recalls (1979:132), Bergmann insisted that Israel was capable of meeting almost all her needs, and "of developing within the country technological assets preferable to anything that could be imported from abroad. . . . Independence would not be just a new declaration, but a new reality." Other scientists decried wasteful, expensive, "futile and unproductive adventures" over pragmatic reliance on science and technology developed elsewhere (Peres 1979:130). Even defense experts reportedly mistrusted Bergmann's futuristic schemes, but Peres believed that much of the opposition to Bergmann stemmed from "the fact that in many cases he has been right, *and the only one who has been right*" (Peres 1979:127; emphasis in the original).

The IDF itself was kept at arm's length in the program's early stages. Ben-Gurion separated nuclear funding from the defense budget to avoid

IDF perceptions of competition for resources. Private funding for the nuclear program also enabled Ben-Gurion and his allies to keep opponents—particularly within the cabinet—largely uninformed.[41] Neither the Knesset's Foreign Affairs and Security or Finance committees were asked to approve nuclear activities, which were under the exclusive jurisdiction of a new intelligence agency (Lakam) that was separate from the official intelligence community (Bar-Joseph 1982; Raviv and Melman 1990). Given disagreements on conventional versus nuclear deterrence, and the conception of the latter as a last resort, military budgets had to accommodate both. Butter would thus compete heavily with guns, deepening cleavages among cabinet factions and increasing the overall tax burden of the Israeli public.

The nuclear program also became tangentially embroiled with the "Lavon affair," which began with a botched covert operation in Egypt in 1954 that pitted Ben-Gurion, Dayan, and Peres against Defense Minister Lavon and his supporters.[42] Lavon had been forced to resign and absorb the blame for the operation, but a 1960 disclosure later revealed his innocence. Ben-Gurion refused to exonerate him and resigned when a ministerial committee vindicated Lavon, but returned soon thereafter to face additional internal challenges regarding Dimona. The affair cost Mapai a few seats in the 1961 elections. A prominent former Mapai legislator, Eliezer Livne, soon thereafter founded the Committee for Denuclearization of the Middle East with prestigious Israeli scientists and wide access to high-level Labor and opposition figures. Mapam adopted the committee's program—which urged a nuclear-free Middle East and invoked international guarantees—in its official platform. Although Ben-Gurion's influence over nuclear policy had declined somewhat, antagonism on the nuclear issue remained. Furthermore, the competition between conventional defense and the nuclear program was becoming more evident. According to Allon (1990:305), an IDF budget request for a new armored brigade nearly lost out to "the acceleration of important scientific research," most likely the nuclear program.[43] Ben-Gurion resigned in 1963, discredited and isolated, amidst the legacy of the Lavon affair, debates over relations with West Germany, and unrelenting pressure from President Kennedy regarding Israel's nuclear program.

Soon after becoming premier, Eshkol found himself under severe pressure from Kennedy, who threatened that U.S. support for Israel "could be seriously jeopardized" if U.S. inspections were not allowed in Dimona (Shalom 1996:15; Karpin 2006:232–33). The United States was not yet a major provider of economic support, military aid, or security guarantees, but the cabinet took the threat seriously.[44] There were even proposals to cancel the project, although Peres (1979:67) suggests that Eshkol "stood by us," presumably implying that Eshkol sided with those supporting the project. Although Eshkol had previously challenged nuclear activities, the program had now reached maturity, and he inherited the path-dependent consequences—international and domestic, political, economic, and bureaucratic—of Ben-Gurion's choices. Furthermore, Eshkol was still heavily constrained by Ben-Gurion—who was perceived as ruling from "exile" in his Kibbutz, Sdeh Boker—and by his cabinet and bureaucratic allies (Karpin 2006:239–40). Eshkol was saddled with squaring the circle. He suggested at a crucial cabinet meeting that Israel respond to Kennedy by acknowledging the separation plant while proposing not to do anything with it for a period of up to three years if the United States could provide security guarantees.[45] Dayan immediately opposed that suggestion, and Eshkol, a consummate consensus-seeker, crafted a letter to Kennedy that accepted inspections on Dimona once the French handed the reactor over to Israel, as demanded, but left the timetable for future visits open for subsequent discussion (Shalom 1996:19–20; Cohen 1998; Karpin 2006:239). In one of his first steps as premier, Eshkol signed the Partial Test Ban Treaty (PTBT) in 1963 immediately after its conclusion, conveying Israel's support for banning nuclear tests as well as countering PTBT opponents at home. Eshkol's rift with Ben-Gurion deepened in 1964 when Mapai allowed Lavon's return to the party, and Eshkol gravitated toward Mapai-Ahdut Ha'avoda unification.

Ben-Gurion and his followers left Mapai before the 1965 elections to create Rafi (Israel's Workers List), which some labeled "the atomic party." Rafi's platform emphasized "independence in security affairs" and rejection of "any form of international inspection to which other countries of the world are not submitted" (Brecher 1972:181). Ben-Gurion used a report on U.S. visits to Dimona to undermine Eshkol's fitness as a leader, which right-wing parties echoed with nationalist concerns about sovereignty.[46] Rafi loyalists depicted Ben-Gurion as a staunch protector of the nuclear program against Kennedy's requests for inspections of what were, after all, French-supplied facilities, in contrast to a "weak" Eshkol, who had "given in."[47] In turn, Lavon, close to Ahdut Ha'avoda and Mapam, ridiculed Rafi leaders as self-appointed "defense avant-garde," and Allon (1990) accused Rafi of "defense demagoguery." A declassified U.S. document cites Eshkol and "his associates" as "notably close-mouthed, pleading, at times, the sensitivity of this [nuclear] issue in Israel's domestic politics."[48] Mapai-Ahdut Ha'avoda's 1965 electoral victory forced Dayan and Peres into the opposition, removing their control over the nuclear program. In 1966, Eshkol accepted Rafi supporter Bergmann's resignation from the IAEC, reduced the IAEC's autonomy, transferred it from the Ministry of Defense to the premier's office, assumed IAEC's chairmanship, and broadened its composition to include the Finance Ministry and civilian sectors in energy, medical, and agricultural research. This reshuffling and diversification diluted the IAEC's erstwhile narrow military outlook and arguably helped "freeze" Dimona's pace at that time (Dowty 1978; Inbar 1986; Flapan 1974; Pry 1984; Raviv and Melman 1990; Steinberg 1994).

It should be noted that Eshkol's steps preceded the NPT's conclusion and were embedded in a broader blueprint for a new political economy with attending domestic, regional, and international consequences. Eshkol's (1965:76) motto was, "Our military wherewithal is contingent on our economy." As finance minister (1952–63), Eshkol presided over economic growth rates of 10 percent annually, but by the mid-1960s a serious recession in Israel's statist economy deepened unemployment to about 15 percent in 1966. The crisis was of such historic proportions that old political bargains became overly strained. As premier, Eshkol worked with Finance, Commerce, and Industry Minister Yoseph Sapir (who had sharp reservations over Ben-Gurion's nuclear policy) to launch a new economic model. The model was designed to overcome Israel's serious crises of import-substitution, trade, and payments imbalances by promoting export-led and high-tech industrialization, foreign investment, and privatization. This strategy involved higher levels of dependence on foreign capital under much more restrictive conditions than those that had characterized earlier discretionary capital inflows. As Barnett (1992:233) argued, at the time Israel became "more beholden to foreign actors to stabilize its financial life." Eshkol's model also involved higher levels of political dependence on prospective suppliers, investors, and markets, primarily the United States, and Eshkol also sought accommodation with France, Germany, the Soviet Union, and China. A 1968 U.S. NIE mentioned how Israel's strong orientation toward internal consumption hindered exports and described Eshkol's efforts to expand exports and control inflation.[49] Eshkol, whose chief advisors included Allon and Galili, was extremely uncomfortable with misleading the United States and endangering this nascent strategy by antagonizing Western powers.[50] Furthermore, Eshkol challenged nuclear expenditures on the basis of cost considerations; he named economist Tzvi Dinstein as deputy defense minister to rationalize all military R&D (including the nuclear program); and Yitzhak Rabin—an Allon protégé—as chief of staff.

The account thus far makes clear that nuclear ambiguity had been an equilibrium solution at the outset and, once the program became a reality, remained a compromise that avoided risky international responses and domestic disagreements. In 1968, Eshkol—widely known as a compromiser par excellence (Peres 1979)—and Allon acknowledged that Israel had acquired the know-how to produce nuclear weapons but not the weapons themselves. The formulation that Israel would "not be the first to introduce nuclear weapons to the Middle East" became a Delphic statement with various meanings. In the words of a director-general of the IAEC—Shalhevet Freier—this formulation had the advantage of providing reassurance to some Israelis "in times of gloom" without compelling the government to take a definitive stand on the matter.[51] While implementing a policy that he favored for domestic reasons, Eshkol also hoped that his model would make the United States more receptive to supplying Israel with conventional arms. In exchange for a commitment not to introduce nuclear weapons, the Johnson administration supplied aircraft and tanks, inaugurating closer U.S.-Israel relations. For Eshkol—the compromiser—ambiguity would also provide an optimal domestic compromise regarding policy vis-à-vis Arab neighbors, Egypt in particular. Whereas some thought Nasser should be reassured that Israel had no nuclear weapons to avoid potential preemptive attacks by Egypt, others favored "keeping Egypt guessing."[52] Eshkol, Sapir, and Eban gravitated toward removing Egypt's concerns, but not Meir (Shalom 1996:3; Cohen 1998:239, 405). Eshkol repeatedly emphasized that Middle East nuclearization was not in Israel's interest. He also tried to resolve the crisis preceding the Six-Day War through diplomacy, which invited harsh attacks of "indecisiveness" from Ben-Gurion and his allies (Peres 1979). Eshkol was forced to cede the Defense Ministry back to Dayan, who led the IDF through the war. A complementary aspect of Eshkol's stillborn new model was an immediate effort to reach an agreement with the Palestinians and King Hussein, and promote regional stability and economic transformation. Alas, an ailing Eshkol died in 1968.

In 1969 Rafi merged with Mapai into the Labor alignment. By that time, supporters of an open deterrent had become marginalized. The policy of ambiguity was further "institutionalized" at the 1969 Nixon-Meir meeting. As was clear from the Nixon-Sato meeting, recounted in chapter 3, and from a private National Security Council memorandum, Nixon's broader policy was to avoid pressing allies to join and ratify the NPT.[53] Nixon allegedly promised that the United States would cease its pressure on Israel if Meir pledged "nuclear restraint," defined as no testing, no acknowledgment, and no display of nuclear weapons.[54] Nixon also rejected the proposal to link the sale of F-4s (Phantom) aircraft with Israeli nuclear concessions. In early 1970, Rabin informed the United States that Israel would not sign the NPT in light of the Nixon-Meir understanding. The commitment neither to test nor declare nuclear capabilities pushed those who favored either tests or a declared deterrent beyond the boundaries of consensus. Dayan's occasional references to advantages of open deterrence were not dominant in Golda Meir's cabinet even under the difficult Yom Kippur surprise attack by Egypt and Syria in 1973.[55] In 1974 Rabin declared, in response to Dayan's call for nuclear weapons, that "attempts to rely on mystical weapons are negative trends" (Inbar 1986:64).

President Efraim Katzir declared in December 1974 that "it has always been our intention to provide the potential for nuclear weapons development. We now have the capabilities, we have the potential and we'll defend this country with all means at hand."[56] Rabin reiterated that Israel was not a nuclear power, would not be the first to introduce nuclear weapons into the region, and would cope with all threats with conventional weapons. In 1975, Foreign Minister Allon formally endorsed the NWFZ proposal submitted to the UNGA with considerable support from most political leaders (Karem 1988; Freier 1985).

Dayan eventually joined Labor's competitor Likud and served as its foreign minister. Likud and its predecessors were in the opposition since independence until Premier Menachem Begin assumed power in 1977. Likud supported free-enterprise liberalism in Israel's early years but later became susceptible to populist demands from protectionist and nationalist economic interests, including segments of small business, blue-collar and underemployed workers, development towns, West Bank and Gaza settlers, and orthodox religious and nationalist constituencies. These groups often dismissed international institutions, mistrusted territorial compromise with Palestinians, and advocated self-reliance as a core theme.[57] Begin's government made the strategic decision to bomb Iraq's Osiraq reactor, three weeks before Israel's general elections and with Likud lagging in the polls (Perlmutter, Handel, and Bar-Joseph 1982:80–81; Inbar 1991:105). Significantly, Begin reportedly overruled the chiefs of Mossad and Military Intelligence (Hersh 1993) as well as important Labor leaders such as Peres who, sensitive to potential responses by international allies and institutions, sought more time for diplomacy. Influential Likud ministers—Ariel Sharon and Rafel Eitan—reportedly opposed an NWFZ at the time.[58] Sharon was traditionally associated with conventional deterrence but later declared that "Israel cannot cope with the conventional arms race with the Arabs who have superiority in manpower and capital."[59] This statement echoed statements by Dayan. Breaking the secrecy mold, Dayan as foreign minister acknowledged in 1981 that Israel had "the capacity" to build the bomb "in a short time."[60]

Labor-led coalitions in the 1980s attracted support from the secular urban professional and middle-class, high-tech industrialists, highly skilled labor, and export-oriented cooperative agriculture. Labor's Shimon Peres designed and implemented economic reform and currency stabilization in the mid-1980s in the context of a national unity government with Likud. The Labor-Meretz coalition headed by Rabin, which assumed power in 1992, emphasized territorial compromise, economic reform and competitiveness, international institutions, the global economy, and the futility of technological fixes as solutions to Israel's security dilemma (Klieman and Pedatzur 1991). The Rabin coalition signed the CWC in 1993 and negotiated the Oslo Accords and the September 1993 Declaration of Principles recognizing the PLO. Rewarding the Rabin government for its more flexible positions the United States approved $10 billion in loan guarantees for investments in infrastructure and jobs. Labor's flexibility on security issues was not externally imposed but advanced in its own terms as part of a model of political survival emphasizing Israel's internationalization, echoing some of Eshkol's forgotten themes. The inability of the preceding (Likud) government to prevent Iraqi Scud missiles from landing on Tel Aviv—or the Negev desert, where Dimona is situated—in 1991 had increased popular receptivity to political rather than technical solutions to Israel's security quandary. This new model was reflected in Israel's positions at the multilateral negotiations described earlier, including ACRS. As head of Israel's delegation to the steering committee for these negotiations, Yossi Beilin (1993: 5) revealed the philosophical foundations of this model in December 1993: "As we achieve the status of a region free from nuclear weapons and remove the threat of weapons of mass destruction, we will re-orient our interests as we strengthen our ties to the world around us." In late 1995, Peres declared that Israel would endorse regional denuclearization following a comprehensive peace settlement, at a very fragile political moment domestically when his opponents attacked the Oslo process and a Jewish extremist opposed to concessions assassinated Premier Rabin. Peres's adversaries warned against outstanding unconventional threats from Iraq, Iran, Syria, and Libya, none of whom had joined the multilateral process.[61] ACRS's moderate achievements stalled completely when Egypt pressed for immediate further concessions from a weakened Labor-Meretz coalition.

In early 1996, radical Islamist terrorist attacks on Israeli civilians succeeded in bringing about the demise of this coalition and the election of hard-line Likud competitor Binyamin Netanyahu. Opposition to compromise with the Palestinians remained Netanyahu's coalition's most valued preference, even when unrest exacerbated a slowdown in foreign investment and global economic and diplomatic access at that time. Likud played the populist card to retain constituencies and coalitional partners (such as Shas) opposed to economic liberalization and, no less importantly, to potential economic consequences of peace with Arab neighbors.[62] A new Labor-led coalition, headed by Ehud Barak, assumed power in 1999, seeking to breathe new life into the multilateral process. In 2000 the Knesset held its first public discussion of Israel's nuclear program in more than thirty-five years, following an Arab Knesset member's petition to the Supreme Court. Labor Minister Chaim Ramon declared that "Israel supports the creation of a region free of nuclear weapons and ballistic missiles once there is a 'proven peace over a sustained period of time.' "[63] A new *intifada* in 2000 decimated the Oslo coalition politically.

Sharon's Likud-led coalition confronted several international crises related to nuclear proliferation. First, Saddam's threats in the early 2000s revived memories of the Scud missiles that Iraq had showered on Israel in 1991 and the potential for fitting them with chemical warheads. Second, Sharon warned that Libya was trying to acquire nuclear weapons and might be the first Arab country to attain them.[64] Based on the interception of nuclear equipment headed for Libya and the transfer of bomb designs by the A. Q. Khan network, former chief of intelligence Danny Yatom expressed that Libya could have produced a bomb before Iran.[65] Third, the IAEA uncovered nuclear activities that Iran had failed to report, unleashing another international nuclear crisis with direct consequences for Israel (see chapter 8). Fourth, the North Korean nuclear crisis had important repercussions on Iran and Israel's nuclear status. As discussed in chapter 6, North Korea supplied missiles and related technology to Iran and other Middle East states. Responding to this conundrum, Sharon's statements ranged from asserting that Iran's nuclear program was "the biggest threat to the existence of Israel" and warning that "Israel will not allow Iran to be equipped with a nuclear weapon" to suggestions during a Likud party meeting that "one day when we arrive at a comprehensive peace and everyone disarms completely, we will also be ready to consider taking steps."[66] An Israeli official also quoted Sharon as affirming that "Israel has no intention of attacking Iran and continues to support the diplomatic efforts of the international community."[67] Defense Minister Shaul Mofaz expressed that diplomacy was the correct path with Iran, asserting that a military strike was not on the agenda.[68] In 2005, Sharon engineered a unilateral withdrawal from Gaza, leading some ultra-nationalists from his own party to withdraw from his government. His political future became tied to Labor, and on the nuclear issue he now appeared much closer to Peres. Sharon's high approval rate reinforced his own incentives to move toward more compromising solutions to Israel's security quandaries.

Public opinion polls provide a window into the difficulties that a policy of open nuclear deterrence might have encountered at the popular level. According to the major annual survey on security conducted by Tel Aviv University's Jaffee Center since 1984, public opinion on unconventional weapons had been remarkably dormant—effectively a non-issue—before the 1991 Gulf War. During that war, Saddam launched conventional Scud missiles into Israel after threatening to fit chemical weapons on them. Israel was not a party to the war and refrained from responding to the attack. Until 1991, when respondents were asked what major issues the government should address, nuclear weapons never came up. If asked directly on this topic, however, respondents were willing to answer (Arian 1998a). After 1991, support for nuclear secrecy declined from about 78 percent (1987) to 71 percent (1993) and 66 percent (1998) when U.N. inspectors withdrew from Iraq, raising new fears of Iraq's WMD activities vis-à-vis Israel (Arian 1998b). However, support for secrecy increased from 62 percent (2002) to 72 percent (2003) as Iraq's WMD threats ceased (Arian 2003). Only one-fifth of respondents favored open deterrence or revealing the existence of nuclear weapons.

Like surveys in most countries, these too can render ambiguous interpretations contingent on the questions asked. They also reveal great volatility regarding nuclear deterrence and, naturally, significant responsiveness to external missile attacks and verbal WMD threats. Polls must therefore be assessed with caution and due consideration to issues of validity, reliability, and timing. Furthermore, although the Israeli public is assumed to be well informed on national security issues, only 45 percent of respondents were absolutely certain that Israel was not an NPT signatory in 1995. Nearly one-fourth thought that Israel was *probably* not a signatory, and one-third thought Israel *was* an NPT member (Arian 1995). The complexities and intricacies of nuclear policy and the emergence of new threats such as those posed by Iran introduce additional elements of contingency in gauging public opinion on this issue. In 1986, almost 66 percent of respondents explicitly rejected basing Israel's security on nuclear weapons or their use, under any circumstances (Arian et al. 1988:96; Russett 1989:193; Evron 1991:81). Clearly, leaders who had either opposed nuclearization or settled for ambiguity had read the risks of a public debate on this issue quite clearly, at least up to that point in time. This 66 percent was quite close to the proportion of Japanese opposed to a nuclear-armed Japan according to the 1968 Asahi poll, whereas other polls found only 46 percent of Japanese opposing nuclear weapons (see chapter 3). This comparison has its limits because Japan, unlike Israel, was covered by the U.S. nuclear umbrella, which arguably should have lowered domestic support for an indigenous deterrent. Furthermore, although the proportion of respondents opposed to *pivoting* the country's security on nuclear weapons was roughly equivalent in both cases, it is unclear how many opposed overt, as opposed to ambiguous or virtual nuclearization, or hedging, in either case.

Following Saddam's threats to "incinerate half of Israel" with chemical weapons during the 1991 Gulf War, support for nuclear use "in principle" increased from 36 percent in 1986 to 88 percent in 1991 (Arian 1993), declining to 66 percent by 1993 when UNSCOM dismantled Iraq's WMD. In the aftermath of terrorist attacks on civilians in January 1996, however, 81 percent rejected the idea of relinquishing WMD, possibly associating suicide bombing with a strategic determination to annihilate Israel (Arian 1996). In 1998, Saddam expelled U.N. weapons inspectors from Iraqi nuclear sites, and U.S. and British forces responded with air attacks that might have triggered Saddam's retaliation on Israel, as in 1991. In the aftermath of the U.N. inspectors' expulsion, 92 percent thought Israel should *develop* nuclear weapons (declining to 82 percent in 1999). Yet over 80 percent opposed nuclear *use* even if nuclear weapons would "save many [Israeli] lives" (Arian 1998a; 1999). Some of Israel's neighbors may have read Israel's public quite accurately. Nasser's advisor Haykal acknowledged that "Israel has nuclear weapons but will not use them unless she finds herself being strangled," and the late King Hussein of Jordan declared that Israelis would not use a nuclear device "unless they were in mortal danger" (Feldman 1982:87). Among those justifying nuclear use, the precise context was in response to nuclear attack by another country or, with significantly less support, in response to gas or biological attacks. There was much lower support for nuclear use in the context of avoiding defeat in conventional war. Thus a majority was unwilling to consider nuclear use *even* if Israel was defeated in war, a prospect often depicted by radical Arab and Iranian groups as "drowning Jews in the Mediterranean sea."

Respondents revealed remarkable openness to region-wide denuclearization. In 1993, the year of the breakthrough Oslo Peace Process, 72 percent supported abandoning all WMD if others in the region did so as well. In 1994—at the height of the Oslo era—72 percent *supported the proposition that Israel should sign the NPT* (35 percent strongly supported, 37 percent supported) and only 28 percent opposed it (12 percent strongly opposed, 16 percent opposed; Arian 1998a). In 1998, nearly 82 percent supported prohibiting all sides (including Israel) from having any WMD (Arian 1998b:33). These responses seem to suggest rather strong support for denuclearization under regional conditions of mutual inspections and verifiable elimination of all unconventional weapons, the very conditions that Labor-Meretz had advanced at ACRS. However, Saddam's renewed threats during the prelude to the 2003 Gulf War forced Israelis once again into "safe rooms" and protective gear against chemical weapons.[69] Subsequently, 47 percent favored removing a threatening neighbor's nuclear capability "by any means available." Notably, however, a much lower 19 percent favored open nuclear deterrence *even if another country in the region had nuclear weapons.* Only 16 percent favored requesting U.S. protection, and 18 percent supported a Middle East NWFZ by international agreement (Arian 2003:15).

Finally, identity-based and constructivist approaches enter the analysis of Israel's nuclear policy by linking it to the Holocaust. Thayer (1995) and others regard the Holocaust as a major symbolic source of Israel's nuclear program, connecting it with "the realization that they could depend upon no other state to assist them in a time of peril," rooted in the memory of perceived inaction during the Nazi decimation of European Jewry

and the vow never to allow a repetition of the gas chambers. The Holocaust cannot be discounted as a deep-seated source in the initial development of Dimona, when Israeli leaders were building a new country
against the shadow of unspeakable tragedy and the reality of continued
calls for its destruction. Yet those links remain to be studied more systematically. Such painful memories can lead to contending positions, elic-
iting commitment to complete self-reliance in some—but not necessarily
nuclear weapons—and promotion of humanistic norms and resistance to
WMD in others (Segev 1993; Flapan 1974). Since different interpretations became part of public debates in Israel, attaching a single operational meaning to the Holocaust trauma for nuclear policy could be misleading.[70] Israel's U.N. isolation largely encouraged self-help (Reiss 1988)
and may have had a critical exacerbating effect on the program's evolution. Yet there is no systematic evidence that this sense of abandonment
invariably translated into majority support for replacing conventional deterrence with nuclear weapons. Threats of chemical attacks on Iraq's
Scud missiles during the Gulf War eerily evoked the "darkest times in
Jewish history" in some Israeli minds (Rabin 1993; Brom 1995; FASW;
NTIW). Ahmadinejad's Holocaust denials and threats to "wipe Israel off
the map" led Premier Ehud Olmert to reaffirm that Iran's regime posed
"an existential threat" to Israel.[71] Yet it is unclear whether or not such
threats will lead to dramatic changes in Israel's nuclear policy.

Conclusion

Israel's leaders have intermittently faced very real dilemmas of *state* survival as well as *domestic* political survival. Extreme vulnerability in the
1950s and 1960s—when seminal decisions were taken—make Israel an
easy case for neorealism and hence not strong ground for testing the theory. Said differently, the severe security dilemma of a state attacked by all
its neighbors upon creation, with no external security guarantees, subject
to a conventional weapons boycott and to unfavorable U.N. votes could
easily be construed as an inevitable candidate for nuclearization by theories pivoted on balance of power and self-help (Normark et al. 2005). By
contrast, a much better test for neorealist theory would be provided by a
hypothetical case where a difficult security dilemma was balanced by the
ability to rely on strong international institutional and political support
(NATO, for instance) and by a correspondingly strong domestic opposition
to nuclear weapons. Nuclearization under such conditions would have indeed suggested that *even* strong international institutions and domestic political consensus could not overwhelm the logic of balance of power and
state survival.

As with other cases in this book, however, various self-help options—nuclear and non-nuclear—appeared compatible with Israel's existential dilemmas, defying the notion of a single neorealist understanding or coherent strategic prescription regarding its nuclear choices (Reiss 1988). Given this underdetermination, Israel's ambiguous nuclear policy—as with any other outcome—can be recounted as the product of relative-power considerations. But could ambiguity have been anticipated a priori? As argued in chapter 2, concern with U.S. responses—which might explain ambiguity—failed to deter myriad other cases (including all current nuclear-weapons-states and other aspirants) from developing nuclear weapons. Furthermore, continuous U.S. support was undoubtedly of utmost concern to Israeli decision-makers but, absent this constraint, would Israeli leaders have formulated a different policy? Would ambiguity have been replaced with another policy—such as open deterrence—had Nixon rejected Meir's proposal? Perhaps not, given other regional, identity, and domestic constraints embedded in Middle East conditions that compelled ambiguity.[72]

Ambiguity preserved a modicum of domestic equilibrium in a highly divided society. One should not underestimate the difficulty of reaching domestic consensus in Israeli politics. Egyptian military expert Mohamed Said (2002:2) observed that "there is no more controversial issue in Israel than its nuclear deterrent." Ambiguity prevented a political big-bang by allowing compromises among leaders, party factions, cross-party coalitions, state agencies, and informed popular constituencies that held disparate views about the merits of nuclear deterrence, and by taming disagreements over the normative implications of nuclearization. Ambiguity enabled compromise whereas an open deterrent risked intense contestation. That was not the case in India or Pakistan, where nuclear tests received strong public approval. Ambiguity in the Israeli context also allowed divergent bureaucratic interests some modus vivendi. Many in the influential military establishment and its associated industrial complex reportedly resisted reliance on nuclear deterrence.[73] Maintaining conventional superiority was the IDF's long-standing mission. The nuclear program arguably represented an institutional threat insofar as it exacerbated budgetary competition and threatened the external network of conventional weapons procurement (high-performance combat aircraft in the 1960s) and outsourcing for locally produced equipment.[74] Yet the IDF was still required to maintain conventional deterrence and fight missions under diminished budgets and capabilities at potentially much higher human costs.

Some proponents of the relationship between democracy and international interactions, as examined in chapter 2, may find Israel's democratic nature—within 1967 borders—to have played an important role in deepening its mistrust for neighboring autocracies, perhaps linking it to the need for robust nuclear capabilities. Such tendencies would presumably be even stronger for isolated democracies surrounded by autocracies that threaten it with extinction, as was the case pointedly in the 1950s and 1960s and recurrently, more recently with Ahmadinejad's threats.[75] But such connections, not directly covered by available public opinion polls, remain subject to systematic empirical investigation. This chapter's overview does suggest that, despite secrecy, Israel's democratic politics intruded into the nuclear debate, as Ben-Gurion was well aware.[76] Coalition and party politics defined the context against which threats were received and answered. Ben-Gurion countenanced some U.S. nuclear inspections when in power but used them to encourage Eshkol's ousting when in the opposition. Leaders differed in approaches to international institutions, the merits of conventional deterrence and NWFZ, and conditions that might trigger an overt—rather than an ambiguous—nuclear posture. Yet cleavages over nuclear weapons did not reflect clear-cut party-based partisanship, except perhaps for Rafi. Publicly available evidence suggests that only a small minority across the political spectrum endorsed explicit nuclear deterrence, although some prominent politicians in this minority were associated with Likud.[77] Support for nuclear ambiguity cuts across party lines, but Labor leaders may have contemplated a regionally based NWFZ more actively than Likud leaders, considering Allon's endorsement of the 1974 NWFZ proposed to the UNGA, available public statements in the mid-1990s (by Peres and others), and positions adopted at ACRS (Karsh 2000). Eshkol's policies in the 1960s and the Labor-Meretz coalition of the early 1990s insinuated potential links among a growing orientation to international institutions and the global economy, IAEC budgetary controls and transparency, and efforts to rein in the nuclear program and dilute its centrality. The same coalition that negotiated the Oslo agreements also advanced the ACRS multilateral process that could one day provide the foundations of a NWFZ. Israel's progressive internationalization has retained nuclear ambiguity. As argued in chapter 1, the extent to which others in the region share congruent orientations toward internationalization influences domestic preferences on nuclear issues. Various Middle East leaders have retained inward-looking nationalist, or religious-based models subject to fewer domestic and international disincentives to acquire nuclear weapons.

Sharon explicitly praised the merits of ambiguity during a 2004 visit by IAEA Director El-Baradei: "Israel has to hold in its hand all the elements of power necessary to protect itself by itself. . . . Our policy of ambiguity on nuclear arms has proved its worth, and it will continue."[78] At the same time, Sharon expressed support for establishing a Middle East NWFZ if peace were achieved throughout the region and its neighbors gave up their WMD, to which El-Baradei responded, "It's not a new policy, but affirming that policy at the level of prime minister I thought to be quite a welcome development."[79] In reality, as Dowty (2005) noted, much of the ambiguity of the early years had been eroded by numerous statements of Israeli leaders, although "non-acknowledgment" remained. Whether Iran's apparent steps toward nuclearization will alter this path remains to be seen.

CHAPTER TEN

Libya

LONG-STANDING SUSPICIONS of Libya's nuclear intentions stemmed from both its declaratory statements and activities geared to obtain nuclear weapons. Beginning in 1970, Muammar Qadhafi's lieutenant Major Abdelsalam Jallud visited China repeatedly in an unsuccessful effort to purchase nuclear weapons.[1] In 1973 Libya launched a war aimed at gaining control of the Aouzou Strip in Chad, a region presumed to be rich in uranium deposits. Efforts to obtain nuclear weapons from India in exchange for paying off its entire foreign debt (estimated at $15 billion) failed (NTIW). Cooperation with Pakistan began in 1974, with Libya providing financial support and uranium "yellow cake" from Niger to Pakistan, reportedly expecting an eventual Pakistani reward in the form of nuclear weapons (Bhatia 1988:67; Spector 1990:176). Yet in 1986 Qadhafi declared to an Indian newspaper that Libya would never help Pakistan acquire atomic weapons, because "we consider nuclear weapons production a great mistake against humanity."[2] In 1981, Libya acquired a 10 MW Soviet research reactor under IAEA safeguards. By 1984, about 750 Libyan experts operated the Tajura nuclear research center with Soviet help. Libya sought to acquire additional research facilities, power plants, equipment, and nuclear training from France, Argentina, China, and India, among others (Bhatia 1988). Belgium refused to supply it with a power plant in 1984 under U.S. pressure, but Japan reportedly delivered a pilot uranium conversion facility that year.[3] Notwithstanding these efforts, Libya could not develop an indigenous program, according to Libya's leading nuclear scientist, and Qadhafi sought foreign assistance to develop nuclear weapons.[4] Libya's chief nuclear scientist acknowledged efforts to obtain nuclear weapons from the Soviets, China, India, Pakistan, France, and Argentina. Qadhafi also voiced concerns over Israel's nuclear capability, publicly expressing desire to obtain nuclear weapons, yet in interviews in 1981 and 1984 he proclaimed that Libya was only interested in peaceful applications of nuclear energy, ridiculing the idea of "an Islamic bomb."

Qadhafi's contradictory statements on nuclear issues were perhaps more extreme than in other cases, but his actions pointed toward nuclear weapons acquisition. Since efforts during the 1970s and 1980s did not yield impressive results, Libya covertly acquired thousands of gas centrifuges, machine tools to produce additional ones, and the design for a nuclear weapon in the 1990s. By 2000 it sought more sophisticated (L-2) centrifuges that would enable production of ten bombs per year from the A. Q. Khan network. Yet in 2003 Libya requested discussions with the United States and Britain regarding its WMD, which began in earnest in March 2003 following earlier incipient contacts. In October the United States and Britain interdicted a Libya-bound German vessel—the BBC *China*—with enrichment components, including thousands of centrifuge parts. It remains unclear whether the interdiction caught Libya in a game of deception or whether Libya had disclosed the shipment to the United States and Britain prior to interdiction. On December 19, 2003, Libya proclaimed its intention to destroy all WMD facilities and abide by the NPT. In January 2004, the U.S. military airlifted Libya's nuclear equipment to the United States. Some argued Libya's program was in its infancy, whereas others claimed it was "substantially further along than had been publicly disclosed."[5]

Libya thus provides an interesting case of both long-standing efforts to attain nuclear weapons and nuclear reversal. The latter gave rise to a debate over motivations. Was Qadhafi's shift a side effect or demonstration effect of the use of force against Saddam Hussein? Or was it a product of sustained diplomatic pressures from the international community resulting from its terrorist activities? In either case, Qadhafi's motivations to salvage his own regime figured most prominently, compelling an analysis of the conditions that ultimately pushed Qadhafi in that direction.

What Libyan Security Dilemma?

What were Libya's justifications for pursuing nuclear weapons? Libya developed adversarial relations with neighbors since the 1970s, occupying territories in Chad and invading or threatening Sudan, Tunisia, and Malta. Relations with Egypt deteriorated into war in 1977 and minor militarized encounters in the 1980s. Some reports on Libya's search for nuclear weapons mentioned Egypt as a possible target.[6] Yet none of these neighbors posed existential threats to Libya and most of these conflicts were nothing but the product of Qadhafi's own provocations. Egypt was the state most likely to develop a nuclear capability in Libya's vicinity from a neorealist perspective, given an assumed nuclear Israel at its border. Yet Egypt had signed the NPT in 1968 and was widely acknowledged to have abandoned nuclear designs after Nasser's death. Consistent reports of Libya's search for nuclear weapons might have fueled Algeria's nuclear designs. Algeria built a secret sizable research reactor supplied by China in the 1980s, when it was not an NPT member (Spector 1993). In 1991,

Algeria agreed to place the facility under IAEA supervision and in 1995 it joined the NPT, although concerns with Algeria's motivation to acquire a second large research reactor remained (Jones and McDonough 1998; Cirincione et al. 2002). The timing of these efforts, however, suggests that Algeria may have been *reacting* to Libya's nuclear activities rather than triggering Libya's search for nuclear weapons, which preceded Algeria's moves. Furthermore, just as Algeria's facilities came under IAEA supervision in the 1990s, Libya accelerated its search for centrifuges and weapon designs. Libya's search for nuclear weapons also preceded President Reagan's 1986 attack on Libya in response to the latter's terrorist activities.

In sum, of all Middle East nuclear aspirants, Libya arguably provides the least support for neorealism. Qadhafi frequently used a more distant Israel as his main public justification for nuclear weapons. Soon after assuming power in 1969, he supported the most radical forces seeking Israel's eradication and began searching for nuclear weapons. Israel's ambiguous nuclear capabilities provided an excellent target for the young revolutionary and aspiring pan-Arab leader to emulate and counter. He did so *before* Sharon warned Qadhafi in 1973 that Israel could also reach Libya and *before* Israel's 1981 attack on Osiraq. Thus, Qadhafi's symbolic quest for nuclear weapons—as currency to enhance his regime at home and abroad—gained it yet another adversary. In January 2005, Qadhafi acknowledged that Libya's WMD program "started at the very beginning of the revolution. . . . The world was different then." It became apparent, he argued, that nuclear arms were not strategically useful weapons: "We started to ask ourselves, 'by manufacturing nuclear weapons, against whom are we going to use them?' . . . World alliances have changed. *We had no target* [emphasis added]. . . . And then we started thinking about the cost. . . . If someone attacks you and you use a nuclear bomb, you are in effect using it against yourself."[7]

The timings of Libya's efforts to both acquire and relinquish nuclear weapons question the relevance of the Israeli factor further. Libyan authorities stated that Libya made a strategic decision to revive its nuclear program in 1995, after a more dormant period in the 1980s.[8] Between 1992 and 1995, Israel's dovish Labor-led government and the PLO signed the Oslo agreements and were involved in multilateral negotiations with several Arab neighbors, including arms control (see chapters 9 and 11). A decade later Qadhafi's son Saif allegedly implied that Libya had developed WMD for use in a conflict with Israel but that "progress" in the Israeli-Palestinian peace process made such planning unnecessary.[9] Yet since the 2000 Palestinian intifada, the heyday of suicide bombing and forceful Israeli repression in Gaza and the West Bank, there had been less progress in that conflict. In other words, Qadhafi reinvigorated the search for nuclear weapons at the peak of Palestinian-Israeli cooperation in 1995 but discontinued it at its nadir. Clearly, the links between the vagaries of the Palestinian-Israeli conflict and Libya's nuclear decisions seemed spurious. By 2004, Saif declared to Al-jazeera that "Libya no longer considers Israel a security threat nor is his country in a confrontation with Israel."[10] The idea that Israel in the era of Oslo and Shimon Peres threatened Libya more than under Ariel Sharon defies credibility, suggesting that other factors were more likely to drive both Libya's search for nuclear weapons and their subsequent abandonment. As Premier Shokri Ghanem acknowledged, not only are nuclear weapons a financial and political burden, but "you can't use these weapons . . . [they] give you a false sense of power. Can Israel use this arsenal?"[11]

Significant discontinuity between the regimes of King Idris and Qadhafi suggests that no immanent security dilemmas existed between Libya and its neighbors, Libya and the United States, or Libya and Israel. In effect, in 2003 these presumed "threats" must have evanesced since Qadhafi renounced his WMD programs and declared the nuclear arms race "crazy," arguing that Libya should abandon its quest for WMD because they exposed it to "danger" and were no longer needed. "Any national state that will adopt this policy cannot protect itself. On the contrary, it exposes itself to danger," he told African leaders.[12] What Qadhafi left out was why they were needed in earlier decades. His contradictory statements and actions over time, however, reinforce the observation that Libya's nuclear efforts were less likely to stem from structural power considerations than from Qadhafi's domestic needs to buttress his regime and personal power. Regime security rather than state security was his foremost motivation for seeking nuclear weapons since the 1970s and for abandoning them in 2003. Threats would be constructed and deconstructed according to Qadhafi's perceptions of popular receptivity at home and in his region. A year after all sensitive nuclear equipment and material was transferred to the United States, Saif declared that Libya had sought modern weapons to strengthen the Arab world against the West, but since Arabs were constantly conspiring against each other, Libya no longer wanted to bear such costs.[13] "Libya now is a safe country. And I think we are safer without those items."[14] Libya's deputy premier and head of the clandestine nuclear weapons program, Ma'atouq Mohamed Ma'atouq, reportedly acknowledged that in debates with Qadhafi's inner circle he himself had argued that the program did not serve Libya's national interests. "Let's assume we have these weapons," he said. "What would we do with them? Who is the target?" (Miller 2006a).

INTERNATIONAL INSTITUTIONS: FROM A. Q. KHAN TO THE IAEA

Just as Libya's place among its neighbors was defined more by the nature of its regime than by balance of power or immanent threats to its existence, so were Libya's incentives and policies vis-à-vis international institutions. King Idris al-Sanusi signed the NPT in 1968, the year preceding Qadhafi's coup. After assuming power, Qadhafi repeatedly proclaimed his determination to acquire nuclear weapons throughout the 1970s. U.S. intelligence estimates referred to nuclear weapons acquisition as Qadhafi's stated objectives by 1974.[15] A close associate of Pakistan's Premier Zulfikar Ali Bhutto, Altaf Abbasi, reported that former senior member of Libya's Revolutionary Command Council Salem bin Aamer accompanied him to the Netherlands to take A. Q. Khan back to Pakistan. According to Abbasi, Salem provided Khan with financial assistance for the nuclear program; Abbasi "talked to Gaddafi in this regard, and he agreed to extend financial cooperation in Pakistan's nuclear program."[16] Yet, in line with other cases in this region where NPT membership did not preclude blatant violations, Qadhafi also ratified the NPT in 1975. The Soviet Union conditioned its 1975 nuclear agreement to supply Libya with a research reactor on Libya's NPT ratification. Negotiations with the Soviet firm Atomenergoeksport for a much larger facility in Sirte, which began in 1977, were discontinued in response to U.S. pressure, Soviet hesitation, and a decline in Libya's oil profits. A 1980 IAEA agreement placed Libya's nuclear facilities under international inspections and between 1981 and 1983 the smaller Tajura reactor began operating (Spector 1990:176). Private firms from various countries—including the United States, Switzerland, Hungary, and Poland—also supplied equipment to Tajura.

In the 1980s, Libya's nuclear program suffered from mismanagement and foreign suppliers' reluctance to provide it with equipment and assistance. According to El-Baradei, Libya's research program to enrich uranium through centrifuges began in the 1980s but "picked up steam in the 90s."[17] These activities were not subject to IAEA inspections at the time and became known only after Libya reported them to the United States and Britain in 2003. Western intelligence services had also failed to comprehend A. Q. Khan's black market activities for many years.[18] Malaysian police subsequently confirmed that Khan had shipped enriched uranium to Libya in 2001, following a meeting between Khan and Libyan representatives in Istanbul in 1997 at which the Libyans requested centrifuges. According to Malaysian police Pakistan sent enriched uranium to Libya by air around 2001, and "a certain number of centrifuge units were sent in 2001–2002."[19] Malaysia's Deputy Internal Security Minister Noh Omar also revealed that Libyans involved with the nuclear weapons program had been secretly trained in Malaysia. A 2003 IAEA report found that between the early 1980s until the end of 2003 "Libya imported nuclear material and conducted a wide variety of (clandestine) nuclear activities" in violation of its safeguards agreement. It failed to declare imports of uranium hexafluoride (UF6) used in enrichment in 1985, 2000, and 2001, the fabrication and irradiation of uranium targets, and the subsequent separation of a small amount of plutonium.[20]

After incipient conversations with British officials in late 2002, in March 2003 Qadhafi approached Britain and the United States, but not the IAEA, to disclose its nuclear and other WMD projects.[21] The U.N. had removed sanctions in 1999, but Libya's foremost interest was removing U.S. sanctions. In December, Qadhafi agreed to end his nuclear weapons program and allow IAEA inspections. In a 2004 confession, A. Q. Khan admitted to selling nuclear technology to Iran, Libya, and North Korea. Private firms from Malaysia, the United States, UAE, Turkey, and Spain, among others, were under investigation as network suppliers. The IAEA found Libya in non-compliance with the NPT, noting that this finding was "for information purposes only," with no threat of sanctions, while commending Libya for its active cooperation with the agency. Libya ratified the NTBT and signed the Additional Protocol allowing intrusive, short-notice IAEA inspections. Yet in March 2004 a container of components for sophisticated L-2 centrifuges that had "escaped" U.S. attention arrived in Libya by boat.[22] In May the IAEA was also investigating reports that a giant cask of UF6 suitable for enrichment had arrived in Libya from North Korea in 2001. The IAEA suspected the shipment was the first delivery of a larger order that could have yielded ten small nuclear warheads (U.S. scientists later concluded with near certainty the North Korean origins of this shipment). El-Baradei proclaimed Libya guilty of long-term violations of its NPT obligations.[23] The August 2004 IAEA report noted that Libya failed to account for sophisticated enrichment technology that could have been stolen, hidden, or lost, and that some of Libya's responses were not borne out by test results and soil samples. The IAEA spokesman declared that despite Libya's commitments to the United States and Britain, "there are gaping holes in this investigation" regarding acquisition of uranium hexafluoride, uranium conversion, and highly enriched uranium particles found in Libya.[24] A. Q. Khan had also supplied Libya with the blueprints for nuclear weapons designs.[25]

In sum, Libya circumvented the NPR for decades and acquired technology suitable for nuclear weapons, a sign of deficiencies in the design of U.N. inspections but also of Western intelligence failures. Libya, like Egypt, signed the Pelindaba Treaty making Africa a NWFZ in 1996 but did not ratify it. Libya also developed chemical weapons and allegedly used mustard gas near the end of its war with Chad (Boucek 2004). The NPT was of little value for Qadhafi's regime. He could well have arrived at the final product he sought for so many years. Instead he disclosed and abandoned these illicit activities in 2003. Why and how did this happen? The U.N.—separate from the NPR itself—had much to do with that outcome. Libya's extensive involvement in international terrorism culminated in 1988, when two Libyan intelligence agents placed a bomb on Pan Am Flight 103 that killed all 259 passengers and crew over Lockerbie, Scotland. A relatively tight U.N. boycott of Libya for many years had important effects on nuclear decisions and, through their domestic economic and political effects, on Qadhafi's signature model of political survival.[26]

Libya's flouting of the NPR until 2003 and its persistent search for nuclear weapons do not leave much room for the assumption that norms against nuclear acquisition had much resonance in this case. Indeed, alternative identity considerations embedded in a sense of pride, defiance, and aspirations for modernity could have fueled Qadhafi's hunt for nuclear weapons. An address to university students in 1987 hinted at such considerations: "They make bombs daily; why should we not do likewise. The Arabs must possess the atomic bomb to defend themselves until their numbers reach one billion, until they learn to desalinate water, and until they liberate Palestine. . . . We should be like the Chinese—poor and riding donkeys, but respected and possessing an atom bomb" (Spector 1990:178). These themes must have clearly reverberated with Qadhafi's audience. The 2003 reversal, however, raises some challenges for identity-related understandings of nuclear behavior. How could thirty years of forceful pursuit of a nuclear deterrent allegedly compatible with such norms come to an end so abruptly—relative to the normal evolution of norms and identity—in the 2000s? Indeed, negotiations between Ma'atouq Mohamed Ma'atouq, who directed Libya's clandestine nuclear efforts, and A. Q. Khan allegedly continued at least until February 2002, and Qadhafi hesitated to renounce all his WMDs until the very last moment before the December 19, 2003, announcement, which he delegated to his foreign minister (Miller 2006a,b). Qadhafi's expedient manipulation of nuclear themes offers a window onto the place of nuclear weapons in evolving models of political survival.

DOMESTIC POLITICS: FROM THE GREEN BOOK AND *JAMAHIRIYYA* TO "NUKES ARE COSTLY"

Libya's King Idris ruled post-independence Libya in alliance with locally powerful families and corrupt bureaucracies. U.S. and British bases and oil operations provided employment and rents. Free parliamentary elections in 1960 brought to power new businesses, contracting and landowning

interests (Anderson 1986). By the late 1960s, a growing nationalist opposition, including the Royal Libyan Army with Nasserite proclivities,
began challenging royal control. King Idris maintained closed ties with
Britain and the United States, signing the NPT in 1968. A coup by Colo-
nel Qadhafi and his Revolutionary Command Council (RCC) ousted him
in 1969.

The new regime borrowed Arab unity, anti-imperialism, and Arab socialism from Nasserism but also imprinted Qadhafi's own style on its
character, including a particular approach to Islam (Qaddafi 1983; Anderson 1986; Zartman and Kluge 1991). With a rather small and unedu-
cated population and little agricultural potential, Libya's economy was
among the most dependent on oil exports in the Arab world. Foreign oil
companies' reluctance to accept Libyan demands for greater profit shares
provided Qadhafi with a popular reason for nationalizing the oil industry
(Vandewalle 1995; Richard and Waterbury 1990). Shortly after assuming
power, he proclaimed that "people who have lived for five thousand years
without oil can live without it a few more years to achieve their legitimate
rights" (Anderson 1995:226). Yet he retained heavy reliance on oil,
which endowed his ruling coalition with rents and windfall revenues to
provide public services and secure support from mobilized constituencies.
Increased access to education, housing, and medical care, and wage increases enhanced popular support in the early post-revolutionary period.
Revolutionary committees replaced the old administration.

Yet in 1976 Qadhafi aborted a coup by his ministers of Planning and
Foreign Affairs, who opposed military expenditures and foreign entangle-
ments at the expense of domestic development (Anderson 1986:264). In
1977, Qadhafi radicalized Libyan politics by creating the world's first
egalitarian *Jamahiriyya* ("people's power"). The old entrepreneurial class
with its Western ties had been major targets of repression immediately
after the 1969 coup, but now even smaller-scale private activities were
suppressed. Many among the educated, managerial, and technocratic professional class emigrated in response to the evisceration of private economic activities and the state apparatus. This complete social reshuffling,
which threw out state institutions with the bathwater, was dictated by Qadhafi's "survival ethic" of weakening all potential competition for power
(Vandewalle 1995:24). He also sought to coopt and neutralize Muslim clerics by promoting his own brand of Islam, which banned alcohol and Western music but also recognized some women's rights, including education
(Anderson 2003). The regime persecuted the Muslim Brotherhood, as
Nasser had done, and in 1986 it closed down forty-eight Muslim institutions for fomenting Islamic fundamentalism. A vast secret police ensured
that political resistance was met with harsh repression and executions, dec-
imating any potential alternative to Qadhafi from the military or Muslim

clerics, or a possible alliance between the two. He survived several attempts on his life by Muslim radicals.

Qadhafi sought to enhance popular support through nationalistic and xenophobic policies, closing down U.S. foreign bases and expelling Italians (including those in their graves) in retaliation for Mussolini's massacres in the 1920s. Oil exports enabled both populist policies and high military expenditures. The military was Qadhafi's pivotal partner and he nurtured it with equipment and promises of sophisticated weapons technology. According to Qadhafi's own account, his pursuit of nuclear weapons began soon after the 1969 revolution when his deputy Abd Al-Salam Jallud sought tactical nuclear weapons from China (GSW). Qadhafi repeatedly portrayed his search for nuclear weapons as a key aspect of his self-reliant economic model.[27] Nuclear weapons also provided him, as Saddam Hussein also believed, with recognition—at home and abroad—as a modern and powerful pan-Arab leader. According to Muhammad Izzat Abd-al-Aziz, a leading Libyan nuclear scientist who studied in Britain, Nasser's chief promoter of nuclear weapons Minister Salah Hedayat recruited him in the 1960s when he worked in the United States. After working for Egypt's Atomic Energy Organization, Aziz received a letter from President Anwar al-Sadat ordering him to go to Libya and help build Libya's atomic energy "for pan-Arab reasons."[28] Qadhafi promoted several political unifications with Arab and African states and, when these failed, financed armed oppositions in neighboring countries and assassination attempts on their leaders. While wrapped in the mantle of pan-Arabism, Qadhafi fought wars against fellow Arab and African states, and he turned Libya into a safe haven for movements aimed at deposing Arab leaders and for radical Palestinian groups, including Abu Nidal's Fatah Revolutionary Council (Anderson 2003). Although a rabid anti-communist himself, Qadhafi spent billions of dollars on Soviet weaponry and training, and supported guerrilla movements in Angola and Mozambique and terrorist groups in Northern Ireland, Japan, Germany, Spain, and the Philippines, among others.

President Carter imposed economic sanctions on Libya for terrorist acts and closed the U.S. embassy in Tripoli in 1980. President Reagan severed diplomatic relations, ordered all Americans to leave Libya, and declared an embargo on Libyan oil in 1982. In 1983, Qadhafi embraced the terrorist leader who during his hijack of the *Achille Lauro* killed an American passenger. In 1984, Libyan embassy officials killed a British policewoman who was monitoring a peaceful protest against Qadhafi in London. In 1985, there were alleged Libyan terrorist attacks at the Rome and Vienna airports. In 1986, Libyan agents placed a bomb in a West Berlin disco, killing a Turkish woman and two American soldiers. The United States responded with an attack on Qadhafi's homequarters in Bab el-Azziziya that only slightly injured Qadhafi himself but killed his infant daughter. And in 1988, there was the massive terrorist incident at Lockerbie, Scotland. Upon Libya's refusal to extradite the agents who planted the bomb for trial in Scotland, the U.N. imposed sanctions, an embargo against spare parts and technology for the oil industry, and a travel ban on Libya. Qadhafi had managed to translate self-reliance into pariah status for his country.

For all the rhetoric of nationalist self-reliance, however, oil exports continued to account for 95 percent of Libya's foreign exchange necessary to purchase food, technology, and capital equipment (O'Sullivan 2003:187). Industrial investments emphasized heavy industries in steel, petrochemicals, and oil refining, but military expenditures displaced development budgets, with arms imports accounting for one-fourth of all imports (Vandewalle 1995). Revenues declined from about $21 billion in 1980 to $6.5 billion in 1986, the year before Qadhafi introduced a halfhearted form of infitah that was abandoned immediately (Vandewalle 1995, 1998). The 1980s made the model's deficiencies evident, with inefficient agriculture, internationally uncompetitive goods, low growth, high inflation, and sharp decline in oil prices, which deprived Qadhafi of revenue to sustain the very constituencies whom his revolution had mobilized.[29] Eccentric expenditures for exotic weapons and revolutionary movements around the world ceased to attract the imagination of impoverished Libyans. Ironically, Libya had become more rather than less dependent on international markets, but sanctions also made it insolvent and diplomatically isolated even among its neighbors. Rising expectations were met with rising prices and scarcity of goods. Editorials attacked Qadhafi's brand of pan-Arabism and involvement in terrorism (Anderson 1995:232). Discontent against revolutionary committees mounted. Against this explosive background Qadhafi imposed moderate economic reforms emulating Egypt's infitah, transferring light and medium-sized enterprises to self-management committees under state control (Vandewalle 1995). In practice, infitah was minimal but created some beneficiaries who favored international normalization. Yet Qadhafi's creation—the Jamahiriyya—had evolved into an entrenched force against reform, trapping its own creator in it. Institutions born under the revolution that were bound to disappear with an opening to the global economy had every incentive to oppose changes. Jallud orchestrated a coup in 1993—in the midst of incipient concessions to surrender the Lockerbie suspects—resulting in bombings, arrests, and executions.

Domestic agricultural and industrial production plummeted to a minute fraction of the GNP by the 1990s, growth hovered around 1 percent annually, unemployment reached 30 percent, and inflation achieved new heights. The declining legitimacy of Qadhafi's inward-looking model revived domestic groups interested in ending international isolation. At a reported meeting in the mid-1990s, technocrats led by General-Secretary Umar al-Muntasir and Energy Minister Abdallah Salim al-Badri pressed for structural reforms and international investments. Qadhafi's Lieutenant Jallud led the camp opposing domestic reforms and international normalization as a new basis of regime legitimacy. Amidst the sharp exchange between the two camps, Qadhafi remained silent. By 1998, however, Qadhafi began supporting reformers, as articles in the official daily *Al-Jamahiriya* censured opponents of a new model. Qadhafi proclaimed that "we cannot stand in the way of progress . . . the fashion now is the free market and investments," and he accepted U.N. demands regarding Lockerbie in 1999 (Takeyh 2001:63). In 2000 he proclaimed the end of anti-imperialist struggle, and General-Secretary Mubarak al-Shamikh pledged that the oil sector was ready for Americans firms to return. *Without oil revenues neither domestic reforms nor compensatory mechanisms for adversely affected constituencies were possible.* In 2002, Libya unified its exchange rate, devalued its dinar to attract foreign investment and benefit exporters, and reduced customs duties by 50 percent. In March 2003 Qadhafi launched a far more forceful infitah than its earlier precursors, one that included privatization of state enterprises and oil (Vandewalle 2006). Precisely in March 2003, Qadhafi also sought normalization with Britain and the United States—more vigorously than at any time before—in exchange for dismantling his WMD.[30]

Qadhafi's ultimate decision to declare and surrender his nuclear weapons program must be seen against this background of declining resources, domestic challenges to his rule, and the embrace of a new model. The combined effect of his nationalist economic policies and international sanctions had left Libya's economy ruined and his regime vulnerable to subversion (O'Sullivan 2003). The nuclear program was no longer an asset but a costly political liability for reconstituting oil resources. Indeed, nuclear expenditures during the 1990s were competing with other *military* priorities, heightening Qadhafi's fears of a military coup, particularly after a 1993 army uprising that was very harshly suppressed (O'Sullivan 2003:204). "The history of mankind is not fixed," Qadhafi now declared, "and it does not go at one pace. Sometimes it moves at a steady pace, and sometimes it is very fast. It is very flexible all the time. The past stage was the era of nationalism—of the identity of one nation—and now, suddenly, that has changed. It is the era of globalization, and there are many new factors which are mapping out the world" (Anderson 2003). In 2004, Qadhafi pronounced the nuclear arms race "crazy," advancing that "we would like to have a better economy and an improved life."[31] Qadhafi's efforts to rebuild a new supportive coalition were also a product of domestic challenges to his rule by Islamist movements. As elsewhere in the Arab world, Islamist movements capitalized on economic and social malaise in Libya to recruit constituencies through the provision of social services and anti-corruption activities. A militant group, the Libyan Islamic Fighting Group, attempted to assassinate Qadhafi in 1996, and the Islamic Martyrs' Movement waged armed resistance against his regime. Both groups were said to be inspired and funded by al-Qaeda and to represent direct threats to Qadhafi's rule, which explains his readiness to provide intelligence on terrorist activities to the United States and to condemn the 9/11 attacks (Boucek 2004; Anderson 2003).

The links between Qadhafi's new strategy of embracing the global economy and abandoning nuclear weapons are also evident from statements by his political allies, foes, and foreign interlocutors. A European diplomat reported that "from [his] conversations with the Libyans, it appeared that they had determined that it was too expensive to develop nuclear weapons, both in specific terms and in terms of sanctions."[32] Following his visit with Qadhafi, Assistant Secretary of State for Near Eastern Affairs William Burns reported that "Libyan officials highlighted their interest in further integrating into the world economy."[33] Premier Ghanem declared that "Libya abandoned the development of weapons of mass destruction in favour of investing funds in the development of the country's economy. . . . We focused on economic issues and therefore this decision was taken."[34] He added that "weapons of mass destruction are very costly. It's better that we concentrate on our economic development."[35] The decision allowed Libya to expand cooperation with other countries, noting that WMD were not making Libya safe but poorer. Hence "we decided to concentrate our way on our economy. To spend this money on butter rather than guns."[36] Libya's Foreign Minister Mohamed Abd-al-Rahman Shalqam spelled out why the regime's model of political survival had shifted toward internationalization, pointing to the emergence of world economic blocs and lamenting that "unfortunately, we the Arabs have not been able to create a body, an entity, or a new movement that goes along with the reality in the world." Libya, he argued, cannot continue "to submit to backwardness and weakness. We cannot continue to be left out, not only politically and militarily, but also scientifically and economically. You need to take part in or create an entity that motivates you and helps you develop—in a world where muscle counts—your scientific, educational, and economic muscles. . . . I do not wish to talk about this or that Arab country. However, I do not think there is a bare minimum Arab reality or situation that is pulled by awareness for the need to create a language for the 21st Century—the language of science, of blocs, of strength, and the acceptance of each country by the other."[37] Exiled opponent Ibrahim Abd-al-Aziz Sahd defined Qadhafi's objectives as begging Western powers for foreign investments and external legitimacy to "enable him to remain in power."[38]

Saif, Qadhafi's second son and apparent successor as "Guide of the Revolution," was a key architect of this shift. An engineer by training, Saif spent three years at the London School of Economics and headed the Qadhafi International Foundation for Charity Associations, which conducted negotiations over the release of Western hostages in Africa, the Philippines, and Algeria and provided compensation to families of Lockerbie and the French airline UTA victims. According to Shahram Chubin, nuclear decisions seemed related to Qadhafi's recognition that a successful transfer of power to his son required him to "leave Libya in a slightly better position" by getting rid of "these useless weapons, which have created unnecessary distrust and suspicion on the part of its neighbors and, of course, the international community as a whole, including Britain and the United States."[39] Saif himself expressed publicly that "the Libyan people want to modernize their economy, they want to reform their system, [and] they want to deepen direct democracy." Voicing the model advocated by Libyan reformers, Saif predicted an economic boom for Libya in the construction, oil, and tourism sectors, arguing that "Libya in the next few years will be the biggest workshop in the world."[40] "Of course we want to bring foreign capital to Libya and we want to bring investment into our country, but we have our own model regarding privatization."[41] Saif proclaimed the new model's objectives as enhancing Libyans' living standards through an improved economy. Foreign minister Shalqam publicly acknowledged that the nuclear program did not benefit Libya's people.[42]

Qadhafi's shift could not have been undertaken without support from other advocates of economic liberalization and foreign investment within the bureaucracy. Ghanem, a U.S.-trained economist and former Trade and Economy minister appointed premier in 2003, launched an explicit new agenda aided by other supporters of economic reform, including Abdallah Badri, the new chief of the National Oil Corporation (NOC), which had remained relatively protected from the most extreme revolutionary measures (Vandewalle 2004). Ghanem reiterated the reformers' logic regarding nuclear weapons: "We thought this would make us look better in the eyes of the world and set an example for others in the Middle East to follow, especially Israel. . . . Weapons of mass destruction are very costly. It's better that we concentrate on our economic development."[43] Other supporters of the new model included Chief of Intelligence Musa Kusa and Shalqam. Ghanem also disclosed that very powerful people in the upper echelons of Libya's hierarchy, particularly security services and revolutionary committees, resisted both economic liberalization and the decision to abandon the weapons program.[44] Opponents were led by Ahmad Ibrahim, an assistant secretary of the General People's Congress, who had extensive ties to the regime's revolutionary wing, and

Abd al-Qadr al-Baghdadi (Vandewalle 2006). The old guard succeeded in removing Ghanem from the premiership but, as chief of the NOC, he remained considerably influential in a country where oil still accounts for about 85 percent of state revenues.[45]

The future of reform may be uncertain but the budding model had incipient effects. In December 2003, Qadhafi ended the nuclear weapons program; a month later Libya ratified the CTBT; in March 2004, it signed the IAEA's Additional Protocol; in September the United States removed all restrictions on oil imports from Libya and, in October, it lifted most sanctions (some remained until Libya could be cleared from the list of state "sponsors" of terrorism). An IMF report served as the basis for further structural and trade reforms in an effort, in Ghanem's words, to create "a new comprehensive architecture for the national economy" (Vandewalle 2006:187). Legislation on privatization, foreign investment, tax reform, creation of a stock exchange, and tourism development followed. Some of the dialectical contortions to align privatization with the Green Book were reminiscent of juche adaptations under Kim Jong-Il, but went significantly farther in the direction of reform. In January 2005, most oil contracts were awarded to U.S. firms; others went to the UAE, Australian, Canadian, and Brazilian ones; even Algerian companies were to help reconstitute Libya's oil industry. Economic growth in 2005 was over 8 percent, driven by foreign investment and oil production. In February 2006, a former economic advisor to President Reagan, Michael Porter, was invited by Saif to deliver a blueprint for Libya's integration into the global economy.[46] The United States did not restore diplomatic relations until May 2006.

CONCLUSION

Qadhafi's shifting models of political survival explain both Libya's nuclearization and denuclearization. Soon after assuming power he pursued nuclear weapons as a central pillar of his populist, nationalist inward-looking model. Accounts emphasizing structural power to justify nuclear pursuits suffer from far more serious failings here than in any other case in this region, except, perhaps, for Egypt. Qadhafi's own statements acknowledged the absence of strategic threats requiring a nuclear-armed Libya. Qadhafi's model made the attainment of nuclear weapons a centerpiece of his drive for domestic control through Jamahiriyya and related international, grandiose and ultimately personal ambitions. Neither can changes in relative power account for Qadhafi's decision to reverse nuclear course. During the program's early phases, threats to a nuclear Israel were convenient tools for enhancing his regime's credentials at home, in the region, and throughout the Arab and Muslim world. Other statements, however, clearly acknowledged that Israel was not regarded as a threat to Libya. No significant changes in relative power between Libya and Israel had taken place that could explain such transformation. The power gap between the two was wide in the 1970s and remained so. Egypt might have been construed as a threat—given its size, proximity, and status in the Arab world, together with occasional skirmishes between the two countries—but Egypt had denuclearized in the 1970s while Libya forcefully continued to seek nuclear weapons for 30 years. Ironically, from a neorealist perspective, Libya renounced nuclear weapons *after* Egypt's largest research reactor with potential plutonium-producing capabilities had been built in the 1990s, *after* Egypt began alluding to potential changes in its nuclear posture arguably related to Iran's nuclearization, and *after* Algeria opted for a second large research reactor (Ain Oussera) as well.[47] Had the presumed neorealist logic of balance of power and self-help applied, these developments should have led Libya in the opposite direction than the one observed.

Finally, the Reagan administration used *direct* military force in 1986 to punish and deter Qadhafi for his terrorist activities, bombing terrorist and military facilities and Qadhafi's family compound. Yet Qadhafi intensified his support for terrorism and his search for WMD. After 1986, and given the Clinton administration's threats to Libya's alleged chemical weapons facilities in the 1990s, the United States could arguably be construed as the main threat providing justification for Libya's nuclear ambitions. Yet this interpretation begs the question of why that calculation would have changed in 2003. As Levi and O'Hanlon (2005:99) argue, the timing of Qadhafi's decision could suggest that the image of Saddam Hussein's capture by U.S. troops was deeply threatening to Qadhafi personally. Qadhafi came out publicly to surrender his WMD programs in December 2003, after nine months of secret negotiations. Whether or not he was personally shaken is irrelevant in some neorealist analyses, where international power differentials—hegemony in this case—tell the story, presumably without reference to personal or domestic considerations. Nor can such a story tell why presumed fear of hegemony arguably led a state to seek nuclear weapons in 1986 but to abandon them in 2003, without resorting to auxiliary (usually domestic) arguments. Why would a very direct military threat to Libya lead to one outcome in 1986 while a less direct demonstration effect of hegemony—the war on Iraq—would have the opposite effect in 2003? Domestic conditions in 1986 enabled Qadhafi to convert external aggression into rally-round-the-leader support through still-flowing oil and still-powerful revolutionary committees (Jentleson and Whytock 2005/06). Domestic conditions in 2003 reflected the legacy of effective multilateral sanctions, extensive popular opposition, a weakened and unsustainable Jamahiriyya revolutionary coalition, the threat of internal coups and a rising reformist camp.

Iraq's demonstration effect may have certainly exacerbated Qadhafi's fears that his *regime* might be nearing its end if domestic or external forces could do to him what was done to Saddam. However, the threat of force was only one factor (Jentleson and Whytock 2005/06), and one which, as we have seen, had a different effect in the 1980s and 1990s. Former Clinton administration official Martin Indyk revealed that Libya, facing a deepening domestic economic crisis, had offered to give up its WMD arsenal in secret negotiations with the United States as early as 1999.[48] The United States made compensations for Lockerbie and an end to Libya's support for terrorism preconditions for lifting U.N. sanctions, leaving U.S. sanctions in place until WMD issues were resolved. Qadhafi reportedly continued to seek nuclear weapons and obtain proscribed technology and weapons designs from Pakistan on the one hand, while denying such efforts on the other, until late 2003.[49] By this time, multilateral sanctions had magnified the adverse effects of Libya's domestic political economy model, dangerously eroding Qadhafi's ability to maintain political control at home (O'Sullivan 2003:202–3). U.N. sanctions had been removed in 1999, and investments in the energy sector in the midst of rising oil prices had improved by 2001. Libya still faced U.S. sanctions, however, which only denuclearization could end, while Qadhafi reportedly sought American companies to develop Libya's oil fields.[50] Most importantly, negotiations with Libya began before the Iraq war, suggesting that the war may have had an accelerating effect at best.[51] After all, the German ship with nuclear equipment bound for Libya was intercepted months *after* the war had started, in October 2003. In sum, Qadhafi's 2003 decision was in line with steps that had begun in the early 2000s, including negotiations with Britain over WMD. As Anderson (2003) suggests, "This was not an overnight conversion."

In the end, both widely acknowledged economic incentives to reconstitute a supportive domestic coalition and (unacknowledged) concerns with his own personal safety may have worked to persuade Qadhafi and his regime to espouse a new model of political survival, one that turned nuclear weapons into a major liability.[52] Libya would certainly not become a new Taiwan at once, but Qadhafi, despite expected internal opposition, appears more resolved to embrace a new model than North Korea's Kim Jong-Il. The United States, Japan, South Korea, and European states have brandished Libya's nuclear reversal as a blueprint for North Korea. Kim Jong-Il responded with a nuclear test in late 2006, superseded by new commitments that are yet to be tested.

CHAPTER ELEVEN

Egypt

FOLLOWING THE 1952 REVOLUTION that brought him to power, President Nasser launched a nuclear program in 1954 and created the Atomic Energy Authority (AEA) in 1955.[1] Nasser's cabinet secretary and secretary-general of the AEA's governing council, Ibrahim Abdel Rahman, was reportedly informed that the program's focus should be on peaceful applications but also preserve the military option (Walsh 2001; Einhorn 2004:45). According to Free Officer Salah Hedayat, who served as AEA director general, science minister (1965–70), and director of the Inshas Nuclear Research Center under Nasser, Egypt began a secret nuclear weapons program some years before Israel, but abandoned it in the 1970s after Nasser's death.[2] A nuclear scientist who worked for Nasser traced the program's beginnings to 1955.[3] In 1957, Nasser signed a nuclear protocol with the Soviet Union, including a 2.5 MW research reactor that began construction at Inshas in 1958 and went critical in 1961 (not subject to international safeguards at that time). In the 1950s and 1960s, Nasser recruited scientists associated with Nazi Germany who had experience in missile and related projects to aid in Egypt's development of al-Zafir, al-Qahir, and al-Ra'id missiles with projected ranges of 370–1,500 km, potential precursors of delivery systems for nuclear weapons. In 1960, Nasser warned that Arab states would acquire nuclear weapons to maintain Egypt's "superiority."[4]

The United States warned Nasser in 1963 that since Egypt was the first to introduce a surface-to-surface missile program in the region, "Israel might well seek to develop more lethal warheads to provide deterrence against implacable Arab hostility it senses from Arab public statements."[5] None of the missiles ever became operational due to technical and management problems and to Israel's alleged hunt for Nazi scientists. Nasser reportedly requested nuclear weapons from its main protector, the Soviet Union, in 1965 and from China in 1967, who advised Egypt to develop them independently.[6] The Soviets declined to supply nuclear weapons, allegedly granting some form of nuclear guarantee, but Nasser declared that Egypt would develop its own program (Farr 1999). Egypt reportedly sought sensitive nuclear technology from India. In 1965, the U.S. embassy in Cairo obtained evidence of increased Egyptian determination to build a larger reactor than originally intended.[7] Nasser's nuclear program

230 • Chapter Eleven

entailed increased budgetary allocations, training of scientists, thorium and uranium exploration, efforts to produce heavy water and extract plutonium, and uranium fuel fabrication (Einhorn 2004). Nasser also threatened to launch a preventive strike against Israel's nuclear facilities (Saif 1997). Egyptian overflights between 1965 and 1967 over Israel's Dimona were thus perceived by Israel as potential reconnaissance exercises preceding a strike on its facilities (Farr 1999). Nasser's request for U.N. withdrawal from the Suez Canal and other military maneuvers and verbal threats contributed to the outbreak of the 1967 war.

With the ascent of President Anwar el-Sadat, U.S. intelligence still regarded Egypt as a nuclear "candidate country" in late 1974 but assessed the likelihood of Egypt's nuclearization to be lower than Pakistan's and Iran's.[8] Nixon proposed to supply nuclear reactors to Egypt and Israel in 1974, but the proposal faltered because of Israel's refusal to abide by inspection procedures among other reasons.[9] Following Egypt's announcement of a potential agreement with the Soviet Union for a 460 MW power reactor in 1975, the United States offered reactors to Egypt, requiring that plutonium from U.S. reactors and fuel be reprocessed outside Egypt. Egypt rejected what it perceived as overly intrusive U.S. inspection procedures (Selim 1996). A subsequent understanding to purchase a 1,000 MW reactor from France floundered because Egypt had not ratified the NPT. In 1981, Egypt ratified the treaty, prompting agreements with France, the United States, and West Germany for two nuclear reactors, fuel, and technical expertise. These agreements collapsed due to lack of Import-Export bank funding, fear of dependence on the West, high costs, and, in the wake of Chernobyl, concerns with potential environmental hazards. U.S. aid for conventional power stations resulted in indefinite suspension of Egypt's nuclear program. In the aftermath of the 1979 Camp David agreements, U.S. political and economic aid to Egypt increased dramatically.

Egypt's activities in missile development continued. The Soviets, who had trained Egyptian technicians in missile guidance since 1967, supplied Scud-B missiles. Since 1980, North Korea helped Egypt produce its own advanced versions of Scud-B missiles capable of carrying nuclear or chemical warheads.[10] In 1982 Egypt developed a partnership with Argentina and Iraq to build a 1,000 km missile. The Condor-II was to be developed in Argentina and eventually shared with Egypt and Iraq as the Badr-2000. The program benefited from Western technology, primarily supplied by West Germany's Messerschmitt-Boelkow-Blohm. Egypt recruited Egyptian-born scientist Abdelkader Helmy—living in the United States— to obtain materials for the Badr-2000 program (Cordesman 1991). Helmy's efforts to export restricted items from the United States were blocked in 1988, and President Hosni Mubarak fired Defense Minister Abdel Halim Abu Ghazala in 1989 for the gaffe. Egyptian missile experts continued to work in Iraq until the latter's invasion of Kuwait in 1990, when Argentina cancelled participation in the project. Although Egypt's Badr-2000 aspirations never died, priorities shifted to simpler Scud technology, with North Korea reportedly supplying materials for Scud-C missiles in the 1990s (CNSW).

Egypt also continued developing nuclear facilities, including a small French-supplied hot cell complex for plutonium extraction research, the Middle East's first industrial electronic accelerator, and a pilot nuclear fuel factory, completed in 1987, which was used to process natural uranium mined in Egypt. In 1992, Argentina supplied a safeguarded 22 MW research reactor that began operating in 1997. Some interpreted a provision in the Argentine agreement for the eventual construction of a fuel fabrication facility as a potential return to full nuclear cycle aspirations (Gregory 1995). Furthermore, occasional public statements continued to raise questions about the durability of Egypt's commitment to denuclearization. For instance, Sadat expressed that "it must be made clear that we cannot possibly stand idly by if Israel introduces atomic weapons into the area" (Jabber 1981). In 1998, Mubarak suggested that Egypt would not hesitate to acquire nuclear weapons if needed, adding that "we do not think now of entering the nuclear club because we do not want war.... We are not in a hurry.... If the time comes when we need nuclear weapons, we will not hesitate," adding that this was "the last thing we are thinking about" and concluding that "every country is preparing for itself a deterrent weapon that will preserve its integrity and its existence."[11] Despite these warnings, Egypt was widely perceived to have upheld its strategic 1981 decision to ratify the NPT (Landau 2002).

Suspicions about Egypt's NPT commitments resurfaced in 2004 as the IAEA found evidence of nuclear experiments with potential applicability to nuclear weapons that were presumably conducted in the 1980s and 1990s and, arguably, as recently as 2004.[12] Thus far these efforts have not been depicted as challenging Egypt's relatively transparent record as a non-nuclear state since Sadat's decision to ratify the NPT (NTIW, FASW). Egypt is considered to have acquired extensive nuclear capabilities including 850 highly qualified academic scientists working for the AEA, supported by about 650 technical staff.[13] In 2006, Egypt announced new plans for its dormant nuclear industry. The timing fueled suspicions that the announcement may have been a response to Iran's nuclear defiance. The United States declared it would aid Egypt's nuclear energy industry.[14] The first nuclear power plant is expected to be completed in 2015.

BALANCE OF POWER: A MOST LIKELY CASE?

In a neorealist world, Egypt provided a "most likely case" for seeking nuclear weapons prima facie given deep mistrust of British intentions in the early and mid-1950s (Walsh 2001:230), the emergence of Israel as a key adversary suspected of harboring nuclear designs in the early 1960s, and the presence of other regional competitors in the balance-of-power game, such as Iraq, Iran, and adjacent Libya, all of whom were alleged to seek nuclear weapons. The region's multipolar structure reinforced neorealist conditions that some would expect to lead to nuclearization. Furthermore, Egypt did not enjoy the protection of a nuclear umbrella except for a vague Soviet commitment. Its military investments amounted only to a progressively declining conventional deterrent. Finally, Egypt was no common regional power but *the* leading Arab power, expected to be particularly sensitive to changes in relative power. Given all these circumstances, the fact that Egypt renounced nuclear weapons for the past three decades posits a serious challenge for neorealism, and an important anomaly in a region progressively more oriented toward nuclear weapons.[15]

Following the U.N. partition and recognition of Israel's creation, five Arab armies attacked it in 1948, suffering a striking defeat that left an indelible mark on both Arab and Israeli publics and rulers (Nasser commanded an Egyptian battalion in that war). Although Arab rhetoric frequently compared Israel with ephemeral Crusader kingdoms, the 1948 war presaged that Israel was not bound to disappear as quickly as expected. Yet aspirations for a *Salah-ad Din* (Saladdin) that would realize the dream of Muslim victory never completely dissipated. Nasser's 1952 revolution revived that dream, calling for extensive investments in missiles and WMD. Israeli decision-makers interpreted the 1948 attack—three years after the Holocaust—and the loss of 1 percent of its population in the war of independence, as evidence of its own precarious condition. Salah Hedayat traced Egypt's secret nuclear weapons program some years ahead of Israel's, but the latter's rumored program compelled Nasser to redouble efforts to develop a nuclear deterrent, a dynamic that exemplified the logic of "security dilemmas." Furthermore, Israel, Britain, and France attacked Egypt in the 1956 Suez campaign, and Nasser reportedly believed that Israel would have the bomb by 1968 (Van Creveld 1998:174).

No less of a strategic problem were Egypt's efforts to preclude military advantages by other Arab states, including Iraq and, closer to home, Libya.[16] Former Foreign Minister Ismail Fahmy advised against signing the NPT to stem nuclear efforts by both other Arab countries and Israel.[17] Malcolm Kerr describes the 1950s and 1960s as an acute Arab Cold War, with Nasser seeking transparent hegemony over the Arab world. Ironically, according to Kerr (1971:vi), Nasser's relations "with his fellow revolutionaries tended to be more difficult than those with the 'reactionaries.'"[18] After Egypt's perceived victory in 1973, Sadat chose *watanyia* (Egyptian nationalism) over *kawmiya* (pan-Arab nationalism). Yet Egypt still had to contend with nuclear activities by Arab states and Israel. Iran's nuclear capabilities progressively became a core concern. As early as 1995 *al-Ahram* researcher Wahid Abd Al-Magid suggested that if Iran could develop nuclear warheads, "this will represent a threat to the Arabs before it does to Israel" (Feldner 2003c:2). Following Indian and Pakistani 1998 nuclear tests, Mubarak warned that Iran might be next. Subsequent disclosures of Iran's secret nuclear endeavors and IAEA lapses for twenty years triggered further Egyptian concerns.[19] Recent reports on presumed Egyptian IAEA reporting transgressions and alleged new incentives to alter its non-nuclear trajectory are more often than not traced to developments in Iran. As Egypt's Ambassador to the United States Nabil Fahmy stated, "I personally believe that like any other country in the region, the acquisition by Iran of nuclear weapons will be a highly egregious act. Outstanding questions regarding its nuclear capabilities remaining unanswered and unresolved with IAEA inspectors can only fuel further suspicions and concerns."[20]

The logic of balance of power is particularly problematic for understanding Egypt's nuclear behavior. First, Hedayat placed Nasser's secret nuclear weapons efforts in the 1950s as preceding Israel's. If such efforts began in 1954, it was the *prospects* of a future threat that would explain Egypt's preemptive program rather than the reality of a nuclear-capable neighbor (the contract for Dimona was signed in 1956).[21] Rumors of an Israeli effort came to the fore only in the 1960s. Indeed, in 1964 Nasser declared that he thought Dimona was not being used for nuclear weapons.[22] Whatever the case, however, regarding who was reacting to whom, some Egyptian constituencies favored matching Israeli nuclear capabilities; others viewed such effort as a strategic chimera that would not provide Egypt with additional security and would sap it of limited resources. Of special importance was Egypt's vulnerability to a nuclear strike on the Aswan dam that would have endangered most of Egypt's population.[23] Others expressed concerns with the futility of nuclear weapons, given high geographic contiguity between Israel and Arab states that might endanger not only the target (Israel) but the attacker as well.[24] Some argued further that Israel's nuclear capabilities may have played an important role in moderating Egyptian military objectives during conventional wars in 1967 and 1973 and that nuclear weapons would have no compelling value for Egypt.[25] Others pointed to the fact that Israel's presumed nuclear capability did not deter Egypt and Syria from attacking it on Yom Kippur 1973 (Saif 1997). Some Egyptian sources believed in Soviet commitments to provide nuclear protection to Egypt if Israel acquired nuclear weapons, but other authoritative sources contested the existence of such commitment.[26] The Soviets reportedly prepared to send nuclear warheads for Scud-B missiles if Israel deployed nuclear weapons in the 1973 war, but others emphasized dilemmas of commitment and entrapment in the Soviet relationship (NTIW).

This diversity of views resonates with the conclusion of leading Egyptian expert Mohamed K. Said (2002:2) that "there is a lack of consensus among the Egyptian elites over the strategic value of acquiring nuclear weapons capabilities. In the 1960s, Egypt was firmly committed to the search for strategic nuclear balance with Israel. By the 1970s, however, Egypt had become less enthusiastic about the issue." Nasser invested in a nuclear program but Sadat renounced it, and debates on the merits of both positions—as the previous overview suggests—spanned both eras. This wide range of views on the intrinsic value of nuclear weapons for Egypt points, as in the other cases, to the indeterminacy of neorealist accounts in anticipating nuclear outcomes. Whether nuclear weapons would make Egypt less rather than more secure remains a matter of contention within Egypt, as discussed later.

Second, Israel's nuclear efforts arguably became a central consideration for Egypt as a broad *political* rather than strategic issue, much as in Iraq before 1981, Libya, and Iran. As argued, Israel's program was far less documented when Egypt began conceiving of a nuclear program than when it decided to abandon it.[27] On the one hand, had a neorealist logic of "reactive proliferation" been at work, Egypt would have sought nuclear weapons more forcefully *after* the 1970s. On the other hand, the premise that Israel's nuclear designs posed an offensive threat to Egypt was dismissed by no less than Egypt's foremost advocate of nuclear weapons, Nasser's advisor Mohamed Hasanayn Haykal, who acknowledged that "Israel has nuclear weapons but will not use them unless she finds herself being strangled."[28] Even Nasser, who warned against Israel's nuclear capabilities, declared that Dimona was not yet being used for that purpose.[29] Why then did Nasser invest in a nuclear program? As a charismatic leader of the Arab world, he had strong incentives to measure up to Israel's actual or potential nuclear endowments. Nasser's ruling coalition was also acutely aware of its primary audience: domestic and regional Arab constituencies demanding supreme efforts to match Israel's imputed capabilities.[30] Yet even if Israel posed only a serious political rather than strategic threat, why did Egypt abandon its weapons program after the 1970s? Sadat's decision to embark on a peace process and abandon Egypt's nuclear aspirations could not be traced to dramatic changes in Israel's capabilities or perceived intentions, or to any other regional changes in the balance of power. If anything, Israel's capabilities had become more prominent. Sadat favored nuclear transparency as part of a broader shift in the model of political control that he adopted upon breaking sharply with Nasserism, which included a historical trip to Jerusalem. This variability in nuclear behavior from Nasser to Sadat in and of itself suggests that successive regimes differed over the imperative for nuclear weapons and that comparable structural conditions were manipulated accordingly, depending on the logics of domestic models of political survival.

Third, can Egypt's denuclearization be traced to hegemonic U.S. coercion? U.S. efforts in the early 1960s to persuade Nasser to avoid an arms race with Israel that Egypt could arguably not win were not very effective.[31] Nasser's domestic model did not encourage receptivity to U.S. (or Soviet) coercion. Under Sadat, the United States agreed to supply Egypt with eight nuclear power plants in 1975 subject to IAEA safeguards. The United States introduced new conditions in the late 1970s that Egypt found unacceptable (FASW). Sadat ratified the NPT in 1981 to advance a nuclear power program. Undoubtedly the United States played a vital role in Sadat's grand design for Egypt's new path. This is quite different, however, from arguing that the United States brought about Egypt's denuclearization. As I later argue in greater detail, Sadat read international incentives differently from Nasser, sought to build alternative bases of support (domestic and foreign), and made extensive use of U.S. economic, political, and military incentives. Yet U.S. influence was not preordained—it had failed miserably under Nasser—and became relevant only after Sadat's own initiatives were in place to reconstruct his domestic base of support through infitah (economic reform), growth, and Egypt-first policies. As a result, Egypt won a special status in U.S. foreign policy ever since, forcing the United States to tolerate Egypt's domestic repression and some of its international initiatives at odds with U.S. preferences, particularly during the 1995 NPT Review Conference.

Fourth, the neorealist hypothesis that deficiencies in conventional capabilities lead to the search for a nuclear deterrent also fails the Egyptian test. The 1955 Czech-Egyptian arms agreement trebled Egypt's military strength and maintained its superiority in conventional arms. Thus, Egypt considered nuclear weapons even when it was arguably conventionally stronger than Israel, and later, when its conventional gap with Israel was the narrowest. Egypt finally abandoned nuclear aspirations when its conventional capabilities had been dramatically overtaken by Israel. The logic of "more bang for the buck" proved itself extraneous to Egypt's considerations (in any case the view that nuclear weapons were cheaper in industrializing contexts is contestable). Although several former military officers cited nuclear weapons as the only means for closing the capability gap between Egypt and Israel, other officers such as Abd Al-Ghani Al-Gamasi and Major General Ismat Ezz opposed any WMD for balancing Israel, suggesting that missiles with conventional warheads were sufficient.[32]

In sum, these four points suggest that Egypt's nuclear behavior in the past three decades is at odds with core principles of neorealism. More recently Iran's nuclear defiance has become an important factor in Egypt's statements and arguably in its 2006 renewed commitment to revive its nuclear industry. Yet this timing also suggests that Egypt's reactions to Iran's alleged nuclearization become more intelligible when taking into account domestic pressures from constituencies mobilized by Iran's nuclearization. As chapter 8 suggested, Ahmadinejad arguably enjoys greater popularity in the proverbial streets of Cairo than in his own land, which compounds pressures on the Mubarak regime to respond to Iran's nuclear defiance. *If* Egypt does embark on a weapons-related program, structural neorealist accounts would need to provide persuasive evidence that (1) Iran is a *strategic* threat to Egypt rather than a political one; (2) distant Iran is a far more serious threat to Egypt's security than adjacent Israel has been (since dramatic steps would have been taken only after the rise of Iran and not vis-à-vis Israel for decades); (3) the causal mechanisms and consequences of changes in relative power are independent from domestic considerations; (4) Egypt's approach to Iran's nuclear capability is unconnected to Sunni-versus-Shi'a competition, a driver more embedded in constructed understandings of religion than in classical balance-of-power considerations; and (5) Egypt's changed nuclear behavior is not motivated by dramatic deterioration of the NPR in the aftermath of North Korea's test and Iran's alleged violations. Without dismissing these contending arguments, balance-of-power considerations may remain obscure and residual for understanding Egypt's nuclear behavior.

International Institutions: Egypt—Friend or Foe of the NPT?

Egypt was suspected of pursuing nuclear capabilities during the 1960s but signed the NPT in 1968. It abstained from ratifying it for the subsequent twelve years on the grounds that Israel had not signed it, but in 1980 the parliament approved ratification. Over time Egypt also developed a scathing criticism of the entire nonproliferation regime, pointing to the fundamentally discriminatory nature of its two-tiered system of nuclear "haves" and "have nots," as well as to "double standards" that allowed some states (Israel, India, Pakistan) to remain non-members. Egypt seized on this issue as a valuable tool to enhance its own credentials among Arab and non-aligned states and to curtail domestic criticism over its commitment to denuclearize, as discussed later.

In 1974, Egypt supported Iran's proposed UNGA resolution advancing the establishment of a Middle East NWFZ.[33] In 1980, Israel endorsed the idea, and since 1990 Mubarak pursued it forcefully in NPT conferences, IAEA meetings, and various public and private international fora. Only in the aftermath of the 1991 Madrid conference, however, did the idea enter the realm of actual discussions among participants in the Multilateral Middle East Peace Process. The Arms Control and Regional Security (ACRS) Working Group accelerated the pace of cooperation in the aftermath of the September 1993 Oslo agreements. ACRS created an operational basket to enhance military communications and a conceptual basket designed to address longer-term security objectives, consensual principles, and declaratory measures. The latter yielded a "Declaration of Principles" with alternative versions of the paths to a future WMD-free zone. Egypt demanded immediate discussion of WMD and Israel's NPT signature. Israel's version excluded reference to the NPT while endorsing a regional alternative.[34] Israel was reluctant to address arms control prior to achieving peace with all of its neighbors (Fahmy 2001). Sharp disagreements led the United States to cancel an ACRS plenary session scheduled for September 1995 (Benn 1995). Egypt suspended an ACRS meeting scheduled for May 1996, protesting Israel's position on the nuclear issue.[35]

Egypt challenged Israel's nuclear status in ACRS more forcefully than any other Arab state, asserting that Israel's refusal to adhere to the NPT provided justification for others to continue WMD programs.[36] A more accommodating Jordanian position that nonetheless retained the need for a WMDFZ is clear from Article 4(7)(b) of the 1994 Jordanian-Israeli peace treaty.[37] Egypt escalated its leadership role on NPT matters when, backed by Algeria, Libya, and Syria, it threatened to block indefinite NPT extension at the 1995 Review and Extension Conference unless Israel signed it (Cirincione et al. 2005:267). Other Arab states responded half-heartedly to this initiative. Ironically, the replacement of Israel's Labor-Meretz coalition—which had partnered the Oslo Accords and many of the achievements in the Multilateral Peace Process—with a hardline coalition headed by Binyamin Netanyahu in 1996, led Mubarak belatedly to acknowledge that "when we talked with Israel about this issue before the present government took over, their view was to open all the books. But Binyamin Netanyahu is not a man who has fought and does not know what war means."[38]

Although Egypt's NPT membership was regarded in good standing since its 1981 ratification, in 2004 IAEA inspectors found plutonium particles at an Egyptian nuclear facility, a claim that Egyptian officials denied. The experiments were allegedly designed to produce uranium metal (suitable for plutonium production) and uranium tetrafluoride (suitable for uranium-enrichment production), and resulted in three kilograms of uranium metal, with some experiments conducted as recently as 2003.[39]

These experiments were never reported to the IAEA, as required by Egypt's NPT commitments. Foreign Minister Ahmed Aboul Gheit told reporters that Egypt was committed to the NPT and that there was no truth behind reports that Cairo had a hidden nuclear program.[40] The IAEA reprimanded Egypt in a confidential memo for failing to declare nuclear sites and materials but reported no evidence for nuclear weapons procurement.[41] "The repeated failures by Egypt to report nuclear materials and facilities to the agency in a timely manner are a matter of concern," the report stated.[42] IAEA Chief El-Baradei, an Egyptian national, declared that "it is regrettable that some activities have not been reported to us, although . . . we haven't seen a proliferation concern. Yet I'd like to ask all countries to take their reporting obligations, their non-proliferation obligation, with the seriousness it deserves."[43]

A review of Egypt's public and private declarations and actual behavior makes it quite clear that its non-nuclear status can hardly be conceived as the result of normative abhorrence of nuclear weapons. NPT ratification was presented to the People's Assembly as part of a purely pragmatic effort to secure international support for a future nuclear industry. Furthermore, statements by Presidents Nasser, Sadat, and Mubarak—including many cited in the next section—intermittently asserted that Egypt would acquire nuclear weapons if Israel did or if Egypt thought its security demanded it. Ambassador Fahmy warned that continued proliferation in the Middle East would "force others to activate programmes that have so far remained dormant."[44] Amidst alternative pragmatic interpretations of Egypt's nuclear behavior, an Egyptian expert declared that "possessing nuclear weapons had no strategic value because Egypt could not use them in military confrontation with Israel, where Palestinian Arabs live and many surrounding Arab countries would be affected by nuclear fallout" (Said 2002:2). This position reveals no taboo against nuclear acquisition but perhaps a narrower normative base for eschewing nuclear weapons to avoid targeting kin. Yet nuclear efforts in the 1960s render such normative concerns less relevant. Furthermore, Nasser pioneered the use of chemical weapons in the region (tear gas, phosgene, and mustard agents) in the 1963–67 Yemen civil war, well before Saddam Hussein reintroduced them in the 1980s. Egypt was the alleged source of chemical weapons transfers to Syria (1970s) and Iraq (1980s) and it is estimated to hold a stockpile of chemical agents (CNSW, NTIW). Although Egypt has denied allegations that it aided Iraq's chemical weapons program, a former U.N. advisor and the ISG Report confirmed them.[45] Egypt has defended chemical weapons production by Arab states as a response to Israel's nuclear capabilities (Cordesman 1991); has refrained from signing the CWC until Israel accedes to the NPT; and has not ratified the BTWC, suggesting that WMD acquisition may not be taboo in Egypt's strategic toolkit.[46] Egypt has not signed the IAEA Additional Protocol and has not ratified the Pelindaba NWFZ or the CTBT (106 states had signed the Additional Protocol by 2005, but only 69 had enforced it).

DOMESTIC POLITICS: *KAWMIYA* (PAN-ARAB NATIONALISM) OR *INFITAH* (ECONOMIC OPENING)?

The impact of models of political survival on Egypt's nuclear choices can be traced rather clearly. Nasser and his military allies launched a strategy of import-substitution industrialization and domestic redistribution involving massive nationalizations of banking, industry, and infrastructure, including the Suez Canal. Proceeds would endow the revolutionary military regime with monopoly rents to gain and retain populist support. Import-substitution also involved income transfers from agriculture to develop infant industries under state sponsorship. State expansion and forceful suppression of private entrepreneurship eliminated economic and political competitors to the state, sapping private capital of both economic and political strength. By the 1960s, the state owned most enterprises in modern sectors of the economy, contributed 90 percent of value-added by plants employing ten or more workers, accounted for 91 percent of gross fixed investment, and consumed nearly 50 percent of total GNP (Anderson 1987; Binder 1988; Richards and Waterbury 1990:18; Owen and Pamuk 1999). Egypt's trade openness (imports plus exports as a percentage of GNP) declined from over 53 percent in the early 1950s, prior to the 1952 revolution, to 37 percent on average under Nasser ($4.4 billion 1965 GDP) (Heston and Summers 1991, 1995). The military-industrial-complex was a pivotal partner in Nasser's ruling coalition and allocated itself the equivalent of 24 percent of GDP.[47] Nasser actively sought hegemony over the Arab world, launching the short-lived United Arab Republic with Syria (1958–61) and intervening in Yemen against Saudi Arabia.

In tandem with an inward-looking, militarized, and belligerent nationalist policy, Nasser pursued nuclear weapons, increasing nuclear budgets, recruitment, and efforts to acquire a radiochemistry laboratory to learn to extract plutonium (Einhorn 2004:46). In 1961 Nasser declared that if Israel were to obtain nuclear weapons, "we will secure atomic weapons at any costs" (Bhatia 1988:48; NTIW). Haykal, Nasser's advisor and editor of *Al-Ahram*, was an ardent supporter of an Arab nuclear deterrent and reported that Nasser was bent on not missing another technological revolution as Egypt had presumably done with previous ones.[48] In 1965 Haykal said that Israel would probably propose to the United Arab Republic an agreement to ban production of atomic weapons through mutual inspections, but "naturally Egypt will refuse to become a party in any agreement with Israel."[49] Hedayat, backed by his mentor Defense Minister Abdel Hakim Amer, also advised Nasser to develop an independent nuclear fuel cycle. In 1965, Nasser approved and funded Hedayat's creation of the Design Consultants Association, a nuclear engineering consultancy group geared to implement that proposal. Other proponents of nuclear weapons (some of whom were supporters of Soviet political and economic models, even though Nasser suppressed Marxists) included Amer, Ali Sabri, General Mohammed Ahmed Sadeq, and Ahmed Sidki. Foreign Minister Ismail Fahmy was to resign his post later to protest Sadat's peace initiative (Jabber 1971, 1977; Bhatia 1988:57; Gregory 1995).[50] Nasser approached the Soviet Union, China, and India for help with a nuclear weapons program and repeatedly declared in 1966 that he would start a "preventive war" against Israel if he obtained conclusive evidence that Israel was developing nuclear weapons.[51]

Nuclear efforts after Egypt's 1967 military defeat by Israel declined largely as a product of a serious economic contraction. Heavy reliance on imported capital goods and the exhaustion of nationalization windfalls and foreign reserves from the Farouq era—exacerbated by military adventurism in Yemen and permanent war preparations against Israel—had deepened Egypt's balance-of-payments crisis.[52] This led to food and consumer goods shortages, high inflation, and reduced sources of foreign credit and foreign exchange, all in the midst of a population explosion and rising expectations. Ironically, the very model of political survival that made nuclear weapons an attractive feature also shrank available resources to a level that all but precluded them. The nationalist fervor that Nasser's policies had unleashed, however, remained strong and was only invigorated by Nasser's territorial losses in 1967. Given scarce resources and the inability to rely on nuclear weapons to compel Israel's withdrawal from Sinai, Egypt's priorities turned toward more robust conventional capabilities. In 1969, Nasser launched a "war of attrition" against Israel. According to Hedayat, Nasser never abandoned nuclear ambitions until his death in 1971.[53] In 1970, Qadhafi offered to fund Hedayat's plan for a dual-purpose 40 MW nuclear desalination plant, but the plan was later cancelled due to tensions between Egypt and Libya following an attempted coup against Nasser's successor, Sadat, allegedly funded by Qadhafi. Hedayat also recruited a Libyan scientist working in the United States for Egypt's AEO.[54]

Sadat launched the 1973 October/Yom Kippur War, portraying it as an Egyptian victory insofar as Egypt crossed the Suez Canal. This surprise attack on Israel enabled Sadat to launch a strikingly innovative strategy of political survival, compared to predominant models throughout the region. At the heart of the model was infitah—the "economic crossing" launched in 1974—which entailed interrelated domestic, regional, and international dimensions. Facing incalculable political risks, Sadat reversed Nasserism, emphasizing economic growth, foreign investment, exports, military conversion, and a new relationship with international markets and institutions. The requirements for transforming the domestic political economy through infitah compelled Sadat to visit Jerusalem in 1977 and negotiate an unprecedented peace treaty with Israel in 1979 (Handoussa and Shafik 1993:20–24; Karawan 1994). This domestic and regional agenda had synergies with enhanced U.S. economic and political support. *Infitah* increased Egypt's trade openness from 33 percent (average under Nasser) in 1973 to over 61 percent in 1975 and 78 percent in 1979.[55] FDI inflows more than doubled between 1974 and 1976. Most dramatic was Sadat's contraction of Egypt's military expenditures from 52 to 13 percent of GNP between 1975 and 1979, an average decline of 3.86 percent yearly.[56] Infitah, however, also increased Egypt's dependence on foreign loans, raising the debt burden from $1.64 billion in 1970 to $10 billion in 1978 (Barnett 1992:222; Springborg 1989).

Unsurprisingly from the standpoint of this analysis, Sadat launched infitah in 1974, the same year that Egypt joined Iran in advancing for the first time the idea of a NWFZ. Whether or not this was a viable plan likely to be adopted, it was expected to improve Egypt's reputation and ingratiate Sadat with the United States and other Western powers in an issue area (nonproliferation) that they regarded as most important among international regimes. In 1974 Sadat also committed to accepting full-scope IAEA safeguards, disregarding opposition by nationalists including Sabri, Sidki, and Haykal. Sadat 's abandonment of nuclear ambitions was part of his broader challenge of domestic foes, particularly Nasserites and Islamist groups, both of which included prominent nuclear advocates. Sadat cancelled the AEA's autonomy, moving it under the Ministry of Electricity. The precise sequence in which these political, economic, and nuclear steps unfolded in 1974 is less relevant than the fact that Sadat sought to advance them all as components of his new model of political survival. Ending an expensive nuclear arms race with a formidable opponent was an important prerequisite for economic reform and growth, as was advancing a nuclear policy that endeared Sadat to the West, with an eye on a U.S. supply of nuclear reactors. Resolving chronic energy shortages through nuclear power was also seen as an important factor for the long-term sustainability of infitah.[57] Sadat's support for Iran's NWFZ initiative and initial steps toward nuclear transparency paved the way for Nixon's promise of nuclear reactors during his 1974 visit. Egypt began receiving a $2 billion average annual U.S. military and economic subsidy since 1979. Sadat also requested a foreign aid package of $18 billion from the G-7 in 1979. In 1980, his government persuaded the People's

Assembly that NPT ratification was required to obtain international support for nuclear energy.

Sadat's model, particularly its emphasis on relations with Israel and the United States, cost him much capital regionally, including Egypt's ousting from the Arab League. The shift from Nasser to Sadat and its implications for nuclear policies are aptly captured by Egyptian analyst Mohamed Kadry Said (2002:1): "Sadat realized that reaching a settlement to the Arab-Israeli conflict is a precondition for Egyptian development. To achieve this goal, Sadat concentrated his energy towards enhancing U.S.-Egyptian relations and to foster a peace process with Israel. He worked hard to change the Egyptian domestic, regional and international environment in a way conductive to peace. Changing Egyptian attitudes towards arms control arrangements was one of the ways of realizing his aims."

President Mubarak maintained Sadat's political model, including its emphasis on domestic economic reform and renunciation of nuclear weapons. The Inshas reactor was shut down for renovation during the 1980s. Pro-nuclear inward-looking secular and Islamist forces—including nationalist politicians, clerics, and some retired military officers, nuclear scientists, and technologists—continued to challenge Mubarak's economic and nuclear policies alike. Prominent supporters of nuclear weapons on the secular side included parliamentary speaker Ahmad Fathi Srour and parliamentary Foreign Liaison Committee Chief Mustafa Al-Faqi, who, pointing to Egypt's ten scientists working as IAEA inspectors (including director-general El-Baradei) added that "we need to begin a strategic nuclear and deterrence program," and "the question now is would it not be better for us to proceed with possession of Arab nuclear arms? . . . Nuclear usage for peaceful purposes can lead to other usage if the funds and know how are available. We have both."[58] These voices also emphasized the modernization potential of a revived nuclear program and the fact that in Egypt "there is an explosion among the scientific cadres in the nuclear sphere—they have no work."

Salameh Ahmad Salameh and others writing for *Al-Ahram* also encouraged changes in nuclear policy. Mustafa 'Alawi expressed that "Egypt made a gross strategic miscalculation when it chose to ratify the NPT in 1981. . . . Today, Egypt should certainly pursue a peaceful nuclear option, because such capabilities can be transformed to perform nonpeaceful ends in a very short time."[59] Mounir Megahed (1998:1) of Egypt's Nuclear Reactor Authority wrote, "A political decision to revive the Egyptian nuclear program . . . will be similar to President Al-Nasser's decision to nationalize the Suez Canal. It will revive the spirit and the feelings of national pride which would provide the basis of popular support for the development plans and the sacrifices that may be required." The pan-Arab opposition party, established in 2000, declared in its platform that "Egypt should obtain nuclear weapons in order to maintain peace in the region."[60] Former military officers such as Sa'd Al-Din Al-Shadhili, Mahmoud Muhammad Khalaf, and chief of the Arab Industrialization Authority General Salah Halabi also called for Egypt's development of nuclear weapons.[61] Former Minister of Defense and director of intelligence Amin Howeidi wrote to an Egyptian newspaper that Israel's nuclear threat can be adequately countered with conventional, chemical, biological, and incendiary weapons "until Egypt develops its own nuclear deterrent."[62]

On the Islamist side, citing the will of Caliph Abu Bakr, leading Egyptian cleric Moahmmed Sayyid al-Tantawi encouraged Arabs and Muslims in 1999 "to acquire nuclear weapons as an answer to the Israeli threat."[63] A *fatwa* issued by the Al-Azhar Religious Ruling Committee stated that developing nuclear weapons was a "religious obligation" and, in the words of the committee's head, "Muslims must obtain all kinds of weapons, not only nuclear weapons," challenging the argument that some weapons are legitimate and others are not. Another prominent cleric, Muhammad al-Ghazali, prodded Muslims to acquire a nuclear capability greater than that of Israel (Hashmi 2004:345). While the ruling coalition has repressed Islamist radicals, it has also coopted some of its themes to offset domestic opposition. Until the 1970s, Israel's policy of ambiguity provided Egypt with a fig leaf. Sadat and others initially argued that, although they believed Israel was capable of manufacturing nuclear bombs, it [Israel] "does not have nuclear weapons."[64] Acknowledgment of Israel's nuclear capabilities would have added to a sense of impotence, perceived failure to respond in kind, and growing popular dissatisfaction with Israel's nuclear monopoly (Jabber 1977; Shikaki 1985; Karem 1988; Solingen 1994b).

However, particularly after Vanunu's declarations, domestic pressures to confront Israel's nuclear status increased. In its role as "regional entrepreneur," Egypt began emphasizing Israel's nuclear capabilities very effectively to rally domestic and regional support. Relations with Israel, though often cold, provided Egypt with an important brokering role between Israel and Palestine and between Israel and the Arab world more broadly. Observers interpreted Egypt's positions in ACRS as reflecting mutually reinforcing objectives to satisfy domestic constituencies and retain the trappings of leadership in the Arab world.[65] Indian and Pakistani nuclear tests in 1998 increased domestic public opinion pressures on Egypt's nuclear policy. In October 1998, Mubarak expressed that Egypt "will not hesitate" to develop or acquire nuclear weapons should it become necessary.[66] Former Foreign Minister Amr Moussa became a prominent architect of Egypt's nuclear entrepreneurship as Arab League secretary-general. Iran's nuclear defiance—and, indirectly North Korea's

2006 test—have arguably made the task of Arab nuclear coordination ever more pressing. In response, Mubarak and his son and likely successor, Gamal, encouraged Egypt to invest in nuclear power as an integral part of Egypt's national security.[67]

CONCLUSION

Egypt vied for leadership in the Arab world, sometimes going to war against Israel and other Arab states. Faced with the potential for a nuclear-armed Israel, Egypt first considered acquiring nuclear weapons but later renounced them. Neorealist explanations do not work well in explaining Egypt's denuclearization and why it remained an anomaly among Middle East contenders for three decades. First, Israel's capabilities had not declined as Egypt rejected "reactive proliferation." In a balance-of-power and self-help world, a more powerful, nuclear-armed rival over time would have been expected to trigger forceful efforts by Egypt to counter it with its own nuclear deterrent. Nuclear weapons designs by other regional rivals—Iraq, Libya, Iran—should have had the same effects, and yet, as those presumably became more threatening, Egypt retained its non-nuclear status. Second, Egypt considered nuclear weapons when it may have been estimated to enjoy conventional superiority or when the gap with Israel was the narrowest; and abandoned nuclear aspirations when Israel's conventional capabilities had dramatically overtaken Egypt's. Third, Egypt considered nuclear weapons when the Soviets arguably provided it with some protection, and abandoned them in the absence of any external guarantees by external powers.[68] Fourth, it is plausible that, despite Nasser's public rhetoric during the 1950s and 1960s, Egyptian leaders did not perceive external threats as warranting nuclear weapons.[69] That possibility would also undermine the common neorealist argument about what drives nuclear weapons acquisition, namely "reactive proliferation," or responding to adversaries' efforts to acquire nuclear weapons. Egypt, however, has recently expressed concerns with Iran. Were Egypt to embark on a weapons program in the future, a structural perspective would have to show that changes in the balance of power triggered this shift rather than growing domestic pressures from pro-nuclear forces, popular support for Ahmadinejad's nuclear defiance within Egypt, identity concerns with the rise of Shi'ism, or a dramatic decline of the NPR due to challenges by North Korea and Iran. Furthermore, it would have to explain why balance of power compels such action vis-à-vis Iran but has hardly operated vis-à-vis Israel, which Egypt has tolerated as a nuclear weapon state for decades, arguably with the understanding that those capabilities were solely defensive.

Both early efforts by Nasser to develop a weapons program and the subsequent shift by Sadat to renounce it were compatible with the respective models each leader relied on to maintain power. Nuclear decisions were embedded in broader changes in domestic political strategies that led to changes in Egypt's strategic alliances and regional policies. Whereas Nasser's model thrived in an aura of inward-looking self-reliance, hypernationalism, and military-technical prowess, Sadat's emphasis on economic growth, foreign investment, exports, military conversion, and a new relationship with international markets and institutions did not leave much room for an expensive nuclear program. Infitah, however, has not led to the positive cycle observed among East Asian cases that renounced nuclear weapons: high economic growth, high integration into the global political-economy, high legitimacy for internationalizing models, and lower incentives to resort to nuclear weapons. That Egypt has been able to retain denuclearizing status despite what some may consider a faltering economic reform is remarkable. Yet strains in—and barriers to—an internationalizing model also explain a strong lingering revisionist current advocating nuclearization. Whether or not Egypt maintains or overturns its post-1981 nuclear policies hinges, to a significant extent, on whether or not this current can overwhelm standard-bearers of a more open economy in Egypt's political system.

PART FOUR

Conclusions

CHAPTER TWELVE

Findings, Futures, and Policy Implications

THIS BOOK'S OBJECTIVE has been primarily analytical, aiming at a better understanding of why states acquire or renounce nuclear weapons and revisiting how we study this subject. A prolific literature has been largely devoted to supply-side concerns related to international control of sensitive nuclear technologies.[1] The demand side—why nuclear aspirants contemplate or acquire nuclear weapons—has received less systematic attention, neglecting the thirty-year-old warning by Nobel Economics Laureate Thomas Schelling (1976:80) that "the emphasis has to shift from physical denial and technology secrecy to the things that determine incentives and expectations." Three decades later, former chief U.N. weapons inspector Hans Blix acknowledged that removing states' incentives to acquire nuclear weapons remains the most important issue on the nonproliferation agenda: "No incentives, no weapons, no use."[2] IAEA Director-General and Nobel Peace Laureate Mohammad El-Baradei admitted that "technology has come out of the box . . . we need to have a different approach to handling issues of non-proliferation. This should not consist only of controlling the source of the water, but we must look at the reasons why countries are trying to acquire nuclear weapons."[3]

In an effort to shed light on this question, this book has reviewed both traditional and novel approaches to international relations while revisiting conventional wisdoms. As Lebow (2003:388) argues, "The deeper we embed ourselves in a paradigm, the more difficult it becomes to abstract ourselves from it and look at the world afresh." The effort here has been to avoid this conceptual trap and look at the problem kaleidoscopically in Roshomon fashion, from various angles, hoping to generate new insights. A focused comparison between East Asia and the Middle East provides fertile ground to explore old and newer paradigms regarding nuclear behavior. The two regions are at the forefront of the policy debate; they jointly account for a significant proportion of nuclear aspirants since the NPT's inception; despite comparable initial conditions in earlier decades— authoritarian rule, limited economic interdependence, regional security dilemmas, and state-building challenges—their nuclear trajectories have diverged significantly; each region exhibits anomalies that are useful methodologically for understanding regional effects; their disparate nuclear trajectories defy technological determinism since the best endowed in nuclear power and industrial technology (East Asia) were arguably less prone to acquire nuclear weapons; and there have been no systematic attempts to compare these two regions' nuclear behavior despite these and other research design considerations that make them an important analytical puzzle.

The empirical chapters addressed this cross-regional variation, examined different conceptual paths to explaining choices for or against nuclear weapons, transcended the limitations of mono-causal explanations, and pointed to advantages gained from integrating recent scholarship in international relations into the study of nuclear proliferation. In some cases, alternative causal paths were found to lead to the same outcome, making it difficult to assess their respective causal weight and estimate the necessity of a particular factor. As George and Bennett (2005:25) suggest, "Case studies remain much stronger at assessing *whether* and *how* a variable mattered to the outcome than at assessing *how much* it mattered." Yet some cases have clearly revealed the tendency to overestimate particular variables and underestimate others. This chapter begins by recapitulating general findings and possible directions for future research, exploring the prospects for continuity and change through the lenses of theories reviewed, and discussing potential scenarios that might "test" assumptions regarding the effects of structural power, international institutions, norms, democracy, and models of political survival on nuclear choices. The final section begins the task of distilling policy implications for international and regional institutions, major powers, and NGOs in their common efforts to strengthen nonproliferation.

Overview of Findings: Will the Future Resemble the Past?

Neorealism

The cases that we reviewed point to the *perception* of existential security as a very important consideration in some cases. Yet understanding nuclear outcomes as the sole perfunctory reflection of international structure, balance of power, and self-help can come at a high analytical cost. Such perspectives are underdetermining, compete with alternative explanations in what should be their best arena of argumentation, fail to explain some of the outcomes observed, and are incomplete in explaining others. All cases raised the problem of underdetermination, where the theory conjures up multiple possible outcomes. States facing difficult structural conditions had multiple choices compatible with securing their survival, ranging from overt to ambiguous nuclearization and several non-nuclear alternatives. States opted for different solutions—nuclear and non-nuclear—to comparable security predicaments. Thus, self-help as an analytic category did not provide clear markers for likely behavior, was unable to forecast whether nuclear weapons enhanced or undermined security, led to indeterminate predictions about regional outcomes, and invariably required additional information unrelated to power balances.

These shortcomings demand special attention because they relate to the theory's performance in its home court—high national security—where structural realist theory should perform best. Nuclear behavior provides easy grounds for testing theories of relative power, balance of power, and *state* security in an anarchic world. Since nuclear weapons are presumably the heart, or the inner sanctum, of states' security dilemmas, the study of why states acquire or renounce them loads the dice *in favor* of neorealism, constituting the most auspicious domain for corroborating its tenets. An additional consideration tilts explanations toward neorealism when analyzing security outcomes. Leaders, politicians, and bureaucrats are more likely to portray decisions for or against nuclear weapons as dictated by "reasons of state" rather than as domestic political expediency. Thus, much of the public record (and even the private one) often points to more "legitimate" considerations of balance of power and state survival as underlying nuclear decisions. Several consequences stem from this doubly privileged analytical position. First, the very fact that nuclear behavior as a subject matter favors neorealism in principle ironically does *not* make nuclear decisions an optimal arena for validating its canons from a methodological standpoint. A good or crucial test of any theory is one that forces the theory to survive *un*favorable conditions (Eckstein 1975). A theory that can be confirmed despite adverse circumstances gains significant analytical traction. A theory that cannot be easily confirmed even under the best circumstances suggests potentially serious problems. Second, because of its assumed status as "favored theory" in the analysis of nuclear choices, even partial deviations from unalloyed neorealist predictions constitute significant challenges to the theory. In its home turf, a theory must be able to explain the overwhelming majority of cases *with ease and at high levels of confidence* and parsimony, and without problems of underdetermination. Third, as the "most likely" explanation for this subject matter, neorealism should effortlessly crowd out other theories, voiding them of much explanatory value. One should not need to go any further than structural power to understand nuclear outcomes.

The empirical chapters suggest that structural power can be a useful category in some cases but, in its crude form, does not explain the overwhelming majority of cases easily or at high levels of confidence and parsimony, and it certainly does not avoid underdetermination nor obviate the need for exploring other hypotheses. If structural power told the story, then Egypt, adjacent to Israel, would have been far more likely to acquire nuclear weapons in a pattern of "reactive proliferation" than other Middle East states such as Libya. Israel was Egypt's main adversary in several wars and was suspected of developing nuclear weapons by the early 1960s. Furthermore, states with lower external existential threats (Libya and arguably early 1970s Iraq) forcefully pursued nuclear weapons whereas states with much higher threats (Taiwan, South Korea, Egypt, Vietnam, Japan, Syria, or Jordan for that matter) did not. As Betts (2000) argues, insecurity is not a sufficient condition for acquiring nuclear weapons; many insecure states have not. The reverse is also true; the absence of particularly severe external threats has not precluded states from considering or pursuing nuclear weapons. Disagreements over what constitutes a structural threat or a genuine deterioration in the balance of power, and how to measure their dynamics over time and across cases, is precisely one conceptual Achilles heel of structural realism. Do threats derive from changes in relative capabilities, from "rival" states as abstract entities trapped in international anarchy, or from the way particular leaders, regimes, or ruling coalitions interpret and define them? and what explains the latter? The dynamics of security dilemmas differ when particular *regimes* are perceived as proximate sources of threat rather than when threats are perceived to emanate from *states* as fixtures of strategic landscapes. Hence, an important frontier in the study of nuclear behavior entails a proper understanding of analytical distinctions and interplays between *regime* and *state* security, or internal and external political survival, which are often interelated. External threats to states have been quite real for Taiwan, Israel, South Korea, and Japan, and harder to construe solely in terms of domestic regime survival considerations, although the latter provide important information in those cases as well. Leaders in Iraq, Iran, Libya, and North Korea construed state security as co-terminal with their respective regimes' survival. However, it is those regimes' models and policies, not merely their states' locations or relative power endowments, that have created threats where there were none, or enhanced them where they existed.

The cases of denuclearization in Japan, Taiwan, and South Korea are often considered to be among the most closely conforming to neorealism among post-1968 nuclear aspirants identified in chapter 1. Yet problems of underdetermination, incompleteness, lack of parsimony, and powerful competing hypotheses emerge even there. First, unalloyed power-balancing perspectives would have expected at least two of these cases to engage in "reactive proliferation" following China's nuclear test in 1964. Relinquishing nuclear weapons in the face of such threats is counterintuitive for such arguments, particularly in the case of Japan. Second, competing structural arguments lead to disparate predictions about what states in the same situation as these three might do—from renouncing to acquiring nuclear weapons—leaving ample a priori ambiguity about which outcome best reduces vulnerability. Third, these states' choices are often traced to U.S. alliances and commitments, which undeniably played significant roles yet beg the question of why technologically endowed states choose alliances over self-help, considering serious episodes of "abandonment" and "entrapment." Indeed, in all three cases, alliance was chosen over self-reliant deterrence at a historical moment *least* conducive to such decisions. During the 1970s, the hegemon at the other end of the alliance was dramatically weakened by the debacle in Southeast Asia, and Nixon's Guam doctrine spelled less than robust commitments to East Asian allies. Fourth, the United States could still coercively deny indigenous deterrents, as it did in Taiwan and South Korea. Yet U.S. and Soviet efforts to compel nuclear aspirants (allies and foes) failed repeatedly, succeeded with some targets at some points but not others, or played secondary roles in their denuclearization. Superpowers' commitments to North Korea, Iraq, Israel (or Pakistan, France, and Britain) did not lead them to renounce nuclear weapons. Nor did the *absence* of security guarantees play any role in Egypt, Libya (2003), South Africa, Argentina, or Brazil's decisions to reverse nuclear ambitions. Too many cases of denuclearization were not the result of successful hegemonic coercion. Superpowers' coercion on Iraq (until 2003), Argentina, Brazil, India, Pakistan, South Africa, North Korea, Israel, Iran, and Libya for several decades—provide numerous instances of the limits of hegemony (Dunn 1982). As Waltz (2003:38) persuasively argues, "In the past half-century, no country has been able to prevent other countries from going nuclear if they were determined to do so." One logical inference from this statement would be that Japan, Taiwan, and South Korea were not as determined to acquire nuclear weapons as many believe. The empirical chapters provide some support for this proposition, suggesting that domestic models can explain from whence resolve, or lack thereof, comes.

Positive and negative hegemonic inducements seem clearly insufficient to explain outcomes for many nuclear aspirants, making Japan, Taiwan, and South Korea more anomalous than typical. Indeed, in some sense, these three arguably provide hegemonic arguments with "easy" cases most likely to confirm their expectations. Yet even here the mechanisms of hegemony can be understood only by probing into domestic conditions that created acquiescence in these cases where so many others stood firm. Understanding relative receptivity to both coercive and persuasive aspects of U.S. influence requires us to consider reigning domestic models of political survival. In all three cases, indigenous nuclear weapons would have seriously undermined favored strategies of economic growth, international competitiveness, and global access. The choice for alliance *itself* was the product of domestic models that favored it over other options, trumping internal demands for nuclear weapons and generating openness to hegemonic inducements. The links between commitments to internationalized models and renunciation of expensive nuclear competitions—as the respective chapters reveal—are thick in these cases. As Premier Miki expressed to Secretary Schlesinger in the mid-1970s, "Asian countries are feeling the need to strengthen their internal system, stabilize their political situation, and improve the public welfare. Military security is important but cannot be considered in isolation."[4] Thus there was far from the strong demand for nuclear weapons in Japan that would have presumably compelled a strong U.S. denial. South Korea bears the marks of stronger hegemonic coercion, but even without it, nuclear weapons would have endangered Park Chung Hee's domestic model of political survival, risking sharp economic decline, increasing political and economic instability, and isolating South Korea from the regional and international market as well as the political and institutional forces that underpinned Park's model. Taiwan's quintessential external vulnerability stemmed from much weaker U.S. commitments than to Japan and South Korea. Despite signs of some military demand for nuclear weapons, there was no consensus among KMT leaders who pinned their regime's survival on export-led economic growth.

A closer look at Japan illustrates both the utility and limitations of the U.S. alliance for explaining Japan's renunciation of an indigenous deterrent. First, ironically, extending a nuclear umbrella over an ally does not necessarily constitute a "strong case" for validating the claim that alliance explains (the ally's) abstention. As argued earlier, social scientific claims are best corroborated when submitted to "hard" tests, where conditions for the operation of the claim are less easily met. One can be more confident about a theory when its tenets are instantiated under conditions least likely to support the theory. Conversely, our confidence is undermined when the theory does not hold well under conditions that ought to have favored its corroboration. Accordingly, a hard (methodologically "fit") case would be one in which U.S. inducements through alliance are shown to prevail *despite* the target ally's very strong demand for nuclear weapons. Cases where U.S. inducements operate *in the absence* of such demand are much weaker tests of this theory. Chapter 3 suggests that Japan's domestic politics did not generate strong demand for nuclear weapons. Hence, Japan does not seem a robust test of the alliance hypothesis. There was neither demand for a Japanese deterrent nor a supply of U.S. coercion.

Second, Japan's critical NPT decisions took place in the 1970s, at the alliance's lowest point, when dilemmas of commitment would have featured prominently in Japan's calculations. Yet neorealist theory has excelled in raising this inherent *problematique* of alliances—credibility, commitment, entrapment—that nuclear weapons can only compound, even within NATO. Third, such dilemmas reinforce competing unalloyed neorealist hypotheses that self-help precludes great powers like Japan from relying on others for their own security. That the world's second largest economy, with sophisticated industrial and nuclear infrastructures, chose to depend on its ally's nuclear umbrella suggests more an anomaly than a confirmation that structural power calculations rule the world. As Waltz (1993:64) argues regarding Japan, "One may wonder how a state with the economic capability of a great power can refrain from arming itself with the weapons that have served so well as the great deterrent." Yet Japan's predicted imminent acquisition of nuclear weapons has not happened over the past four decades, thus far not even after North Korea's 2006 nuclear test.[5] Fourth, Japan's decisions are even more startling from a neorealist viewpoint considering the sometimes ambiguous U.S. position regarding Japan's nuclear options. How the United States would have responded had there been strong Japanese demand for nuclear weapons remains unclear, entirely in the domain of counterfactuals. Nixon and others certainly signaled forbearance and perhaps encouragement of Japan's nuclearization even during crucial debates over the NPT and subsequently. Even if this position was not dominant in successive U.S. administrations, it had the potential of turning the alliance argument on its head, making it a latent source rather than a barrier to Japan's nuclearization. Finally, if alliances alone (rather than prestige or other considerations) told the story, post–World War II Britain and France might not have acquired nuclear weapons (Rosecrance 1964). At most one could classify the alliance as necessary in this case but certainly not sufficient for explaining nuclear outcomes, and only when one considers the alliance's role in Japan's domestic politics.

The power of hegemons to persuade and coerce states to forgo nuclear weapons should not be underestimated but neither should it be *over*estimated. Hegemonic pressures or inducements do not single-handedly and invariably account for outcomes. North Korea enjoyed the war-tested protection of two superpowers, China and the Soviet Union, yet nurtured nuclear designs early on, well before experiencing severe fears of abandonment with the Soviet Union's collapse. One cannot understand why such dilemmas were so extreme in this case without dwelling on juche, the Kims' autarkic model of domestic political survival since the 1950s. North Korea's search for nuclear weapons, which began in the 1960s, bred changes in relative power that would have predicted reactive nuclearization among neighboring states. Yet neither Japan nor South Korea altered their non-nuclear status for over three decades. Immediate responses to North Korea's 2006 nuclear test were met with reaffirmations that neither would develop nuclear weapons. An unalloyed neorealist logic (skeptical of alliance explanations) could explain why North Korea developed and tested nuclear weapons, but would also need to demonstrate that North Korea faced the most dire structural predicament of all East Asian cases examined in part 2.

Part 3 suggests that of all Middle East cases, Libya and Egypt arguably provide least support for neorealism, as do perhaps Iraq in the early 1970s and Iran since the 1990s. Decisions taken in Iran and Iraq in the 1980s, and Israel in the 1950s and 1960s, provide stronger support. Yet neorealism is underdetermining for all five cases, is problematic and non-parsimonious in most of them, and cannot easily exclude alternative explanations in any of the five. First, structural power accounts of Libya's nuclear pursuits suffer from more serious failings than most other cases. Egypt, the neighboring state most likely to overpower Qadhafi's *regime*, renounced nuclear weapons prior to Qadhafi's most determined efforts to acquire them in the 1990s. Libya accelerated its search for centrifuges and weapons designs just as Algeria's facilities came under IAEA supervision in the 1990s. Ironically for neorealist perspectives, Libya renounced nuclear weapons in the 1990s, *after* Egypt's largest research reactor with potential plutonium-producing capabilities had been built, *after* Egypt began alluding to potential changes in its nuclear posture arguably related to Iran's nuclearization, and *after* Algeria opted for a second large research reactor as well.[6] Had the logic of self-help applied, these developments would have led Libya in the opposite direction than the one observed. As Qadhafi himself reportedly stated (chapter 10), his nuclear weapons "*had no target.*" His initial search for nuclear weapons in the early 1970s preceded the 1986 U.S. attack. Israel provided a useful *political* target, but the timings of both Libya's efforts to acquire and relinquish nuclear weapons question the relevance of the Israeli factor from a structural power-balancing standpoint. Qadhafi heightened the search for nuclear weapons when Israel was least menacing (1990s), but Israel was declared no security threat after its fighter jets flew over Libya's skies and during Ariel Sharon's premiership. No significant changes in relative power between Libya and Israel can explain such transformation. The gap between the two—despite Libya's abundant oil resources—was and has remained wide. Threats were constructed and deconstructed according to Qadhafi's evolving domestic models and regional implications.

Second, changes in the balance of power do not provide coherent, parsimonious, accounts of Egypt's denuclearization. Despite the rise in the conventional military power of Israel and other regional rivals with nuclear ambitions (Iraq, Libya, Iran), Egypt has rejected "reactive proliferation" since the 1970s. Egypt (under Nasser) considered nuclear weapons when its conventional gap with Israel was the narrowest, and it abandoned nuclear aspirations (under Sadat) when the gap widened. Egypt considered nuclear weapons when it arguably enjoyed stronger external (Soviet) security guarantees but abandoned them in their absence (the United States never provided Egypt with equivalent guarantees).

Third, Iraq's early nuclear efforts during the 1970s—prior to the war with Iran and Israel's attack on Osiraq—are much less compatible with neorealism than its nuclear behavior in the late 1980s. Saddam asserted that WMD helped him reverse the fate of wars (that he had initiated), presumably halting Iranian ground troops and deterring allied forces from entering Baghdad in 1991. Yet other Iraqis, including Saddam's cousin and former Minister of Defense Adnan Khayr Allah, thought nuclear weapons made Iraq more vulnerable. Other Iraqi officials confirmed that Saddam wielded nuclear weapons as symbols of dominance designed to intimidate domestic rivals no less than foreign ones. Saddam himself acknowledged that the mere threat of chemical weapons helped him crush internal revolts.

Fourth, the war with Iraq provides some support for balance-of-power considerations as a source of Iran's nuclearization but less so after 1991 and U.N. containment of Saddam (Chubin 2006). The 2003 war in Iraq eliminated Saddam altogether, although concerns with Pakistan arguably remained. Following Pakistan's 1998 test, Rafsanjani stressed that Iran "must be concerned" (Taykeh 2006:144). Yet Pakistan's president Pervez Musharaf met with Khamene'i and Ahmadinejad in Tehran in early 2007, and discussed an Indo-Iranian natural gas pipeline that would cross Pakistan. Whether the United States became a genuine motive for Iran's sustained nuclear efforts remains contested. U.S. overextension (Afghanistan, Iraq, North Korea, and other challenges) and concerns with Iran's terrorist networks are arguably more powerful deterrents against U.S. attack than are any budding Iranian nuclear capabilities. Israel provides another important ideological and political justification that Iranian leaders have used instrumentally for domestic purposes. In the end, however, as Chubin and Litwak (2003:105) argue, Iran has no existential threats requiring it to compensate for military imbalances with nuclear weapons. While others may reject this premise, the variability of means consistent with coping with external threats—evident in Iran's public debates—calls into question nuclearization as the only outcome compatible with neorealism. Competing Iranian leaders have defined threats and appropriate responses to them differently.

Fifth, Israel's concerns with its survival as a state are widely accepted as a source of alleged nuclearization. Extreme conditions of vulnerability in the 1950s and 1960s—a U.N. conventional weapons boycott, no external security guarantees—make it an easier case for neorealism, but not strong ground for testing the theory. As with other cases, however, even in Israel, balance-of-power considerations led to various possible outcomes, from an acknowledged nuclear deterrent to ambiguity and non-nuclear alternatives. This defies the notion of a single neorealist understanding or coherent strategic prescription regarding its nuclear choices (Reiss 1988). Given this underdetermination, Israel's ambiguous nuclear policy—as any other outcome—can be recounted as the product of relative power considerations a posteriori. But could ambiguity have been anticipated a priori? As argued in chapter 2, the same concerns with U.S. responses that might explain ambiguity in this case failed to deter myriad other cases of nuclear aspirants that did not respond with ambiguity but with nuclear tests, defiance, or nuclear renunciation. Israel's choice for ambiguity had sources not only in external constraints but also in domestic ones. Said differently, although continuous U.S. support was undoubtedly of utmost concern to Israeli decision-makers, it is unclear whether or not Israeli leaders would have formulated a different policy in the absence of that consideration. Other sources of ambiguity existed, and are recounted later in this chapter. Finally, the search for an ultimate deterrent—ambiguous or explicit—is amenable to constructivist interpretations that are quite different conceptually from balance-of-power arguments. Such interpretations emphasize Israel's search for security not merely as a result of shifts in relative power but more as the product of a resolve to avoid another Holocaust. Similarly, Israel's precarious status at the U.N.—where it saw Arab- and Muslim-backed initiatives prevail via the power of arithmetic majority, if not always on the basis of merit— deepened Israel's sense of isolation in a way not captured by balance-of-power considerations.

Sixth, Arab-Arab and Arab-Iranian disputes have arguably been a more fundamental motivating force for nuclear capabilities—from a neorealist standpoint—than have changes in Arab-Israeli and Iranian-Israeli relative power. The historical analyses of Iraq, Iran, and Libya, as well as Egypt's more recent concerns with Iran, suggest that Israel has provided a secondary layer of incentives at best.[7] Neither Israel's nor China's nuclearization in the 1960s turned these countries into the *primary* targets of reactive nuclear programs respectively in Iraq, Iran, Libya, or North Korea. Egypt, Taiwan, and Japan would have arguably had Israel or China as primary targets, but all three refrained from acquiring them.

Cumulatively, these findings pose significant challenges to neorealism. Ironically, as Sigal (1998:249) has argued, "Realism seems to be the secular religion of the foreign policy establishment. Those who want to play a part in policy-making believe in it, or at least pay lip service to it by acting as if they believe in it, even if they do not." Yet predictions of proliferation do not necessarily flow automatically from systemic incentives, to which different states respond differently (Bueno de Mesquita et al. 1993). Competing hypotheses examined in the remainder of this chapter suggest additional limitations and caveats to an overemphasis on international power distribution as a source of denuclearization. At issue is not to question this theory's applicability in some cases but rather its nearly universal acceptance as the driving force of all or most nuclear programs. It is as important to recognize enduring contributions as is, borrowing from Mahoney (2005:20), to "break out of a reigning theoretical straightjacket." Neorealism's contributions can be enhanced by specifying a priori the precise underlying measures of relative power and thresholds that lead to nuclearization, so as to avoid circularity and ex post facto rationalizations (such as "state x went nuclear because of acute insecurity," whereby the acuteness threshold is detected by a nuclear test). Sharpening core concepts will help cast the argument in falsifiable terms and enable more clearly defined and testable propositions. These improvements should include a better specification of when, how, and why hegemony may or may not account for nuclear outcomes. The task for unalloyed neorealism also entails explaining variation in nuclear outcomes independently of domestic or international institutional and normative considerations. Alternatively, studies can follow neoclassical realist variants (Christensen 1996; Glaser 2000) more open to domestic politics as filters defining geo-strategic threats.

Without such amendments and improvements, the inherent difficulties of a crude neorealist logic encumber our ability to extend its use into the future. Unalloyed neorealism considers great powers like Japan to be structural anomalies difficult to sustain: "How long can Japan . . . live alongside other nuclear states while denying [itself] similar capabilities?" (Waltz 1993:66). Many scenarios have held China first and North Korea subsequently as sources of chain reactions.[8] Yet the structural power thresholds that would trigger an East Asian nuclear domino are unclear, and constantly shifting. Different imputed thresholds in North Korea's ascendance as a nuclear weapons state have already been crossed, from its expulsion of IAEA inspectors in 1993 to its plutonium extraction, discovery of alleged enrichment activities, repeated verbal threats to Japan and South Korea, declaration of "nukes" possession, and missile tests. The 2006 nuclear test has renewed predictions of Japan's nuclearization, yet Premier Abe responded that he "would like to clearly state that there will be no change regarding the three nonnuclear principles," reaffirming Japan's non-nuclear status.[9] If this response is sustained, Japan would have renounced nuclear weapons even as it witnessed three of its neighbors acquire nuclear weapons: the Soviet Union, China, and North Korea. Furthermore, an unalloyed neorealist analysis of China's rise in the past two decades would have portended further pressures on Japan to nuclearize. Japan's continued resistance to such presumed temptations have provided and will continue to provide crucial tests of unalloyed structural neorealism's predictive power. Conversely, Japan's hypothetical turn toward an indigenous nuclear deterrent would deal a nearly fatal blow (a conceptual "friendly fire" of sorts) to competing neorealist theories that, for many decades, regarded the U.S. alliance as obviating the need for a Japanese deterrent.[10] Explanations relying on alliance would have to elucidate why balance of power mattered more for Japan vis-à-vis North Korea than vis-à-vis other nuclear-armed neighbors (including the Soviet Union/Russia and China), why a rising (internationalizing) China might be more of a threat than a radical Maoist one (to which Japan did not respond with an indigenous deterrent), and why U.S. guarantees might be considered weaker today than ever before (as during the U.S. debacle in Indochina and Nixon's Guam doctrine). The last condition does not sit well with the reality of a very strong U.S.-Japan alliance as of 2006. A nuclear umbrella constitutes a hegemon's ultimate inducement, and Secretary Rice was quick to reiterate the U.S.-extended deterrence commitment following North Korea's test. If alliance does not work in as strong a context as the U.S.-Japan relationship, one might doubt its relevance under much less optimal conditions.

Such conditions seem to increasingly apply to South Korea, where the alliance has weakened significantly, potentially freeing South Korea's hand to pursue nuclear weapons. Yet South Korea's official response to North Korea's nuclear test dismissed such a turn away from the alliance, for reasons related no less to South Korea's domestic considerations than to alliance robustness. South Korea's attitudes toward both the U.S. alliance and North Korea appeared to shift more in tandem with the relative power of domestic ruling coalitions than with changes in structural (international) power. The latter would anticipate Japan's nuclearization to drive South Korea willy-nilly into nuclear status (and vice versa), eroding restraints imposed by alliances. This possible nuclear domino effect or "breakout" in East Asia would strengthen unalloyed neorealism at the expense of alliance-based arguments. U.S. commitments to Taiwan are arguably weaker, much less codified, far more contingent, and frequent subjects of contention within both Taiwan and the United States.[11] Rising existential threats to Taiwan from China, and fluctuating, conditional U.S. commitments to Taiwan in the context of a hypothetical attack by China, would arguably make Taiwan a strong candidate for nuclearization. It is doubtful, however, that Taiwan will opt for this path, given alternative readings of what drives Taiwan's behavior vis-à-vis China and the density of economic and political interests at stake. I return to this scenario later.

Iran's alleged nuclearization has triggered concerns with similar nuclear snowball effects in the Middle East. Saudi Arabia, Turkey, and Egypt, some have argued, may be tempted to respond in kind (Campbell et al. 2004). As Egyptian researcher Wahid Abd Al-Magid suggested, Iran's nuclear warheads "will represent a threat to the Arabs before it does to Israel" (Feldner 2003c:2). Nuclear programs in Iraq and Israel did not drive Turkey or Egypt down the reactive proliferation path in the past, but in 2006 a defiant Iranian nuclear program has allegedly led Turkey, Algeria, Egypt, Morocco, Saudi Arabia, Tunisia, and the UAE to embark on nuclear power programs, potential precursors of a nuclear weapons race.[12] A weakened U.S. military presence in Iraq hardly creates strong conditions for hegemonic denial of further nuclearization in the Middle East. Furthermore, the record of hegemonic success in preventing proliferation within and beyond this region suggests only moderate expectations for such a scenario. The United States has maintained relatively stable bilateral alliances with Egypt, Israel, Jordan, Turkey, Saudi Arabia, and other GCC countries, although none has been as formally encoded as the U.S.-Japan alliance, except perhaps for Turkey as part of NATO.[13] Recent reports alleging a potential Turkish drive to acquire nuclear weapons could provide yet another challenge to alliance-based and hegemony arguments.

Finally, *contra* neorealism, Egypt has avoided nuclearization for decades as Israel's relative power has increased dramatically. Signs of possible revisions in Egypt's policy have been strongest as the threat of Iran's nuclearization has grown higher. The likelihood of this turn is, once again, hard to estimate, given unclear thresholds for changes in relative power to yield expected effects. If indeed Egypt embarks on a weapons-related program in the future, unalloyed neorealist perspectives would need to establish that Iran has been a strategic threat to Egypt rather than a political one, that it has been a more serious threat to Egypt's security than Israel has been (since dramatic steps were taken only after the rise of Iran as a threat and not vis-à-vis Israel for decades), and that the causal mechanisms and consequences of changes in relative power are independent from domestic considerations, such as popular pressures for emulating Ahmadinejad's defiance, which are unrelated to changes in the balance of power between Iran and Egypt. A Middle East nuclear domino would put to rest the notion of a common search for a Muslim bomb, suggesting instead multiple bids for nuclear weapons in the Muslim world from Pakistan to Iran, Egypt, Saudi Arabia, and Turkey. Such prospects would be more connected to domestic circumstances and to Sunni versus Shi'a identity-based competition—or constructed understandings of religion—than to classical balance-of-power considerations. Finally, the dramatic deterioration of the NPR following the South Asian tests, North Korea's test, and Iran's defiance of the IAEA might also play important roles in Egypt's future nuclear behavior.

Rational-institutionalism

Rational-institutionalism forces attention to the NPR as an important dimension weighing on nuclear decisions. That most states have abrogated their right to acquire nuclear weapons by ratifying the NPT is certainly a *potentially* powerful indication that the international regime matters. It is also plausible, however, that normative, security, or domestic considerations might have driven states' decisions for or against nuclear weapons. Such prior concerns could thus explain both nuclear decisions and NPT compliance. Egypt's ambassador to the United States Nabil Fahmy pointed out that

> in the spirit of candid and clear sighted analysis, one must be obliged to acknowledge that very few non-nuclear weapons states—parties—actually joined the treaty because it responded to their immediate security concerns. Most of the parties that joined NPT did so for political or economic reasons or circumstances, or because they had no reason to pursue nuclear weapons or nuclear programs from the beginning. Some parties did join because they assumed the NPT would generate a wider nuclear nonproliferation regime and disarmament effort, ultimately dealing effectively with nuclear weapons concerns. This was particularly true of states that initially had peaceful nuclear programs and the potential to develop them.

More systematic research on nuclear aspirants that abstained or indulged, as well as on non-nuclear aspirants, are needed to validate premises that cost-benefit calculations associated with the NPR indeed influenced nuclear behavior. This broader agenda remains a matter of empirical investigation.

As for the cases reviewed here, few provided strong support for the NPR as the *main* determinant for renouncing nuclear weapons. State-centric rational-institutionalist perspectives proved compatible in a few cases but inadequate, incomplete, or unnecessary for explaining nuclear choices and outcomes in several others. Persuasive institutionalist accounts would have had to establish that—had the NPR not existed at the time—Japan's domestic politics would have likely yielded an alternative decision, that is, to develop nuclear weapons. The historical record does not provide strong evidence for such a counterfactual. The NPT itself had limited currency in Japan's domestic debate, according to important participants. The decision to remain non-nuclear was logically prior to, not a consequence of, the decision to ratify the NPT. Ratification itself and Japan's subsequent receptivity to NPT injunctions were corollaries of a domestic consensus around the "economy first" Yoshida doctrine, which blunted potential domestic demand for nuclear weapons. Similar considerations operated in South Korea, which went beyond its NPT commitments by agreeing not to develop indigenous enrichment and reprocessing facilities despite strong economic incentives for an energy-starved economy and despite strong security demands from nationalist sectors. Park and his allies had their eyes on the prize, and the prize was not nuclear weapons but an economic miracle that would undercut both domestic and North Korean challengers. Chiang Kai-shek's decision to forego nuclear weapons had even less to do with the NPT, which granted nuclear status to its archenemy (China) while denying Taiwan statehood itself. Domestic considerations of economic growth—which was highly dependent on international markets, technology, investments, and political support—greatly influenced the KMT's nuclear policies. Absent this domestic model of political survival, Taiwan might have gone the North Korean way. Other potential institutionalist considerations—regional regimes capable of constraining East Asian powers—did not exist in the 1960s and 1970s, and thus could not explain decisions to renounce nuclear weapons either. New security institutions—the ASEAN Regional Forum (ARF), KEDO, and Six-Party Talks—did not emerge until the 1990s and, as of mid-2006, had failed to denuclearize North Korea. None of these institutions has had any bearing on Taiwan, which has been effectively excluded even from the most inclusive institution in the region, the ARF (Solingen 2008).

The NPT clearly did not prevent Middle East nuclearization. The region's NPT-compliance record has been dismal. As chapters on Iraq, Libya, and Iran document, these NPT members violated commitments and deceived the IAEA, approaching international institutions and international law with contempt, and not just on nuclear matters. The NPR raised barriers to sensitive technology transfers but not high enough to prevent clandestine acquisitions on a grand scale. Furthermore, the IAEA was unable to detect defections in pre-1991 Iraq, pre-2002 Iran, and pre-2003 Libya, although UNSCOM dismantled Iraq's WMD, and UN-MOVIC read Iraq's nonexistent nuclear capabilities in 2003 accurately. Israel never signed the NPT, and so its nuclear activities were not violations of formal commitments. Since Israel perceived the U.N. as biased toward automatic majorities mustered by Arab, Islamic, and non-aligned states and by the Soviet bloc, its abstention from the NPT seemed consistent with a rational-institutionalist logic of states as unified entities weighing the costs and benefits of joining institutions. An institution that was unwilling or unable to monitor compliance and detect defections adequately, and that could enable withdrawals ("legal" defections through Article X) was considered ill suited to improve Israel's security, according to Israel's Atomic Energy Commission director-general (Freier 1985). Yet Israel supported regionally based, mutually verifiable, and fully inclusive NWFZ as an institutional alternative to the NPT, conditioned on prior peace agreements with all regional parties.

Egypt's behavior seems compatible with institutionalist expectations insofar as it signed, ratified, and largely complied with NPT injunctions. That it did so despite its status as the foremost Arab regional power and in the presence of nuclear-armed Israel (presumably to induce Israel to follow suit) certainly seems more consistent with institutionalism than with neorealism. Yet Egypt weighed ratification for nearly twelve years, and its timing suggested that domestic political instrumentalities were at play no less than aggregate state-level considerations. Sadat was receptive to U.S. economic inducements for NPT ratification and needed those resources to compensate domestic constituencies in the midst of efforts to liberalize the economy (infitah). The prospects of obtaining assistance for its nuclear energy program, which required NPT ratification, were also deemed important for a sustainable infitah. Sadat could also wield NPT membership as an external constraint to counter domestic criticism over Egypt's unwillingness to match Israel's nuclear capabilities. Such criticism subsided but never disappeared, compelling Egyptian leaders to mount progressively more defiant condemnations of the NPT for unfulfilled promises of Article VI and for "double standards" allowing Israel, India, and Pakistan to remain non-members. Egypt also consistently demanded a Middle East NWFZ that would compel all parties to abide by the NPT and threatened to block indefinite extension in 1995 unless Israel signed it. Egypt's NPT compliance has generally been acknowledged by the IAEA, although some remained skeptical.[14] In 2004, the IAEA reprimanded Egypt for failing to declare nuclear sites and materials as "a matter of concern" but reported no evidence of nuclear weapons procurement.[15] Egypt never signed the IAEA Additional Protocol or ratified the Pelindaba NWFZ and the CTBT.

Regarding detection failures (notably of defections incurred by Iraq prior to 1991, by Iran for nearly two decades, and by North Korea and Libya for decades), they may stem more from flawed institutional design than poor implementation, as discussed in chapter 2. Former Iraqi scientist Hamza (1998:3), however, argues a different perspective: "The understanding that gradually emerged from a closer relationship to the IAEA was how weak and easily manipulated the agency was. . . . Further, according to Al-Saji and Mahmoud, if an inspector gained a reputation as antagonistic or aggressive, few states would allow him to inspect their facilities. Overall, the IAEA proved extremely useful to the Iraqi weapons program in obtaining nuclear technology." In the end, Hamza added, "the IAEA accepted and promoted power reactor programs in both Iraq and Iran—two oil-rich countries with high military expenditures, centuries-old antagonisms, and many possibilities for conflict. Under cover of safeguarded civil nuclear programs, Iraq managed to purchase the basic components of plutonium production, with full training included, despite the risk that the technology could be replicated or misused."

As a tool to deny nuclear capabilities to potential aspirants, the NPR suffered from a classic problem identified by rational-institutionalism: persistent difficulties in achieving collective action. As Feinstein and Slaughter (2004) argue, rifts and paralysis within the UNSC allowed states to pursue WMD under the cover of NPT membership, as with Iraq, North Korea, and arguably Iran. Former U.N. Under-Secretary General for Disarmament Affairs Nobuyasu Abe has claimed that "many voices in recent years have questioned either the ability or the readiness of the members of the Security Council to perform its responsibility concerning a wide range of challenges related to WMD."[16] In his view, the UNSC's inability to force Iraqi compliance despite several resolutions, its reluctance to act on North Korean violations, and its failure to implement the 1998 unanimous resolution condemning Indian and Pakistani nuclear tests validated these concerns. Even when collective action yielded sanctions, problems of disparate interpretations and resolve remained. Whereas some considered sanctions on Iraq as means to compel inspections others regarded them in more restrictive terms, as merely designed to deny Iraq the ability to import items for military use (Blix 2005:56). Russia and France have had a tendency to "defect" in the application of effective sanctions, which cannot be understood through state-level considerations more typical of rational-institutionalist theory but rather through domestic pressures leading to uneven implementation of sanctions. French and Russian firms had agreements to develop oil fields in Iraq and pressed their governments for expanded activities. Iraq's neighbors promptly exploited sanctions "fatigue" to expand exchanges with Baghdad favored by their domestic constituencies adversely affected by sanctions. By 2001, Egypt, Syria, and the UAE had signed free trade-agreements with Iraq.

Collective-action problems have also been rampant regarding Iran and North Korea (Samore 2004) with occasional successes, which are reported in chapters 6 and 8. Russia, France and China were reluctant to refer the cases to the UNSC, acceding eventually, although conflicting approaches to sanctions due to members' internal constraints have remained. Additional concerns have included the ability of dictatorships to deflect the pain inflicted by sanctions onto vulnerable constituencies (Lebovic 2007). Saddam's war adventures against Iran and Kuwait, for example, had already created deplorable economic and social conditions, which sanctions only worsened. The Oil-for-Food program alleviated these conditions somewhat but also channeled vast proceeds to Saddam's military industrial complex, missile development, palaces, and political allies. Many of the same considerations have applied to North Korea, Libya, and Iran, forcing greater attention to domestic distributional effects of sanctions (Solingen 1995; O'Sullivan 2003). Libya has provided a seemingly successful case, but sanctions there have been related to terrorism rather than denial of nuclear weapons. Indeed, Libya continued nuclear purchases from the A. Q. Khan network after U.N. sanctions regarding Lockerbie were suspended.

Notwithstanding some shortcomings of rational-institutionalism, the empirical chapters suggest that the NPR can be credited with some successes. Export controls raised the costs of acquiring sensitive technologies and equipment; inspection regimes were tightened following the IAEA's discovery of extensive prescribed activities by Iraq prior to 1991; the IAEA also stood firm during the North Korean 1993 crisis; NPT Review Conferences and UNSC resolutions arguably changed the context against which states formulated decisions regarding nuclear weapons; institutional processes increased opportunities for cooperation and offered new focal points such as the Additional Protocol, the NPT's indefinite extension, and the CTBT. Efforts to provide the IAEA with the authority to collect its own information, to revamp the entire safeguards system, and to create incentives to forgo the development of sensitive technologies are under consideration. These and other achievements could be significant given that the NPR operates in the thorniest domain of national security, where the emergence and functioning of international institutions command Sisyphean efforts. From this standpoint, rational-institutionalism faces vast disadvantages—particularly relative to neorealism—as a theory explaining nuclear choices and outcomes. As argued, nuclear issues load the dice in favor of theories hinged on self-help and unilateral pursuit of security. Achieving institutional cooperation, enforcing rules, and punishing non-compliance are arguably far more difficult in this arena than in economic, environmental, or other functional issues (Lipson 1984). Nuclear behavior does not constitute a "most likely case" for overcoming prisoner's dilemma situations and problems of collective action. Hence, to the extent that a significant number of states may have rejected nuclearization at least partly due to NPT positive inducements (technology provision) and disincentives (export controls, denial, monitoring, and punishment for non-compliance), the theory achieves significant analytical scores. This recognition should not ignore that a sometimes unquestioned lore often assigns far more weight to the NPT as the chief motive for nuclear decisions and outcomes than is warranted by extant empirical findings.

This book has examined nuclear decisions by nine states over forty years in light of five major theories of international relations, an effort that could not permit detailed examination of counterfactuals. Controlled studies of what might have happened in the absence of the NPR could improve our understanding of mechanisms linking institutional constraints to choice. How many of these cases might have decided differently absent the NPR?[17] The future is likely to provide additional tests of regime effects. Ambassador Fahmy argued in 2005 that "some states are bound to reassess their [NPT] commitments or hesitate to make new ones without a change of course by the international community and more rigorous disarmament and nonproliferation efforts."[18] A rational-institutionalist research agenda would hold future compliance to be contingent on states' calculations under unfolding rules and procedures. Were such calculations to override relative power or domestic tendencies toward defection, regime effects might be considered strong. Were balance-of-power or internal tendencies to defect to coincide with regime disincentives, our confidence in regime effects might be lower. Either way, institutional reasoning must be able to explain why we observe such significant variation in East Asian and Middle Eastern compliance patterns.

If the NPR's dramatic deterioration does not alter the number of nuclear aspirants, this could suggest that its impact is marginal. Alternatively, the NPR's significant deterioration, exacerbated by North Korea's 2006 nuclear test and Iran's defiance, could presage additional departures from NPT commitments. Either way, the task of separating institutional effects from responses to changes in relative power or increased domestic pressures could be challenging. Understanding the mechanisms through which the NPR operates requires a theory of domestic politics that remains largely absent from much of the institutional literature on the NPT. This book has proposed one such framework, linking compliance and defection to domestic models of political survival, but other domestic theories can be developed. States are not monolithic abstractions and identification of underlying domestic forces provides better a priori specifications of state interests to comply/defect from international regimes. Prospects that regional institutional arrangements may reaffirm East Asia's denuclearizing trend or induce similar trends in the Middle East hinge largely on the continuity (in East Asia) and emergence (in the Middle East) of compatible models of domestic political survival.[19]

Norms and Constructivism

A different institutionalist argument traces nuclear-weapons-abstention to states' socialization into NPR norms, where a "logic of appropriateness" rather than interests or rational expectations explains denuclearization (Finnemore and Sikkink 1998; March and Olsen 1998). Part 2 does not provide much evidence that anti-nuclear-weapons-acquisition norms played critical roles in most historic decisions. Japan's renunciation is often explained through the taboo engendered by Hiroshima and Nagasaki. Since this taboo was home-grown and preceded the NPT, it could not be traced to international socialization but could well have nurtured anti-nuclear norms worldwide.[20] Japan's unique experience with nuclear Holocaust arguably makes it a "most likely case" to support normative accounts of denuclearization. Its important pacifist movement sensitized Japanese leaders to opposition to nuclear weapons. Yet the fateful decisions of the 1960s–1970s may not be so easily traced to the "nuclear allergy," which—perhaps counterintuitively—was much stronger subsequently than during the first two decades of the postwar era (Imai 1975; Calder 1996; Akiyama 2003). Japan signed the NPT eighteen months after its adoption and delayed ratification by nearly seven years. Furthermore, the conduct of various government studies on Japan's nuclear options since 1968 suggests that nuclear weapons acquisition—although unlikely—was less than a taboo, particularly given special sensitivity to secret contingency studies following the 1965 *Mitsuya Kenkyū Jiken* simulation exercise (Okimoto 1978). Most important, Japanese opponents of nuclear weapons regarded the U.S.-Japan alliance as "embedded nuclearization," where Japan's defense rested on the U.S. nuclear umbrella, as was reiterated after North Korea's nuclear test. Nor do the surveys and government studies analyzed in chapter 3 suggest that nuclear weapons were "unthinkable." Institutional restraints such as the Atomic Energy Law and the Three Non-Nuclear Principles had significant force. However, there was continuous contestation over interpretations of Article IX of the Constitution (renouncing the right of belligerency but not referring specifically to nuclear weapons), which may explain why the Principles never became law (Chai 1997). Furthermore, compromises over the U.S. introduction of nuclear weapons into Japan were another expression of nuclear embeddedness. As Mochizuki (2006) argues, "Japan's pacifism has always been pragmatic." Further research on Japan's anti-nuclear norms must come to terms with the fact that Japan took nearly seven years to ratify the NPT; both forceful proponents and opponents of nuclear weapons invoked memories of Hiroshima and Nagasaki (Harrison 2002); Japan's acceptance of nuclear embeddedness in U.S. nuclear deterrence; and difficulties in extricating normative from rationalistic sources of Japan's opposition to nuclear weapons, as examined in chapter 3 and summarized below.

Japan was not alone in substituting U.S. nuclear weapons for its own. South Korea and Taiwan also relied on U.S. commitments, suggesting additional pragmatic compromises rather than principled condemnations of nuclear weapons. Indeed, all three countries encouraged the alliance and extracted repeated U.S. pledges by occasionally insinuating that without them they might be forced to acquire indigenous deterrents. There was some support for a national deterrent in South Korea in the 1970s, countered by public statements reiterating that the alliance—not normative considerations—obviated that need. Furthermore, U.S. nuclear weapons remained the South's favored deterrent for decades despite kinship ties with North Korea, a factor that calls into question the operation of nuclear taboos related to common identity or ancestry. Nor were such concerns dominant when Taiwan weighed its nuclear options against China in the 1960s and 1970s while pressing for protection by the U.S. umbrella.

Even important opponents of an indigenous deterrent, who included scientist Wu Ta-you, made their case on other than normative grounds. The experience of China's civil war, the KMT's massacre of 10,000–20,000 Taiwanese, the demands for extended deterrence, and the nature of war plans against China also question the strength of kin-related taboos as barriers to warfare. A North Korean official's threat to turn Seoul into "a sea of fire," other such implacable warnings, and its consistent search for—and threats with—nuclear weapons belies any influence of anti-acquisition norms.

That anti-nuclear-weapons-acquisition norms were not central in East Asia is far from anomalous, since they were not fundamental considerations in other cases of abstention or reversal either, including Argentina, Brazil, Libya, and South Africa. It should thus not be surprising that part 3 finds little evidence of such norms having taken deep roots in the Middle East, given this region's poor record of NPT compliance and the actual *use* of chemical weapons by Egypt, Iraq, Iran, and Libya. The evidence thus far might suggest that norms *favoring* nuclear acquisition are more common in some areas of the Middle East and South Asia. Derived from nationalist, religious, and other identities, such norms invested nuclear weapons with redemptive value as tools of modernization and defiance of the international order. As part 3 suggests, statements by leaders and "norm entrepreneurs" from Iraq to Iran and Libya revealed far less reluctance to advocate nuclear weapons as politically and normatively valuable than in East Asia (except North Korea). Identity themes were malleable tools that could lead to contradictory prescriptions. WMD *use* was proclaimed contrary to Islam in Iran's early post-revolutionary period. Following the painful war with Iraq, Rafsanjani encouraged WMD development, declaring that "the moral teachings of the world are not very effective when war reaches a serious stage." Ahmadinejad's spiritual mentor, Ayatollah Yazdi, proclaimed that *shari'a* does not forbid nuclear *use*, let alone acquisition, contradicting other religious interpretations. Islam thus provided a flexible normative foundation that could be marshaled to justify competing arguments. This selective and opportunistic use of identity themes—not unique to the Middle East—compels the need to ground their role on nuclear decisions in a theory explaining the sources of domestic receptivity to such themes. Even for the important case of NPT compliance in this region, the record does not suggest that Egypt's denuclearization resulted from abhorrence of nuclear weapons. NPT ratification was justified in the People's Assembly in purely pragmatic terms, as part of efforts to secure international support for a nuclear industry. Furthermore, statements by Nasser, Sadat, Mubarak, and other officials asserted that Egypt would acquire nuclear weapons if its security demanded it; and "norm entrepreneurs" advocating nuclear weapons on identity grounds have certainly not been absent in Egypt, as chapter 11 documents.

Some identity-based perspectives have linked Israel's nuclearization to memories of the Holocaust and perceptions of international abandonment during those crucial years. Although quite plausible, this connection remains to be studied more systematically in light of competing normative corollaries from the Holocaust experience. Ben-Gurion and Bergman at one extreme, and members of the Committee for Denuclearization at the other, with various views in between, all shared a common desire to prevent another Holocaust but differed in means-ends prescriptions. Surveys showing apparent widespread support for a mutually verifiable, regionally based, and fully inclusive NWFZ based on prior peace agreements with all parties suggests that nuclear weapons are certainly not the only, or even the ranking, normative preference stemming from the Holocaust experience. To some extent this may be reflected in extensive support for nuclear non-acknowledgment rather than open deterrence, since the former could arguably be more amenable, symbolically, to be superseded by effective alternative arrangements that can assuage anxieties about physical survival. Such arrangements become more concrete in the context of a regional transformation of leading models of political survival along internationalizing lines, as I discuss below. The essentializing treatments of both Japan and Israel as facile derivatives of traumatic historical experiences must be eschewed in favor of further empirical research on identity and norms that is also sensitive to other variables, from formal alliances providing a nuclear umbrella (Japan) to U.N. isolation (Israel), to the democratic nature of institutions at home and across the border, much sparser in the Middle East than in East Asia, with different implications for Japan and Israel.

Where does constructivist analysis of denuclearization go from here? Developments over the past four decades compel norm-based studies to take stock of how, why, and to what extent have norms condemning the consideration, development, acquisition, or transfer of nuclear weapons (as distinct from use) diffused throughout the world; whether and why those norms may have declined or atrophied; how and when do we know that this has taken place (or what constitutes a critical mass of anomalies); what may explain sudden departures from such norms; and why have competing norms valuing nuclear weapons acquisition emerged. Norms emerge and evolve through reflection and analysis, through following established mores, through public discussion, and through evolutionary selection that favors certain norms because of their consequential role (Sen 1999:273). These four mechanisms provide good foundations for exploring the dynamics of both anti-acquisition norms and their competitors. The NPR, NPT review conferences, ancillary NGO, and track-two processes offer valuable contexts for exploring norm diffusion through analysis, reflection, and public discussion. Detailed tracing of socialization experiences (Johnston 2001) may improve our understanding of nuclear choices and the relative effectiveness of different contexts in strengthening or weakening norms. Constructivist accounts would be particularly valuable if they could isolate the effects of socialization from those of hegemonic coercion or rational nuclear learning. They could explore clustered behavior toward or away from nuclearization in different regions and why such differences obtain under the shadow of presumably shared anti-nuclear-weapons-acquisition norms. They could apply evolutionary selection to explain why anti-acquisition norms may or may not decline relative to competing norms favoring nuclear weapons on the basis of identity, modernity, or redemption. The cases in this book also suggest that a theory of domestic politics would help reveal whether, when, and how norms can play important and even decisive roles in nuclear decisions (Checkel 1997). Such theories may help clarify when and why agents promoting anti-acquisition norms may be more effective than those advocating competing norms, and would force greater attention to the interplay between international norms and the domestic conditions that reaffirm, modify, or weaken them.

Constructivist approaches rely on different epistemological and ontological tools than rationalist alternatives and are sometimes less concerned with strict causation and prediction. Furthermore, more constructivist work today seems concerned with human-security issues than with regional nuclear trajectories. Nonetheless, the preceding discussion suggests ways in which constructivist tools may help estimate future nuclear developments in East Asia and the Middle East in response to norms and identity shifts. For instance, many fear that rising nationalism in China, Japan, the Koreas, and Taiwan could lead to a more fragile regional order. The literature on the shadow cast by history and memory on relations among East Asian states might suggest that the sustainability of the region's evolution toward denuclearization could be tenuous. At an extreme those shadows would arguably turn East Asia into a "most likely" case for nuclearization, a perception that might be stronger among some scholars attentive to memory, history, and changing power balances than among those focusing on East Asia as a nascent security community or as the economic dynamo of the early twenty-first century. Some constructivist accounts may be able to propose tipping points while others would not. Yet all would need to identify the mechanisms leading from nationalism, memory, or identity to nuclear weapons, particularly since many other states have sublimated such emotions unto alternative paths. Identifying the direction and strength of those effects might be helped by an improved understanding of the role of democratic or authoritarian contexts in amplifying or reducing the instrumentalities of—and cultural receptivity to—history, norms, and identity.

Democracy and Nuclear Choices

Chapter 2 extended democratic peace analysis to infer that, since nuclear weapons symbolize most violent and extreme solutions, democracies may arguably shy away from acquiring nuclear capabilities to resolve disputes with fellow democracies. This conjecture may be validated by this book's cases, given that no democracy developed nuclear weapons to deter another democracy in East Asia or the Middle East thus far. Beyond these cases, however, it is unclear whether India and Pakistan conform to this generalization, since both shared democratic regimes at some points but only India remained consistently democratic since independence. Furthermore, the first five nuclear-weapons-states included three democracies (United States, France, and Britain). Some might explain their nuclearization as efforts to confront autocratic rivals (fascism first, communism later), but extant evidence supports prestige and power balancing as more crucial considerations during the first nuclear age (Rosecrance 1964; Dunn 1982; Husbands 1982). The Southern Cone also raises questions regarding the relationship between interactive democracies and nuclear weapons, since joint democracies in Argentina and Brazil overlapped with periods of ambiguous nuclear programs until the early 1990s, when leaders advocating internationalizing models signed mutual inspection agreements and ratified the NPT.

The proposition that democracies may be less prone to violate international agreements than non-democracies gains some validation. Few democracies were found to have violated the NPT in the way that Iraq, Libya, North Korea, and arguably Iran did, the small incident with South Korea notwithstanding. Yet several democracies (and autocracies) have not fully complied with Article VI of the NPT. Autocracies have conducted most flagrant deceptions of the IAEA, supporting expectations from Gaubatz (1996). This poor record of compliance also provides one—yet untested—hypothesis for why India and Israel might have been deterred from entering denuclearization agreements or signing the NPT with adversarial autocracies (Pakistan had democratic interludes), as democracies facing problems of uncertainty over ratification and implementation of agreements by autocratic adversaries. Israel within 1967 borders was the only continuous Middle East democracy since its creation, and it abstained from the NPT but favored a mutually verifiable and comprehensive regional NWFZ.[21] It is plausible, but unconfirmed by systematic research, that Israel's democratic nature played an important role in deepening its mistrust for neighboring autocracies, perhaps leading it to search for robust nuclear capabilities in the 1950s and 1960s.[22] Ironically, more recent threats of extinction by Ahmadinejad have emerged from one of the least autocratic regimes in the region, although certainly not a democracy. In Israel's early years, extreme secrecy precluded democratic politics from intruding into the nuclear debate at the popular level, with some exceptions.[23] Leading journalist Dan Margalit (1997:7) argues that Israel's democracy in the 1990s would have jailed Ben-Gurion's group, and Dimona would have never been built, another potential subject for a good counterfactual analysis. The limited available evidence at the popular level suggests that only a small minority across the political spectrum endorsed explicit nuclear deterrence. Disagreements within ruling coalitions—resulting from an unwieldy electoral system— are discussed later.

Beyond that, regime type does not seem too germane a consideration for explaining nuclear behavior. Both regions had mixed clusters (democracies and autocracies), which might have led to similar outcomes regarding nuclear trajectories but didn't. Except for Japan, all other East Asian nuclear claimants were non-democratic at the time they decided to eschew (South Korea, Taiwan) or acquire nuclear weapons (North Korea). All three lacked democratic institutional restraints and might have gone either way without having to account to domestic publics for their nuclear decisions. Non-democratic Taiwan, South Korea, and several autocratic Southeast Asian states largely abided by NPT commitments. Since the late 1980s, democracies in Japan, South Korea, and Taiwan maintained their commitments despite North Korea's repeated threats to the first two and China's intermittent threats to attack Taiwan.

Even dictatorships must sustain supportive coalitions, and the military has been a key player in sustaining dictators and voicing positions on nuclear weapons. Yet in Taiwan and South Korea the military was cajoled into supporting denuclearization, while in North Korea and the Middle East cases some military agencies were the heart of nuclear weapons programs. The key difference was in the model of political survival within which military institutions were embedded: export-led versus juche and Middle East equivalents. The advent of democracy in Taiwan and South Korea did not alter these fundamental differences, except for eroding even further the military's political role. Even prior to the inception of democracy, domestic groups in Taiwan—including the Atomic Energy Commission's highest echelons—foiled nuclear efforts such as the 1967 plan. While most Middle East nuclear aspirants were autocracies (Iraq, Libya, Iran, Nasser's Egypt), most autocracies also avoided nuclearization in both regions. Some even reversed course and abandoned nuclear weapons programs (Egypt, Libya). Autocracies have thus not exhibited uniform nuclear behavior. A possible testable hypothesis is the extent to which democracies in Japan, Taiwan, and South Korea may have posed higher barriers to nuclearization than did autocracies in Iraq, Libya, Iran, or North Korea.

In the end, many international regimes, including the NPR, are subscribed to by various regime types. NWFZ were concluded in temporal and spatial domains with few democracies (Latin America, the South-Pacific, Africa, and Southeast Asia). Autocratic leaders initiated unilateral denuclearization in Argentina, Brazil, Egypt, Kazakhstan, Belarus, Ukraine, South Korea, Taiwan, and other cases. The vast majority of democracies and autocracies have abided by their NPT commitments. Two out of three non-NPT states as of 2006 are long-standing democracies that face threats from autocracies, India and Israel (Pakistan has been an unstable, intermittent democracy). However, as non-members, India and Israel have not legally violated the NPT. Recent agreements with India despite its nuclear tests, and countenance of Israel's nuclear status, have raised allegations of "double standards," suggesting that democratic states may regard nuclear weapons in the hands of other democracies as arguably more legitimate than in the hands of autocracies. Shaker Al-Nabulsi explains this potential bias as follows: "The world is silent with regard to nuclear weapons in the hands of countries with constitutional institutions that do not make war-and-peace decisions in accordance with a leader's temper, a ruler's dream, or a cleric's fatwa, but by means of constitutional, rational, democratic, and modern institutions. This is why the world is silent in the face of Israel's nuclear weapons, for example, but goes berserk when North Korea and Iran possess these dangerous weapons, which could spark World War III, leading to the destruction [of the world]—all because of a fatwa by Ayatollah 'Ali Khamene'i, the supreme spiritual leader of the Iranian republic, or a decision based on the midsummer night's dream of the North Korean dictator."[24] Whether or not there is greater tolerance for democracies acquiring nuclear weapons remains subject to empirical investigation. Democracies and autocracies are also hypothesized to differ with respect to illegal transfers of WMD technology to other states or terrorist organizations (India and Israel, as opposed to Pakistan, China, North Korea, and arguably Iran). Yet private firms from democratic states have been quite involved in such transfers. Democracies and autocracies may respond differently to international sanctions and positive inducements regarding nuclear weapons. Democracies may approach nuclear issues under strong domestic identity and normative constraints (Japan and arguably Israel) or under widespread domestic support (India).

Future scenarios will test many of these hypotheses. The proposition that democracies would not be likely to develop nuclear weapons in disputes with other democracies could be falsified if, for instance, Japan were to develop nuclear weapons in response to a unified (democratic) nuclear Korea. Refutability requires clear a priori definitions of both democracy and nuclear status.[25] Regarding definitions of democracy, Iran is not South

Korea. Regarding definitions of nuclear status, South Korea—without indigenous reprocessing and enrichment facilities—may not be Japan (some experts consider "hedging" to blur definitional clarity). Either way, the behavior of both regime-types may be contingent on the nature of their ties to the global political economy, to which I turn now.

Domestic Approaches to Political Survival

Given the limits of alternative understandings of nuclear behavior, the lack of rigorous examination of domestic sources of nuclear postures is particularly puzzling. Singh and Way (2004) have corroborated an empirical connection between involvement in the world economy and nuclear abstinence.[26] Whereas nuclear behavior provides neorealism with "most likely" conditions for supporting its tenets, it also offers "least likely" conditions for corroborating domestic political survival approaches. As discussed in part 1, evidence for the weight of domestic political considerations in nuclear outcomes is much harder to garner. Leaders are far more likely to cast decisions favoring or rejecting nuclear weapons as "reasons of state," invoking national security, international institutional incentives, and normative considerations (for or against such weapons) rather than ulterior domestic political motivations or expediency. Hence, available historical sources document "reasons of state" more frequently and thoroughly, loading the evidentiary dice against domestic political justifications. Precisely because nuclear issues are least likely to validate the role of domestic politics, they provide a tough, crucial arena for investigating such effects. Consequently, even partial substantiation for the importance of domestic considerations gains particular significance in this unfriendly terrain for this theory. One might argue that the threshold for gaining confidence in this argument should be lower than for theories advantaged by leaders' needs to justify nuclear decisions as national security imperatives. Yet as the empirical probes suggest, there is no need to lower the bar. Models of political survival and nuclear policies are not merely loosely associated but indeed joined at the hip. Their omission may have led to an overestimation of other causal variables and to potential spurious effects (Brady and Collier 2004). Their inclusion may improve our understanding of the actual effects of security dilemmas, international norms, and institutions when interacting with domestic models.

Leaders vary in their tolerance for domestic and international, political and economic (including opportunity) costs entailed by nuclear weapons. What specific aspects of models that emphasize economic growth and openness to the global economy as tools of political survival make certain leaders more receptive to denuclearization than others? The answer ranges from the need to appeal to foreign investors with an interest in domestic economic growth and stability; to the related need to reassure neighbors in order to preserve regional cooperation and stability; to the requirement of securing access to international markets for exports, capital, technology, and raw materials; to the related aversion to risking reputational losses at home and abroad for uncertain nuclear gains; to the costs of alienating domestic agents of internationalization—both within and outside state structures—which would be adversely affected by nuclear weapons development. Clearly, there are several causal pathways linking the renunciation of nuclear weapons to models that emphasize economic growth through global integration. Nuclearization burdens efforts to enhance exports, economic competitiveness, macroeconomic and political stability, and global access—all objectives of internationalizing models—while strengthening state bureaucracies, agencies, and industrial complexes opposed to economic transformation.[27] As part 2 suggests, denuclearization has often been related to broader programs of internationalization designed to strengthen market-oriented forces, leaders, and institutions—state and private—favoring export-led growth. Beyond these cases, the profile of nearly all nuclear aspirants who steered their countries away from nuclearization matches these expectations.[28]

Conversely, leaders and ruling coalitions relying on or promoting inward-looking bases of support have had greater tolerance—and in some cases strong incentives—for developing nuclear weapons. Nuclearization has entailed considerable domestic advantages for foes of internationalizing models in inward-looking, import-substituting regimes that favor extreme nationalism, religious radicalism, or autarky. Nuclearization has also borne lower international costs for leaders advancing models less dependent on external markets, investment, capital, and technology. Such leaders and their political allies have often relied on extreme language to compel and threaten regional adversaries, wielding potential nuclear and other WMD as means to coerce and intimidate. Statements such as North Korea's repeated threats to Seoul and Tokyo, Saddam Hussein's threats to Iran and Saudi Arabia together with his vow to "incinerate half of Israel," and Iran's warning that "the use of even one nuclear bomb inside Israel will destroy everything" are certainly more rare in domestic political contexts driven by internationalizing objectives. Most inward-looking nuclear aspirants have been NPT members who have misled IAEA inspectors or have violated NPR commitments. As a region, the Middle East has gravitated toward the inward-looking end of the spectrum for many years, although there have also been efforts to transcend that path (Lebanon, Turkey, Jordan, and, more recently, some GCC countries). North Korea's dominant political survival strategy has more affinity with that of post-1979 Iran, Saddam's Iraq, and Libya than with most of its neighbors. For all of the presumed devotion to brotherly unification with kin states (pan-Arabism or pan-Islamism in the cases of Saddam, Qadhafi, and Nasser, *Koryo* for Kim Il-Sung), inward-looking leaders have promoted extreme nationalist platforms of political survival.

Restating the argument, nuclearization has been less attractive and much more costly for leaders and coalitions pursuing integration into the global economy in order to advance domestic, regional, and international objectives. From this point of view, Middle East leaders faced lower barriers to, and stronger incentives for, nuclearization than East Asian ones. Whereas inward-looking models might have regarded nuclear weapons as assets in the arsenal of building regime legitimacy, outward-oriented ones regarded them as liabilities. The heavy regional concentration of internationalizing models in East Asia reinforced domestic incentives across the border for rejecting nuclearization.[29] The heavy regional concentration of inward-looking models in much of the Middle East had opposite effects, exacerbating individual incentives to develop nuclear weapons. As gleaned from the experience of an overwhelming number of nuclear aspirants in the second nuclear age, domestic survival models should be treated as more fundamental considerations in explaining nuclear choices than has been the case, not merely as afterthoughts or residual factors. The nuclear choices of all pertinent cases in the Middle East and East Asia since the 1960s are compatible with domestic survival models, which provide crucial information about which leaders and ruling coalitions are more sensitive to certain pressures and inducements but not others. Such receptivity may change over time even for the same state, as a result of changes in leadership, coalitions, and survival models, as in Egypt and Libya. In both of these cases, infitah and steps toward denuclearization were introduced in tandem, sometimes the same year (Egypt) or the same month (Libya). Regime survival has been a crucial logic in North Korea, Libya, Iraq, and Iran's nuclear efforts, and it explains domestic receptivity to denuclearization—with or without alliances—in Egypt, South Korea, and Taiwan, and many other cases from South Africa to Argentina, Brazil, and Turkey.

In many ways East Asia and the Middle East provide the toughest tests for hypotheses related to domestic models of political survival, because both regions are ridden with security dilemmas and a history of militarized rivalries. The latter, as argued, should make these regions easy cases for hypotheses emphasizing balance of power. By contrast, cases from Latin America, South Africa, and Europe in the second nuclear age could arguably provide more favorable grounds for domestic survival hypotheses (Solingen 1996, 1998; Liberman 2001). The challenge, as always, is to scrutinize the viability of hypotheses precisely where they are least likely to be validated. On those grounds, how do domestic survival models fare across the individual cases examined in East Asia and the Middle East, which provide difficult cases indeed for this argument? Japan's nuclear status has frequently been traced to its U.S. alliance or the nuclear allergy, but both require a model of domestic politics that explains their respective roles. The alliance was a critical component of the Yoshida model of political survival, not an end in itself but a means to enable concentration on economic growth through global access, while avoiding militarization. Such a model also provided special receptivity—at the societal and leadership level—to anti-nuclear acquisition norms. In a specific rejection of the war-oriented autarkic and militarized model of the 1930s, Japan's postwar leaders sought domestic political legitimacy and electoral approval through export-led economic growth and recovery. As Berger (1998:29) notes, Japan's population "was more concerned with the task of rebuilding the economy than dwelling on the past." This created significant space for Yoshida Shigeru's model hinging on Japan as "merchant nation" (*chōnin kokka*). Prominent advocates of a denuclearized Japan (Nagai, Kōsaka, Kishida, Momoi among many others) could rely heavily on the alliance and the NPT as disincentives to be emphasized in domestic debates.[30] Regardless of their deep personal preferences, nuclear weapons were a political liability for leaders advancing a model of national security that was "economic in nature" (Inoguchi 1993:36).

A 1957 U.S. NIE got it fundamentally right: "Japanese policy with respect to the production of nuclear weapons is likely to be determined primarily by domestic and regional considerations."[31] An expert on Japan's nuclear policy asserted that "for the Japanese people, nuclear issues were more or less subjects for domestic politics or domestic social movements, which seemed to be rather insulated from the reality of international security" (Akiyama 2003:89). Another suggested that "Japan may have likely remained non-nuclear regardless of any external security developments" (Kase 2001:56). The Yoshida model, the nuclear allergy, the 1955 system, and institutional restraints were all part of the domestic landscape that trumped nuclearization. An emphasis on the alliance and anti-nuclear norms has obscured the importance of the domestic political-economy model on Japan's nuclear decisions, deprived the account of the nuts and bolts of politics underlying early nuclear choices and their path-dependent consequences, and overlooked domestic receptivity to certain solutions but not others. The model embraced by Japan's postwar politicians and the requirements of a "trading state" at peace with its region provide a powerful account for the absence of demand for nuclear weapons in Japan, and explains why Japan embraced the alliance to begin with. The nuclear umbrella is thus endogenous to Japan's forgoing of a national nuclear deterrent, insofar as the alliance itself was a derivative of a domestic compromise. Some domestic opponents of nuclear weapons regarded this compromise as a form of "embedded nuclearization" that contradicted nuclear norms. In sum, the Yoshida model—its expections, achievements, and its legacy—arguably constituted necessary conditions for Japan's non-nuclear status. The alliance and the nuclear allergy made the outcome even more likely, but it is plausible that domestic considerations might have been sufficient in and of themselves.

Both the alliance and coercion may have been necessary for South Korea's denuclearization, but one can fully understand their respective roles only in the context of domestic survival models, which explain why alliance was chosen over autarkic juche in the first place, with ensuing consequences for relative receptivity to external inducements, positive and negative. What would have been the fate of the alliance had Park relied on North Korea's brand of juche? Park's model was not the result of external imposition alone; earlier U.S. pressures on Rhee Syngman for economic reform rarely yielded fruit. U.S. pressures and Park's own model worked in the same direction. As Reiss (1988:95) argues, Park's objectives were to ensure political stability and economic growth. The two were symbiotic and left little room for nuclear weapons, which would have endangered growth, stability, and access to global markets, capital, and technology; alienated domestic support; risked sharp economic decline; and isolated South Korea from the regional and international, market and institutional forces that underpinned the model. The alliance enabled the model's core objectives in addition to providing protection. Park could skillfully wield domestic pressures for both an alternative model and an indigenous deterrent in the 1970s to extract concessions from the United States. Yet he was not ready to sacrifice a 10 percent average growth rate on the altar of nuclear weapons. Park even deployed the threat from the North to consolidate support for his model: "There is an even more important reason for seeking high economic growth, and that is the need for us to maintain a position superior to North Korea in our present state of confrontation. . . . Unless a policy of high economic growth is sustained, there will be no way to meet increased defense spending" (Park 1979:94–96). Subsequent democratization strengthened the model and overwhelmed the few advocates of nuclear weapons. Roh Moo-Huyn, presiding over one of South Korea's least friendly administrations vis-à-vis the United States since the 1960s, reaffirmed his intention not to develop or possess nuclear weapons.

Meeting most definitions of existential insecurity, Taiwan did not resort to nuclear weapons either. U.S. pressures were certainly important here as well but, as Yager (1985:192) suggests, "The unanswered question is, Why did the ROC authorities yield so readily to U.S. demands?" The KMT's favored model of political survival—which hinged on economic growth, prosperity, and domestic stability—explains widespread receptivity to U.S. demands and inducements. Nuclear weapons would have introduced massive stress at home, among neighboring countries and worldwide, with negative consequences for domestic growth and stability. KMT leaders had strong incentives to avoid regional conflict and instability in order to sustain attractiveness to foreign investors, controlled military expenditures, and ample foreign reserves (thanks to successful exports), given Taiwan's international isolation. Access to preferential export markets, international capital, investments, and nuclear technology to fuel the economic miracle required nuclear restraint. Without it, the political prospects of the KMT and its successors were fragile. Opponents of nuclear weapons could thus overwhelm domestic adversaries, as economic growth propelled Taiwan from among the poorest to among the most dynamic economies worldwide. The model also explains severe anomalies for neorealism, such as Taiwan's impressive embrace of the mainland—its presumed archrival—as a vital trading partner. While unveiling Taiwan's first formal national security policy, the deputy secretary-general of Taiwan's National Security Council, Michael Tsai, provided further reassurance: "We're not pursuing preemptive capabilities, and we will not develop nuclear weapons or weapons of mass destruction."[32]

Part 3 provides significant support for links between inward-looking models and pursuit of nuclear weapons. Saddam's model was anchored in the entrenched combined power of militarized state bureaucracies and enterprises, import-substituting interests, and the military-industrial-complex, as well as their respective beneficiaries in state-controlled professional and labor organizations. The state dominated infrastructure, manufacturing, trade and services, employing at least half of the workforce and, together with the military-industrial-complex, absorbed progressively more resources. The prominence assigned to oil and the military-industrial-complex trumped manufacturing, industrial diversification, and non-oil exports. Saddam was much less preoccupied with fiscal policy, macroeconomic stability, export-competitiveness in manufacturing, or servicing foreign debts. He derided the international economic order. His nuclear program cannot be understood in isolation from these priorities. It became a core symbol of his broader strategy of self-reliance and a major tool to enhance his personal power and boost his model of political control at home and throughout the region. As Saddam acknowledged and his lieutenants confirmed, WMD kept his domestic and external enemies at bay, portraying an aura of invincibility. Chapter 7's account on pre-delegation of authority corroborates that he regarded the potential passing of his regime as co-terminal with Iraq's integrity. The structure, function, budgets, and manning of Iraq's nuclear program—the roots of which preceded both the Iran-Iraq war and the 1981 Israeli attack on Osiraq—point to its central role in Saddam's model of regime survival against domestic and foreign threats.

Iran's alleged nuclear weapons program can be more readily justified as a response to Saddam's 1980 invasion and Iraq's use of chemical weapons and missiles on Iranian troops and cities. Even in Iran, however, the domestic underpinnings of the nuclear weapons program are brought to relief by statements from one of the program's alleged "fathers." Asgar-Khani acknowledged that the program was needed also "for Iran's social cohesion and prestige. . . . Internally Iran is in a state of disarray. I would now argue that, only by becoming a nuclear weapons state, can Iran consolidate its social coherence. Iran needs both soft and hard power to regain its national identity and prestige."[33] The program was advanced by a coalition of radical inward-looking forces largely opposed to internationalization, from radical mullahs (including Khamene'i) to the Ministry of Defense, Pasdaran, and massive state enterprises (bonyads) controlled by top clerics and the military. The inability of reformist leaders to overpower the ancien régime and change Iran's approach to the global political economy had significant consequences for the program's acceleration. Ancien régime supporters regard nuclear weapons "as an insurance policy against a forced change in the government," in other words, as a guarantee of regime survival and continued protection of vast state corporations and military privileges.[34] As Milani (2005b:48) argues, Iran's "regime has sought the bomb for the same reason that it does everything: its monomaniacal commitment to self-preservation," namely, "self-preservation at home" (Milani et al. 2005:9). In the 1990s, the revolution had lost its luster for supporters at home and abroad. According to Chubin (2006:8), the nuclear option, initially an insurance against Iraq, was in search of a rationale and offered a way out for rallying nationalist opposition and providing legitimacy to a failing regime hinged on economic and military self-sufficiency. Once coalitions and constituencies favoring nuclear weapons have developed, "a state can cross the point of political no return [and] this phenomenon is becoming all too evident in the case of Iran" (Takeyh 2004).[35]

Immediately after assuming power Qadhafi pursued nuclear weapons as a central pillar of his inward-looking model, wielding nationalistic and xenophobic objectives. He nationalized the oil industry and used windfall revenues to secure popular support while virtually eliminating private economic activities. The military was his core constituency and he nurtured it with promises of sophisticated weapons technology. In time, declining oil prices deprived Qadhafi of revenues needed to maintain the very constituencies his revolution had mobilized. Eccentric terrorist activities leading to international sanctions diluted his resources further at a time when expenditures for exotic weapons ceased to attract the imagination of an impoverished population. Feeble initial efforts to reform the economy in the 1980s made way for a more forceful statement by 2000 that "now is the era of economy, consumption, markets, and investment" (chapter 10). Private and public statements provide significant evidence that Qadhafi's 2003 decision to surrender his nuclear weapons program was made under conditions of declining resources for compensating domestic political allies and amidst continued domestic challenges to his rule. Both Qadhafi's most forceful attempt at economic reform (infitah) and his boldest approach to Britain and the United States in negotiating the surrender of his WMD programs took place in March 2003. Negotiations for the terms of denuclearization began prior to the 2003 Iraq war, although personal safety concerns may have furthered Qadhafi's extant incentives to trade WMD programs for external support for implementing an internationalizing shift. In the end, both external economic incentives that would enable him to reconstitute supportive domestic coalitions and concerns with his own fate compelled Qadhafi to adopt a new model, which turned nuclear weapons into a major liability. A political survival approach can thus explain both Qadhafi's efforts to seek nuclear weapons since the 1970s and his 2003 reversal.

The origins of Israel's nuclear program in the 1950s is often discussed within the context of the Holocaust, the 1948 military attack by all its neighbors, its conventional weapons inferiority compounded by arms embargoes, extensive Soviet military and political support to Arab regimes committed to destroying Israel, and its adversaries' early search for missile and chemical weapons and their actual use in battle. Decision-makers faced genuine dilemmas of state survival but domestic politics provided an important background for how the program emerged and developed. Mapai-led ruling coalitions advanced their political survival on explicit socialist principles that kept markets and private enterprise at arm's length, favored extensive economic controls and import-substitution, but—in the absence of natural resources—also depended on foreign capital and agricultural exports. A small group around Ben-Gurion embodying Mamlachtiut (statism) and autonomy from "sectarian" social forces launched the nuclear program in the late 1950s. Their emphasis on self-reliance was compatible with the political and economic foundations of Ben-Gurion's model and the development of a military-industrial-complex. International economic access and external guarantees were in scarce supply (Reiss 1988; Dunn 1998). Domestic political survival hinged on the ability to provide both fail-safe assurances against external threats and adequate welfare for remnants of concentration camps and refugees from Arab states. Yet that left room for significant differences across factions on guns-versus-butter, economic self-reliance versus dependence, conventional versus nuclear deterrence, and domestic versus external guarantees of survival. Ben-Gurion guarded the nuclear program even from partners in the coalition who were more skeptical of his program. A policy of nuclear ambiguity became an equilibrium solution that circumvented risky external responses and serious domestic conflicts in a highly divided polity and society. Furthermore, Israel was not merely the only democracy in the region in the 1950s in the midst of autocracies that threatened it with extinction, but also part of a region dominated by inward-looking models suspicious of the global political economy and heavily rooted in military-industrial-complexes. In this last respect, Israel was no exception. Nuclear ambiguity eventually eroded with certain statements by Israeli leaders, but "non-acknowledgement" lingered (Dowty 2005).

Finally, both Nasser's early efforts to acquire nuclear weapons and Sadat's subsequent shift to renounce them were compatible with their respective models of political survival. Nasser and the Free Officers introduced import-substituting industrialization and massive nationalizations of banking, industry, and infrastructure (including the Suez Canal), a model emulated by Saddam, Qadhafi, and others in the region. State expansion and forceful suppression of private entrepreneurship eliminated economic and political competitors to the state. Trade openness declined from over 53 percent in the early 1950s—prior to the revolution—to 33 percent average under Nasser. The military-industrial-complex was Nasser's crucial partner, allocating itself nearly 24 percent of GDP. Nasser's search for hegemony over the Arab world led him to pursue unification schemes and to intervene in Yemen's civil war, including use of chemical weapons. In tandem with aspirations for economic self-sufficiency, militarization of the economy, and belligerent pan-Arab nationalism, Nasser's ruling coalition also sought nuclear weapons and delivery systems as early as the 1950s, a step that was encouraged by supporters of Soviet-style models of political control among others. Economic policies and foreign adventurism led to balance-of-payments crises, food and consumer goods shortages, high inflation, and reduced foreign credit and foreign exchange, all in the midst of population explosion and rising expectations. Ironically, the very model of political survival that made nuclear weapons an attractive feature also shrank available resources to levels that all but precluded them. Nuclear weapons proponents advocated self-reliance over Soviet nuclear guarantees. Among them, Nasser's advisor Haykal rejected possible mutual inspections with Israel, because "naturally Egypt will refuse to become a party in any agreement with Israel."[36]

Whereas Nasser's model thrived in this aura of inward-looking self-reliance, hypernationalism, and military-technical prowess, Sadat's emphasis on economic growth, foreign investment, exports, military conversion, and a new relationship with international markets and institutions did not leave much room for an expensive nuclear program. The economic prerequisites of Sadat's model required regional stability (peace with Israel) and precluded nuclear arms races with regional competitors. Transparent nuclear policies were also expected to endear Egypt to the West. In 1974, Egypt supported the NWFZ proposed by Iran and committed to accept full-scope IAEA safeguards, all with an eye on receiving economic benefits and nuclear power reactors from the United States. Resolving chronic energy shortages through nuclear power was deemed important for sustaining a planned infitah (economic opening). Nixon's 1974 visit to Egypt delivered an agreement to provide the power plants and solidified U.S.-Egyptian relations. Infitah, also launched in 1974, increased Egypt's trade openness from an average of 33 percent under Nasser to over 61 percent in 1975 and 78 percent in 1979. FDI inflows more than doubled between 1974 and 1976, and military expenditures declined from 52 to 13 percent of GNP between 1975 and 1979. Infitah also increased Egypt's dependence on foreign loans and aid. Egypt received about $2 billion average annual military and economic aid since 1979, reaching nearly $60 billion in cumulative aid by 2005. Sadat also requested a foreign aid package of $18 billion from the G-7 in 1979. Abandoning a nuclear weapons program also meant challenging Sadat's domestic political foes, particularly Nasserites and Islamist groups with prominent nuclear advocates. Sadat cancelled the Atomic Energy Authority's autonomy, transferring it to the Ministry of Electricity. In 1981, he persuaded the People's Assembly that NPT ratification was needed to secure international support for nuclear energy. Sadat's model, particularly relations with Israel and the United States, cost him much capital regionally, including Egypt's ousting from the Arab League.

The shift from Nasser to Sadat and its implications for nuclear policies are well summarized by Egyptian analyst Mohamed Kadry Said (2002:1): "Sadat realized that reaching a settlement to the Arab-Israeli conflict is a precondition for Egyptian development. To achieve this goal, Sadat concentrated his energy towards enhancing U.S.-Egyptian relations and to foster a peace process with Israel. He worked hard to change the Egyptian domestic, regional and international environment in a way conducive to peace. Changing Egyptian attitudes towards arms control arrangements was one of the ways of realizing his aims." Yet infitah never led to the kind of positive cycle observed among East Asian cases that renounced nuclear weapons: high economic growth, high integration in the global political-economy, high legitimacy for the internationalizing model, and lower incentives to resort to nuclear weapons.[37] Furthermore, heavy regional concentration of inward-looking models in much of the Middle East has exacerbated incentives of individual leaders, parties, and ruling coalitions to develop nuclear weapons, creating additional barriers to foreign investment and economic reform throughout most of the region. The strains and barriers to internationalization within Egypt explain strong lingering revisionist currents advocating nuclearization. The continuity of

Egypt's current nuclear policies depends, to a significant extent, on whether or not this revisionist current can overwhelm a struggling ruling coalition with stronger internationalizing orientations.

In sum, identifying domestic models that underlie nuclear shifts in these nine cases takes us several steps beyond structural power explanations in understanding how external and internal factors interact to produce changes in nuclear behavior. Furthermore, the relative incidence of different models in each region certainly magnifies domestic incentives of leaders in one direction or another. Regions more highly integrated in the global economy enhance the prospects of internationalizing models, whereas regions less integrated pose more serious difficulties for denuclearization. The argument may not be equally supported in all cases, but it consistently sheds light on how domestic models regarding integration in the global political-economy have created different constraints, incentives, receptivity, and compliance patterns, and have conditioned the role that international power, institutions, and democracy played in nuclear decisions. Understanding domestic survival models thus provides fuller explanations for why security dilemmas are sometimes seen as more (or less) intractable, why some states rank alliance higher than self-reliance but not others, when and how hegemonic coercion and inducements are effective and when they play a secondary or marginal role, why nuclear weapons programs surfaced where there was little need for them (Libya), why such programs were abandoned where unalloyed neorealist structural perspectives would have expected them (Egypt), and how leaders filter different concepts of security through their preferred approach to political survival.[38] As Meyer's (1984:47) landmark study of nonproliferation put it, "*all* the motive conditions will be filtered through the domestic political system. . . . Therefore all the motive conditions are in some way tied to domestic politics."

The existence of an association between domestic models and nuclear policies gains support from different regions, making it an analytically indispensable category that should be integral to explanations of denuclearization. However, a framework contingent on evolving political survival models implies, by its very nature, no linear or irreversible trajectories in either direction. Leaders and ruling coalitions may reverse courses in response to domestic pressures and external contingencies, including global or regional economic and security developments.[39] Thus, Qadhafi's incentives changed in response to well-coordinated international sanctions, lower oil prices, the inducements of a globalizing economy, and the war in Iraq, all of which undermined his old would-be autarkic model. Propositions derived from this framework are also bounded—as noted in chapter 1—in three ways: with respect to conditions of necessity and sufficiency in developing nuclear weapons, by the incidence of compatible models in the region, and by temporal sequences in the acquisition of nuclear weapons. This last scope condition implies that eliminating existing weapons may be more costly politically than eradicating precursor programs, and that the incentives emanating from the global political economy may operate more forcefully at earlier stages in the inception of internationalizing models and early stages in the consideration of nuclear weapons. These, as many other hypotheses proposed in this book, remain subject to further investigation.

Furthermore, the political survival argument is only probabilistic, as are most arguments in the social sciences. Internationalizing leaders may embrace nuclear weapons.[40] Inward-oriented leaders may decide to abandon them. Both instances would prove the argument falsifiable (subject to empirical refutation), a healthy attribute provided that anomalies do not overwhelm corroborations. But even if one finds this approach reasonably persuasive in explaining the past, it does not necessarily follow that it will also apply in the future (Hirschman 1986). Different dynamics could be at work, triggering conditions under which internationalizing models may no longer provide sufficient conditions for continued denuclearization. As Campbell et al. (2004:13) suggest, "There is widespread concern that the calculus of incentives and disincentives has shifted during the past decade, with incentives increasing and disincentives declining. New threats have arisen while the nuclear taboo has weakened. And it is not just a single factor in this new strategic landscape that gives pause. Rather, it is the accumulation of multiple factors and their interplay and mutual reinforcement that account for many of these new dangers."

The framework proposed here provides a roadmap for considering the conditions under which its expectations might be corroborated or refuted. Figure 1 suggests four possible scenarios. The vertical axis refers to the two basic models, internationalizing and inward-looking. The horizontal axis maps two basic trends: toward nuclearization and away from it. Scenario 1 suggests a situation where leaders and coalitions continue to steer internationalizing models in their respective countries and, at the same time, retain commitments to denuclearization. This joint outcome would be compatible with the framework's expectations. This scenario matches the reality of most of East Asia in the early twenty-first century and has a reasonable likelihood to persist, provided that most central features analyzed in part 2 remain in place, including regional and global conditions propitious for these models' survival. This scenario is supported, among many other considerations, by the presence of some 28,000 Japanese companies employing over a million workers in China as of 2005, double the number merely a decade ago, and of over one million Taiwanese entrepreneurs in the mainland.[41] Former MOFA official Kaneko Kumao (1996:46) draws attention to another requisite for the continuity of Japan's model: "Japan main-

	Internationalizing	Inward-looking
Denuclearization	1 Compatible	2 Anomaly
Nuclearization	3 Anomaly	4 Compatible

Figure 1. Models of political survival and nuclear outcomes: Four scenarios

tains cooperative nuclear agreements with six countries, the United States, Britain, France, Canada, Australia, and China. I personally negotiated . . . most of these. . . . If Japan misuses its civilian nuclear program for military purposes, a set of stringent sanctions will be imposed on it, including the immediate return of all imported materials and equipment to the original exporting country. Should that ever happen, nuclear power plants in Japan [would] come to a grinding halt, crippling economic and industrial activities. It is simply unthinkable that the nation would be willing to make such a heavy sacrifice—unless it [was] really prepared to start a war. In this sense, the bilateral nuclear energy agreements provide a rather effective deterrent, certainly more effective than the NPT."[42]

Scenario 3 entails the continuity of internationalizing models accompanied by discontinuities in nuclear policies. In other words, internationalizers go nuclear, which would constitute an anomaly for political survival arguments. This may be less likely under the current circumstances of a strongly internationalizing East Asia (including China) considered to be the locomotive of an expanding global economy. Should others backtrack on internationalizing models, however, such prospects could be higher. For instance, a Chinese leadership that does not cope appropriately with domestic challenges of economic transformation could be weakened or replaced by inward-looking opponents, with attending regional consequences. Furthermore, internationalizing leaders everywhere are not immune to miscalculating by overplaying nationalist cards or falling victim to "blowback" and entrapment by constituencies more favorable to nuclearization.[43] The 2005 Chinese legislation codifying a declaration of war against Taiwan if the latter claims independence could provide an example of unintended effects of such miscalculations. In the Middle East, recent reports suggested that Turkey could, under certain circumstances, reconsider its nuclear status (Fuerth 2004). In the past two decades, Turkish leaders appeared to have transcended the Middle East's modal inward-looking path, consolidating an internationalizing model and renouncing nuclear weapons. If this choice were reversed while Turkey sustains the current model, the domestic survival argument would be refuted. If, however, Turkey were to reverse its nuclear commitments in tandem with the rise of progressively more inward-looking domestic models—exacerbated by E.U. exclusion—the argument would be sustained. Such domestic changes could also involve deterioration in Turkey's relationship with NATO, highlighting the importance of domestic considerations in shaping security policies.

Scenario 2 points to conditions where inward-looking models dominate within a nuclear aspirant which nonetheless embraces denuclearization. The past record of nuclear aspirants shows that this joint occurrence has been rare if not nonexistent. This scenario would constitute another anomaly for the basic argument and could be illustrated by situations where inward-looking regimes in North Korea and the Middle East join and implement durable, transparent, mutually and unconditionally verifiable agreements renouncing nuclear capabilities as part of broader peace settlements.[44] The prospects for this outcome do not seem very likely under current circumstances. However, if, for instance, Iran's and North Korea's nuclear policies change in tandem with domestic survival models, as in Egypt and Libya, the argument would be corroborated.[45] In East Asia, scenario 2 would similarly involve the rise of domestic inward-looking models in pivotal states that nonetheless retain NPT commitments and compliance. This situation might be explained by path dependency or increasing returns of a three-decade-old legacy of shunning nuclear weapons (except for North Korea).

Scenario 4 suggests the presence of resilient inward-looking leaders resistant to internationalization, a defining characteristic of much of the Middle East for many decades, accompanied by intermittent efforts to acquire nuclear weapons. This scenario is compatible with the basic framework of regime survival, and its permanence does not bode well for denuclearizing shifts in that region. In East Asia, the widespread replacement of internationalizing models of political survival is certainly plausible but seems to be a low-probability event as of 2006. The Asian crisis signaled more resilience than anticipated and, despite some political turnovers, did not lead to significant departures from internationalizing strategies. Such turns remain nonetheless plausible in conjunction with global recessions or other regional and domestic downward economic or nationalist spirals. Significant domestic evolutions away from internationalizing trajectories—from

China to South Korea, Indonesia, and Japan—might encourage nuclear dominos. This outcome, although unlikely under present conditions in the world's most economically dynamic region, would be compatible with predictions in scenario 4.

These scenarios offer some guidance regarding continuity and change in nuclear trajectories on the basis of evolving domestic models of political survival. More complex scenarios can be developed by supplementing them with propositions derived from other approaches to nuclear behavior. As the independent, non-partisan Commission on the Intelligence Capabilities of the United States Regarding Weapons of Mass Destruction acknowledged, strengthening competitive analysis and competing hypotheses must be a sine qua non in the analysis of WMD programs of other countries (see http://www.whitehouse.gov/wmd/index.html). It would be misleading to conclude that policies of engagement in the global economy make states less secure because they arguably thwart nuclear capabilities. Japan, Taiwan, and South Korea, without natural resources or nuclear weapons, seem far less vulnerable or insecure than North Korea, Iran, or pre-2003 Iraq. Internationalizing models have turned them into engines of the twenty-first global economy, with much higher levels of domestic political stability, social equity, human rights, expected life-spans, employment, and educational endowments than nuclear-equipped but unstable Middle East models, despite rich natural and human resources.

POLICY IMPLICATIONS

As George (1993) suggested, theoretical analysis may be more helpful in conceptualizing the formulation of policy strategies than in providing detailed policy plans, or detailed elements of particular policies. This section thus offers very preliminary steps in the direction of translating what we know into what can be done. Clearly, different understandings of nuclear incentives can lead to different policy implications. No single approach opens the gate to the holy grail of denuclearization. Furthermore, every approach raises the problem of causal versus manipulative variables in policy formulation. Even if the leading causal variable driving or discouraging proliferation could be identified (relative power, norms and institutions, democracy, or domestic survival models), that variable may not be easily manipulable. Furthermore, as Lebow (2003:384) argues, "Our ability to predict, explain, control or manipulate social phenomena has been consistently confounded by the complexity and openness of social systems, and the ability of human beings to plan around and undermine any temporarily valid generalization." The challenge involved in outlining gaps between causal variables at work, and assessing what might be done with them to steer policy in more efficient directions, remains. Since policy-relevant studies along neorealist and neoliberal-institutionalist lines have been the staple in nonproliferation, I survey them only briefly and concentrate on tentative propositions that disaggregate the domestic context of nuclear aspirants.

The strategic circumstances of states vary from very threatening and precarious to relatively benign, setting up some background conditions but also raising an array of operational limitations. As different chapters suggested, hegemons and other powerful states with many resources can find it very difficult to translate them into preferred outcomes. Hegemons have relied on both forceful coercion and attractive enticements to discourage nuclearization, but those efforts have failed in a non-trivial number of cases. The specific domestic receptivity of targets to selected negative and positive inducements is a critical intervening factor between hegemonic efforts and responses by nuclear aspirants. Policies that assume states as unified entities inexorably buffeted by changes in the balance of power, and that rely on coercion or inducements without considering domestic political landscapes, are less likely to succeed. Ironically, acting on the assumption that states are monolithic structures under threat tends to reproduce such assumptions in target states, enabling their regimes to widen domestic sympathy. Surgical attacks on Iran's nuclear facilities could bring about just such rallying-round-the-flag effects. Milani (2005) also cautions against granting "security assurances" to Iran's regime that would forestall its inevitable demise by Iran's own disgruntled citizens. Yet granting such assurances can also prevent such regimes from wielding external threats to unify their publics, provided the public can learn about the existence of such assurances. Construing nuclear aspirants as monolithic states can thus subvert the successful design of positive and negative inducements. Furthermore, as studies in this book suggest, single-handed emphasis on structural power does not necessarily lead to any particular policy equilibrium but to a cacophony of options. Whereas some advocate forceful, including military, prevention or preemption as tools of nuclear denial, others regard the diffusion of nuclear capabilities as potentially stabilizing, requiring only that those newcomers be helped to transition into nuclear balance (Intriligator and Brito 1981; Waltz 1981; Bueno de Mesquita and Riker 1982). Additional prescriptions compatible with relative-power considerations that emphasize the dangers of diffusion point to export controls and economic sanctions.

For the most part, international institutions enjoy greater international legitimacy as agents of nonproliferation than any single state or any group of states that has already acquired nuclear weapons. The Nobel Peace Prize award to the IAEA is perhaps a reflection of that recognition. Chapter 2 discussed NPR-related mechanisms designed to prevent diffusion of sensitive technologies for military uses. The Fissile Material Cut-Off Treaty, for instance, was conceived to prohibit use of fissile materials in nuclear weapons while enabling civilian use. New forms of control of enrichment and reprocessing technologies are being considered.[46] Most institutional solutions are crafted from the perspective of technological denial and supply of coercion. A major deficiency of the NPR, however, even when it can overcome problems of collective action, has been its lack of effective means of enforcement. Beyond their multilateral essence, rational-institutionalist approaches to the NPT have shared with neorealism explicit or implicit assumptions about unified states, without providing a coherent account of the sources of state preferences. As the chapters on Iraq, Libya, and North Korea suggest, measures that could be considered rational for application on target states as a whole may be far less rational when domestic distributional consequences are considered, creating unintended victims and strengthening already powerful dictators. Many such lessons have been learned in the past two decades by states, multilateral institutions, and NGOs. Policy instruments have all too often neglected domestic factors in the crystallization of nuclear preferences until relatively recently. Widespread economic sanctions, indiscriminating blockades, and exclusion from membership in international institutions can sometimes help uncompromising leaders coalesce national opposition. Lessons from Iraq and North Korea suggest that sanctions have not been effective in producing popular uprisings.

In sum, approaches pivoted on the concept of balance of power ignored, by definition, the domestic nature of states, and those pivoted on the NPR have similarly been inattentive to systematic domestic sources of demand for nuclear weapons. In both cases the basic problem has been, as Feinstein and Slaughter (2004:144) note, "to treat North Korea as if it were Norway." Even studies emphasizing normative persuasion have overlooked domestic political conditions as integral and constitutive, rather than residual. This task would involve calibrating dominant domestic receptivity to norms against nuclear weapons acquisition as opposed to norms advocating nuclear weapons on prestige, modernization, or identity-related grounds. Sometimes even well-meaning critiques of globalization and the NPR as "Western constructs" have the unintended effect of strengthening domestic forces and "moral entrepreneurs" with nuclear weapons agendas as redemptive symbols. Normative-legal perspectives such as Feinstein and Slaughter's (2004:140) reveal greater sensitivity to domestic drivers of nuclear proliferation when, for example, they argue that "it is not states that are the danger, but their rulers." Indeed, they go as far as suggesting that the international community—through multilateral or regional frameworks—has a "duty to prevent" rulers of closed societies from acquiring and using nuclear weapons.

A domestic political survival approach may provide a window into the internal currents that sustain demands for such weapons.[47] Efforts to untangle how domestic political-economy agents and structures overlap with, reinforce, or undermine nuclear policy can help craft more effective policies. This is different from ad hoc depictions of the domestic scene in one country or another, often drawn without reference to an overarching comparative framework. It is also different from simply modeling the domestic politics of target states cleavaged between "moderates" and "hardliners" on the basis of inductive "who's who" approaches. Such efforts are very useful and indeed progressive moves in the direction of disaggregating the domestic context of target states, but they do not always provide an underlying logic for what makes some leaders, institutions, and coalitions "moderates" or "hardliners." The framework suggested here provides one way to endogenize the question of who is likely to be a moderate or a hardliner, or to make it an integral part of the explanation. Understanding the deep psychological, philosophical, political, and normative sources leading individuals toward "moderate" or "hardline" nuclear choices can be both interesting and helpful but also a potentially open-ended and protracted enterprise with unknown universal applicability. This should nonetheless be part of the research agenda ahead. However, the pressing policy relevance of nuclear proliferation highlights the value of more discrete markers, shortcuts, or rules-of-thumb for identifying the motivations of leaders and constituencies in states aspiring to acquire nuclear weapons. Models of political survival provide a systematic tool, with premises backed by considerable preliminary evidence that are potentionally applicable worldwide.

These models may not capture all the correlates of nuclear preferences and are, after all, only ideal-types, conceptual constructs, and not historical or "true" realities. As such, they need not fit every case or indeed any particular case completely (Eckstein 1975) but instead provide a heuristic, a helpful shortcut, and a comparative framework capable of reducing complex reality—and different cases—down to some fundamentals. Models of political survival can explain why different actors within the same state vary in their approaches and preferences regarding nuclear policy; why nuclear policies within states may vary over time as a function of the relative power of particular domestic forces; and why different states vary in their commitments to increase information, transparency, and compliance with the NPR. This heuristic provides a different foundation for the design of positive and negative inducements to encourage denuclearization than those conceiving of states as unified actors. At the broadest level, positive inducements would aim at strengthening models of political survival pivoted on economic growth and integration in the global economy, which also curb domestic demand for nuclear weapons.

Negative inducements would be directed at domestic actors with stakes in nuclear-industrial-complexes and ancillary political-economic structures that thrive under protection and state control. Iran's largest conglomerates (bonyads)—fiefdoms of radical clerics and Pasdaran—may be cases in point.

Translating models of political survival into a more detailed set of policies requires a dedicated effort that goes beyond the already packed agenda for this book. That effort should take account of unintended effects of policies, informed by expert knowledge of domestic landscapes of nuclear aspirants. Some unintended effects can be anticipated whereas others cannot. Unintended effects can be positive and negative (Sen 1999:257). Some attempts to shore up private sectors, for instance, may alienate groups who, while favoring other dimensions of internationalization, transfer their support to prophets of economic self-sufficiency. Research along these lines must also craft policies suitable to different institutional environments within which models thrive or decline. Iran is certainly not North Korea, even though both are authoritarian. Different institutional contexts may require different mixes of aid, trade benefits, investments, debt-relief, food, and selective removal from export control lists. The financial community may be allied with internationalizing or inward-looking camps under different conditions; carrots and sticks must thus be fine-tuned according to the circumstances of particular models. Policies must also countenance the fact that the ascendancy, design, and fate of domestic models of political survival have powerful internal dynamics that do not always render themselves open to external intervention. Finally, disaggregating the roles of different senders of positive and negative inducements (international institutions, great powers, and NGOs) can help create complementarities among them and reduce the potential for cross-purpose or neutralizing tensions. With all these caveats in mind, we can outline preliminary considerations that might guide further policy-oriented research:

REWARDING NATURAL CONSTITUENCIES OF INTERNATIONALIZING MODELS

International institutions may provide incentives—positive and negative—to influence the relative appeal of different models. For instance, international economic institutions provide credit and define terms of trade and investment that may in principle strengthen internationalizing models. Their effects are mediated by the extent to which such institutions and their domestic beneficiaries in target states are able to advance economic growth and reform with an eye on broad redistribution, equity, and low tolerance for corruption (particularly regarding privatization). External intervention can encourage health, education, and welfare and discourage oversized military-industrial-complexes. Myopic policies insensitive to these objectives decrease political support for internationalization, plant the seeds of inward-looking reversals, and weaken the prospects for developing open economies with lower incentives to acquire nuclear weapons.[48] Externally induced structural adjustment can strengthen state and private actors involved in economic reform, privatization, export promotion, finance ministries, and central banks but can also weaken agents of reform if designed with indifference to distributional, including equity, effects. International pressures for human rights standards empower domestic groups responsible for monitoring compliance with international agreements at the expense of repressive agencies, even if they also can trigger cycles of reprisal, which have recrudesced in Iran under Ahmadinejad. Nonetheless, awarding the Nobel Peace Prize to Iranian lawyer Shirin Ebadi was undoubtedly intended to strengthen human rights groups under assault by the Iranian judiciary. International environmental regimes entrust local civil networks with legitimacy to challenge industrial activities that damage the environment, including those resulting from nuclear-industrial-complexes.

These examples are only suggestive of how broad constituencies opposed to nuclear weapons for different reasons can aggregate (logroll) as a consequence of ostensibly unrelated international influences. The stronger these constituencies become, the less willing they will be to bear the economic, social, and political consequences of nuclear programs and the external instability that they often induce. Clearly, the ability to encourage the path toward internationalizing models is itself a function of existing relative openness and of the relative strength of its political carriers, particularly in the private sector. Although unrelated to the nuclear program, sanctions on South Africa were effective at least partly because they consolidated opposition against apartheid among important segments of the outward-oriented financial and industrial community (Liberman 2001). As on other issues, Iran is not North Korea with respect to existing constituencies potentially oriented to an international economy. Iran's WTO membership can benefit a private sector—small and medium-size firms—that was once thriving but has been adversely affected or coopted by the massive statization that followed the Islamic Revolution. Under near-total closure and without a critical mass of current beneficiaries from internationalization, the path in North Korea may be more difficult but not impossible. After all, current beneficiaries of Kim Jong-Il's model are not legion either.[49] Furthermore, the dominance of internationalizing models throughout East Asia provides not only a blueprint but also regional incentives for North Korea's leadership to soft-land by emulating the historical experience of its neighbors. Policies supporting North Korea's economic reform and export-processing zones help strengthen domestic reformers vis-à-vis their opponents.

STRIPPING AUTARKIC OR INWARD-LOOKING REGIMES OF THE
MEANS TO CONCENTRATE POWER

Many policies cited in the previous paragraph have adverse effects on inward-looking domestic actors. The introduction of markets, openness, transparency, foreign investment, conditionality, structural adjustment, and export-led industrialization harms state and private institutions and monopolistic enterprises that thrive under closure. Thus Milani (2005b: 50) suggests that an end to Iran's embargo will reduce the power of protectionist rackets, vigilantes, and monopolies such as bonyads, Mo'talefe, and Pasdaran.[50] UNSC resolutions banning exports of luxury items to North Korea—imposed after its nuclear test—punish Kim Jong-Il's associates most directly. Conditionality arrangements by some international institutions often threaten military-industrial-complexes insofar as economic rationalization deprives the latter of resources and rents. The military, however, is not *invariably* pro-nuclear, and selected segments develop interests that can become intertwined with internationalizing agendas, as in China, and to a much more limited extent, in North Korea. Furthermore, conventional military establishments may weigh the costs of nuclear defiance today against the viability of conventional modernization in the longer run, as well as the opportunity costs of nuclearization for maintaining conventional capabilities (Betts 1980:136). Alleged tensions in Iran between the regular military and Pasdaran bear on some of these considerations.

Iraq's experience suggests that the Oil-for-Food program benefited Saddam's military-industrial-complex and security services even if U.N. inspections prevented reconstitution of WMD programs. Monopoly agencies, corrupt officials, smugglers, and black-market profiteers (state and private) also thrived, strengthening their control of the economy and the means of coercion. North Korea provides another example of difficulties in preventing dictatorships from shifting the burden of sanctions to innocent victims, and of the need to maximize efforts to deny control of aid allocation and distribution to domestic actors poised to gain from economic closure. Foreign providers to protectionist rackets can themselves be rogue state agencies or private profiteers whose operations are sometimes tacitly sanctioned by government officials, from Russia to Pakistan and Europe. However, even some legitimate trade, including that between Japan and North Korea, arguably benefits the military and party elite.[51] Sanctions imposed on North Korean money laundering, counterfeiting and narcotics trade activities in Macao's Banco Delta Asia are said to have directly disrupted a secretive North Korean agency (Unit 39) that provided Kim Jong-Il with patronage funds.[52] Furthermore, over two dozen other banks have also severed ties with North Korea. Sanctions on Yog'aksan General Trading Company targeted North Korea's main producer and exporter of missiles and the Korea Ch'anggwang Credit Bank, which manages finances and payments for missile exports (Pinkston 2003). According to ICG (2005), most revenue from missiles and drugs is accrued by the military directly, not the government. Active targeting of individual and corporate architects of nuclearizing policies can involve freezing personal bank accounts, canceling travel visas, and depriving them of diplomatic immunity. The UNSC resolution following North Korea's nuclear test banned trade related to WMD and luxury items, and authorized cargo inspections. The December 24, 2006, UNSC resolution following Iran's defiance of a previous UNSC resolution banned trade in materials and technology for uranium enrichment, reprocessing, heavy water, and ballistic missiles, and froze assets of twelve Iranians (including Pasdaran commander Yahya Rahim Safavi) and ten companies involved in those activities. Russia's and China's economic interests (including Russia's interests in the Bushehr reactor) precluded the inclusion of a mandatory travel ban on people involved in nuclear activities. In addition to these multilateral measures, the U.S. Treasury Department has began barring American banks from transactions with Iranian banks with reputed ties to terrorism, such as Bank Saderat, triggering similar steps by some European banks, lest they too might suffer adverse consequences from their own ties to Iranian banks.[53] A second major Iranian bank (most major banks in Iran are state-owned or controlled)—Bank Sepah—became the second target of sanctions for activities related to missiles or WMD. These measures will hurt projects under the purview of Pasdaran, bonyads, and other government interests. Despite its heavy dependence on foreign oil, Japan has supported some of these measures and downgraded its stake in the Azadegan oil field.

CRAFTING PACKAGES OF SANCTIONS AND INDUCEMENTS THAT ARE SENSITIVE TO DIFFERENCES BETWEEN ENERGY-RICH AND ENERGY-POOR TARGETS

The cases analyzed here point to considerable differences in the way in which leaders and coalitions from oil-rich versus oil-poor countries sustain inward-looking models. Rentier states such as Iran, Iraq, and Libya were able to rely on both coercion and extensive oil revenues to develop wide clientelistic networks supporting the regime (to some extent the Iraqi insurgency showed determined resistance by some Sunni elements to relinquish these privileges). Such resources have been far more limited for Kim Jong-Il, presiding over an energy-poor economy in dire need of external support. This key difference suggests an important research agenda in the study of positive and negative inducements. Such an agenda must understand the influence of the oil industry's power structure and its clientelistic networks on economic liberalization, their respective position on the nuclear program, and the presumed barriers posed by the "oil

curse" for export-led strategies (through "Dutch disease" effects), democratization, and denuclearization (Komaie and Solingen 2007). East
Asia's limited natural resources are thought to have provided better conditions for adopting export-led models and democratic institutions. Although these assumptions are not unchallenged, North Korea's demise of
juche could arguably render the country more fit for markets, democracy,
and denuclearization. Evolving realities in Iraq, Libya, Iran, and the GCC
will enable further research on connections between the oil sector, economic reform, and nuclear programs.

USING DEMOCRACY—WHERE AVAILABLE—AS AN ALLY OF DENUCLEARIZATION

Democracies and autocracies respond differently to international sanctions and inducements. The responses of both, however, are often contingent on the nature of their ties to the global political economy. Chapter 2
hypothesized that democracies may have been less likely to acquire nuclear weapons to face democratic opponents. Yet democratic regimes appear neither necessary nor sufficient for denuclearization. Some democracies have been highly favorable to nuclear weapons (India), and many
autocracies have not pursued them. Nonetheless, democratic contexts
offer much better opportunities for the international community to reach
domestic groups favoring denuclearization. Democratization challenges
the conditions that allow nuclear programs to thrive beyond public
scrutiny by media, political parties, and interest groups and allows these
groups to help verify compliance with international agreements. The
more democratic the state, the greater the opportunities for suasion, perhaps with diminishing returns for democracies surrounded by autocratic
adversaries, particularly neighbors with nuclear designs.[54] Promoting domestic allies of denuclearization is much harder under autocratic controls,
yet new mass technologies have enabled greater external access to disen-
franchised populations, more so in Iran than in North Korea. Milani
(2005b:4) proposes a tacit grand alliance between the West and the pre-
dominantly pro-American Iranian people. In his view, popular support
for the nuclear program is ephemeral and contingent, whereas the crisis
of leadership is structural and deepening. Without patronizing or coopting reformist leaders, external supporters of democracy can help raise the
political, strategic, and economic costs of Iran's nuclear program, which
Milani argues would be far more effective in mobilizing Iran's domestic
opposition. In a country where a million new jobs are needed every year,
some conclude that nuclear weapons may be of less vital importance to
Iran's population than concrete economic benefits.[55] Highlighting these
opportunity costs is as effective as pointing to the high actual costs of
defiant nuclear programs. Limited access to domestic audiences in North
Korea makes it much more difficult to advance similar objectives, but

such efforts are becoming increasingly less impossible in an era of mobile phones and a porous China border. By contrast, Qadhafi's shift encountered mixed reception in a regional context that retains an emphasis on inward-looking models and defiance of internationalization.[56]

These considerations offer a foundation upon which more detailed strategies can be crafted, not as substitutes for, but rather in conjunction with, other multilateral policies including denial of weapons technologies to NPT violators and a verifiable fissile material ban.[57] No single instrument can yield immediate results or guarantee absolute compliance. As Blix (2005:81–82) noted prior to the 2003 war, "A clause signaling forceful action in case of non-compliance would be valuable. Iraq did not move without forceful, sustained pressure, and it simply shrugged off economic sanctions." But this is different from overemphasizing threats of force that have unintended, although easily foreseen, domestic effects in target states. Effective policies should convert nuclear programs from rallying points to lightning rods, not the other way round. Some positive inducements take longer to yield results. U.S. reassurances at the Six-Party Talks that it had "no intention to attack or invade the DPRK" and that it "respects [its] sovereignty" are a case in point.[58] North Korea's subsequent nuclear test can be traced to many factors but cannot be construed as "proof" that such statements are ineffective. Though not sufficient to produce immediate outcomes, such commitments deprive inward-looking leaders from opportunities to exploit external threats to strengthen internal unity. Even if positive commitments are precluded from immediately reaching the wider population, they could make elements of the ruling coalition more susceptible to compromise. The Libyan experience suggests that even inward-looking regimes with long histories of radical self-sufficiency and nuclear weapons aspirations can be brought back from isolation. As Jentleson and Whytock (2005/06:81–82) argue, "The combination of internal pressures and the coercive diplomacy strategy helped bring Qaddafi to a point where his hold on power was better served by global engagement than global radicalism."

Libya's experience also suggests that multilateral cooperation is of the essence in bringing about positive outcomes, even if such cooperation crystallized as a consequence of Libya's terrorist rather than nuclear activities. The adverse effects of multilateral steps by the IAEA on Tehran's stock market, Iranian businesses, and consumers were tangible and sharpened domestic debates over Ahmadinejad's policies. Yet consistent multilateral cooperation on Iran and North Korea has been hard to obtain, inspite of the fact that their nuclear programs are more advanced than were Libya's.[59] French and Russian military-industrial- and energy-complexes are undoubtedly strong political forces to contend with but have sometimes been defeated by their domestic opponents and by strong external, including E.U., pressure for collective action. North Korea's nuclear test drove the point home to Chinese leaders that China too can be adversely affected by failures of collective action, launching a domestic reassessment of its own policies. Certain U.S. policies have undermined collective action no less, including withholding CTBT ratification and discussions of new generations of nuclear weapons and bunker-busting devices. The failure of all nuclear weapons states to make progress on Article VI, a contractual obligation under the NPT, may not be the main driver of nuclearization. Yet it certainly provides inward-looking proponents of such weapons worldwide with additional pretexts while weakening domestic constituencies receptive to denuclearization and internationalization.[60] Carter (2005) summarized eight "Ds" that have become part of the toolkit to prevent nuclear proliferation: dissuasion, disarmament, diplomacy, denial, defusing, deterrence, defenses, and destruction.[61] A ninth "D" should be added for "domestic" (or "DD," for "disaggregating domestic" effects), reminding architects of nonproliferation policy that each tool should be evaluated in light of distributional consequences within target states. Designing appropriate mixes of Ds, as well as their sequence and timetable, must be inextricably linked to the careful analysis of "qui bono?" or how each mix could affect the relevant internal constituencies that—in the end—shape nuclear logics.

Notes

1. I use the terms "nuclearization" to suggest movement *toward* nuclear weapons acquisition, even if it does not result in actual acquisition, and "denuclearization" to suggest renunciation. Although discussions throughout the book address a wide range of nuclear behavior, sometimes I rely on this binary formulation as shorthand.

2. I adopt Bracken's (2003) characterization of the "second nuclear age" as involving proliferation dynamics unrelated to superpower rivalries, starting after China's 1964 tests. For an alternative application, see Gray (1999). My concern is with state actors, not with nuclear terrorism, which stems from different sources and dynamics (Schelling 1976; Allison 2004; Ferguson and Potter 2005). Nuclear aspirants like Iran and North Korea are considered potential suppliers of sensitive technologies to terrorists (Carter 2005).

3. Carnegie Endowment website (CEW henceforth); Arms Control Association website (ACAW); Nuclear Threat Initiative website (NTIW henceforth); Federation of American Scientists website (FASW henceforth); Global Security website (GSW henceforth); Institute for Science and International Security website (ISISW henceforth); Campbell et al. (2004); Richelson (2006). Egypt, Iraq, Iran, and Libya have also produced and used chemical weapons (Cordesman 2000; Center for Nonproliferation Studies website, CNSW henceforth).

4. (London) *Times*, November 4, 2006:2.

5. Chanlett-Avery and Squassoni (2006); Dafna Linzer, "Optimism Turns to Anxiety on Curbing Nuclear Arms," *Washington Post*, Nov. 3, 2006: A23. Concerns with potential covert efforts by South Korea, Taiwan, and Egypt are addressed in respective chapters. Japan explored the theoretical merits and drawbacks of nuclear weapons in the late 1960s and 1970s but never established a nuclear weapons program. Early efforts by Taiwan and South Korea in the 1970s are certainly not comparable to those in the Middle East cases and were largely superseded by compliant nonproliferation commitments.

6. The literature has differentiated between "offensive realism," predicting balancing or "buckpassing" (Mearsheimer 2002), and "defensive realism" (Waltz 1979), predicting only a tendency to balance; and between neorealism, a purely structural theory of outcomes, and neoclassical realism, sensitive to domestic influences on state behavior (Snyder 1991; Brooks 1997; Rose 1998; Rosecrance 2006). Much of the critique of neorealism in different chapters is directed at offensive neorealism (its rather crude version), which presumes inevitable aggression and expansionism.

7. Internationalization involves the expansion of global markets, institutions, and norms, which progressively reduces the purely domestic aspects of politics (Solingen 2001a).

8. "Political survival" is used here to connote efforts by political leaders to gain or remain in power in the face of domestic challenges and external threats (Bueno de Mesquita et al. 2003).

9. Eckstein (1975). Crucial tests are well positioned to corroborate or reject a theory, offering least or most likely conditions for either to take place.

10. A poll found that 84 percent of respondents regarded the prevention of the spread of nuclear weapons as very important and 13 percent as somewhat important for U.S. priorities (Kull 2004).

11. John Kerry declared that nuclear proliferation was the most serious threat facing U.S. national security (GSN, October 1, 2004). For official statements under the Clinton administration citing nuclear proliferation as the gravest potential threat to security in the twenty-first century, see Halperin (1999). Keller (2003) noted that "a dozen years after the Soviet Union crumbled, nuclear weapons have not receded to the margins of our interest, as many expected. On the contrary, in this second nuclear age, such weapons govern our foreign policy more than they have in decades." On the *Bulletin of Atomic Scientists*, see the bulletin.org.

12. "Intelligence Chiefs Paint Grim Picture of Proliferation," *Arms Control Today*, March 2003:19; Keller (2003); Campbell and Sunohara (2004:238). On "hedging," "virtual weapons," or capabilities that could quickly be converted into weapons, see Levite (2002/03); Campbell et al. (2004); and Reiss (2003).

13. (London) *Times*, November 4, 2006:1.

14. *New York Times*, March 23, 1963:1.

15. For extensive references to Israel's program, see chapter 9.

16. On the paucity of efforts and gaps in the scholarly understanding of nuclear proliferation, see Sagan (1996/97) and Levite (2002/03:59). Some early theoretical treatments include, inter alia, Betts (1977a); Reiss (1988, 1995); Intriligator and Brito (1981); Waltz (1981); Bueno de Mesquita and Riker (1982); Meyer (1984); Solingen (1994a,b, 1995). More recent additions include Paul (2000); Walsh (2001); and Hymans (2006).

17. For an expanded treatment of theoretical and methodological considerations underpinning this study, including case selection, theory-testing, and identification of crucial cases, see Solingen (2007b).

18. Most sources agree that these included Argentina, Brazil, Egypt, India, Iran, Iraq, Israel, Japan, Libya, North Korea, Pakistan, South Africa, South Korea, and Taiwan. There is much less consensus on Algeria, Syria, Romania, Indonesia, and Yugoslavia. For circumstantial evidence on Yugoslavia, see Potter <http://www .cns.miis.edu>. Ukraine, Belarus, and Kazakhstan are in a different category, having inherited nuclear weapons from the former Soviet Union and returned them to Russia soon after independence. Industrialized countries in the 1960s include Italy, Norway, Sweden, and Switzerland (Foreign diplomats, personal communications, Washington, DC, November 8, 2005; Zurich, Switzerland, October 25–27, 2006); Australia may have ended consideration in the early 1970s (Levite 2002/03).

19. The tighter comparison between these two regions would be diluted if the two South Asian cases were included, contributing only residual and potentially confounding effects. Three features set South Asia apart: (1) its bipolar regional structure at least in most recent decades (versus multipolar in the Middle East and East Asia, as discussed later); (2) its non-NPT membership (versus wide member-

ship in the other two regions, except Israel), which made it subject to different institutional constraints; and (3) nuclear tests in India and Pakistan (1974, 1998) as opposed to no tests in the other two regions (until North Korea's test in 2006).

20. At the same time, the historical analysis delves into pre-NPT nuclear deliberations in each of these countries, providing within-case analyses and a quasi-experimental design where the NPT's inception arguably produced a discontinuity between pre-institutional and post-institutional eras.

21. For an early exploration of this variable, see Solingen (1994a, b, 1995).

22. Process-tracing is designed to identify steps in a causal chain in a particular historical context. Such intervening variables and causal mechanisms are "ultimately unobservable physical, social, or psychological processes through which agents with causal capacities operate, but only in specific contexts or conditions" (George and Bennett 2005:176).

23. "Approximating" implies a more relaxed form of Mill's method, known for its inherent difficulty in the social sciences (Brady and Collier 2004; George and Bennett 2005).

24. The "hedging" hypothesis induces a more tentative formulation of this last proposition, but the fact remains that many countries with latent capabilities have not ostensibly converted them into military ones.

25. On the difficulty of identifying least and most likely conditions for any theory, see George and Bennett (2005). Truly crucial cases are rare but tough tests are useful (Eckstein 1975).

26. There are important differences between neorealism and neoclassical realism; the latter is more open to domestic considerations (Rose 1998). The deficiencies noted throughout this book are mostly directed at neorealism, particularly its offensive variant, rather than at neoclassical realism. Security dilemmas stem from states' efforts to resolve their insecurities by arming themselves, which, in turn, leaves them less secure in that others interpret such efforts as offensive rather than defensive (Jervis 1976).

27. For three excellent but competing neorealist responses to this question, see Ross (1999); Mastanduno (2003); and Gilpin (2000).

28. Neorealism has significantly declined in conceptual and empirical studies in the broader field of international relations (Vazquez 1998; Legro and Moravcsik 1999; Stein 2005; Walker and Morton 2005).

29. As Beck (2005) suggests, the question is not what decision-makers claimed was important but rather why they decided one way or another, which may be two related but different questions. On the strategic role of deception in public statements, see Kowert and Legro (1996).

30. Systematic attention to domestic contexts in this academic subfield has lagged behind a broader turn to domestic sources of international behavior in the discipline, pioneered by Rosenau (1969) among others.

31. For early analytical efforts in this direction, see Solingen (1994a, 2001b) and for subsequent applications, Liberman (2001); Walsh (2001); and Singh and Way (2004).

32. It should be noted that a theory may be necessary or sufficient to explain a specific case.

33. Rentier states relied on oil exports but pointedly not on internationally competitive export-led manufacturing. Rentier states that had undergone revolutions (Ba'th, Islamist, Libyan) stepped up efforts to reduce reliance on oil exports but were ultimately unsuccessful.

34. Yet they operated in the South African case (Liberman 2001).

35. Saddam Hussein practically acknowledged as much, but only after being deposed (see chapter 7).

NOTES TO CHAPTER TWO

1. Campbell et al. (2004). For an early overview of incentives and disincentives, see Rosecrance (1964); Betts (1977a); Potter (1982); and Dunn (1982).

2. The classic statement is in Waltz (1981). See also Mearsheimer (1990) and critiques by Rosecrance (1964, 1986); Solingen (1994a, 1994b); Betts (2000); Sagan (1996/97), Stein (2005), and Mueller (1988, 1995), who argues that nuclear weapons may not have had much impact on world affairs since World War II and that they were not necessary to deter world war, shape alliance patterns, or induce caution.

3. The *force de frappe* was not a reaction to declining U.S. alliance commitments but "the product of prior nationalism for which declining U.S. involvement is given as justification" (Rosecrance 1964:301).

4. These also include West Germany, Italy, and Spain. Scarce resources can be significant but not insuperable barriers to nuclear weapons, as the cases of Pakistan and North Korea suggest. A 1963 National Intelligence Estimate (NIE) argued that "political and military considerations are likely to prove more important in determining the pace and scope of nuclear diffusion than differences in national wealth and technical skill. Where the motivation is strong enough, a country might attempt to overcome a lack of native resources by importing materials, technology, and technicians, or even weapons themselves" (Burr 2005).

5. As Dunn (1982:122) predicted, superpower postures did not affect nuclear decisions in Pakistan, India, South Africa, Israel, Argentina, or Brazil.

6. As Waltz (2003:40) argues, the more vulnerable states feel, the more strenuously they will pursue a nuclear program.

7. On neorealism's move from an emphasis on balance of power as its core principle to more "generalist" formulations with opaque and indistinct claims, see Rosecrance (2001). On neorealism as indeterminate, see Stein (2005). According to George and Bennett (2005:191), structural neorealism is not designed to make highly specific predictions anyway. Mearsheimer (1990, 1993, 2001) has made specific predictions that Japan, Germany, and Ukraine were highly likely to acquire nuclear weapons. So far none has. On Japan, see also Waltz (1981). On how neorealist theories engage in foreign-policy predictions, see Elman (1996).

8. George and Bennett (2005). As Collier, Seawright, and Munck (2004:39) suggest, the quality of causal inferences is improved when theories are posed with sufficient clarity and linked to appropriate observable implications. On the lack of clarity of what it means for states "to seek to ensure their survival," see Powell (2002).

9. See also Christensen (1996).

10. The scope of this book does not enable more than a summary of this vast literature, which includes, inter alia, Nye (1981); Potter (1982); Scheinman (1987); Smith (1987); and WMDC (2006).

11. Samore (1994), Reiss (2003), Campbell et al. (2004). A 1996 IAEA report suggested that Iraq could have had nuclear weapons by 1992 had the first Gulf War not happened.

12. India, Pakistan, and Israel have remained outside the NPT. See http://disarmament2.un.org/wmd/.

13. Von Stein (2005) alludes to this generic problem of "selection bias," which can overstate the effects of treaty obligations.

14. Kahler (1995). Counterfactuals are assessments of "what might have happened" in the absence of a proposed causal factor (Tetlock and Belkin 1996; Tetlock and Lebow 2001). Counterfactual analysis cannot prove or disprove a proposition but can be valuable for developing theory, gaining deeper understandings of decisions, dispelling cognitive misconceptions, and relaxing rigid theoretical commitments, although it also entails the risk of assigning too much subjective probability to too many scenarios.

15. Indeed, Libya's leader Mu'ammar Qadhafi declared that "the Arabs are waging a fierce campaign against us for deciding to get rid of WMD. I hope they are not successful in taking revenge against us" (Hearing Before the Subcommittee on International Terrorism, Nonproliferation and Human Rights of the Committee on International Relations, House of Representatives, 108th Congress, Second Session, September 22, 2004, Serial No. 108–145; see http://www.house.gov/international_relations/108/95978.pdf). Arab League Secretary-General Amr Moussa, bemoaning "vain attempts to divide" the Arab world, stated that illicit weapons should be negotiated only "within the structure of the Arab League" (William J. Broad and David E. Sanger, "Warhead Designs Tie Libya Nuclear Project to Pakistani Scientist," New York Times, February 4, 2004:A9). On the role of the Arab League in deepening intra-regional competition, see Barnett and Solingen (2007).

16. On NPT norms, see Nye (1981); Scheinman (1990); and Quester (1991). On the limited nuclear test ban as having placed a "moral imprimatur" upon renunciation of nuclear weapons in the 1960s, see Rosecrance (1964). On "inhibitions" regarding the use of nuclear weapons, see Schelling (1976); Dunn (1982); and Tannenwald (1999, 2005), and on the inability to rule out alternative explanations for non-use, Beck (2005).

17. Mazarr (1995a); Campbell et al. (2004). On Japan as a "virtual" nuclear weapons state, see FASW.

18. "Japanese Leader's Nuclear Remarks Slammed," United Press, June 18, 1994 (in Mack 1996:23).

19. William J. Broad and David E. Sanger, "Restraints Fray and Risks Grow as Nuclear Club Gains Members," New York Times, October 15, 2006.

20. "China refuses to back down on general's nuclear threat over Taiwan," Agence France-Presse (AFP henceforth), July 16, 2005.

21. Ariane Bernard, "Chirac Hints at Nuclear Reply to State-Sponsored Terrorism," New York Times, January 20, 2006: A8.

22. "Russia and Threats of WMD Proliferation and Terrorism," PIR Center Report, Moscow, Human Rights Publishers, 2006:16.

23. Tannenwald (2005:8) defines a taboo as "a particularly forceful kind of normative prohibition that is concerned with the protection of individuals and societies from behavior that is defined or perceived to be dangerous."

24. Schelling (1976:81) notes that "the stronger the perceived limitations on the usefulness of nuclear weapons, the stronger will be the considerations militating against acquisition."

25. Nuclearfiles.org, Nuclear Age Peace Foundation, at http://www.nuclear files.org.

26. This and next citation are from AmericanCatholic.org.

27. On the Islamic or Hindu bomb, see Keller (2003). On nuclear weapons as redemptive anti-colonial tools in the Muslim world, see Mazrui (1989) and Hoodbhoy (1993). On the compatibility between nuclear use and shari'a, see Ayatollah Mesbah Yazdi's "fatwa" (chapter 8). Hashmi (2004) reports that the majority view in Islamic intellectual circles holds that nuclear proliferation is both inevitable and morally acceptable because of India's and Israel's nuclear weapons. In efforts to attract Libyan, Saudi, and Iranian funds for his own program, Pakistan's Zulfiqar Ali Bhutto emphasized an "Islamic bomb" to counter Christian, Jewish, and Hindu capabilities (see B. Raman, "The Nuclear Jihad," *The Kashmir Telegraph,* February 2004, at http://www.kashmirtelegraph.com). On the media's warm reception of Pakistan's "Islamic bomb" in the Arab world and on calls for an "Arab nuclear bomb," see Abdus Sattar Ghazali, "Pak Nuclear Tests: Fallout on the Arab World," July 1998, at http://www.toluislam.com.

28. Rosecrance (1964, 1966); Scheinman (1965); Husbands (1982); May (1994); Thayer (1995). A 1957 NIE ranks prestige higher than deterrence as an incentive for "fourth countries" (following the United States, Soviet, and British bombs; see Burr 2005).

29. Waltz (1989:48). Blix (2005:17) argued that nuclear-weapons-states deterred each other from using them during the Cold War through "mutual assured destruction."

30. Reiss (1988). For Mueller (1988), it is not nuclear weapons that have made war obsolete among developed states but the latter's emphasis on prosperity and economic growth. Others argue that conventional weapons have been "perfected" in ways that obviate nuclear weapons.

31. For an identity-based explanation of Argentina's restraint, see Hymans (2006).

32. Alani (2005:7). Chemical weapons have been used by Egypt in Yemen, Saddam Hussein against Iran and Iraq's civilian Kurdish population, Iran against Iraq, and Libya against Chad (Cordesman 2000; Hashmi 2004; Boucek 2004; NTIW).

33. The "hedging" hypothesis (Levite 2002/03) might place these cases closer to each other (except for NPT membership).

34. Autocracies exhibit a concentrated monopoly of political power, praetorian domestic structures, the absence of electoral cycles, and restrictive individual rights.

35. On normative contradictions between democracy (accountability, transparency, decentralization of authority) and nuclear weapons, see Lifton and Falk

(1982); Dahl (1985). On nuclear weapons sponsoring peace and hence democracy in the Western world, see Joffe (1993).

36. British Premier Macmillan stated that nuclear weapons provided Britain with "a better position in the world . . . a better position with respect to the United States. It puts us where we ought to be, in the position of a great power . . . [making the United States] pay a greater regard to our point of view" (Husbands 1982:131).

37. A 1986 poll found that 64 percent of Israel's public opposed reliance on, or use of, nuclear weapons, under any circumstances (Arian, Talmud, and Hermann 1988:96; Russett 1989:193). Yet unilateral missile attacks by Iraq (1991) and subsequent threats by Iraq and Iran to "burn half of Israel" and "wipe it off the map" appear to have increased acceptance of implicit nuclear deterrence (see chapter 9).

38. For a seminal contribution, see Rosecrance (1986).

39. For early exploratory efforts in the context of nuclear policy, see Solingen (1994a, 1994b, 1995). This section draws on more elaborate theoretical frameworks applied more broadly to regional conflict and cooperation in economics and security (Solingen 1998, 2001a).

40. Bruno (1988). On sectoral and factoral (land, labor, capital) analysis, see Baldwin (1988), Frieden and Rogowski (1996); on internationalized firms, Milner (1988); and on labor, Garrett and Lange (1996:57–60).

41. In addition to multilateral measures imposed by the U.N., the United States applied unilateral sanctions through the Symington Amendment (1976), Glenn Amendment (1977), the Non-proliferation Act (1979), the Pressler Amendment (1985), and the Arms Control Export Act (1994), which terminates credits and loan guarantees to states that conduct nuclear tests. Other countries, including the second and third largest economies for many years (Japan and Germany), adopted their own legislation tying aid and trade to nuclear behavior.

42. On the large size of such complexes in Iran and Iraq, see chapters 7 and 8.

43. On Iran's inward-oriented coalition and its rejection of foreign investment and economic reform while advancing a defiant nuclear program, see Nazila Fathi, "Conservatives in Iran Battle the Spread of Foreign Investment," *New York Times*, October 10, 2004:16.

44. Several studies debunk the conventional wisdom that nuclear programs are universally cheap (Rosecrance 1964), particularly in the industrializing world (Knopf 2002; Reiss 1988). On how costs increase sharply with sophisticated delivery systems and compatible weaponization, and how these costs compete directly with other military and non-military needs, see 1963 NIE in Burr (2005).

45. On Weberian ideal types as deliberately one-sided abstractions from social reality that are useful as "heuristic" devices in the "imputation" of causality, see Ruggie (1998:31–32). "Internationalizing" points to processes, paths, or empirical approximations to the ideal-type, which always remains an abstraction.

46. Liberman (2001) and Singh and Way (2004) address nuclear outcomes specifically. The latter found support for the proposition that, for all countries that explored the nuclear option, trade liberalization has provided the most statistically significant predictor of whether or not they would acquire nuclear weapons. Solingen (1998); Lobell (1999); Peceny and Stanley (2001:156); and

Herrmann and Keller (2004) focus on additional dependent variables. A quantitative analysis of ninety-eight coalitions in nineteen states in five regions between 1948 and 1993 suggests that internationalizing coalitions deepened trade openness, expanded exports, attracted foreign investments, restrained military-industrial-complexes, initiated fewer international crises, deferred to international economic and security regimes, and strove for regional cooperative orders that reinforced those objectives. Inward-oriented coalitions were found to reduce trade openness and exports, curb foreign investment, build expansive military complexes, challenge international regimes, exacerbate civic-nationalist, religious, or ethnic differentiation, and initiate international crises (Solingen 2001a).

47. As George and Bennett (2005:26) suggest, "Few nontrivial single-variable relationships of necessity or sufficiency have been found to hold for large populations or wide-scope conditions in the social world." Necessary conditions can be cast in probabilistic, not just deterministic, terms. Hence theories cannot be assailed by single disconfirming instances (Goertz 2005).

48. According to prospect theory's endowment effect, the psychological costs of relinquishing a good are greater than the psychological benefits of acquiring it (Levy 2000).

49. Some consider India to fit this case, although India became a nuclear power in 1974 under Indira Ghandi's inward-looking era and long before India's effective economic reforms of the 1990s. Nonetheless, if India were to be found an anomaly, it would prove the argument's refutability. Alternatively, India could also be explained by the higher costs that leaders arguably incur when renouncing actual weapons capabilities rather than potential ones, as with China and Israel. In all three cases, such capabilities preceded the inception of internationalizing models.

50. Socialization processes are hard to trace, burdening causal inferences (Jervis 2002), but see also the novel contribution by Johnston (2001).

51. Liberman (2001); Solingen (2001b). The inclusion of earlier cases, including those of trading states such as Sweden, Germany, and Switzerland, would make the claim even more robust.

52. Notice that internationalizing leaders need not be personally averse to nuclear weapons to reject them; their preference order may simply rank other objectives higher than nuclear weapons. This may have clearly been the case with Premier Sato (see chapter 3).

53. In such circumstances, models of political survival can be considered a condition variable (Van Evera 1997:11) that affects the size of the impact of security dilemmas on nuclear choices. Condition variables can significantly magnify or *reduce* the impact of other variables. Some neoclassical realist frameworks (Glaser 2000) are entirely compatible with this formulation. On domestic politics as filters between international politics, decisions, and security outcomes, see Solingen (1998:273). More recently Schweller (2006:5) also resorted to the concept of filter, or domestic politics serving as transmission belts that mediate between systemic considerations and policy decisions.

NOTES TO CHAPTER THREE

1. Rosecrance (1966:25); Makoto (1977). On Foreign Minister Abe Shintaro and others' enduring perception of a Soviet threat as late as the 1980s, see Akaha (1984:865).

2. DNSA January 7, 1965, JU00423; DNSA October 2, 1974, NP01382; NIE July 1, 1958 (NSA NSAEBB155). In 1994 Premier Hata Tsutomu acknowledged that Japan had the capability to possess nuclear weapons but had not made them. He was later forced to clarify his statement.

3. In most cases such predictions were based on deductions from neorealism rather than close acquaintance with Japanese politics (Okimoto 1978:149). French strategist Pierre Gallois predicted in 1964 that Japan would acquire its own nuclear arsenal; and so did Herman Khan (Okimoto 1978:146–7). In a 1967 article, none other than Richard Nixon (1967:121) argued in reference to Japan that "looking toward the future, one must recognize that it simply is not realistic to expect a nation moving into the first rank of major powers to be totally dependent for its own security on another nation, however close the ties." Waltz (1993) and Mearsheimer (2001) have predicted Japan's nuclearization to be highly likely.

4. Campbell and Sunohara (2004:221). The June 18, 1957, NIE (NSA NSAEBB155) asserted that Kishi would be "successful in strengthening the overall conservative party position, and that the Japanese government will probably take the initiative in building public support for nuclear weapons production. Thus the chances now appear at least even that Japan will undertake the initial steps in a nuclear weapons production program within five years."

5. On these two dilemmas, see Snyder (1984). On Japan's concerns with the reliability of U.S. security guarantees, see Makoto (1978) and Waltz (1993), and on entrapment, Imai (1974).

6. Makoto (1978); Okimoto (1978). The 1968–70 study referred to such vulnerabilities as well, as did the September 21, 1961 NIE (NSA NSAEBB155).

7. Green (1995:23). Nagai was one of the authors of the 1968–70 study.

8. Kamiya (2002–03); Calder (1988); Harrison (1996); personal interviews (Tokyo November 2004).

9. Ambassador Reischauer indicated that Sato considered it "only common sense for Japan to have nuclear weapons," but that he also recognized public opinion was not ready, although the younger generation could be "educated" (DNSA, December 29, 1964, JU00400). On Sato's conversation with Johnson, see DNSA, January 13, 1965, JU00455. Declassified documents also point out that Sato's "common sense" was shared only by a narrow circle of conservatives and that domestic opposition would not be overcome for years (DNSA, January 7, 1965, JU00423).

10. DNSA, January 12, 1965, JU00437. At a 1966 meeting with Rusk, Sato said emphatically that there was no de Gaulle in Japan (DNSA July 7, 1966, JU00589).

11. Sato was quite precise: "The President [Johnson] said the Prime Minister . . . had asked whether the United States would come to Japan's assistance under the Treaty in the event of nuclear, no less than conventional, attack on Japan." Johnson replied that the United States understood Japan's position, would

provide Japan with a nuclear deterrent, and did not want to see an increase in the number of nuclear powers (DNSA, January 12, 1965, JU00437).

12. DNSA, January 6, 1972, 01499.

13. DNSA, January 7, 1972, 01500. On the absence of U.S. pressure on Japan to ratify the NPT quickly, see also U.S. Secret Memorandum, February 20, 1975 (DNSA JU01921) and Endicott (1975:69). Nixon was said to have acknowledged using the "nuclear Japan" card to extract concessions from Zhou Enlai.

14. Schaller (1996). A White House official allegedly told *Nihon Keizai* editor Takeyama Yasuo in November 1971 that the United States could provide Japan with nuclear weapons or the know-how to produce them (Harrison 1996:15–17). On Kissinger's favorable position regarding nuclear weapons in the hands of friendly states (West Germany, Israel, India), see Kissinger (1957).

15. Schaller (1996). On Kissinger's alleged statements that Japan might find advantages in becoming a nuclear power, see also Okimoto (1978:146). On Laird's "nuclear Japan" scenarios, see Harrison (1996:15) and Pempel (1975). On Rusk's ambiguity regarding Japan's nuclear states in the mid-1960s, and on internal U.S. debates on this issue, see Gavin (2004–05:116).

16. In reviewing declassified documents from the 1960s, Kitamura (1996:7) suggests that "the United States could not forcefully or directly stop Japan if it were to obtain nuclear bombs, since such an attitude would disgust Tokyo and poison the bilateral partnership, including the military relationship." See also "Report on Japan's Prospects in the Nuclear Weapons Field" (DNSA, June 15, 1965, JU00485).

17. DNSA, January 7, 1965, JU00423.

18. Hughes (2004a, b). Japan signed the Biological Weapons Convention in 1972 (ratified in 1982) and the Chemical Weapons Convention in 1993 (ratified in 1995).

19. NIE, June 18, 1957 (NSA *NSAEBB155*); Endicott (1975:49–75); Imai (1975).

20. Central participants in those debates claimed there was discernible apathy toward the NPT (Imai 1974:245) and limited knowledge among the public (including some Diet members), suggesting it could have hardly been an instrument of persuasion domestically (personal interviews, Tokyo, November 2004, March 2005).

21. Imai (1974:250). On Imai's extraordinary expertise, knowledge, and influence in nuclear policy despite being an outside consultant, see Okimoto (1978:318).

22. Kurosaki (2003:2). In 1963 the socialists left Gensuikyo against the background of Soviet nuclear tests supported by the communists, and founded Gensuikin (Japanese Congress Against A and H Bombs). The LDP used communist support of Gensuikyo to discredit the latter.

23. Calder (1996:76). Okimoto (1978:197) reports that 45 percent found nuclear weapons "extremely undesirable" and 22 percent "rather undesirable" in a 1970 Yomiuri poll. According to Passin (1977:83) and Kamiya (2002–03:66), a 1969 Yomiuri Shinbun poll found 72 percent opposing nuclear weapons.

24. A 1965 report by the bipartisan National Security Research Council noted that as China and others developed nuclear weapons, the pressure on Japan to do likewise would grow. Another report (1968–70) was submitted to the Cabinet Information Research Office. An internal MOFA study (1969) argued that Japan

could not rely indefinitely on the U.S. nuclear umbrella given U.S. continued economic decline, and recommended maintaining capabilities to produce nuclear weapons if they became necessary (Mack 1996:22; Campbell and Sunohara 2004; Harrison 2002:234). There was also a 1970 internal study by JDA under Nakasone and a subsequent JDA study in 1995 (FASW; Calder 1996).

25. Pempel (1975:173) reports that in 1972 over 51 percent thought Japan would eventually acquire nuclear weapons. See also Passin (1977:73). Akaha (1984:870) also notes that 67 percent supported the Non-Nuclear Principles in 1975. Endicott (1999) cites a *Sankei Shimbun* 1975 poll with only 54 percent favoring NPT ratification and 17 percent opposing it.

26. U.S. intelligence sources support this contention, arguing as far back as 1958 that "despite the unique sensitivity of the Japanese people to nuclear weapons . . . popular acquiescence in such a program can be obtained" (NIE, July 1, 1958, Secret, NSA NSAEBB155). See also earlier citation on Kishi in 1957 NIE. By 1964 another intelligence source suggested that the United States should recognize that psychological restraints on Japan's nuclearization will "tend to disappear" (DNSA, December 12, 1964, NP01079).

27. NIE, November 4, 1965 (NSA, NSAEBB155); DNSA, October 16, 1975, JU01959.

28. Glosserman and Nakagawa (2002); Calder (1988:419; 1996:80).

29. Calder (1996:78). On the "Hiroshima mentality" as a rather late development of the 1970s and, only "to an extent," as an "afterthought" of events thirty years earlier, see Imai (1975:2). On the ambiguous role of anti-nuclear norms in deterring Japan from going nuclear, see Akiyama (2003). On antimilitarist norms as a rather weak explanation for Japan's non-nuclear status, see Lind (2004).

30. On the role of social norms regarding the military and police, see Berger (1993) and Katzenstein (1996).

31. Boyd and Samuels (2005:16) argue that Yoshida and other centrists justified their policies by emphasizing practical considerations rather than norms or identity.

32. Endicott (1975:44–5). The Atomic Law, unlike the constitution, can be changed through simple majority vote.

33. Account by Wakaizumi Kei, Sato's advisor and founder of the Four-Nuclear-Policies, as reported in Kase (2001):140–41.

34. Reiss (1988:121). A U.S. ambassador quoted Sato as arguing in 1969 that while the Three Non-Nuclear Principles were "nonsense," "this should not be interpreted to mean Japan wants to have nuclear weapons" (DNSA, January 14, 1969, JU01039). On the Three Principles as an effort by Sato to appease opposition parties and enable log-rolling compromises on other issues, see Okimoto (1978:494). In 1967, Sato sent Wakaizumi as a confidential representative to Washington, where he inquired about possible distinctions between defensive and offensive nuclear weapons (DNSA, November 11, 1967, JU00829).

35. Disclosed in Nakasone's memoirs, published in 2004 ("Ex-Japanese Premier Once Challenged Japan's Non-nuclear Taboo: Report," AFP June 18, 2004). In 1971, however, he allegedly proposed nuclear weapons in times of emergency (Endicott 1975:62). Japan's Atomic Energy Commission Chairman Arisawa Hiromi

asserted in 1972 that although pressured repeatedly (presumably by Nakasone) to conduct research on atomic weapons, he refused (Harrison 1996:12).

36. According to a late-1960s college student poll, only 26 percent did not foresee a nuclear Japan; nearly 17 percent traced that to the nuclear allergy and only 2.6 percent to Article IX (Okimoto 1978:219).

37. As JDA chief under Sato, Nakasone allegedly agreed to allow U.S. nuclear weapons into Japan in 1970. (*AFP*, "Japan Had Secret Deal with U.S. to Host Nuclear Bombs," December 12/20/00, NAPSNET Daily Report).

38. The July 1, 1958, NIE (NSA NSAEBB155) argued that even Kishi considered Japan's future "greatness" to rest primarily on economic rather than military strength and that there was "nothing to suggest" that "responsible conservative leaders" were "seriously considering an independent nuclear weapons program." On how mainstream conservative politicians did not favor guns over butter, see Calder (1988).

39. Yoshida, who served as premier in 1946–47 and 1948–54, persuaded U.S. occupation forces to endorse his growth strategy after they had initially opposed strengthening Japan's economy (Kosaka 1982:91–92). For an insightful assessment of Yoshida, see Samuels (2003). Yoshida later allegedly regretted the sweeping success of his own doctrine in discouraging changes in defense policy (Chai 1997). On Yoshida's personal traits as "equivocal," "ambiguous and evasive," "erratic," "devious," "dictatorial," and prone to "philosophical double-talk," see Dower (1993:209–212) and Kosaka (1982).

40. On the "iron triangle" (LDP, business, bureaucracy), see Johnson (1982); Muramatsu and Krauss (1984); Samuels (1986); Uriu (1996); Pempel (1998); and Fukai (1999), inter alia. On how perceptions of crisis during the first postwar decade influenced the distributive grassroots-oriented policies of the 1950s–70s, see Calder (1988). On the LDP as a coalition of factions, see Curtis (1988) and Boyd and Samuels (2005).

41. Green (1995:17–20); Samuels (1994); Pempel (1998); Calder (1988). Opposition to an expansive military-industrial-complex came not only from the left but also from the Ministry of Finance and the private financial sector (Berger 1998:77), wary of undermining export-led domestic growth and global access. On cleavages within the business community on this issue, see Samuels (1994).

42. On how the alliance was as much an interest of U.S. policy as of Yoshida's calculations, see Tsuchiyama (2000).

43. Japan devoted 99 percent of its R&D to civilian industries in contrast to nearly 50 percent of R&D spent by the United States on defense (Rosecrance 1986:138–39, 155). Military expenditures relative to GNP and as percentages of the budget were between three and four times higher in Germany and France than in Japan (Calder 1988:412; Inoguchi 1993:26). The yen's appreciation made Japan's defense budget rank among the highest worldwide in the 1990s in current dollars, but, as Katzenstein (1996:194) points out, this is a misleading measure of Japan's postwar military investments, which were not geared to turn Japan into a world-class military power.

44. Samuels (2003). Yoshida's own memoirs (1962:146, 265) make it clear that he opposed rearmament because of "the burden of national expenditure that the people of Japan already have to bear" and not because of normative concerns

with Japan's militarization. Indeed, Yoshida envisaged that rearmament should not be precluded in the long run. While reviewing factors explaining Japan's "miracle," Tanaka's memoirs (1973) listed restraint on arms expenditures in first place.

45. On the broad consensus that economic policies must take priority in safeguarding security, that cultivating relations with all nations was of first-order importance, and that nuclear weapons would harm Japan's international relations and "trading state" status through potential sanctions, see Okimoto (1978:194, 202). On Japan's vulnerability to external energy supplies, see Makoto (1978).

46. Endicott (1975:69–89); Reiss (1988:117–34). On the domestic coalition behind the nuclear energy industry, from local to national economic, political, industrial, banking, and construction interests, see Kitamura (1996:5).

47. On power companies and the LDP, see Imai (1975:7). On the nuclear energy and general industrial sector's support for the NPT, see Imai (1974:251).

48. Imai (1974:251); Green (1995:78). On Yoshida's acute sensitivity to neighbors' hostility to even conventional rearmament by Japan, see Dower (1993:190) and Samuels (2003). According to Inoguchi, "If the United States gives its permission to Japan to go nuclear, it might have very negative consequences for many countries" (Sieg 2003).

49. Endicott (1975:169). On how neighbors' responses could pose very serious threats to Japan's *economic* and security goals, see Halperin (1999). On drivers of Japan's regional policies, see Inoguchi (1991, 2002); Vogel (1994); Pempel (1997); and Katzenstein and Shiraishi (1997).

50. Calder (1988:102), Endicott (1975:59). Labor and opposition parties criticized the LDP largely on defense rather than economic matters (Pempel 1998: 78–79).

51. Other compensatory mechanisms included support for agriculture, public works, and depressed regions. These political forces dwarfed the power of the defense "zoku" (tribe) in the Diet (Calder 1988:104–7, 423). See also Inoguchi (1993).

52. NIE, September 21, 1961 (NSA NSAEBB155). On Sato's concern with socialists' gains in public opinion and a false sense of security regarding China, see DNSA, November 14, 1967, JU00840.

53. On the domestic sources of Japan's reactive foreign policy, see Curtis (1984) and Tanaka (2000).

54. "Defense Agency Concluded in '95 that Nuclear Arms Aren't Worth It," *Japan Times*, February 20, 2003; Kurosawa (2004:112).

55. "Reports: Opposition Leader Says Japan Could Easily Go Nuclear," Associated Press, April 7, 2002; Smith (2003:4).

56. "Shinzo Abe: Japan's Policy Remains: No Nuclear Weapons," *Asahi Shimbun*, June 12, 2002.

57. Howard W. French, "Nuclear Arms Taboo Is Challenged in Japan," *New York Times*, June 9, 2002. Kamiya (2002–03:72) suggests that the word "likely" was an incorrect translation of something that "could" take place.

58. NAPSNet *Daily Report*, June 3, 2002.

59. On December 12, 1964, Koizumi's father, then JDA Director, expressed that Japan depends on the U.S. umbrella and that "there is no need to change the defense setup as a result of the Communist Chinese success in the nuclear test."

60. NAPSNet *Daily Report*, May 31, 2002.

61. NAPSNet *Daily Report*, December 17, 2002.

62. Fukuyama (2005). On the small number of extremists favoring nuclear weapons, see Kamiya (2003). Other observers suggest that any Japanese government that declared Japan's intention to go nuclear would be toppled immediately (personal interviews, Tokyo, March 2005). A popular poll, however, found 37 percent of respondents ready to consider acquiring nuclear weapons if North Korea declared that it had them (Campbell and Sunohara 2004:242). On politicians' calculations as an obstacle to nuclear weapons, see Oros (2003:52).

63. Hara Manabu, "Arms Curb," *Asahi Shimbun*, August 2, 2004:15. Others suggest that the alliance helps moderate domestic arguments on defense and that without it Japan would split sharply into pro-nuclear and anti-nuclear camps and, in the process, harm Japan's very democracy (Personal interviews, Tokyo, March 2005; Okimoto 1978:201).

64. Yukio Aoki, "IAEA to Cut Japan Nuclear Inspections," *Asahi Shimbun*, in *International Herald Tribune*, June 16, 2004.

65. "Editorial: Nuke Tests in South Korea," *Asahi Shimbun*, in *International Herald Tribune*, September 16, 2004. Mack (1996:25) acknowledged that "Japan generally has been scrupulous in its observation of nuclear safeguards" but questioned Japan's preference for breeder reactors, given their diseconomies.

66. "Japanese Nuclear Arsenal Looks Unlikely," *Japan Times*, August 10, 2003.

67. Takashi Hiraoka, "Point of View: Host A-bomb Exhibitions Around the World," *Asahi Shimbun*, June 25, 2004.

68. Kahn (1970:165) predicted that Japan would likely become a nuclear power by the 1980s. Waltz (1993) regarded Japan's transformation into a nuclear power as likely and inevitable. Kissinger (2003) suggested that failure to resolve North Korea's nuclear threat would result in Japan's nuclear armament. A FASW report considers Japan a "virtual" NWS and others a case of nuclear "hedging" (Levite 2002/03:71). Imai was an early proponent of the hedging strategy labeled "nuclear weapons minus two years" (Okimoto 1978:246). Although Japan's capabilities would enable hedging, its verbal commitments have never endorsed it or anything short of a non-nuclear status. Many countries have latent capabilities but have no intention to convert them into military ones.

69. On Yoshida's view of the United States as the best conduit to "promote the prosperity of the Japanese people," see Kosaka (1982:107).

70. Reiss (1988:129) sees the focus on economic growth as key to Japan's security as a necessary but insufficient condition, complemented by the alliance. Green (1995:3) considers independent nuclear capabilities to have been politically or constitutionally problematic—if not impossible—for Japan.

71. On how Japanese officials sometimes *encouraged* U.S. pressure on Japan to ratify the NPT, to counter domestic opposition (including Nakasone), see Secret Memorandum, February 20, 1975 (DNSA JU01921). This memorandum from Philip Habib and Winston Lord to Kissinger also makes clear that Japanese officials sensed ambiguity in the U.S. position (which had yielded no U.S. pressure for ratification) and acknowledges that the United States would not be the determining factor in Japan's decisions; the interests of Japanese leaders would.

72. NIE, June 18, 1957 (NSA, NSAEBB155).

73. On North Korea's threats, see James Brooke, "Japan Raises Defenses on Signs North Korea Plans Missile Test," *New York Times*, September 24, 2004:A6.

74. Eric Prideaux and Akemi Nakamura, "Japan May not Want to Go Nuclear but It's No Technical Hurdle: Analysts," *Japan Times*, October 11, 2006. Professor Yasuhiko Yoshida, a former IAEA public information director, argued that Japan has enough plutonium and uranium that it could make a nuclear weapon in six months, that going nuclear "was preferable to relying on the United States for protection," and that the Japanese public would support such a move although legal restrictions would put off weapons indefinitely.

NOTES TO CHAPTER FOUR

1. Russian Federation Foreign Intelligence Service, at http://www.fas.org/irp/threat/svr_nuke.htm#rok.

2. On the impact that U.S. withdrawal of an infantry division had on Park, see Park (1979:48, 132) and Pollack and Reiss (2004). On Park's relation with the United States as "fundamentally lacking in trust," see Oberdorfer (2001:33).

3. Dunn (1982:110); DNSA, November 10, 1975, NP01442; Hayes (1993); Calder (1996:76).

4. The average for developing countries in that period was 4 to 6 percent (West 1992:25, 31; ACDA 1995–1997).

5. IAEA, at http://www.iaea.org; ISISW, September 27, 2004.

6. Global Security Newswire (GSN), October 6, 2004; Korean Institute for National Unification, at http://www.kinu.or.kr.

7. On U.S. skepticism about Park's 1961 economic policies, see DNSA, October 30–November 5, 1961, JU00134.

8. Park (1971, 1976, 1979); Solingen (1998:223–30).

9. For different perspectives, see Cumings (1984); Haggard and Cheng (1987); Haggard and Moon (1993); Haggard et al. (1994); Cooper (1994).

10. Koh (1984); DNSA, October 30, 1961, JU00133.

11. Haggard and Kaufman (1995). On the military's commitment to private enterprise and its decisive role in the switch from import-substitution to export-led growth, see Cumings (1984:26), Johnson (1987:153), and Amsden (1989:48–52).

12. Gillette (1978); Dunn (1982); Hayes (1993); Investigation of Korean-American Relations (1978); Yager (1985). There is no hard evidence that this amounted to an effort to acquire full-blown nuclear weapons capability (Siler 1998). A national security report and a National Assembly Defense Committee report in 1970 recommended the consideration of a bilateral defense treaty with Japan, and in his 1971 New Year's address, Park argued that he did not perceive Japan as a threat or oppose a larger Japanese defense presence (Hwang 2003).

13. DNSA, March 20, 1970, PD01201; Pollack and Reiss (2004).

14. Reliance on IMF funds had been minimal in the early 1970s, but Park sought to increase it. A decade later, IMF borrowing had reached about 300 percent of South Korea's quota.

15. On the concern among some South Korean scientists that a nuclear weapons program would harm efforts to obtain nuclear fuel-cycle technology for power generation, see Hymans, Kim, and Riecke (2001:101).

16. This and the next citation are from Rowland Evans and Robert Novak, "Korea: Park's Inflexibility," *Washington Post*, June 12, 1975. On the pressure from certain military quarters for an indigenous deterrent, see Hymans et al. (2001:99).

17. A 1974 CIA assessment did not include South Korea among those with the strongest impulse to acquire nuclear weapons (DNSA, October 2, 1974, NP01382). Another intelligence memorandum documented that South Korea's nuclear program was extremely limited and its expenditures very small until 1975 ("South Korean Economy and Nuclear Capability," January 9, 1975, at http://www.foia.cia.gov).

18. DNSA, August 1972, JU01590.

19. *Time* magazine, June 30, 1975.

20. DNSA, June 17, 1977, NP01543.

21. Pollack and Reiss (2004:263); personal interviews in Seoul (February 2006), Washington, D.C. (June 2004), and Tokyo (July 2004). For a more skeptical view, see Pinkston (2004). Park reportedly declared at a Defense Ministry meeting in January 1977 that South Korea would not go nuclear (Ha 1978:1142). Oh Won-chul, who was in charge of the defense and heavy chemical industries as second senior economic secretary to Park, recalled that the goal was to attain capabilities but not an actual weapon (Hymans et al. 2001:98).

22. Reiss (1988:96); Chung-in Moon (personal communication March 13, 2006).

23. Chun sought to purge the business community, which resisted neoliberal reforms in the 1980s (Moon 1994).

24. On Chun's definitive steps to dismantle residual nuclear weapons potential, see Pollack and Reiss (2004). For a clearly articulated official statement of South Korea's rejection of nuclear weapons, see Moon Young-Park (1994–95).

25. David E. Sanger, "Furor in Seoul Over North's Atom Plant," *New York Times*, April 16, 1991:A3.

26. Steven R. Weisman, "South Korea to Keep Out All Atom Arms," *New York Times,* November 9, 1991:3. The U.S. submarine-based nuclear umbrella would remain.

27. Sam Jameson, "No A-Arms for South Korea, Leader Pledges." *Los Angeles Times*, November 14, 1993:A8.

28. See South Korea's Foreign Minister Han Sung-chu's formal response to the Agreed Framework (*FBIS-EAS*, October 31, 1994:57–59).

29. *FBIS-EAS*, March 21, 1994:14–24, 39–47. The North Korean official was later removed.

30. Sam Jameson, "Dictator's Death Upsets South Korean Policy," *Los Angeles Times*, July 31, 1994:A4 and Andrew Pollack, "Nuclear Fears? Noodle Sales Say No," *New York Times*, May 9, 1994. On foreign investors' concern with instability in the peninsula as a barrier to investing in South Korea, see Paul Lewis, "World Markets: Is South Korea Poised to Rise Again?" *New York Times*, March 12, 1995:15. KOTRA is the national trade promotion organization created in the 1960s to facilitate South Korea's rapid export-led economic development.

31. Bernard Kirshner, "Kim Dae-Jung: Linking Liberal Democracy to Economic Growth in South Korea," *Los Angeles Times*, January 11, 1998: M3.

32. "South Korean President Asks West to End Sanctions on North Korea," *New York Times*, June 2, 1998:A8.

33. James Brooke, "Tentatively, North Korea Solicits Foreign Investment and Tourism," *New York Times*, February 19, 2002:C1. John Chambers, managing director for sovereign ratings at Standard & Poor's, cited North Korea's nuclear weapons and its economic backwardness for not raising South Korea's bond rating (James Brooke, "Quietly, North Korea Opens Markets," *New York Times*, November 19, 2003:W7).

34. James Brooke, "South Korea Stakes Its Future on Keeping Peace with North," *New York Times*, May 25, 2004:A3.

35. James Brooke, "In Koreas, High Hopes for an Industrial Marriage," *New York Times*, October 20, 2004:W1.

36. Ibid.

37. William Pesek, Jr., "Will Kim Learn to Love the Bond?" *International Herald Tribune*, July 26, 2004:B2; Lee Han-deuk, *Asia Pulse*, September 19, 2005.

38. South Korea ratified the NPT in April 1975, as North Vietnamese forces overwhelmed the South unimpeded by U.S. forces (Yager 1985:188). Both the alliance and the model account for South Korea's policies vis-à-vis the NPT.

39. All quotes in this paragraph are from Park Chung Hee (1979:94–96).

40. Even the most conservative voices were not calling for nuclearization (Pollack and Reiss 2004). Mazarr (1995) confirms very marginal support for a nuclear deterrent. Popular attitudes, however, are volatile (ICG 2004). As for economic globalization, a 2004 study found that 81 percent of respondents regarded it as good for South Korea and 81 percent supported the Sunshine Policy ("Global Views 2004," The East Asia Institute [September] at http://www.ccfr.org/globalviews2004/sub/pdf/south_korea_topline_report.pdf).

41. More South Koreans found the United States more threatening to South Korea than North Korea despite the fact that 75 percent of respondents believed North Korea had nuclear weapons ("Global Views"; Anthony Faiola, "Despite U.S. Attempts, North Korea Anything but Isolated; Regional Trade Boom Reflects Division between Bush Priorities, Asian Interests," *Washington Post*, May 12, 2005. On the view in South Korea that North Korea's nuclear weapons were designed to distract attention from domestic problems, and not to be used against South Korea, see ICG (2004).

42. James Brooke, "6-Nation North Korean Nuclear Talks in Doubt," *New York Times*, September 26, 2004:6.

43. "The agreement will be good news for both foreign and domestic investors since it can greatly reduce inherent risks in the market," said Kang Gyong-dong, an analyst monitoring the KOSDAQ market (*Asia Pulse*, September 19, 2005). On South Korea's bond ratings as dependent on a perception of stability in military terms, see ICG (2004). See also Noland (2006b).

44. Chosun Ilbo, "North Korean Demands Freeze Moody's Rating of South Korea," September 21, 2005 (NAPSNET Daily Report, September 21, 2005).

45. See http://daccessdds.un.org/doc/UNDOC/GEN/N06/572/07/PDF/N0657207.pdf?OpenElement.

46. Donald Kirk, "Koreans Take Dimmer View of 'Sunshine,' " *Christian Science Monitor*, October 13, 2006.

NOTES TO CHAPTER FIVE

1. The shorter name is used here for convenience, unrelated to the political meanings of "ROC" and "Taiwan" respectively.

2. The Pact committed both parties to "maintain and develop their individual and collective capacity to resist armed attack and communist subversive activities . . . against their territorial integrity and political stability" (University of Tokyo, Institute of Oriental Culture, at http://avatoli.ioc.u-tokyo.ac.jp). Chiang Kai-shek reportedly used Quemoy and Matsu as bases for hostile activities on the mainland (Taylor 2000:243).

3. Wu (1988). "Atom for Peace," *China Post*, April 3, 1988:2; FBIS-CHI-88-070, April 12, 1988.

4. Burr (1999), Richelson (2006). According to Taylor (2000:323), Chiang Kai-shek vetoed Ching-kuo's proposal. Hsu was a protégé of Wang Shih-chieh, reportedly a member of Chungshan.

5. Burr (1999) document dated April 8, 1966, DEF 12-1.

6. Ibid., February 24, 1973.

7. Ibid., January 31, 1973.

8. Ibid., April 5, 1973.

9. Ibid., February 14, 1973.

10. Ibid., September 11, 1976.

11. Burr (1999); Dunn (1982:111); Yager (1980:80). Taiwan also returned 863 grams of plutonium in 1978 (Albright and Gay 1998).

12. Mack (1996); Albright and Gay (1998); "Vice Foreign Minister Says Nuclear Armament Proposal Rejected," Hong Kong AFP, December 20, 1978. Diplomats close to the IAEA argued that plutonium-separation experiments might have been carried out in the 1980s, but the IAEA never confirmed this (George Jahn, "Taiwan Said to Conduct Plutonium Tests in 1980s," Associated Press, October 14, 2004).

13. See previous citations and Taylor (2000:431).

14. NTIW; "Concern about Possible Nuclear Weapons Activity in Taiwan," *AFX Asia*, October 17, 2005.

15. Sofia Wu, "Taiwan: Defense Ministry on 'Non-Nuclear Arms' Policy, Defector," Taiwan Central News Agency, January 20, 1998 (FBIS-CHI-98-020).

16. "Defense Ministry Denies Producing Atomic Bomb," *China Post*, March 9, 1988:16 (FBIS-CHI-88-051, March 16, 1988); "Cabinet Denies Nuclear Official's Connections," Central News Agency, May 13, 1988 (FBIS-CHI-88-096, May 18, 1988). A Taiwanese spokesman acknowledged that a warrant for Chang's arrest had been issued, but he did not elaborate.

17. Edward Chen, "Former Military Head: Taiwan Had Nuke Weapons Capability," Central News Agency, January 7, 2000 (FBIS-CHI-2000-0107). According to Taylor (2000:324), citing a source on Hao's diary, the reprocessing program was put on hold in 1977, but research continued.

18. Victor Lai, "Taiwan Reiterates 'Never' to Develop Nuclear Arms," Central News Agency, January 5, 2000 (FBIS-CHI-2000-0105).

19. "The Nuclear Potential of Individual Countries," Russian Federation Foreign Intelligence Service, April 6, 1995 (FASW).

20. On Taiwan's efforts to cope with what he defined as "Peiping's nuclear blackmail" and "Mao's nuclear threat," see Chiang Kai-shek (1967:7–8).

21. All citations in this paragraph are from documents in Burr and Richelson (2001), October 24, 1964.

22. NSA (NSAEBB41 October 6, 1969).

23. NSA Electronic Briefing Book No. 20 May 1, 1974.

24. "Taiwan Slammed on Lax Defense," *Washington Times*, September 20, 2005.

25. An annual computer war game at the U.S. Naval War College usually ended with a successful invasion of Taiwan by China (David DeVoss, "The US Won't Take Yes for An Answer From Taiwan." *Los Angeles Times*, May 16, 2004:M3). Szu-yin Ho, KMT director for overseas affairs, posed this question: "[I]f China attacks, are Americans willing to shed blood for Taiwan? I'm not sure they are."

26. Martin Walker, "Can Taiwan Truly Rely on the US?" United Press International, February 8, 2006.

27. Gerald Segal, "Taiwan's Nuclear Card," *Asian Wall Street Journal*, August 5, 1998. On Taiwan's technical capabilities, see Quester (1974).

28. "Taiwan: Defense Ministry Vows Not To Develop Nuclear Weapons," Central News Agency, August 4, 1998 (FBIS-CHI-98-219, August 8, 1998).

29. *Taipei Times*, August 13, 2004:8.

30. An important study by Betts et al. (1980:317) argued that the United States had a limited ability to weaken Taiwan's incentives to acquire nuclear weapons.

31. Quester (1974); Betts et al. (1980:315); Yager (1980). In 1968, Taiwan had diplomatic relations with sixty-four states, and China only with forty-five states. By mid-1975, only twenty-six states recognized Taiwan, while China enjoyed diplomatic relations with 112, including the major powers (Roy 2003:132).

32. Ching Cheong, "Talk of Nuclear Risk in Taiwan Conflict," *The Straits Times*, August 7, 2004:6.

33. See also "Atom for Peace," *China Post*, April 3, 1988:2; and retired Lt.Gral. Shuai Hua-min in AFP, October 18, 2004.

34. *China Post*, March 11, 1988:16 (FBIS Chi-88-051, March 16, 1988); Mitchell (2004:313); FBIS November 10, 1998:A7.

35. Digital National Security Archives (DNSA), January 23, 1969, PR00327.

36. Chan (1992:167); Jacoby (1966:118–26); UNDP (1994:170); IISS 1995/96:266–67.

37. U.S. estimates of China's amphibious and other conventional capabilities have already reached that point (Jim Yardley and Thom Shanker, "Chinese Navy Buildup Gives Pentagon New Worries," *New York Times*, April 8, 2005:A3). See also Shambaugh (2000).

38. Albright and Gay (1998:58); Burr (1999:2); "U.S. Strategist Suggests Taiwan Develop Nuclear Weapons," AFP, January 17, 1979.

39. Although Taiwan signed the BTWC in 1972, it no longer enjoys formal status and could not join the CWC.

40. Jacoby (1966:138); Chan and Clark (1992). On the early years of the postwar era in Taiwan, see Cumings (1984).

41. Jacoby (1966:134–44); Nordhaug (1998:142) concurs that the KMT's own orientation toward economic reform has been underestimated and the role of U.S. coercion overestimated.

42. Roy (2003), Burr and Richelson (2001) September 1, 1963, Doc. 9. On his persistent predictions of the demise of Maoist China, see Chiang Kai-shek (1970).

43. DNSA, January 23, 1969, PR00327.

44. Edward Schumacher, "Taiwan Seen Reprocessing Nuclear Fuel," *Washington Post*, August 29, 1976:1.

45. Cheng (1990). Amsden (1985) and Lo (2001) discuss the decline of the military institution in Taiwan's political economy.

46. DNSA, January 23, 1969, PR00327.

47. On U.S. warnings that reprocessing could jeopardize Taiwan's nuclear industry and the economy more generally, see Burr (1999), particularly cable 685 January 31, 1973.

48. Burr (1999), August 29, 1973, AE 1.

49. "Official Stresses Nuclear Energy, Not Weapons," Taipei Domestic Service, April 25, 1988 (FBIS-CHI-88-086, May 4, 1988).

50. Personal interviews (Taipei, February 2006).

51. Albright and Gay (1998).

52. "Peaceful Nuclear Stance Reiterated," *China Post*, January 22, 1991:11 (FBIS-CHI-91-019, January 29, 1991).

53. Hong Kong AFP, July 28, 1995.

54. *China Economic News Service*, September 4, 2006, at http://taiwansecurity.org; Taiwan, Bureau of Foreign Trade, at http://cus93.trade.gov.tw.

55. "Taiwan Standing Firm on Opposition to Nuclear Weapons," *Taipei Times*, June 27, 2004.

56. BBC Monitoring, Asia Pacific, October 13, 2004.

57. Chen's foreign minister Tan Sun-chen acknowledged that in Taiwan, as elsewhere, "all politics are local" (Speech at Taipei Economic and Cultural Office and Asia Society, Los Angeles, June 16, 2004).

58. Tu Ho-ting, "The Real Threat to Taiwan's Security," *Taipei Times*, September 15, 2006.

59. Mainland Affairs Council, Public Opinion on Cross-Strait Relations, Republic of China, at http://www.mac.gov.tw.

60. Private interviews (Taipei, February 2006).

61. Vice Foreign Minister Frederick Chien acknowledged internal divisions even within the KMT in the 1970s (AFP, December 20, 1978).

62. Edward Cody, "Taiwan Sets Self-Defense Objectives," *Washington Post*, May 21, 2006:A19.

63. S. C. Chang, "CNA: Taiwan Will 'Definitely Not' Develop Nuclear Weapons: Premier," Central News Agency, November 10, 2006 (WNC).

Notes to Chapter Six

1. Wampler (2003, document 8). North Korean archives are certainly not open for research, but declassified documents from Soviet bloc sources offer important information. See Cold War International History Project, North Korea in the Cold War (CWIHP). Most declassified NIE on nonproliferation from the 1960s to the early 1980s fail to refer to North Korea as a potential nuclear weapon state

(Wampler 2003). Independent data can be gleaned from published accounts by defectors, foreigners, NGOs with access to North Korea, and foreign media. China's influence on North Korea's nuclear behavior is hard to gauge even today (private interviews in Beijing, August 2004; Tokyo, August 2004; Washington, D.C., June 2004; Shanghai, August 2005 and February 2006; Seoul, February 2006).

2. IISS (2004:48) estimated North Korea's nuclear arsenal at six to twelve weapons over the next several years.

3. CWIHP, November 25, 1967. On North Korea's 1960s interest in nuclear weapons, see Oberdorfer (2001) and Wit et al. (2004). On the 1960s as least threatening, see also Hymans et al. (2001).

4. President Clinton (2004:591) admitted that he was "determined to stop North Korea from developing a nuclear arsenal, even at the risk of war."

5. The text of the Agreed Framework is in Wampler (2003, document 17). Shortly before that, Kim reportedly told Selig Harrison at the height of the 1993 crisis, "What would be the point of making one or two nuclear weapons when you have ten thousand-plus delivery systems that we don't have. We would be a laughing-stock" (Oberdorfer 2001:322). This suggests that Kim Il-Sung's primary objective for his nuclear program may have been less as a deterrent than as a bargaining chip. North Korea's chief nuclear negotiator Kang Sok-Ju privately described nuclear components and facilities as "our chips" (Oberdorfer 2001:351; Wit et al. 2004).

6. Kim (2006). Kim Il-Sung declared in 1977 that the United States and South Korea could not use nuclear weapons on the peninsula because they too would be killed (Ha 1978:1142). See also Hayes (1991).

7. "Hwang Jang-yop Holds Press Conference to Explain Why He Defected from North Korea" (FASW).

8. For the texts of both treaties, see University of Tokyo, Institute of Oriental Culture, at http://avatoli.ioc.u-tokyo.ac.jp/~worldjpn/documents/indices/docs/index-ENG.html.

9. Archival Russian and East German research (CWIHP) concluded that Kim Il-Sung was always as wary of Soviet great-power chauvinism and Chinese nationalism as he was of American imperialism, despite Soviet diplomatic, economic, and military aid. In 1984, Kim Il-Sung vividly described to East Germany's Erich Honecker how serious the late 1960s' threat from China's Cultural Revolution was to his *regime* (as opposed to North Korea as a *state*).

10. This presumes a widely held view that both superpowers preferred a nonnuclear North Korea. For the view that they may not have done enough to restrain it either, see Sigal (1998:20). On the uneasy relationship between China and North Korea as early as the 1950s, see Jian (2003).

11. Kim (2006); personal interviews (Shanghai, February 13–15, 2006).

12. As Kang (1998:261–62) argued, nuclear weapons in the hands of North Korea "would be capable of virtually nothing that conventional weapons cannot already do . . . destroy Seoul," and "North Korea is no more likely to win a war with nuclear weapons than without them."

13. North Korea's resistance to bilateral mutual inspections led South Korea to renew Team Spirit exercises with the United States—vehemently objected to by North Korea—in 1993.

14. Clinton (2004); Cha and Kang (2003); Reiss and Gallucci (2005). Personal interviews (Washington, D.C., June 2004; Tokyo, July 2004).

15. David E. Sanger, "U.S. Failing in Effort to Slow Arms Programs," *International Herald Tribune*, August 9, 2004:1,7.

16. Personal interviews (Washington, D.C., June 2004; Tokyo, July 2004; Seoul, February 2006; Shanghai, February 2006).

17. Foot (1990:41). On North Korea's belligerent rhetoric and near-war footing since Soviet troops departed in 1948, see Cumings (1990:374).

18. On revolution and war in North Korea's context, see also Walt (1996: 19–23).

19. Han S. Park (1996:2). On North Korea as a corporate, nepotistic, self-reliant state, and Kim Il-Sung's depiction of Koreans as "a superior people," see Cumings (1993:204–7, 214–15, 223–24).

20. Quoted in Smith (1994:100). See also Mikheev (1996:92); Solingen (1998); and Official DPRK website at http://www.korea-dpr.com/politics2.htm.

21. Scalapino (1963a); Paige and Lee (1963:24–25). On the centrality of nationalism to North Korea's regime and how it overwhelmed the uses of nationalism in South Korea, see Koh (1984).

22. Chung (1963:110). On the regime's unwavering commitment to military victory over South Korea and efforts to provoke a war, as recorded in communist countries' archival records, see CWIHP.

23. Kim (1988:137); Yoon Kuark (1963). Economic data on North Korea is far from robust. Amsden (1989:40) reports that North Korea was growing roughly three times faster than South Korea in the late 1950s.

24. "Blowback" refers to using particular symbols or policies for mobilizing nationalistic support, which create self-entrapment by heightening the political costs of renouncing the myth. As Snyder (1991) points out, the instrumentality that gives life to myths can be forgotten eventually and leaders then fall victim to their own deceptions.

25. Baek (1988:167). Hostile incidents grew from fifty in 1965 to 629 in 1968 (Koh 1984). On the assassination of Park's wife as an effort to trigger an invitation by South Korea to invade, see CWIHP.

26. CWIHP, March 13, 1967.

27. Kang (1998:241); CWIHP, February 15, 1963.

28. Soviet sources maintain that a deputy minister of the People's Armed Forces in Pyongyang discussed possible Chinese supply of tactical nuclear weapons to North Korea to offset nuclear forces in South Korea (CWIHP, July 30, 1975).

29. CWIHP, February 16, 1976.

30. Ibid., February 18, 1976.

31. Ibid., February 23, 1979.

32. Russian Federation Foreign Intelligence Service, at http://www.fas.org/, and CNSW. For demands from the Soviets, see CWIHP, April 15, 1976.

33. Pollack (1994:A3); Hayes (1993); Cho (2004); South Korea, Ministry of Unification, "Statistics of North Korea Administrative District: Trends in Foreign Trade," April 22, 2005, at http://www.unikorea.go.kr/en/.

34. David E. Sanger, "Pakistan Leader Confirms Nuclear Exports," *New York Times*, September 13, 2005.

35. Park (1996:226) and FBIS-EAS, February 24, 1992:18. By 1993, South Korea's GDP was over $300 billion, whereas North Korea's was $21 billion; in per capita terms the gap was about $9,200 to $1,000 (Sigal 1998:22; Cho 2004).

36. Kihl and Kim (2006); Sigal (1998:23); South Korea, Ministry of Unification at http://www.unikorea.go.kr/en.

37. Reformers in the relatively independent Institute of Peace and Disarmament allegedly played an important role in 1991, urging the International Department of the WP to normalize relations and improve economic ties with the West; advance a comprehensive security, political, economic, and cultural dialogue with South Korea; cooperate with the IAEA; and change policy on the nuclear issue (Mansourov 1994).

38. "Source on ROK Firms Outside of Special Zones," FBIS-EAS, October, 31, 1994:56–57. This analysis makes no assumption that reformers necessarily acted in coordination as a tight faction, since such modus operandi would doom them in North Korea's highly centralized system.

39. "Can Kim's Son Rule—and Last?" *World Press Review* 49, no. 9 (September 1994):16–21; "Hyundai 'Secretly' Meets North Officials in PRC," FBIS-EAS, October 24, 1994:59–60; "Businesses Prepare for North South Economic Cooperation," FBIS-EAS, October 27, 1994:35; Harrison (2002:34). On reformers' emphasis on light industry, see Carlin and Wit (2006).

40. On North Korea's domestic and bureaucratic politics, see Mikheev (1996).

41. Divisions within the military led to an attempted coup by generals from the Ministry of People's Armed Forces in 1992, successfully suppressed by Kim Il-Sung (Oh and Hassig 2004).

42. According to Hayes (n/d:7–10), reporting an interview with Kim Yong-Sun, former head of the International Affairs Department of the WP and alleged architect of a breakthrough in Japanese–North Korean relations, and Harrison (2002:204). Hayes links nuclear hardliners or "conservatives" with the coalition seeking to freeze economic reform, and "pragmatists" with those working to undo North Korea's withdrawal from the NPT. Oh and Hassig (2004: II24) identify a similar divide; Harrison (2002, 2005) describes struggles between moderates and hardliners or pragmatic technocrats and WP ideologues; Banchev (1996:203) speaks of a "red" versus "expert" cleavage; and Oberdorfer (2001:360) points to the thinning of the glue binding together disparate interest groups, particularly the Foreign Ministry versus the KPA. See also International Crisis Group (2005).

43. United States Institute of Peace, *Special Report*, n/d:15.

44. Oberdorfer (2001:337). See also Kim Jong-Il's website at http://www.korea dpr.com.

45. Editorial Bureau Special Article, "Military-First Ideology Is an Ever-Victorious, Invincible Banner for Our Era's Cause of Independence," *Nodong Sinmun*, March 21, 2003 (NIW).

46. For a comprehensive analysis of family, institutional, military, political, and bureaucratic dimensions of Kim Jong-Il's regime, see Oh Hassig (2004). For Kim's role in the bomb incidents and NPT withdrawal, see Ahn (1994:96) and "Who Is Kim Jong Il," *World Press Review* 41, no. 9 (September 1994):18–20. On his supportive coalition, see Sakai (1996), and on his leanings toward reformers, Mazarr (1995c:166–67).

47. Mazarr (1995c:101, 107, 152) also discusses the military's psychological buildup toward a war option. See also FBIS-EAS, February 22, 1993:11–13.

48. "Kim Il Sung and the Specter of War: North Korea's Leader Has Nothing to Lose," *World Press Review* 41, no. 4 (April 1994):18–20.

49. "Kim Chong-Il's 'Pragmatist Diplomacy' Analyzed," Chungang Ilbo, FBIS-EAS, October 20, 1994:41.

50. "Foreign Ministry Communique on U.S.-North Accord," Pyongyang Korean Central Broadcasting Network, FBIS-EAS, October 20, 1994:25.

51. According to Mansourov (1995), the military and Public Security services lost ground in domestic control over the nuclear program, whereas officials in the energy, foreign trade, banking, and telecommunications sectors enhanced their position. Obsolete manufacturing sectors feared the lifting of trade restrictions that would accompany implementation of the Agreed Framework.

52. "18 October U.S.-ROK 'Air War Game' Reported," FBIS-EAS, October 20, 1994:27–28.

53. Cho (2004); Babson (2003). Other estimates of famine casualties were much higher, reaching more than two million, according to the International Federation of Human Rights, 2003 Report on Economic, Social, and Cultural Rights Violations (NIW).

54. Nicholas D. Kristof, "U.S. and North Koreans Begin a Wary Dialogue," *New York Times*, July 6, 1996:3.

55. Andrew Pollack, "A Philosophical Marxist Ideologist," *New York Times*, March 19, 1997:A9; "Hwang Jang-yop Holds Press Conference," op. cit.

56. Oberdorfer (2001:411). A suspected testing site in Kumchangri was discovered in 1999.

57. Frank (2003). On economic growth since 1999, see "North Korean Economy Grew 2.2 Pct in 2004," *Yonhap News*, May 31, 2005 (FBIS no. 208400092). On statements supportive of economic reforms in North Korea's quarterly economic journal *Kyongje Yongu*, see Carlin and Wit (2006).

58. Howard W. French, "North Korea Experiments, with China as Its Model," *New York Times*, March 28, 2005:A5. About 700,000 people were estimated to engage in private entrepreneurial activities by the late1990s (Kim 2006). See also Anna Fifield, "North Korea Toys with Risk and Reward—The Zeal of the Workers Has Increased," *Financial Times*, September 2, 2005:9. On the very limited nature of these reforms, see Eberstad (2006).

59. Harrison (2002:26). Perhaps this effort to avert doctrinal warfare (or difficulties in squaring out internal contradictions within the regime) account for the fact that Kim Jong-Il's web-posted personal history ends in 1997; see http://www.korea-dpr.

60. Cha (2004). According to Haggard and Noland (2005), annual inflation was over 100 percent, unemployment in nonagricultural sectors about 30 percent, and wage reductions between 50 and 80 percent.

61. Barbara Demick, "North Korea, Without Rancor," *Los Angeles Times World Report*, reprinted in *Yomiuri Shimbun*, March 15, 2005:18.

62. *Nodong Sinmun* Editorial Bureau, "Military-First Ideology Is an Ever-Victorious, Invincible Banner for Our Era's Cause of Independence," March 21–22, 2003, at http://www.nautilus.org.

63. Peter Maass, "The Last Emperor, Kim Jong Il," *New York Times Magazine*, October 19, 2003:38–47; Noland (2002).

64. *Nodong Sinmun*, "Military-First Ideology," op. cit.

65. Kim Jong-Il's awareness that an image of continuity with his father still constitutes political currency is evident from North Korea's homepage, occupied by Kim Jong-Il's picture adjacent to that of his father in identical posture; see http://www.korea-dpr.com.

66. Mansourov (2004). The estimated flight to China of 130 generals from North Korea—10 percent of the military elite—may be evidence of dissent within the military (James Brooke, "Japanese Official Warns of Fissures in North Korea," *New York Times*, November 22, 2005:A3.

67. Gordon Fairclough, "China's Beacon of Hope for North Korea," *Asian Wall Street Journal*, July 21, 2005:A3; Harrison (2002:38); Kihl and Kim (2006); Haggard and Noland (2007). Military exports, drug trafficking, counterfeiting, and smuggling account for about one-third of all balance-of-payments revenue (Noland 2006a).

68. *Nodong Sinmun*, "Military-First Ideology," op. cit.

69. Ibid.

70. Dwor-Frécaut (2004); Sano (2005). The weakness of reformers is also evident from the fact that Pak did not mention market reforms even once in his 2004 speech to the Supreme People's Assembly. See also Pinkston (2003).

71. Dwor-Frécaut (2004); Lee Kyo-kwan, "North Korean Deputy Trade Minister Executed," *Chosun Ilbo*, January 23, 2002. On the allergy of world financial markets and investors to North Korea's projects, see James Brooke, "Quietly, North Korea Opens Markets," *New York Times*, November 19, 2003:W7.

72. James Brooke, "South Korea Casts Wary Glance to North," *New York Times*, April 29, 2004:W1,W7. Kim Yong-Ryong headed the export-oriented enterprises under the State Security Agency's control (Oh and Hassig 2004).

73. For well-argued statements on the centrality of regime survival and the incompleteness (at best) and incorrectness (at worst) of the external security interpretation of North Korea's behavior, see Cotton (1993); Mazarr (1995c); and Mansourov (1994).

74. Personal interviews, Seoul and Shanghai (February 2006). On the symbolic domestic importance of nuclear weapons in North Korea, see Kim (2003) and Moon (2007).

75. GSN, August 3, 2004; Mansourov (2004).

76. Harrison (2005) learned during a visit to North Korea that in early February a showdown over nuclear policy had occurred between the "dealers," led by First Deputy Foreign Minister Kang Sok-Ju, principal foreign policy advisor to Kim, and a coalition of hardline generals and party leaders. The hardliners prevailed, Harrison contends, leading to pronouncements that North Korea had "manufactured nukes" and is a "nuclear weapons state" and to demands for economic and diplomatic relations with the United States before engaging in any discussions of dismantling North Korea's nuclear weapons capabilities. For the full statement, see BBC News, February 10, 2005.

77. "Interview: Samore: North Korean Atomic Test 'A Purely Political Act,' " October 17, 2006, Council on Foreign Relations; see http://www.cfr.org. The eight Macau Delta Asia branches were allegedly used to launder counterfeit

money and drug sales as well as the personal wealth of North Korean leaders (see www.treas.gov/press/releases/js2720.htm).

78. Benjamin Robertson, "Hardliners' Control North Korea Policy," Aljazeera .net, October 11, 2006.

79. "Text of North Korea's Announcement," BBC News, October 9, 2006.

80. On the bottom-up nature of economic reform in North Korea, see Haggard and Noland (2007).

NOTES TO CHAPTER SEVEN

1. UNSCOM/IAEA, "Transcript of Deposition by Huseyn Kamil to UNSCOM and IAEA Officials," February 26, 2003, at http://www.fair.org/pressreleases/kamel.pdf.

2. NSA, NSAEBB167 Documents 3 and 4.

3. Saddam personally negotiated a Treaty of Friendship and Cooperation with the Soviet Union in 1972. Article 9 promised cooperation in defense and hinted at an enlarged Soviet military presence in Iraq with Gulf-based support facilities, extensive technical assistance, and military equipment (U.S. Department of State, Foreign Relations, 1969–72, vol. E-4, Iran and Iraq, at http://www.state.gov/r/pa/ho/frus/nixon/e4/72108.htm).

4. ISG (2004) Transmittal Message (TM):4. ISG and Duelfer report are henceforth used interchangeably. The report includes first-hand interviews with Saddam and his officials, and original documents captured after the war. All references are to the Comprehensive Report unless noted with the TM prefix.

5. Hamza, in Cirincione (2000). Hamza participated in the early 1970s' weapons program, became chairman of the Physics Department of the Nuclear Research Center at al-Tuwaitha, chief of Fuel Division in the 1970s, head of the Theoretical Division of the Enrichment Program, scientific advisor to the IAEC chairman in the 1980s, and—for a brief period in 1987—director of weaponization. He left Iraq in 1994. Some, including Saddam's son-in-law Huseyn Kamil who oversaw the nuclear program, questioned Hamza's centrality to the program (UNSCOM/IAEA, "Transcript of deposition"). Yet as a participant in many events and processes since 1971, his account provides important background on the politics and sociology of nuclear weapons-making in Iraq.

6. Nuclear Weapon Archive at http://nuclearweaponarchive.org/Iraq/Iraq AtoZ.html.

7. "Interview With Saddam's Bomb Maker," CNN Crossfire, February 7, 2003.

8. UNSCOM/IAEA, "Transcript."

9. Ibid.

10. ISG (2004:27). On the existence of about twenty-five missile warheads equipped with bacteriological weapons in December 1990, see UNSCOM/IAEA, "Transcript."

11. UNSCOM/IAEA, "Transcript."

12. According to Iraqi nuclear scientist Hussain Al-Shahristani, "The chief of the Iraqi security organisation at that time, Barazan Al Tikriti, Saddam's half-brother, came to visit me after I was initially tortured for twenty-two days and nights. He

told me that Saddam wanted me to work on developing nuclear weapons, because he needed "a long arm to reshape the map of the Middle-East." This was in June 1980, before waging war on Iran and before Israel's destruction of Osiraq (Dorothy Hodgkin Memorial Lecture, 54th Pugwash Conference, Seoul, 7 October 2005), available at http://www.ciaonet.org/pbei/pug/dec_04/dec_04_04.pdf.

13. "Iraq's Nuclear Weapons Program, From Aflaq to Tammuz," 2001, at http://nuclearweaponarchive.org/Iraq/IraqAtoZ.html.

14. The IAEA list of targets for inspection included two nuclear facilities, whereas UNSCOM eventually uncovered more than twenty nuclear sites described as "main facilities" (http://www.fas.org/nuke/guide/iraq/nuke/when.htm).

15. Obeidi and Pitzer (2004); UNSCOM/IAEA, "Transcript." See also declarations by Iraqi nuclear scientist Ja'afar Dhiya Ja'afar, who fled Iraq during the U.S. invasion in 2003 and had declared in 1991 that Iraq was "three years away, give or take a year," from nuclear weapons (*New York Times*, January 27, 2005).

16. "Unresolved Disarmament Issues—Iraq's Proscribed Weapons Programmes," UNMOVIC Working Document, March 6, 2003 (FASW; NTIW). Blix (2005) acknowledged that because he himself believed that Iraq concealed weapons, he favored the *threat* of *multilateral* military action to enforce compliance.

17. *NTIW*. Shahristani, a Shi'a, accused Hussein of hiding chemical and biological weapons, stating he had knowledge of Sarin, possibly anthrax, and the nerve agent VX ("Saddam's Deadly Subway Scheming," *CBS News*, February 21, 2003).

18. Mahdi Obeidi, former director of the pre-1991 centrifuge program, buried documents and small prototypes of the centrifuge program that could have helped restart enrichment once sanctions were lifted (Obeidi and Pitzer 2004).

19. See http://nuclearweaponarchive.org.

20. Over 100,000 Kurds were killed or vanished in the 1980s alone, some in attacks with mustard and nerve gas ("The Struggle for Iraq: High Crimes to Be Tried," *New York Times*, June 7, 2005:A10). About 400,000 Shi'a and unknown numbers of Kurds were massacred in March 1991 after the war.

21. Heston and Summers (1991, 1995); U.N., *Human Development Report* (1991–96); U.N. *Statistical Yearbook* (1999a); World Bank, *World Development Indicators* (1998), *World Development Report* (1991–97), and *World Tables* (1980, 1989–90, 1995).

22. Testimony by 'Ali Hasan Al Majid (also known as "Chemical 'Ali" for his role in chemical weapons), (ISG 2004:18).

23. Sipri Yearbooks (1975–96), IISS, (1995–96:266–67); U.N.D.P. *Human Development Report* (HDR) (1994:170; 1996:174–75), ACDA (1976, 1982, 1990, 1996); World Bank, *World Development Indicators* (1998:279).

24. Niblock (1993) challenges Chaudhry's (1991) thesis that privatization led to the invasion of Kuwait. Instead, he argues that social problems spawned by very incipient economic liberalization were significant but did not require a war with Kuwait and could have been solved if Saddam's attention and resources had not been directed elsewhere. Ibrahim (1994:79) explains the invasion as a response to domestic threats to the regime from a new middle class, a modern working class, and the urban proletariat.

25. This paragraph builds on Hamza (1998).

26. See http://nuclearweaponarchive.org/Iraq/IraqAtoZ.html.

27. On corruption in the Oil-for-Food program, see report by independent Volker Commission at http://www.iic-offp.org/documents/IIC%20Final%20Report%2027Oct2005.pdf.

28. Much has been written on the intelligence and political dimensions of these events. For a selection of relevant documents and accounts, see CEW, ISG (2005); Blix (2005); and Richelson (2004, 2006).

29. UNSCOM/IAEA, "Transcript." See also Obeidi and Pitzer (2004:152, 168, 184).

30. According to Huwaysh, Saddam had told his generals that he had "something in his hand" (or "something up his sleeve"). According to Hassan al-Majid, many within Saddam's ruling circle never stopped believing the weapon still existed (Woods et al. 2006). According to Tariq 'Aziz, only in December 2002 did Saddam surprise his own generals, informing them that he had no WMD and they would have to fight the United States without them (ISG 2004:65).

31. ISG (2004, Regime Strategic Intent:62). Cirincione, Wolfsthal, and Rajkumar (2005:332) believe some of Saddam's bluster against inspections may have been directed at Iran but that "much of it may have been for the benefit of his domestic audience." On Saddam's view of his nuclear weapons as tools of coercion and guarantees of regime survival, see also Baram (2001).

32. As quoted from former presidential secretary Mahmud, who also wrote while a detainee that Saddam "would say if only Iraq possessed the nuclear weapon then no one would commit acts of aggression on it or any other Arab country, and the Palestinian issue would be solved peacefully because of Iraq."

Notes to Chapter Eight

1. DNSA, April 1, 1975, NP01401.

2. CEW; see also http://www.wilsoncenter.org.

3. NTIW; Sayigh (1993); PBS, *Frontline*, April 13, 1993.

4. Steve Coll, "U.S. Halted Nuclear Bid By Iran," *Washington Post*, November 17, 1992.

5. Carnegie Endowment Annual Conference, Washington, D.C., June 23, 2004 (CEW); ICG (2003). According to Aleksey Arbatov, head of the International Security Centre of the Russian Academy of Sciences, "The Iranian leadership wants to have technological opportunities for creating nuclear weapons" ("Russian Academician: Iran Wants to Leave Door Open for Creating Nuclear Weapons," ITAR-TASS, October 11, 2005 (NTIS Doc. 200510111477.1_112c0018956dce7c).

6. "Controlling Weapons of Mass Destruction—Lessons from Iraq," Lecture at the University of California, Irvine, May 5, 2005. See also WMDC (2006). On suspicions of Iran's nuclear program's military objectives by France's foreign minister, Germany's chancellor, Russia's president, and Chinese, Saudi, and Jordanian officials, see references in Amuzegar (2006: 96, 109).

7. DNSA, May 5, 1976, NP01466.

8. FBIS-NES October 7, 1988:52; CEW. On chemical weapons use in the Iran-Iraq war, see Karsh (1993).

9. "U.S. Attack 'Madness,' Says Khatami," *BBC*, January 20, 2005. Ahmadine-jad's Deputy Interior Minister for Security Affairs Muhammad Baqer Zolqadr declared to the official IRNA news agency that the United States was only capable of soft threats, but incapable of launching a military operation against Iran (*Jerusalem Post*, April 27, 2007:9).

10. A 2005 book published in Tehran by Khamene'i's representative at the Kayhan Institute, citing classified Iranian documents, asserted that neither Israel nor the United States opposed Iran's nuclearization under the Shah (Hoseyn Shar-i'atmadari, "Daily Views Changed Stance of Israel Regarding Iran's Nuclear Activities," *Kayhan*, January 31, 2005). Even as unconfirmed claims, these suggest recognition that the same structural power relationship can lead to dramatically different definitions of threats by different domestic regimes.

11. On U.S. sensitivity to such cooperation, see DNSA, July 18, 1977, IR01199.

12. IRNA, October 23, 1991 (*FBIS*, JPRS-TND-91-017, November 7, 1991: 23–24); *Milavnews*, November 1991:3.

13. Carnegie Endowment 2005 Nonproliferation Conference (CEW).

14. Wahid Abd Al-Magid, a well-known researcher at the Al-Ahram Center for Strategic Studies, suggested in 1995 that "even if we suppose that Iran can develop nuclear warheads, this will represent a threat to the Arabs before it does to Israel" (cited in Feldner 2003c).

15. Joseph Cirincione, "Time for Clear Public Understanding of Iranian Threat" (CEW).

16. "Saudi Arabia: Gulf Official Says GCC States Sense Gravity of Iran Nuclear Armament," MENA, January 3, 2005. For similar statements of concern, see *Khaleej Times Online*, May 23, 2006.

17. MEMRI, Special Dispatch 586, October 10, 2003.

18. "Iranian Missile Program, Threat Against Turkey," *Istanbul Milliyet*, July 19, 2000 (FBIS Daily Report).

19. NTI Iran Profile, May 24, 1993 (NTIW).

20. Oliver Burkeman, "Iran Rules Out Nuclear Weapons," *The Guardian*, February 6, 2002.

21. 'Nuclear Armed Iran Would Be More Vulnerable', *AFP*, June 9, 2004.

22. *E'TEMAD-E MELLI*, October 7, 2006.

23. MEMRI, Special Dispatch Series 1316, October 11, 2006.

24. Mark Hibbs, *Nucleonics Week*, November 21, 1991:2–3, in NTIW.

25. Michael Z. Wise, "Atomic Team Reports On Iran Probe," *Washington Post*, February 15, 1992:A29–A30.

26. "Iran and Libya 'Bought Nuclear Goods,'" *Aljazeera*, February 20, 2004.

27. David E. Sanger and William J. Broad, "From Rogue Nuclear Programs, Web of Trails Leads to Pakistan," *New York Times*, January 4, 2004.

28. William J. Broad and Elaine Sciolino, "Iran's Secrecy Widens Gap in Nuclear Intelligence," *New York Times*, May 19, 2006:A1, A14.

29. In 2004, Khan acknowledged selling nuclear secrets to Iran, Libya, and North Korea ("Iranian FM Arrives in Pakistan for Talks With Leaders," Hong Kong, AFP, December 27, 2004. All IAEA reports cited in this section are available at http://www.iaea.org/NewsCenter/Focus/IaeaIran/index.shtml.

30. Scott Peterson, "Tough US Rhetoric as Iran's Nuclear Intent Remains Unclear," *Christian Science Monitor*, June 3, 2004.

31. "Iran's Nuclear Stance Criticized," BBC News, March 8, 2004.

32. ABC News at http://abcnews.go.com/images/International/iran_eu_objectives.pdf.

33. See http://www.iaea.org/Publications/Documents/Board/2005/gov2005-67.pdf; "Iranian Nuclear Chief Ali Larijani: The West Should Learn the Lesson of North Korea," IRINN TV, September 20, 2005, at http://memri.org.

34. Alissa Rubin, "Iran Admits More Nuclear Activity," *New York Times*, June 16, 2005; see also http://www.iaea.org/NewsCenter/Statements/2005/ebsp2005n007.html#iran.

35. See http://www.iaea.org/Publications/Documents/Board/2006/gov2006-15.pdf.

36. "Chief Iranian Nuclear Affairs Negotiator Hosein Musavian: The Negotiations with Europe Bought Us Time to Complete the Esfahan UCF Project and the Work on the Centrifuges in Natanz," Iranian TV, Channel 2, August 4, 2005, at http://memri.org.

37. Only Venezuela opposed and twelve abstained, including Russia and China (NTIW); see http://www.iaea.org.

38. "Iran's Nuclear Program is 'Irreversible,'" *CNN*, April 23, 2006.

39. See http://www.iaea.org/Publications/Documents/Board/2006/gov2006-15.pdf.

40. See http://www.iaea.org/Publications/Documents/Board/2006/gov2006-27.pdf.

41. Elaine Sciolino, "U.N. Agency Says Iran Falls Short on Nuclear Data," *New York Times*, April 29, 2006:A1.

42. William J. Broad, "U.N. Finds New Uranium Traces in Iran," *New York Times*, May 13, 2006:A8.

43. GSN, January 3, 2007; Nazila Fathi, "Iran's Leader Stands by Nuclear Plans; Military to Hold Exercises," January 22, 2007 and Nazila Fathi and Michael Slackman, "Rebuke in Iran to Its President on Nuclear Role," *New York Times*, January 19, 2007.

44. Joseph Cirincione, "The Clock's Ticking: Stopping Iran Before It's Too Late," *Arms Control Today*, November 2006.

45. *SIPRI Yearbooks* (1975–96); Khosrokhavar (2004). About 70 percent of total public expenditures since 1979 is estimated to have been channeled through extra-budgetary mechanisms to military, security, and other state enterprises under the Supreme Leader's supervision (Esfahani and Taheripour 2002:693).

46. Official Iranian news agency, in R. Jeffry Smith, "Officials Say Iran Is Seeking Nuclear Weapons Capability," *Washington Post*, October 30, 1991:A1; Hoodbhoy (1993:43).

47. Spector (1990:208) traces the source to a recording smuggled out of Iran.

48. Takeyh (2006b); DeSutter (1997); Sayigh (1993); PBS, *Frontline*, April 13, 1993. The Defense Ministry allegedly used front organizations like Sharif University to obtain nuclear equipment (CEW).

49. Jane's world armies profile: Iran, August 29, 2006 at www.janes.co.uk. Alex Vatanka, *Jane's Intelligence Review*, November 2, 2004; NTIW; Albright and Hibbs (1992).

50. Private interests in insurance, construction, shipbuilding, aircraft, and banking have grown in size and influence but remain weak relative to state enterprises (Hamid Ahadi, "Government Pushes Largest Private Bank Out of Business," *Rooz*, October 10, 2006, at http://www.roozonline.com).

51. Hugh Carnegy, *Financial Times*, January 29, 1992:4, in NTIW.

52. Caryle Murphy, "Iranian Sees No Breakthrough On U.S. Ties," *Washington Post*, February 1, 1993:A12, A15, in NTIW.

53. Perkovich (2005b). Pragmatic elements reportedly approached U.S. officials to negotiate a "grand bargain" (Flynt Leverett, "Why Libya Gave Up on the Bomb," *New York Times*, January 23, 2004:A25). By contrast, Carter (2005) argues that "reformers and mullahs alike think that it might be a good idea for Iran to have a bomb."

54. Pasdaran theoretician Hassan Abassi reportedly proposed to eradicate Anglo-Saxon civilization using missiles and suicide bombers at a secret meeting with the terrorist group *Ansar-e Hizbullah* (*Al-Sharq Al-Awsat*, May 28, 2004, at http://memri.org).

55. *GSN*, September 8, 2006. For Khatami's statements on globalization and the need to stop the "monopolistic activity" of state enterprises, see Aftab-e Yazd (Iran), December 7, 2005.

56. A Tehran analyst reported that according to the Social Security Organization, 30 percent live under the poverty line, whereas the top 20 percent controls 80 percent of the total wealth and 50 percent of national income ("Ahmadinejad's Domestic Troubles," *The Intelligence Summit*, October 4, 2006, at http://intelligence-summit.blogspot.com). On the gas contract, see Khalaji (2006).

57. Milani (2005a:2); Shirzad Bozorgmehr, "Iran Leader Plays Populist Game," *BBC News*, May 9, 2006. On alleged elections fraud, see Michael Slackman, "Iran's Leaders Warn Candidate Who Charged Vote Fraud," *New York Times*, June 21, 2005:A3.

58. Michael Ignatieff, "Iranian Lessons," *New York Times Magazine*, July 17, 2005:51.

59. The Intelligence Ministry owns telecommunications and information-technology companies; the Agricultural Ministry owns agribusiness, and so on (Molavi 2004).

60. Both views in "Live at Carnegie: Iran—What Next?" November 5, 2004 (CEW).

61. Tarek Al-Issawi, "Threat of International Sanctions Not a Major Concern for Iran," Associated Press, April 26, 2005. On Iran's inward-oriented coalition's rejection of foreign investment and economic reform, and its support for a defiant nuclear program, see Fathi, "Conservatives." The United States imposed additional trade sanctions on Iran in 1995, prohibiting purchases of Iranian oil and goods and banning all dual-use exports.

62. "Live at Carnegie: Iran."

63. Over 80 percent allegedly support nuclear *energy* ("Iranians Defend Nuclear Rights," *Los Angeles Times*, March 7, 2006). Vakil (2005:187) is skeptical of government surveys, arguing that people are far more motivated by economic incentives than by ambiguous nuclear posturing. In an informal probe, a young Iranian feared that "if these guys [the regime] get the bomb they will be able to hold on to power

for another 25 years. . . . Nobody wants that" (ICG 2003:19). See also Perkovich (2005b). On government censorship and threats to silence reformist media critical of the nuclear program, see MEMRI, Special Dispatch Series-No-1127, March 30, 2006.

64. Mahan Abedin, "Iranian Public Opinion and the Nuclear Stand-Off," *Mideast Monitor* 1, no. 2 (April/May 2006).

65. Joel Brinkley, "Iranian Leader Refuses to End Nuclear Effort," *New York Times*, September 18, 2005:10.

66. "Iran: Mardom Salari Leader on Guardian Council Disqualifications, Ties With US," *Mardom Salari*, December 18, 2004 (FBIS IAP20041220000026).

67. Mohamed Semati, Carnegie Endowment Annual Conference, Washington, DC, June 22, 2004. For a clearly articulated position against nuclear technology, see statement by former Majlis Isfahan representative Ahmad Shirzad, "The Mirage of Nuclear Power," *Rooz*, November 6, 2006.

68. "Iran: Analytical Article Views Conservatives' Efforts to 'Monopolize' Power," *Sharq*, December 28, 2004 (FBIS- IAP20041230000086).

69. Parisa Hafezi, "Iranian Hardliners Unhappy with Nuclear Deal," Reuters, November 16, 2004.

70. "Iran Warns EU of 'Response' If Nuclear Pressure Too High," AFP, September 8, 2004; "Iran Will Never Compromise on Nuclear Fuel Cycle: Rowhani," *Tehran Times*, September 9, 2004, at http://www.tehrantimes.com.

71. Ali Akbar Dareini, "Khatami: Iran Will Pursue Nuclear Program," Associated Press, September 21, 2004.

72. Ali Akbar Dareini, "Iran Hard-Liners Drafting Bill to Force Resumption of Uranium Enrichment," Associated Press, October 4, 2004.

73. Mahan Abedin, "Iranian Public Opinion and the Nuclear Stand-Off," *Mideast Monitor* 1, no. 2 (April/May 2006); Marie Colvin and Leila Asgharzadeh, "Iran's strongman loses grip as ayatollah offers nuclear deal," [London] *Sunday Times*, January 21, 2007.

74. *BBC News*, May 9, 2006. Rafsanjani expressed that "If there [are] domestic and foreign conflicts, foreign capital will not flow into the country. . . . In fact, such conflicts will lead to the flight of capital from this country" (Pollack and Takeyh 2005).

75. Milani (2005a:3); Nazila Fathi, "Iran's Stocks Plunge After Vote for U.N. Review of Nuclear Program," *New York Times*, October 9, 2005:5. One economist estimates that the stock market declined at 50 percent of its value relative to its peak ("Ahmadinejad's Domestic Troubles").

76. Nazila Fathi, "Iranian President Stands By Call to Wipe Israel Off Map," *New York Times*, October 29, 2005:A3; Ali Akbar Dareini, "Ahmadinejad's Israel Remarks Split Iran," AP, October 30, 2005; Nazila Fathi, "Iran's Leader Stands by Nuclear Plans; Military to Hold Exercises," *New York Times*, January 22, 2007:A4. See also Salama and Salch (2006).

77. Hamid Ahadi, "New Political Linings in Iran," *Rooz*, October 10, 2006.

78. Nazila Fathi, "Iranian Plans for Economy Spur Widespread Concern," *New York Times*, May 1, 2006:A8; Geoffrey Kemp, "Iran and Iraq: The Shia Connection, Soft Power, and the Nuclear Factor," United States Institute of Peace, Special Report 156, November 2005.

79. Saeed Leylaz and Ahmad Tavakoli, in Fathi, "Iranian Plans."

80. Simon Tisdall, "Ahmadinejad's rivals jockeying for position," *The Guardian*, June 22, 2006.

81. "Economists Send Ahmadinejad Letter Urging Economic Policy Change," *E'TEMAD-E MELLI*, June 21, 2006. Iran's OECD country risk classification worsened in 2006, in tandem with its nuclear defiance (www.oecd.org).

82. Nazila Fathi and Michael Slackman, "Rebuke in Iran"; Nazila Fathi, "Results of Elections Reflect Poorly on Ahmadinejad," *New York Times*, December 22, 2006:A14.

83. Shaker Al-Nabulsi's suggested that the Shi'ite bomb is a "substitute for the legendary power of the Mahdi that [the Shi'ites] await, who will subjugate Asia and the Islamic and Arab world to the hegemony of a Shi'ite Persian empire by force of weapons." Al-Arabiyya TV's director Al-Rashed argued that the Gulf countries are the only likely targets of Iran's nuclear nuclear weapons: "It is inconceivable that Iran will drop the bomb on Syria and target Jordan or Egypt. . . . It is incomprehensible that Iran will bomb Israel, which has a shield of missiles, tremendous firepower, and nuclear weapons artillery sufficient to eradicate every city in Iran. In addition, any attack on Israel would mean the immediate, widescale destruction of the Palestinians. . . . This means that if this destructive weapon is used, the only option for a target is the Arab Gulf [countries]. . . . Fear will plunge the region into an arms race" (both citations in H. Avraham, "Arab Media Reactions to Iran's Nuclear Project," *MEMRI* 277 (May 23, 2006).

84. Indeed an internal Iranian analysis points out that, leaving aside the nuclear issue, Iran is in a much stronger relative power position regionally and vis-à-vis the United States in 2006, just as Iran resists relinquishing a nuclear option (Abbas Abdi, "Will the Nuclear Issue Explode?" *Rooz*, June 26, 2006, at http://roozonline .com). On internal differences in threat perceptions and the need for nuclear weapons, see Kibaroglu (2006), who argues that the most likely consensus will emerge from groups that regard nuclear weapons as detrimental to Iran's security, making Iran a target and furthering regional proliferation.

85. Extremist clerics from Qom, led by Mohsen Gharavian, disciple of Mesbah Yazdi (Ahmadinejad's spiritual mentor), issued a new fatwa claiming that "shari'a does not forbid the use of nuclear weapons" (Shahram Rafizadeh, "Iranian Cleric Okays Use of Nuclear Weapons!" *Rooz*, February 21, 2006).

86. Neil MacFarquhar, "Across Iran, Nuclear Power Is a Matter of Pride," *New York Times*, May 29, 2005:A1; Brent Scowcroft and Daniel Poneman, "An Offer that Iran Cannot Refuse," *Financial Times*, March 9, 2005:13.

87. At a meeting between academics and Khamene'i, Chancellor Ahmad Fahimifar of Amir Kabir Industrial University acknowledged that "huge human and financial resources have been invested in this program" and hence the government "should not retreat at all." Khamene'i reassured them that there will be no retreat ("Iranian Academics Support Nuclear Program at Meeting with Khamene'i," Tehran Vision of the Islamic Republic of Iran, Network 1, December 19, 2004). On strong support for nuclear projects among bureaucrats, scientists, and technicians employed in the nuclear sector, see Kibaroglu (2006).

88. Con Coughlin, "North Korea Helping Iran with Nuclear Testing," Telegraph .co.uk, January 26, 2007 at www.telegraph.co.uk.

NOTES TO CHAPTER NINE

1. DNSA, November 18, 1986, NPO2380; Spector (1988).

2. DNSA, December 21, 1960, NP00721.

3. NSA Document 1 at http://www.gwu.edu/~nsarchiv/israel/documents/hebrew/index.html. Different sources attribute the formula to Ben-Gurion or Eshkol (Horowitz 1993).

4. DNSA, October 2, 1974, NP01382.

5. "Revealed: The Secrets of Israel Nuclear Arsenal," (London) *Sunday Times*, October 5, 1986. The FASW estimated Israel's arsenal at 75 to 130 weapons and Normark et al. (2005) at 100 to 200.

6. See Nasser's statements in chapter 11 and Dunn (1982). Ben-Gurion conveyed to Kennedy his belief that Egypt would develop nuclear weapons, that the conventional balance favored Egypt, and that Nasser's declared aim was to destroy, not defeat, Israel, adding that "he would do to the Jews what Hitler did" (NSA, June 29, 1961, Documents 15 and 16) at http://www.gwu.edu/~nsarchiv/israel/documents/first/16-02.htm. On his chief scientist Bergman's belief that Arab countries would probably achieve nuclear capabilities, see Segev (1993:370). On Dayan's statement that "no one would stop the United Arab Republic from developing nuclear weapons," see Hedrick Smith, "Soviet Said to Offer Cairo Atomic Defense," *New York Times*, February 3, 1966:1,12. On "the arms embargo that threatened to choke the country," see Peres (1995–88).

7. See www.gwu.edu/%7Ensarchiv/israel/documents/first/15-01.htm; and www.gwu.edu/%7Ensarchiv/israel/documents/first/16-02.htm. Ben-Gurion also mentioned to Kennedy that Israel might want to develop a pilot plutonium separation plant in the future, but there was no intention to develop a weapons capacity at that time. See http://www.gwu.edu/%7Ensarchiv/israel/documents/first/1602.htm. Shalom (2004:62–9) argues that in so doing, Ben-Gurion "put his cards on the table," as he did in meetings with Canadian and British officials.

8. "Nasser Threatens Israel on A-Bomb," *New York Times*, December 23, 1960:1,8.

9. Shikaki (1985:11); Hedrick Smith, "Warning on Bomb Given by Nasser," *New York Times*, February 21, 1966:8.

10. Farr (1999); global security newswire (GSN), January 16, 2002; Dunn (1982:49); Aronson (1992). A Soviet ship allegedly carrying nuclear weapons to be fitted on Russian Scud missiles stationed in Egypt docked in Alexandria (Egypt) during the 1973 war ("How Israel Got the Bomb," *Time Magazine*, April 12, 1976:39–40); Freedman 1975:118.

11. *GSN*, January 16, 2002; Melman (2006).

12. See chapter 11. In 1998, Peres declared in Amman that Israel had built a nuclear option "not in order to have a Hiroshima, but to have an Oslo" (NTIW).

13. Interview with former head of Iraqi Military Intelligence Wafic al-Samarrai, *Frontline, The Gulf War*, January 9, 1996, at http://www.pbs.org.

14. *The Jerusalem Report*, September 21, 1995:8. Maoz (2003) refutes the value of Israel's nuclear deterrent.

15. "Iranian leader: Wipe out Israel," October 27, 2005, at http://www.cnn.com; Menashri (1998:33). A top Pasdaran commander, Mohammad Ebrahim

Dehghani, stated, "We have announced that wherever (in Iran) America does make any mischief, the first place we target will be Israel" (Elaine Sciolino, "U.S., Britain and France Draft U.N. Resolution on Iran's Nuclear Ambitions," *New York Times*, May 3, 2006:A12). Iran's Lebanese ally Hassan Nasrallah said, "If they (Jews) all gather in Israel, it will save us the trouble of going after them worldwide" and "if we searched the entire world for a person more cowardly, despicable, weak and feeble in psyche, mind, ideology and religion, we would not find anyone like the Jew. Notice, I do not say the Israeli," quoted in *Daily Star*, October 23, 2002, and *New Yorker* October 14, 2002, respectively; also in Deborah Passner, "Hassan Nasrallah in His Own Words," July 26, 2006, at http://www.camera.org.

16. During Khatami's presidency, Iran's military paraded missiles painted with the slogan "Israel must be wiped off the map" (Dan De Luce, "Iran parades new missiles daubed with threats to wipe Israel off the map," *The Guardian*, September 23, 2003). Rafsanjani threatened that "the use of even one nuclear bomb inside Israel will destroy everything" (see chapter 8).

17. Ze'ev Schiff, "Israel Urges U.S. Diplomacy on Iran," May 30, 2006 (CEW).

18. *GSN*, January 16, 2002.

19. NSA at http://www.gwu.edu/~nsarchiv/israel/documents/hebrew/04-23.htm.

20. DNSA, December 12, 1964, NP01079. See also Karpin (2006:238, 373), who discusses Dayan's preference for "the product of Dimona" over a less reliable U.S. guarantee.

21. A bilateral U.S.-Israel cooperation agreement strictly regarding the Soviet Union existed between 1981 and 1991. In 1987, Israel was "upgraded" to non-NATO ally—not a mutual defense treaty—the same status granted to Egypt, Kuwait, Morocco, Bahrain, Jordan, Argentina, and others. In 1998, President Clinton pledged to assist Israel against direct threats stemming from regional deployment of ballistic missiles of intermediate range or greater. This memorandum does not enjoy the legal status of a treaty and does not guarantee U.S. military intervention in all cases of missile attacks on Israel. U.S. reluctance prior to 1967 was unrelated to occupied territories since it preceded their acquisition in the Six-Day War and Israel's subsequent illegitimate rule over the West Bank and Gaza.

22. U.S. Department of State, Foreign Relations, 1961–63, vol. 18, Near East, 1962–63, at http://www.state.gov/r/pa/ho/frus/kennedyjf/xviii/26209.htm; NSA Doc. 1, July 5, 1963, at http://www.gwu.edu/~nsarchiv/israel/documents/exchange/index.html.

23. DNSA, October 30, 1983, NPO2087. On Nixon's belief that Israel's nuclear ambitions were justified and understandable, see Ellsberg (2005).

24. According to a source close to Secretary of Defense James Schlesinger, Kissinger's strategy was allegedly to "let Israel come out ahead, but bleed" (UPI, September 17, 2002).

25. NSA, September 10, 1968, at http://www.gwu.edu/~nsarchiv/israel/documents/battle/03-01.htm.

26. NSA, October 28, 1968, Document 7, at http://www2.gwu.edu/~nsarchiv/israel/documents/battle/07-01.htm.

27. Freier (1985); Brecher (1972:555, 559). Mitchell Bard, The United Nations and Israel, available at http://www.jewishvirtuallibrary.org/jsource/UN/israel_un.html#1. Many years later Secretary-General Kofi Annan called on the U.N. to

acknowledge that its record on anti-Semitism had "fallen short" of U.N. ideals (Warren Hoge, "U.N. Is Gradually Becoming More Hospitable to Israel," *New York Times*, October 11, 2005:A3).

28. Brecher (1980:104, 230–31). On the eve of the Six-Day War, Egyptian authorities covered Cairo with posters demanding "the death of the poisonous viper of imperialism, Arab reaction, and Zionism" (Jansen 1997:158).

29. Cirincione et al. (2005:266); CNSW, NTIW, ACAW, FASW. Israel never signed the BTWC.

30. DNSA, August 8, 1988, NP02605; Freier (1985).

31. Feldman and Toukan (1997); Peters (1994, 1996); Jentleson (1996); Jentleson and Kaye (1997); Solingen (2000); Kaye (2001).

32. "Israel's Approach to Regional Security, Arms Control, and Disarmament," Geneva, September 4 ,1997, at http://www.israel-mfa.gov.il. Israel also signed (but did not ratify) the CTBT and represented the Middle East and South Asian region at the CTBT's Executive Council.

33. ISISW (1997); Karsh and Sayigh (1994); Solingen (2001b).

34. Israel TV Channel 1, December 22, 1995.

35. Guy Bechor, "The Nuclear Scarecrow Is Less Threatening," *Ha'aretz*, January 3, 1996:B2.

36. In 1968, Eban, one of the least enthusiastic cabinet members regarding the nuclear program, expressed concerns with bias against Israel in the IAEA inspection system (Cohen 1998:305). On U.N. bias against Israel, see also Peres (1970:105) and Eshkol (1967).

37. Several studies cited in this section describe the domestic history of Israel's nuclear program. For a preliminary application of international relations theory to understanding the domestic functions of nuclear ambiguity, see Solingen (1994b), upon which segments of this section build. Subsequent, more historical accounts include Shalom (1966, 2004); Cohen (1998); and Karpin (2006).

38. Incoming soft loans and grants with few political and military strings attached allowed high allocative autonomy at this time (Barnett 1992).

39. Bialer (1991); Shalev (1992). Mapam and Ahdut-Ha'avoda challenged Mapai in the 1955 elections, calling for pro-Soviet neutralism and abolition of nuclear weapons (Brecher 1972:165, 171). Ben-Gurion's hostility to Mapam played a central role in his policies even as he recognized Mapam's electoral strength.

40. Allon's memoirs (1990:191) went as far as favoring coercive prevention of nuclear proliferation by nuclear powers. On nuclear debates within Allon's party, see *Ha'aretz*, March 14, 1962; Evron (1974); Flapan (1974); and Segev (1993).

41. According to Hersh (1993:93), "There were too many critics of the nuclear program inside and outside Israel to raise money any other way."

42. As defense minister, Lavon deeply mistrusted both his Director General Peres and the IDF Chief of Staff Dayan as capable of keeping things from him, acting without his authority, and of concluding arms deals with France behind his back, even though in Lavon's view it was "crazy to hitch ourselves to the French wagon" (Peres 1995:89). Peres was advancing the French nuclear connection against this background.

43. The censorship code on nuclear issues would not have allowed explicit

identification. Allon (1990:200) acknowledged that the topic could not be discussed publicly.

44. Peres (1979:66–67) recalls Eshkol's demand that "in the matter of the atomic plant in Dimona [Eshkol] made clear to [Peres] that he did not want any detail, any conceivable doubt kept from him." Eshkol added, "Aren't you wasting good money? Experts don't tell you the truth and you can't find it out for yourself."

45. NSA, Document 3, at http://www.gwu.edu/~nsarchiv/israel/documents/hebrew/index.html.

46. John W. Finney, "Israel Permits U.S. to Inspect Atomic Reactor," *New York Times*, March 15, 1965:1.

47. On U.S. awareness of intense domestic fights between factions, see DNSA, March 22, 1965, NP01112.

48. NSA, Document 1, at http://www2.gwu.edu/~nsarchiv/israel/documents/battle. Although this document finds Eshkol's concerns with domestic challenges "of limited validity," Israeli newspapers had turned attacks on Eshkol's performance on the nuclear issue into a key electoral issue.

49. DNSA, April 11, 1968, NP01229.

50. On Eshkol's concerns with misleading the United States, see NSA, Miscelaneous Hebrew Documents, at http://www.gwu.edu/~nsarchiv/israel/documents/hebrew/04-01.htm. Sapir, Education Minister Zalman Aran, and Eban, among others, had been willing to accept Kennedy's demands for biannual visits to Dimona, which would have arguably effectively precluded a future weapons option (Cohen 1998:142, 162).

51. Freier (1993) is credited with elaborating nuclear ambiguity into a political doctrine geared to achieve deterrence against enemies, a responsible image vis-à-vis friends, and self-confidence at home (Karpin 1996:343; personal interview in January 1994 with Shalhevet Freier).

52. DNSA, April 9, 1965, NP01114.

53. NSA, Document 4, at http://www.gwu.edu/~nsarchiv/NSAEBB/NSAEBB189/index.htm.

54. NSA, "Israel Crosses the Threshold," at http://www.gwu.edu/~nsarchiv/NSAEBB/NSAEBB189/index.htm. Karpin (2006:318).

55. Under Dayan's prodding, Meir allegedly ordered the assembly of nuclear weapons during the war's early stages. No specific evidence for that allegation is available (UPI, September 17, 2002).

56. Danish TV, December 17, 1974 (U.S. National Archives COPENH03577 231723Z). See also Freedman (1975).

57. Harkabi (1988); Inbar (1991:105). On several of these constituencies' proclivity to regard the threat of war as much more probable than peace, see Arian et al. (1988:72).

58. Nimrod (1991); Bar-Joseph (1982). On Likud's forerunner Gahal's support for a nuclear option, see Flapan (1974). Ne'eman, a key nuclear scientist, was originally a Ben-Gurion and Peres protégé, an advisor to Dayan, and "chief scientist" in the Defense Ministry, but not necessarily supportive of replacing conventional with nuclear deterrence.

59. Quoted in Hewedi (1989:21). See also Bar-Joseph (1982); Inbar (1986);

and Yaniv (1987). According to Nimrod (1991), Sharon opposed both an open deterrent and a NWFZ.

60. "Dayan Says Israelis Have the Capacity to Produce A-Bombs," *New York Times*, June 25, 1981.

61. On internal opposition to Peres on nuclear issues, particularly among the "nuclear bureaucracy," see Oren (1995). Syria and Lebanon, though nominally part of the multilateral process, often boycotted its meetings.

62. Likud advanced privatization but initially limited it mainly to eliminating old Labor fiefdoms.

63. Deborah Sontag, "Israeli Lawmakers Hold Quick Debate on Nuclear Arms," *New York Times*, February 3, 2000:A3.

64. "Israeli PM Says Libya Trying to Acquire Nuclear Weapons at Talks with Envoys," *Financial Times Global News Wire*, October 14, 2003, at http://www.nti .org. See also chapter 10.

65. Leslie Susser, "Ex-Mossad Chief Yatom: Libya was Closer than Iran to Nuclear Bomb," *Jerusalem Report*, January 12, 2004, at http://www.nti.org.

66. Israel Targets Iran Nuclear Plant," *Sunday Times (London)*, July 18, 2004; GSN July 30, 2004; Normark et al. 2005:24. During the 1981 Osiraq attack, as Minister of Defense, Sharon stated that "Israel cannot afford the introduction of the nuclear weapon. For us it is not a question of balance of terror but a question of survival. We shall therefore have to prevent such a threat at its inception" (visit www.globalsecurity.org/wmd/world/israel/nuke.htm). In an oblique reference to Israel's capabilities, Sharon pointed out that "if you read the foreign press you will see that they talk about a whole complex of defensive tools, which Israel needs in its hands" ("Sharon Hints at Israel Nuclear Deterrent," *The Miami Herald*, April 24, 2004).

67. "Israel Has No Intention of Striking Iranian Nuclear Sites: Sharon," AFP, March 22, 2005; "Sharon Puts Diplomacy First in Dealing With Iranian Nuke Row," *Xinhua*, April 21, 2005.

68. Arieh O'Sullivan, "Mofaz: No Attack on Iran for Now," *Jerusalem Post*, February 8, 2005.

69. There was also a mass vaccination of cattle against possible Iraqi use of biological agents (Normark et al. 2005).

70. Notably, only 33 percent of those who favored use of nuclear weapons in 1988 mentioned the Holocaust as a reason (Arian 1998a:4). IAEC's first chairman, Ernst D. Bergmann, a refugee from Nazi Germany, is reported to have favored nuclear deterrence as the best way to ensure "that we shall never again be led as lambs to the slaughter" (Peres 1979:132). Eliezer Livne, who spearheaded the Committee for Denuclearization in the 1960s, also called for a forceful response to Nasser's May 1967 threats to annihilate Israel, saying "Nasser *is* Hitler" (*Ha'aretz*, May 31, 1967).

71. Address to Joint Session of Congress, May 24, 2006 (CNN). See also Normark et al. (2005). Olmert also provoked a storm when he stated that "Israel is a democracy, Israel doesn't threaten any country with anything, never did," he said. "The most that we tried to get for ourselves is to try to live without terror, but we never threaten another nation with annihilation. Iran openly, explicitly and publicly threatens to wipe Israel off the map. Can you say that this is the same level, when

they [Iran] are aspiring to have nuclear weapons, as America, France, Israel, Russia?" Perceived as a veiled acknowledgment of Israel's nuclear capabilities, Olmert was attacked by politicians across the political spectrum. Yuval Steinitz (Likud) called for his resignation and Meretz-Yahad Chairman Yossi Beilin called Olmert's remarks "irresponsible to the point of recklessness." See Herb Keinon, "PMO denies that Olmert disclosed Israel's nuclear hand," *Jerusalem Post*, December 11, 2006.

72. Jabber (1977); Shikaki (1985); Reiss (1988), and others have argued that an open Israeli deterrent would have compelled Arab leaders to admit impotence, would have demoralized the Arab world, and would have jeopardized these regimes' stability. Hence, several Arab leaders initially favored Israel's ambiguity as a mitigating solution or partial fig leaf. These factors relate ambiguity to constructivist categories and domestic political considerations.

73. These included Chiefs of Staff Yigal Yadin, Yitzhak Rabin, and Chaim Barlev, and head of Military Intelligence Aharon Yariv (Rosen 1976; Inbar 1986:66; Horowitz 1993:45; Cohen 1998:240). Israel's nuclear industrial infrastructure (private and public) was estimated to be relatively small compared to the extensive network of conventional arms producers (Steinberg 1990). On the domestic context underlying Israel's conventional strategy, see Mandelbaum (1988) and Barnett (1992).

74. On the expressed link between Israel's nuclear restraint and U.S. commitments to supply it with conventional weapons, see Evron (1974:1338). The military establishment has been particularly sensitive to its dependence on U.S. aid, at times for about 50 percent of Israel's defense budget.

75. Nobel Economics Laureate Robert J. Aumann argued in a panel on WMD in the Middle East that Israel as a democracy cannot violate its international commitments, but that Israel's counterparts would not be equally bound (Panel on Removal of Weapons of Mass Destruction from the Middle East, National Security Studies Center, University of Haifa, at http://video.haifa.ac.il/HTML/HTMLEng/NationalSecurityStudiesCenter).

76. Leading Israeli journalist Dan Margalit (1997:7) argued that Israel's democracy in the 1990s would have jailed Ben-Gurion's group and Dimona would have never been built.

77. In 2001, Netanyahu publicly urged Israel to replace its official policy of ambiguity in light of Iran's nuclear program (Aluf Benn, *Ha'aretz*, March 13, 2001). For a dovish position on Israel's withdrawal from the Palestinian territories that also favored an open nuclear deterrent, see Feldman (1982) and Yovel (2000). Anti-nuclear activist Livne opposed withdrawal from the occupied territories.

78. "Israel Will Not Discuss Nuclear Issue Until Overall Peace Secured—IAEA Head," BBC, July 7, 2004.

79. NTIW, July 9, 2004.

NOTES TO CHAPTER TEN

1. Richelson (2006:325); Haykal (1975:76); Dunn (1982:30–1); Bhatia (1988:66). See also allegations by former CIA officer in "Writer Reports Libya A-Bomb Bid," *Washington Post*, April 16, 1979. Qadhafi also insinuated that Libya could be transformed into a nuclear power because "nuclear weapons are

no longer a secret" ("Rumors of Libyan Atomic Bomb Quest Raise Fears," *Washington Post*, July 30, 1979).

2. See http://globalsecurity.org.

3. A Japanese diplomat suggested the government must have been apprised of that transfer ("Japan Company Sold Atomic Plant to Libya," AP, March 12, 2004).

4. "Libya: Tajura Nuclear Reactor Senior Scientist on Its Construction, Capabilities," interview with Dr. Muhammad Izzat Abd-al-Aziz, *Al-Majallah*, February 1–7, 2004:26–29 (FBIS-NES-2004-0206). In 1983, the Organization of African Unity reported that Libya had "the ability to deploy nuclear weapons" ("Africans Are Advised to Develop Atom Arms," *New York Times*, June 10, 1983).

5. Boucek (2004); see also http://globalsecurity.org. Saif al-Islam, Qadhafi's son, claimed that in late 2003 "Libya was in a state where it was possible to make nuclear weapons in five years" ("Ties with U.S. 'Before End of Year'," BBC, April 8, 2005).

6. "Qadhafi's Great Aim for Libya Is a Nuclear Capability of Its Own," *Christian Science Monitor*, November 12, 1980.

7. NTIW, January 31, 2005:1.

8. See IAEA document at www.iaea.org/Publications/Documents/Board/2004/gov2004-12.pdf.

9. Robert Kerr, "IAEA Praises Libya for Disarmament Efforts" (ACAW).

10. Ahmed Sheikh, "Al-Qadhafi Son: Israel Is Not a Threat," *Aljazeera,* January 9, 2004.

11. Stephen Fidler, Roula Khalaf, and Mark Huband, "Return to the Fold: How Gadaffi Was Persuaded to Give Up His Nuclear Goals," *Financial Times*, January 27, 2004.

12. Sudarsan Raghavan, "Libyan Leader Says the Race to Develop Nuclear Weapons Is 'Crazy'," Knight Ridder/Tribune News Service, February 29, 2004.

13. NTIS, December 23, 2003, FBIS-WEU-2003-1221.

14. Raghavan, "Libyan leader."

15. Central Intelligence Agency (CIA), Intelligence Memorandum No. 279, "Qadhafi's Nuclear Weapons Aims" (May 1975). Interestingly, this memorandum established as early as 1975 that Libya may attempt to leap-frog some normal steps by acquiring nuclear technology from the most advanced nuclear program in the Moslem world, that of Pakistan.

16. "Dr. Khan's Friend Speaks on Libyan Involvement in Pakistan's Nuclear Program," February 20, 2004:1, 7, AFS SAP20040221000030, FBIS-NES-2004-0221.

17. George Jahn, "Gadhafi: We Don't Want to Hide Anything," Associated Press Online, December 23, 2003.

18. "German Report Notes Existence of 'Nuclear Black Market' for Weapons," *Munich Sueddeutsche Zeitung*, January 2, 2004 (FBIS-WEU-2004-0101).

19. "Iran and Libya 'Bought Nuclear Goods'," *Aljazeera*, February 20, 2004:20.

20. "IAEA: Libya Could Make Plutonium," *Aljazeera*, February 21, 2004; "IAEA Says Libya Refined Small Amount of Plutonium," AFP, February 20, 2004.

21. Full transcript: Blair's Libya statement, BBC News, Friday, December 19, 2003; Miller (2006a).

22. "IAEA Says Libya Received Clandestine Nuclear Shipments as Late as March," AFP, May 29, 2004.

23. "IAEA Says Iran, Libya Broke Nuke Rules," *Aljazeera*, March 8, 2004; David E. Sanger and William J. Broad, "Using Clues from Libya to Study a Nuclear Mystery," *New York Times*, March 31, 2005:A10.

24. "Libya Praised for IAEA Cooperation," *Aljazeera*, August 30, 2004; "IAEA to Investigate Libya's Nuclear Program Further," AFP, June 16, 2004.

25. William J. Broad and David E. Sanger, "Warhead Designs Tie Libya Nuclear Project to Pakistani Scientist," *New York Times*, February 4, 2004:A9.

26. On the international dimensions of the boycott, which was unrelated to Libya's nuclear program, see Hurd (2005).

27. "Libya Neared Nuclear Bomb, Qaddafi Says," *New York Times*, July 7, 2006:A8.

28. "Libya: Tajura." According to Bhatia (1988:64–66), Egyptian nuclear scientists gravitated toward cooperation with Libya's well-financed program, with Nasser's consent. Sadat removed that formal collaboration after discovering a Libyan-backed coup against Sadat.

29. It is crucially important to understand the independent effects of Qadhafi's model of political survival on this state of affairs, over and beyond the role of sanctions (O'Sullivan 2003:193–95).

30. There had been earlier approaches during the Clinton administration and Libya's intelligence chief's Musa Kusa's 2002 meeting in London with U.S. Assistant Secretary of State for Near Eastern Affairs William Burns, which allegedly focused on accepting responsibility for Lockerbie (*[London] Times*, January 15, 2002).

31. Raghavan, "Libyan leader," op cit. For Qadhafi's view of globalization, see his personal web page at http://www.algathafi.org/en/index_en.htm.

32. Douglas Frantz and Josh Meyer, "The Deal to Disarm Kadafi," *Los Angeles Times*, March 13, 2005:A1.

33. "Ambassador Richard A. Boucher holds State Department regular news briefing," Federal Document Clearing House, April 20, 2004; Personal interviews with U.S. government officials (Washington, D.C., June 18–22, 2004).

34. "Prime Minister Says Libya Abandoned Nuclear Weapons Development in Favor of Development," ITAR-TASS, April 6, 2004 (FBIS-NES-2004-04060).

35. Peter Biles, "Slow and Painful Change for Libya," BBC News, December 30, 2003.

36. "The New Gadhafi," *60 Minutes*, CBS News, March 10, 2004.

37. "Libyan Foreign Minister Explains Libya's Stance on Africa," *Al-Arabiyah*, February 27, 2004 (FBIS-NES-2004-0228). These views echo Qadhafi's web page: "The so-called Arab World or Arab Homeland is . . . based on very dangerous probabilities of countless ethnic and sectarian divisions because of the nature of the present age, the age of major spaces, the age of minority fever. . . . Any attempt to talk about mutual Arab work, league structure, or practical measures will fail in the face of reality. . . . Clinging to the Arab League is mere negligence or ignorance of reality" (at http://www.algathafi.org/en/arab_en.htm).

38. "Libyan Opponent Says There Are Political Prisoners in Country-Algerian paper," *BBC Monitoring*, June 8, 2004.

39. Golnaz Esfandiari, "Libya: Analysts Say Decision on WMD Inspired by Economics, Worries about Succession," Radio Free Europe/Radio Liberty, December 22, 2003 (GSW).

40. BBC World Service, November 18, 2004.

41. "Saif Gaddafi's Vision for Libya," BBC News, November 16, 2004.

42. Laurie Kassman, "Libya Wrap," December 20, 2003 (GSW).

43. *Al-Ahram Weekly Online*, no. 673, January 15–21, 2004.

44. Jad Mouawad, "Libya Is Enticing U.S. Executives with Its Abundant Oil Reserves," *New York Times*, January 2, 2005:1; Craig S. Smith, "Qaddafi's Modern-Sounding Sin is a Riddle to the West," *New York Times*, December 14, 2004:A3; Broad and Sanger, "Warhead Designs."

45. Editorial, "Liberalising Libya," March 9, 2006, *Khaleej Time Online*; EIU, CRS, Libya, August 2006.

46. William Wallis, "New Blueprint for Overhaul of Libyan Economy," *Financial Times*, February 9, 2006:5.

47. Henry Sokolski, "President Bush's Global Nonproliferation Policy: Seven More Proposals," The Heritage Lectures, no. 829, April 19, 2004.

48. Martin Indyk, "Was Kadafi Scared Straight? The Record Says No," *Los Angeles Times*, March 23, 2004:M3.

49. "Libyan Leader Urges Speed on Nation's Atom Bomb," *Toronto Star*, June 18, 1990; website at http://www.iaea.org/Publications/Documents/Board/2004/gov2004-12.pdf; Douglas Frantz and Josh Meyer, "The Deal to Disarm Kadafi," *Los Angeles Times*, March 13, 2005:A1.

50. Martin S. Indyk and Edward S. Walker, "What Does Libya's Disarmament Teach About Rogue States?" Middle East Institute, April 7, 2004, available at http://mideasti.org/articles/doc192.html.

51. Saif al-Islam, "The New Gadhafi," *60 Minutes*, CBS News, March 10, 2004.

52. Personal interviews with U.S. officials (Washington, D.C. June 18–20, 2004). A Libyan opposition leader traced Qadhafi's nuclear "confessions" to his effort to retain power and pass it on to his children. "Libyan opponent," *BBC Monitoring*. See statement by the Honorable Paula A. DeSutter, Assistant Secretary, Bureau of Verification and Compliance, U.S. Department of State, at http://www.state.gov/t/np.

NOTES TO CHAPTER ELEVEN

1. "Consultative Council Discusses Nuclear Energy," *Middle East News Agency*, June 28, 1987 (see NTIW). This source informs this general introduction. See also NIE (1966); Shaker (1980); Shikaki (1985); Lavoy (2004); Jabber (1981:34); FASW; and Bhatia (1988).

2. Salah Hedayat, interview in *Al Arabi*, reported in "Egypt Unveils Nasser's Secret Nuclear Weapons Programme," *Deutsche Presse-Agentur*, July 24, 1995. Hedayat was a graduate in chemistry but not a scientist.

3. "Libya: Tajura Nuclear Reactor Senior Scientist on Its Construction, Capabilities," interview with Muhammad Izzat Abd-al-Aziz, *Al-Majallah*, February, 1–7, 2004:26–29 (FBIS-NES-2004-0206).

4. "Nasser Threatens Israel on A-Bomb," *New York Times*, December 23, 1960:1,8.

5. DNSA, May 29, 1964 NP00979. See also Haykal (1973:207–9).

6. Mohammed Hassanein Haykal, editorial in *Al Ahram*, cited in Raymond H. Anderson, "Top Cairo Editor Urges Nuclear Arms for Arabs," *New York Times*, November 23,1973; DNSA, December 12, 1964, NP01079; Bhatia (1988:56).

7. DNSA, January 17, 1965, NP01098; Gregory (1995).

8. DNSA, October 2, 1974, NP01382.

9. DNSA, July 16, 1974, NP01370.

10. This account builds on "Egypt's Missile Efforts Succeed with Help from North Korea," *The Risk Report* 2, no. 5 (September–October 1996). Wisconsin Project on Nuclear arms Control at http://www.wisconsinproject.org.

11. *Al-Hayat*, October 5, 1998, cited in Feldner (2003a:1).

12. "UN nuclear watchdog investigating Egypt for atomic experiments," AFP, January 5, 2005.

13. Egypt, Atomic Energy Authority, at http://www.frcu.eun.eg/www/home page/aea/about.htm.

14. GSN, September 21, 2006.

15. According to Meyers (1984:109), Egypt had latent capabilities to build nuclear weapons had it chosen to. See also Bhatia (1988:47). According to a 1963 proliferation estimate by Secretary of Defense Robert McNamara, Egypt's motivations to obtain nuclear weapons were "moderate to high" at the time (Lavoy 2004).

16. In 1977, Egypt and Libya engaged in armed attacks, artillery fire, and border-crossings by tanks and aircraft (Brecher, Wilkenfeld, and Moser 1988).

17. See quotes from *A-Sha'ab* in Bar-Joseph (1982:208).

18. On how Pan-Arabism became more of a threat to Arab regimes than to Israel, see Walt (1987:267) and Noble (1991:74).

19. Saif (1997). According to Perkovich (2005a:3), an Egyptian official declared that "the Iranian nuclear program is an existential threat to Egypt."

20. Carnegie Endowment 2005 Nonproliferation Conference (CEW).

21. The FASW places the beginnings of Egypt's program in 1954.

22. Robert Stephens and Patrick Seale, "Nasser: We Want to Be Friends with Britain," *London Observer*, July 5, 1964:1.

23. DNSA, December 12, 1964, NP01079.

24. U.S. Department of State, "Background Paper"; Saif (1997).

25. GSN, January 16, 2002. See also chapter 9.

26. Haykal doubted Soviet nuclear guarantees, according to Shikaki (1985:11). See also Haykal (1978). Nasser publicly denied such guarantees (Walsh 2001: 232–33). See also Hedrick Smith, "Soviet Said to Offer Cairo Atomic Defense," *New York Times*, February 4, 1966:1; Feldman (1982:68).

27. Ben-Gurion hid Israel's nuclear activities even from his cabinet members until challenged by the United States in December 1960 (see chapter 9). Dimona's activities were only revealed in 1960 (Bhatia 1988:54).

28. Feldman (1982:87). For the alternative view that Israel's nuclear designs involve compellence rather than deterrence, see Said (2002).

29. *London Observer*, July 5, 1964.

30. Saif (1997) believes Nasser's nuclear efforts were for public consumption alone and revealed a rather weak substantive commitment.

31. DNSA, May 29, 1964, NP00979. Walsh's (2001) comprehensive study of Egypt discounts hegemonic coercion as a reason for Egypt's non-nuclear status.

32. *Al-Ahram Weekly*, October 22, 1998, (cited in Feldner 2003b:2).

33. "Egypt and weapons of mass destruction in the Middle East," Egypt State Information Service, at http://www.sis.gov.eg/En/Politics/Foreign/issues/mass_de struction/040308050000000001.htm.

34. See chapter 9, n. 31.

35. Private interviews (Petra, Jordan, December 1995; Tel Aviv, Israel, August 1997; Washington, D.C., September 1997; Cairo, Egypt, March 1998).

36. Jones (1997b:60) argued that none of the other Arab delegations was as vocal as Egypt's.

37. *Journal of Palestine Studies* 24, no. 2 (winter 1995):128.

38. *Proliferation News*, October 3–6, 1998.

39. *GSN*, February 14, 2005.

40. "Egypt Says Nuclear Programme Peaceful," *Khaleej Times Online*, January 6, 2005.

41. "U.N. Nuclear Watchdog Chides Egypt," *New York Times*, February 15, 2005:A6.

42. GSN, February 14, 2005.

43. See http://www.iaea.org.

44. Nabil Fahmy, Special Comment, *Disarmament Forum: The Middle East 2001*, no. 2:3–5, available at http://www.unidir.org.

45. GSN, March 14, 2005.

46. GSN, October 4, 2001. Official Egyptian proposals called for non-WMD *use* but explicitly prohibited only nuclear *acquisition* ("Egypt and weapons," see n. 33).

47. IISS, 1992–93, Bill and Springborg (1990:247); Richards and Waterbury (1990:354, 362); Korany and Dessouki (1991:38); Sadowski (1993).

48. *Al-Ahram*, November 23, 1973 (FBIS, November 26,1973:GI, G2). On Haykal as the "anointed prophet of Nasserism," see Haykal (1973:xii).

49. "Cairo Editor Says Israel Plans to Test Nuclear Device Soon," *New York Times*, August 21, 1965:2.

50. Fahmy demanded that Israel's adherence to the NPT be made a pre-condition for Egypt's relations with Israel (Shikaki 1985).

51. "Nasser Threatens to War on a Nuclear-Armed Israel," *New York Times*, April 18, 1966:6; Hedrick Smith, "Warning on Bomb Given by Nasser," *New York Times*, February 21, 1966:8.

52. Barnett (1992). On Nasser's acknowledgment that no resources were available for nuclear weapons, see DNSA, December 12, 1964, NP01079.

53. Hedayat, "Egypt Unveils." Others contend that pressures for conventional weapons from Egypt's military in the aftermath of the 1967 debacle effectively forced the program's discontinuation. Bhatia (1988:56) argues that, after the 1967 war, Nasser sent a delegation to China led by Abdel Maaboud El Guibaily that reportedly inquired about purchasing nuclear weapons.

54. Bhatia (1988:57); see also chapter 10.

55. Heston and Summers' Penn World Tables (1991, 1995); U.N. Statistical Yearbook (1999); *World Development Indicators* (1998:310); *World Development Reports* (1991–97).

56. Military expenditures relative to central government expenditures declined from highs of 30 percent under Nasser and 48 percent under Sadat's inward-looking period down to 34 percent with Sadat's infitah and 16 percent under Mubarak in the 1980s (Solingen 2001a).

57. Gregory (1995:24) cites Egyptian ambassador Mohamed Shaker regarding the link between energy considerations and NPT ratification. Walsh (2001:279) agrees that the period between 1973 and 1981 witnessed a change in both economic and nuclear policies but regards "the link between liberalization and [NPT] regime participation [as] not a strong one." Walsh (2001:277) correctly points out that the results of infitah by 1980 were disappointing. However, whether or not infitah eventually worked out as Sadat initially envisaged is a completely separate question from what his objectives and expectations in 1974 were.

58. *Al-Ahram Weekly*, July 2, 2002, translated in Feldner (2003b:1), and Mustafa al-Faqi, "Nuclear Arms and the Middle East Conflict," *Al-Ahram Weekly*, May 21, 2002, in "Middle East Nuclear Strategic Balance Viewed" (NTIW).

59. *Al-Ahram Weekly*, January 18, 2001, translated in Feldner (2003a:2).

60. *Al-Ahram Weekly*, March 9, 2000, translated in Feldner (2003a:2).

61. *Al-Bayan*, April 23, 2002, and August 7, 2002; *Al-Ahram Weekly*, October 21, 1999, both translated in Feldner (2003b:2). On Egyptian military's refusal to accept Israeli monopoly of nuclear weapons, see Said (2002:2), who was himself a military advisor.

62. "Egypt's Former Defense Minister: How to Counter the Israeli Nuclear Deterrent," *Mideast Mirror* 9, no. 21 (January 31, 1995) (NTIW).

63. For Arabic originals of all citations henceforth, see http://www.islamon line.net/Arabic/news/2002-12/23/article06.shtml and http://www.islamonline-.net/iol-arabic/dowalia/alhadath-17-11/alhadath2.asp. This Islamist website cites only U.S.-based clerics among those opposing nuclear arms from an Islamist standpoint. For English translations, see Feldner (2003c:1).

64. For this and other public denials, see Feldman (1982). Shikaki (1985:9) cites statements by Sadat reflecting ambiguity about Israel's capabilities.

65. See, for instance, Jones (1997b: 59–60), citing Egyptian official Mahmoud Karem; statements in "Panel Discussion on Nuclear Threat from Israel," reported by *Al-Musawwar*, January 13, 1995: 54–58 (FBIS Near East and South Asia, November 18, 1995), particularly by Ambassador Mahmud Murtada, Deputy Assistant Foreign Minister; "Jalal Duwaydar, Interview with President Husni Mubarak," *Al-Akhbar*, January 1, 1995:3–6 (*FBIS* Near East and South Asia, November 19, 1995); Elaine Sciolino, "Christopher Plunges into Israel-Egypt Nuclear Dispute," *New York Times*, March 9, 1995:A3.

66. George Sam'an, "Egypt's Mubarak on Current Issues," *Al-Hayath* (London), October 5, 1998, via FBIS, FTS19981006000309, October 6, 1998, at NTIW.

67. "Egypt Needs No Permission to Seek Nuclear Energy: Mubarak," AFP, November 19, 2006.

68. In 1971, Egypt and the Soviet Union signed a defense consultation Treaty on Friendship and Cooperation, which Sadat denounced unilaterally in 1976.

69. This view was expressed in private interviews with Egyptian and other officials (see note 35 in addition to interviews in Washington, D.C., November and

December 2006), which emphasized that Nasser's primordial concern was with "anti-imperialism" from great powers, not Israel, but even then, Nasser is said to have never feared that Egypt's survival was at stake. Furthermore, as cited earlier, even Haykal reportedly acknowledged that Israel would not use nuclear weapons "unless she finds herself being strangled."

NOTES TO CHAPTER TWELVE

1. See, for instance, National Academy of Sciences, Committee on International Security and Arms Control, *Monitoring Nuclear Weapons and Nuclear-Explosive Materials: An Assessment of Methods and Capabilities* (Washington, D.C. 2005).

2. Carnegie Endowment Conference, Washington, D.C., June 21, 2004.

3. "Al-Arabiyah Interviews IAEA Chief on Libya's Cooperation, Iran, Proliferation," Al-Arabiyah TV, February 24, 2004.

4. NSA, September 17, 1975, 01946.

5. Such predictions include those by Kahn (1970), Mearsheimer (2001), and Kissinger, who argued, "We must have no illusion: Failure to resolve the North Korean nuclear threat in a clear-cut way will sooner or later lead to the nuclear armament of Japan—regardless of assurances each side offers the other" (Henry Kissinger, "Why We Can't Withdraw from Asia," *Washington Post*, June 15, 2003). Others consider Japan a virtual nuclear state (Levite 2002/03:71).

6. Henry Sokolski, "President Bush's Global Nonproliferation Policy: Seven More Proposals," The Heritage Lectures, no. 829, April 19, 2004.

7. Jones (1997a); Fahmy (2001); Chubin (2006); Takeyh (2006a). Jones (1997b) outright repudiates the argument that all other regional WMD programs are related to Israel's nuclear status.

8. Among many others, Vice President Richard Cheney speculated that Pyongyang's ambitions could trigger regional arms races (Yuri Kageyama, "Japan Rethinks Nuclear Taboo," *Washington Times*, August 15, 2003). Inoguchi Takashi suggested that "a loss of U.S. self-confidence in Iraq is a threat to Japan, because it would prompt isolationism in America and a U.S. withdrawal from South Korea, and that would expose Japan to a threat very, very directly. . . . Then public opinion in the United States and Japan might get more favourable to the option of Japan going nuclear. . . . Aggressive South Korean pursuit of unification with the North could have a similar result by prompting a U.S. withdrawal from the peninsula" (Sieg, "North Korea"). Notice that Inoguchi's scenarios are sensitive to domestic dynamics.

9. Eric Prideaux and Akemi Nakamura, "Japan May Not Want to Go Nuclear but It's No Technical Hurdle," *Japan Times*, October 11, 2006.

10. Some consider Japan to be only months or moments away from becoming a nuclear weapons state, but the fact remains that it has not done so for over three decades.

11. In an implicit critique of U.S. commitment to Taiwan, Lee Teng-Hui invoked the threat of Munich and Yalta ("A Strategy of Freedom in Asia," lecture hosted by the Formosa Foundation, Los Angeles, October 21, 2005).

12. London *Times*, November 4, 2006:2.

13. Private voices in the Gulf have raised demands for U.S. extended deterrence if Iran acquires nuclear weapons (Alani 2005).

14. Fawaz Gerges expressed that "I know that the official Egyptian line is to deny. But common sense and history tell me that the Egyptians, the Syrians, the Iraqis have either acquired or experimented with acquiring nuclear weapons" and "when Libya, which had been one of Khan's clients, agreed in 2003 to dismantle its nuclear weapons program, some Arabs grumbled publicly that closing the program would only be to Israel's advantage—and perhaps they worried privately that Libya's revelations would focus attention on their own secrets" (Donna Bryson, "Arab Nuclear Ambitions Spurred by Israel, Yes, but Iran, Other Concerns, Too," Associated Press, January 10, 2005).

15. See http://www.iaea.org/NewsCenter/Statements/2005/ebsp2005n002.html.

16. Second Moscow International Nonproliferation Conference, Hotel Metropol, September 19, 2003 (CEW).

17. According to Timerbaev (2005), "If there had been no NPT, the total number of nuclear-weapon-states . . . might have reached 30 or 40 by now." For eight useful guides for conducting counterfactual analysis in international relations, see Lebow (2000).

18. See http://www.carnegieendowment.org.

19. On the relationship between domestic models and regional institutions, see Solingen (2008).

20. Japan submitted resolutions advocating total elimination of nuclear weapons to the UNGA since 1994, which the United States has opposed since 2001.

21. Although positions on WMD hardened after Iraq's missile attacks on Israel in 1991, 82 percent of the Israeli public in 1998 supported a NWFZ if it included all states in the region; only 19 percent favored open nuclear deterrence despite continued tension with most neighbors (Arian 2003). A 1994 survey during the Oslo era found 72 percent supporting Israel's accession to the NPT if all states in the region abandoned WMD.

22. Economics Nobel laureate Robert J. Aumann argued that as a democracy Israel cannot violate its international commitments, although its neighbors are not equally bound ("Removal of Weapons of Mass Destruction from the Middle East," National Security Studies Center, Haifa University, available at http://video.haifa.ac.il).

23. Ben-Gurion countenanced U.S. inspections when in power but used them publicly against Eshkol to encourage his ousting prior to elections.

24. See Al-Siyassa (Kuwait), May 3, 2006 at http://memri.org/bin/articles.cgi?Page=archives&Area=ia&ID=IA27706.

25. Roberts (1993) and Mansfield and Snyder (2005) suggest that weak and unstable democracies may lead to outcomes that differ from those expected for full-fledged liberal democracies.

26. The connection might arguably be even stronger if one includes cases that abandoned nuclear programs, excluded in Singh and Way (2004).

27. Bloated nuclear-industrial-complexes have come to symbolize the excesses of state expansion among virtually all nuclear aspirants who developed nuclear weapons.

28. Solingen (1994a, 2001b); Liberman (2001). Testing an hypothesis along these lines, Singh and Way (2004:876, 878) find that "the process of economic liberalization is associated with a reduced likelihood of exploring nuclear weapons" and that economic openness "has a statistically significant negative effect" on exploring, pursuing, or acquiring nuclear weapons.

29. East Asian states' economic, political, and institutional structures varied widely but all shared commitments to export-led growth (more centralized in South Korea, decentralized in Taiwan, and oligopolostic in Japan). Japan's model was more reliant on domestic markets initially (Pempel 1999). State bureaucracies played important roles in steering integration in the global economy in most cases.

30. On how Japanese officials sometimes *encouraged* U.S. pressure on Japan to ratify the NPT in order to counter domestic opponents (including Nakasone), see memorandum from Philip Habib and Winston Lord to Secretary Kissinger (DNSA, February 20, 1975, JU01921). This source also makes clear that Japanese officials sensed ambiguity in the U.S. position, which entailed little pressure for ratification at that point, and acknowledges that U.S. preferences would not be the determining factor in Japan's decisions; the interests of Japanese leaders would.

31. NIE, June 18, 1957 (NSA, NSAEBB155).

32. Edward Cody, "Taiwan Sets Self-Defense Objectives," *Washington Post*, May 21, 2006:A19.

33. Asgarkhani, Abumohammad. Iran, Sept. 11 and the Repercussions of 'Regime Change.' *The Daily Star*, September 15, 2003. Available at http://yaleglobal .yale.edu/display.article?id=2459.

34. Neil MacFarquhar, "Across Iran, Nuclear Power Is a Matter of Pride," *New York Times*, May 29, 2005:A1.

35. The chancellor of Amir Kabir Industrial University, Ahmad Fahimifar, acknowledged that "huge human and financial resources have been invested in this program" and hence the government "should not retreat at all." Khamene'i reassured him that there would be no retreat ("Iranian Academics Support Nuclear Program at Meeting with Khamene'i," Network 1, December 19, 2004).

36. "Cairo Editor Says Israel Plans to Test Nuclear Device Soon," *New York Times*, August 21, 1965:2.

37. Why internationalizing models had difficulties taking root in the Middle East is outside the scope of this book but is discussed in Solingen (2007a).

38. On domestic politics as filtering external considerations, see Solingen (1998). A recent study by Schweller (2006:5) also resorts to the concept of *filter* or domestic politics as mediating between systemic considerations and actual decisions. Neoclassical realist studies sensitive to domestic politics include Snyder (1991); Christensen (1996); and Glaser (2000).

39. On how international crises of capitalism lead to realignments of domestic political structures, see Gourevitch (1986).

40. Some consider India to fit this case, although India became a nuclear power in 1974 under Indira Ghandi's inward-looking era and long before India's economic reforms of the 1990s. If India were to be found an anomaly, it would prove the argument's refutability. Alternatively, it could also be explained by the third scope condition, pointing to the higher political costs incurred in renouncing actual weapons rather than precursor programs, as with China and Israel.

41. Mark Magnier, "China and Japan Try to Ease Strain," *Los Angeles Times*, April 24, 2005:A3. For a competing argument, see Kitamura (1996:11). Bueno de Mesquita et al. (1993) predicted that pro-nuclear groups in Taiwan would face a strong coalition of internal and external actors opposed to indigenous nuclear weapons. Domestic opponents of nuclearization within and outside the government would be sensitive to its economic and political consequences.

42. As of 2005, few Japanese experts and politicians believed Japan would go nuclear but some think it should. Interviews (Tokyo, June 2003, July–August 2004, March 2005); Kamiya (2002–03); Keller (2003); Hughes (2004:93–94); Oros (2003); Kurosawa (2004). For a pro-nuclear view, see Nakanishi Terumasa, "Goals for Japan in Its 'Second Postwar' Period," *Japan Echo* 30, no. 5 (October 2003). This book goes to press under the fog of North Korea's nuclear test, too early to evaluate its repercussions.

43. "Blowback" entails using symbols (such as visits to Yasukuni) or policies (reciting historical grievances) to mobilize nationalistic support. While this may be done instrumentally and tactically, it can create self-entrapment, heightening the costs of renouncing such practices and, even worse, engraining them as valid strategic concepts (Snyder 1991; Van Evera 1994:32–33).

44. For such a scenario, labeled a "bold switchover," see Eberstadt, Ellings, Babson, and Noland (2006).

45. According to Takeyh (2004a:8), this may be unlikely because "The emergence of bureaucratic and nationalist pressures in Iran is generating its own proliferation momentum, empowering those seeking a nuclear breakout. As time passes, the pragmatic voices calling for hedging are likely to be marginalised and lose their influence within the regime. The notion that the United States has the luxury of time is belied by Iran's internal domestic alignments on the nuclear issue."

46. For updated accounts on an extensive literature on technology denial, see inter alia Levi and O'Hanlon (2005) and Goldschmidt (2003, 2007).

47. For a preliminary effort to derive policy guidelines akin to "smart sanctions" and positive inducements sensitive to domestic politics, see Solingen (1995). In the intervening decade, experiences in Iraq, North Korea, Iran, and Libya led to additional efforts to disaggregate the domestic context, including those by Drezner (1999); Haas and O'Sullivan (2000); Niblock (2001); O'Sullivan (2003); and Lopez and Cortright (2004).

48. Solingen (1998, chap. 8) provides further elaboration on these effects.

49. According to Carlin and Wit (2006), about three million people constitute a "court economy" of beneficiaries of special goods and services. It is unclear, however, how many among this selected tier perceive the status quo to be preferable to economic reforms, including the demise of the "second (military) economy." For a balanced view of the advantages and difficulties of various scenarios concerning evolutionary economic and political transformation in North Korea rather than "regime change," see Haggard and Noland (2007).

50. According to O'Sullivan (2003:74), U.S. sanctions added to domestic sources of weakness faced by Iran's reformers.

51. Richard Armitage, "Japan-U.S. ties crucial in changing world," *Daily Yomiuri*, March 16, 2005:20.

52. David E. Sanger, "US Said to Weight a New Approach on North Korea," *New York Times*, May 18, 2006:A10; Steven R. Weisman, "U.S. Pursues Tactic of Financial Isolation," *New York Times*, October 16, 2006:A10.

53. Weisman, "U.S. Pursues Tactics"; Steven R. Weisman, "U.S. Prohibits All Transactions With a Major Iranian Bank," *New York Times*, January 10, 2007:3.

54. According to Cox and Cooper (2006), democracies are less likely to sanction each other although they employ sanctions more than other regime types, advancing human rights and democratization through economic sanctions.

55. Abbas Maleki, BCSIA News, Summer 2006, at www.belfercenter.org. By some estimates, only 15 percent of voters actively support Ahmadinejad's model and the extremist religious parties that promote it. His executive powers are limited by Iran's constitution and by the coalition of interests represented in the government (see Simon Tisdall, "This Is More about National Pride than Nuclear Weapons," *The Guardian*, September 8, 2006).

56. Qadhafi's 2003 moves were denounced by some not only in the Arab world. Iran's nuclear negotiator Rowhani stated that "Iran is Iran. It is neither South Korea nor Libya. . . . Both of them submitted themselves to America" ("Iran's Nuclear Negotiator Rowhani Holds News Conference," Islamic Republic of Iran News Network, November 30, 2004, in FBIS December 1, 2004 IAP20041201000099).

57. As Kimball argues, "A close reading of the NPT makes it clear that peaceful nuclear endeavors are a benefit that accrues only to those non-weapons NPT states that credibly fulfill their obligation not to divert nuclear material and technology for weapons" (see Daryl G. Kimball, "Iran: Getting Back on Track," *Arms Control Today*, October 2004).

58. "Joint Statement from Nuclear Talks," *New York Times*, September 19, 2005.

59. Samore (2005) estimated that it would take Iran at least five years to produce enough fissile material for a single weapon. More recent estimates suggest Iran is closer to that goal (David E. Sanger, "Atomic Agency Confirms Advances by Iran's Nuclear Program," *New York Times*, April 19, 2007:A10). According to a Pentagon report, Iran could have enough nuclear material for a nuclear weapon by 2010 (David Martin, *CBS News*, April 26, 2007)

60. A new proposal by very high former U.S. officials suggests steps in the direction of a world free of nuclear weapons (George P. Shultz, William J. Perry, Henry A. Kissinger, and Sam Nunn, "A World Free of Nuclear Weapons," *Wall Street Journal*, January 4, 2007).

61. Carter (2005) and Testimony of Ashton B. Carter, House Armed Services Committee, United States House of Representatives, Regarding Seven Steps to Overhaul Counterproliferation, March 17, 2004, available at http://www.house.gov.

References

Abedin, Mahan. 2006. Iranian public opinion and the nuclear stand-off. *Mideast Monitor* 1 (2).

Abrahamian, Ervand. 1993. *Khomeinism: Essays of the Islamic Republic*. Berkeley and Los Angeles: University of California Press.

ACAW (Arms Control Association). Visit website at http://www.armscontrol.org.

ACDA (U.S. Arms Control and Disarmament Agency). 1976, 1982, 1990, 1996. *World military expenditures and arms transfers*. Washington, D.C.: U.S. Government Printing Office.

Ahmad, Yousef A. 1991. The dialectics of domestic environment and role performance: The foreign policy of Iraq. Pp. 186–215 in *The foreign policy of Arab states*, ed. Baghat Korany and Ali E. Hillal Dessouki. Boulder, Colo.: Westview.

Ahn, Byung-joon. 1994. The man who would be Kim. *Foreign Affairs* 73 (6): 94–108.

Akaha, Tsuneo. 1984. Japan's non-nuclear policy. *Asian Survey* 24 (8):852–77.

Akiyama, Nobumasa. 2003. The socio-political roots of Japan's non-nuclear posture. Pp. 64–91 in *Japan's nuclear option: Security, politics, and policy in the 21st century*, ed. Benjamin L. Self and Jeffrey W. Thompson. Washington, D.C.: Henry L. Stimson Center.

Alani, Mustafa. 2005. The case for a Gulf weapons of mass destruction free zone. *Security and Terrorism Issue* 1 (October). Available at www.grc.ae.

Albright, David. 1995. An Iranian bomb? *The Bulletin of the Atomic Scientists* 51 (4):20–26.

Albright, David, Frans Berkhout, and William Walker. 1997. *Plutonium and highly enriched uranium, 1996: World inventories, capabilities, and policies*. New York: Oxford University Press.

Albright, David, and Corey Gay. 1998. Taiwan: Nuclear nightmare averted. *Bulletin of the Atomic Scientists* 54 (1):54–60.

Albright, David, and Mark Hibbs. 1992. Spotlight shifts to Iran. *The Bulletin of Atomic Scientists* (March):9–11.

Aljazeera. Visit website at http://english.aljazeera.net.

Al-Khalil, Samir. 1989. *The republic of fear: The politics of modern Iraq*. Berkeley: University of California Press.

Allison, Graham T. 2004. *Nuclear terrorism: The ultimate preventable catastrophe*. New York: Times Books/Henry Holt.

Allon, Yigal. 1990. *Betachbulot milhama—Sugiyot be-iniyanei bitachon*. Tel Aviv: Hakibutz Hameuchad.

Amsden, Alice H. 1985. The state and Taiwan's economic development. Pp. 78–106 in *Bringing the state back in*, ed. Peter Evans, Dietrich Rueschemeyer, and Theda Skocpol. New York: Cambridge University Press.

———. 1989. *Asia's next giant: South Korea and late industrialization*. New York: Oxford University Press.

————. 1993. *Structural macroeconomic underpinnings of effective industrial policy: Fast growth in the 1980s in five Asian countries.* Geneva: United Nations Conference on Trade and Development.

Amuzegar, Jahangir. 2006. Nuclear Iran: Perils and prospects. *Middle East Policy* 13 (2):90–112.

Anderson, Lisa. 1986. *The state and social transformation in Tunisia and Libya, 1830–1980.* Princeton: Princeton University Press.

————. 1987. The state in the Middle East and North Africa. *Comparative Politics* 29 (2): 1–18.

————. 1995. Qadhafi's legacy: An evaluation of a political experiment. Pp. 223–37 in *Qadhafi's Libya, 1969–1994*, ed. Dirk Vandewalle. New York: St. Martin's.

————. 2003. Libyan Expert: Qaddafi, Desperate to End Libya's Isolation, Sends a 'Gift' to President Bush. Interview with Bernard Gwertzman. Council on Foreign Relations, December 22. Available at http://www.cfr.org/publication/6617/libyan_expert.htmlhttp://www.cfr.org.

Arian, Asher. 1993. Israel and the peace process: Security and Political Attitudes in 1993. Jaffee Center for Strategic Studies. Memorandum no. 39 (February). Available at http://www.tau.ac.il/jcss/publications.html#memoranda.

————. 1995. The Peace Process and Terror: Conflicting trends in Israeli Public Opinion in 1995. Jaffee Center for Strategic Studies. Memorandum no. 45. (February)

————. 1996. Israeli Security Opinion. Center for Strategic Studies. Memorandum no. 46. (February).

————. 1998a. Public Opinion and Nuclear Weapons. *Jaffee Center-Strategic Assessment* 1, no. 3 (November).

————. 1998b. Israeli Public Opinion on National Security 1998. Center for Strategic Studies. Memorandum no. 49 (July).

————. 2003. Israeli Public Opinion on National Security 1998. Center for Strategic Studies. Memorandum no. 67 (October).

Arian, Asher, Ilan Talmud, and Tamar Hermann. 1988. *National security and public opinion in Israel.* Boulder, Colo.: Westview Press.

Arms Control and Disarmament Agency (U.S.). 1995–97. World military expenditures and arms transfers. Available at http://dosfan.lib.uic.edu/acda/reports1.htm.

Aronson, Shlomo. 1992. *The politics and strategy of nuclear weapons in the Middle East: Opacity, theory, and reality, 1960–1991: An Israeli perspective.* Albany: State University of New York Press.

Avraham H. 2006. Arab media reactions to Iran's nuclear project. *MEMRI*, no. 277 (May 23). Available at http://memri.org/bin/articles.cgi?Page=countries&Area=iran&ID=IA27706.

Babson, Bradley O. 2003. The potential future role for the multilateral development banks on the Korean peninsula. Pp. 33–52 in *North Korea in the world economy*, ed. Kwan E. Choi, E. Han Kim, and Yesook Merrill. New York: RoutledgeCurzon.

Baek, Jong-Chun. 1988. North Korea's military strategies for reunification: Hypotheses and policies. Pp. 159–78 in *Northeast Asia security and peace:*

Toward the 1990s, ed. J. H. Shin, K. Tae-Hwan, and E. A. Olsen. Seoul, Korea: Kyung Hee University Press.

Baldwin, David A. 1985. *Economic statecraft*. Princeton: Princeton University Press.

————. 1988. *Trade policy in a changing world economy*. Chicago: University of Chicago Press.

Ballard, Col. William T. 1973. *Strategic power: On balance*, USAF *Air University Review* 24, no. 4 (May–June). Available at http://www.airpower.maxwell.af.mil.

Banchev, Iuli. 1996. Prerogatives of the new foreign economic policy making. Pp. 189–204 in *North Korea: Ideology politics, economics*, ed. Han S. Park. Englewood Cliffs, N.J.: Prentice-Hall.

Bar-Joseph, Uri. 1982. The hidden debate: The formation of nuclear doctrines in the Middle East. *The Journal of Strategic Studies* 5 (2):205–27.

Baram, Amatzia. 1998. *Building toward crisis: Saddam Hussein's strategy for survival*. Washington, D.C.: Washington Institute for Near East Policy.

————. 2001. An analysis of Iraqi WMD strategy. *The Nonproliferation Review* 8 (2):25–39.

Barnett, Michael N. 1992. *Confronting the costs of war: Military power, state and society in Egypt and Israel*. Princeton: Princeton University Press.

Barnett, Michael, and Martha Finnemore. 1999. The politics, power, and pathologies of international organizations. *International Organization* 53 (4): 699–732.

Barnett, Michael, and Etel Solingen. 2007. Designed to fail or failure of design? The sources and institutional effects of the Arab League. In *Crafting cooperation: The design and effect of regional institutions in comparative perspective*, ed. Alastair Iain Johnston and Amitav Acharya. Cambridge: Cambridge University Press.

Beck, Nathaniel. 2005. Multilevel analyses of comparative data: A comment. *Political Analysis* 13:457–58.

Beilin, Yossi. 1993. *A vision of the Middle East*. State of Israel.

Benn, Aluf. 1995. Hasichot le-bakarat neshek hukpeu ekev hamachloket im mitzraim. *Ha'aretz* 1 (December):1.

Beres, Louis Rene, ed. 1986. *Security or Armageddon: Israel's nuclear strategy*. Lexington, Mass.: Lexington Books.

Berger, Thomas U. 1993. From sword to chrysanthemum: Japan's culture of anti-militarism. Pp. 300–331 in *East Asian security*, ed. Michael E. Brown, Sean M. Lynn-Jones, and Steven E. Miller. Cambridge: MIT Press.

————. 1998. *Cultures of antimilitarism: National security in Germany and Japan*. Baltimore: Johns Hopkins University Press.

Betts, Richard K. 1977a. Paranoids, pygmies, pariahs and nonproliferation. *Foreign Policy* 26:157–83.

————. 1977b. *Soldiers, statesmen, and Cold War crises*. Cambridge: Harvard University Press.

————. 1980. Incentives for nuclear weapons. Pp. 85–175 in *Nonproliferation and U.S. foreign policy*, ed. Joseph A. Yager. Washington, D.C.: Brookings Institution.

————. 1993/94. Wealth, power, and instability: East Asia and the United States after the Cold War. *International Security* 18 (3):34–77.

———. 2000. Universal deterrence or conceptual collapse? Liberal pessimism and utopian realism. Pp. 51–86 in *The coming crisis: Nuclear proliferation, U.S. interests, and world order*, ed. Victor A. Utgoff. Cambridge: MIT Press.

Bhatia, Shyam. 1988. *Nuclear rivals in the Middle East*. New York: Routledge.

Bialer, U. 1991. Facts and pacts: Ben-Gurion and Israel's international orientation, 1948–1956. In *David Ben-Gurion—Politics and leadership in Israel*, ed. R. W. Zweig. London: Frank Cass.

Bill, James A., and Robert Springborg. 1990. *Politics in the Middle East*. New York: HarperCollins.

Binder, Leonard. 1988. *Islamic liberalism: A critique of development ideologies*. Chicago: University of Chicago Press.

Blix, Hans. 2005. *Disarming Iraq: The search for weapons of mass destruction*. London: Bloomsbury.

Boucek, Christopher. 2004. Libya's Return to the Fold? *Strategic Insights* 3 (3).

Boyd, J. Patrick, and Richard J. Samuels. 2005. Nine lives: The politics of constitutional reform in Japan. East-West Center, Policy Studies no. 19.

Bracken, Paul. 2003. The Structure of the Second Nuclear Age. *Foreign Policy Research Institute* (September 25). Available at www.fpri.org.

Bradford, Colin I., Jr. 1990. Policy interventions and markets: Development strategy typologies and policy options. Pp. 32–54 in *Manufacturing miracles: Paths of industrialization in Latin America and East Asia*, ed. Gary Gereffi and Donald L. Wyman. Princeton: Princeton University Press.

Brady, Henry E., and David Collier, eds. 2004. *Rethinking social inquiry: Diverse tools, shared standards*. Lanham, Md.: Rowman and Littlefield.

Brecher, Michael. 1972. *The foreign policy system of Israel: Setting, images, process*. New Haven: Yale University Press.

———. 1980. *Decisions in crisis: Israel, 1967 and 1973*. Berkeley: University of California Press.

Brecher, Michael, Jonathan Wilkenfeld, and Sheila Moser. 1988. *Crisis in the twentieth century*. New York: Pergamon.

Brom, Shlomo. 2005. Is the Begin Doctrine still a viable option for Israel? In *Ready for a nuclear-ready Iran*, ed. Henry Sokolski and Patrick Clawson, Strategic Studies Institute at http://www.strategicstudiesinstitute.army.mil/pdf files/pub629.pdf.

Brooks, Stephen G. 1997. Dueling realisms. *International Organization* 51 (3): 445–47.

Bruno, Michael. 1988. Opening up: Liberalization with stabilization. Pp. 223–48 in *The open economy: Tools for policymakers in developing countries*, ed. Rudiger Dornbusch and F. Leslie Hemers. New York: Oxford University Press.

Bueno de Mesquita, Bruce, and David Lalman. 1992. *War and reason: Domestic and international imperatives*. New Haven: Yale University Press.

Bueno de Mesquita, Bruce, James D. Morrow, and Samuel S.G. Wu. 1993. Forecasting the risk of nuclear proliferation: Taiwan as an illustration of the method. Pp. 311–31 in *The proliferation puzzle: Why nuclear weapons spread (and what results)*, ed. Zachary S. Davis and Benjamin Frankel. London: Frank Cass.

Bueno de Mesquita, Bruce, and William H. Riker. 1982. An assessment of the merits of selective nuclear proliferation. *Journal of Conflict Resolution* 26 (2):283–306.

Bueno de Mesquita, Bruce, Alastair Smith, Randolph M. Siverson, and James D. Morrow. 2003. *The logic of political survival.* Cambridge: MIT Press.

Bunn, Matthew. 2004. Nonproliferation, safeguards, and export controls. Belfer Center for Science and International Affairs, April. Available at http://bcsia.ksg-.harvard.edu/publication.cfm?program=CORE&ctype=paper&item_id=452.

Burr, William, ed. 1999. New archival evidence on Taiwanese 'Nuclear Intentions,' 1966–1976. National Security Archive Electronic Briefing Book, no. 19. October 13. Available at http://www2.gwu.edu/~nsarchiv/NSAEBB/NSAEBB20.

———. 2005. National intelligence estimates of the nuclear proliferation problem: The first ten years, 1957–1967. National Security Archive Electronic Briefing Book, no. 155. Posted June 1, 2005. Available at http://www.gwu.edu/~nsarchiv/NSAEBB/NSAEBB155/index.htm.

Burr, William, and Jeffrey T. Richelson, eds. 2001. The United States and the Chinese Nuclear Program—1960–1964. National Security Archive, January 12. Available at http://www2.gwu.edu/~nsarchiv/NSAEBB/NSAEBB38/NSAEBB38/index.html.

Burrows, William E., and Robert Windrem. 1994. *Critical mass: The dangerous race for superweapons in a fragmenting world.* New York: Simon and Schuster.

Bush, Richard C. 2004. *At cross purposes: U.S.-Taiwan relations since 1942.* New York: M. E. Sharpe.

Calder, Kent E. 1988. *Crisis and compensation: Public policy and political stability in Japan 1949–1986.* Princeton: Princeton University Press.

———. 1996. *Pacific defense: Arms, energy, and America's future in Asia.* New York: William Morrow.

Campbell, Kurt M., Robert J. Einhorn, and Mitchell B. Reiss, eds. 2004. *The nuclear tipping point: Why states reconsider their nuclear choices.* Washington, D.C.: Brookings Institution Press.

Campbell, Kurt M., and Tsuyoshi Sunohara. 2004. Japan: Thinking the unthinkable. Pp. 218–53 in *The nuclear tipping point,* ed. Campbell et al.

Carasales, Julio C. 1995. The Argentine-Brazilian nuclear rapprochement. *The Non-Proliferation Review* 2 (3):39–48.

Carlin, Robert L., and Joel S. Wit. 2006. North Korean reform: Politics, economics and security. *Adelphi Papers* 46, no. 382 (July):1–65.

Carter, Ashton B. 2004. Seven steps to overhaul counterproliferation. Statement before the House Armed Services Committee, March 17. Available at http://bcsia.ksg.harvard.edu/publication.cfm?program=CORE&ctype=testimony&item_id=39.

———. 2005. Panel: New approaches for addressing the threat of WMD proliferation. Presentation at Non-Proliferation of Weapons of Mass Destruction: Current Challenges and New Approaches, Tufts University, Fletcher School of Law and Diplomacy, October 21. Available at http://bcsia.ksg.harvard.edu/publication.cfm?program=CORE&ctype=presentation&item_id=104.

CEW (Carnegie Endowment for International Peace). Visit website at http://www.carnegieendowment.org.

Cha, Victor. 2004. North Korea's economic reforms and security intentions. Testimony for Senate Foreign Relations Committee, March 2. Available at http://69 .44.62.160/archives/DPRKbriefingbook/transition/ChaTestimony040302.html.

Cha, Victor, and David C. Kang. 2003. *Nuclear North Korea: A debate on engagement strategies*. New York: Columbia University Press.

Chai, Sun-ki. 1997. Entrenching the Yoshida defense doctrine: Three techniques for institutionalization. *International Organization* 51 (3):389–412.

Chan, Steve. 1988. Defense burden and economic growth: Unraveling the Taiwanese enigma. *American Political Science Review* 82 (3):913–20.

———. 1992. Military burden, economic growth, and income inequality: The Taiwan exception. Pp. 163–78 in *Defense, welfare, and growth*, ed. Steve Chan and Alex Mintz. New York: Routledge.

Chan, Steve, and Cal Clark. 1992. *Flexibility, foresight, and fortune in Taiwan's development*. New York: Routledge.

Chanlett-Avery, Emma, and Sharon Squassoni. 2006. *North Korea's nuclear test: Motivations, implications, and U.S. options*. Washington, D.C.: Congressional Research Service.

Chaudhry, Kiren Aziz. 1991. On the way to market: Economic liberalization and Iraq's invasion of Kuwait. *Middle East Report* 170:14–23.

Checkel, Jeffrey T. 1997. *Ideas and international political change: Soviet/Russian behavior and the end of the Cold War*. New Haven: Yale University Press.

Chen, Jian. 2003. Uneasy allies: Fifty years of China-North Korea relations. Woodrow Wilson International Center for Scholars. Asia Program Special Report no. 115.

Cheng, Tun-jen. 1990. Political regimes and development strategies: South Korea and Taiwan. Pp. 139–78 in *Manufacturing miracles: Paths of industrialization in Latin America and East Asia*, ed. Gary Gereffi and Donald L. Wyman, Princeton: Princeton University Press.

———. 2005. China-Taiwan economic linkage: Between insulation and superconductivity. Pp. 92–130 in *Dangerous strait: The U.S.-Taiwan-China crisis*, ed. Nancy Bernkopf Tucker. New York: Columbia University Press.

———. 2006. Washington's policies toward North Korea and the Taiwan Strait: The role of US domestic politics. Pp. 61–84 in *Regional cooperation and its enemies in Northeast Asia: The impact of domestic forces*, ed. Edward Friedman and Sung Chull Kim. New York: Routledge.

Chiang, Kai-shek. 1967. *Selected speeches and messages in 1967*. Republic of China, Taipei, Government Information Office.

———. 1970. President Chiang Kai-shek's selected speeches and messages in 1970. Taipei: Government Information Office.

Cho, M. A. 2004. North Korea's 2003 Foreign Trade (Abstract). Digital KOTRA, North Korean Economy. Available at http://crm.kotra.or.kr/main/info/nk/eng/main.php3.

Choi, Jang Jip. 1993. Political cleavages in South Korea. Pp. 13–50 in *State and society in contemporary Korea*, ed. Hagen Koo. Ithaca: Cornell University Press.

Christensen, Thomas. 1996. *Useful adversaries: Grand strategy, domestic mobilization, and Sino-American conflict, 1947–1958*. Princeton: Princeton University Press.

———. 1999. China, the U.S.-Japan alliance, and the security dilemma in East Asia. *International Security* 23 (4):49–80.

———. 2003. China, the U.S.-Japan alliance and the security dilemma in East Asia. Pp. 25–26 in *International relations theory and the Asia-Pacific*, ed. G. John Ikenberry and Michael Mastanduno. New York: Columbia University Press.

Chubin, Shahram. 2006. *Iran's nuclear ambitions*. Washington, D.C.: Carnegie Endowment for International Peace.

Chubin, Shahram, and Robert S. Litwak. 2003. Debating Iran's nuclear aspirations. *Washington Quarterly* 26 (4):99–114.

Chung, Kiwon. 1963. The North Korean People's Army and the Party. Pp. 105–24 in *North Korea today*, ed. Robert A. Scalapino. New York: Praeger.

CIA (Central Intelligence Agency). 2004. *Iraq Survey Group Final Report*. Comprehensive Report of the Special Advisor to the DCI on Iraq's WMD. Washington, D.C., September 30, 2004.

Cirincione, Joseph. 2000. Querying Saddam's bombmaker. *Carnegie Endowment Proliferation Brief* 3, no. 34 (November 21). Available at http://www.carnegieendowment.org/publications/index.cfm?fa=view&id=562&prog=zgp&proj=znpp.

Cirincione, Joseph, Jon B. Wolfsthal, and Miriam Rajkumar. 2002. *Deadly arsenals: Tracking weapons of mass destruction*. Washington, D.C.: Carnegie Endowment for International Peace.

———. 2005. *Deadly arsenals: Nuclear, biological and chemical threats*. 2nd ed. Washington, D.C.: Carnegie Endowment for International Peace.

Cliff, Roger. 1998. Taiwan: In the dragon's shadow. Pp. 288–314 in *Asian security practice: Material and ideational influences*, ed. Muthiah Alagappa. Stanford: Stanford University Press.

Clinton, Bill. 2004. *My life*. New York: Knopf.

CNSW (Center for Nonproliferation Studies). Visit website at http://cns.miis.edu.

Cohen, Avner. 1998. *Israel and the bomb*. New York: Columbia University Press.

Collier, David, Jason Seawright, and Gerardo L. Munck. 2004. Pp. 21–52 in *Rethinking social inquiry*, ed. Brady and Collier. Lanham, Md.: Rowman and Littlefield.

Congressional Resolution 21. 2007. 110th Congress, House of Representatives, January 9. Available at http://frwebgate.access.gpo.gov/cgi-bin/getdoc.cgi?dbname=110_cong_bills&docid=f:hc21ih.txt.pdf.

Cooper, John F. 1979. Taiwan's options. *Asian Affairs* 5:282–94.

Cooper, Richard. 1994. Korea's balance of international payments. Pp. 261–94 in *Macroeconomic policy and adjustment in Korea, 1970–1990*, ed. Stephan Haggard et al. Cambridge: Harvard University Press.

Cordesman, Anthony H. 1991. *Weapons of mass destruction in the Middle East*. London: Brassey's.

———. 2000. Iranian arms transfers: The facts. Center for Strategic and International Studies, October 30. Available at http://search.msn.com/results.aspx?q=csis-iranarmstransf&FORM=MSNH.

———. 2004. Weapons of mass destruction in the Middle East. Paper. Center for International and Strategic Studies. Available at http://www.csis.org/index.php?option=com_csis_pubs&task=view&id=1714.

Cotton, James. 1993. North Korea's nuclear ambitions. Pp. 94–106 in *Asia's international role in the post-Cold War era*, Adelphi Paper no. 275, part I. London: IISS.

Cox, Dan and Drury A. Cooper. 2006. Democratic sanctions: Connecting the democratic peace and economic sanctions. *Journal of Peace Research* 43 (6):709–22.

Cumings, Bruce. 1984. The origins and development of the Northeast Asian political economy: Industrial sectors, product cycles, and political consequences. *International Organization* 38 (1):1–40.

———. 1990. *The origins of the Korean War. Vol. II: The roaring of the cataract 1947–1950*. Princeton: Princeton University Press.

———. 1993. The corporate state in North Korea. Pp. 197–230 in *State and society in contemporary Korea*, ed. Hagen Koo. Ithaca: Cornell University Press.

———. 2004. *North Korea: Another country*. New York: New Press.

Curtis, Gerald. 1984. The domestic roots of Japanese foreign policy. Working paper no. 31. Toronto: Joint Centre of Modern East Asia's Canada and the Pacific Programme, University of Toronto-York University.

———. 1988. *The Japanese way of politics*. Washington, D.C.: Columbia Books.

CWIHP (Cold War International History Project). Visit website at http://www .wilsoncenter.org/index.cfm?topic_id=1409&fuseaction=topics.home.

Dahl, Robert. 1985. *Controlling nuclear weapons: Democracy versus guardianship*. Syracuse, N.Y.: Syracuse University Press.

DeSutter, Paula A. 1997. *Denial and jeopardy: Deterring Iranian use of NBC weapons*. Washington, D.C.: National Defense University Press.

Dower, John W. 1993. *Japan in war and peace*. New York: New Press.

Dowty, Alan. 1978. Nuclear proliferation: The Israeli case. *International Studies Quarterly* 22 (1):79–120.

———. 1995. The enigma of opacity: Israel's nuclear weapons program as a field of study. *Israel Studies Forum* 20 (2):3–21.

———. 1998. *The Jewish state: A century later*. Berkeley: University of California Press.

———. 2005. *Israel/Palestine*. Cambridge: Polity.

Doyle, Michael W. 1983. Kant, liberal legacies, and foreign affairs. *Philosophy and Public Affairs* 12 (3):205–35.

———. 1986. Liberalism and world politics. *American Political Science Review* 80 (4):1151–69.

DNSA (Digital National Security Archive). Visit website at http://nsarchive.chad wyck.com.

Drezner, Daniel. 1999. *The sanctions paradox: Economic statecraft and international relations*. Cambridge: Cambridge University Press.

Dunn, Lewis A. 1982. *Controlling the bomb*. New Haven: Yale University Press.

———. 1998. On proliferation watch: Some reflections on the past quarter century. *The Nonproliferation Review* 5 (3). Available at http://cns.miis.edu/pubs/ npr/vol05/53/dunn53.pdf.

Dwor-Frécaut, Dominique. 2004. Korea: Long-term decline in the DPRK Premium. Paper. Barclays Capital Research. Available at http://69.44.62.160/ archives/DPRKbriefingbook/transition/index.html.

Eberstadt, Nicholas. 2006. Why hasn't North Korea collapsed? Pp. 268–98 in *North Korea: The politics of regime survival*, ed. Young Whan Kihl and Hong Nack Kim. New York: M. E. Sharp.

Eckstein, Harry. 1975. Case studies and theory in political science. Pp. 79–138 in *Strategies of inquiry*, vol. 7, ed. Fred Greenstein and Nelson Polsby. Reading, Mass.: Addison-Wesley.

Einhorn, Robert J. 2004. Egypt: Frustrated but still on a non-nuclear course. In *The nuclear tipping point: Why states reconsider their nuclear choices*, ed. Kurt M. Campbell et al. Washington, D.C.: Brookings Institution Press.

Eisenstadt, Michael. 1998. The military dimension. Pp. 71–98 in *Iran under Khatami: A political, economic, and military assessment*, ed. Patrick Clawson, Michael Eisenstadt, Eliyahu Kanovsky, and David Menashri. Washington, D.C.: Washington Institute for Near East Policy.

Ellsberg, Daniel. 2005. Vanunu's threat to "ambiguity" and to Israel's national security. April 17, 2005. Available at http://www.nonviolence.org/vanunu/20050417ellsberg.html.

Elman, Miriam Fendius, ed. 1997. *Paths to peace: Is democracy the answer?* Cambridge: MIT Press.

Endicott, John E. 1975. *Japan's nuclear option: Political, technical, and strategic factors*. New York: Praeger.

———. 1999. In Morton H. Halperin: The nuclear dimension of the U.S.-Japan alliance. Posted on the Nautilus Institute. Available at http://www.nautilus.org/archives/library/security/papers/US-Japan-1.html.

Esfahani, Hadi S., and Farzad Taheripour. 2002. Hidden public expenditures and the economy in Iran. *International Journal of Middle East Studies* 34:691–718.

Eshkol, Levi. 1965. *Amarot : mivhar amarot mi-tokh ha-ketavim, ha-maamarim veha-neumim*. Ed. Aleksander Manor. Tel Aviv: Orli.

———. 1967. *Be-itsumo shel maavak*. Jerusalem: Merkaz ha-hasbarah be-Misrad Rosh ha-Memshalah.

Evron, Yair. 1974. Israel and the atom: The uses and misuses of ambiguity, 1957–1967. *Orbis* 17 (4):1330.

———. 1991. Israel. In *Security with nuclear weapons?* ed. R. C. Karp. Oxford: Oxford University Press.

———. 1994. *Israel's nuclear dilemma*. Ithaca: Cornell University Press.

Fahmy, Nabil. 2001. Prospects for arms control and proliferation in the Middle East. *Nonproliferation Review* (Summer):1–6.

Farr, Warner D. 1999. The third temple's holy of holies: Israel's nuclear weapons. *Counterproliferation Papers*, Future Warfare Series, no. 2 (September).

FASW (Federation of American Scientists). Visit website at http://www.fas.org.

Feinstein, Lee, and Anne-Marie Slaughter. 2004. A duty to prevent. *Foreign Affairs* 83 (1):136–55.

Feldman, Shai. 1982. *Israeli nuclear deterrence: A strategy for the 1980s*. New York: Columbia University Press.

Feldman, Shai, and Abdullah Toukan, eds. 1997. *Bridging the gap: A future security architecture for the Middle East*. Lanham, Md.: Rowman and Littlefield.

Feldner, Yotam. 2003a. Egypt rethinks its nuclear program. Part I: Scientific and technological capability vs. international commitments. Middle East Media

Research Institute Inquiry and Analysis Series no. 118. January 17. Available at http://memri.org/bin/articles.cgi?Page=archives&Area=ia&ID=IA11803#_edn4.

———. 2003b. Egypt rethinks its nuclear program. Part II: The egyptian nuclear lobby. Middle East Media Research Institute Inquiry and Analysis Series no. 118. January 17. Available at http://memri.org/bin/articles.cgi?Page=archives&Area=ia&ID=IA11903#_edn3.

———. 2003c. Egypt rethinks its nuclear program. Part III: The nuclear lobby (continued). The Middle East Media Research Institute Inquiry and Analysis Series no. 120. January 22. Available at http://memri.org/bin/articles.cgi?Page=archives&Area=ia&ID=IA12003.

Ferguson, Charles D., and William C. Potter. 2005. *The four faces of nuclear terrorism*. New York: Routledge.

Finnemore, Martha, and Kathryn Sikkink. 1998. International norm dynamics and political change. *International Organization* 52 (4):887–917.

Flapan, Simha. 1974. Nuclear power in the Middle East. *New Outlook* (July):46–54.

Foot, Rosemary. 1990. *A substitute for victory: The politics of peacemaking at the Korean armistice talks*. Ithaca: Cornell University Press.

Freedman, Lawrence. 1975. "Israel's Nuclear Policy." *Survival* 17, no. 3 (May–June):114–20.

———. 2004. *Deterrence*. Malden, Mass.: Polity.

Freier, Shalhevet. 1985. Israel. In *Non-proliferation: The why and the wherefore*, ed. Josef Goldblat. London: Taylor and Francis.

———. 1993. A nuclear-weapon-free-zone (NWFZ) in the Middle East and its ambience. Paper. Washington Institute for Near East Policy. July 14.

Frieden, Jeffry A., and Ronald Rogowski. 1996. The impact of the international economy on national policies: An analytic overview. Pp. 25–47 in *Internationalization and domestic politics*, ed. Robert O. Keohane and Helen V. Milner. Cambridge: Cambridge University Press.

Fukai, Shigeko N. 1999. The impact of changes in the international system on domestic politics: Japan in the 1990s. Pp. 199–225 in *Globalism, regionalism, and nationalism: Asia in search of its role in the twenty-first century*, ed. Yoshinobu Yamamoto. Oxford: Blackwell.

Fukuyama, Francis. 2005. Re-envisioning Asia. *Foreign Affairs* 84 (1).

Garrett, Geoffrey, and Peter Lange. 1996. Internationalization, institutions and political change. Pp. 48–75 in *Internationalization and domestic politics*, ed. Robert O. Keohane and Helen V. Milner. Cambridge: Cambridge University Press.

Gaubatz, Kurt T. 1996. Democratic states and commitment in international relations. *International Organization* 50 (1):109–39.

Gavin, Francis J. 2004/05. Blasts from the past: Proliferation lessons from the 1960s. *International Security* 29 (3):100–135.

Gehring, Verna. 2004. The nuclear taboo. Manuscript, Institute for Philosophy and Public Policy. Available at http://www.publicpolicy.umd.edu/IPPP/Summer00/nuclear_taboo.htm.

George, Alexander L. 1993. *Bridging the gap: Theory and practice in foreign policy*. Washington, D.C.: United States Institute of Peace Press.

George, Alexander L., and Andrew Bennett. 2005. *Case studies and theory development in the social sciences*. Cambridge: MIT Press.

George, Alexander, and Tim McKeown. 1985. Case studies and theories of organizational decision making. Pp. 43–68 in *Advances in information processing in organizations*, ed. Robert Coulam and Richard Smith. Greenwich, Conn.: JAI Press.

Gereffi, Gary, and Donald L. Wyman, eds. 1990. *Manufacturing miracles: Paths of industrialization in Latin America and East Asia*. Princeton: Princeton University Press.

Gillette, Robert. 1978. U.S. squelched apparent S. Korea A-bomb drive. *Los Angeles Times* (November 4):A1.

Gilpin, Robert. 2000. *The challenge of global capitalism: The world economy in the 21st century*. Princeton: Princeton University Press.

Glaser, Charles L. 2000. The causes and consequences of arms races. *Annual Review of Political Science* 3:251–76.

Gleysteen, William H. 1999. *Massive entanglement, marginal influence: Carter and Korea in crisis*. Washington, D.C.: Brookings Institution Press.

Glosserman, Brad. 2004. Nuclear sword of Damocles. *Japan Times*, August 3. Available at http://www.japantimes.co.jp.

Glosserman, Brad, and Yumiko Nakagawa. 2002. Trust Japanese democracy. *PacNet Newsletter* 28, no. 26 (June). Available at http://www.csis.org.

Goertz, Gary. 2005. *Social science concepts: A user's guide*. Princeton: Princeton University Press.

Goldschmidt, Pierre. 2003. The increasing risk of nuclear proliferation: Lessons learned. *International Atomic Energy Agency Bulletin* 45 (2):24–27.

———. 2007. Priority steps to strengthen the nonproliferation regime. Carnegie Endowment, Policy Outlook No. 33 (January). Available at http://www.carnegie endowment.org/files/goldschmidt_priority_steps_final.pdf.

Gourevitch, Peter. 1978. The second image reversed: The international sources of domestic politics. *International Organization* 32 (4):881–911.

———. 1986. *Politics in hard times: Comparative responses to international economic crises*. Ithaca: Cornell University Press.

———. 1999. The governance problem in strategic interaction. Pp. 115–36 in *Strategic choice and international relations*, ed. David Lake and Robert Powell. Princeton: Princeton University Press.

Gray, Colin S. 1999. *The second nuclear age*. Boulder, Colo.: Lynne Rienner.

Green, Michael J. 1995. *Arming Japan: Defense production, alliance politics, and the postwar search for autonomy*. New York: Columbia University Press.

Gregory, Barbara M. 1995. Egypt's nuclear program: Assessing supplier-based and other developments constraints. *Nonproliferation Review* (Fall):20–27.

GSN (Global Security Newswire). Visit website at http://www.nti.org/d_newswire/issues.

GSW (GlobalSecurity.org). Visit website at http://www.globalsecurity.org.

Ha, Young-sun. 1978. Nuclearization of small states and world order: The case of Korea. *Asian Survey* 18 (11):1134–51.

Haas, Ernst. 1953. The balance of power: Prescription, concept, or propaganda? *World Politics* 5 (4):442–77.

Haggard, Stephan. 1994a. Macroeconomic policy through the first oil shock, 1970–75. Pp. 23–48 in *Macroeconomic policy and adjustment in Korea, 1970–1990*, ed. Stephan Haggard et al.

———. 1994b. From the heavy industry plan to stabilization: Macroeconomic policy, 1976–1980. Pp. 49–74. *Macroeconomic policy and adjustment in Korea, 1970–1990*, ed. Stephan Haggard et al.

———. 1995. Inflation and stabilization. Pp. 447–59 in *International political economy: Perspectives on global power and wealth*, ed. Jeffry A. Frieden and David A. Lake. London: Routledge.

Haggard, Stephan, and Tun-Jen Cheng. 1987. State and foreign capital in East Asian NICs. Pp. 84–135 in *The political economy of the new Asian industrialism*, ed. by Frederic Deyo. Ithaca: Cornell University Press.

Haggard, Stephan, Richard N. Cooper, and Chung-in Moon. 1993. Policy reform in Korea. Pp. 294–332 in *Political and economic interactions in economic policy reform: Evidence from eight countries*, ed. Robert H. Bates and Anne O. Krueger. Oxford: Blackwell.

Haggard, Stephan, Richard Cooper, Susan Collins, Choongso Kim, and Sung-Tae Ro. 1994. *Macroeconomic policy and adjustment in Korea, 1970–1990*. Cambridge: Harvard University Press.

Haggard, Stephan, and Robert R. Kaufman. 1995. *The political economy of democratic transitions*. Princeton: Princeton University Press.

Haggard, Stephan, Byung-Kook Kim, and Chung-In Moon. 1990. *The transition to export-led growth in South Korea: 1954–66*. Washington, D.C.: World Bank.

Haggard, Stephan, and Chung-in Moon. 1993. The State, politics, and economic development in postwar South Korea. Pp. 51–94 in *State and society in contemporary Korea*, ed. Hagen Koo. Ithaca: Cornell University Press.

Haggard, Stephan, and Marcus Noland. 2005. Hearings on the North Korean Human Rights Act of 2004: Issues and implementation. Subcommittee on Africa, Global Human Rights, and International Operations, United States House of Representatives, April 28. Available at http://66.39.74.146/wpcontent/uploads/2006/07/Noland042805Hearing.pdf.

———. 2007. *Famine in North Korea: Markets, aid, and reform*. New York: Columbia University Press.

Halliday, Fred. 2005. *The Middle East in international relations: Power, politics and ideology*. New York: Cambridge.

Halperin, Morton H. 1999. The Nuclear Dimension of the U.S.-Japan Alliance. Paper. Nautilus Institute. Available at http://www.nautilus.org/archives/library/security/papers/US-Japan-1.html.

Hamm, Taik-young. 2005. "North Korea: Economic foundations of military capability and the inter-Korean balance." Pp. 167–96 in *North Korea: 2005 and beyond*, ed. Philip W. Yun and Gi-Wok Shin. Stanford University: The Walter H. Shorenstein Asia-Pacific Research Center.

Hamza, Khidir. 1998. Inside Saddam's secret nuclear program. *Bulletin of the Atomic Scientists* 54 (5):26–33.

Hamza, Khidir, and Jeff Stein. 2000. Presentation. Carnegie Endowment Nonproliferation Project. Available at http://www.ceip.org/files/projects/npp/resources/hamzatranscript.htm.

Handoussa, Heba, and Nemat Shafik. 1993. The economics of peace: The Egyptian case. Pp. 19–54 in *The economics of Middle East peace: Views from the region*, ed. Stanley Fischer, Dani Rodrik, and Elias Tuma. Cambridge: MIT Press.

Hardin, Russell, ed. 1985. *Nuclear deterrence: Ethics and strategy.* Chicago: Chicago University Press.

Harkabi, Yehoshafat. 1988. *Israel's fateful hour.* New York: Harper and Row.

Harkavy, Robert E. 1977a. Spectre of a Middle Eastern holocaust: The strategic and diplomatic implications of the Israeli nuclear weapons program. Monograph Series in World Affairs, University of Denver Graduate School of International Studies 14 (4).

———. 1977b. The pariah state syndrome. *Orbis* 21 (3):623–49.

———. 1981. Pariah states and nuclear proliferation. *International Organization* 35 (1):135–63.

Harrison, Selig S., ed. 1996. *Japan's nuclear future: The plutonium debate and East Asia security.* Washington, D.C.: Carnegie Endowment for International Peace.

———. 2002. *Korean endgame: A strategy for reunification and U.S. disengagement.* Princeton: Princeton University Press.

———. 2005. Getting around Pyongyang's hard-liners. Nautilus Institute Policy Forum Online 5 (55A), July 2005. Available at http://www.nautilus.org/fora/security/0555Harrison.html.

Hashmi, Sohail H. 2004. Islamic ethics and weapons of mass destruction: An argument for nonproliferation. Pp. 321–52 in *Ethics and weapons of mass destruction: Religious and secular perspectives,* ed. Sohail H. Hashmi and Steven P. Lee. New York: Cambridge University Press.

Hayes, Peter. 1991. *Pacific powderkeg: American nuclear dilemmas in Korea.* Seoul: Han-ul Press.

———. 1993. The Republic of Korea and the nuclear issue. Pp. 51–83 in *Asian flashback: Security and the Korean peninsula,* ed. Andrew Mack. Canberra: Australian National University and Allen & Unwin.

———. nd. North Korea's challenge to the nuclear non-proliferation treaty. Unpublished paper.

Haykal, Mohamed Hasanayn. 1973. *The Cairo documents; The inside story of Nasser and his relationship with world leaders, rebels, and statesmen.* Garden City, N.Y.: Doubleday.

———. 1975. *The road to Ramadan.* London: Collins.

———. 1978. *Sphinx and commissar: The rise and fall of Soviet influence in the Arab world.* London: Collins.

HDR (Human Development Report). 1994. United Nations Development Program: Human Development Report. Oxford: Oxford University Press.

Herrmann, Richard K., and Jonathan W. Keller. 2004. Beliefs, values and strategic choice: U.S. leaders' decisions to engage, contain and use force in an era of globalization. *Journal of Politics* 66 (2):557–80.

Hersh, Seymour M. 1993. *The Samson option: Israel's nuclear arsenal and American foreign policy.* New York: Vintage.

Heston, Alan, and Robert Summers. 1991. 1995. Penn World Table. Available at http://pwt.econ.upenn.edu/php_site/pwt_index.php.

Hewedi, A. 1989. *Militarization and security in the Middle East.* London: Frances Pinter.

Hirschman, Albert O. 1986. *Rival views of market societies and other recent essays.* New York: Viking.

Hoodbhoy, Pervez. 1993. Myth-building: The 'Islamic' bomb. *Bulletin of the Atomic Scientists* 49 (5):42–49.

Horowitz, D. 1993. The Israeli concept of national security. Pp. 11–54 in *National security and democracy in Israel*, ed. Avner Yaniv. Boulder, Colo.: Lynne Rienner.

Hosokawa, Morihiro. 1998. Are U.S. troops in Japan still needed? Reforming the alliance. *Foreign Affairs* (July/August):2–5.

Hufbauer, Gary C., Jeffrey J. Schott, and Kimberly Ann Elliott. 1990. *Economic sanctions reconsidered*. Washington, D.C.: Institute for International Economics.

Hughes, Christopher W. 2004a. *Japan's security agenda: Military, economic, and environmental dimensions*. Boulder, Colo.: Lynne Rienner.

———. 2004b. Japan's re-emergence as a 'Normal' military power. *Adelphi Paper* 368: 9.

Hurd, Ian. 2005. The strategic use of liberal internationalism: Libya and the UN sanctions, 1992–2003. *International Organization* 59 (3):495–526.

Husbands, Jo L. 1982. The Prestige States. Pp. 112–38 in *Nuclear proliferation in the 1980s*, ed. William H. Kincade and Christoph Bertram. New York: St. Martin's.

Hwang, Balbina Y. 2003. Curtailing North Korea's illicit activities: Backgrounder #1679. Paper, The Heritage Foundation. Available at http://www .heritage.org.

Hwang, Jihwan. 2003. Rethinking the East Asian balance of power: historical antagonism, internal balancing, and the Korean-Japanese security relationship. *World Affairs*, September 22, 2003.

Hymans, Jacques. 2006. *The psychology of nuclear proliferation: Identity, emotions, and foreign policy*. New York: Cambridge University Press.

Hymans, Jacques, Seung-young Kim, and Henning Riecke. 2001. To go or not to go: South and North Korea's nuclear decisions in comparative context. *Journal of East Asian Studies* 1 (1):91–153.

IAEA (International Atomic Energy Agency). Visit website at http://www.iaea .org.

Ibrahim, Saad Eddin. 1994. Arab elites and societies after the Gulf crisis. Pp. 77–90 in *The Arab world today*, ed. Dan Tschirgi. Boulder, Colo.: Lynne Rienner.

ICG (International Crisis Group). 2004. Korea backgrounder: How the South views its brother from another planet. Asia Report 89, December 14.

ICG (International Crisis Group). 2005a. North Korea: Can the iron fist accept the invisible hand? Asia Report, no. 96, April 25. Available at http://www .crisisgroup.org/home/index.cfm?id=3388&l=1.

———. 2005b. Iran: What does Ahmadi-Nejad's victory mean? *Middle East Briefing*, no.18, August 4.

IISS (International Institute for Strategic Studies). 1992–93, 1995–96. *The Military Balance*. London: Brassey's.

Ikenberry, G. John, and Michael Mastanduno, eds. 2003. *International relations theory and the Asia-Pacific*. New York: Columbia University Press.

Imai, Ryūkichi. 1974. Plutonium issues: The view from Japan. *Asia Pacific Review* 1 (1).

———. 1975. *The outlook for Japan's nuclear future.* Discussion paper no. 63. Santa Monica: California Seminar on Arms Control and Foreign Policy.

Inbar, Efraim. 1986. Israel and nuclear weapons since October 1973. In *Security or Armageddon: Israel's nuclear strategy,* ed. Louis Rene Beres. Lexington, Mass.: Lexington Books.

———. 1991. *War and peace in Israeli politics: Labor party positions on national security.* Boulder, Colo.: Lynne Rienner.

Inoguchi, Takashi. 1991. *Japan's international relations.* London: Pinter.

———. 1993. *Japan's foreign policy in an era of global change.* London: Pinter.

———. 1997. A peace-and-security taxonomy. In *North-east Asian regional security: The role of international institutions,* ed. Takashi Inoguchi and Grant B. Stillman. New York: United Nations University Press.

———, ed. 2002. *Japan's Asian policy: Revival and response.* New York: Palgrave Macmillan.

———. 2004. "Tinkering every 15 Years: A new major turn in Japan's foreign policy?" *Japan Spotlight* (March-April):38–39.

Intriligator, Michael D., and Dagobert L. Brito. 1981. Nuclear proliferation and the probability of nuclear war. *Public Choice* 37 (2):247–60.

Investigation of Korean-American Relations. 1978. Report of the Subcommittee on International Organizations of the Committee on International Relations, U.S. House of Representatives. Washington, D.C.: U.S. Government Printing Office.

ISG (Iraq Survey Group). 2004. Comprehensive report of the Special Advisor to the DCI on Iraq's WMD, by Charles Duelfer, Central Intelligence Agency. Available at http://www.cia.gov/cia/reports/iraq_wmd_2004/index.html.

ISISW (Institute for Science and International Security). Visit website at http://www.isis-online.org/.

Jabber, Paul. 1971. *Israel and nuclear weapons: Present option and future strategies.* London: Chatto and Windus for the International Institute for Strategic Studies.

———. 1977. A nuclear Middle East: Infrastructure, likely military postures, and prospects for strategic stability. Los Angeles: Central for Arms Control and International Security.

———. 1981. *Not by war alone: Security and arms control in the Middle East.* Berkeley: University of California Press.

Jacoby, Neil H. 1966. *U.S. aid to Taiwan: A study of foreign aid, self-help, and development.* New York: Praeger.

Jansen, Johannes J. G. 1997. *The dual nature of Islamic fundamentalism.* Ithaca: Cornell University Press.

Jeon, Jei Guk. 1995. Exploring the three varieties of East Asia's state-guided development model: Korea, Singapore, and Taiwan. *Studies in Comparative International Development* 30 (3):70–88.

Jentleson, Bruce W. 1996. The Middle East arms control and regional security (ACRS) talks: Progress, problems, and prospects. La Jolla, Calif.: Institute on Global Conflict and Cooperation.

Jentleson, Bruce W., and Dalia Kaye. 1997. Explaining the limits of regional security cooperation: The Middle East ACRS Case. Presented at the Annual Conference of the American Political Science Association, Washington, D.C., August 28–31.

Jentleson, Bruce W., and Christopher A. Whytock. 2005/06. Who "won" Libya: The force-diplomacy debate and its implications for theory and policy. *International Security* 30 (3):47–86.

Jervis, Robert. 1976. *Perception and misperception in international politics.* Princeton: Princeton University Press.

———. 1982. Security regimes. *International Organization* 36 (2):357–78.

———. 2002. Correspondence: Institutionalized disagreement. *International Security* 27 (1):174–85.

Joffe, Josef. 1993. Democracy and deterrence: What have they done to each other? Pp. 108–25 in *Ideas and ideals: Essays on politics in honor of Stanley Hoffmann*, ed. Linda B. Miller and Michael J. Smith. Boulder, Colo.: Westview.

Johnson, Chalmers. 1982. *MITI and the Japanese miracle: The growth of industrial policy, 1925–1975.* Stanford: Stanford University Press.

———. 1987. Political institutions and economic performance: The government-business relationship in Japan, South Korea, and Taiwan. Pp. 136–64 in *The political economy of the new Asian industrialism*, ed. Frederic Deyo. Ithaca: Cornell University Press.

Johnston, Alastair I. 1995. *Cultural realism: Strategic culture and grand strategy in Chinese history.* Princeton: Princeton University Press.

———. 1999. *Engaging China: The management of an emerging power.* New York: Routledge.

———. 2001. Treating international institutions as social environments. *International Studies Quarterly* 45 (4):487–515.

Jones, Leroy P., and Il Sakong. 1980. *Government, business, and entrepreneurship in economic development: The Korean case.* Cambridge: Harvard University Press.

Jones, Peter. 1997a. New directions in Middle East deterrence: Implications for arms control. *Middle East Review of International Affairs* 1 (4). Available at http://meria.idc.ac.il/journal/1997/issue4/jv1n4a4.html.

———. 1997b. Arms control in the Middle East: Some reflections on ACRS. *Security Dialogue* 28 (1):57–70.

———. 1998. Iran's threat perceptions and arms control policies. *The Nonproliferation Review* (Fall):39–55.

Jones, Rodney W., and Mark G. McDonough. 1998. *Tracking nuclear proliferation.* Washington, D.C.: Carnegie Endowment for International Peace.

Junnosuke, Kishida. 1973. Japan's non-nuclear policy. *Survival* 15, no. 1 (January/February):15–20.

Kahler, Miles. 1995. *International institutions and the political economy of integration.* Washington, D.C.: Brookings Institution.

———. 2000. Conclusion: The causes and consequences of legalization. *International Organization* 54 (3):661–83.

———. 2002. The state of the state in world politics. Pp. 56–83 in *Political science: The state of the discipline*, ed. Ira Katznelson and Helen Milner. New York: Norton.

Kahn, Herman. 1970. *The emerging Japanese super-state: Challenge and response*. Englewood Cliffs, N.J.: Prentice-Hall.

Kakuei, Tanaka. 1973. *Building a new Japan: A plan for remodeling the Japanese archipelago*. Tokyo: Simul Press.

Kamiya, Matake. 2002–3. Nuclear Japan: Oxymoron or coming soon? *Washington Quarterly* 26 (1):63–75.

———. 2003. A disillusioned Japan confronts North Korea. *Arms Control Today* (May).

Kaneko, Kumao. 1996. Japan needs no umbrella. *Bulletin of the Atomic Scientists* 53 (2):46–51.

Kang, David. 1998. North Korea: Deterrence through danger. Pp. 234–63 in *Asian security practice: Material and ideational influences*, ed. Muthiah Alagappa. Stanford: Stanford University Press.

Kang, Jungmin, Peter Hayes, Li Bin, Tatsujiro Suzuki, and Richard Tanter. 2005. South Korea's nuclear surprise. *Bulletin of the Atomic Scientists* 61 (1):40–50.

Karawan, Ibrahim A. 1994. Sadat and the Egyptian-Israeli peace revisited. *International Journal of Middle East Studies* 26 (2):249–66.

Karem, M. 1988. *A nuclear-weapon-free-zone in the Middle East: Problems and prospects*. New York: Greenwood.

Karpin, Michael I. 2006. *The bomb in the basement: How Israel went nuclear and what that means for the rest of the world*. New York: Simon and Schuster.

Karsh, Efraim. 1993. Rational ruthlessness: Non-conventional and missile warfare in the Iran-Iraq War. Pp. 31–48 in *Non-conventional weapons proliferation in the Middle East*, ed. Efraim Karsh, Martin Navias, and Philip Sabin. Oxford: Clarendon Press.

———. 2000. "Nuclear weapons and the post-Cold-War Middle East: Business as usual." In *Alternative nuclear futures*, ed. John Baylis and Robert O'Neill. Oxford: Oxford University Press.

Karsh, Efraim, and Yezid Sayigh. 1994. A cooperative security approach to Arab-Israeli peace. *Survival* 36 (1):114–25.

Kase, Yuri. 2001. The costs and benefits of Japan's nuclearization: An insight into the 1968/70 Internal Report. *Nonproliferation Review* (Summer):55–68.

Katzenstein, Peter J., ed. 1996. *Cultural norms and national security: Police and military in postwar Japan*. Ithaca: Cornell University Press.

Katzenstein, Peter, and Takashi Shiraishi, eds. 1997. *Network power: Japan and Asia*. Ithaca: Cornell University Press.

Kay, David. 1993. Iraqi inspections: Lessons learned. *Eye on Supply* (Winter):89.

Kaye, Dalia Dassa. 2001. *Beyond the handshake: Multilateral cooperation in the Arab-Israeli peace process, 1991–1996*. New York: Columbia University Press.

Keck, Margaret E., and Kathryn Sikkink. 1998. *Activists beyond borders: Advocacy networks in international politics*. Ithaca: Cornell University Press.

Keddie, Nikki R. 2006. *Modern Iran: Roots and results of revolution*. New Haven: Yale University Press.

Kedourie, Elie. 1992. *Politics in the Middle East*. New York: Oxford University Press.

Keller, Bill. 2003. The thinkable. *New York Times Magazine*, May 4.

Keohane, Robert O. 1984. *After hegemony: Cooperation and discord in the world political economy*. Princeton: Princeton University Press.

Keohane, Robert O., and Helen V. Milner, eds. 1996. *Internationalization and domestic politics*. Cambridge: Cambridge University Press.

Kerr, Malcolm H. 1971. *The Arab cold war: Gamal 'Abd al-Nasir and his rivals, 1958–1970*. New York: Royal Institute of International Affairs.

Khadduri, Imad. 2003. *Iraq's nuclear mirage: Memoirs and delusions*. Toronto: Springhead.

Khalaf, Roula. 2004. Iranian nuclear ambitions worry Gulf Arab states. *Financial Times,* December 18.

Khalaji, Mehdi. 2006. Iranian President Ahmadinezhad's relations with Supreme Leader Khamenei. Washington Institute of Near East Policy, Policy Watch #1147, September 12. Available at http://www.washingtoninstitute.org/templateC05.php?CID=2514.

Khosrokhavar, Farhad. 2004. The new conservatives take a turn. Middle East Report Online at http://www.merip.org/mer/mer233/khosrokhavar.html.

Kibaroglu, Mustafa. 2006. Good for the Shah, banned for the mullahs: The West and Iran's quest for nuclear power. *Middle East Journal* 60 (2):207–33.

Kihl, Young Whan, and Hong Nack Kim, eds. 2006. *North Korea—The politics of regime survival*. New York: M. E. Sharpe.

Kim, C. I. Eugene. 1988. North Korea's perspective on northeast Asian security. Pp. 133–58 in *Northeast Asia security and peace: Toward the 1990s*, ed. Jung Hyun Shin, Tae-Hwan Kwak, and Edward Olsen. Seoul: Kyung Hee University Press.

Kim, Sung-Chull. 2006. *North Korea under Kim Jong Il: From consolidation to systemic dissonance*. Albany: State University of New York Press.

Kim, Taewoo. 2003. Living with North Korean bomb: Current debate in and future options for South Korea. *KIDA Papers*, no. 2 (June).

King, Gary, Robert O. Keohane, and Sidney Verba. 1994. *Designing social inquiry: Scientific inference in qualitative research*. Princeton: Princeton University Press.

Kissinger, Henry. 1957. *Nuclear weapons and foreign policy*. New York: Harper.

———. 2003. Why we can't withdraw from Asia." *Washington Post,* June 15.

Kitamura, Motoya. 1996. Japan's plutonium program: A proliferation threat." *Nonproliferation Review* 3 (Winter 1996).

Kleiman, Aharon, and Reuven Pedatzur. 1991. *Rearming Israel: Defense procurement through the 1990s*. Boulder, Colo.: Westview.

Klotz, Audie, and Cecelia M. Lynch. 2007. *Strategies for research in constructivist international relations*. New York: M. E. Sharpe.

Koh, Byung Chul. 1984. *The foreign policy systems of North and South Korea*. Berkeley and Los Angeles: University of California Press.

Komaie, Maryam, and Etel Solingen. 2007. Carrots, sticks, and nonproliferation: The case of rentier states. Manuscript. Department of Political Science, University of California Irvine.

Koo, Hagen, ed. 1993. *State and society in contemporary Korea*. Ithaca: Cornell University Press.

Korany, Bahgat, and Ali E. Hillal Dessouki, eds. 1991. *The foreign policies of Arab states: The challenge of change*. 2nd ed. Boulder, Colo.: Westview.

Kosaka, Masataka. 1982. *A history of postwar Japan*. New York: Harper and Row.

———. 1986. Theater nuclear weapons and Japan's defense policy. Pp. 123–40 in *The Soviet Far East military buildup: Nuclear dilemmas and Asian security*, ed. Richard H. Solomon and Masataka Kosaka. Dover, Mass.: Auburn House.

Kowert, Paul, and Jeffrey Legro. 1996. "Norms, identity and their limits: A theoretical reprise." Pp. 451–97 in *Cultural norms and national security: Police and military in postwar Japan*, ed. Peter Katzenstein. Ithaca: Cornell University Press.

Kratochwil, Friedrich, and John G. Ruggie. 1986. International organization: A state of the art on an art of the state. *International Organization* 40 (4):753–75.

Krueger, Anne O. 1993. *Political economy of policy reform in developing countries*. Cambridge: MIT Press.

Kuark, Yoon T. 1963. North Korea's industrial development during the post-war period. *China Quarterly* 14:51–64.

Kull, Steven. 2004. Survey says: Americans back arms control. *Arms Control Today* (June). Available at http://www.armscontrol.org/act/2004_06/Kull.asp.

Kurosaki, Akira. 2003. Domestic politics and nuclear disarmament diplomacy: Limits of the Japanese antinuclear movement. 44th Annual International Studies Association Convention, Portland, Oregon, February 27.

Kurosawa, Mitsuru. 2004. Moving beyond the debate on a nuclear Japan. *Nonproliferation Review* 11 (3):110–37.

Kwark, Yoon T. 1963. North Korea's industrial development during the post-war period. Pp. 51–64 in *North Korea today*, ed. Robert A. Scalapino. New York: Praeger.

Landau, Emily. 2002. Egypt's nuclear dilemma. *Strategic Assessment* 5 (3). Available at http://www.tau.ac.il/jcss/sa/v5n3p5Lan.html.

Lavoy, Peter. 1993. Nuclear myths and the causes of nuclear proliferation. *Security Studies* 2 (2):192–212.

———. 2004. Predicting nuclear proliferation: A declassified documentary record. *Strategic Insights* 3 (1). Available at http://www.fas.org/man/eprint/lavoy.pdf.

Lebovic, James. 2007 *Deterring international terrorism and rogue states: U.S. National Security Policy after 9/11*. New York: Routledge.

Lebow, Richard N. 2000. What's so different about a counterfactual? *World Politics* 52 (4):550–85.

———. 2003. *The tragic vision of politics: Ethics, interests and orders*. New York: Cambridge University Press.

Legro, Jeffrey W., and Andrew Moravcsik. 1999. Is anyone still a realist? *International Security* 24 (2):5–55.

Levi, Michael A., and Michael E. O'Hanlon. 2005. *The future of arms control*. Washington, D.C.: Brookings Institution Press.

Levite, Ariel E. 2002/03. Never say never again: Nuclear reversal revisited. *International Security* 27 (3):59–88.

Levy, Jack S. 2000. The implications of framing and loss aversion for international conflict. Pp. 193–221 in *Handbook of War Studies II*, ed. Manus I. Midlarsky. Ann Arbor: University of Michigan Press.

———. 2002. Qualitative methods in international relations. Pp. 131–60 in *Millennial reflections on international studies: Evaluating methodology in international studies*, ed. Frank P. Harvey and Michael Brecher. Ann Arbor: University of Michigan Press.

Liberman, Peter. 2001. The rise and fall of the South African bomb. *International Security* 26 (2):45–86.

Lifton, Robert Jay, and Richard Falk. 1982. *Indefensible weapons.* New York: Basic Books.

Lind, Jennifer M. 2004. Pacifism or passing the buck? Testing theories of Japanese security policy. *International Security* 29 (1):92–121.

Lipson, Charles. 1984. International cooperation in economic and security affairs. *World Politics* 37 (1):1–23.

———. 2003. *Reliable partners: How democracies have made a separate peace.* Princeton: Princeton University Press.

Lo, Chih-cheng. 2001. Taiwan: The remaining challenges. Pp. 143–64 in *Coercion and governance: The declining political role of the military in Asia,* ed. Muthiah Alagappa. Stanford: Stanford University Press.

Lobell, Steven E. 1999. Second image reversed politics: Britain's choice of freer trade or imperial preferences, 1903–1906, 1917–1923, 1930–1932. *International Studies Quarterly* 43:671–94.

Lopez, George A., and David Cortright. 2004. Containing Iraq: Sanctions worked. *Foreign Affairs* 83 (4):90–103.

Mack, Andrew. 1996. Proliferation in Northeast Asia. The Henry L. Stimson Center, Occasional Paper Series 28 (July). Available at http://www.stimson.org/wmd/pdf/mack.pdf.

Mahoney, James. 2005. Clarifying comparative historical methodology. *Qualitative Methods: Newsletter of the American Political Science Association Organized Section on Qualitative Methods* 3 (1):19–22.

Makoto, Momoi. 1977. "Basic Trends in Japanese Security Policies." Pp. 341–64 in *The Foreign Policy of Modern Japan,* ed. Robert A. Scalapino. Berkeley: University of California Press.

———. 1978. Are there any alternative strategies for the defense of Japan?" Pp. 71–92 in *US-Japan relations and the security of East Asia: The next decade,* ed. Franklin B. Weinstein. Boulder, Colo.: Westview.

Mandelbaum, Michael. 1988. *The fate of nations—The search for national security in the nineteenth and twentieth centuries.* Cambridge: Cambridge University Press.

Mansfield, Edward D., and Jack Snyder. 1995. The dangers of democratization. *International Security* 20 (1):1–33.

———. 2005. *Elected to fight: Why emerging democracies go to war.* Cambridge: MIT Press.

Mansourov, Alexandre. 1994. North Korean decision-making processes regarding the nuclear issue. The Nautilus Institute, commissioned paper. Available at http://www.nautilus.org.

———. 1995. In search of a new identity: Revival of traditional politics and modernisation in post Kim Il Sung North Korea. Canberra, Australia: Research School of Pacific Studies, Australian National University.

———. 2004. Inside North Korea's black box: Reversing the optics. Pp. 160–225 in *North Korean policy elites,* ed. Oh Hassig, Kongdan. Alexandria, Va.: Institute for Defense Analyses.

———. 2006. Emergence of the Second Republic: The Kim regime adapts to the challenges of modernity. In Kihl and Kim, eds. 2006, 37–58.

Maoz, Zeev. 2003. The mixed blessing of Israel's nuclear policy. *International Security* 28 (2):44–77.

March, James G., and Johan P. Olson. 1998. The institutional dynamics of international political orders. *International Organization* 52 (4):943–69.

Margalit, Dan. 1997. *Raiti otam.* Tel-Aviv: Zemorah-Betan.

Marr, Phebe. 1985. *The modern history of Iraq.* Boulder, Colo.: Westview.

Mastanduno, Michael. 2003. Incomplete hegemony: The United States and security order in Asia. Pp. 141–70 in *Asian security order*, ed. Muthiah Alagappa. Stanford: Stanford University Press.

May, Michael. 1994. Nuclear weapons supply and demand. *American Scientist* 82 (6):526–37.

Mazarr, Michael J. 1995a. Going just a little nuclear: Nonproliferation lessons from North Korea. *International Security* 20 (2):92–122.

———. 1995b. Virtual nuclear arsenals. *Survival* 37 (3):7–26.

———. 1995c. *North Korea and the bomb: A case study in nonproliferation.* New York: St. Martin's.

Mazrui, Ali. 1989. The political culture of war and nuclear proliferation: A third world perspective. In *The study of international relations*, ed. Hugh C. Dyer and Leon Mangasanan. London: Macmillan.

McDermott, Rose. 1998. *Risk-taking in international politics: prospect theory in American foreign policy.* Ann Arbor: University of Michigan Press.

Mearsheimer, John J. 1990. Back to the future: Instability in Europe after the Cold War. *International Security* 15 (1):5–56.

———. 1993. The case for a Ukrainian nuclear deterrent. *Foreign Affairs* 72 (3):50–66.

———. 2001. *The tragedy of great power politics.* New York: Norton.

Megahed, Mounir. 1998. A Nuclear Boost. Al-Ahram Weekly Online 380 (June 4–10). Available at http://weekly.ahram.org.eg/1998/380/op4htm.

Melman, Yossi. 2006. Let the world worry. PostGlobal, December 14, 2006, at newsweek.washingtonpost.com/postglobal.

Menashri, David. 1988. Introduction: Is there a new Middle East? In *Central Asia meets the Middle East*, ed. David Menashri. London: Frank Cass.

Mercer, Jonathan. 2005. Prospect theory and political science. *Annual Review of Political Science* 8:1–21.

Meyer, Stephen M. 1984. *The dynamics of nuclear proliferation.* Chicago: University of Chicago Press.

Mikheev, Vasily. 1996. Politics and ideology in the post–Cold War era. Pp. 88–104 in *North Korea: Ideology, politics, economics*, ed. Han S. Park. Englewood Cliffs, N. J.: Prentice-Hall.

Milani, Abbas. 2005a. Iran's new president. *Hoover Digest* 4:1–5.

———. 2005b. U.S. Policy and the future of democracy in Iran. *Washington Quarterly* 28 (3):41–56.

Miller, Judith. 2006a. How Gadhafi lost his groove. OpinionJournal, May 16, 2006, at WSJ.com.

———. 2006b. Gadhafi's leap of faith. OpinionJournal, May 17, 2006, at WSJ.com.

Milner, Helen V. 1988. *Resisting protectionism: Global industries and the politics of international trade.* Princeton: Princeton University Press.

Mitchell, Derek J. 2004. Taiwan's Hsin Chu program: Deterrence, abandonment, and honor. Pp. 293–316 in *The nuclear tipping point*, ed. Campbell et al. Washington, D.C.: Brookings Institution Press.

Mochizuki, Mike. 2006. Japan's drift away from pacifist policy. *Los Angeles Times,* September 22.

Molavi, Afshin. 2004. Buying time in Tehran—Iran and the China model. *Foreign Affairs* 83 (6):9–16.

Moon, Chung-in. 1990. Beyond statism: Rethinking the political economy of growth in South Korea. *International Studies Notes* 15 (1):24–27.

———. 1994. Changing patterns of business-government relations in South Korea. Pp. 142–66 in *Business and government in industrializing Asia*, ed. Andrew MacIntyre. Ithaca: Cornell University Press.

———. 2007. The North Korean nuclear problem: Motives, impacts, and management strategies. In *The United States and East Asia*, ed. John Ikenberry and Chung-in Moon. Lanham, Md.: Rowman and Littlefield.

Mueller, John. 1988. The essential irrelevance of nuclear weapons. *International Security* 13 (2):55–79.

———. 1995. *Quiet cataclysm: Reflections on the recent transformation of world politics.* New York: Harper Collins.

Muramatsu, Michio, and Ellis Krauss. 1984. Bureaucrats and politicians in policy-making: The case of Japan. *American Political Science Review* 78 (1):126–46.

Nakagawa, Tatsuhiro. 1980. Why Japan should let nuclear arms. *Japan Echo* 7 (4):99–110 (translated from 'Kaku no mochikomi' igai ni michi wa nai in *Shokun,* September 1980:62–85).

NAPSNet (Northeast Asia Peace and Security Network). Daily Report. Available at http://www.nautilus.org/napsnet/dr/index.html.

Nasr, Vali, and Ali Gheissari. 2004. The debate in Iran. *Middle East Policy Journal* 11 (2):94–106.

NA (National Archives). Visit website at http://www.archives.gov.

Nelson, Joan M. 1992. Poverty, equity, and the politics of adjustment. Pp. 221–69 in *The politics of economic adjustment*, ed. Stephan Haggard and Robert R. Kaufman. Princeton: Princeton University Press.

Niblock, Tim. 1993. International and domestic factors in the economic liberalization process in Arab countries. Pp. 55–87 in *Economic and political liberalization in the Middle East,* ed. Tim Niblock and Emma Murphy. London: British Academic Press.

———. 2001. *"Pariah states" and sanctions in the Middle East: Iraq, Libya, Sudan.* Boulder, Colo.: Lynne Rienner.

Nimrod, Yoram. 1991. Arms control or arms race? *New Outlook* (September/October):15–18.

NIW (Nautilus Institute). Visit website at http://www.nautilus.org.

Nixon, Richard M. 1967. Asia after Viet Nam. *Foreign Affairs* 46 (1):111–25.

Noble, Paul C. 1991. The Arab system: Pressures, constraints and opportunities. Pp. 49–102 in *The foreign policies of Arab states*, ed. Korany and Dessouki. Boulder, Colo.: Westview.

Noland, Marcus. 2002. West-bound train leaving the station: Pyongyang on the reform track. Paper Prepared for the Council on U.S.-Korea Security Studies

(October 14–15). Available at http://www.iie.com/publications/papers/noland1002.htm.

———. 2006a. How North Korea funds its regime. Testimony before the Subcommittee on Federal Financial Management, Government Information, and International Security, Committee on Homeland Security and Governmental Affairs, United States Senate, April 25.

———. 2006b. The economic implications of a North Korean nuclear test. *Asia Policy* 2 (July):25–39.

Nordhaug, Kristen. 1998. Development through want of security: The case of Taiwan. *Forum for Development Studies* 1:129–61.

Normark, Magnus, Anders Lindblad, Anders Norqvist, Björn Sandström, and Louise Waldenström. 2005. Israel and WMD: Incentives and capabilities. NBC Defence, FOI-R-1734-SE, December. FOI. Stockholm: Swedish Defence Research Agency.

North, Douglass C. 1981. *Structure and change in economic history*. New York: Norton.

NSA (The National Security Archive). Visit website at http://www.gwu.edu/~nsarchiv.

(NTIW) Nuclear Threat Initiative. Visit website at http://www.nti.org.

Nye, Joseph S., Jr. 1981. Maintaining a nonproliferation regime. *International Organization* 35 (1):15–38.

———. 1986. *Nuclear ethics*. New York: Free Press.

———. 1988. U.S.-Soviet cooperation in a nonproliferation regime. Pp. 336–52 in *U.S. Soviet Security Cooperation* edited by A. L. George, P. J. Farley, and A. Dallin. New York: Oxford University Press.

NuclearFiles.org. Project of the Nuclear Age Peace Foundation. Visit website at http://www.nuclearfiles.org.

Nuclear Weapon Archive. Visit website at http://nuclearweaponarchive.org.

Obeidi, Mahdi, and Kurt Pitzer. 2004. *The bomb in my garden—The secrets of Saddam's nuclear mastermind*. Hoboken, N.J.: John Wiley.

Oberdorfer, Don. 2001. *The two Koreas: A contemporary history*. New York: Basic Books.

Ogilvie-White, Tanya. 1996. Is there a theory of nuclear proliferation? An analysis of the contemporary debate. *Nonproliferation Review* 4 (1):43–60.

Ogle, George E. 1990. *South Korea: Dissent within the economic miracle*. London: Zed.

Oh, Kongdan, and Ralph C. Hassig. 2004. North Korea's nuclear politics. *Current History* 103:273–79.

Oh Hassig, Kongdan. 2004. *North Korean policy elites*. Alexandria, Va.: Institute for Defense Analyses.

Okimoto, Daniel I. 1978. *Ideas, intellectuals, and institutions: National security and the question of nuclear armament in Japan*. Ph.D. diss., University of Michigan.

O'Neill, Barry. 1999. *Honor, symbols, and war*. Ann Arbor: University of Michigan Press.

Oren, Amir. 1995. Darush: Meturgeman dover peresit. *Ha'aretz*, December 8:17.

Oros, Andrew L. 2003. Godzilla's return: The new nuclear politics in an insecure Japan. Pp. 49–63 in *Japan's nuclear option: Security, politics, and policy in the*

21st century, ed. Benjamin L. Self and Jeffrey W. Thompson. Washington, D.C.: Henry L. Stimson Center.

O'Sullivan, Meghan L. 2003. *Shrewd sanctions: Statecraft and state sponsors of terrorism*. Washington, D.C.: Brookings Institution.

Owen, Roger. 2000. *State, power, and politics in the making of the modern Middle East*. New York: Routledge.

Owen, Roger, and Şevket Pamuk. 1999. *A history of Middle East economies in the twentieth century*. Cambridge: Harvard University Press.

Paige, Glenn D., and Dong Jun Lee. 1963. The post-war politics of communist Korea. Pp. 17–29 in *North Korea today*, ed. Robert A. Scalapino. New York: Praeger.

Park, Chung Hee. 1971. *To build a nation*. Washington, D.C.: Acropolis.

———. 1976. *Toward peaceful unification*. Seoul: Kwangmyong.

———. 1979. *Korea reborn: A model for development*. Englewood Cliffs, N.J.: Prentice-Hall.

Park, Han S., ed. 1996. *North Korea: Ideology, politics, economics*. Englewood Cliffs, N.J.: Prentice-Hall.

Park, Moon Young. 1994/1995. Corking the nuclear bottle: "Lure" North Korea. *Foreign Policy* 97:97–105.

Passin, Herbert. 1977. Nuclear arms and Japan. Pp. 67–132 in *Asia's nuclear future*, ed. William H. Overholt. Boulder, Colo.: Westview.

Paul, T. V. 2000. *Power versus prudence: Why nations forgo nuclear weapons*. Montreal: McGill-Queens University Press.

Peceny, Mark, and William Stanley. 2001. Liberal social reconstruction and the resolution of civil wars in Central America. *International Organization* 55 (1):149–82.

Pekkanen, Robert, and Ellis S. Krauss. 2005. Japan's 'Coalition of the Willing' on security policies. *Orbis* 49 (3):429–44.

Pempel, T. J. 1975. Japan's nuclear allergy. *Current History* 68 (404):169–73.

———. 1997. Transpacific Torii: Japan and the emerging Asian regionalism. Pp. 47–82 in *Network Power*, ed. Katzenstein and Shiraishi. Ithaca: Cornell University Press.

———. 1998. *Regime shift: Comparative dynamics of the Japanese political economy*. Ithaca: Cornell University Press.

———. 1999. The developmental regime in a changing world economy. Pp. 137–81 in *The developmental state in historical perspective*, ed. Meredith Woo-Cumings. Ithaca: Cornell University Press.

Peres, Shimon. 1970. *David's Sling*. London: Weidenfeld and Nicolson.

———. 1979. *From these men: Seven portraits*. Translated by Philip Simpson. London: Weidenfeld and Nicolson.

———. 1993. *The new Middle East*. New York: Henry Holt.

———. 1995. *Battling for peace: Memoirs*. Edited by David Landau. London: Weidenfeld and Nicolson.

Perkovich, George. 2005a. Iran is not an island: A strategy to mobilize the neighbors. Carnegie Endowment for International Peace, Policy Brief 34, February.

———. 2005b. For Tehran, nuclear program is a matter of pride. Yale Global, March 21, at http://www.carnegieendowment.org/publications/index.cfm?fa=view&id=16694.

Perkovich, George, Joseph Cirincione, Rose Gottemoeller, Jessica T. Mattews, and Jon B. Wolfsthal. 2005. *Universal compliance: A strategy for nuclear security*. Washington, D.C.: Carnegie Endowment for International Peace.

Perlmutter, Amos, Michael Handel, and Uri Bar-Joseph. 1982. *Two minutes over Baghdad*. London: Vallentine Mitchell.

Peters, Joel. 1994. *Building bridges: The Arab-Israeli multilateral talks*. London: Royal Institute of International Affairs.

——. 1996. *Pathways to peace: The multilateral Arab-Israeli peace talks*. London: Royal Institute of International Affairs.

Pinkston, Daniel A. 2003. Domestic politics and stakeholders in the North Korean missile development program. *Nonproliferation Review* 10 (2):1–15.

——. 2004. South Korea's nu clear experiments. Center for Nonproliferation Studies. Available at http://cns.miis.edu/pubs/week/041109.htm.

Pollack, A. 1994. North Korea said to dip into rice reserves to bar unrest. *New York Times*, July 18, 1994:A3.

Pollack, Jonathan D., and Mitchell B. Reiss. 2004. South Korea: The tyranny of geography and the vexations of history. Pp. 254–92 in *The nuclear tipping point*, ed. Campbell, Einhorn, and Reiss. Washington, D.C.: Brookings Institution Press.

Pollack, Kenneth, and Ray Takeyh. 2005. Taking on Tehran. *Foreign Affairs* (March/April). Available at http://www.foreignaffairs.org/2005/2.html.

Potter, William C. 1982. *Nuclear power and nonproliferation: An interdisciplinary perspective*. Cambridge: Oelgeschlager, Gunn, and Hain.

Powell, Robert. 2002. Game theory, international relations theory, and the Hobbesian stylization. Pp. 755–83 in *Political Science: The State of the Discipline*, ed. Ira Katznelson and Helen V. Milner. New York: Norton.

Price, Richard. 1997. *The chemical weapons taboo*. Ithaca: Cornell University Press.

Pry, Peter Vincent. 1984. *Israel's nuclear arsenal*. Boulder, Colo.: Westview.

Qaddafi, Muammar Al-. 1983. *The Green Book*. Canada: The Green Book World Center for Research and Study.

Quandt, William. 1996. The Middle East on the brink: Prospects for change in the 21st Century. *Middle East Journal* 50 (1):9–17.

Quester, George. 1974. Taiwan and nuclear weapons. *Orbis* 18 (1):140–50.

——. 1991. Conceptions of nuclear threshold status. In *Security with nuclear weapons?* ed. R. C. Karp. New York: Oxford University Press.

Rabin, Yitzhak. 1993. Deterrence in an Israeli security context. In *Deterrence in the Middle East: Where theory and practice converge*, ed. Aharon Klieman and Ariel Levite. Boulder, Colo.: Westview.

Raghavan, Sudarsan. 2004. Libyan leader says the race to develop nuclear weapons is "crazy." Knight Ridder/Tribune News Service. Washington Bureau, February 29, 2004.

Raviv, Daniel, and Yossi Melman. 1990. *Every spy a prince: The complete history of Israel's intelligence community*. Boston: Houghton Mifflin.

Rawls, John. 1999. *The law of peoples*. Cambridge: Harvard University Press.

Razin, Assaf, and Efraim Sadka. 1993. *The economy of modern Israel: Malaise and promise*. Chicago: University of Chicago Press.

Reiss, Mitchell B. 1988. *Without the bomb*. New York: Columbia University Press.

———. 1995. *Bridled ambition: Why countries constrain their nuclear capabilities.* Washington, D.C.: Woodrow Wilson Center Press.

———. 2003. Atoms for peace: A future after fifty years? Remarks to the conference hosted by Los Alamos National Laboratory, the Woodrow Wilson International Center for Scholars, and the College of William and Mary, December 9, Washington, D.C. Available at http://www.state.gov/s/p/rem/2003/27035.htm.

Reiss, Mitchell B., and Robert L. Gallucci. 2005. Red-Handed. *Foreign Affairs* 84 (2):142–45.

Richards, Alan, and John Waterbury. 1990. *A political economy of the Middle East: State, class, and economic development.* Boulder, Colo.: Westview.

Richelson, Jeffrey, ed. 2004. Iraq and weapons of mass destruction. National Security Archive, Electronic Briefing Book No. 80 (February 11). Available at http://www.gwu.edu/~nsarchiv/NSAEBB/NSAEBB80/.

———. 2006. *Spying on the bomb: American nuclear intelligence from Nazi Germany to Iran to North Korea.* New York: Norton.

Ritter, Scott. 1999. *Endgame: Solving the Iraq problem—once and for all.* New York: Simon and Schuster.

Roberts, Brad. 1993. From nonproliferation to antiproliferation. *International Security* 18 (1):139–73.

———. 1995. Rethinking the proliferation debate: A Commentary. *Security Studies* 4 (4).

Rose, Gideon. 1998. Neoclassical realism and theories of foreign policy. *World Politics* 51 (1):144–72.

Rosecrance, Richard N., ed. 1964. *The dispersion of nuclear weapons: Strategy and politics.* New York: Columbia University Press.

———. 1966. *Problems of nuclear proliferation; technology and politics.* Los Angeles: University of California Press.

———. 1986. *The rise of the trading state: Commerce and conquest in the modern world.* New York: Basic Books.

———. 2001. Has realism become a cost-benefit analysis? A review essay. *International Security* 26 (2):132–54.

———. 2006. Power and international relations: The rise of China and its effects. *International Studies Perspectives* 7(1): 31–35.

Rosen, S. J. 1976. Nuclearization and stability in the Middle East. *Jerusalem Journal of International Relations* 1.

Rosenau, James, ed. 1969. *Linkage politics.* New York: Free Press.

Ross, Robert S. 1999. The geography of the peace: East Asia in the twenty-first century. *International Security* 23 (4):81–118.

Roy, Denny. 2003. *Taiwan: A political history.* Ithaca: Cornell University Press.

Rubinstein, Murray A, ed. 1999. *Taiwan.* Armonk, N.Y.: M. E. Sharpe.

Ruggie, John G. 1998. *Constructing the world polity: Essays on international institutionalization.* New York: Routledge.

Russett, Bruce M. 1989. Democracy, public opinion, and nuclear weapons. In *Behavior, society, and nuclear war*, vol. 1, ed. Philip E Tetlock et al. Oxford: Oxford University Press.

———, and John R. Oneal. 2001. *Triangulating peace: Democracy, interdependence and international organizations.* New York: Norton.

Sadowski, Yahya M. 1993. *Scuds or butter? The political economy of arms control in the Middle East.* Washington, D.C.: Brookings Institution.

Sagan, Scott D. 1996/97. Why do states build nuclear weapons: Three models in search of a bomb. *International Security* 21 (3):54–86.

———. 2003. More will be worse. Pp. 46–87 in *The spread of nuclear weapons: A debate renewed*, ed. Scott D. Sagan and Kenneth N. Waltz. New York: Norton.

Said, Mohamed Kadry. 2002. Security and defense dilemmas in the Middle East: The nuclear dimension. Pugwash Meeting No. 279. Pugwash OnLine, November 15–17. Available at http://www.pugwash.org/reports/nw/kadrysaid.htm#1.

Saif, Mostafa Elwi. 1997. Nuclear weapons and arms control in the Middle East: An Egyptian view. Unione Scienziati per il Disarmo. Available at http://www.uspid.dsi.unimi.it/proceed/cast97/elwisaif.html.

Sakai, Takashi. 1996. The power base of Kim Jong Il: Focusing on its formation process. Pp. 106–22 in *North Korea*, ed. Park. Englewood Cliffs, N.J.: Prentice-Hall.

Salama, Sammy, and Cameron Hunter. 2005. Leading Iraqi nuclear scientist, once imprisoned, elected to prominent post. Center for Nonproliferation Studies, June 7.

Salama, Sammy, and Elizabeth Salch. 2006. Iran's nuclear impasse: Give negotiations a chance. *Center for Nonproliferation Studies* (June 2). Available at http://www.cns.miis.edu.

Samore, Gary. 1994. Iraq. Pp. 15–32 in *Nuclear proliferation after the Cold War*, ed. Mitchell Reiss and Robert S. Litwak. Washington, D.C.: Woodrow Wilson Center Press.

———. 2004. Meeting Iran's nuclear challenge. Stockholm: The Weapons of Mass Destruction Commission, no. 21 (October).

———. 2005. Diplomacy at a loss over Iran's nuclear program. The International Institute for Strategic Studies, March 24, 2005. Available at http://www.iiss.org.

Samuels, Richard. 1994. *Rich nation, strong army: National security and the technological transformation of Japan.* Ithaca: Cornell University Press.

———. *Machiavelli's children: Leaders and their legacies in Italy and Japan.* Ithaca: Cornell University Press.

Sano, Yoel. 2005. "N. Korea's reformist PM may be shooting star," Asia Times Online, April 9, 2005. Available at http://www.atimes.com.

Sato, Yukio. 1982. The evolution of Japanese security policy. *Adelphi Papers* (178):1–41.

Sayed, Abdulhay. 1997. The future of the Israeli nuclear force and the Middle East peace process. *Security Dialogue* 28 (1):31–48.

Sayigh, Yezid. 1992. *Arab military industry: Capability, performance, and impact.* London: Brassey's.

———. 1993. Middle Eastern stability and the proliferation of weapons of mass destruction. In *Non-conventional weapons proliferation in the Middle East*, ed. Efraim Karsh, Martin Navias, and Philip Sabin. Oxford: Clarendon Press.

Scalapino, Robert A. 1963a. The foreign policy of North Korea. Pp. 30–50 in *North Korea today*, ed. Robert A. Scalapino. New York: Praeger.

———, ed. 1963b. *North Korea today.* New York: Praeger.

Schaller, Michael. 1996. The Nixon shocks and U.S.-Japan Strategic Relations, 1969–74. Working Paper 2. Washington, D.C.: NSA.

Scheinman, Lawrence. 1965. *Atomic energy policy in France under the Fourth Republic*. Princeton: Princeton University Press.

———. 1987. *The International Atomic Energy Agency and world nuclear order*. Washington, D.C.: Resources for the Future.

———. 1990. Does the NPT matter? In *Beyond 1995: The future of the NPT regime*, ed. Joseph Pilat and Robert Pendley. New York: Plenum.

Schell, Jonathan. 1984. *The abolition*. New York: Knopf.

Schelling, Thomas C. 1976. Who will have the bomb? *International Security* 1 (1):77–91.

———. 2000. A half-century without nuclear war. *Key Reporter* (spring). Available at http://www.pbk.org/pubs/Keyreporter/Spring2000/Schelling.htm.

Schiff, Ze'ev. 2006. Israel urges U.S. diplomacy on Iran. Carnegie Endowment for International Peace, May 30.

Schweller, Randall L. 2006. *Unanswered threats: Political constraints on the balance of power*. Princeton: Princeton University Press.

Segev, Tom. 1993. *The seventh million: The Israelis and the Holocaust*. New York: Hill and Wang.

Selim, Mohammad El-Sayed. 1996. Egypt and the Middle Eastern nuclear issue. *Strategic Analysis*, January 1. Available at http://www.nti.org/db/nuclear/1996/n9614112.htm.

Semati, Hadi. 2004. Dealing with Iran: A panel discussion with Robert J. Einhorn of the Center for Strategic and International Studies (CSIS), Philippe Errera of the French Ministry of Foreign Affairs, and M. Hadi Semati of Tehran University. Carnegie Endowment for International Peace, June 21 and 22. Available at http://www.ceip.org.

Sen, Amartya. 1999. *Development as freedom*. New York: Knopf.

Shaffer, Brenda. 2003. Iran at the nuclear threshold. *Arms Control Today* (November):7–12.

Shaker, Mohamed I. 1980. *The nuclear non-proliferation treaty: Origin and implementation, 1959–1979*. London: Oceana.

Shalev, Michael. 1992. *Labour and the political economy in Israel*. Oxford: Oxford University Press.

Shalom, Zaki. 1996. Israel's nuclear policy in historical perspective: Kennedy, Ben-Gurion and the Dimona Project 1960–1963. *Israel Studies* 1, no. 1 (Spring): 3–33.

———. 2004. *Bein Dimona le-Washington: Hama'avak al Pituach Ha'optzia Hagarinit shel Israel 1960–1968*. Be'er Sheva: Hotza'at Hasfarim shel Universitat Ben-Gurion Ba-Neguev.

Shambaugh, David. 2000. A matter of Taiwan: Taiwan's eroding military advantage. *Washington Quarterly* 23 (2):119–33.

Shikaki, Khalil. 1985. The nuclearization debates: The cases of Israel and Egypt. *Journal of Palestine Studies* 14 (4):77–91.

Shirk, Susan L. 1994. Chinese views on Asia-Pacific regional security cooperation. *NBR Analysis* 5 (5). Seattle: WA: The National Bureau of Asian Research.

Sick, Gary. 1995. An interview by J. Javid. "Open Wounds." *The Iranian*, December 1995. Available at http://www.iranian.com/Jan96/Features/OpenWounds.html.

Sieg, Linda. 2003. North Korea fears erode Japan's nuclear arms taboo. *Planet Ark*, March 28. Available at http://www.planetark.org/dailynewsstory.cfm/newsid/20303/story.htm.

Sigal, Leon. 1998. *Disarming strangers: Nuclear diplomacy with North Korea*. Princeton: Princeton University Press.

Siler, Michael J. 1998. U.S. nuclear nonproliferation policy in the Northeast Asian region during the Cold War: The South Korean case. *East Asia: An International Quarterly*, Pp. 41–78.

Singh, Sonali, and Christopher R. Way. 2004. The correlates of nuclear proliferation: A quantitative test. *Journal of Conflict Resolution* 48 (6):859–85.

SIPRI (Stockholm International Peace Research Institute). 1975–96. *SIPRI yearbook of world armaments and disarmament*. New York: Humanities Press.

Smith, Hazel. 1994. The Democratic People's Republic of North Korea and its foreign policy in the 1990s. Pp. 96–116 in *Renegade states: The evolution of revolutionary foreign policy*, ed. Stephen Chan and Andrew J. Williams. Manchester and New York: Manchester University Press.

Smith, Roger K. 1987. Explaining the non-proliferation regime: Anomalies for contemporary international relations theory. *International Organization* 41 (2):253–81.

Smith, Sheila A. 2003. Japan's future strategic options and the US–Japan Alliance. Pp. 4–23 in *Japan's nuclear option: Security, politics, and policy in the 21st Century*, ed. Benjamin L. Self and Jeffrey W. Thompson. Washington, D.C.: Henry L. Stimson Center.

Snyder, Glenn H. 1984. The security dilemma in alliance politics. *World Politics* 36 (4):461–95.

Snyder, Jack. 1984. *The ideology of the offensive: Military decision making and the disasters of 1914*. Ithaca: Cornell University Press.

———. 1991. *Myths of empire—Domestic politics and international ambition*. Ithaca: Cornell University Press.

Sokolski, Henry. 2004. President Bush's global nonproliferation policy: Seven more proposals. The Heritage Lectures No. 829, April 19. Available at http://www.heritage.org/Research/NationalSecurity/hl829.cfm.

Solingen, Etel. 1994a. The political economy of nuclear restraint. *International Security* 19 (2):126–69.

———. 1994b. The domestic sources of international regimes: The evolution of nuclear ambiguity in the Middle East. *International Studies Quarterly* 38 (4): 305–37.

———. 1995. The new multilateralism and nonproliferation: Bringing domestic politics in. *Global Governance* 1 (2):205–27.

———. 1998. *Regional orders at century's dawn*. Princeton: Princeton University Press.

———. 2000. The multilateral Arab-Israeli negotiations: Genesis, institutionalization, pause, future. *Journal of Peace Research* 37 (2):167–87.

———. 2001a. Mapping internationalization: Domestic and regional impacts. *International Studies Quarterly* 45 (4): 517–56.

———. 2001b. Middle East denuclearization? Lessons from Latin America's Southern Cone. *Review of International Studies* 27 (3):375–94.

———. 2007a. Pax Asiatica versus Bella Levantina: The foundations of war and peace in East Asia and the Middle East. *American Political Science Review* 101 (4).

———. 2007b. Why some do and others don't: Theory and method in the study of nuclear proliferation. Manuscript, Department of Political Science, University of California, Irvine.

———. 2008. The genesis, design, and effects of regional institutions: Lessons from East Asia and the Middle East. *International Studies Quarterly* 52(1).

Spector, Leonard. 1987. *Going nuclear: The spread of nuclear weapons 1986–1987.* Cambridge, Mass.: Ballinger.

———. 1988. *The undeclared bomb.* Cambridge, Mass.: Ballinger.

———. 1990. *Nuclear ambitions.* Boulder, Colo.: Westview.

———. 1993. Nuclear proliferation in the Middle East: The next chapter begins. Pp. 135–60 in *Non-conventional weapons proliferation in the Middle East,* ed. Efraim Karsh, Martin S. Navias, and Philip Sabin. New York: Oxford University Press.

Spector, Leonard, and Jacqueline Smith. 1990. *Nuclear ambitions: The spread of nuclear weapons, 1989–1990.* Boulder, Colo.: Westview.

Springborg, Robert. 1989. *Mubarak's Egypt: Fragmentation of the political order.* Boulder, Colo.: Westview.

Stein, Arthur. 2005. The realist peace and the anomaly of war. Manuscript, Department of Political Science, University of California, Los Angeles, April 20.

Steinberg, Gerald M. 1990. Israel: An unlikely nuclear supplier. In *International nuclear trade and nonproliferation,* ed. W. C. Potter. Lexington, Mass.: Lexington.

———. 1994. Middle East arms control and regional security. *Survival* 36 (1): 126–41.

Takagi, Jinzaburo. 1996. Japan's plutonium program: A critical review. Pp. 69–86 in *Japan's nuclear future,* ed. Harrison. Washington, D.C.: Carnegie Endowment for International Peace.

Takeyh, Ray. 2001. The rogue who came in from the cold. *Foreign Affairs* 80 (3):62–72.

———. 2004a. Iran: From reform to revolution. *Survival* 46 (1):133–41.

———. 2004b. Iran builds the bomb. *Survival* 46 (4):51–64.

———. 2005. It's not Israel that's driving Tehran to nukes. *International Herald Tribune,* August 27:6.

———. 2006a. Prepared testimony before the Subcomittee on Federal Financial Management, Government Information, and International Security, July 20. Available at http://www.cfr.org.

———. 2006b. *Hidden Iran: Paradox and power in the Islamic Republic.* New York: Henry Holt.

Tanaka, Akihiko. 2000. Domestic politics and foreign policy. Pp. 3–17 in *Japanese foreign policy today,* ed. Takashi and Jain. New York: St. Martin's.

Tanaka, Akihiko, and Koji Murata. 1995. Kusuda Minoru oral history interview. *National Security Archives,* November 16. Available at http://www.gwu.edu/~nsarchiv/japan/kusudaohinterview.htm.

Tannenwald, Nina. 1999. The nuclear taboo: The United States and the normative basis of nuclear non-use. *International Organization* 53 (3):433–68.

———. 2005. Stigmatizing the bomb: Origins of the nuclear taboo. *International Security* 29 (4):5–49.

Taylor, Jay. 2000. *The Generalissimo's son*. Cambridge: Harvard University Press.

Tetlock, Philip E., and Aaron Belkin. 1996. *Counterfactual thought experiments in world politics: Logical, methodological, and psychological perspectives*. Princeton: Princeton University Press.

Tetlock, Philip E., and Richard N. Lebow. 2001. Poking counterfactual holes in covering laws: Cognitive styles and historical reasoning. *American Political Science Review* 95 (3):829–43.

Thayer, Bradley. 1995. The causes of nuclear proliferation and the utility of the nuclear nonproliferation regime. *Security Studies* 4 (3):463–519.

Timerbaev, Roland. 2005. What next for the NPT? Facing the moment of truth. *IAEA Bulletin* 46 (2):4–7.

Toukan, Abdullah. 1997. Arab national security issues: perceptions and policies. Pp. 33–72 in *Bridging the gap*, ed. Feldman and Toukan. Lanham, Md.: Rowman and Littlefield.

Trigubenko, Marina Ye. 1996. Economic characteristics and prospect for development: With emphasis on agriculture. Pp. 142–59 in *North Korea: Ideology, politics, economics*, ed. Han S. Park. Englewood Cliffs, N.J.: Prentice Hall.

Tsuchiyama, Jitsuo. 2000. Ironies in Japan's defense and disarmament policies. In *Japanese foreign policy today*, ed. Takashi and Jain. New York: St. Martin's.

United Nations. 1991–1996. *Human development report*. New York: Oxford University Press.

———. 1999. *Statistical Yearbook*. New York: United Nations.

Uriu, Robert M. 1996. *Troubled industries: Confronting economic change in Japan*. Ithaca: Cornell University Press.

Vakil, Sanam. 2005. The Persian dilemma: Will Iran go nuclear? *Current History* 103:183–88.

Van Creveld, Martin L. 1993. *Nuclear proliferation and the future of conflict*. New York: Free Press.

———. 1998. *The sword and the olive: A critical history of the Israeli defense force*. New York: Public Affairs.

Van Evera, Stephen. 1994. Hypotheses on nationalism and war. *International Security* 18 (4):5–39.

———. 1997. *Guide to methods for students of political science*. Ithaca: Cornell University Press.

Vandewalle, Dirk. 1995. The failure of liberalization in the Jamahiriyya. Pp. 203–22 in *Qadhafi's Libya, 1969–1994*, ed. Dirk Vandewalle. New York: St. Martin's.

———. 1998. *Libya since independence: Oil and state-building*. Ithaca: Cornell University Press.

———. 2004. The origins and parameters of Libya's recent actions. *Arab Reform Bulletin* (Carnegie Endowment for International Peace) 2, no. 3 (March).

———. 2006. *A history of modern Libya*. New York: Cambridge University Press.

Vasquez, John. 1998. *The power of power politics: From classical realism to neo-traditionalism*. Cambridge: Cambridge University Press.

Viorst, Milton. 1991. Report from Baghdad. *The New Yorker*, June 14.

Vision of the Islamic Republic of Iran, Network 1. 2004. Iranian academics support nuclear program at meeting with Khamene'i. December 19. Available at http://wnc.dialong.com.

Vogel, Ezra F. 1987. Korea in 2000: From social Instability to consensus? Pp. 1987 in Han and Myers, eds. 1987.

———. 1994. Japan as number one in Asia. Pp. 159–83 in *The United States, Japan, and Asia*, ed. Gerald L. Curtis. New York: Norton.

Von Stein, Jana. 2005. Do treaties constrain or screen? Selection bias and treaty compliance. *American Political Science Review* 99 (4):611–22.

Walker, Thomas C., and Jeffrey S. Morton. 2005. *International Studies Review* 7 (2):341–56.

Walsh, James J. 2001. *Bombs unbuilt: Power, ideas, and institutions in International Politics*. Ph.D. diss., Massachusetts Institute of Technology.

Walt, Stephen M. 1987. *The origins of alliances*. Ithaca: Cornell University Press.

———. 1996. *Revolution and war*. Ithaca: Cornell University Press.

Waltz, Kenneth N. 1981. The spread of nuclear weapons: More may be better. *Adelphi Papers* 171.

———. 1989. The origins of war in neorealist theory. Pp. 39–52 in *The origins and prevention of major wars*, ed. Robert I. Rotberg and Theodore K. Rabb. New York: Cambridge University Press.

———. 1993. The emerging structure of international politics. *International Security* 18 (2):44–79.

———. 2003. More may be better. In *The spread of nuclear weapons*, ed. Scott D. Sagan and Kenneth N. Waltz. New York: Norton.

Walzer, Michael. 1977. Just and unjust wars: A moral argument with historical illustrations. New York: Basic Books.

Ward, Michael D., David Davis, and Steve Chan. 1993. Economic growth and military spending in Taiwan. *Armed Forces and Society* 19 (4):533–51.

Wampler, Robert A., ed. 2003. North Korea and nuclear weapons: The declassified U.S. record. *National Security Archive Electronic Briefing Book* 87, April 25. Available at http://www.gwu.edu/~nsarchiv/NSAEBB/NSAEBB87/#3.

Weber, Max. 1949. *Max Weber on the methodology of the social sciences*. Translated and edited by Edward A. Shils and Henry A. Finch. Glencoe, Ill: Free Press.

West, Robert L. 1992. Determinants of military expenditure in developing countries: Review of academic research. Pp. 113–46 in *Military expenditure and economic development: A symposium on research issues*, ed. Geoffrey Lamb and Valeriana Kallab. Washington, D.C.: World Bank.

Wit, Joel S., Daniel B. Poneman, and Robert L. Gallucci. 2004. *Going critical: The first North Korean nuclear crisis*. Washington, D.C.: Brookings Institution Press.

WMDC (Weapons of Mass Destruction Commission). 2006. *Weapons of terror: Freeing the world of nuclear, biological and chemical arms*. Stockholm: EO Grafiska.

Wolfsthal, Jon B. 2004. The next nuclear wave. *Foreign Affairs* 84 (1):156–61.

Woods, Kevin, James Lacey, and Murray Williamson. 2006. Saddam's delusions: The view from the inside. *Foreign Affairs* 85, no. 3 (May/June):2–26.

World Bank. 1980, 1989–1990, 1995. *World tables.* Baltimore and London: Johns Hopkins University Press.

———. 1991–1997. *World development report.* New York: Oxford University Press.

———. 1998. *World development indicators.* Washington, D.C.: World Bank.

———. 2006a. *World Development Indicators.* Washington, D.C.: World Bank. Available at http://devdata.worldbank.org/data-query.

———. 2006b. *World Development Report.* Washington, D.C.: World Bank.

Wortzel, Larry M. 2003. North Korea's connection to international trade in drugs, counterfeiting, and arms. Testimony before the Governmental Affairs Subcommittee on Financial Management, Budget, and International Security, May 20.

Wu, Sofia. 1998. Taiwan: Defense Ministry on "non-nuclear arms" policy, defector. Taiwan Central News Agency, January 20, 1998.

Wu,Ta-you. 1988. A historical document—A footnote to the history of our country's "nuclear energy" policies. English translation from *Biographical Literature,* May. Available at http://www.isis-online.org/publications/taiwan/ta-youwu.html.

Yager, Joseph A., ed. 1980. *Nonproliferation and U.S. foreign policy.* Washington, D.C.: Brookings Institution.

———. 1985. Nuclear supplies and the policies of South Korea and Taiwan toward nuclear weapons. Pp. 187–95 *The nuclear suppliers and nonproliferation: International policy choices,* ed. Rodney W. Jones et al. Lexington, Mass.: Lexington Books.

———. 1989. *Nuclear proliferation strategy in Asia.* Center for National Security Negotiations: Science Applications International Corporation.

Yaniv, Avner. 1987. *Deterrence without the bomb: The politics of Israeli strategy.* Lexington, Mass.: Lexington Books.

Yoshida, Shigeru. 1962. *The Yoshida memoirs: The story of Japan in crisis,* trans. Kenichi Yoshida. Boston: Houghton Mifflin.

Yovel, Yirmiyahu. 2000. "Blast, from the past to the present." *Ha'aretz,* July 28, 2000.

Zartman, William, and A. G. Kluge. 1991. Heroic politics: The foreign policy of Libya. Pp. 236–59 in *The foreign policies of Arab states: The challenge of change,* ed. Ali Dessouki and Bahgat Korany. Boulder, Colo.: Westview.

Index

Aamer, Salem bin, 217
abandonment in alliances, 60, 80, 253
Abbasi, Altaf, 217
Abe, Nobuyasu, 265
Abe Shinzo, 77, 81, 259
Abu Bakr, 243
Abu Nidal, 221
Achille Lauro hijacking (1985), 221
ACRS (Arms Control and Regional
  Security Group), 195–96, 205, 208,
  237, 243, 344n.36
AEA (Atomic Energy Authority; Egypt),
  229, 241
AEC (Atomic Energy Council; Taiwan),
  100–103, 108, 113
AEOI (Atomic Energy Organization of
  Iran), 164, 177, 179
Afarideh, Hossein, 182
Agency for Accounting and Control of Nu-
  clear Materials (Argentina and Brazil), 38
Agency for Defense Development (South
  Korea), 90
Agency for International Development
  (AID), 110
Aghazadeh, Gholam Reza, 179
Agreed Framework, 120, 123, 133–34,
  321n.5
Agreement on Reconciliation, Nonaggres-
  sion, and Exchanges and Cooperation
  (North/South Korea), 131
Ahdut-Ha'avoda (Israel), 198–99, 201,
  336n.39
Ahmadinejad, Mahmoud: blogging by, xi;
  election of, 44, 180; Holocaust denied
  by, 209; human rights under, 294; and
  Iranian finances, 184–85; Israel threat-
  ened by, 184, 209, 211, 272–73; vs.
  Khamene'i, 183; and Musharaf, 257;
  nuclear policy of, 174, 182, 183, 186;
  popularity of, 186, 236, 354n.54; on
  potential for Iranian global power, 169
AID (Agency for International Development), 110
Ain Ousseara (Algeria), 227
Akaha, Tsuneo, 311n.25

'Alawi, Mustafa, 242
Albright, David, 102
Alfonsín, Raúl, 38
Algeria: NPT membership of, 214–15;
  nuclearization by, 3, 260–61, 302n.18;
  nuclear research reactors of, 214–15,
  227, 256
Allah, Adnan Khayr, 149, 257
alliances: and abandonment, 60, 80, 253;
  vs. deterrence, 253; and entrapment, 60,
  80, 253; vs. self-help, 25, 59–60, 82,
  253; of vulnerable states, 25–26. *See also
  specific countries*
Allon, Yigal: on conventional weapons,
  192, 200; and Eshkol, 202; memoirs of,
  xi, 336n.40; on the NPT, 193; on nuclear deterrence/weapons, 190, 199, 200,
  202, 336n.40; on nuclear secrecy,
  336n.43; NWFZ endorsed by, 204, 211;
  on Rafi, 201
Amer, Abdel Hakim, 240
Amrollahi, Reza, 171, 179
Anderson, Lisa, 228
Annan, Kofi, 6, 33, 159, 335–36n.27
Aouzou Strip (Chad), 213
APEC (Asia Pacific Economic Cooperation), 124
approximating (ideal types), 9, 303n.23
Arab-Israeli wars/conflict/competition, 187,
  189
Al-Arabiyya TV, 168
Arab League: Egypt ousted from, 242; inaction on nuclear weapons, 15; ineffectiveness of, 32; nuclearization's spread
  not prevented by, 22
Arak (Iraq), 172
Arakatsu Bunsaku, 57
Aran, Zalman, 337n.50
ARF (ASEAN Regional Forum), 30–31,
  123–24, 263
Argentina: in Badr-2000 program, 230–31;
  democracy in, 38, 272; inspections
  regime approved by, 196; nuclearization
  by, 302n.18; U.S. nuclear technology
  exported to, 192

Arisawa Hiromi, 311–12n.35
Arms Control and Regional Security
  Group. See ACRS
Arms Control Export Act (U.S., 1994),
  307n.41
Asahi Shimbun, 59, 78, 207, 314n.65
ASEAN Regional Forum (ARF), 30–31,
  123–24, 263
Asgar-Khani, Abu Mohammed, 180, 181,
  281
Asia Pacific Economic Cooperation
  (APEC), 124
Aswan dam (Egypt), 233
Atomenergoeksport (Soviet Union), 217
Atomic Energy Authority (AEA; Egypt),
  229, 241
Atomic Energy Commission (Japan), 75
Atomic Energy Council (AEC; Taiwan),
  100–103, 108, 113
Atomic Energy Development Promoting
  Committee (South Korea), 88
Atomic Energy Law (Japan, 1955), 68, 72,
  268, 311n.32
Atomic Energy Organization of Iran
  (AEOI), 164, 177, 179
al-Attiyah, Abdul-Rahman bin Hamad,
  168
Aumann, Robert J., 339n.75, 347n.22
autarky, 46, 97, 121, 124, 125, 276. See
  also juche
autocracies: compliance with international
  agreements by, 37–38, 273–74; vs.
  democracies, 37–40, 50–51; described,
  306n.34; IAEA deceptions by, 272; and
  nuclear weapons, 16–17, 37
axis of evil, 37, 119, 165–66
Al-Azhar Religious Ruling Committee, 243
al-Aziz, Muhammad Izzat Abd-, xi, 221
Aziz, Tariq, 146, 148, 156, 160–61
Al 'Azzawi, Hikmat Mizban Ibrahim, 155

Badr-2000 program (Egypt), 230–31
al-Badri, Abdallah Salim, 222–23, 225
al-Baghadi, Abd al-Qadr, 225–26
balance of power, 4, 6, 9, 20, 21, 277;
  vs. constructivism, 258; definitions/
  conceptions of, 25, 119; and Egypt,
  149, 232–36, 244, 256, 343n.19,
  343nn.15–16; and Iran, 146, 257; and
  Iraq, 146; and Israel, 209, 257; and
  Japan, 259–60; measuring, 252; and

national security, 11–14, 24, 119, 209,
  250–51, 256–57, 303nn.29–30; out-
  comes of considerations of, 192–93; pol-
  icy implications, 290, 291–92; and po-
  litical survival models, 18; and regime
  effects, 267; and structural realism, 48,
  188; and Taiwan, 106
Banco Delta Asia, 140, 325–26n.77
Bandar-e-Abbas project, 178
Bank Saderat (Iran), 296
Bank Sepah (Iran), 296
Barak, Ehud, 196, 205
Bar-lev, Chaim, 339n.73
Barnett, Michael, 32, 202
Basic Principles of National Defense
  (Japan), 76
Beck, Nathaniel, 303n.29
Begin, Menachem, 204
Beilin, Yossi, 205, 339n.71
Belarus, 302n.18
Belgium, 213
Ben-Gurion, David: ruling coalition of,
  192, 197, 211, 282, 339n.76; on con-
  ventional deterrence, 192; Dimona facil-
  ity ordered constructed by, 187; and
  Eshkol, 200–201, 211, 347n.23; on the
  Histadrut, 198–99; Israeli nuclear activi-
  ties hidden by, 343n.27; and Kennedy,
  188, 191, 334n.7; and Lavon, 200; vs.
  Mapam, 336n.39; memoirs of, xi; on
  Nasser, 334n.6; on nuclear energy,
  197–98; Rafi formed by, 201; resignation
  of, 200; role in Israel's nuclear weapons
  program, 188, 192, 198; treaties sought
  by, 198–99
Bennett, Andrew, 250, 303n.22, 304n.7,
  308n.47
Berger, Thomas U., 69–70, 75, 278
Bergmann, Ernst David, 199, 338n.70
Betts, Richard K., 12–13, 14, 252
Bhak Byong-Won, 96
Bhatia, Shyam, 344n.54
Bhutto, Zulfiqar Ali, 306n.27
Billing, Bruce, 101
Biological and Toxin Weapons Convention.
  See BTWC
Blix, Hans: on deterrence, 306n.29; on
  incentives/demand for proliferation, 7–8,
  154, 249; on Iran, 6–7, 165, 171; on
  Iraq, 151, 152, 153, 298, 327n.16; and
  Kim Dal-Hyon, 131

blowback, 126, 287, 322, 349n.43
Bonyad-e Mostaz'afi, 176
bonyads, 44, 176–81, 281, 293, 295, 296
Boyd, J. Patrick, 311n.31
Brazil: democracy in, 38, 272; inspections regime approved by, 196; nuclearization by, 302n.18
Britain, 38, 307n.36
BTWC (Biological and Toxin Weapons Convention), 86, 124–25, 170–71, 238–39, 319n.39, 336n.29
Bueno de Mesquita, Bruce, 40, 348–49n.41
Burns, William, 224, 341n.30
Burr, William, 112, 116
Burrows, William E., 188
Bush, George W., 6, 37, 165
Bush, G.H.W., 95
Bushehr (Iran), 164–65, 179
Butler, Richard, 151–52

Cabinet Information Research Office (Japan), 72
Campbell, Kurt M., 6, 286
Camp David agreements (1979), 156, 230
Carlin, Robert, 349n.48
Carter, Jimmy: Agreed Framework led by, 123; Iranian "most favored nation" status for fuel reprocessing granted by, 164, 170; and Kim Il-Sung, 120, 132; Libyan sanctions imposed by, 221; on preventing proliferation, 299; troop withdrawal from South Korea proposed by, 83, 93–94
Catholic Bishops' Pastoral Letter on War and Peace (U.S.), 34–35
Ceausescu, Nicolae, 130
Central Reform Committee (Taiwan), 109
Chai, Sun-ki, 68
Chang Hsien-yi, 102, 108, 116
Chang Myon, 87
Chang Song-taek, 131
chemical weapons, 188–89, 195, 218, 238, 269, 306n.32
Chemical Weapons Convention. *See* CWC
Chen Cheng, 109
Cheney, Richard, 346n.8
Cheng, Victor, 101
Chen Shui-bian, 114–15
Chernobyl, 230
Chiang Ching-kuo, 100–102, 106, 110, 113, 116

Chiang Kai-shek, 100–101, 103, 106–7, 109–13, 262–63
Chieng Chi-peng, 101
China: conventional capabilities of, 319n.37; CTBT obstructed by, 29; economy of, 121, 135, 296; Japanese workers in, 286; Japan's relations with, 73; "no first use" policy of, 33; North Korea's commitment from, 255; nuclearization by, 3–4, 19, 259; nuclear test by, 252; Taiwanese entrepreneurs in, 286; Taiwan threatened by, 287–88; U.S. relations with, 58
Chirac, Jacques, 33, 143
Choe-Kwang, 133
Zhou Enlai, 128, 310n.13
Chubin, Shahram, 225, 257, 281
Chun Doo-Hwan, 93–94, 128
Chung In-Moon, 96
Chungshan Institute of Science and Technology, 100
Clinton, Bill, 33, 80, 95, 104, 178, 179, 227, 302, 321; commitment to Israel, 335n.21; democratic-enlargement policy of, 37; on Japan, 80; relations with Libya, 341n.30
coercion, effectiveness of, 12, 13–14, 25, 253, 255, 304n.5. *See under specific countries*
collective action, 264–65, 266, 298–99
Commission on the Intelligence Capabilities of the United States Regarding Weapons of Mass Destruction, 289
Committee for the Denuclearization of the Middle East (Israel), 190, 200
Committee of Four (Iraq), 160–61
Communist Party (Israel), 197
Communist Party (Japan), 64, 66, 74, 75
competing perspectives on denuclearization, 23–53; democratic peace hypothesis, 37–40, 50–51, 307nn.36–37; deterrence as a factor, 34–35, 39, 51, 299, 306nn.28–29, 307n.37; domestic-political-survival models, 40–47, 51–53, 307n.41, 307–8nn.44–49, 308nn.52–53 (see also *juche*); neoliberal institutionalist account, 28–32, 48–49, 305nn.13–15; norm-based/constructivist account, 32–37, 49–50, 306nn.23–24, 306nn.27–33; overview of/conclusions, 23–24, 47–53; prestige as a factor, 35,

competing perspectives (*continued*)
306n.28; scarcity of resources as a factor, 304n.4; self-help, 25, 26, 48, 253 (*see also* self-help); structural power/neorealist account, 24–28, 48, 251–52, 304nn.2–7. *See also* Middle Eastern vs. East Asian nuclear policies
Comprehensive Nuclear Test Ban Treaty. *See* CTBT
condition variables, 308n.53
Constitution (Japan), 58, 62, 65, 68–69, 70, 74, 77–78, 80, 268, 311n.32
constructivism: definition of, 32; findings on, 271; norm-based/constructivist account of denuclearization, 32–37, 49–50, 306nn.23–24, 306nn.27–33; and norms, 15–16, 267–71
conventional deterrence/weapons/capabilities: Allon on, 192, 200; Ben-Gurion on, 188, 192; boycott of, 191, 209, 257; Chinese, 319n.37; Egyptian, 235, 240, 243, 244, 344n.54; exports of weapons, 136; Iranian, 145, 167, 168, 182; Iraqi, 206; Israeli, 191–92, 198–200, 203–4, 209–11, 244, 256, 282, 339n.73; Israel's vulnerability, 24, 192; Japanese, 62–63, 74; North Korean, 84, 121, 130, 321n.12; and nuclear abstention, 62, 105–6; vs. nuclear weapons, 32, 182, 295; as obviating nuclear weapons, 84, 85, 306n.30; Pakistan's vulnerability, 24; research on weapons, 153; South Korean, 84, 91, 130; Soviet, 232; Taiwanese, 105–6, 110; value of, 188–89
Cooper, Drury A., 350n.53
costs of nuclear programs, 43, 307n.44
counterfactuals, 14–15, 30, 31, 49, 80, 255, 262, 266, 273, 305n.14, 347n.17
Cox, Dan, 350n.53
CTBT (Comprehensive Nuclear Test Ban Treaty): effectiveness of, 14; obstruction of, 29; signing/ratification of, 29, 171, 226
Curtis, Gerald, 75
CWC (Chemical Weapons Convention), 86, 124, 171, 179, 195, 204–5
Czech-Egyptian arms agreement (1955), 235

Davis, David, 111
Dayan, Moshe, 167, 192, 198, 200–201, 203, 204, 334n.6, 335n.20, 336n.42, 337n.55

Declaration of Principles (1993), 195, 204–5, 237
de Gaulle, Charles, 187, 191, 309n.10
Dehghani, Mohammad Ebrahim, 334–35n.15
democracies: vs. autocracies, 37–40, 50–51; citizens' consent under, 37; compliance with international agreements by, 37; definitions of democracy, 274–75; findings on, 272–75; and nuclear weapons, 16–17; policy implications, 297–99, 350nn.53–54; transparency in, 37, 38; weak/unstable vs. full-fledged liberal, 347n.25
Democratic Progressive Party (DPP; Taiwan), 114–15
Democratic Socialist Party (Japan), 74
denuclearization, 38, 301n.1. *See also under specific countries*
Desert Storm, 143, 145
Design Consultants Association (Egypt), 240
deterrence: and acquisition vs. use of weapons, 15, 35, 50; vs. alliances, 253; Allon on, 190, 199, 200, 202, 336n.40; via ambiguity, 337n.51 (*see also under* Israel); Ben-Gurion on, 192; Bergmann on, 338n.70; demands for/popularity of, 269, 273, 347n.13, 347n.21; by Egypt, 242; as a factor in denuclearization, 34–35, 39, 51, 299, 306nn.28–29, 307n.37; by Iran, 166, 168, 169; by Israel, 189–90, 192, 198, 200, 203, 206–11, 229, 307n.37, 339n.73; by Japan, 66; by Kim Jong-Il, 105; moral/religious view of, 34–35; via mutual assured destruction, 306n.29; by North Korea, 120, 121; vs. nuclear non-acknowledgment, 270; by South Korea, 82; by Taiwan, 105; theory of, 15; U.S. commitment to, 59, 260, 268, 347n.13. *See also* conventional deterrence/weapons/capabilities
Deutsch, John M., 165, 172
Dimona nuclear facility (Israel): Ben-Gurion's role in, 187, 273, 339n.76; contract for, 233; Egyptian overflights over, 189, 230; Eshkol on, 337n.44; Holocaust memories' role in building, 209; as impractical/costly, 199; inspections of, 191, 200–201; Iraqi missile

strikes at, 205; and the Lavon affair, 200; Nasser on, 233, 234; secrecy surrounding, 343n.27; and U.S.-Israeli relations, 198, 200, 337n.50
Dinstein, Tzvi, 202
"Doctrine for Joint Nuclear Operations" (U.S., 1995), 33
domestic approaches to political survival: findings on, 255, 275–89, 287 (table), 348n.35, 348n.38, 348nn.28–30, 349n.41; Middle Eastern vs. East Asian nuclear policies, 17–20, 277–78, 304nn.33–35; policy implications, 292–93. *See also* internationalizing models of political survival; inward-looking models of political survival
domino effect, 33, 259–61, 346n.8. *See also* reactive proliferation
Doomsday Clock, 6
Dower, John W., 70
Dowty, Alan, 212
DPP (Democratic Progressive Party; Taiwan), 114–15
"Ds" for preventing proliferation, 299
Duelfer report, 146, 153, 326. *See also* ISG
Dulles, John Foster, 66, 107
Dunn, Lewis A., 191, 304n.5
Al-Duri, Izzat Ibrahim, 160

Ebadi, Shirin, 294
Eban, Abba, 193–94, 198, 203, 336n.36, 337n.50
Economic Planning Board (EPB; South Korea), 87, 89, 93
economy: global, orientation to, 5, 9, 11, 17–20, 24, 39–40, 42, 275–76, 277, 285–89, 292–93, 304nn.33–35, 347n.26; international economic institutions, 293–94; positive-sum vs. zero-sum, 75; reform policies, 42–44 (see also *infitah*); sanctions, 290–91, 298; and self-help, 53. *See also under specific countries*
Egypt, 229–45; in ACRS, 196, 237, 243, 344n.36; Arab League ousting of, 242; Argentina's relations with/aid to, 230–31; Atomic Energy Authority, 229, 241; and balance of power, 149, 232–36, 244, 256, 343n.19, 343nn.15–16; BTWC rejected by, 238–39, 344n.46; chemical weapons of, 188–89, 195, 238, 269, 306n.32; conventional capabilities of, 235, 240,

243, 244, 344n.54; denuclearization by, 9–10, 12, 214, 227, 231–32, 235, 238, 244, 256, 261, 269, 344n.54; deterrence by, generally, 242; domestic politics of, 234–35, 239–44; economy of, 44, 46, 230, 235, 239–42, 245, 262, 264, 283–84; free-trade agreements with Iraq, 265; IAEA inspections in, 233; IAEA's reprimand of, 238, 264; *infitah* (economic reform) in, 44, 222, 235, 240–41, 245, 264, 277, 284, 345nn.56–57; Iranian threat to, 233, 236, 243–44, 343n.19; Islamists on nuclear weapons, 242, 243; Israeli threat to, 237, 240, 243, 251–52, 344n.50, 346n.69; Israel threatened by, 188–89, 194, 203, 230, 334n.6, 336n.28 (*see also under* Nasser, Gamal Abdul); *kawmiya* (pan-Arabism) in, 233, 242–43, 283; Libya's relations with, 214, 221, 240, 341n.28, 343n.16; military expenditures in, 241, 345n.56; missile program of, 229, 230–31; as "most likely" to acquire nuclear weapons, 10, 232, 343n.15; NPR criticized by, 236, 264; NPT signed/ratified by, 214, 230–31, 235, 236–38, 241–42, 263–64, 345n.57; NPT violations by, 237–38, 347n.14; nuclear industry in, 231; nuclearization by, 3, 4, 229–30, 242–44, 260–61, 302n.18; NWFZ endorsed by, 236–37, 241; overflights over Dimona by, 189, 230; overview of/conclusions, 21–22, 229–31, 244–45, 345–46n.69; secret nuclear weapons program in, 229, 232, 233, 343n.21; self-help in, 244; Soviet Union's relations with, 229, 230, 232, 233–34, 244, 256, 343n.26, 345n.68; U.S. relations with/aid to, 230, 235, 241, 261. *See also* Mubarak, Hosni; Nasser, Gamal Abdul; al-Sadat, Anwar; Six-Day War; Yom Kippur War
Einhorn, Robert J., 6, 286
Eitan, Rafel, 204
El-Baradei, Mohammed: on Egypt's NPT violations, 238; on incentives for proliferation, 249; on Iran's nuclear capability, 172–74; on Iraq's nuclear capability, 152; on Israel's nuclear capability, 118; Nobel Peace Prize awarded to, 30; on nuclear ambiguity, 211–12; on nuclear proliferation, 7, 35

El Guibaily, Abdel Maaboud, 344n.54
EMIS, 150–51
Endicott, John E., 78
Endo Tetsuya, 77
EPB (Economic Planning Board; South Korea), 87, 89, 93
equifinality, 52, 80
Esfahan (Iran), 164, 173
Eshkol, Levi, 191, 197, 198, 200–203, 211, 337n.44, 337n.48, 347n.23
EU3 (Britain, Germany, France), 172–73, 180, 182–83
EURATOM, 64
EURENCO, 151
Ezz, Ismat, 235

Fahimifar, Ahmad, 348n.35
Fahmy, Ismail, 232, 240, 344n.50
Fahmy, Nabil, 4, 14, 167, 233, 238, 262, 266
al-Faisal, Prince Saud, 3
Al-Faqi, Mustafa, 242
FASW (Federation of American Scientists), 334n.5, 343n.21
Fatah Revolutionary Council, 221
Fedayeen Saddam, 154
Federation of American Scientists (FASW), 334n.5, 343n.21
Federation of Korean Industries, 89
Feinstein, Lee, 264–65, 291–92
Feldman, Shai, 190
Fesharaki, Fereydun, 177
findings, 249–99; on democracy/nuclear choices, 272–75; on domestic approaches to political survival, 255, 275–89, 287 (table), 348n.35, 348n.38, 348nn.28–30, 349n.41; on neorealism, 250–61, 346n.7; on norms/constructivism, 267–71; overview of, 249–50; on rational-institutionalism, 261–67
Finnemore, Martha, 32
Fissile Material Cut-Off Treaty, 291
Five-Year Plan (North Korea), 126
Ford, Gerald, 91–92
Four Nuclear Principles (Japan), 68
Fourth Defense Build-Up (Japan), 73
France, 38, 187, 191
Freier, Shalhevet, viii, 203, 337n.51
Fukuda Takeo, 64, 68, 75
Fukuda Yasuo, 77
Fukuryu Maru, 66

Funakoshi, Takehiro, 77–78
Furukawa, 72

Galili, Israel, 190, 192, 202
Gallois, Pierre, 309n.3
Al-Gamasi, Abd Al-Ghani, 235
Gaubatz, Kurt T., 272
Gay, Corey, 186
Gaza, 194, 206, 215, 335n.21
GCC (Gulf Cooperation Council), 168
General People's Congress (Libya), 225–26
Gensuikin (Japanese Congress Against A and H Bombs), 310n.22
Gensuikyo (Japanese Council Against A and H Bombs), 66, 310n.22
George, Alexander L., 250, 289, 303n.22, 304n.7, 308n.47
Gerges, Fawaz, 347n.14
al-Ghafour, Humam, 158
Ghandi, Indira, 308n.49, 348n.40
Ghanem, Shokri, 216, 224, 225, 226
Ghazala, Abdel Halim Abu, 230–31
al-Ghazali, Muhammad, 243
Gheit, Ahmed Aboul, 238
Glaser, Charles L., 26
Glenn Amendment (U.S., 1977), 307n.41
global economy, orientation to, 17–20, 275, 304nn.33–35, 347n.26
Glosserman, Brad, 8
Green, Michael J., 70, 314n.70
Green Book, 226
Gregory, Barbara M., 345n.57
Guam doctrine (U.S.), 25, 83, 253
Guardian Council (Iran), 182
Gulf Cooperation Council (GCC), 168
Gulf War (1991), 189, 195, 206
Gulf War (1993), 208

Habib, Philip, 314n.71
Halabi, Salah, 243
Hamza, Khidir, xi, 145, 149, 157, 264
Hao Pei-tsun, 102
Harel, Isser, 198
Hashmi, Sohail H., 306n.27
Hassig, Ralph C., 121–22, 127
Hata Tsutomu, 309n.2
Haykal, Mohamed Hasanayn, xi, 208, 234, 239–40, 343n.26, 346n.69
Al-Hazen Ibn Al-Haytham Center for Research, 158

Hedayat, Salah, 221, 229, 232, 233, 240, 342n.2
hedging, nuclear, 207, 275, 303n.24, 306n.33, 314n.68, 349n.44
hegemony. *See* coercion, effectiveness of; *and specific countries*
Helmy, Abdelkader, 230–31
Herter, Christian, 187
Herut (Israel), 197
Hezbollah, 167
Hiroshima, 15, 32, 36, 66–68, 267–68
Hojatiyye, 180
Holocaust, 188, 197, 208–9, 258, 270, 282, 338n.70
Honecker, Erich, 130
Hong Song-nam, 135
Hosokawa Morihiro, 59
Howeidi, Amin, 243
Hsia Hsin, 101
Hsin Chu program (Taiwan), 100
Hsu Cho-yun, 100, 112
Hu Chen-pu, 104
Hu Jintao, 115
Hussein, King, 203, 208
Hussein Uday, 158
Huwaysh, 'Abd-al-Tawab 'Abdallah Al-Mullah, 156, 159
Hwang Jang-yop, 120, 134
Hyundai, 135

IAEA (International Atomic Energy Agency): inspections by, 29, 78, 217–18, 233; and Iran, 165, 170–75, 178, 180, 182–84, 186; Iran's weapons program undetected by, 29–30, 194–95, 263; and Iraq, 143, 146, 149–53; Iraq's weapons program undetected by, 29–30, 194–95, 263, 305n.11; Libya's weapons program undetected by, 29–30, 194–95, 263; Nobel Peace Prize awarded to, 290–91; and North Korea, 118, 122–24, 130–32; North Korea's weapons program detected by, 30; Quadripartite Agreement with, 38; reprimand of Egypt, 238, 264; safeguards agreement, 64; and South Korea, 85–86, 95; and Taiwan, 102, 107–8, 113
IAEC (Iraqi Atomic Energy Commission), 143, 149, 153, 157–58
IAEC (Israel Atomic Energy Commission), 190, 199, 201, 206, 211

Ibrahim, Ahmad, 225–26
ideal types, 44, 292, 307n.45
Idris al-Sanusi, King, 216, 217, 219–20
Ikeda Hayato, 70, 71, 75
Imai, Ryūkichi, 62, 65, 72
IMF (International Monetary Fund), 87, 89–90, 96
"Independent Defense" slogan (*Jishu bōei*; Japan), 76
India: democracy in, 38, 272; domestic support for nuclear weapons in, 33–34; economic reforms in, 308n.49; "no first use" policy of, 33; NPT rejected by, 7, 305n.12; nuclearization by, 302n.18, 308n.49, 348n.40; nuclear tests by, 7, 30, 32–34, 210, 243; U.S. nuclear technology exported to, 192
Indonesia, 302n.18
industrial/technological infrastructures, 9–10
Indyk, Martin, 228
INER (Institute for Nuclear Energy Research; Taiwan), 101–2, 108
infitah (economic reform): in Egypt, 44, 222, 235, 240–41, 245, 264, 277, 284, 345nn.56–57; in Iraq, 155; in Libya, 222–23, 277, 282
Inoguchi Takashi, 313n.48, 346n.8
Inshas (Egypt), 229, 242
Institute for Nuclear Energy Research (INER; Taiwan), 101–2, 108
International Atomic Energy Agency. *See* IAEA
International Court of Justice on the Legality of Nuclear Weapons, 34
international institutions, legitimacy of, 28–32, 261–67, 290–91. *See also specific institutions*
internationalization, 5, 18–19, 301n.7, 348n.29; effects on domestic policy, 40–47, 51–53, 307–8nn.44–49, 307n.41, 308nn.52–53; findings on, 276–77, 286–87, 287–88, 347n.27; and ideal types, 44, 307n.45; rewarding, 293–95
internationalizing models of political survival, 307n.41, 308nn.52–53; affinity with denuclearization, 17, 18–19, 21, 22, 38, 40–47, 51–53, 245, 308n.52; characteristics of, 276; in China, 260; findings regarding, 270, 272, 276–77,

internationalizing (*continued*)
282, 284–89, 308n.46; and ideal types, 307n.45; in Japan, 46; policy implications regarding, 293–95; in South Korea, 46, 94; in Taiwan, 46, 110, 111. *See also* global economy, orientation to; *infitah*; *juche*

International Monetary Fund (IMF), 87, 89–90, 96

intifada, 215

inward-looking models of political survival: affinity with nuclear weapons, 5, 17, 19, 21–22, 46, 51–52, 211; characteristics of, 41; in Egypt, 239, 242, 245; findings regarding, 276–77, 280–81, 283–84, 286–88; in India, 308n.49, 348n.40; in Iran, 44, 175–76, 180, 182, 186; in Iraq, 154–56, 160; in Libya, 222–23; in North Korea, 138; policy implications regarding, 293–96, 298–99; in South Korea, 87, 89, 94–95, 97. *See also* autarky; *juche*

Iran, 164–86; as axis of evil member, 165–66; and balance of power, 146, 257; banks in, sanctions against, 296; chemical weapons used by, 195, 269, 306n.32; conventional capabilities of, 145, 167, 168, 182; CTBT signed by, 171; defiant nuclear behavior of, x, 3, 7, 30; deterrence by, generally, 166, 168, 169; domestic opposition to the NPT in, 177–79, 182; domestic politics of, 175–85, 349n.44; economy of, 46, 166, 174, 175–77, 178–80, 181–82, 183–85, 186, 281, 294, 297; Egypt threatened by, 233, 236, 243–44, 343n.19; IAEA misses weapons program in, 29–30, 194–95, 263; IAEA's promotion of nuclear reactor programs in, 264; and international institutions, 170–75; Israel threatened by, 189–90, 192, 206, 207, 208, 209, 334–35nn.15–16 (*see also under* Ahmadinejad, Mahmoud); military expenditures of, 175; as "most likely" to acquire nuclear weapons, 11; NPT signed/ratified by, 145, 164, 170; NPT violations by, 7, 165, 172–73, 186, 194, 263, 301n.2; nuclear capabilities of, 350n.58; nuclearization by, 33, 260–61, 302n.18, 347n.13; and nuclear weapons development, 164, 170–75, 177; NWFZ

endorsed by, 241; overview of/conclusions, 21–22, 164–65, 185–86; Pakistan's relations with, 257; as potentially supplying technologies to terrorists, 301n.2; reformers vs. radicals in, 43–44, 178–82, 184, 186; and shifting logics of relative power, 165–70; as threat to other Arab states, 1, 233, 236, 343n.19; U.S. sanctions against, 349n.49. *See also* Ahmadinejad, Mahmoud

Iran-Iraq war (1980–88), 9, 14, 147, 280–81, 328

Iraq, 143–63; and balance of power, 146; and biological/chemical weapons, 145, 147–48, 195, 238, 269, 281; conventional capabilities of, 206; domestic politics of, 154–61; economy of, 46, 145, 154–55, 157, 159, 161, 265, 280, 295; free-trade agreements of, 265; IAEA misses weapons program in, 29–30, 194–95, 263, 305n.11; IAEA's promotion of nuclear reactor programs in, 264; *infitah* (economic reform) in, 155; and international institutions, 149–54; Israel threatened by, 189, 205, 206–7, 209; Kuwait invaded by, 231; military expenditures of, 156; as "most likely" to acquire nuclear weapons, 11; and the NPT, 143, 149; NPT violations by, 194, 263, 347n.14; nuclearization by, 3, 257, 302n.18; and nuclear weapons development, 143, 145–47, 156–57; overview of/conclusions, 21–22, 143–44, 161–63; and relations with neighboring states, 144–45; self-help in, 144–49; WMD dismantled by UNSCOM, 207. *See also* Saddam Hussein

Iraqi Atomic Energy Commission. *See* IAEC (Iraqi Atomic Energy Commission)

Iraqi Special Security Organization, 162

Iraq Survey Group. *See* Duelfer report; ISG

Iraq War (2003), 6, 228, 257

Isfahan facility (Iran), 171

ISG (Iraq Survey Group), 144–45, 148, 152–53, 155, 159–62. *See also* Duelfer report

Ishiba Shigeru, 78

Ishihara Shintaro, 75–76, 77

Ishii factions, 75

Isis (Tammuz-2), 143

Islamic bomb, 213, 261, 306n.27

Islamic fundamentalists, 220–21
Islamic Martyrs' Group, 224
Islamic Revolution, 294
Islamist terrorist attacks on Israeli civilians, 205, 207
Israel, 187–212; on ACRS, 195–96, 205, 208, 237; ambiguous nuclear policy of, 193, 196–212, 243, 257–58, 282–83, 337n.51, 338–39nn.71–72, 338n.66, 339n.77; Arab states' attacks on/threats to, generally, 187, 193, 208–9, 232, 339n.75 (see also specific countries below); and balance of power, 209, 257; BTWC rejected by, 336n.29; chemical weapons, protective measures against, 208, 338n.69; conventional capabilities of, 191–92, 198–200, 203–4, 209–11, 244, 256, 282, 339n.73; CTBT ratification opposed by, 29; CTBT signed by, 29, 336n.32; CWC signed by, 204–5; democracy in, 210–11, 272–73, 339n.76, 347n.22; deterrence by, generally, 189–90, 192, 198, 200, 203, 206–11, 210, 229, 307n.37, 339n.73; dilemmas of international survival, 188–93, 334–35nn.15–16, 334n.10, 334n.12, 334nn.6–7; domestic coalitions in, 197, 204–5, 211; domestic politics of, 197–209, 336–37nn.38–44, 337n.48, 337nn.50–51, 337nn.58–59, 338n.62, 338–39nn.70–71, economic recession in, 202; economy of, 46, 197–98, 201, 202–3, 204, 205, 211, 282; Egyptian threat to, 188–89, 194, 203, 230, 334n.6, 336n.28 (see also under Nasser, Gamal Abdul); Egypt threatened by, 237, 240, 243, 251–52, 344n.50, 346n.69; France's relations with, 191; France's secret nuclear agreement with, 187; Gaza occupied by, 194, 215, 335n.21; and Gaza withdrawal, 206; Holocaust memories in, 208–9, 258, 270, 282, 338n.70; independence of, 187; industrial/technological infrastructure of, 9; internationalization of, 211; Iranian threat to, 189–90, 192, 206, 207, 208, 209, 334–35nn.15–16 (see also under Ahmadinejad, Mahmoud); Iraqi threat to, 189, 205, 206–7, 209; Islamist terrorist attacks on civilians in, 205, 207; Libya's relations with, 215–16, 226–27; Nazi scientists hunted by, 229; NPT rejected by, 7, 193–95, 203, 237, 263, 272, 305n.12; nuclear capabilities/arsenal of, 187, 232, 334n.5; nuclear-energy needs of, 197–98; nuclearization by, 3, 302n.18; nuclearization by, launch of, 19, 32–33, 282; nuclear secrecy in, 200, 204, 206–7, 336n.43, 338–39n.71, 343n.27; NWFZ endorsed by, 195–96, 204, 211, 236–37, 263, 272, 347n.21; Osiraq reactor bombed by, 204, 215, 280, 338n.66; overview of/conclusions, 21–22, 187, 209–12, 339nn.72–77; Palestinian relations with (see Oslo agreements); public reluctance/acceptance of nuclear deterrence by, 207-8, 307n.37; second-strike capabilities of, 190; self-help in, 190, 192–93, 208–10; size of, 190, 198; U.N. bias against/isolation of, 194, 196, 209, 258, 263, 335–36n.27, 336n.36; U.N. embargo of, 192; UNESCO's expulsion of, 194; U.S. coercion of, 191–92, 193–94, 200–201, 335n.24, 337n.50; U.S. commitments to/relations with, 190–91, 198, 202–3, 205, 261, 335n.21; U.S. nuclear technology/aid to, 192, 339n.74; vulnerability of, 24, 26, 188, 192, 209, 232, 257–58; West Bank occupied by, 194, 215, 335n.21. See also Ben-Gurion, David; Dimona nuclear facility; Six-Day War; Yom Kippur War
Israel Atomic Energy Commission. See IAEC (Israel Atomic Energy Commission)

Ja'afar, Ja'afar Dhiya, xi, 153, 157
Jaffee Center (Tel Aviv University), 206
Jallud, Abd Al-Salam, 213, 221, 222–23
Jamahiriyya (people's power; Libya), 220, 222, 227–28
al-Janabi, Fadil, 160
Jannati, Ahmad, 182
Japan, 57–81, 302n.18; Atomic Energy Law, 68, 72, 268, 311n.32; and balance of power, 259–60; China's relations with, 73; Constitution of, 58, 62, 65, 68–69, 70, 74, 77–78, 80, 268, 311n.32; conventional capabilities of, 62–63, 74; denuclearization in, 252–53; deterrence by, generally, 66; domestic politics of, 68–79, 310–11nn.22–26,

Japan (*continued*)
  311nn.31–32, 311–12nn.34–38,
  312n.41, 312–13nn.43–44, 313n.48,
  313nn.50–51, 313n.59, 314nn.62–63,
  314n.65 (*see also* "nuclear allergy";
  Yoshida doctrine); economic growth in,
  70–72, 312n.43, 314n.70 (*see also*
  Yoshida doctrine); economy of, 57, 58,
  59–60, 62–63, 69–74, 75–76, 77–80,
  254–55, 262, 278, 287; embedded nuclearization of, 16, 74, 268, 278–79;
  Four Nuclear Principles, 68; *kokusanka*
  plan, 58, 62, 64, 70, 74; LDP, 64, 66–76,
  78, 80, 310n.22, 313n.50; on legality of
  using nuclear weapons, 33, 65, 68; military expenditures/forces of, 62–63,
  71–72, 312–13nn.43–44; as "most" vs.
  "least likely" to acquire nuclear
  weapons, 10–11; natural resources vs.
  nuclear technological capabilities in, 10;
  norm-based constraints on, 16; North
  Korean threat to, 76–77, 78, 80, 255,
  259, 314n.68, 346n.5; NPT membership
  of, 3, 57–58, 62, 63, 69, 76, 262, 268;
  NPT ratification debate in, 60, 63–67,
  72–73, 74–76, 268, 310n.20, 311n.25,
  314n.71, 348n.30; "nuclear allergy" of,
  36, 60, 66–68, 80, 267–68, 278–79,
  312n.36; nuclear energy agreements of,
  287; as nuclear-free, 3, 255, 301n.5,
  346n.8 (*see also* Three Non-Nuclear
  Principles); nuclearization predicted for,
  66, 79, 255, 259, 304n.7, 309n.3,
  314n.68, 346n.5, 346n.10; nuclearization
  prescribed for, 349n.42; Okinawa's
  reversion to, 61–62, 76; overview of/
  conclusions, 21, 57–58, 79–81, 309n.2,
  314n.68, 314nn.70–71, 315n.74; South
  Korea's relations with, 73; structural
  power and dilemmas of, 58–63,
  309nn.3–4, 309n.9, 309–10n.11,
  310nn.13–14, 310n.16; uranium
  conversion facility supplied to Libya by,
  213; U.S. alliance with/commitments to,
  13, 25, 57–61, 70, 74, 79–80, 207,
  254–55, 259–61, 268, 278, 310n.14,
  314n.70; U.S. coercion of, 61, 62,
  253–54, 310n.16, 314n.71, 348n.30;
  Yoshida doctrine, 70, 73–74, 79, 80, 262,
  278–79, 312n.39. *See also* Three Non-
  Nuclear Principles

Japan Atomic Industrial Forum, 72, 75
JDA (Japan Defense Agency), 58–60,
  68–69, 75–76
Jennekens, Jon, 171
Jentleson, Bruce W., 298
Jericho II (missile), 167
John Paul II, Pope, 34–35
Johnson, Lyndon B., 61, 203, 309–10n.11
Joint Declaration for the Denuclearizaton
  of the Korean Peninsula, 131, 323n.37
Joint Venture Law (North Korea, 1984),
  105
Jones, Peter, 188, 344n.36, 346n.7
Jordan, 44
Jordanian-Israeli peace treaty (1994), 237
juche (autarky; North Korea), 44–45, 89,
  97, 121, 124–27, 130, 134, 138, 255,
  279
Junnosuke, Kishida, 60

Kaesong Industrial Park, 96, 99, 135, 137
Kahler, Miles, 40
Kahn, Herman, 314n.68, 346n.5
Kamil, Husseyn, 147, 158–60
Kamiya, Matake, 313n.57
Kaneko Kumao, 59, 286–87
Kang Song-san, 129, 131
Kant, Immanuel, 37
Katzenstein, Peter J., 311n.30, 312n.43,
  313n.49
Katzir, Efraim, 204
Kawasaki, 72
kawmiya (pan-Arabism), 233, 242–43, 283
Kazakhstan, 302n.18
KEDO (Korean Peninsula Energy Develop-
  ment Organization), 30–31, 123–24, 263
Keidanren (Federation of Economic Orga-
  nizations; Japan), 73
Keller, Bill, 43, 302n.11
Kennedy, John F., 7, 187, 188, 191,
  200–201, 337n.50
Kerr, Malcolm, 232–33
Kerry, John, 302n.11
Khadduri, Imad, xi
Khalaf, Mahmoud Muhammad, 243
Khamene'i, 177, 179, 180, 183, 257,
  348n.35
Khan, A. Q., 9, 30, 164, 172, 206, 214,
  217–18, 219, 265
Khan, Herman, 309n.3
Kharazi, Kamal, 171

Khatami, Mohammed, 178–80, 184, 190, 335n.16
Khomeini, Ayatollah Ruholla, 164, 166, 177, 184
Kimball, Daryl G., 354n.56
Kim Dae-Jung, 89, 93, 95, 96, 120, 125
Kim Dal-hyon, 131–32
Kim Il-Sung, 118–21, 123, 125–27, 130, 132, 136–37
Kim Jong-Il, 294; Agreed Framework signed by, 120; deterrence by, 105; and domestic politics, 125, 131; Internet use by, xi; Joint Venture Law spearheaded by, 129; *juche* adaptations under, 226, 255, 279; and Kim Dae-Jung, 96, 125; military rule of, 134–35, 137; nuclear policy of, 133; nuclear test by, 140, 228; patronage funds of, 295–96; purges by, 137–38; reform by, 132–33, 135, 140; *songun* policy of, 132–33, 136; support for/opposition to, 131–32
Kim Jong-U, 131, 137
Kim Kyong-hui, 131
Kim Mun-sung, 137
Kim Su-yong, 137
Kim Yong-ryong, 137, 325n.72
Kim Young-sam, 95
Kishi Nobusuke, 58, 68, 70, 309n.4, 312n.38
Kissinger, Henry, 61, 62, 91, 192, 314n.68, 335n.24, 346n.5
Kitamura, Motoya, 67, 310n.16
KMT (Kuomintang), 101, 106–7, 109–17, 254, 269, 279–80
Koizumi, Junichiro, 77, 78–80
kokusanka plan (import-substitution of weapons systems; Japan), 58, 62, 64, 70, 74
Komeito (Japan), 66, 74
Kono Fumihiko, 73
Kono Taro, 78
Korea Ch'anggwang Credit Bank, 296
Korean Peninsula Energy Development Organization (KEDO), 30–31, 123–24, 263
Korean Trade Promotion Corporation (KOTRA), 95, 316n.30
Kosaka, Masataka, 71
KOTRA (Korean Trade Promotion Corporation), 95, 316n.30
Kubo Takuya, 69
Kumgang Project, 99

Kuomintang. *See* KMT
Kuraishi Tadao, 68
Kusa, Musa, 225, 341n.30
Kusuda Minoru, xi, 58
Kyoto Imperial University, 57

Labor-Meretz (Israel), 204, 205, 208, 237
Labor Party (Israel), 203, 204–5, 211, 338n.62
Lacey, James, 163
Lakam (Israel), 200
La Rocque, Gene, 75
Lavizan-Shian (Iran), 174
Lavon, Pinhas, 198, 200, 201, 336n.42
LDP (Liberal Democratic Party; Japan), 64, 66–76, 78, 80, 310n.22, 313n.50
Lebanon, 44, 338n.61
Lebow, Richard N., 249, 289–90, 347n.17
Lee Jye, 117
Lee Teng-Hui, 102, 113–14
Lien Chan, 115
Levi, Michael A., 227
Liberal Democratic Party. *See* LDP
Libya, 213–28; chemical weapons of, 195, 218, 269, 306n.32; CIA report on, 217, 340n.15; CTBT ratified by, 218, 226; denuclearization by, 215, 216, 218–19, 223–25, 226–28, 256; domestic politics/reform in, 219–26, 227–28, 341n.29; economy of, 46, 219, 220, 221, 222–24, 225–26, 228, 281–82, 285; Egypt's relations with, 214, 221, 240, 341n.28, 343n.16; external security as justification for nuclearization, 214–16; IAEA inspections in, 217–18; IAEA misses weapons program in, 29–30, 194–95, 263; *infitah* (economic reform) in, 222–23, 277, 282; and international institutions, 217–19; Islam/Islamists in, 220–21, 223–24; Israel's relations with, 215–16, 226–27; Jamahiriyya in, 220, 222, 227–28; military expenditures in, 222; as "most" vs. "least likely" to acquire nuclear weapons, 10–11; NPR flouted by, 218–19; NPT signed/ratified by, 217, 220; NPT violations by, 194, 218, 263; nuclearization by, 3, 4, 206, 213–15, 302n.18, 339–40n.1, 340n.3, 340n.5; oil industry in, 220, 221, 222, 223, 226, 228; overview of/conclusions, 21–22,

Libya (*continued*)
213–14, 226–28; Pakistan's relations
with, 213, 340n.15; Pelindaba Treaty
signed by, 218; Reagan's attack on, 215;
repression/executions in, 220–21; Soviet
Union's relations with, 217; terrorism by,
215, 219, 221–22, 226, 228, 265; U.N.
boycott of/sanctions against, 219, 222,
228, 265; U.S. sanctions against/bombing
of, 218, 221–22, 226, 227, 228. *See also*
Qadhafi, Muammar
Libyan Islamic Fighting Group, 224
Likud (Israel), 204, 205–6, 211, 338n.62
Litwak, Robert S., 257
Livne, Eliezer, 200, 338n.70, 339n.77
Lockerbie disaster (Scotland, 1988), 219,
222, 223, 225, 228, 265, 341n.30
Lockheed scandal, 75
London Suppliers Group, 29
Lord, Winston, 314n.71

Ma'atouq, Ma'atouq Mohamed, 216, 219
Macmillan, Alexander S., 307n.36
Al-Magid, Wahid Abd, 233, 260
Mahoney, James, 258–59
Al-Majid (chemical 'Ali), 160, 162
Makoto Momoi, 59, 73
Malaysia, 217
Al-Mallah, Moyesser, 149
Mamlachtiut (statism; Israel), 197, 282
Mansfield, Edward D., 347n.25
MAN Technologie AG, 150
Mapai (Workers' Party; Israel), 197, 198,
200, 201, 203, 282, 336n.39
Mapam (Israel), 198–99, 336n.39
Margalit, Dan, 273, 339n.76
Mazarr, Michael J., 139, 317, 323
McNamara, Robert, 343n.15
Mearsheimer, John J., 304n.7, 309n.3,
346n.5
Megahed, Mounir, 242
Meir, Golda, 191, 194, 198, 203, 337n.55
Messerschmitt-Boelkow-Blohm, 230
methodology, 5–6, 8–11, 19–22, 23, 31,
35, 249–50, 251, 302–3nn.18–20,
303n.23, 303nn.22–24
Meyer, Stephen M., 6, 104, 285, 343n.15
MIC (Military Industrial Commission;
Iraq), 153–54, 158–61
Middle Eastern vs. East Asian nuclear poli-
cies: democracy as an account of, 16–17;

domestic political survival models of,
17–20, 277–78, 304nn.33–35; internationalizing model in East Asia, 18–19,
276–77, 348n.29; neoliberal institutionalist account of, 14–15; norm-based/
constructivist account of, 15–16, 36–37;
overview of, 249–50; and predictions of
rise in NWS, 6–7; quandary over, 3–6,
301n.5; research on/methodological issues, 8–11, 20–22, 302–3nn.18–20,
303nn.22–24; structural power/
neorealist account of, 11–14, 27–28,
251–52, 303nn.29–30; U.S. alliances'
role in, 12, 13–14. *See also* competing
perspectives on denuclearization
Miki Takeo, 62, 75, 254
Milani, Abbas, 281, 290, 295, 297
Military Industrial Commission (MIC;
Iraq), 153–54, 158–61
Military Intelligence (Israel), 204
Ministry of Foreign Affairs (MOFA;
Japan), 65, 72, 310–11n.24
Mirza, Suroor Mahmoud, 150
Missile Technology Control Regime
(MTCR), 29
Mitchell, Derek J., 105
Mitsubishi, 72, 73
Mitsui, 72
Mitsuya Kenkyū Jiken simulation exercise
(1965), 268
Miyazawa Kiichi, 59
Mochizuki, Mike, 69, 268
MOFA (Ministry of Foreign Affairs;
Japan), 65, 72, 310–11n.24
Mofaz, Shaul, 206
Mohajerani, Ayatollah, 177
Mohtashemi, Ali-Akbar, 178
Morocco, 3, 260–61
Morrow, James D., 40, 348–49n.41
Mossad (Israel), 204
Mossadegh, Muhammad, 166, 175
Mo'talefe, 180
Moussa, Amr, 243, 305n.15
MTCR (Missile Technology Control
Regime), 29
Mubarak, Gamal, 244
Mubarak, Hosni, 230–31, 233, 236–37,
238, 242, 243–44
Mueller, John, 304n.2, 306n.30
Mukhabarat (Iraqi intelligence), 22, 155,
157

Multilateral Middle East Peace Process
(1990s), 22, 32, 46, 195, 237
multipolarity, 9, 12, 27
al-Muntasir, Umar, 222–23
Muramatsu Takeshi, 58
Musharaf, Pervez, 130, 257
Muslim Brotherhood (Libya), 220
Muslim Brotherhood (Syria), 144
Mutual Security Treaty (U.S.-Japan, 1952),
57, 61

Al-Nabulsi, Shaker, 274
Nagai Yōnosuke, 60
Nagasaki, 15, 32, 36, 49–50, 66–68,
267–68
Naji, Muayad, 157
Nakasone Yasuhiro: on Japan's nuclearization, 69, 74, 76, 311–12n.35; memoirs
of, xi; in the NPT debate, 64; on Okinawa's reversion to Japan, 76; U.S. nuclear weapons allowed into Japan by,
312n.37
Nasrallah, Hassan, 335n.15
Nasser, Gamal Abdul: AEA created by,
229; anti-Israeli stance of, 188, 191,
194, 203, 230, 283, 334n.6, 338n.70;
chemical weapons use pioneered by, 238;
death of, 229, 240; on the Dimona nuclear facility, 233, 234; nationalizations
by, 239, 283; nuclear policy of, 229,
234, 238, 239, 240, 343n.30, 344n.54,
345–46n.69; pan-Arab commitment of,
162; relations with other Arab states,
232–33; on Soviet nuclear guarantees,
343n.26
Natanz (Iraq), 172
National Defence Programme Outline
(Japan, 1976), 62
National Intelligence Estimate. See NIE
National Oil Corporation (NOC; Libya),
225–26
National Security Council (U.S.), 62
National Security Research Council
(Japan), 68, 310n.24
National Unification Board
(South Korea), 93
Nazis, 208–9, 229. See also Holocaust
Ne'eman, Yuval, 190, 337n.58
neoclassical realism, 26, 259, 308n.53
neoliberal institutionalism, 14–15, 28–32,
305nn.13–15; findings on, 261–67,

neorealism: falsifiability of, 26, 27; findings
on, 250–61, 346n.7; on national security/
balance of power, 11–14, 250–51,
256–57, 303nn.29–30; vs. neoclassical
realism, 26, 259, 303n.26; offensive, 11,
301n.6; as open-ended (indeterminate),
63; overview of, 4–5, 301n.6; specificity
of predictions by, 304n.7
Netanyahu, Benjamin, 205, 237, 339n.77
nezam, 176
NI (Ni-go Kenkyū), 57
NIE (National Intelligence Estimate), 79,
164, 202, 278, 304n.4, 306, 307, 309,
312n.38, 320
Ni-go Kenkyū (NI), 57
Nimrod, Yoram, 337n.59
9/11 attacks (U.S., 2001), 224
Nishihara Masashi, 78
Nishimura Shingo, 77, 78
Nishina Yoshio, 57
Nixon, Richard M., 85, 89–90; China visit
by, 58–59, 83, 89, 103; Guam doctrine
of, 25, 83, 253; Israeli policy of,
191–92; on Japan, 61–62, 255, 309n.3,
310n.13; and Meir, 191, 194, 203; and
Sato, 61, 76, 203; on supplying nuclear
reactors to Egypt/Israel, 230, 241; and
Zhou Enlai, 310n.13
NOC (National Oil Corporation; Libya),
225–26
Non-Nuclear Principles. See Three Non-
Nuclear Principles
Non-proliferation Act (U.S., 1977),
307n.41
nonproliferation regime. See NPR
Normark, Magnus, 190, 334n.5
norms: against acquisition vs. use, 35; and
constructivism, 15–16, 267–71;
mobilizing capacity of, 41; norm-based/
constructivist account of denuclearization,
32–37, 49–50, 306nn.23–24,
306nn.27–33; nuclear taboos, 34–35,
37, 49, 267, 347n.20; violators of,
33–34
North Korea, 118–40; as axis of evil member, 119; China's commitment to, 255;
conventional capabilities of, 84, 121,
130, 321n.12; deterrence by, generally,
120, 121; deterring friendly/rival hegemons, 118–22; domestic politics of,
125–38; economy of, 44–45, 124,

North Korea (*continued*)
125–33, 134–35, 136–37, 138, 139–40, 279, 294–95; IAEA finds weapons program in, 30; industrial/technological infrastructure of, 9; and international institutions, 122–25; Japan threatened by, 76–77, 78, 80, 255, 259, 314n.68, 346n.5; Libya supplied with nuclear components by, 218; luxury imports to, ban on, 295, 296; military expenditures of, 121, 126, 130; as "most likely" to acquire nuclear weapons, 11; natural resources vs. nuclear technological capabilities in, 10; NPT rejected by, 123, 132, 139; NPT signed/ratified by, 122, 124, 133, 140, 320–21n.1; NPT violations by, 7, 76, 118, 194; nuclearization by, 302n.18; nuclearization by, influence of, 33, 259; nuclear missiles launched by, 67, 76–77, 80; nuclear tests by, x, 3–4, 7, 30, 118; nuclear tests by, reaction to, 34; and nuclear weapons development, 118–19, 127–29; as a nuclear weapons state, 118, 139, 321n.2, 321n.5, 325n.76; overview of/conclusions, 118, 138–40; as potentially supplying technologies to terrorists, 301n.2; sanctions on, 295–96; self-help in, 121; South Korea threatened by, 260; Soviet Union's commitment to, 255

NPR (nonproliferation regime), 107, 124, 174–75; anti-nuclear norms as origin of, 15, 32; collapse predicted for, 6; enforcement of, 291; ineffectiveness of, 264–65; influence of, 14, 261–62, 267

NPT (Nonproliferation Treaty, 1968): Additional Protocol, 15, 29, 85–86, 239; Article VI, 28–29, 30, 31, 39; beneficiaries of, 354n.56; counterfactual scenarios without NPT, 266–67, 347n.17; international institutional order represented by, 8, 303n.20; opt-out prerogative of, 193, 195; preventive influence of, 14–15, 28–29, 48–49; ratification of, 30–31, 38, 48–49, 305n.12; Review and Extension Conference, 196; sanctions against violators of, 298; second nuclear age following, 3, 301n.2; successes of, 266; two-tier system of, 14; widespread acceptance of, 7. *See also under specific countries*

"nuclear allergy" (Japan), 36, 60, 66–68, 80, 267–68, 278–79, 312n.36
nuclear energy industry, Japanese, 72, 75
nuclearization: costs of, 43, 307n.44; definition of, 301n.1; domino effect of, 33, 259–61, 346n.8. *See also* competing perspectives on denuclearization; Middle Eastern vs. East Asian nuclear policies; *and specific countries*
nuclear learning, 36
nuclear policies: international security affected by, 6–8, 302nn.10–11; political sensitivity of, 19–20; secrecy surrounding, xi, 7, 67–68. *See also* Middle Eastern vs. East Asian nuclear policies
Nuclear Posture Review (U.S., 1994), 33, 120
nuclear proliferation. *See* domino effect; NPR; NPT; reactive proliferation
nuclear status, definitions of, 274–75
nuclear taboos, 34–35, 37, 49, 106–7, 267, 347n.20
Nuclear Weapons Free Zone. *See* NWFZ
nuclear-weapons-states. *See* NWS
nuclear weapons tests: by China, 252; by India, 7, 30, 32–34, 210, 243; by Kim Jong-Il, 140, 228; by North Korea, x, 3–4, 7, 30, 118; by Pakistan, 7, 30, 32–34, 210, 243; U.N. sanctions against, 307n.41; by the United States, 66; U.S. sanctions against, 307n.41
NWFZ (Nuclear Weapons Free Zone): Egypt's endorsement of, 236–37, 241; Iran's endorsement of, 241; Israel's endorsement of, 195–96, 204, 211, 236–37, 263, 272, 347n.21; Middle East, 170, 171; South Korea, 94
NWS (nuclear-weapons-states): commitment to advance nuclear disarmament, 28; CTBT signed by, 29; NPT violations by, 30; rise in, 6–7; virtual, 33
Nye, Joseph S., Jr., 28

Obeidi, Mahdi, xi, 147, 161
October Revitalizing Reforms, 89
Office of Policy and International Relations (Iraq), 157
Ogilvie-White, Tanya, 27
Oh, Kongdan, 121–22, 127
O'Hanlon, Michael E., 227
Oil-for-Food program, 159–60, 265, 295

oil-rich vs. oil-poor countries, 10, 296–97
Okimoto, Daniel I., 66, 67, 310n.23
Okinawa, 61–62, 76
Olmert, Ehud, 209, 338–39n.71
Omar, Noh, 217
OPEC (Organization for Petroleum Export-
    ing Countries), 156
Organization of African Unity, 340n.3
Oros, Andrew L., 64
Osiraq (Iraq), 143, 146, 158, 204, 215,
    280, 338n.66
Oslo process/agreements (1993), 44, 46,
    147, 190, 195, 204–5, 211, 215, 237,
    338n.61
O'Sullivan, Meghan L., 349n.49
Ozawa Ichiro, 76, 77

Pakistan: democracy in, 272; domestic sup-
    port for nuclear weapons in, 33–34;
    Iran's relations with, 257; Libya's rela-
    tions with, 213, 340n.15; NPT rejected
    by, 7, 305n.12; nuclearization by,
    302n.18; nuclear tests by, 7, 30, 32–34,
    210, 243; vulnerability to massive con-
    ventional attacks, 24
Pak Pong-ju, 137
Palestine Liberation Organization. See PLO
Palestinians, 205, 215. See also Oslo agree-
    ments; PLO
Pan Am Flight 103 bombing. See Lockerbie
    disaster
Park Chung Hee, xi, 83–93, 97–98, 135
Park Keun-hye, 135
Partial Test Ban Treaty (PTBT), 201
Pasdaran, 176–84, 281, 293, 295–96. See
    also Revolutionary Guards
Pelindaba Treaty (1996), 218
Pempel, T. J., 311n.25
People First Party (PFP; Taiwan), 115
Peres, Shimon, xi, 187, 190, 192, 196,
    198–206, 216, 334n.12, 336n.42,
    337n.44
Perkovich, George, 343n.19
Perry, William, 119
perspectives on denuclearization. See com-
    peting perspectives on denuclearization
PFP (People First Party; Taiwan), 115
PLO (Palestine Liberation Organization),
    195, 204–5, 215, 237
policy implications, 289–99; and balance of
    power, 291–92; democracy as an ally of

denuclearization, 297–99, 350nn.53–54;
    and domestic political survival, 292–93;
    and international institutions, 290–91;
    rewarding natural constituencies of
    internationalizing models, 293–95;
    sanctions sensitive to differences between
    energy-rich/energy-poor targets, 296–97;
    stripping autarkic regimes from means to
    concentrate power, 295–96, 349n.49
political-survival models, 5, 40–47, 51–53,
    277–78, 302n.8, 307n.41,
    307–8nn.44–49, 308nn.52–53. See also
    domestic approaches to political survival;
    juche
Porter, Michael, 226
Pressler Amendment (U.S., 1985), 307n.41
prestige, 24, 33, 35, 138, 157, 162,
    168–69, 181, 272, 306n.28
process-tracing, 9, 303n.22
Program 93+2 (IAEA, 1992), 29
proliferation, nuclear. See domino effect;
    NPR; NPT; reactive proliferation
Proliferation Security Initiative, 99
prospect theory, 19, 46, 308n.48
PTBT (Partial Test Ban Treaty), 201
Pueblo (ship), 83, 127

Qadhafi, Saif al-Islam, 215, 216, 225, 226,
    340n.5
Qadhafi, Muammar: on Arab response to
    Libya's WMD removal, 305n.15; assassi-
    nation attempt on, 224; coup by, 220;
    coup feared by, 223; criticism of policy
    shift of, 298, 354n.55; daughter killed dur-
    ing U.S. bombing, 221–22; Internet use by,
    xi; on Israel's nuclear capability, 213, 215;
    on Libya's nuclearization, 339–40n.1; mo-
    tivations of, 228, 282, 342n.52; Muslim
    extremists repressed by, 220–21; on na-
    tionalism vs. globalization, 223; nationalis-
    tic/xenophobic policies of, 221, 226, 281;
    9/11 attacks condemned by, 224; nuclear
    weapons sought by, 213–15, 219, 221,
    226–28, 256, 281; on Pakistan, 213; pan-
    Arabism of, 162, 221, 222, 341n.37; pres-
    tige sought by, 221; reform resisted/sup-
    ported by, 222–23; terrorists/guerrilla
    movements supported by, 221–22, 227,
    281; U.S./Britain courted by, 223–24
Qadhafi International Foundation for
    Charity Associations, 225

Quandt, William, 194
Quemoy-Matsu incident, 100, 103

Rabin, Yitzhak, 195, 202, 203–5, 339n.73
Rafi (Israel), 201, 203, 211
Rafsanjani, Hashemi, 164–65, 169–70,
  175, 177–78, 180, 257, 269, 335n.16;
  blogging by, xi
Rahman, Ibrahim Abdel, 229
Ramadan, Taha Yasin, 147, 160
Ramon, Chaim, 205
Al-Rashed, Abd Al-Rahman, 168
rational (neoliberal) institutionalism find-
  ings, 261–67
RCC (Revolutionary Command Council;
  Iraq), 154, 157
RCC (Revolutionary Command Council;
  Libya), 217, 220
reactive proliferation, 24, 36, 244–45,
  251–52, 260. See also domino effect
Reagan, Ronald, 102, 192, 215, 221, 227
reasons of state, 5, 13, 19–20, 46–47, 181,
  251, 275
regional security institutions, 30–31. See
  also specific institutions
Reischauer, Edwin O., 61, 309n.9
Reiss, Mitchell B., 6, 71, 97–98, 188, 191,
  194, 279, 286, 314n.70
relative power, 4, 53, 58, 63, 103, 149,
  210, 333n.84; changes in, 49, 120,
  166–67, 186, 226–27, 232, 236,
  255–56, 257–58, 260–61, 267; definitional problems with, 25, 119; effects of,
  39, 51; policy implications regarding,
  290, 292; in structural theory (neorealism), 5, 24, 27, 165, 251–52, 259. See
  also balance of power; neorealism
rentier states, 10, 175, 178, 185, 296,
  303n.32
Republican Guard, 154
Revolutionary Command Council (RCC;
  Iraq), 154, 157
Revolutionary Command Council (RCC;
  Libya), 217, 220
Revolutionary Guards (Iran), 44, 166, 176.
  See also Pasdaran
Rezai, Mohsen, 166
Rhee, Syngman, 86–87, 110, 125, 279
Rho Tae-Woo, 94–95
Rice, Condoleezza, 260
Ri Jong-ok, 129

Ri Kunmo, 129
Roberts, Brad, 347n.25
Roh Moo-Huyn, 83, 96–97, 99, 279
Romania, 302n.18
Rometsch, Rudolf, 108
Rosecrance, Richard N., 7, 11, 28, 35,
  304n.1–2, 304n.7, 305n.16, 307n.38
Rosenau, James, 303n.30
Rowhani, Hassan, 183
Royal Libyan Army, 219
Rusk, Dean, 61, 193
Russia, 33, 296. See also Soviet Union

Al-Sa'adi, 'Amir Hamudi Hasan, 160
Sabri, Ali, 240
al-Sadat, Anwar, 264, 269, 283–84; assas-
  sin of, 176; coup attempt against, 240;
  infitah launched by, 240–41, 245, 264,
  345nn.56–57; isolation following economic reform, 44; Jerusalem trip by,
  234–35, 241; on nuclearization, 231;
  nuclear policy of, 234–35, 238, 241–42;
  peace initiative of, 189, 234, 240,
  241–42, 283–84; relations with Libya,
  221, 341n.28; Treaty on Friendship and
  Cooperation with Soviet Union denounced by, 345n.68; wataniyia (Egyptian nationalism) policy of, 233; Yom
  Kippur war launched by, 240
Saddam Hussein, 42, 143–63, 176; chemical weapons used by/threatened, 195,
  206, 238, 306n.32; missile attacks on Israel, 189, 192, 206; nuclear policy of, xi,
  257, 280, 304n.35; ousting of, 166, 168,
  170; prestige sought by, 221; threatens
  to destroy Israel, 195, 206, 207, 208;
  U.N. containment of, 167; U.N.
  weapons inspectors expelled by, 207–8;
  U.S. capture of, 227, 228, 257; war ad-
  ventures against Iran/Kuwait, 265
Sadek, Mohammed Ahmed, 240
Sahd, Ibrahim Abd-al-Aziz, 224
Sa'id, Khalid Ibrahim, 160
Said, Mohamed Kadry, 210, 234,
  242, 283
Saif, Mostafa Elwi, 343n.30
al-Saji, Abdul-Wahid, 149
Salah-ad Din (Saladdin), 232
Salameh, Salameh Ahmad, 242
Salehi, Ali Akbar, 169
Samore, Gary, 350n.58

Samuels, Richard J., 311n.31, 312n.39, 312n.41, 313n.48
Sanken (Industrial Problems Study Council; Japan), 73
Sapir, Pinhas, 198, 202, 203, 337n.50
Sarney, José, 38
al-Satidah, Serwan, 158
Sato Eisaku, 57–58, 61–62, 68–69, 71, 73–76, 308n.52, 309–10nn.9–11, 311n.34
Sato-Johnson communiqué (1965), 57, 61, 309–10n.11
Saudi Arabia, nuclearization by, 3, 260–61
Schelling, Thomas, 7, 32, 249, 305n.16, 306n.24
Schiff, Ze'ev, 190
Schlesinger, James, 119, 254
Schweller, Randall L., 27, 308n.53
second nuclear age, 3, 6, 14, 37–38, 47, 277, 301, 302
selection bias, 305n.13
self-help, 26, 48, 250–51, 256, 266; vs. alliances, 25, 59–60, 82, 253; definitions of, 27, 53; and the economy, 53; in Egypt, 244; in Iraq, 144–49; in Israel, 190, 192–93, 208–10; neorealist account of, 4, 24, 25–28, 60, 63, 82, 250–51, 253, 254–56; in North Korea, 121; in South Korea, 82, 97; structural realist account of, 48; in Taiwan, 105, 106
Semati, Mohamed, 181
September 11 attacks (U.S., 2001), 224
Al-Shadhili, Sa'd Al-Din, 243
Shah of Iran, 144, 145, 164–67, 170, 175–76
Al-Shahristani, Hussain, xi, 157
Shalom, Zaki, 334n.7
Shalqam, Mohamed Abd-al-Rahman, 224
al-Shamikh, Mubarak, 223
Shamkhani, Ali, 169
Sharon, Ariel, 204, 206, 211, 215, 216, 338n.59, 338n.66
Shatt-el-Arab, 144–45
Al-Shawi, Hisham, 149, 158
Sidki, Ahmed, 240
Sigal, Leon, 258, 321n.10
Singh, Sonali, 23, 275, 307n.46, 348n.28
Sirte (Libya), 217
Six-Day War (1967), 189, 194, 203, 230, 335n.21, 336n.28

Six-Party Talks (SPT), 30–31, 99, 124–25, 140, 263, 298
Slaughter, Anne-Marie, 264–65, 291–92
Snyder, Jack, 309n.5, 322n.24, 347n.25, 348n.38
Socialist Party (Japan), 64, 66, 74
son'gun chŏngch'i (military first; North Korea), 132–33, 136
Soong, James, 115
Soshinkai (Pure Hearts Association; Japan), 64, 68, 75
South Africa, 192, 294, 302n.18
South Asia, 302–3n.19
South Korea, 82–99; Agency for Defense Development, 90; Agreed Framework, 95; alternatives to nuclear proliferation, 83–85; Communist groups in, 87; conventional capabilities of, 84, 91, 130; democracy in, 273; denuclearization in, 252–53; deterrence by, generally, 82; domestic politics of, 86–94; economy of, 84–85, 86–94, 95–97, 98, 99, 254, 262; Force Modernization Plan, 84, 90; Japan's relations with, 73; "Joint Declaration for a Non-Nuclear Korean Peninsula," 95; as "least likely" to acquire nuclear weapons, 11; military expenditures of, 84, 90; Mutual Defense Treaty, 82; natural resources vs. nuclear technological capabilities in, 10; as a non-nuclear state, 82, 95, 316n.26; North Korean threat to, 260; and the NPT, 82, 84–86, 88, 90–91, 95; NPT joined by, 3, 262, 301n.5; as nuclear-free, 3; nuclearization by, 302n.18; overview of/conclusions, 21, 82, 97–99; peace and prosperity policy of, 97; reconciliation and non-aggression pact by, 95; self-help in, 82, 97; and structural power/alliance dilemmas, 82; sunshine policy of, 96; transition to democracy, 94–97; U.S. abandonment of, 82–83; U.S. alliance with/aid to, 13, 25, 84, 91, 260, 268; U.S. coercion of, 83–84, 91–92, 253–54
Soviet Union: collapse of, 255; conventional capabilities of, 232; Egypt's relations with, 229, 230, 232, 233–34, 244, 256, 343n.26, 345n.68; Libya's relations with, 217; military assistance to Arab states by, 192; "no first use" policy of, 33; North Korea's commitment from,

Soviet Union (*continued*)
255; and the Yom Kippur War, 189,
334n.10
SPT. *See* Six-Party Talks
Stalin, Joseph, 119
Steinitz, Yuval, 339n.71
Straits of Tiran, 188, 189, 194
structural realism, 48, 52, 58, 188, 252.
See also neorealism
Suez Canal, 230, 239, 242
suicide bombing, 207, 215
Sumitomo, 72
Su Tseng-chang, 117
Symington Amendment (U.S., 1976),
307n.41
Syria: chemical weapons of, 195; free-trade
agreements with Iraq, 265; NPT viola-
tions by, 347n.14; potential nucleariza-
tion by, 3, 302n.18; Oslo process meet-
ings boycotted by, 338n.61. *See also*
Yom Kippur War

taboo, definition of, 306n.23. *See also* nuclear taboos
Taiwan, 100–117; and balance of power,
106; Chinese threat to, 287–88; conventional capabilities of, 105–6, 110;
democracy in, 113–15, 273; denuclearization in, 252–53; and dependence on external energy resources, 112; deterrence
by, generally, 105; domestic politics of,
109–13, 349n.41; and doubts of U.S.
commitment, 103–4, 319n.25; economy
of, 106, 108–10, 111–13, 114, 115, 116,
260, 263, 279–80; independence of,
287–88; KMT massacres civilians in,
107, 269; as "least likely" to acquire nuclear weapons, 11; military expenditures
of, 105–6; natural resources vs. nuclear
technological capabilities in, 10; neorealist perspectives on, 104–6; and the NPT,
102, 108; NPT joined by, 3, 301n.5; as
nuclear-free, 3, 262–63; nuclearization
by, 302n.18; and nuclear weapons as
taboo, 106–7; overview of/conclusions,
21, 100–103, 115–17; self-help in, 105,
106; and structural power/existential
threats, 103–6; U.S. coercion of, 13,
104–5, 108, 253–54; U.S. commitment
to, 25, 260, 268; vulnerability to massive
conventional attacks, 24–25, 26

Taiwan Research Reactor (TRR),
101–2
Tajura (Libya), 217
Takemi Keizo, 78
Takeyama Yasuo, 310n.14
Takeyh, Ray, 349n.44
Taliban, 166
Tanaka Kakuei: memoirs of, xi, 313n.44;
on military expenditures, 313n.44; recession under, 75; on the Three Non-
Nuclear Principles, 64, 69
Tang Chun-po, 100
Tang Fei, 102
Tannenwald, Nina, 306n.23
al-Tantawi, Moahmmed Sayyid, 243
Tel Aviv, 205
Tel Aviv University, 206
terrorists: Israeli civilians attacked by, 205,
207; Libyan, 215, 219, 221–22, 226,
228, 265; Qadhafi's support of, 221–22,
227, 281; technologies supplied to,
301n.2
Thant, U, 194
theories, generally: clarity/observable
implications of, 304n.8; counterfactuals'
role in, 305n.14; necessary/sufficient
conditions, 303n.32, 308n.47; testing
of, 5–6, 251, 302n.9. *See also* counterfactuals
Three Arrows Study Incident (1965), 67
Three Non-Nuclear Principles (Japan): Abe
on, 81, 259; force of, 69, 268; Fukuda
Yasuo on, 77; Koizumi on, 77, 78–79;
Nakasone on, 76; and NPT ratification,
57–58, 64, 311n.25; Sato on, 61–62, 68,
71, 76, 311n.34; Tanaka on, 69; violations of, 69, 74, 76–77, 312n.37
Timerbaev, Roland, 347n.17
Tōjō Hideki, 57
Togo Fumihiko, 64
Tokyo Institute of Physical and Chemical
Research (Riken), 57
Toshiba, 72
Toufanian, Hasan, 167
trade liberalization, 307–8n.46. *See also*
economy; internationalization; *infitah*;
and under individual countries
Treaty of Mutual Cooperation and Security
(1960), 57
Treaty on Friendship and Cooperation
(1971), 345n.68

TRR (Taiwan Research Reactor), 101–2
Truman, Harry S., 119
Tsai, Michael, 117, 280
Tunisia, nuclearization by, 3, 260–61
Turkey, nuclearization by, 3, 260–61, 287–88
al-Tuwaitha, 149, 158

UAE (United Arab Emirates), 3, 260–61, 265
Ukraine, 302n.18
UNESCO, 194
Unger, Leonard, 101
United Arab Emirates (UAE), 3, 260–61, 265
United Arab Republic, 239–40
United Nations, 107–8, 143–44; Israel's isolation in, 194, 196, 209, 258, 263, 335–36n.27, 336n.36; sanctions against nuclear tests, 307n.41; Sinai peacekeepers withdrawn by, 194 (see also Six-Day War); on Zionism as racism, 194
United Nations Security Council. See UNSC
United Nations Special Commission. See UNSCOM
United States: alliances'/coercion's effects on nuclear behavior, generally, 12, 13–14, 25, 253–54 (see also under specific countries); extended deterrence (nuclear umbrella), 16, 38, 59, 61, 63, 68–71, 75, 91, 120, 191, 194, 207, 232, 254–255, 260, 268, 270, 311n.24, 347n.13; CTBT obstructed by, 29; on Egyptian nuclearization, likelihood of, 230; Egypt's relations with/aid from, 230, 235, 241, 261; hydrogen bomb tests by, 66; "no first use" policy of, 33; nuclearization by, 38; sanctions against nuclear tests, 307n.41. See also Carter, Jimmy; Clinton, Bill; Nixon, Richard M.; and under individual countries
UNMOVIC, 152–53, 263
UNSC (United Nations Security Council): collective action problems in, 264–65; and Iranian non-compliance, 173–74, 181, 183–86; and Iraqi non-compliance, 151–52, 159; luxury imports to North Korea banned by, 295, 296; Resolution 1540, 29; sanctions on North Korea by, 99

UNSCOM (United Nations Special Commission), 143, 151–53, 158–60, 207, 263
US-ROC Defense Pact, 100, 318n.2

Vaezi, Mahmud, 178
Vanunu, Mordechai, 187, 243
Velayati, 'Ali Akbar, 166
Von Stein, Jana, 305n.13

Walsh, James J., 302n.16, 343n.31, 345n.57
Walt, Stephen M., 25–26, 314n.68
Waltz, Kenneth N., 12, 25, 60, 104, 253, 255, 304, 309n.3, 314
Wang Shih-chieh, 112
Ward, Michael D., 111
Washington-Taipei Mutual Security Treaty, 25
watanyia (Egyptian nationalism), 233
Way, Christopher R., 23, 275, 307n.46, 348n.28
Weapons Exploitation Committee (South Korea), 90
Weber, Max, 44, 307n.45
West Bank, 194, 215, 335n.21
Whytock, Christopher A., 298
Williamson, Murray, 163
Windrem, Robert, 188
Wit, Joel S., 349n.48
Woods, Kevin, 163
Worker's Party (North Korea), 120, 125, 131
WTO (World Trade Organization), 42, 173, 182, 294
Wu, Samuel S. G., 40, 348–49n.41
Wu Ta-you, xi, 100, 105, 107, 112, 116, 269

Yaari, Meir, 190
Yadin, Yigal, 339n.73
Yager, Joseph A., 279
Yang Chao-yie, 102
Yariv, Aharon, 339n.73
Yatom, Danny, 206
Yazdi, Ayatollah Mesbah, 180, 269
Yemen civil war (1963–67), 238
Yen Chen-hsing, 101, 113
Yi Song-nok, 131
Yog'aksan General Trading Company (North Korea), 296

Yomiuri Shimbun, 66, 310n.23
Yom Kippur War (1973), 189, 192, 203, 233, 240, 334n.10
Yongbyong nuclear research facility (North Korea), 30, 95, 127–28, 130
Yon Hyong-muk, 129
Yoshida, Yasuhiko, 315n.74
Yoshida doctrine (Japan), 70, 73–74, 79, 80, 262, 278–79, 312n.39

Yoshida Shigeru: anti-nuclear policies of, 68, 311n.31; on Japan as a merchant nation, 70, 278; memoirs of, xi, 312–13n.44; on rearmament, 312–13n.44
Yugoslavia, 302n.18
Yu Shyi-kun, 115

Zhu Chenghu, 33
Zionism, 187, 189–90, 194. *See also* Israel

PRINCETON STUDIES IN
INTERNATIONAL HISTORY AND POLITICS

Nuclear Logics: Contrasting Paths in East Asia and the Middle East
by Etel Solingen

Social States: China in International Institutions, 1980–2000
by Alastair Iain Johnston

Appeasing Bankers: Financial Caution on the Road to War
by Jonathan Kirshner

The Politics of Secularism in International Relations
by Elizabeth Shakman Hurd

Unanswered Threats: Political Constraints on the Balance of Power
by Randall L. Schweller

Producing Security: Multinational Corporations, Globalization, and the Changing Calculus of Conflict
by Stephen G. Brooks

Driving the Soviets up the Wall: Soviet-East German Relations, 1953–1961
by Hope M. Harrison

Legitimacy and Power Politics: The American and French Revolutions in International Political Culture
by Mlada Bukovansky

Rhetoric and Reality in Air Warfare: The Evolution of British and American Ideas about Strategic Bombing, 1914–1945
by Tami Davis Biddle

Revolutions in Sovereignty: How Ideas Shaped Modern International Relations
by Daniel Philpott

After Victory: Institutions, Strategic Restraint, and the Rebuilding of Order after Major Wars
by G. John Ikenberry

Stay the Hand of Vengeance: The Politics of War Crimes Tribunals
by Gary Jonathan Bass

War and Punishment: The Causes of War Termination and the First World War
by H.E. Goemans

In the Shadow of the Garrison State: America's Anti-Statism and Its Cold War Grand Strategy
by Aaron L. Friedberg

States and Power in Africa: Comparative Lessons in Authority and Control
by Jeffrey Herbst

The Moral Purpose of the State: Culture, Social Identity, and Institutional Rationality in International Relations
by Christian Reus-Smit

Entangling Relations: American Foreign Policy in Its Century
by David A. Lake

A Constructed Peace: The Making of the European Settlement, 1945–1963
by Marc Trachtenberg

Regional Orders at Century's Dawn: Global and Domestic Influences on Grand Strategy
by Etel Solingen

From Wealth to Power: The Unusual Origins of America's World Role
by Fareed Zakaria

Changing Course: Ideas, Politics, and the Soviet Withdrawal from Afghanistan
by Sarah E. Mendelson

Disarming Strangers: Nuclear Diplomacy with North Korea
by Leon V. Sigal

Imagining War: French and British Military Doctrine between the Wars
by Elizabeth Kier

Roosevelt and the Munich Crisis: A Study of Political Decision-Making
by Barbara Rearden Farnham

Producing Security: Multinational Corporations, Globalization, and the Changing Calculus of Conflict
by Stephen G. Brooks